THE PROTESTANT TEMPERAMENT

THE PROTESTANT TEMPERAMENT

Patterns of Child-Rearing, Religious Experience, and the Self in Early America

Philip Greven

The University of Chicago Press

THE UNIVERSITY OF CHICAGO PRESS, CHICAGO 60637

Published by arrangement with Alfred A. Knopf, Inc.

Library of Congress Cataloging in Publication Data

Greven, Philip J.
    The Protestant temperament : patterns of child-rearing, religious
experience, and the self in early America / Philip Greven. —
University of Chicago Press ed.
        p.   cm.
Reprint. Originally published: New York : Knopf, 1977.
Bibliography: p.
Includes index.
    1. Protestantism.   2. Child development.   3. Temperament—
Religious aspects—Christianity.   4. Experience (Religion)
5. Religious thought—United States.   I. Title.
[BR515.G75   1988]   87-25966
305.6—dc19   CIP
ISBN 0-226-30830-8 (pbk.)

Acknowledgments can be found on pages 402–3.

For my grandmother
JULIA OSBORN HAWKINS

For we know in part, and we prophesy in part.
But when that which is perfect is come, then that
*   which is in part shall be done away.*
When I was a child, I spake as a child, I under-
*   stood as a child, I thought as a child: but*
*   when I became a man, I put away childish*
*   things.*
For now we see through a glass, darkly; but then
*   face to face: now I know in part; but then*
*   shall I know even as also I am known.*

I CORINTHIANS 13:9–12

✥§ CONTENTS ✥

Part Five

EPILOGUE

✒ ACKNOWLEDGMENTS ᗌ

READERS FAMILIAR WITH MY FIRST BOOK, *Four Generations*, may wonder how I came to write a book called *The Protestant Temperament*. Although the reasons undoubtedly are rooted in my own childhood, life experiences, and psyche, I can at least locate the moment when I became preoccupied with some of the issues explored in the following pages: William R. Taylor's colloquium on revivalism in which I participated at Harvard during the spring of 1959. The questions we raised in that remarkable course (but rarely answered satisfactorily) have continued to intrigue me.

One of the great pleasures of scholarship is the opportunity to share ideas and concerns with others and to benefit from the assistance, advice, suggestions, and criticisms of students, colleagues, and friends. I am grateful to the many students in my courses over the years who have listened and responded to my hypotheses, intuitions, and interpretations. I have appreciated the assistance of Denis Johnson and Louis Kern in locating sources and doing some research, and of Charles Carmony, who helped with the task of putting the final manuscript in order and doing the index. At various stages, drafts of the manuscript have been read, commented upon, and criticized most helpfully by Mary Maples Dunn, Richard S. Dunn, Jane N. Garrett, Helen Stokes Greven, Michael G. Kammen, Elizabeth D. Kirk, Gerald F. Moran, Carol M. Petillo, and Michael G. Vaught. In addition, Rhys Isaac and Warren I. Susman scrutinized one of the late drafts of the manuscript with particular care and provided me with invaluable commentaries. I wish to thank all of these individuals for their encouragement and the candor with which they expressed their disagreements and suggestions. None is responsible, however, for the book that I have written. This is a responsibility they cannot be asked to share, since this book, more than many, is very much the result of a personal interpretation of the meaning of the evidence that I have gathered and sought to understand.

Thanks to invitations by Irwin Pollack, Chairman of the Department of Psychiatry at the Rutgers Medical School—College of Medicine and Dentistry of New Jersey, and by Iradj Siassi, formerly the Chief of the Adult Psychiatric Service of the Rutgers Medical School, I was able to participate as a volunteer trainee in an adult outpatient treatment program for nearly a year and a half. The experience, both theoretical and practical, was extraordinarily valuable to me and has had an important impact upon my awareness of the ways in which the human psyche shapes our experience and thought.

Without the generous support of grants from the National Endowment for the Humanities (1970–1971), the American Council of Learned Societies (1974–1975), and Rutgers–The State University of New Jersey, I would not have been able to do the research and to write the book as freely and as expeditiously as I have. I am very grateful to Clifford Geertz and Carl Kaysen for the invitation to the Institute for Advanced Study at Princeton as a Visiting Fellow in 1974–1975. The Institute provided a beautiful and supportive setting for the writing of the manuscript for this book as well as excellent secretarial assistance and typing. In addition, I have been most appreciative of the generosity of Elsie Perkins Youngman, who graciously offered me the use of a cabin in the New Hampshire woods for several summers while I wrote and revised various parts of this book. I also wish to thank the editorial staff of Alfred A. Knopf, Inc. (especially Jane Garrett, Alice Quinn, and Sally Rogers), for their suggestions and help.

Every scholar shares an abiding sense of gratitude for the generous and invaluable assistance of the librarians, archivists, and members of the staffs of university libraries and historical societies throughout the country. My own indebtedness to particular libraries is acknowledged elsewhere in this book.

Given my concerns with the history of childhood and the family, I am acutely aware of the subtle but profoundly important ways in which personal experience always shapes our historical concerns. As always, Helen, my wife, has encouraged and supported me in my work even when her own work left little time for involvement with mine. Hannah (who is seven now) cannot remember a time when I was not at work on this book, and undoubtedly will be relieved to see it completed. Philip (who is ten) has been generous in his willingness to have me spend so much time for so many years upon this project. My children have taught me far more than I can ever acknowledge, and the responsibilities of parenthood have constantly sharpened my sensitivity to the varied responses of other parents whose choices, actions, and values are explored in this book. To each of the members of my own family, I continue to be permanently indebted for their understanding, support, and love.

By dedicating this book to my grandmother Julia Osborn Hawkins, I wish to acknowledge the enduring influence that she has had upon my life and upon my awareness of the significance which religious beliefs and experience can have in a person's life. My grandmother has always been a very special person to me, and I shall always be grateful that she was so much a part of my own personal past and that she continues even now as part of my present life.

P.J.G.

May 4, 1977

PART ONE

PROLOGUE

❧ I ❧

Patterns for the Past

MOST HISTORIANS are preoccupied with the outer life of people in the past. Numerous studies of the economic, social, political, religious, ideological, and, most recently, demographic aspects of American history during the seventeenth and eighteenth centuries have stressed the public events and the public expressions of behavior, thought, and belief. The new emphasis by some historians upon quantitative and collective studies of families, groups, and communities has augmented the traditional concern with the exterior world of public actions and ideas. These studies have provided us with an unparalleled amount of evidence for the historical experiences of many people and regions in early America, and, cumulatively, they provide an extraordinary range of insights and illuminating perspectives upon our nation's early past. Yet, at the same time, these studies often seem to be curiously remote from the inner life of the people who are being scrutinized so precisely and in such detail. Although we know much about their behavior in public, their institutions, their theologies, and their ideologies, we rarely are able to discover the ways in which these aspects of their lives are connected to their psyches and selves, to bring both the public and the private spheres of expression and experience together into a more coherent and meaningful whole.*

---

* In an earlier study, I explored the actions and behavior of people in one small New England town in an analysis that focused, because of the nature of the evidence, upon the outer life of the people; see Philip J. Greven, Jr., *Four Generations: Population, Land, and Family in Colonial Andover, Massachusetts* (Ithaca, N.Y., 1970), especially pp. 1–18, 41–2.
    Although most biographers primarily describe the outer life of individuals, there are some notable exceptions. See, for instance, Erik H. Erikson, *Young Man Luther: A Study in Psychoanalysis and History* (New York, 1958); Robert Middlekauff's study of Cotton Mather in *The Mathers: Three Generations of Puritan Intellectuals, 1596–1728* (New York, 1971); Fawn M. Brodie, *Thomas Jefferson: An Intimate History* (New York, 1974); Peter Shaw, *The Character of John Adams* (Chapel Hill, N.C., 1976); Frank E. Manuel, *A Portrait of Isaac Newton* (Cambridge, Mass., 1968); John Clive, *Macaulay: The Shaping of the Historian* (New York, 1973); Bruce Mazlish, *James and John*

By seeking to understand people's temperaments, we can begin to comprehend the nature of the self that took shape during the years of infancy, childhood, and youth, and to observe some of the ways in which the sense of self was expressed and manifested in the consciousness, sensibilities, beliefs, and behavior of people as adults. Through an exploration of the religious experiences of many early American Protestants, we can begin to discover the innermost realms of feelings, desires, anxieties, and hopes, both conscious and unconscious, that were expressed in recurrent themes in the life experiences of particular individuals and that linked them meaningfully to others. Beliefs and behavior were never divorced from feelings and perceptions. The self always shaped the responses of individuals to the world in which they lived.

A Historian's Past: Patterns of Thought and Religious Belief in Early America

FOR NEARLY FOUR DECADES, historians of early America have been influenced profoundly by a paradigm for religious thought and development so massive in scope and detail, so brilliant in conceptualization, and so persuasive that most of the work done during this period by other historians has been done within its boundaries. Perry Miller's *The New England Mind*, one of the truly great historical creations of this century, established the "anatomy of the Puritan mind" in New England and provided the "map of the intellectual terrain of the seventeenth century" that has continued to guide scholars in their own, more detailed studies of the religious history of the region. Indeed, Miller's claim to have provided his readers with "a sort of working model for American history" was amply justified.

In the first volume of his study, Miller pursued a topical rather than a chronological analysis, seeking always to discern and describe the central themes and patterns of thought that formed the core of Puritan belief and piety and demonstrating the ways in which this thought was connected to the entire context of the ideas and world views of early New Englanders. In the second volume, he placed his paradigm in motion, tracing the slow and subtle transformation of the Puritan mind of the mid-seventeenth century as it interacted with the changing society of New England from the 1630's to the 1730's. In both volumes, however, Miller

---

Stuart Mill: Father and Son in the Nineteenth Century (New York, 1975), among others. Biographies, however, rarely seem to be influential in shaping the general perspectives of most historians.

always was intent upon the clarification of the overarching design, the central configurations of ideas that gave meaning to the public mind of New Englanders.[1]

Perry Miller's paradigm rests upon three governing assumptions. The first is that "the mind of man is the basic factor in human history," a conviction that dominated Miller's vision of intellectual history and persuaded him of the centrality of thought in any proper account of the past. While he recognized that "in the history of thought what is spoken is less important than what is felt," and that religious doctrines "were not embraced for their logic, but out of a hunger of the human spirit and an anxiety of the soul," Miller insisted nevertheless that piety "is only a half of Puritanism." In general, he, like so many scholars, preferred to focus most closely upon thought rather than feelings, upon theology rather than piety. This assumption continues to be shared widely among students of early American religious history, with the result that we know far more now about what people believed and thought in the seventeenth and eighteenth centuries than what they felt and experienced inwardly. Miller's assumption thus has encouraged the concentration by historians upon religious doctrines at the expense of religious experience.[2]

Miller's second assumption, central to his paradigm, is that New England Puritanism in the seventeenth century represented a unique synthesis, a harmonious balance of thought and piety, which provided a *single*, consistent, and almost universally shared mode of belief and experience. At the heart of this mode of thought was the theology of the Covenant, which became nothing less than "the theoretical foundation both for metaphysics and for the state and the church in New England." The doctrines of the Covenant, which Miller also called the federal theology, provided the starting point for subsequent developments in both doctrine and piety. According to Miller, the Covenant offered New Englanders the means of achieving salvation by entering voluntarily and freely into a binding agreement, virtually a legal contract, with God, who promised to give them the faith which He required in return for their acceptance of the Covenant. Miller emphasized that New England Puritans were not Calvinists who believed in an absolute, unbounded, and sovereign God, the utter impotence of humanity, the total inability of unregenerate sinners to do anything toward achieving their own personal salvation. For these New Englanders, reason, logic, and method were to be far more decisive in the quest for salvation than most Calvinists could allow.[3]

Throughout Miller's work, the theme of declension, forming his third major assumption, dominated the historical processes he sought to illuminate. Miller was convinced that even in the first generation, "piety was on the wane," so that the "colonists thenceforward" were to be "progressively more swayed by factors in the intellectual heritage than by the hunger of the spirit." The decline of piety, however, only foreshadowed the still more

dramatic disintegration of the ideology of the Covenant: "The history of
New England, from Winthrop to Otis, from Cotton to Emerson . . . and
the intellectual career of the communities might be most succinctly described as a progressive disintegration of the federal theology." By 1730,
he believed, New England was "a parched land, crying for deliverance
from the hold of ideas that had served their purpose and died."[4]

With the public appearance of Jonathan Edwards, "the first consistent and authentic Calvinist in New England," a new era in the history
of the New England mind began, the start of an age of Calvinist evangelicalism that, Miller believed, was fated to run its course, too, within a
century. By insisting that Calvinism appeared in New England only during the 1730's and 1740's, a period of intense revivalism known as the
Great Awakening, Miller was able to argue that the process which transformed the theology of the Covenant in seventeenth-century New England
was both linear and irreversible—that it involved nothing less than the
disintegration and demise of one systematic pattern of thought and the
sudden and surprising emergence of a fundamentally new pattern of
thought.[5]

The Persistence of Piety

IN STRIKING CONTRAST to Perry Miller's broad and comprehensive studies
of religious thought and development in America, ranging across two and
a half centuries even when they focused upon the minds of New Englanders, most studies of American religious thought, institutions, and
practices done subsequently by other historians have been far more concentrated, more intensively explored, and far more narrowly conceived
than Miller's work. The result has been the accumulation of a series of
disconnected essays and monographs devoted to particular periods,
places, churches, or issues, each of which individually has contributed
significantly to our knowledge and understanding of the past without
providing overarching themes or conceptualizations that might suggest
alternatives to Miller's vision.[6]

By compartmentalizing the past this way, we have inhibited the
development of our own vision of early American religious, intellectual,
and social history even though in actuality much of the analysis done by
other historians in recent decades has diverged, often sharply, from the
paths first sighted and charted by Perry Miller. A close reading of a
number of important studies by younger historians indicates, however,
that we must reckon with the consequences of recent observations, and

begin to sketch out an alternative paradigm to complement, if not sup-
plant altogether, the paradigm invented by Miller so long ago.*

Instead of demonstrating a sudden transformation of piety and
thought, a number of separate studies by historians over the past two
decades concerned with specific periods, groups, and issues in these centuries suggest the *persistence* of at least two distinctive, symbiotically
related modes of experience and thought. From one perspective, the
pattern seems to be one of recurrence—the reappearance in different
periods and places of modes of piety and belief that resemble the piety
and beliefs of other periods and places in many important ways. From
another perspective, the pattern seems to be one of continuities, with
clear linkages between the modes of piety and belief in successive generations of people in particular places. Yet even when these modes of piety
and belief are so closely intertwined and associated that they are difficult
to disentangle, they usually reveal themselves as two perceptibly different
ways of being, behaving, and thinking, distinct and ever present.†

* There are several notable exceptions to this observation. For a general
interpretation, see Lazer Ziff, *Puritanism in America: New Culture in a New
World* (New York, 1973). Two significant studies have sought to create
paradigms for understanding Puritanism: Michael Walzer's *The Revolution of
the Saints: A Study in the Origins of Radical Politics* (Cambridge, Mass.,
1965) and Darrett B. Rutman's *American Puritanism: Faith and Practice*
(Philadelphia, 1970). While both are imaginative and suggestive, I have always
found Walzer's analysis to be more directly relevant to my own central concerns.

Since completing my manuscript, I have had an opportunity to read
Henry F. May's *The Enlightenment in America* (New York, 1976), which provides
four new categories for the analysis and the understanding of the enlightenment during the second half of the eighteenth century. The first category, "The
Moderate Enlightenment," corresponds remarkably well to my own interpretation of the moderates (a term which we each invented independently). It is
an important study and a suggestive complement to mine.

In addition, see the following studies by sociologists and anthropologists
concerned with paradigms: Max Weber, *The Protestant Ethic and the Spirit
of Capitalism*, Talcott Parsons, trans. (New York, 1956; orig. ed. 1930); Ernst
Troeltsch, *The Social Teaching of the Christian Churches*, Olive Wyon, trans.,
2 vols. (New York, 1931); Werner Stark, *The Sociology of Religion: A Study
of Christendom*, 3 vols. (London, 1966); H. H. Gerth and C. Wright Mills,
eds. and trans., *From Max Weber: Essays in Sociology* (New York, 1946),
especially Part III; and Clifford Geertz, *The Interpretation of Cultures:
Selected Essays* (New York, 1973).

† One of the most fascinating and important implications of the work done
by several historians in recent years is that, contrary to Perry Miller's assumption, there was no significant decline of piety during the course of the
seventeenth century. Two quantitative analyses of church membership—
Robert G. Pope's study of *The Half-Way Covenant: Church Membership in
Puritan New England* (Princeton, N.J., 1969) and Gerald Francis Moran's
"The Puritan Saint: Religious Experience, Church Membership, and Piety in
Connecticut, 1636–1776" (Ph.D. thesis, Rutgers University, 1973)—have provided abundant evidence to demonstrate that revivalism, with its dramatic
increases in conversions and consequent admissions to full membership in
Congregational churches, was not only evident during the 1630's, the peak
of piety during the first decade of settlement in Massachusetts, but continued

Norman Pettit has illuminated the controversies among Anglo-American Puritans throughout the seventeenth century over the nature and the process of conversion. In considerable detail, he has traced the specific views of particular ministers and theologians, including one group whom he designates "preparationists" and a second group whom he terms "predestinarians." Both groups were Puritans and were in agreement on many issues, yet on the central issues of regeneration and grace, they clearly were always at odds. According to Pettit, the predestinarians, such as the Reverend John Cotton of Boston, insisted that grace was a free gift given by God to those whom He chose for salvation without any prior efforts on their own behalf, and insisted also that conversion usually was instantaneous, a new birth that made individuals into gracious Christian saints with no dependence upon any prior preparations. The preparationists, like Miller's federalists, insisted that individuals not only could prepare themselves to receive Divine grace but ought to do so, and argued that the infusion of grace was a gradual, often almost imperceptible process which slowly and imperfectly regenerated human nature. The preparationists usually insisted that God made active preparation possible by giving humans free wills which would permit them to choose to obey the Divine will voluntarily. Although Pettit focuses upon the preparationists, his study makes it evident that *both* points of view and modes of thought were present among Anglo-American Puritans throughout the seventeenth century, forming an ongoing debate without ever resolving it.[7]

The persistence of a profound difference of opinion and beliefs is evident also in Norman Fiering's erudite study "Will and Intellect in the New England Mind." Whereas Pettit concentrates upon one of the central issues of religious thought—the process of conversion—Fiering focuses upon an equally crucial issue—the nature of the human will and its role in the process of regeneration. In general, Fiering argues that there were two philosophical positions evident among Harvard students and others—the "intellectualist" and the "voluntarist"—with the intellectualist position being "the most common opinion in the seventeenth century and the centuries preceding." The intellectualists, who traced their position back to Thomas Aquinas, believed in the primacy of the intellect over the will, of reason over the passions, for the will was seen as dependent upon the understanding in making a choice. The alternative position, which derived from St. Augustine, did not identify the will "as a rational appetite at all,"

---

to occur frequently throughout the towns in Massachusetts and Connecticut during the entire course of the seventeenth century. Moran, in particular, has insisted that piety did not wane after the first decade of settlement, but continued to be evident in Connecticut throughout the century.

For a wider perspective upon the process of declension, see Daniel Walker Howe's essay "The Decline of Calvinism: An Approach to Its Study," *Comparative Studies in Society and History*, 14 (1972), pp. 306–27.

but instead saw the will as "almost synonymous with the inner essence of the whole man, the battleground of God and the devil." "The personal drama of salvation is enacted in the will," Fiering notes, "and on the will's ultimate orientation depends one's entire fate with God." Thus the will became dominant in the "Augustinian or pietistic voluntarism," for this position insisted that "Man's sinful nature is primarily a matter of perverse will, not intellectual error." Both viewpoints were expressed continuously, and both were to be of profound importance for religious thought and the early American (or at least the New England) mind. As Fiering observes, "it becomes readily evident that intellectualism can lead rather easily to a belief in salvation by effort and endeavor, whereas the pietistic voluntarist can only wait on divine grace for redemption." Both views were present consistently, however, despite their divergent implications.[8]

The dichotomy between "preparationists" and "predestinarians," or between "intellectualists" and "voluntarists," is evident also in the dualism of "moderates" and "purists" that David Hall has explored in his careful study of the New England ministry in the seventeenth century. Hall discerned an enduring split among the ministers in terms of those who emphasized nurture and growth in grace and those who emphasized conversion or the new birth.[9]

This dichotomy is amplified by the juxtaposition of two biographies of leading ministers in the late seventeenth and early eighteenth centuries, representative of a generation prior to that of Jonathan Edwards: Samuel Willard and Cotton Mather. Willard epitomizes the exponents of the Covenant, the perfect exemplar of Perry Miller's seventeenth-century New England Puritan, while Cotton Mather, his contemporary, is virtually the antithesis, being instead an ardent evangelical pietist. Robert Middlekauff's probing and sensitive analysis of Mather's personality and religious experience demonstrates the inadequacy of Miller's thesis about the uniqueness of Jonathan Edwards and the innovations of the 1730's. Certainly, as Middlekauff has revealed, evangelical piety was visible in New England long before Perry Miller discerned its presence. The fact that Cotton Mather was the grandson of John Cotton (perhaps the most evangelical preacher among the first generation of ministers in New England and closely associated with the Antinomianism of Anne Hutchinson and her followers) suggests some of the hidden continuities of religious experience and belief which escaped Miller's otherwise perceptive scrutiny. What is crucial, however, is the recognition that *both* Willard and Mather were present simultaneously in Boston, and that both represented distinctive forms of experience, sensibility, and belief. Born in the seventeenth century and living into the opening decades of the eighteenth century, these two prominent figures among the New England ministry thus demonstrate the persistence of the dichotomies observed among first-

and second-generation New Englanders and provide us with vital links between the beliefs and experiences of people in earlier and later generations.[10]

Some of the possible connections between different periods, so often obscured by the narrow chronological focus and the isolation inherent in monographic research, have been suggested by several historians. Norman Pettit, for instance, noted that the debate in the seventeenth century over preparation persisted into the eighteenth-century controversies over the revivals. He also observed that the rival persuasions which distinguished predestinarians from preparationists also carried into the next century: "From [John] Norton's position there is a clear line of development which can readily be traced through the next few generations, through figures such as Increase Mather and Solomon Stoddard down to Jonathan Edwards." "It is a line," he notes, "that would continue into the nineteenth century through a series of evangelical revivals." Similarly, from the other position "there emerged a different tradition," which was a "line that cannot be so accurately traced in terms of immediate influence, but one that would continue into the next two centuries as a moving force in the development of a more 'liberal' theology." Norman Fiering also pointed out that "it is remarkable how close the correspondence is between the seventeenth-century Augustinian voluntarist position and the ideas of Jonathan Edwards, and the seventeenth-century intellectualist position and the ideas, for example, of Edwards's opponent, Charles Chauncy." Indeed, Fiering notes, "All of the disputants in the Great Awakening debate were relying on well-established older arguments," of which the "voluntarist/intellectualist debate of the seventeenth century was possibly the most central."[11]

The sustained symbiosis of two distinctive forms of religious experience and thought that has become increasingly apparent for the period from 1630 to 1730 is also seen in the period from 1730 to 1830. Alan Heimert's massive (and controversial) study of "Calvinists" and "Liberals," or "evangelicals" and "rationalists," provides the evidence needed to extend the patterns discerned in the seventeenth century into the early nineteenth century, although his own assumptions prevented him from realizing this. Heimert began his study where Perry Miller left off, and shared Miller's conviction that the developments after 1730 represented something altogether new. For Heimert, as for Miller, the Great Awakening marked a pivotal divide in American religious history. "There were in substance only *two* parties on the American religious scene in the period after the Great Awakening," each of which "marked the independent fulfillment of one of the strains that in Puritanism had been held in precarious balance: 'piety' and 'reason.' " Thenceforth, there were to be "only two viable intellectual options," forming "conflicting ideologies" that were "presented to the American people as alternative patterns of thought and behavior." In the years since Heimert published his analysis *Religion and* *the American Mind,* however, the continuities between the dichotomies observed after the Awakening and those observed before the Awakening have become evident. Seen from this new perspective, Heimert's work provides the indispensable link between the seventeenth century and the nineteenth century.[12] *

While some studies of early American religious thought and piety thus have been demonstrating the continuation of patterns of belief and values from the early seventeenth to the early nineteenth centuries, other studies by historians concerned with early American political ideology have been discovering that many of the ideas associated with the Revolution in the mid-eighteenth century were present, in fact, decades earlier. Bernard Bailyn, for instance, has observed that "the configuration of ideas and attitudes" which he "had described . . . as the Revolutionary ideology could be found intact—completely formed—as far back as the 1730's; in partial form it could be found even farther back, at the turn of the seventeenth century." Similarly, Gordon Wood has noted that "There was nothing really new about these republican principles" of the 1760's and 1770's. "John Winthrop would have found them congenial." "In fact," he observed, "republicanism as the Americans expressed it in 1776 possessed a decidedly reactionary tone." Concurrently, studies of political parties in New England have been demonstrating the persistence of two distinct forms of political groupings from the 1680's to the 1770's: the "country" and the "court" parties that divided New Englanders into two distinct camps, as both Timothy Breen and Stephen Patterson have shown. Thus the links between the seventeenth century and the late eighteenth century have become as visible through the analysis of political ideas and behavior as they have through the analysis of religious ideas and attitudes.[13]

Once we have recognized the persistence of particular patterns of thought and action, we must begin to ask if these public expressions of continuities were also mirrored in the private experiences of people throughout these centuries. Was there an inner history which corresponded to the outer history that has become so familiar to us? Only by

* The intensity of the opposition to Heimert's interpretations and methodology is remarkable. So effective were the critics, however, that Heimert's analysis has never received the attention that it deserves. For negative readings, see Edmund S. Morgan's review in the *William and Mary Quarterly,* XXIV (1967), pp. 454–9, and Sidney E. Mead, "Through and Beyond the Lines," *Journal of Religion,* 48 (1968), pp. 274–88; for positive readings, see William G. McLoughlin, "The American Revolution as a Religious Revival: 'The Millennium in One Country,'" *New England Quarterly,* 40 (1967), pp. 99–110, and Harry S. Stout, "Religion, Communications, and the Ideological Origins of the Revolution," *William and Mary Quarterly,* forthcoming. Heimert, nevertheless, has had an influence upon several important studies, including Gordon S. Wood, *The Creation of the American Republic, 1776–1787* (Chapel Hill, N.C., 1969), and May's *Enlightenment in America.* My own views have shifted several times with respect to Heimert's arguments and interpretations, but on balance, while I remain diametrically opposed to some of his central propositions, I also share many of his basic assumptions.

turning our attention from the exterior worlds of ideas and actions will
it be possible to discover some of the ways in which the less visible but no
less significant personal worlds of individuals interconnected with the
historical past that we have sought to explore and to illuminate.

Temperament and the Self

WHEN WE BEGIN to listen for the recurrent and the significant themes
that emerge from the private as well as the public writings of people in
the past—many of whom were remarkably sensitive and self-knowing,
conscious of their feelings and thoughts and aware of the implications
of their inner experience for their outer lives and future destinies—we
can discern patterns of feeling, thought, and sensibility that formed three
distinctive expressions of temperament, and shaped three distinctive
forms of self throughout the seventeenth and eighteenth centuries. These
three patterns of temperament—which I have chosen to call the "evangelical," the "moderate," and the "genteel" modes—not only existed at
certain times and among particular groups, but also persisted over the
course of many generations and centuries among numerous groups in
many different places throughout the Anglo-American world. Evangelicals, for example, could be found in many religious denominations, including Anglicans, Congregationalists, Presbyterians, Baptists, and
Quakers. Moderates also could be found in all of these denominations at
the same time. The genteel, too were present throughout the Anglo-
American world during this period, and were members of many of the
principal religious denominations.*

The temperaments of evangelicals were dominated by a persistent
and virtually inescapable hostility to the self and all of its manifestations.

---

* To some extent, these distinctive modes of temperament may have corresponded to particular levels of economic or social rank, with the genteel
ordinarily being the wealthiest, most prominent, and most prestigious, the
moderates often among the middling ranks, and the evangelicals among the
lower-middle ranks. But no one has yet demonstrated such clear socioeconomic
distinctions in relation to these particular types of temperament, nor have I
sought to do so in this study. The issue, however, merits further attention. See,
for instance, H. Richard Niebuhr, *The Social Sources of Denominationalism*
(New York, 1957; orig. ed. 1929); James Walsh, "The Great Awakening in the
First Congregational Church of Woodbury, Connecticut," *William and Mary
Quarterly*, XXVIII (1971), pp. 543–652; J. M. Bumsted, "Religion, Finance,
and Democracy in Massachusetts: The Town of Norton as a Case Study, *Journal
of American History*, LVII (1971), pp. 817–31. Alan Heimert, *Religion and the
American Mind*, p. 10, discounts the importance of social and economic factors,
insisting instead that the basic differences were "not of income but, in substance, of taste."

Thus evangelicals were preoccupied with ways to abase, to deny, and to annihilate their own enduring sense of self-worth and selfhood, convinced that only by destroying the self could they conform absolutely and unquestioningly to the sovereign will of God. They shared the experience of the new birth, a transforming crisis which seemed to reshape their innermost selves into radically new and more acceptable forms, for they believed that regeneration could be accomplished only when the self had been conquered. Evangelicals thus were people always at war with the self yet never able to escape the self, even, as most discovered, after the new birth. They often felt themselves to be liberated, however, by the sense of self-denial and self-annihilation which had preceded their conversion experience, and took heart from the inner assurance that their personal wills had been broken so they could at last follow the will of God wherever it might lead, no matter what the cost might be in personal suffering. Once reborn, evangelicals often felt themselves freed from the burdens of their sinful past, and able finally to war with the sins of the unconverted, who seemed always to be so numerous. Evangelicals thus often became extremists and purists, eager to restore their inner and outer worlds to a primitive order of harmony, unity, and self-lessness.*

The moderates, on the other hand, were rarely extremists, forever feeling caught between the poles of duty and of desire, seeking a middle way in their lives that necessitated an extraordinary range of compromises and of controls both within and without in order to achieve the harmony between opposites which tugged at them. They, too, believed in the need for self-denial, but they never accepted the evangelicals' insistence upon the virtual annihilation of the corrupted and sinful self. Moderates were self-approving people, on the whole, while also always guarding themselves against excess of any kind. They were more often anxious and ambivalent temperamentally than they were extremists or

---

* My concern with patterns of religious experience and temperament has much in common with the fascinating and still unequaled study by William James, *The Varieties of Religious Experience: A Study in Human Nature* (New York, 1929; orig. ed. 1902), which focused upon "personal religion pure and simple" rather than upon institutional or doctrinal history (p. 30). James sought to analyze the experiences of both Catholics and Protestants from St. Augustine to the present in terms of a fundamental dichotomy between "the two ways of looking at life which are characteristic respectively" of what he called "the healthy-minded, who need to be born only once, and of the sick souls, who must be twice-born in order to be happy." "The result," he said, "is two different conceptions of the universe of our experience" (p. 163). Like James, I am drawn most toward the twice-born as subjects for my analysis, and the evangelicals always have been at the center of my inquiry. But like James, I also have found that in order to understand the twice-born, it is essential to understand the once-born, those who were not evangelicals. As a result, I have sought to contrast and to compare the evangelicals with others whose temperaments and religious experiences were quite different. See also Baird Tipson, "How Can the Religious Experience of the Past Be Recovered? The Examples of Puritanism and Pietism," *Journal of the American Academy of Religion*, XLIII (1975), pp. 695–707.

purists, for their perceptions of the self and the world were rarely polarized into the rigid dichotomies of sin and grace that dominated the evangelical consciousness. Moderates frequently shared the desire for regeneration and grace, but they generally denied the necessity of a dramatic emotional transformation, preferring to believe that grace could develop gradually, and that moral behavior and good works could be efficacious in bringing about a person's salvation. Moderates also were preoccupied with virtue and with morality, keeping themselves within fairly narrow boundaries of feeling and behavior. Their central concern was always self-control.

The genteel were notably indifferent to most of the issues that concerned both evangelicals and moderates, feeling very comfortable about themselves and indeed experiencing a sense of self-confidence that set them apart from most people. They were far more at ease with themselves, their desires, and their pleasures than were others, for they lived without the burdens of conscience and guilt that so often shaped the sensibilities and the self of evangelicals and moderates. The genteel took their state of grace for granted, when they cared about such matters at all, and were generally confident that the church and the sacraments, which they acknowledged, sufficed to ensure their personal salvation. On the whole, the genteel were the least concerned about inner piety and private religious experience of the three groups, content to enjoy the world they lived in and to minimize their concerns about the world to come. Self-assertion rather than self-control or self-suppression was to be the central theme of many of their lives, thus revealing just how different they were from those who were moderates or evangelicals.*

Childhood, Temperament, and Religious Experience

IN ORDER TO UNDERSTAND the temperaments of early Americans, and in order to account for some of the substantive differences of character and of religious experience that distinguished evangelicals from moderates and both from the genteel, we must seek to understand the ways in which their psyches were shaped by the formative experiences of childhood.

* Among the notable studies of temperament, character, or personality in early America, apart from extended biographies, are: Richard L. Bushman, *From Puritan to Yankee: Character and the Social Order in Connecticut, 1690–1765* (Cambridge, Mass., 1967); Bernard Bailyn, "Religion and Revolution: Three Biographical Studies," *Perspectives in American History*, IV (1970), pp. 85–110; Richard D. Brown, "Modernization and the Modern Personality in Early America, 1600–1865: A Sketch of a Synthesis," *The Journal of Interdisciplinary History*, II (1972), pp. 201–28.

Given the nature of the sources, both personal and public, that have survived from the seventeenth and eighteenth centuries, the connections between childhood experience, temperament, and religious experience must emerge from the analysis of evidence from adults. To discern this evidence requires that we learn to listen carefully for themes that recur and become dominant in the personal lives of innumerable adults. Until we begin to hear such themes of childhood experience, we will continue to be unable to bridge the gap between the public and private realms of consciousness and thought.*

In the seventeenth and eighteenth centuries, many people recognized the profound importance of childhood in the shaping of temperament and religious experience in subsequent years of life, even though they knew, long before Sigmund Freud reminded us, that such experiences generally are forgotten. John Locke, for instance, noted late in the seventeenth century that a "compliance, and suppleness" of children's "wills, being by a steady hand introduced by parents, before children have memories to retain the beginnings of it, will seem natural to them, and work afterward in them, as if it were so." He knew, of course, that such compliance was anything but natural, requiring the most conscientious and sustained efforts on the part of Christian parents if their goals for the education of their offspring were to be successful. A century and a half later, Horace Bushnell also recognized, with respect to many Christian converts, that they "are now born into that by the assent of their own will, which they were in before, without their will. What they do not remember still re-

* Historians can learn much from students of the human psyche, especially by becoming sensitive to the recurrent themes and patterns of feeling and thought that emerge from the discrete and confusing details of ordinary existence. I have found the writings of a number of psychologists and psychiatrists most helpful and suggestive. See, for example, Sigmund Freud, *Collected Papers*, Ernest Jones, ed., and Joan Riviere, trans., 5 vols. (New York, 1959), and Sigmund Freud, *The Complete Introductory Lectures on Psychoanalysis*, James Strachey, ed. and trans. (New York, 1966); Otto Fenichel, *The Psychoanalytic Theory of Neurosis* (New York, 1945); Erik H. Erikson, *Childhood and Society*, 2nd ed. (New York, 1963), and Erik H. Erikson, "Identity and the Life Cycle: Selected Papers," *Psychological Issues*, I (1959); Kenneth Kenniston, *The Uncommitted: Alienated Youth in American Society* (New York, 1965); Philip M. Helfaer, *The Psychology of Religious Doubt* (Boston, 1972); David Shapiro, *Neurotic Styles* (New York, 1965); Liam Hudson, *Contrary Imaginations: A Psychological Study of the Young Student* (New York, 1966); Samuel Novey, *The Second Look: The Reconstruction of Personal History in Psychiatry and Psychoanalysis* (Baltimore, 1968).

Among the notable psychological studies by historians are several by Richard L. Bushman: "On the Uses of Psychology: Conflict and Conciliation in Benjamin Franklin," *History and Theory*, V (1966), pp. 225–40; "Jonathan Edwards and Puritan Consciousness," *Journal for the Scientific Study of Religion*, V (1966), pp. 383–96; "Jonathan Edwards as Great Man: Identity, Conversion, and Leadership in the Great Awakening," *Soundings: An Interdisciplinary Journal*, LII (1969), pp. 15–46. I also find Manuel's sensitive and illuminating analysis of Isaac Newton to be one of the most persuasive psychological studies yet done by a historian.

members them, and now claims a right in them. What was before unconscious, flames out into consciousness." As these and other men and women realized, the experiences of infancy and early childhood were of enduring importance for the formation of the self and the creation of proper modes of religious experience and belief in later life.[14]

In infancy, childhood, and youth lay the sources for many of the enduring traits of temperament and many of the most intimate personal feelings, needs, and desires that were to mold the religious experiences and beliefs of people into such distinctive patterns of piety and thought. Childhood was the matrix within which the sense of self, shaping consciousness and convictions, was being formed, not only because many parents set about to ensure the inculcation of particular modes of behavior, values, and beliefs, but also because the accumulation of personal experiences in the earliest years of life had an enduring influence upon the development of the temperaments and religious experiences of people in adulthood. By discovering how differently people of different temperaments reared their children, by seeing how they chose to feed, to clothe, to discipline, and to educate their children, by recognizing the issues that seemed to many parents to be of decisive importance for the development of character and the fostering of piety, we can begin to perceive the recurrent patterns of early life experiences associated with each of these three distinctive patterns of adult temperament and piety.*

Toward a New Paradigm

THE CENTRAL GOAL OF MY BOOK is to suggest a set of patterns or configurations that will clarify and enrich our analysis of the American past. Thus the study that follows is not to be read as "a history of" childhood,

---

* Although my emphasis in *Child-Rearing Concepts, 1628–1861: Historical Sources* (Itasca, Ill., 1973) was upon the transformation of child-rearing modes during the first half of the nineteenth century, subsequent research and analysis have persuaded me of the necessity to stress continuities of child-rearing methods over long periods of time (corresponding to particular types of religious temperaments) rather than constant evolution. However, I do hope that the analysis of changes, too, will become a major focus of attention by others, so that we can begin to discern the patterns *and* the processes, the continuities *and* the changes, that shaped the temperaments and piety of successive generations. As I suggested in *Four Generations*, both aspects of the history of the family are essential.

In a subsequent study, I hope to extend the interpretations set forth in this book by the analysis of the social sources of religious experience, exploring patterns of family structure, religious institutions, and communities. I will be concerned with the impact of mobility upon the formation of sectarian forms of religious associations and try to work out a typology suited to the public expression of shared religious experience.

temperament, or religious experience in the sense of tracing these topics as they might have developed or changed over the course of time. Chronology always is subordinated to the quest for patterns. My concern is with enduring themes that transcend time and space and denominations and bind people together into meaningful associations through personal experiences which can be discerned and illuminated by the juxtaposition of people from different periods, places, and religious groups.

Unlike Perry Miller and others, I am persuaded that there never was a single consistent set of beliefs or one mode of piety characteristic of Protestants anywhere at any time. On the contrary, the studies which have been done by so many other scholars have suggested to me that each of the modes of piety and thought explored in this book—the evangelical, the moderate, and the genteel—could be found throughout the seventeenth, eighteenth, and early nineteenth centuries, sufficiently distinctive as to be visible and significant factors in the historical experiences of people throughout the Anglo-American world. Each had a separate but interconnected history that we have only begun to discern and to explore.

Also unlike Miller and others, I have always sought to analyze and to understand religious *experience* or piety rather than theology or sacraments. I have found assumptions such as Miller's ("The real life of Jonathan Edwards was the life of his mind") to be inadequate for the kind of understanding that I seek: to discover the ways in which personal experience and religious experience and thought were interconnected. I cannot accept the proposition that a person can be understood by focusing almost exclusively upon ideas and regarding biography as "external." The mind cannot be divorced from the self if we are to understand the whole person. Thus I believe that historians, too, must begin to explore the inner realms of feelings, emotions, perceptions, and consciousness, to discover the unconscious as well as the more rational dimensions of the human personality.[15]

An understanding of temperament is indispensable for our understanding of the past. The nature, the experience, and the expression of the self provide us with a key to the integration of the disparate pieces of information, insight, and interpretation emerging from the past several decades of historical research in the field of early American history. Since I have found that knowledge about each of the three temperaments analyzed in this book often supplies the crucial linkage between thought and behavior, I hope that an awareness of these three distinctive forms of self will help us to begin to create new paradigms more consonant with the implications of our research and observations than the paradigm invented by Perry Miller. But any new paradigm must strive to accomplish what Miller achieved: the integrated vision of the ways in which theology, politics, and religious institutions in early America formed coherent patterns of thought and behavior. My ambition is to contribute some insight into the way in which the temperaments of individuals mediated between thought and behavior, always shaping the perceptions, values, ideas, and actions of people in distinctive ways.

I hope, however, that readers will remember that these three studies of temperament represent composite portraits. They are based upon a wide and varied array of personal experiences, self-perceptions, and self-expressions, but they reflect only some of the many possible themes that people's lives could reveal. I trust that no one will be surprised by the acknowledgment that particular individuals often were much more complex and varied in their experiences, feelings, and convictions than these collective portraits might seem to suggest. Individuals could and often did combine aspects of more than one of these basic patterns of temperament and religious experience. My purpose in this book, however, is simply to observe and to establish some of the dominant motifs or themes of certain enduring patterns of human experience, self-consciousness, and thought that can serve us henceforth as models in our continuous quest for an understanding of people in the past and that can help us comprehend the infinite diversity and richness of human lives. By learning to understand these people better, we cannot fail to learn about ourselves as well.

~§ *PART TWO* §~

THE EVANGELICALS:
The Self Suppressed

Except ye be converted, and become as little children, ye shall not enter into the kingdom of heaven.

MATTHEW 18:3

⋖§ II §⋗

Authoritarian Families:
Modes of Evangelical Child-Rearing

OVER AND OVER AGAIN for more than two centuries on both sides of the Atlantic Ocean, the same phrase was repeated, forming the recurrent theme of evangelical childhood: Children were to "love and fear" both their parents and their God. The Reverend John Wesley, striving to define the nature of a true Christian and the essence of "real, genuine Christianity," noted that "the ruling temper" of a Christian's heart was "the most absolute submission, and the tenderest gratitude to his Sovereign Benefactor. And this grateful love creates filial fear: an awful reverence toward him, and an earnest care not to give place to any disposition, not to admit an action, word, or thought, which might in any degree displease that indulgent Power to whom he owes his life, breath, and all things." Wesley's use of parental imagery for Divinity evokes the central configurations of the child's relationship both to parents and to God, the parent of all mankind. Love and fear evoke some of the central and recurrent themes of evangelicalism and of the fundamental patterns of nurture, socialization, and discipline that marked evangelical families with common experiences and common convictions generation after generation. Forming two persistent poles within the psyches and the beliefs of evangelicals, love and fear were rooted in the processes of child-rearing that shaped the evangelical character and gave emotional sustenance to evangelical piety throughout the centuries. Not only did evangelicals believe that children should develop an intense sense of both love and fear for their parents and for their God—beliefs that shaped their writings and musings about the best and most effective ways in which to rear children —but the effective practice of these beliefs is revealed in the intimate details of their lives, their relationships with their children, and in the methods they used to rear those children from infancy to maturity.[1]

Pious Parents, Precious Mothers

EVANGELICALS USUALLY RECALLED being raised by pious parents, who had sought conscientiously to bring their children up in the ways of the Lord, with a proper sense of love and fear for Him. Their early memories of their parents thus provided evangelicals with images of parenthood and with standards of parental piety that endured throughout their lives. The combination of effective discipline, powerful consciences, and complete subjection of children to the wills of parents ensured that evangelical children would sustain a sense of the power, authority, and piety of their parents, making it exceedingly difficult for them to acknowledge any feelings toward their parents other than those of obedience and love. Yet their recollections, however brief, were often distinguished according to parent, the father being more usually associated with authority and the mother with love.

The impression left by the accounts of pious lives and religious experiences from evangelicals is of an intensely religious family background and of early religious training by very pious parents. Many evangelicals could have said of their own parents and ancestors what Samuel Hopkins said of his: "My parents were professors of religion; and I descended from christian ancestors, both by my father and my mother, as far back as I have been able to trace my descent. I conclude I and my ancestors descended from those called *Puritans* in the days of queen Elizabeth, above two hundred years ago, and have continued to bear that denomination, since, and were the first settlers of New-England. This I have considered to be the most honourable and happy descent, to spring from ancestors, who have been professors of religion, without interruption during the course of two hundred years, and more: and many of them, if not all *real christians*." Even if evangelicals could not trace their religious piety back through more than two centuries of ancestors, most recalled having been reared by pious parents.[2]

In Cambridge, Massachusetts, during the 1630's and 1640's, many of the newly admitted members of the congregation of the Reverend Thomas Shepard recalled the impressions made upon them by pious parents during their childhoods in England. Mr. Eaton stated that "My education was in a religious manner from a cradle that I was raised up to hear Scripture." Mr. Sanders was "religiously brought up." Mr. Andrews was "brought up of godly parents," with whom he "remained till 17 years of age, instructed in the principles of religion." Richard Cutter observed that "The Lord was pleased for to give my parents hearts to bring me up in the fear of the Lord though I had much opposition of heart against my parents and those that were over me." Similar recollections mark some of the relations of religious experiences by members of the Reverend John Fiske's congregation in Wenham, Massachusetts, during the mid-seventeenth century. Mrs. Farwel said that "Her education was godly," as did Mr. Farwel. Thomas Hincksman's wife "was first convinced of her estate by nature by means of her godly parent oft instructing of her and telling her what her condition by nature was and how to get out of the same." Goodman Foster could not "call to mind all matters from his childhood," but he did state that "He was brought up of godly parents."[3]

Early Quakers also remembered pious parents who shaped their consciences and formed their characters in childhood. Elizabeth Stirredge, who was born in 1634, said that her "parents were people fearing God, and very zealous in their day." She recalled that her father's "honest and chaste life is often in my remembrance, and his fervent and zealous prayers amongst his family, are not forgotten by me." George Fox said that his father "was by profession a weaver, an honest man, and there was a Seed of God in him. The neighbours called him Righteous Christer." His mother "was an upright woman" who descended from "the stock of the martyrs." William Caton, born about 1636, recalled: "When I was a child I was nurtured and tutored with such fatherly care and motherly affection, as my parents at that day were endued with." The distinction he makes between his father's "care" and his mother's "affection" was felt by other evangelicals as well.[4]

As important as both parents were for the shaping of piety and of character, evangelicals often placed particular emphasis in their memories upon their mothers. Characteristically, the Reverend Thomas Shepard, one of the leading evangelical preachers of the first generation of Puritans in New England, remembered that his mother "was a woman much afflicted in conscience, sometimes even unto . . . distraction of mind, yet was sweetly recovered again before she died," which occurred when he was "about four years old." As he recalled, "I being the youngest she did bear exceeding great love to me and made many prayers for me," who was "best beloved of my mother." The Reverend Increase Mather, an imminent preacher of the second generation in Massachusetts and son of one of the most respected ministers of the new colony, recalled that his mother "was a very Holy praying woman" who "had a peculiar love for me," he noted, "and her affection caused her to be the more earnest in prayer to God for me day and night. I remember she has sometimes sayd to me, when I was a child, that she prayed but for 2 things on my behalfe, first that God would give me grace, secondly that Hee would give me learning." On her deathbed, she exhorted him to serve God "in the work of the ministry." The last words his "dear and precious mother" spoke to him made a deep and lasting impression upon him. The Reverend John Cleaveland, an ardent New Light minister reared in Connecticut, educated at Yale, and preaching in Ipswich, Massachusetts, recalled in his uncompleted autobiography that his mother "being a Woman of Experimental Piety—took a Considerable Deal of pains not only to Teach us to Read but also, to Shew us the Danger of an unconverted State or a State of unregeneracy; how we were Children of wrath and Exposed to Hell Fire and also Set forth to us the Necessity of having an Interest in Jesus Christ in Order to be Save[d] and hapy." The Reverend Isaac Backus, who became the leading minister among the New Light Baptists in the mid-eighteenth century, also recalled that he "was often warned and Exorted (especially by my godly mother), To fly from the Wrath to come." Susanna Anthony, who was reared as a Quaker in Newport but converted to Congregationalism during the Great Awakening of the early 1740's, recalled that she was "early taught to love, fear and serve the Lord. My dear mother took great pains to form my mind for God." George Whitefield, the most charismatic evangelical preacher of the eighteenth century, recalled that although his father died when he was only two years old, his mother remained alive and "was used to say, even when I was an infant, that she expected more comfort from me than any other of her children." "This," he added, "with the circumstance of my being born in an inn, has been often of service to me in exciting my endeavours to make good my mother's expectations."[5]

Similarly, Joseph Pike, an early Quaker, remembered that his own mother and father were "virtuous and godly people, who endeavoured to educate their children in the same steps." He believed firmly that parents in general "should keep a very strict hand over" children, adding that "had not my parents been careful over me, I had been worse than I was. And although my dear mother would never indulge me in any evil practice, being a prudent, discreet woman; yet she loved me exceedingly, which I well knew," a knowledge and conviction which "in some measure" he "presumed upon" and "ventured abroad at some times, which I should not have done, had she corrected me oftener." When his mother died, he observed: "I loved her very tenderly, and carried myself towards her with dutifulness; this she fully expressed on her death-bed, and of her dear love of me." "I can say in truth," he added, "that I have very often looked back, and seriously reflected upon the whole course of my behaviour towards her, and have found great peace and satisfaction of mind; my conscience on the nicest scrutiny has not reproached me." For these evangelicals, as for so many others, pious parents, and in particular devoted mothers, shaped their earliest consciousness and character and remained fixed in their memories for the rest of their lives.[6]

The Household

IDEALLY, EVANGELICAL FAMILIES consisted only of parents and children. Parents needed exclusive influence and control over their children in order to accomplish their goals. The distance that they maintained between their households and the surrounding community and the distance that characterized their relationships with other adults who might be present at various times within their households—servants and occasionally grandparents—served to intensify the relationship binding parents to their children and children to their parents. Within relatively isolated and self-contained households, the focus of authority and the source of love were united in the parents, who dominated the household and determined the principles and practices that were to shape the temperaments of their offspring. Within the confines of the nuclear family, children found no alternatives, no defenses, no mitigation, no escape from the assertion of power and the rigorous repressiveness of their parents. The self-enclosed household thus provided a setting that augmented the goals and methods of nurture and of discipline characteristic of evangelical families.

For many evangelicals, migration often served as an initial step in the process of cutting ties to other people and places, and the experience of being uprooted, or removing from one place to another, emerges as a factor of considerable importance in the early lives of many individuals throughout the seventeenth and eighteenth centuries. A restless moving about from village to village characterized the lives of thousands of people both in England and in the colonies, so that there was nothing unusual about migration. Many children would grow up with memories of moving from one place to another, and sometimes to several new communities before resettling.[7]

John Dane, who immigrated from England to Ipswich, Massachusetts, in the late 1630's, recalled that "In my infansy, and yet I veary well Remember it," his father removed "his habetation" from Berkhampstead to Stortford, where his mother and her children found themselves utterly alone, "not being among anie aquaintans" when their father returned briefly to their former place of residence. Later, he would journey restlessly about, thinking of himself as one who might "goe and work Jurney work" through "all the Counties in ingland, and so walk as a pilgrim up and doune on the earth," thus evoking the imagery of pilgrimage as the most appropriate description for his own rootless life in England.[8]

Migration and the isolation so often inherent in the experience of moving to new communities augmented the sense of being separated from neighbors and familiar places. Women, especially, were liable to be removed from their birthplaces and their own immediate families by virtue of marriage to men in other towns and places. Hannah Heaton, who became an ardent evangelical after the Great Awakening, found herself utterly isolated and lonely after moving from Long Island, where her parents lived and she had been reared, to Connecticut, where her husband lived. In 1751, she took her only child across the Sound to visit her relatives, whom she had not seen in eight years. For years she suffered because she felt herself to be totally alone, without support even from her husband or children, who scoffed at her and scorned her for her piety. At one point, she found herself "distracted" because, she said, "I am a stranger alone none to take me by the hand in soul matters and my dear poor husband knows not what I ail poor heart he has no other breath but threatening and slaughter against christs religion." The sense of anguish which she felt at being so far removed from her pious parents and old friends, living in the midst of strangers and hostile people, was partly due to the experience of isolation that arose from moving to a new community. The early Quakers also were notably mobile. Few seemed to stay in the places where they were born. Evangelicals did not always remove themselves to new residences, of course, but evangelicalism generally flourished when individuals and households were most separate and self-contained, whatever the reason might be.[9]

In part, the sense of isolation and distance from the surrounding community that might stem from the experiences of migration could also be fostered self-consciously under any circumstances, since evangelicals constantly sought to ensure that their own immediate households would remain separated from the surrounding world and as free as possible of pernicious influences. They always knew that corruption and sinful influences could come not only from the outside world but also from within the household itself, owing to the presence of outsiders—usually domestic servants—who worked and often lived within the family's dwelling place. John Wesley urged parents to control their children's diet rigorously, but warned them that "Your servants who will not understand your plan, will be continually giving little things to your children, and thereby undoing all your work. This you must prevent, if possible, by warning them when they first come into your house, and repeating the warning from time to time. If they *will* do it notwithstanding, you must turn them away. Better lose a good servant," he noted, than spoil a good child." In a series of letters on education written in the late eighteenth century, the Reverend John Witherspoon, a Presbyterian president of the college at Princeton, New Jersey, told parents: "You will find it extremely difficult to educate children properly, if the servants of the family do not conspire in it; and impossible, if they are inclined to hinder it. . . . It is a known and very common way for servants to insinuate themselves into the affections of children, by granting them such indulgencies as would be refused them by their parents, as well as concealing the faults which ought to be punished by parents." The presence of servants within the household posed a perpetual danger to the inculcation of values and the designs of parents for their children's lives. Constant vigilance over these subversive but indispensable outsiders was essential.[10]

Sometimes even members of the family could pose dangers for children and for parents, particularly when they resided within the household itself. Grandparents were a particular problem for evangelical parents, caught between the principle of obedience of younger generations to older generations and the necessity for shaping and disciplining their own children according to the dictates of their consciences. Over the centuries, writers cautioned parents about the possibility of a pernicious influence being exerted over children by overly indulgent grandparents. As the Reverend John Robinson, pastor to the Pilgrims in Holland before their departure for Plymouth in 1620, commented: "grandfathers are more affectionate towards their children's children, than to their immediates. . . . And hence it is, that children brought up with their grandfathers or grandmothers, seldom do well, but are usually corrupted by their too great indulgence." A century and a half later, John Wesley warned mothers that "Your mother, or your husband's mother, may live with you; and you will do well to shew her all possible respect. But let her on no account have the least share in the management of your children. She would undo all that you have done; she would give them their own will in all things. She would humour them to the destruction of their souls, if not their bodies too." "In four-score years," he added, "I have not met with one woman that knew how to manage grand-children. My own mother," the notable Susanna, "who governed her children so well, could never govern one grand-child. In every other point obey your mother. Give up your will to her's. But with regard to the management of your children, steadily keep the reins in your own hands." The message was clear: the presence of grandparents within the household or very close by could have a powerful effect upon the character of growing children, providing them with alternatives to the firm discipline and rigorous training insisted upon by evangelical parents, corrupting them with indulgence, and offering them alternative authorities and standards of behavior. Grandparents, like servants, could be dangerous. It would be best to keep them at a distance—either spatial or emotional—to ensure that children were not corrupted. Their presence within the household could only complicate and confuse relationships between parents and their own immediate offspring.[11]

The nucleated household provided an ideal setting for the authoritarian methods of child-rearing that were to be characteristic of evangelicals throughout these centuries. Within the self-enclosed households of evangelicals, children would grow up without other people present to

provide them with different voices of authority, or to shield them effectively from the full force of the parental control, influence, and discipline
that shaped their temperaments from infancy to adulthood. Growing up
in such households ensured that children would know from experience
that parental power and authority were absolute and unquestionable. And
within these enclosed households, the relationships binding parents and
children together could become very intense, creating the emotional bases
of the love and the fear that were to be characteristic of evangelicals, and
providing the setting for the development of both the psychological and
the behavioral foundations of their subsequent religious experiences and
temperaments.

Embryo-Angels or Infant Fiends?

ALTHOUGH THE EXPERIENCES of infancy have profound and enduring
consequences for the development of temperament and for the responses
of individuals to themselves, to other people, and to the world in which
they live, very little evidence has survived to tell us about the first year or
so of life for evangelical children during the seventeenth and eighteenth
centuries. Yet running throughout the sources is a persistent theme of
ambivalence toward infancy, which suggests that many evangelical parents experienced both a sense of love and affection for their infant children and a sense of distrust and fear as well. "They are a blessing great,
but dangerous," observed the Reverend John Robinson, minister to the
Pilgrims, who had seen the dangers of childbirth for both the mother and
the infant, as well as the subsequent dangers to health and growth that
could threaten children throughout their infancy and early years of life.
More than a century later, Samuel Davies, a prominent New Light Presbyterian preacher in Virginia, celebrated the birth of his third son with a
poem that captured the ambivalence of so many toward infancy. He observed the "little wound'rous miniature of man,/Form'd by unerring
Wisdom's perfect plan," who was to be a "candidate/For an important
everlasting state," and obviously hoped that his son would win "the prize
immense," no matter how "severe the strife." When he looked at his
infant son, seeing before him "Thou embryo-angel, or thou infant fiend,/
A being now begun, but ne'er to end," he had to acknowledge "What
boding fears a Father's heart torment" as he contemplated the life ahead
and the future destiny in the life to come of his newly born offspring.[12]

 The preoccupation of many evangelicals with the issue of infant
depravity and damnation suggests the strength of the negative side of

parental perceptions of infancy. This negative perception undoubtedly shaped the responses of many evangelical parents to their offspring from the outset, and may have encouraged some parents to establish an emotional distance between themselves and their children during the first months of life. Anne Bradstreet portrayed infancy and early childhood in the somber imagery of innate depravity: "Stained from birth with *Adams* sinfull fact,/Thence I began to sin as soon as act:/A perverse will, a love to what's forbid,/A serpents sting in pleasing face lay hid." Echoing Bradstreet's image of the serpent's sting hidden "in pleasing face," an anonymous writer in a staunchly Calvinist magazine acknowledged early in the nineteenth century that "we often hear parents calling their children 'harmless creatures,' 'pretty innocent,' and other fond and endearing names which *figuratively* denote the same thing, such as 'little doves,' 'harmless birds,' with a thousand other equivalent appellations"; but, he confessed, "I never hear them without trembling, lest those, their unfledged offspring, should prove birds of evil omen, if not birds of prey." This grim and mistrustful imagery was pursued by a dire prediction, a fantasy which revealed the profoundly fearful perception of infancy that shaped the responses of this particular writer toward childhood generally: "Were infants from their birth endowed with strength and activity like the young of some animals, the most fatal effects would follow." Readers were warned that infants, were they to be given "the strength of manhood," would not hesitate "to take your life, were you the cause of his exasperation." Only "his impotence, and not his gratitude, will prove his own restraint, and your protection." Infants indeed seemed to be dangerous little animals, bent upon the aggrandizement of their own wills and their own gratification. All they lacked was power to make themselves truly frightening. For this particular evangelical, there was nothing innocent, charming, or appealing about these small creatures. When asked the question "from what can such a disposition proceed," the answer to any Calvinist was clear—"the most deep-rooted depravity."[13]

Although the theme of mistrust, fear; and perhaps even more often indifference toward infants persists through the centuries in the attitudes of evangelicals, another response toward infants and very small children is evident as well—one of pleasure and appreciation. Anne Bradstreet, as if unconsciously confirming the warnings about the shifting sensibilities of grandparents toward grandchildren, felt very differently about her infant grandchildren than she evidently felt about her immediate progeny. When her granddaughter, Elizabeth Bradstreet, died in August 1665 at the age of a year and a half, she wrote: "Farewel dear babe, my hearts too much content,/Farewel sweet babe, the pleasure of mine eye,/Farewel fair flower that for a space was lent,/Then ta'en away unto Eternity./Blest babe why should I once bewail thy fate,/Or sigh the days so soon were terminate;/Sith thou art setled in an Everlasting state." Four years later, she lost two more grandchildren—Anne, who died at three years and seven months, and Simon, who died at one month, one day. Of Anne she wrote, "More fool then I to look on that was lent,/As if mine own, when thus impermanent./Farewel dear child, thou ne're shall come to me,/But yet a while, and I shall go to thee;/Mean time my throbbing heart's chear'd up with this/Thou with thy Saviour art in endless bliss." And of Simon, dead so soon after his birth: "No sooner come, but gone, and fal'n asleep,/Acquaintance short, yet parting caus'd us weep,/Three flours, two scarcely blown, the last i'th' bud,/Cropt by th' Almighties hand; yet is he good,/ . . . Go pretty babe, go rest with Sisters twain/Among the blest in endless joyes remain." In these lamentations, Bradstreet's imagery is of beauty, innocence, and flowers; her assumption clearly is that these infant children are already in Heaven with their Saviour, gracious even in their earliest days on earth.[14]

The themes of parental affection and a sense of the innocence of infancy appear in the recollections and writings of evangelicals with notable persistence. While trying to escape from England to New England, the Reverend Thomas Shepard found that, as soon as he and his family began their voyage, "my first-born child, very precious to my soul and dearly beloved of me, was smitten with sickness," and he felt that the Lord had struck at him because of his "immoderate love of creatures and of my child especially." Ten years later, another son by his second wife died at sixteen weeks of age, going, Shepard said, "To the bosom of rest to him who gave it, which was no small affliction and heartbreaking to me that I should provoke the Lord to strike at my innocent children for my sake."[15]

Cotton Mather also looked upon his infant children as innocent and lovely. His daughter Hannah was a "very hearty and comely Infant" at birth; his first son, Increase, was "an hearty, lusty and comely Infant," his "only and lovely Son"; his second son, Samuel, "a lovely and a lusty Infant"; his third son, also Samuel, was "to appearance, an hearty and an handsome Infant" at birth. When his eleven-month-old daughter lay sick, Mather noted that "My pretty little Daughter *Jerusha*, on whom we have been so fond, as to make me fear whether we should not lose her, now lies very sick of a Fever. I would endeavour exceedingly to glorify God, by making a Sacrifice of the lovely Child." In 1693, his wife delivered a son who died soon after birth "unbaptised." Yet Mather preached the child's funeral sermon, buried his son, "and on one of the Grave-stones, I write only that Epitaph, RESERVED FOR A GLORIOUS RESURRECTION." Even an unbaptized child thus was presumed innocent by Mather, who seemed confident that his son in due time would be among the saints in Heaven. Yet Mather also felt intensely the inevitable sinfulness of infants and small children. In May 1709, as his young son Samuel lay in danger of imminent death, Mather "bewayled the Sins, by which the Life of my

Children, and of this desireable Child," had been "forfeited." He "resigned the Child unto the Lord; submitted unto whatever Disposal, the infinite Sovereignty and Faithfulness of God, should make of the Child," and then "declared, that I did not aske, that the Child might live, and be a Rebel and a Traitor to God; no, I had rather have him dy in his Infancy, than live in cursed and lothsome Wickedness." Thus the ambiguities of response emerged once again. However innocent and "desireable" his infant children might seem, they were still subject to the sin and depravity that merited death.[16]

The innocence of infancy and the presumption that infants went to Heaven immediately upon their deaths thus shaped the attitudes of many evangelicals, even though the predominant views—of mistrust and depravity—were current. When the brilliant evangelical preacher Jonathan Edwards warned against the tendency to view children as innocent, he confirmed that even evangelical parents often felt too benignly toward their own offspring:

> What has more especially given offense to many, and raised a loud cry against some preachers, as though their conduct were intolerable, is their frighting poor innocent children with talk of hell fire and eternal damnation. But if those that complain so loudly of this really believe what is the general profession of the country, viz. that all are by nature the children of wrath and heirs of hell; and that every one that has not been born again, whether he be young or old, is exposed every moment to eternal destruction, under the wrath of Almighty God; I say, if they really believe this, then such a complaint and cry as this be[t]rays a great deal of weakness and inconsideration. *As innocent as children seem to be to us*, yet if they are out of Christ, they are not so in God's sight, but are young vipers, and are infinitely more hateful than vipers, and are in a most miserable condition, as well as grown persons; and they are naturally very senseless and stupid . . . and need much to awaken them. Why should we conceal the truth from them?[17]

But the truths that emerged from the feelings of many evangelical parents did not always conform to the truths that were taught by the Bible and the doctrines they also believed and acted upon. They both loved their infant children and feared for their souls. Indeed, it was because they did love their children so much that they cared so intensely about what became of them not only in this life but, even more, in the life to come. Infancy was only the beginning of a long process of training and experience which ultimately could result in regeneration and the second birth.

Broken Wills:
Discipline and Parental Control

EVANGELICAL FAMILY GOVERNMENT was authoritarian and rigorously repressive. Parental authority was absolute, and exercised without check or control by anyone else within the household. Obedience and submission were the only acceptable responses for children. Over and over again, from the early seventeenth century through at least the early nineteenth century, the same themes appear in the writings of evangelicals about discipline and family government.[18]

The domestic rule of the Reverend Jonathan Edwards, the most influential evangelical theologian in eighteenth-century America, was observed by Samuel Hopkins, one of Edwards's students and his most ardent follower, who wrote in his biography of Edwards: "He was careful and thorough in the government of his children; and, as a consequence of this, they reverenced, esteemed, and loved him. He took special care to begin his government of them in season. When they first discovered any considerable degree of will and stubbornness, he would attend to them till he had thoroughly subdued them and brought them to submit. And such prudent thorough discipline, exercised with the greatest calmness, and commonly without striking a blow, being repeated once or twice, was generally sufficient for that child; and effectually established his parental authority, and produced a cheerful obedience ever after."[19]

Another perspective upon family government within the Edwards household emerges from the description of Sarah Edwards's role in the family contained in their grandson's biography, written early in the nineteenth century:

> She had an excellent way of governing her children; she knew how to make them regard and obey her cheerfully, without loud angry words, much less heavy blows. She seldom punished them; and in speaking to them, used gentle and pleasant words. If any correction was necessary, she did not administer it in a passion; and when she had occasion to reprove and rebuke, she would do it in few words, without warmth and noise, and with all calmness and gentleness of mind. In her directions and reproofs in matters of importance, she would address herself to the reason of her children, that they might not only know her inclination and will, but at the same time be convinced of the reasonableness of it. She had need to speak but once; she was cheerfully obeyed: murmur-

ing and answering again, were not known among them. . . . Her system of discipline, was begun at a very early age, and it was her rule, to resist the first, as well as every subsequent exhibition of temper or disobedience in the child, however young, until its will was brought into submission to the will of its parents: wisely reflecting, that until a child will obey his parents, he can never be brought to obey God.[20]

Very similar advice was offered to readers of the *Panoplist* by an anonymous author in 1814, whose views on "the proper government of children" echoed earlier generations of evangelicals. In order "to insure, as far as may be, the proper behavior of his children, let every parent make it his inflexible determination, that he will be obeyed—*invariably* obeyed." "An uniform adherence to this resolution," the author assured his readers, "will save him from a multitude of difficulties, and produce incalculable good. The sum and substance of good government is to *be obeyed*; not now and then, when the humor suits; but always, and *invariably.* . . . The connexion between *your* command, and *his* obedience, should be as certain as that between cause and effect; the one should be the unfailing consequent of the other." The authoritarianism of evangelical family government—unquestioning obedience on the part of the ruled—did not imply that parents had to "play the tyrant in order to enforce their [children's] obedience," however. "Habitual obedience has no need of such severities; it is yielded readily, and as a matter of course. Nothing short of very obstinate and habitual disobedience can bring matters to such extremities." As was clear to other evangelicals also, "Parents, who govern well, never suffer their children to arrive at such a pass, that nothing short of torture will coerce them. They commence the business in season, and enforce obedience by gentler methods; they master the disease at its first appearance, and so avoid the necessity of desperate remedies."[21]

The consequences of disobedience were set forth with vivid specificity by Jonathan Edwards: "And let children obey their parents, and yield to their instructions, and submit to their orders, as they would inherit a blessing, and not a curse. For we have reason to think, from many things in the word of God, that nothing has a greater tendency to bring a curse on persons, in this world, and on all their temporal concerns, than an undutiful, unsubmissive, disorderly behaviour in children towards their parents." Disobedience would be punished in this world; but its ultimate consequence, as Edwards and others knew, was nothing less than eternal damnation.[22]

Jonathan Edwards's message was scarcely novel, yet the anxiety underlying his words reveals the central fear lurking beneath his admonitions and threats: that family government would fail, authority not be maintained, and disobedience flourish. The perpetual threat to absolutism is moderation; and the tendency always is present for parents to lessen the rigors of their discipline and the thoroughness of their oversight of the daily lives of their children. Edwards knew this—and so did all evangelicals who maintained the necessity for strict authority and unhesitating obedience within their families. This fear, which produced a constant tension within evangelicals who sought to adhere to the rigorous authoritarianism essential for family government in spite of constant temptation to act otherwise out of deep love for their children, was evident in a ministerial injunction (very possibly by Jonathan Edwards himself) written during a period of unparalleled mortality among the children of New England: "May we not think the Design of God in the Great Sickness and Mortality there has been among Children to be a Testimony against our Immoderate Love to, and Doating upon our Children, and sinful neglect of our Duty towards them in Educating them in the Ways of Virtue and Religion, Bringing them up for God, and Exercising the Authority we have over them to Restrain them from Sin and Wickedness . . . the Sinfull Tenderness, and Indulgence of Parents, is the Ruin of Many Children."[23]

Tenderness and indulgence were the Achilles heel of discipline in evangelical families. Evangelicals constantly had to guard themselves against these subversive inner tendencies—which would overthrow all order and authority within families. Evangelicalism depended for its success upon an unrelenting defense against these perpetual threats. There could be no relaxation, no toleration, no accommodation. Salvation itself depended upon their ability to maintain family discipline, authority, and order, uncompromised by too much tenderness.

From the earliest months of life through the subsequent years of childhood, evangelical parents acted upon the assumption that parental authority was unlimited and incontrovertible. Parents systematically imposed their own wills upon their infants and small children without interference from servants or grandparents. Total power of parents, total dependency and obedience of children—this was the persistent polarity. The parent-child relationship thus was shaped by a stark and sharply defined gulf between the generations—an enormous and unbridgeable distance between parents and children, which implicitly denied to children any rights to their own desires, needs, or wishes that might be at odds with those designed for them by their parents.

As John Witherspoon noted of the "successful education of children," it was imperative "that husband and wife ought to be entirely one upon this subject, not only agreed as to the end, but as to the means to be used, and the plan to be followed in order to attain it." "When this is the case," he said, "every thing is enforced by a double authority, and recommended by a double example; but when it is otherwise, the pains taken are commonly more than lost, not being able to do any good, and certainly producing very much evil." The central point of Witherspoon's advice to like-minded parents was that they must "establish, as soon as possible, an entire and absolute authority" over their children. "I would have it early," he said, "that it may be absolute, and absolute, that it may not be severe. If parents are too long in beginning to exert their authority, they will find the task very difficult. Children, habituated to indulgence for a few of their first years, are exceedingly impatient of restraint; and if they happen to be of stiff or obstinate tempers, can hardly be brought to an entire, at least to a quiet and placid submission; whereas, if they are taken in time, there is hardly any temper but what may be made to yield, and by early habit the subjection becomes quite easy to themselves."[24]

With remarkable consistency and persistence, evangelicals through the centuries insisted that parents must control and break the emerging will of children in the first few years of life. The central issue, as they perceived it, was this: the autonomous will and self-assertiveness of the child must be reduced to impotency, be utterly suppressed and contained, or the child ultimately would be damned for eternity. "Break their wills," urged John Wesley, "that you may save their souls." This simple injunction, reiterated again and again, was the keystone to the evangelical method of child-rearing. Everything in the subsequent lives of these children depended upon the success or failure of this policy of unrelenting repression, which shaped their personalities and provided the foundations in experience early in life of the denial of self and self-will that formed the innermost core of evangelical religious experience and belief. To understand evangelicals and evangelicalism, it is imperative to understand the goals and practices of discipline that dominated the earliest years for the children of evangelical families. As the Reverend George Whitefield observed, when only twenty-three years old himself, if parents "would but have resolution to break their [children's] wills thoroughly when young, the work of conversion would be much easier, and they would not be so troubled with perverse children when they are old."[25]

The imposition of parental wills, and the disciplining of children's wills, undoubtedly began very early in life, often within the first year, although very few sources survive to describe precisely how such control might have been exerted. Two mothers, one English and the other American, one the mother of evangelicals and the other the daughter of an evangelical, did leave a few observations about their practices during the infancies of their children. Esther Edwards Burr, a daughter of Jonathan Edwards and the wife of the Reverend Aaron Burr, an early president of Princeton, wrote in 1754 to her intimate friend Sarah Prince (daughter of the Reverend Thomas Prince of Boston) that "I had almost forgot to tell you that I have begun to govourn Sally [her firstborn child]. She has been Whip'd once on *Old Adams* account, and she knows the differance between a Smile and a frown as well as I do. When She has done any thing that She Suspects is wrong, will look with concern to See what Mamma Says, and if I only knit my brow, She will cry till I Smile, and altho She is not quite Ten months old, yet when She knows so much, I think tis time

She should be taught." Such discipline and early government of an infant was not always easy for a parent, essential though it was deemed to be. As Esther Burr added, "none but a parent can conceive how hard it is to chastise your *own most tender self*, I confess I never had a right idea of the mothers heart at such a time before, I did it my Self too, and it did her a vast deal of good. If you was here I would tell you the effect it had on her." For all her affection for her child, she was too much the daughter of an evangelical Christian not to know that a beginning must be made early, in order to subdue sin and self-will in the child while still in the cradle.[26]

Similarly, Susanna Wesley recalled her own methodical ways of nursing, rocking, and disciplining her children from their infancy—but with none of the tenderness and affection evident in the comments by Esther Burr:

> The children were always put into a regular method of living, in such things as they were capable of, from their birth; as in dressing and undressing, changing their linen, etc. The first quarter commonly passes in sleep. After that they were, if possible, laid into their cradle awake, and rocked to sleep, and so they were kept rocking till it was time for them to awake. This was done to bring them to a regular course of sleeping, which at first was three hours in the morning and three in the afternoon: afterwards two hours, till they needed none at all. When turned a year old (and some before) they were taught to fear the rod and to cry softly, by which means they escaped abundance of correction which they might otherwise have had: and that most odious noise of the crying of children was rarely heard in the house, but the family usually lived in as much quietness as if there had not been a child among them.

From the mother of the founder of "Methodism," these words leap off the page as testimony to the carefully controlled pattern of daily life governing the infants in her family from the day of their birth. "A regular method of living," "a regular course of sleeping" require no imagination to infer the imposition of parental goals. Every aspect of the infant's life was controlled by the mother, or by the servants who did her bidding. Strictly maintained schedules of sleep and feeding assured that the infant's needs and desires would be shaped into conformity with the intentions and plans of the parents. In the Wesley household, at least, there was to be no such thing as demand feeding or uninterrupted sleep. The shaping and breaking of the child's will had begun during the first months of life.[27]

Like Susanna Wesley and Esther Edwards Burr before him, John Witherspoon knew that the process of subjugation had to begin as early as possible, starting in infancy. "I would therefore recommend to every parent to begin the establishment of authority much more early than is commonly supposed to be possible; that is to say, from about the age of eight or nine months." "You will perhaps smile at this," he acknowledged, "but I do assure you from experience, that by setting about it with prudence, deliberation, and attention, it may be in a manner completed by the age of twelve or fourteen months."[28]

Nevertheless, successive generations of evangelicals knew that breaking a child's will, even in infancy, was not easy. The imagery of repression and conquest which persists through the centuries in evangelical discussions of early childhood testifies to the difficulties and the constant challenges posed by the necessity of breaking children's wills. As John Wesley observed, "A wise parent . . . should begin to break their [children's] will, the first moment it appears. In the whole art of Christian education there is nothing more important than this. The will of a parent is to a little child in the place of the will of God. Therefore, studiously teach them to submit to this while they are children, that they may be ready to submit to his will, when they are men." "But in order to carry this point," he acknowledged, "you will need incredible firmness and resolution. For after you have once begun, you must never more give way."[29]

Evangelical parents were engaged in war with their children, a war which could end only with total victory by the parents and unconditional surrender by the child. The imagery of their warfare is the language of conflict, of conquest, of breaking, crushing, subduing, destroying; the language of power unchecked and of resistance quelled. Might and right—the prerogatives of parenthood—faced defiance and rebellious willfulness—the characteristics of the unbroken child. Generation after generation of evangelical parents wrote about their battles with the pride and contentment that sprang from success. Their children, conquered, submitted and forgot their own early efforts at independence and selfhood.

Early in the seventeenth century, John Robinson observed that "surely there is in all children, though not alike, a stubbornness, and stoutness of mind arising from natural pride, which must, in the first place, be broken and beaten down; that so the foundation of their education being laid in humility and tractableness, other virtues may, in their time, be built thereon. This fruit of natural corruption and root of actual rebellion both against God and man must be destroyed, and no manner nourished, except we will plant a nursery of contempt of all good persons and things, and of obstinacy therein." In order to do this, he said that parents must see to it that "children's wills and wilfulness be restrained and repressed, and that, in time."[30]

A century later, the same assumptions and similar imagery pervade the advice offered by Susanna Wesley to her son John for rearing children as she herself had raised her own:

In order to form the minds of children, the first thing to be done
is to conquer their will and bring them to an obedient temper. To
inform the understanding is a work of time, and must with children proceed by slow degrees, as they are able to bear it; but the
subjecting the will is a thing that must be done at once, and the
sooner the better; for by neglecting timely correction they will
contract a stubbornness and obstinacy which are hardly ever after
conquered, and never without using such severity as would be as
painful to me as to the child. . . . When a child is corrected it must
be conquered, and this will be no hard matter to do, if it be not
grown headstrong by too much indulgence. And when the will of
a child is totally subdued, and it is brought to revere and stand in
awe of the parents, then a great many childish follies and inad-
vertencies may be passed by. Some should be overlooked and
taken no notice of, and others mildly reproved; but no wilful
transgression ought ever to be forgiven children without chastisement less or more, as the nature of circumstances of the case may
require. I insist on the conquering of the will of children betimes,
because this is the only strong and rational foundation of a religious education, without which both precept and example will be
ineffectual. But when this is thoroughly done, then a child is
capable of being governed by the reason and piety of its parents
till its own understanding comes to maturity, and the principles
of religion have taken root in the mind.[31]

What is most striking about successive generations of evangelicals is
their exceptionally fierce response to the emergent will of their children,
and their insistence, over and over again, that parents must break the
child's will in order to make the child obedient. The injunction is repeated
time and again—but remarkably little was ever said to parents about *how*
the child's will might be conquered. To be sure, Susanna Wesley suggested the method of perpetually denying the child's wishes in everything
whatsoever if they conflicted with the goals of the parents. And many
writers seemed to feel that their children's wills might be broken without
the use of too much physical punishment or beatings with the infamous
rod. The Edwardses, seemingly, chose to conquer their children's wills
without employing force; but at some point, fear of spanking or the rod
may have played a role in the consciousness of their infants, as in the
case of Esther Edwards Burr's daughter. Yet the sources are curiously
silent about the actual practices by parents in their conquest of their
children's wills. What survives is mostly a literature of advice and injunctions, which testifies to the conviction and intention but only occasionally
hints at the methodology of conquest.

Recently, however, one remarkably explicit firsthand account of the
breaking of a child's will was discovered in the *American Baptist Maga-*

zine of 1831, which printed an anonymous account by the Reverend Francis Wayland, an early president of Brown University and a Baptist minister, of the experience of conquering the will of his fifteen-month-old son, Heman Lincoln Wayland, who was born in 1830. President Wayland's father also was a Baptist minister, who was converted during the second Great Awakening at the turn of the nineteenth century. Wayland recalled that "My father was a man of very fixed ideas of family government," who "required of his children implicit obedience. I have no recollection of ever disobeying him deliberately but once." Like most other evangelical parents through the centuries, Wayland was convinced that "The *right* of the parent is to *command*; the *duty* of the child is to *obey*. Authority belongs to the one, submission to the other." He was explicit in his view that "In infancy the control of the parent over the child is absolute; that is, it is exercised without any due respect to the wishes of the child." These were Wayland's public views, published in his influential college textbook *The Elements of Moral Science*, which appeared four years after his account of his battle with his own small son.[32]

After reading Wayland's anonymous report, one can have little doubt that his general principles were grounded in personal experience—or confirmed by it. The account itself deserves close attention:

> My youngest child is an infant about 15 months old, with about the intelligence common to children of that age. It has for some months been evident, that he was more than usually self willed, but the several attempts to subdue him, had been thus far relinquished, from the fear that he did not fully understand what was said to him. It so happened, however, that I had never been brought into collision with him myself, until the incident occurred which I am about to relate. Still I had seen enough to convince me of the necessity of subduing his temper, and resolved to seize upon the first favorable opportunity which presented, for settling the question of authority between us.
>
> On Friday last before breakfast, on my taking him from his nurse, he began to cry violently. I determined to hold him in my arms until he ceased. As he had a piece of bread in his hand, I took it away, intending to give it to him again after he became quiet. In a few minutes he ceased, but when I offered him the bread he threw it away, although he was very hungry. He had, in fact, taken no nourishment except a cup of milk since 5 o'clock on the preceding afternoon. I considered this a fit opportunity for attempting to subdue his temper, and resolved to embrace it. I thought it necessary to change his disposition, so that he would receive the bread *from me*, and also be so reconciled to me that he would *voluntarily* come to me. The task I found more difficult than I had expected.

I put him into a room by himself, and desired that no one should speak to him, or give him any food or drink whatever. This was about 8 o'clock in the morning. I visited him every hour or two during the day, and spoke to him in the kindest tones, offering him the bread and putting out my arms to take him. But throughout the whole day he remained inflexibly obstinate. He did not yield a hair's breadth. I put a cup of water to his mouth, and he drank it greedily, but would not touch it with his hands. If a crumb was dropped on the floor he would eat it, but if I offered him the piece of bread, he would push it away from him. When I told him to come to me, he would turn away and cry bitterly. He went to bed supperless. It was now twenty-four hours since he had eaten anything.

He woke the next morning in the same state. He would take nothing that I offered him, and shunned all my offers of kindness. He was now truly an object of pity. He had fasted thirty-six hours. His eyes were wan and sunken. His breath hot and feverish, and his voice feeble and wailing. Yet he remained obstinate. He continued thus, till 10 o'clock, A.M. when hunger overcame him, and he took from me a piece of bread, to which I added a cup of milk, and hoped that the labor was at last accomplished.

In this however I had not rightly judged. He ate his bread greedily, but when I offered to take him, he still refused as pertinaciously as ever. I therefore ceased feeding him, and recommenced my course of discipline.

He was again left alone in his crib, and I visited him as before, at intervals. About one o'clock, Saturday, I found that he began to view his condition in its true light. The tones of his voice in weeping were graver and less passionate, and had more the appearance of one bemoaning himself. Yet when I went to him he still remained obstinate. You could clearly see in him the abortive efforts of the will. Frequently he would raise his hands an inch or two, and then suddenly put them down again. He would look at me, and then hiding his face in the bedclothes weep most sorrowfully. During all this time I was addressing him, whenever I came into the room, with invariable kindness. But my kindness met with no suitable return. All I required of him was, that he should come to me. This he would not do, and he began now to see that it had become a serious business. Hence his distress increased. He would not submit, and he found that there was no help without it. It was truly surprising to behold how much agony so young a being could inflict upon himself.

About three o'clock I visited him again. He continued in the state I have described. I was going away, and had opened the door, when I thought that he looked somewhat softened, and returning, put out my hands, again requesting him to come to me. To my joy, and I hope gratitude, he rose up and put forth his hands immediately. The agony was over. He was completely subdued. He repeatedly kissed me, and would do so whenever I commanded. He would kiss any one when I directed him, so full of love was he to all the family. Indeed, so entirely and instantaneously were his feelings towards me changed, that he preferred me now to any of the family. As he had never done before, he moaned after me when he saw that I was going away.

Since this event several slight revivals of his former temper have occurred, but they have all been easily subdued. His disposition is, as it never has been before, mild and obedient. He is kind and affectionate, and evidently much happier than he was, when he was determined to have his own way. I hope and pray that it may prove that an effect has been produced upon him for life.*

Wayland's hope and prayers were to be fulfilled, for his successfully subdued young son grew up to be affectionate, dutiful, and always obedient. He proved a truly evangelical Christian, who experienced conversion in college, became a Baptist minister like his father, and also a teacher and college president. The "effect" of this early conquest and total subjugation of Heman's will evidently was "produced upon him for life."

Yet Wayland was not content merely to describe the details of his successful battle of wills with his infant son. He also felt compelled to justify it to his readers, as the tone of some of his subsequent remarks indicates. "It will be remembered," presumably by his audience, "that I offered my child food, and he would not take it. I offered to receive him to my arms, if he would renounce his hostility to me, and evince it by simply putting forth his arms to come to me." "I would not force him to come," he said, "nor would I treat him with favor until he submitted." The fundamental assumption governing Wayland's actions, however, is revealed by his simple assertion that "I was right and he was wrong." Parents always are right, children always are in the wrong. Authority is

---

* "A Case of Conviction," *The America.ı Baptist Magazine*, XI (1831), pp. 296–8. The entire account is reprinted in William G. McLoughlin, "Evangelical Child-Rearing in the Age of Jackson," *Journal of Social History*, 9 (1975), Appendix 1, pp. 35–9. I am most grateful to Professor McLoughlin for bringing this document to my attention and for his generosity in permitting me to read the manuscript for his important essay on Francis Wayland and child-rearing in the early nineteenth century prior to its publication. I find McLoughlin's observations (p. 21) about the relevance of the concept of "reaction formation" to be significant for evangelicals generally. For a psychological analysis of Wayland's account, see the comments by Lewis P. Lipsitt, Appendix 2, pp. 40–3. For other psychological analyses of this early emergence of a sense of autonomy and self-will, see: Erik Erikson, *Childhood and Society*, 2nd ed. (New York, 1963), pp. 76–81, 222–4; David Hunt, *Parents and Children in History* (New York, 1970), ch. 7; John Demos, *A Little Commonwealth* (New York, 1970), p. 134–9.

absolute and must be obeyed without reservation or questioning. Besides, the father is kindly and the child is hostile—so that clearly the infant is at fault in persisting in asserting his own individual will in opposition to the will of his parent. After all, as Wayland said, his son "might at any moment have put an end to the controversy. He was therefore inflicting all this misery voluntarily upon himself." Yet still Wayland seems to have felt further need for self-justification for his "controversy" with his fifteen-month-old child. "The terms I offered him were perfectly kind," he noted. "I was willing to pass by all that he had done," beginning with throwing away a piece of bread, "if he would only evince a right disposition." Upon the ability of his son to "evince a right disposition" turned the entire battle, of course, which is why Wayland said that "I could offer him no other terms." Total victory, complete surrender; these alone would suffice. "To have received him on any other terms would have been to allow that his will was to be my rule of action, and whenever he set out to have his own way, I must have obliged my whole family to have conformed in all their arrangements to his wishes. He must have been made the centre of the whole system. A whole family under the control of a child 15 months old! How unjust this would have been to all the rest, is evident."

Echoes of the tyrannical infant envisaged by the anonymous writer of the *Panoplist* essay reverberate through Wayland's self-justification. Certainly he was confident that his son "did not *know enough* to be able to secure his own happiness. Had I let him do as he pleased, he would have burnt and scalded himself a dozen times a day, and would very soon have destroyed his life." Without total control, it seemed, there could be only total license and self-destruction. There were no gradations between these domestic extremes. Being persuaded of this dire prospect, and "Seeking, therefore, his good, and the good of the family," Wayland felt that "I could do nothing else than I did. Kindness to him as much as to them, taught me not to yield to him on any other terms than a change of disposition." This was the key—"a change of disposition"—behind Wayland's and every other evangelical's systematic efforts to break the wills of their children. As Wayland noted, "by yielding to me, my whole family has been restored to order; he is happier by far than he has ever been before, and he is acquiring a disposition which will fit him for the wide world, which, if he lives, he will enter upon."[33]

This expectation, which Wayland shared with virtually every evangelical parent, justified the rigors of repression. Only because evangelical parents like Wayland believed that what they did to their children would have permanent consequences could they satisfy themselves about the righteousness of parental discipline. Breaking the child's will was the crucial step toward a lifelong experience of submission and self-denial.

Submission extended beyond the initial confrontations of infancy and very early childhood to dominate the lives of children throughout the years in which they remained under their parents' roof and tutelage. Parental discipline and the constant control exercised by parents over their children's lives never ceased entirely. As John Wesley noted, not even marriage "cancels or lessens the general obligation of filial duty," nor did obedience cease or lessen "by our having lived one-and-twenty years." "I never understood it so in my case," he acknowledged. "When I had lived upwards of thirty years, I looked upon myself to stand just in the same relation to my father as I did when I was ten years old. And when I was between forty and fifty, I judged myself full as much obliged to obey my mother in everything lawful, as I did when I was in my leading-strings"—from the time he could first walk. Obedience, first securely obtained by the successful conquest of the child's will, remained the central preoccupation of both parents and children in evangelical families.[34]

Regular Methods of Living: External Discipline in Evangelical Households

BREAKING CHILDREN'S WILLS was vital for discipline within evangelical families. But it was only the first stage in the imposition of rigorous parental control over the lives of children as they emerged from infancy and passed through childhood. From the time children could walk and talk, their outward lives were subject to daily discipline in diet, dress, and manner. Outward appearances counted even when parents acknowledged that godliness was not subject to external confirmation. But their actions implied over the generations that they were intent upon seeing that the outward lives of their children bore witness to the discipline and the self-denial which marked the true Christian. What one ate, how much one ate, how one dressed, and how one behaved mattered profoundly to evangelical parents, who sought to govern the outer lives of their children according to the values which dominated their inner lives as well.

Restrictions upon food and habits of eating probably began in infancy for many evangelicals, but little information has survived about the first year or so of life. The more general attitudes toward food as an agency of discipline, however, are apparent in some of the writings by evangelicals. John Robinson recommended that parents inure their children "from the first, to such a meanness in all things, as may rather pluck

them down, than lift them up: as by plain, and homely diet, and apparel."
Susanna Wesley, too, knew the importance of food in shaping the character of her children, and used it as a basic weapon in her armory of
domestic discipline. Her description of her method of feeding her own
children merits close attention:

> As soon as they were grown pretty strong they were confined to
> three meals a day. At dinner their little table and chairs were set
> by ours, where they could be overlooked; and they were suffered
> to eat and drink [small beer] as much as they would, but not to
> call for anything. If they wanted aught they used to whisper to
> the maid that attended them, who came and spake to me; and as
> soon as they could handle a knife and fork they were set to our
> table. They were never suffered to choose their meat, but always
> made to eat such things as were provided for the family. Morn-
> ings they always had spoon meat; sometimes at nights. But
> whatever they had, they were never permitted at those meals to
> eat of more than one thing, and of that sparingly enough.
> Drinking or eating between meals was never allowed, unless
> in case of sickness, which seldom happened. Nor were they
> suffered to go into the kitchen to ask anything of the servants
> when they were at meat: if it was known they did so, they were
> certainly beat, and the servants severely reprimanded. . . .
>
> They were so constantly used to eat and drink what was
> given them, that when any of them was ill there was no diffi-
> culty in making them take the most unpleasant medicine; for
> they durst not refuse it, though some of them would presently
> throw it up. This I mention to show that a person may be taught
> to take anything, though it be never so much against his stomach.

Her words tell it all: "confined," "suffered," "never permitted,"
"never allowed," "made to eat"—the language of control and conscious
repressiveness. Food was a focal point for discipline in the Wesley household, as it undoubtedly was in other evangelical households as well.
The advice of her son, in later years, simply confirmed her own practices.
Noting that "Next to self-will and pride, the most fatal disease with
which we are born, is *love of the world*," John Wesley observed disapprovingly that many parents "cherish 'the desire of the flesh,' . . . by
studying to *enlarge the pleasure of tasting* in their children to the
uttermost: not only giving them before they are weaned other things
besides milk, the natural food of children, but giving them both before
and after, any sort of meat or drink that they will take." To take pleasure
in eating was an invitation to lust and unbridled sensuality in general.
To discipline the palate and to govern the stomach, therefore, were
important elements in shaping character. That was why evangelicals

assumed that food was too important to permit children from infancy on to determine their own wishes and needs in this respect.[35]

Clothing, too, was an indispensable focal point of discipline in evangelical households. Quakers, of course, beginning in the first generation of the mid-seventeenth century and persisting for generations thereafter, were particularly concerned about dress, as their plain style testified over the years. But the same was true of other evangelicals as well. As John Wesley said, "Whenever . . . I see the fine-dressed daughter of a plain-dressed mother, I see at once the mother is defective either in knowledge or religion." Since clothing provided visible clues to the inner person, rich and costly clothing could only mean one thing. "I am pained continually," Wesley said again, "at seeing religious parents suffer their children to run into the same folly of dress, as if they had no religion at all." "In God's name," he implored parents, "why do you suffer them to vary a hair's breadth from *your* example? 'Why, they will do it.' They will! Whose fault is that? Why did not you break their will from their infancy? At least, do it now; better late than never. It should have been done before they were two years old: It may be done at eight or ten, though with far more difficulty." Christian parents, he insisted, must "Instil diligently into them the love of plain dress, and hatred of finery. Show them the reason of your own plainness of dress, and show it is equally reasonable for them. Bid defiance to indolence, to cowardice, to foolish fondness, and, at all events, carry your point; if you love their souls, make and keep them just as plain as yourselves." Wesley was not alone in his conviction that plain dress was an indispensable outward sign of inner grace, for the Edwardses also dressed simply. After a visit with the Edwards family in Northampton, Massachusetts, in 1740, George Whitefield noted in his journal that "Their children were not dressed in silks and satins, but plain, as become the children of those who, in all things, ought to be examples of Christian simplicity."[36]

While simplicity was considered to be indispensable to evangelicals, the actual clothing which their children wore was taken so much for granted by parents that the issue was rarely discussed in letters or diaries. Yet for the purposes of both discipline and the formation of temperament, the clothing of infants and small children was actually of profound importance. Throughout the Anglo-American world, probably at all levels of society from the poorest to the wealthiest, children were dressed in the clothing of females regardless of their actual gender. From infancy until about the age of six, both girls and boys wore petticoats or gowns, thus appearing almost indistinguishable on the basis of their clothing until boys were breeched, when they abruptly shifted to the clothes characteristic of young and adult men, giving up forever the feminine dresses and gowns they had worn throughout the formative years of childhood. The portraits of children from genteel and wealthy families which survive from the seventeenth and the eighteenth centuries (discussed on pp. 282–6) provide clear evidence of this practice among the upper ranks of early American society—a practice that continued throughout at least the first half of the nineteenth century and, in some families until the early twentieth century. There is no reason to assume that evangelicals and others did not share these practices, for rural families with large numbers of children would have found it very easy to pass the gowns from one child to the next, regardless of gender, as they were still doing in the late nineteenth century in the Middle West and probably elsewhere as well. Gowns of simple homespun were the clothing of farmers' boys and girls, while the genteel dressed in silks and satins. But every child before the age of six seems to have been dressed in clothing appropriate to females.[37]

Clothing symbolized the feminization of children; and since being female meant being perceived as weaker, inferior, submissive, and obedient, the clothing of children became a part of the overall process of discipline by parents who sought to control and dominate the wills of their offspring. By having both boys and girls wear long dresses, with aprons and petticoats, their physical movements would be restricted and inhibited from the first stages of motion—crawling, walking, running, and climbing. Perhaps one of the major purposes of such clothing was to limit the play of very young children, as dresses so clearly limited the activities of girls and young women for the rest of their lives. Only boys eventually would be freed from these encumbering clothes, enabled to participate actively in the physical life of the world outside and beyond the household.

The choice of identical clothing for boys and girls also suggests that, by beginning life as visibly female, all children could be governed in the same ways and with the same goals in mind. All had wills that needed breaking and desires that needed to be subdued and suppressed. Girls would never have any outward sign of release from the submission of early childhood. Boys, once they took off their gowns, would see that they were different—and superior. Clothing was only a facet of these deeply engrained assumptions and beliefs; but the original experience of being conquered, broken, and feminine bound both sexes together in ways that would continue to shape their temperaments, values, and experiences throughout their lifetimes.

The attitudes toward food and clothing were symptomatic of a pervasive preoccupation with discipline that governed all aspects of children's lives. Their manners and deportment toward parents, siblings, and other persons both within and outside the household were also constantly subject to parental injunctions and oversight. Children's behavior in general was shaped by parental discipline long after the initial confrontations had been resolved successfully in favor of parental authority and the child's submission.

Evangelical children appeared to be notably obedient, respectful, sober, quiet, and responsive to their parents' will. Of the children in the Edwards family, it was said that "In their manners, they were uncommonly respect[ful] to their parents. When their parents came into the room, they all rose instinctively from their seats, and never resumed them until their parents were seated; and when either parent was speaking, no matter with whom they had been conversing, they were all immediately silent and attentive. The kind and gentle treatment they received from their mother, while she strictly and punctiliously maintained her parental authority, seemed naturally to beget and promote a filial respect and affection, and to lead them to a mild tender treatment of each other." Jonathan Edwards, who always "practised that conscientious exactness which was perspicuous in all his ways" in the "conduct" of his family affairs, never ceased to oversee and to govern the outward behavior of his children. "He kept a watchful eye over his children, that he might admonish them of the *first* wrong step, and direct them in the right way." Like so many other evangelical parents, he was careful to catechise his children and instruct them in the principles of religion that infused their household. He also "was a great enemy to young people's unseasonable company-keeping and frolicking, as he looked upon it as a great means of corrupting and ruining youth. And he thought the excuse many parents make for tolerating their children in it (viz., that it is the custom, and others children practice it, which renders it difficult, and even impossible to restrain theirs), was insufficient and frivolous; and manifested a great degree of stupidity, on supposition the practice was hurtful and pernicious to their souls. And when some of his children grew up he found no difficulty in restraining them from this pernicious practice; but they cheerfully complied with the will of their parents herein." From early childhood through youth, the Edwards children experienced constant supervision, admonition, and control by their parents over their behavior, even outside the household. There could be no deviations from the pattern of discipline and manner maintained by parents and children alike.[38]

Many of the men and women who became evangelical Quakers recalled being raised in strict and orderly households. Elizabeth Stirredge, who was born in Thornbury in Gloucestershire in 1634, observed that "My parents brought me up after a very strict manner, so that I was much a stranger to the world and its ways." William Caton, born in the mid-1630's in England, recollected that he "had also a fear upon me of reproof and chastisement from my parents, who according to their knowledge endeavoured to educate me in virtue and godliness." "Great was their care to being me up in the fear of the Lord, according to their ability and understanding," he said. Charles Marshall, who was born in Bristol in 1637, recalled that "My education and bringing up was after the strictest manner of religion, my parents being such as feared the Lord. I was kept much from the company of other children," and taught early to read the Scriptures. These recurring recollections suggest the importance of strictly governed families for many who were later to become evangelicals.[39]

The close regulation of the daily lives of children also marked the Wesley household, as might be expected from the pattern of control established from their infancies. Susanna Wesley's children were "taught as soon as they could speak, the Lord's prayer, which they were made to say at rising and at bedtime constantly; to which, as they grew bigger, were added a short prayer for their parents, and some collects, a short catechism, and some portion of Scripture, as their memories could bear. They were very early made to distinguish the Sabbath from other days, before they could well speak or go. They were as soon taught to be still at family prayers, and to ask a blessing immediately after, which they used to do by signs, before they could kneel or speak." Religious training, of course, was characteristic of virtually all evangelical families, although Susanna Wesley typically was preoccupied with "making" her children perform their religious duties according to a strict routine.[40]

In addition, she also saw to it that "Taking God's name in vain, cursing and swearing, profanity, obscenity, rude, ill-bred names, were never heard among" her children, "nor were they ever permitted to call each other by their proper names without the addition of brother or sister." Manners counted even amongst the children themselves, and her own offspring were forbidden the language of their contemporaries in Ely. Since her children were taught at home, she made certain that "There was no such thing as loud playing or talking allowed of, but every_ one was kept close to business for the six hours of school. . . . Rising out of their places, or going out of the room, was not permitted except for good cause; and running into the yard, garden, or street, without leave, was always esteemed a capital offence." Permission obviously had to be given by parents even for play, and such permission presumably could always be withheld.

"For some years," Susanna commented, "we went on very well. Never were children in better order. Never were children better disposed to piety, or in more subjection to their parents." But all of this—order, piety, and subjection—was overturned suddenly by the destruction of the Wesley house by fire, which forced "that fatal dispersion" of the children into neighboring households. She noted: "In these they were left at full liberty to converse with servants, which before they had always been restrained from, and to run abroad to play with any children, bad or good. They soon learned to neglect a strict observance of the Sabbath, and got knowledge of several songs and bad things which before they had no notion of. That civil behavior which made them admired when they were at home by all who saw them was in a great measure lost, and a clownish accent and many rude ways were learned which were not reformed without some difficulty." Without the continual oversight and rules of parents, children's behavior might not be perfect or conform to the wills of their parents. External discipline, as Wesley's observations imply, had to be maintained unrelentingly throughout childhood if behavior was to be always orderly and mannerly, and children to be kept pious and in subjection to their parents. Evangelical parents must have concurred, on the whole, with the convictions of the Wesleys and the Edwardses, for they maintained strict watch and rigorous control over the outward behavior of their children from the time they were in their cradles to the time—if not beyond—that they married and established families of their own.[41]

Shaping the Evangelical Conscience: Shame, Guilt, and Inner Discipline

THE ENDURING SYMBOL of the exercise of external authority and discipline by early American parents was the rod, the use of which is often thought to have been characteristic of discipline in evangelical families century after century. Severity did mark the conduct of some parents, of course, and the rod or physical punishment of various kinds were manifestations of discipline, sometimes even from infancy. Anne Bradstreet's poetry suggests the reliance upon physical beatings as a chief method of discipline for many children, and her own religious experiences are described in the imagery of harsh physical correction. She often felt that she had "been with God like an untoward child, that no longer then the rod has been on my back (or at least in sight) but I have been apt to forgett him and myself too." "Before I was afflicted," she said, "I went astray, but now I keep thy statutes." In one of her meditations, she observed that "some children (like sowre land) are of so tough and morose a dispo[si]tion, that the plough of correction must make long furrows on their back, and the Harrow of discipline goe often over them, before they bee fit soile to sow the seed of morality, much lesse of grace in them." "But when by prudent nurture they are brought into a fit capacity," she noted, "let the seed of good instruction and exhortation be sown in the spring of their youth, and a plentiful crop may be expected in the harvest of their yeares." Yet Anne Bradstreet also recognized that "Diverse children have their different natures; some are like flesh which nothing but salt will keep from putrefaction; some again like tender fruits that are best preserved with sugar: those parents are wise that can fit their nurture according to their nature."

Undoubtedly parents used the rod as a weapon or as a threat against disobedience and misbehavior by their children generation after generation. Even though John Robinson noted in the early 1620's that "It is much controverted, whether it be better, in the general, to bring up children under the severity of discipline, and the rod, or no," he himself did not hesitate to recommend the use of the rod to break children's wills.[42]

Yet the use of the rod in fact usually testified to the failure of discipline rather than its success. The rod punished disobedience and external behavior which did not conform to the wishes of parents; but the actions themselves revealed a failure of parental discipline. The whole point of breaking a child's will early, as evangelicals knew, was to make the child's obedience habitual and "natural" from infancy, so that physical punishments and the use of the rod would be rarely necessary. If a child's will were broken successfully, obedience would not depend upon external coercions and threats. As John Witherspoon recognized, "The more complete and uniform a parent's authority is, the offences will be more rare, punishment will be less needed, and the more gentle kind of correction will be abundantly sufficient." "We see every where about us examples of this," he noted. "A parent that has once obtained, and knows how to preserve authority, will do more by a look of displeasure, than another by the most passionate words, and even blows." Successfully imposed discipline implemented from the earliest years of childhood minimized the need for the rod.[43]

The most effective discipline of all, however, was not external—in response to parental punishments—but internal—in response to self-discipline. The use of the rod in discipline, which has been exaggerated in our portraits of the early American past, was probably the *least* effective method of all for the encouragement of self-discipline and conformity to the standards of behavior set by evangelical parents for their children. Important as outward behavior was to evangelicals, and preoccupied as they always were with the obedience of their children, their principal methods of discipline, once the children's wills had been conquered, focused upon the most effective source of control over their children's actions, feelings, and thoughts: their consciences.

The continuous pressure exerted by parents upon their children for perfect compliance with parental standards was augmented, from a very early age, by the pressures exerted by children upon themselves. Evangelical discipline was most successful when it was least dependent upon external commands and oversight. What made most evangelical children behave properly—whether or not any adult was around to notice—was their continuously active conscience, the inescapable inner disciplinarian, which governed their lives from early childhood through adulthood, monitoring, checking, censuring, and controlling their thoughts, feelings, and behavior. True discipline, for evangelicals, was self-discipline, and self-discipline was internal and inescapable. For this, a powerful conscience was essential, and the methods of child-rearing characteristic of evangelical families were designed to ensure the formation of such a conscience.[44]

The interplay between conscience as an inner disciplinarian and parents as outer disciplinarians shapes the recollections of John Dane, the Ipswich tailor, who remembered: "When I was but a lettell boy, being edicated under godly parents, my Conshans was veary apt to tell me of evells that I should not doe. Being now about aight yers ould, I was given mutch to play and to run out without my fathers Consent and againe his comand. One a time, I haveing gone out most parte of the day, when my father saw me cum home, he toke me and basted me. I then cept home, and followed my busenes two or thre[e] dase. My father and mother Comended me, and tould me that god would bles me if I obeyed my parents, and what the contrary would ishew in. I then thout in my harte, o that my father would beat me more when I did amis. I fard, if he did not, I should not be good." In fact, Dane need not have been overly afraid of being disobedient, for his conscience was strong, active, and persistent, despite his fears that it would not suffice against his own inclination to play and to sin. Another memory confirms the power of his conscience in his early childhood: "Not longe after, I being alone on the shopbord Repping open a payer of bretches of a Gintilmans who had had a hole in his pocut and sewed up againe, thorow [through] which hole he had lost or dropt into his knes of his linings a pese of gould, which, when I saw, I thought I myt have it, for I thout nobody knew of it, nor could know of it. I toke the Gould and hed it, and sat upon the shopboard to worke; but, thinking of it, I thout it is none of myne. I fetcht it againe, but upone more pondring I went and hed it againe. When I had dun so, I could not be quiet in my mynd, but fetcht it againe, and thout thow nobody could know of it, yet god, he knew of it. So I gave it to my fatther, hoe gave it to the gintelman." Thus his conscience was eased and he could once more "be quiet" in his "mynd."[45]

Thomas Story, who later became a Quaker after having been "educated in the way of the national church of England" during the midseventeenth century, recalled that he "was not naturally addicted to much vice or evil" in his "early days," although "through the conversation of rude boys at school," he "had acquired some things by imitation, tending that way." But "as I came to put them in practice, by word or action," he said, "I found something in myself at such times, suddenly surprising me with a sense of the evil, and making me ashamed when alone; though what I had said or done was not evil in the common account of such as I conversed with, or among men, in a common acceptation." "And though I did not know, or consider what this reprover was," he added, "yet it had so much influence and power with me that I was much reformed thereby from those habits, which, in time, might have been foundations for greater evils." Like Story, most evangelicals carried about an inner "reprover," which monitored their behavior and checked their words and actions even when they seemed to be no different in their behavior from other children.[46]

For evangelical children, conscience served as the inner voice for external authority—the expectations and commands of both parents and God. Their obedience was thus assured by the permanent presence within themselves of the internalized rules and restrictions upon feelings, thoughts, and behavior constantly invoked and enforced by their own consciences. But conscience often was a stricter disciplinarian than even parents, so that self-discipline proved much more effective in shaping the behavior of evangelical children than the prospects of punishment by parents.

The techniques used by Cotton Mather to shape the consciences and temperaments of his children were designed to foster both a sense of guilt and of shame. As he observed in 1706,

> I first begett in them an high Opinion of their Father's Love to them, and of his being best able to judge, what shall be good for them.
>
> Then I make them sensible, tis a Folly for them to pretend unto any Witt and Will of their own; they must resign all to me, who will be sure to do what is best; my word must be their Law.
>
> I cause them to understand, that it is an *hurtful* and a *shameful* thing to do amiss. I aggravate this, on all Occasions; and lett them see how *amiable* they will render themselves by well doing.

Mather's basic premise of discipline was the absolutism of his own paternal authority within the family, and the totality of submission on the part of children to their parent's will and wishes: "my word must be their law." But Mather knew that the most effective method for ensuring the compliance of children with the wills of their parents was not beatings but guilt and shame. The hurtfulness of doing "amiss" would be felt both by the parents and by the children, whose consciences would cause them intense inner pain; while the shamefulness of doing amiss would embarrass them in their own eyes and make them eager to be accepted once more by conforming to the will of their parents. Only by so doing could they ensure that they would be loved.[47]

Love and fear were a potent combination in the disciplining of children. Jonathan Edwards's grandfather, Richard Edwards, ruled his own family on these principles. As his son, Timothy Edwards, recalled: "God gave him not only wisdome to Govern himself, but also to Govern others, that he in his providence had put in Subjection to him. His Children and Servants, always both Lov'd and fear'd him, and never despis'd him." Fear arose not from the use of the rod, but from the awesomeness of parental power directed against misbehavior. Richard Edwards "hated vice and wickedness wherever he Saw it. He abhorr'd to plead for, Justify, or make Light of Sin, because Committed by them that were nearly Related to him. . . . If his Children did amiss they must expect no favour from him, no more then if they were Strangers. Yea his Spirit (though he Lov'd them dearly) was more Stir'd against that which is evil in them then in Such as were but Neighbours." The Reverend Thomas Prince of Boston recalled that his own father had been "a very affectionate Husband and Father: In his former years, pretty severe in Governing his Family; of later, rul'd them with great ease and Gentleness." As Cotton Mather said, "I wish that my *children* may as soon as may be, feel the principles of *reason* and *honor*, working in them, and that I may carry on their education, very much upon those principles. Therefore, first, I will wholly avoid, that harsh, fierce, crabbed usage of the children, that would make them tremble, and abhor to come into my presence." "I will so use them," he added, "that they shall *fear* to offend me, and yet mightily *love* to see me, and be glad of my coming home, if I have been abroad at any time."[48]

The same theme of severity and gentleness, of fear and of love, as alternating elements in the disciplining of children recurs in the advice offered by John Abbott to evangelical mothers during the early 1830's. "Fear is a useful and a necessary principle in family government," he acknowledged. "God makes use of it in governing his creatures." "But," he cautioned, "it is ruinous to the disposition of a child, exclusively to control him by this motive. How unhappy must be that family where the parent always sits with a face deformed with scowls, and where the voice is always uttered in tones of severity and command! Such parents we do see. Their children fear them. They are always under restraint in their presence; and home becomes to them an irksome prison, instead of the happy retreat of peace and joy." Accordingly, Abbott urged mothers to smile, caress, and reward their children, addressing them "in tones of mildness and affection" so as to touch "those chords in the human heart which vibrate in sweet harmony," and to call "into action the noblest and the loveliest principles of our nature." "And thus," he said, does a mother "prepare the way for every painful act of discipline to come with effectual power upon the heart. The children know that she does not love to punish. In all cases where it can be done, children should thus be governed by kindness." "But when kindness fails, and disobedience ensues," he admonished, echoing earlier generations of similar advice, "let not the mother hesitate for a moment to fall back upon her last resort, and punish as severely as is necessary." Though love should predominate, there was no question in Abbott's mind that it was founded upon absolute obedience established in infancy and sustained, subliminally, by fear of punishment. Effective fear, however, was a response not so much to the prospect of physical punishments—

beatings and the pains of the rod—as to the disapproval of parents and the withdrawal of their love.[49]

There are hints throughout the generations that evangelical parents—and others too—used the threat of disownment as an ultimate weapon against disobedient children. This technique of discipline is suggested, for instance, in the example of Richard Edwards dealing with his disobedient children as if "they were Strangers." Cotton Mather noted that "I would have it looked upon as a severe and awful *punishment* for a crime in the family, to be *forbidden for awhile to come into my presence*." Given the intensity of the relationship between parents and children, such a threat, even briefly and infrequently made, could evoke profound fear in a small child. There is no way of knowing how significant such threats and such techniques might have been. But a reasonable guess is that the frequent experience of anguish and terror reported by evangelicals who felt themselves cast out or banished from the sustaining presence of God implies that banishment from the presence of one's parents, and the withdrawal of their love, could be potent sources of fear indeed.[50]

The reactions of Joseph Pike to his children suggest the power of the withdrawal of love and approval, as well as the potency of reproof and correction. "I love those of them who deserve it, very dearly; and, when I have observed them sober and religiously inclined, I thought them as near and dear to me as my own life"; "on the other hand," he added, "when I have observed anything in them that tended to hurt, such as wildness, rudeness, evil words, or actions, bad company, or an inclination to pride or height, or to this, or the other new fashion,— these things, I could not see in my children, without duly discountenancing, and advising, reproving, or correcting, as the nature of the offence required." And he continued—significantly for the impact of parental disapproval on their children's behavior—that "I bear my dear wife witness, that she has been of the same mind with me, in all these respects." When both parents joined together in offering love to children on the condition of exact compliance with their wishes and wills, the impact upon the child could be profound.[51]

If displeasure came from the parents themselves, and no grandparents were around to intercede on the child's behalf, the loss of parental love and parental approval left children bereft of support, isolated within the family and totally at the mercy of their own desires and their own self-will, which got them punished in the first place. When their wills could only exist in conformity to the wills of their parents, who alone could decide "what shall be good for them," evangelical children left on their own and disapproved of by their parents could feel utterly devastated and destroyed. The loss of love left only fear. The options presented to children were clear and simple: either obey the wills of parents, or be cast away— left alone without other wills to guide and sustain them. For children whose wills had been broken early, such punishment—which focused upon their inner need to obey without deviation—indeed would be severe. What ultimately guaranteed their obedience was their inability to exist comfortably on their own. Conscience therefore provided them with internalized rules, which mirrored their parents' wishes and wills more faithfully than even parents might have thought possible. The methods of discipline most favored by evangelicals therefore had their most profound impact upon the moral consciences of evangelical children. For the rest of their lives, they would never be entirely freed from the pangs of guilt and the embarrassments of shame implanted within them during their earliest years.

The Vanities, Pleasures, and Sins of Youth: The Emergence of Self and Self-Will

MEMORIES OF THE LATER YEARS of childhood and youth often were painful and embarrassing for evangelicals to recall, since they catalogued the sins of disobedience and rebelliousness, of playfulness, worldliness, and sensuality, of pride and self-confidence. The specifics varied from individual to individual, of course; but the themes which recur in the recollections by evangelicals of their childhood and youth form a general pattern over the generations—a pattern of the rejection (either willfully or inadvertently) of the standards of behavior, morality, and character set forth by their parents in their earliest years, and of the discovery and fulfillment of their own personal desires and needs. As they grew up and became increasingly aware of their own selfhood and self-will, as they came increasingly to have a sense of their own autonomy and power, their ability to act on their own behalf and to do what pleased themselves, they felt increasingly at odds with their parents and with the standards of behavior implanted within their own consciences.

The sins of childhood and youth were sharp in the memory of George Whitefield. "I can truly say I was froward from my mother's womb. I was so brutish as to hate instruction, and used purposely to shun all opportunities of receiving it. I can date some very early acts of uncleanness," or masturbation, which continued to trouble him through his youth. "I soon gave pregnant proof of an impudent temper. Lying, filthy talking, and foolish jesting I was much addicted to, even when very young. Sometimes I used to curse, if not swear. Stealing from my mother I thought no theft at all . . . and have more than once spent money I took in the house, in buying fruits, tarts, etc., to satisfy my sensual appetite. Numbers of Sabbaths have I broken, and generally used to behave myself very irreverently in God's sanctuary. Much money have I spent in plays, and in the common entertainments of the age. Cards, and reading romances, were my heart's delight. Often have I joined with others in playing roguish tricks, but was generally, if not always, *happily detected.*" These recollections, however, were only the beginning, for "It would be endless to recount the sins and offences of my younger days. They are more in number than the hairs of my head." As Whitefield noted, "However the young man in the Gospel might boast how he had kept the commandments from his youth, with shame and confusion of face I confess that I have broken them all from my youth."[52]

The same sense of "shame and confusion" was present in the memories of Thomas Shepard's youthful sins while in college at Cambridge in England, a period in which he "fell from God to loose and lewd company, to lust and pride and gaming and bowling and drinking." One day, he recalled, "I drank so much . . . that I was dead drunk." He was carried to another student's rooms to sleep. "And when I awakened I went from him in shame and confusion, and went out into the fields and there spent that Sabbath lying hid in the cornfields where the Lord, who might justly have cut me off in the midst of my sin, did meet me with much sadness of heart and troubled my soul for this and other my sins which then I had cause and leisure to think of." He also recalled that he had "lived in unnatural uncleanesses not to be named and in speculative wantonness and filthiness with all sorts of persons which pleased my eye (yet still restrained from the gross act of whoredom which some of my own familiars were to their horror and shame overtaken with)." For many evangelicals like Thomas Shepard, the years of childhood and youth provided the experiential basis for their knowledge of active sinning as they made their way in the world of school, friends, and communities beyond their parents' household.[53]

Although Joseph Pike remembered being a sober child until about the age of nine, he soon "began by degrees to lose this condition," as "the enemy" of his "soul" insinuated into his mind: " 'What harm or evil is there in things, which are accounted innocent diversions?' " "And being of a lively, active temper," he recalled, "this bait took with me. . . . Beginning to love playful pastimes, I lost that inward sweetness and peace which I had before enjoyed; and by endeavouring to stifle these secret reproofs, I grew harder, until, from a desire to keep company with other wild boys, I took delight in getting out into the streets to play with them, so that I grew very wanton, although my dear parents endeavoured to restrain me." By the age of twelve, "although, to the praise of the Lord, I was preserved from any very wicked or gross actions, or even very bad words, yet my mind was drawn away into vanity and wildness, and I was far from being so sober as I ought to have been." After John Banks was converted in 1654, he recalled that when "about sixteen years of age," he found himself "very much bowed down and perplexed, my sins being set in order before me; and the time I had spent in wildness and wantonness, out of the fear of God, in vanity, sport, and pastime, came into my view and remembrance. The book of my conscience was opened, for I was by nature wild and wanton." Like others whose consciences were very active, John Gratton felt throughout his childhood "two spirits working in me, both striving to gain me, the one from the other; but I found the good Spirit, for so it was, always counselled me to do good things, and when I was obedient to it, then I found the evil spirit could not break my peace." When he "was about ten or eleven years old," he recalled, "the Lord visited me with the light of his Son, and gave me to see the vain life and way I lived in, being much given to play amongst rude boys, and took great delight in playing at cards, and shooting at butts, and ringing of bells, for which I was reproved. I came to see that vain sports and pleasures were displeasing to the Lord." And Alice Hayes, after leaving her father and stepmother, found herself being followed by the Lord "with his reproofs in my conscience for the sins of my youth; which were dancing, singing, telling idle stories, and some other pastimes, into which youth are too liable to run"; but, she added with evident relief, "through the Lord's great mercy and goodness to me, I was addicted to no worse evils in all my life."[54]

For other evangelicals, too, the sins of youth were restrained, so that their outward conduct seemed pious and proper. Samuel Hopkins recalled that "I from my youth was not volatile and wild, but rather of a sober and steady make, and was not guilty of external irregularities, such as disobedience to parents, profanation of the sabbath, lying, foolish jesting, quarrelling, passion and anger, or rash and profane words; and was disposed to be diligent and faithful in whatever business I was employed; so that as I advanced in age, I gained the notice, esteem and respect of the neighbourhood." David Brainerd remembered: "I was, I think, from my Youth, something sober, and inclined rather to Melancholy, than the contrary Extreme." At seven or eight years of age, he "became something concern'd for my Soul, and terrified at the Thoughts of Death; and was driven to the Performance of Duties: But it appeared a melancholy Business, and destroyed my Eagerness for Play." Evidently he never did enjoy playing or joining in the amusements of his contemporaries. "I was not exceedingly addicted to young Company, or Frolicking (as it is called) But this I know, that when I did go into Company, I never returned from a Frolick in my Life, with so good a Conscience as I went with; It always added new Guilt to me." For many youths like Brainerd, conscience kept their activities in close check, always providing them with an inward testimony to the sinfulness of their desires for play and other self-indulgent activities. As Mr. Eaton recalled in his confession before Thomas Shepard's congregation, after leaving "the wings of parents," the "hidden corruption" of his heart was discovered to him by his "Sabbath breaking and company keeping." "Yet in all this time," he said, "I was not left without a testimony within. My conscience was convinced that my ways were of death."[55]

Similarly, Samuel Gray, who wished to become a student under the tutelage of the Reverend Eleazer Wheelock, wrote from Boston in 1762 about his own religious experiences, being as yet unconverted, and his memories of early sinfulness. "I have ever since my Childhood through God's restraining Grace been kept from many gross Outbreakings of Sin in Life which some are guilty of, Yet in my Younger years [he was then in his mid-twenties] my whole Soul was bent to Sports and Play to the total neglect of my Soul's Salvation—Revenge in Words calling Names . . . was sweet to me, and I could curse bitterly in my heart though not in words—I had checks of Conscience some times when very young so that I was afraid to run the length others did." Clearly his inward sins were rarely evident from his outward behavior, which he recalled as being carefully controlled. Yet, as he confessed, "I have I think been the very chief of Sinners," a person who "gratify'd my carnal Inclinations in secret though my outward behaviour has been in many Respects blameless."[56]

Despite the restraints upon their daily behavior by parents and by their consciences, evangelical children usually felt guilty and ashamed for the sins of thought, of feeling, and of act which they knew from experience. But their sins, they also knew, were the sins of nature, which arose almost unavoidably from their own innate corruption and the depravity of human nature itself. It made little difference to them whether or not their outward sins were visible and obvious to others or only to themselves, for the inward feelings of guilt and of shame were the same in both cases.

One of the most persistent and disturbing sins experienced by many evangelicals was the sin of disobedience to parents. Joseph Bean, who thought his parents had been wise for not sparing the rod on him when he was young, because they were "aduing of me the gratest kindness that an Earthly Parent is capable of bestowing on their Children for tu much Indulgence of[t] in times ruens them both for soul and body," also recalled that he had had a passionate fondness for playing with his friends, often saying to his "Companions that I would tak my ful of play which was uterly aganst my Parents will which was a hored brech of the 5 Command[ments]." James Gough, whose parents were Quakers and reared him very strictly, recalled that in his youth, during the early 1720's, "I was sensible of my mother's anxious care for my preservation from evil, and attainment of good; but I eluded as much as I could, the confinement which she thought conducive thereto, in keeping me under her own eye, and out of the way of corrupting company." "I loved liberty," he remembered. "I sought it with eagerness, frequently got it by craft, and abused it to my hurt, as inexperienced young people are apt to do." Jonathan Edwards was outwardly always careful to maintain his own filial obedience to his parents, while inwardly he was intensely concerned lest he be guilty of the least degree of disobedience. Early in 1723, at the age of twenty, Edwards resolved in the privacy of his diary "Never to allow the least measure of any fretting or uneasiness at my father or mother." In addition, he resolved "To suffer no effects of it, so much as in the least alteration of speech, or motion of my eye; and to be especially careful of it with respect to any of our family." There should be no visible sign of any inward discontent over the duties of obedience and honor due parents. Not too long after recording these personal resolutions, Edwards noted in his diary that "I now plainly perceive, what great obligations I am under, to love and honour my parents. I have great reason to believe, that their counsel and education, have been my making; though, in the time of it, it seemed to do me so little good." About three months later, he noted cryptically: "Have sinned, in not being careful enough to please my parents." In Edwards's experience, gross and overt disobedience was not the issue, for the mere displeasure of his parents sufficed to make him feel guilty for his sins.[57]

Disobedience to parents preyed on the minds of many evangelicals, as in the case of John Collins, a member of Michael Wigglesworth's congregation in the mid-seventeenth century. Collins acknowledged God's grace in causing him "to be educated under such parents and tutors whose care it was to commend me to be conversant in the holy will." "Hence," he said, "I had never been suffered to lie at ease in security in my natural estate as those that are out of God's hope and from his ordinances but that from 9 years old and upward the Lord has been working on me sometimes by his word and sometimes by his rod to show me what my Christless condition was by nature." His parents sought to bring him to Christ, but he resisted. In time, though, he felt that he was doomed to Hell and that "God left me to great and gross disobedience to my parents and so to myself he inflicted the greatest affliction that ever I had." And he thought, "how foolish I had been to disobey my parents and put them to so much trouble and grief and myself with so much pain." Another confession by John Green, presumably before the same congregation, also noted that "Considering of all my disobedience to parents my sabbath breakings and my many sins which the Lord help me to mourn for I saw that I was far from God and God far from me." Whatever the specific actions or thoughts of children might be that they considered sinful, they were all facets of the general sin of disobedience. By disobeying their parents' wills and standards of behavior, evangelical children felt themselves at odds with them and separated from them by both thoughts and deeds.[58]

The sense of disobedience which disturbed the consciences of most evangelicals was symptomatic of a much broader pattern of experience that set the wills of children against the wills of their parents and other superior adults in their schools, churches, and communities. Over and over again, the recollections of evangelicals reveal the emergence during youth and early adulthood of a growing sense of selfhood and self-will, an increasing confidence that they could act on their own behalf and for their own purposes apart from the expectations set for them by parents and others. Characteristically, the terms used by evangelicals to describe these feelings of independence, self-worth, and autonomy were "pride," "self-love," "self-righteousness," and "self-will." Yet in the vocabulary of evangelicalism, each of these terms, apt though they were as descriptions of inner feelings and consciousness, carried pejorative connotations, for they were synonymous with sin. Nevertheless, evangelicals usually experienced a period of their lives between childhood and the time of their rebirth and conversion during which they felt inwardly self-confident, self-assured, and self-approving, conscious of their ability to act on their own behalf for their own ends.

The recollections of the vanities and sins of youth that dominate so many of the accounts by evangelicals of their experiences prior to conversion are vivid confirmations of the development of a sense of self and self-worth. The pleasures, however simple or excessive, which they allowed themselves were evidence of their desire to please themselves alone—and not their parents or consciences. As they grew in years, some came to perceive that they had desires and interests of their own which they wished to fulfill, even when these conflicted with the acknowledged disapproval of parents. They began to discover that they had developed a self, and that they liked and approved of the self they saw emerging. Samuel Hopkins remembered that in his youth he "was often plotting for something, which then appeared to me good and great in this life; and often indulged and pleased myself with vain and foolish imaginations of what I should be and do in this world." Joseph Pike recalled that when he was about fourteen or fifteen, early in the 1670's, he found that the "enemy" of his soul "tempted me with the pleasures and vanities of the world, so that my mind was allured and drawn towards them, and I did love and delight therein." "Among the rest," he said, "I was inclined to take pleasure in fine apparel, and the like, as I could get them, according to my station, of which I remember a particular instance. Having got a pretty fine new coat, the spirit of pride arose in me, and passing along the street, (I remember the place,) I thought myself, as the saying is, somebody." Instantly, however, he felt "struck as with an arrow from the Lord," and his pleasure dissolved. Yet the experience left him with the enduring memory of being "somebody"—and that was what mattered.[59]

For many youths in early America, being "somebody" was only the beginning of a lifetime of experiences sustaining the emerging sense of self and self-will that so often began to appear in adolescence. But not for those who were to become evangelicals. For people whose wills had been broken early in childhood, and whose sense of self had been suppressed and denied by the powerful controls and governance of parents, the emergence of a sense of self and self-will in youth, which could stretch from the early teens to the mid- to late twenties, proved impossible to accept. Their temperaments had been shaped in ways which made selfhood too dangerous, too frightening, too difficult to be sought and attained. Their consciences left little room for the freedom of experience and of uncertainty. And when they felt, as most did, that they were beginning to become separate, independent, and self-governing individuals, they also began to feel intensely unhappy and anxious. Yet without some sense of self, some experience of self-will, however brief and limited, evangelicals probably would never have been able to achieve the central goal of their lives: the new birth, or conversion, which was to be the indispensable sign to them of their personal regeneration. Without a new birth, they had no hope and no future. Adulthood, for evangelicals, began with the experience of being reborn. And for that experience, childhood and youth provided the indispensable foundations which were to create the distinctive patterns of temperament and piety that made evangelicals into the people they became.

"A Habitation of Dragons": Themes of Evangelical Temperaments and Piety

The New Birth

EVANGELICALS WERE BORN not once but twice. "I was born Feb[ruary] 15th 1711 and born again Octo[ber] 1741," said Nathan Cole, a Connecticut farmer. Similarly, when John Gratton awoke one morning in the mid-seventeenth century, he found a "secret cry" in his heart: "Oh! that this day may be my birth day: for I saw that I wanted to be born again, and to be made a new creature." For every evangelical of whatever denomination, the experience of being reborn was the central event in their lives, indispensable for their salvation and essential for the fulfillment of their innermost needs, desires, and expectations. "Conversion," said Solomon Stoddard, one of the most powerful and influential evangelical preachers in western Massachusetts during the late seventeenth and early eighteenth centuries, "is a great change, from darkness to light, from death to life, from the borders of despair to a spirit of faith in Christ." "Conversion is the greatest change that men undergo in this world," he added, as countless numbers of evangelicals in the British Isles and the British colonies on the American continent could affirm by their own personal experiences. As Stoddard's grandson, Jonathan Edwards, later declared: "They that are truly converted are new men, new creatures; new, not only within, but without; they are sanctified throughout, in spirit, soul and body; old things are passed away, all things are become new; they have new hearts, and new eyes, new ears, new tongues, new hands, new feet . . . a new conversation and practice; and they walk in newness of life, and continue to do so to the end of life." Personal experience confirmed Edwards's observations and convictions, as Francis Howgill, one of the early Quaker evangelists in mid-seventeenth-century England, could testify: "As soon as I heard one declare . . . the Light of

Christ in Man was the Way to Christ, I believed . . . and then my Eyes
were opened, and all things were brought to remembrance that ever I
had done. . . . All was overturned. . . . The Lord . . . rejoyced . . . the
Captive came forth out of his Prison . . . and the new Man was made."
For every evangelical, conversion was experienced as the crucial turning
point in their lives—a new beginning, a second chance to become a
perfect child again.[1]

Anyone whose life was not transformed by the second birth was
liable to confront damnation. Outward morality, seeming virtue, even
the performance of religious duties and participation in the sacraments
of churches were meaningless without the experience of the new birth.
John Wesley spoke directly to the issue when he observed that:

> Men may indeed flatter themselves (so desperately wicked and
> so deceitful is the heart of man!) that they may live in their sins
> till they come to the last gasp, and yet afterwards live with God;
> and thousands do really believe, that they have found a broad
> way which leadeth not to destruction. "What danger," say they,
> "can a woman be in that is so *harmless* and so *virtuous*? What
> fear is there that so *honest* a man, one of so strict *morality*,
> should miss of heaven; especially if, over and above all this, they
> constantly attend on church and sacrament?" One of these will
> ask with all assurance, "What! shall not I do as well as my
> neighbours?" Yes, as well as your unholy neighbours; as well as
> your neighbours that die in their sins! For you will all drop into
> the pit together, into the nethermost hell! You will all lie together
> in the lake of fire; "the lake of fire burning with brimstone."
> Then, at length, you will see (but God grant you may see it
> before!) the necessity of holiness in order to glory; and, conse-
> quently, of the new birth, since none can be holy, except he be
> born again.[2]

The same message was propounded in New England by Jonathan
Edwards, the most powerful and brilliant exponent of evangelicalism in
eighteenth-century America and Wesley's counterpart in the New World.
In his famous sermon on "Sinners in the Hands of an Angry God,"
Edwards warned his congregation that "Almost every natural man that
hears of hell, flatters himself that he shall escape it; he depends upon
himself for his own security; he flatters himself in what he has done,
in what he is now doing, or what he intends to do. Every one lays out
matters in his own mind how he shall avoid damnation, and flatters
himself that he contrives well for himself, and that his schemes will not
fail." But all such natural men were self-deceivers, and likely to find
that they, like others before them, were doomed to damnation. As
Edwards warned, "all you that never passed under a great change of

heart, by the mighty power of the Spirit of God upon your souls; all you that were never born again, and made new creatures, and raised from being dead in sin, to a state of new, and before altogether unexperienced light and life, are in the hands of an angry God." Only by being born again and becoming children of God could they escape the punishments to come.[3]

The experience of rebirth marked a profound transformation from a state of nature and of sin to a state of grace and of ultimate salvation. The necessity for rebirth or conversion, evangelicals agreed, was to be traced to its original source: the fall of Adam and the legacy of sin which he bequeathed to mankind. John Wesley made the point cogently: " 'in Adam all died,' all human-kind, all the children of men who were then in Adam's loins. The natural consequence of this is, that every one descended from him, comes into the world spiritually dead, dead to God, wholly dead in sin; entirely void of the life of God, void of the image of God, of all that righteousness and holiness, wherein Adam was created. Instead of this, every man born into the world, now bears the image of the devil, in pride and self-will; the image of the beast, in sensual appetites and desires. This then is the foundation of the New Birth, the entire corruption of our nature. Hence it is, that being 'born in sin,' we must be 'born again.' Hence every one that is born of a woman, must be born of the Spirit of God." For Wesley, as for all evangelicals, there could be no doubt whatsoever of the fact that "the new birth is absolutely necessary" for "eternal salvation." This was the conviction which bound together evangelicals of all periods, places, and persuasions, the bedrock of their religious beliefs, and the central experience of their lives.[4]

Experience confirmed the sense of a profound change in life—from sin to grace, from damnation to salvation—and the testimonies of evangelicals through the centuries dwell continually upon the transformations wrought in their lives by the experience of the second birth. But in an equally profound if often less visible way, conversion or the new birth was less a transformation than a fulfillment, less a radical break with the personal past than the elaboration, in youth and adulthood, of the central modes of past experience and past behavior characteristic of evangelical childhoods. Far from being a rejection of their complete past, conversion marked the acceptance of their earliest past— the past of their formative years in infancy and early childhood. Evangelicals did not remember their own earliest experiences, and few ever reported their earliest memories; yet their actions, their beliefs, and their temperaments reveal, as nothing else could, that their earliest and most formative experiences still shaped and influenced their lives throughout youth and adulthood.

The new birth brought assurance to evangelicals that they had become children of God. The second childhood, which lasted for the remainder of their lives, elaborated the themes and sustained the central experiences of the first childhood. The relationships that henceforth united individuals with their God mirrored those relationships that had been characteristic of childhood among evangelical families. In both cases, total power and authority were attached to the persons in the role of parents, including both actual parents and God as Father of all humanity. But conversion proved essential for most evangelicals as a result of the experiences that caused them to feel they had departed from the pattern of strict and undeviating obedience to parental authority and parental will. By once again experiencing the breaking and sub-jection of their own personal wills through the powerful intervention of God, by once again feeling that they themselves were utterly unable to govern their own lives and to fulfill their own desires and wills, evangelicals accepted the basic conditions of love and acceptance instilled into them during their formative years. By becoming children again, evangelicals found themselves able to accept roles and feelings that only seemingly had been denied during the years which preceded their con-versions. The traumas of the new birth demonstrated, however, that the acceptance of these roles and feelings, which meant self-denial and a state of will-lessness, could be achieved only after internal battles causing the most intense pain and anguish. By surrendering themselves to the omnipotent power and authority of God, by reducing the self to a state of utter impotency, by feeling their own wills breaking once more, evangelicals knew from experience that they had become true children of God.*

"Our Loathsome Corruption and Pollution": Attitudes Toward the Body

AT THE VERY CORE of evangelical experience, the foundation upon which piety was based, there existed a profound alienation of individuals from their own bodies and an intense hostility toward their own innermost natures. The doctrines of original sin and of innate depravity were grounded in the feelings evangelicals had toward their inner selves. Again and again, evangelicals insisted that human nature was corrupt, not in part but totally. Sinful men, said Jonathan Edwards, "are totally cor-

* For an exploration of the connections between the experiences of child-hood and the adult religious experience of male seminarians, see the fascinat-ing study by Philip M. Helfaer, *The Psychology of Religious Doubt* (Boston, 1972), an analysis which I have found to be immensely suggestive and cor-roborative of my assumptions about the connections between childhood and adult religious experience in early America.

rupt, in every part, in all their faculties, and all the principles of their nature, their understandings, and wills; and in all their dispositions and
affections, their heads, their hearts, are totally depraved, all the members
of their bodies are only instruments of sin; and all their senses, seeing,
hearing, tasting, &c., are only inlets and outlets of sin, channels of
corruption. There is nothing but sin, no good at all." And John Wesley
declared: "Our nature is altogether corrupt, in every power and faculty.
And our will, depraved equally with the rest, is wholly bent to indulge
our natural corruption." As Wesley noted with respect to heathens, "none
of them knew his total corruption. They knew not, that all men were
empty of all good, and filled with all manner of evil. They were wholly
ignorant of the entire depravation of the whole human nature, of every
man born into the world, in every faculty of his soul." Christians, however, knew that "all men are conceived in sin, and shapen in wickedness: that hence there is in every man a carnal mind, which is enmity
against God, which is not, cannot be subject to his law, and which so
infects the whole soul, that there dwelleth in him, in his flesh, in his
natural state, no good thing; but all the imagination of the thoughts of
his heart, is evil, only evil, and that continually." This basic view of
human nature in general, as well as of each specific individual, provided
the underpinnings for evangelical doctrine and piety. But the experience
of corruption was not limited to the unregenerated and sinful person.
It often remained an integral part of evangelical experience after conversion as well, the inescapable reality of personal corruption, which
generated a sustained hostility toward the body and all its manifestations and demands.[5]

The perception of the inner self and body as being polluted and
filthy, and the conviction that the bodily functions of urination and
defecation were daily reminders of the inner corruption of human nature,
are evident in the life of the Reverend Cotton Mather, whose career in
Boston as minister and prolific writer made him one of the most influential evangelicals in the later seventeenth and early eighteenth centuries. On the occasion of his forty-sixth birthday in 1709, he gave thanks
to the Lord "For His using me in what Services to the evangelical
Interests, I have had Opportunity to pursue, in my Life hitherto; and this
notwithstanding my being so foolish and shallow a Creature . . . and so
filthy a Creature as tis known to Him that I am." Twenty-eight years
earlier, the same preoccupations had been recorded in his diary. "Alas,"
he wrote, "I have the Seed of all Corruption in mee." "*Lord*, why have
not the Outbreakings of my *corrupt Nature*, been as hideous as any
whatsoever! My *Nature* is as *corrupt*, as any Man's in the World." He
desired "to walk humbly before the Lord, all my Dayes, in the Remembrance of the lothsome Corruptions, which my Soul has been from my
Youth polluted withal. . . . Altho' I have been kept from such Outbreakings of Sin, in Actions towards others, as have undone many in

the World, yett I have certainly been one of the filthiest Creatures upon Earth." In July 1700, Mather observed the close affinities of men and beasts in their bodily functions and needs:

> I was once emptying the *Cistern of Nature*, and making *Water* at the Wall. At the same Time, there came a Dog, who did so too, before me. Thought I; "What mean, and vile Things are the Children of Men, in this mortal State! How much do our natural Necessities abase us, and place us in some regard, on the same Level with the very Dogs!"
>
> My Thought proceeded. "Yet I will be a more noble Creature; and at the very Time, when my natural Necessities debase me into the Condition of the Beast, my Spirit shall (I say, at that very Time!) rise and soar, and fly up, towards the Employment of the Angel."
>
> Accordingly, I resolved, that it should be my ordinary Practice, whenever I step to answer the one or other Necessity of Nature, to make it an Opportunity of shaping in my Mind, some holy, noble, divine Thought. . . .

He added that "the loathsome and filthy Nature of SIN" would be part of his thoughts on such occasions. A similar preoccupation with and response to natural necessities recurred again in 1711, when Mather noted that "There are with me, in common with all the Children of Men, the usual Evacuations of Nature, to be daily attended." He wanted to use these occasions "to form some Thoughts of Piety, wherein I may differ from the Brutes, (which in the Actions themselves I do very little)" and to observe that his thoughts at the time had "some abasing Tendency." "The actions themselves carry Humiliations in them," he felt, "and a Christian ought alwayes to think humbly of himself, and be full of self-abasing and self-abhorring Reflections. By loathing of himself continually, and Being very sensible of what are his own loathsome Circumstances, a Christian does what is very pleasing to Heaven." For Cotton Mather, bodily functions were daily reminders of the beastliness of human nature, and the loathsomeness of the inner man. Left to himself, he could only despair for his own corruptions.[6]

For Jonathan Edwards, too, both the inner and the outer worlds were filthy and polluted, corrupt and sinful. "The inside of the body of man is full of filthiness," he said, "contains his bowels that are full of dung, which represents the corruption and filthiness that the heart of man is naturally full of." Just as the inner man is filled with dirt and defilement, so, too, is the outer world. "This world is all over dirty. Everywhere it is covered with that which tends to defile the feet of the traveller. Our streets are dirty and muddy, intimating that the world is full of that which tends to defile the soul, that worldly objects and worldly concerns and worldly company tend to pollute us." The realities of ordinary life in eighteenth-century New England thus had implications that went far beyond themselves and spoke to the innermost nature of mankind, as well as to daily experience. "We can't go about the world but our feet will grow dirty. So in whatever sort of worldly business men do with their hands," Edwards said, "their hands will grow dirty and will need washing from time to time, which is to represent the fulness of this world of pollution. It is full of sin and temptations. In all their goings they are imperfect and polluted with sin, every step they take is attended with sin. So all the works that they do are polluted. They can perform no service, no business, but they contract their guilt and defilement, that they need the renewed washing of the blood of Christ." Even with the renewal of the new birth, many evangelicals thus continued to experience within themselves just such corruption, inner filthiness, and pollution as Edwards described.[7]

The experiences of Susanna Anthony, for instance, bore witness to the inescapable sense of inner corruption and sin long after her own conversion. "I have seen sin to be the worst of evils; myself the worst of sinners, a transgressor from the womb. I have been convinced of the sinfulness of my nature, the corrupt fountain from whence proceeded every sinful act. . . ." "My heart," she noted, "has looked like a sink of sin, more loathsome than the most offensive carrion that swarms with hateful vermin! My understanding dark and ignorant; my will stubborn; my affections carnal, corrupt and disordered; every faculty depraved and vitiated; my whole soul deformed and polluted, filled with pride, enmity, carnality, hypocrisy, self-confidence, and all manner of sins." "Woe is me," she cried out in her diary, "because of the leprosy of sin, by which I am so defiled, that I pollute all I touch!" In September 1763, at the age of almost thirty-seven years, she still felt the pangs of inner corruption as intensely as in her earlier years: "O, in what a depraved state is fallen man! And what a wretched heart have I! Good God, what a leprous soul is this! How polluted, how defiled! What a running sore, that pollutes all I touch! I stain and spoil every thing, I have any concern with. Sin, this worst of leprosy, defiles, and ruins holy ordinances and duties. . . . O how does it pollute prayer; that sacred thing, which we never touch, but we defile, and leave the print of our loathsome corruption and pollution upon it! . . . Thus does sin spoil all it comes near to. And thus do we, as sinners, pollute all we have any thing to [do] with, whether ordinances or providences." The only hope Susanna Anthony had for escape from her inner corruption and persistent sinfulness was to be cleansed and purified by the blood of Christ; but the defilement within and the defilements of the world outside made escape from corruption virtually impossible in this life. As she noted in her diary in 1754, "O methinks I never knew the plague of my heart. It bursts out like a putrid sore, that never was truly healed." "Lord," she cried, "rip open the inmost sides, and let me be ashamed and confounded, because there are yet such horrid remains of the abominable thing, which thy soul hates; and which is for ever rebelling, and going contrary to thee; which is not subject to thy law, nor can it be. And O let the Lamb of God, who takes away the sins of the world, be more than ever precious to me: that blessed Redeemer, who takes away not only the guilt, but the filth; not only the power, but the pollution of sin. O blessed Savior, dearest Jesus, thou Son of God, I come, I come to thee; for I have heart thy blood cleanseth from all sin." Yet, knowing that the pollutions of her inner world could never be overcome fully in this life, she prayed, "O take me out of this defiling world. . . . I am almost impatient to get rid of this defiling heart and world."[8]

For other evangelicals, daily experience confirmed the sense of inner corruption and defilement felt by Mather, Edwards, and Anthony. Joseph Bean believed that he had been born in sin and was full of corruption in every part of his body, which "so Convade the dismal and most hored Infection through every Vein and artary of my body and so defiled me in every power . . . thare is nothing but wounds and bruses and putrifieng soers." In early 1741, he felt that God "has bin Pleasd of late to make such de[s]coviries of my hart unto me and I See such Corruptions Continualy Proceding from the Corrupt fountane I have within that I am ever Surprised at my one [own] vileness." "Lord," he said, "I See that I Cannot Speke one good woord nor do one go[o]d action nor think a good thought I am so Univarsally Corrupted in every power and facalty of my Soule." While at Exeter, New Hampshire, Daniel Rogers, an itinerant preacher, found that "the Lord was pleased to give me a further Sense of the hateful Nature of Sin from a View of the Working of It in my own Heart. So that I did Sensibly loath and abhorr It as the vilest filthiest Thing in all the World— I hate It with a perfect Hatred—It is nauseous." As his fellow evangelical preacher in Durham, New Hampshire, Nicholas Gilman, noted in his diary early in March 1743, "This day is Witness to My Sloth, My Unbelief My Ingratitude, Enmity to God and Hardness of Heart, what am I by Nature but a Very Lump of Sin and Image of the Devill, what reason have I to loath My Self and Repent in dust and ashes." And Benjamin Lyon, who was an ardent New Light, wrote of himself in 1762, "O Lord I am Destitute of all good, a most lothsome polluted Creature, Unworthy of the least of all thy mercies, Lord make me really Sensible I am So, I that am a Sinner by nature and more So by practice. What a monster of Wickedness am I, who so vile as I am." Another Connecticut New Light and separatist from the standing churches of her neighborhood, Hannah Heaton, also found that she "was troubled again with sin it seemed as if I had nothing nor was nothing but sin from the crown of my head to the soles of my feet no clean part in me. I felt a body of death."[9]

Michael Wigglesworth, too, felt himself to be totally corrupt and unclean within. "Look down and see my plague sores which I spread before thee my saviour," he wrote in his diary during the mid-1650's, "wounds and old putrifyd sores which provoke the Lord, stink in his nosthrils, and poison the peace and comfort of my own soul." "Behold I am vile," he exclaimed, "when thou showest me my face I abhor my self. Who can bring a clean thing out of filthiness," he asked. "I was conceived bred brought up in sin. O redeem from these devouring Lyons the hopeless shiftless soul that thou hast purchased." When David Brainerd woke up on the morning of February 22, 1744, he found that he "had as clear a Sense of the exceeding Pollution of my Nature, as ever I remember to have had in my Life. I then appear'd to my self inexpressibly loathsome, and defiled: Sins of Childhood, of early Youth, and such Follies as I had not thought of for Years together . . . came now fresh to my View, as if committed but Yesterday, and appeared in the most odious Colours." The following December, he once more felt that his "Soul appeared exceedingly polluted, my Heart," he recalled, "seem'd like a Nest of Vipers, or a Cage of unclean and hateful Birds: And therefore I wanted to be purified *by the Blood of Sprinkling*, that *cleanseth from all Sin*." Again and again, evangelicals such as these felt themselves to be diseased and dirty within their innermost selves, imprisoned within bodies of death until death itself freed their souls.[10]

The body was a perpetual reminder of the persistence of sin, the source of unending anguish, suffering, and dismay. Corruption and depravity were not abstractions; they were daily experiences as evangelicals felt themselves at war with their own flesh. While Daniel Rogers was riding toward New Brunswick, New Jersey, in 1741, he "had many of the Sins of my youth brought to remembrance and God enabled me to mourn over them and to loath them and my self for them." "It appeared plain to me," he noted, "that I was by Nature a Beast and Devil—I felt my self to be so." Jonathan Edwards noted, as many evangelicals could confirm from their own intense personal experience, that "Though Christian fortitude appears, in withstanding and counteracting the enemies that are without us; yet it much more appears, in resisting and suppressing the enemies that are within us"; "because," he added, "they are our worst and strongest enemies, and have greatest advantage against us." When the worst enemies were "within us," the body itself had to be attacked and, if possible, conquered and subdued.[11]

Characteristically, evangelicals sought to deny the sins of the flesh through the mortification of the body. Edwards as a youth of nineteen was frequently preoccupied with the necessity and comfort of self-mortification. Early in January 1723, he noted his intention "to live in continual mortification, without ceasing, and even to weary myself thereby, as long as I am in this world, and never to expect or desire any worldly ease or pleasure." Four days later, he assured himself: "I think I find myself much more sprightly and healthy, both in body and mind, for my self-denial in eating, drinking and sleeping." The following week, he noted that "Great instances of mortification, are deep wounds, given to the body of sin; hard blows, which make him stagger and reel. We thereby get strong ground and footing against him, he is the weaker ever after, and we have easier work with him the next time. He grows cowardly; and we can easily cause him to give way, until at length, we find it easy work with him, and can kill him at pleasure." "While we live without great instances of mortification and self-denial," Edwards observed, "the old man keeps about where he was; for he is sturdy and obstinate, and will not stir for small blows. This, without doubt, is one great reason why many Christians do not sensibly increase in grace. After the greatest mortifications, I always find the greatest comfort." Edwards thus not only sought to "kill" the "body of sin" but also felt himself dissociated from his own body. In attacking his own flesh, it was as though he were at war with someone else. The same sense of dissociation of self and body was apparent the following July, when Edwards noted that he could "count it all joy, when I have occasions of great self-denial; because, then, I have a glorious opportunity of giving deadly wounds to the body of sin, and of greatly confirming, and establishing the new creature. I seek to mortify sin, and to increase in holiness."[12]

Self-denial in every aspect of life was one of the most frequent methods of self-mortification, a way of keeping the body in constant subjection through constant rationing and denial of food and drink, occasionally through fasting, always through severe restrictions on diet. Edwards evidently kept to his regimen throughout his lifetime, since his student, Samuel Hopkins, who resided with the Edwards family for some time and visited thereafter, observed that "Agreeable to his Resolutions," Edwards "was very careful and abstemious in eating and drinking, as doubtless it was necessary so great a student, and a person of so delicate and tender a bodily make as he was, should be, in order to be comfortable and useful. When he had, by careful observation, found what kind and what quantity of diet best suited his constitution, and rendered him most fit to pursue his work, he was very strict and exact in complying with it; and in this respect *lived by rule*; and herein constantly practiced great self-denial, which he also did in his constant early rising, in order to redeem time for his study. He used himself to rise by four, or between four and five in the morning," and "commonly spent thirteen hours every day in his study." The resolutions for self-denial and mortification made by Edwards as a youth were practiced daily for the remainder of his life.[13]

The intensified consciousness of inner corruption and total depravity, together with a heightened sense of worthlessness, prepared evangelicals who were in the process of being born again for the denial and sometimes virtually the annihilation of the self that preceded conversion. The experiences of nineteen-year-old George Whitefield during the months at college "when religion began to take root" in his "heart," and he was "fully convinced that my soul must totally be renewed ere it could see God," exemplify the multiple levels of self-denial characteristic of many evangelicals before conversion. He joined with the Wesleys and their small group of young Methodists, and "chose rather to bear contempt with those people of God, than to enjoy the applause of almost-Christians for a season." He found his tutors, friends, and relations all dismayed by his behavior and hostile toward him when they saw him "resolved to deny myself, take up my cross daily, and follow Jesus Christ." The experiences of his daily life and the increasing isolation in which he placed himself "inured me," he said, "to contempt, lessened self-love, and taught me to die daily." He felt that his "whole soul was barren and dry," and he fancied himself "to be like nothing so much as a man locked up in iron armour." For many weeks, he battled with his inward nature and begged "for freedom from those proud hellish thoughts that used to crowd in upon and distract" his soul, but he found that "these thoughts and suggestions created such a self-abhorrence within me, that I never ceased wrestling with God, till He blessed me with a victory over them."

Whitefield's inner battles, however, were mirrored in his daily battles with his outer life. He discovered "what a slave" he had been to "sensual appetite," and began to fast twice a week and eat "the worst sort of food" he could find. "My apparel was mean. I thought it unbecoming a penitent to have his hair powdered. I wore woollen gloves, a patched gown and dirty shoes." Eventually, after fasting for the six weeks of Lent and inflicting his body with the cold morning air "till part of one of my hands was quite black," he "so emaciated" his body" by his "continued abstinence, and inward conflicts" that he "could scarce creep upstairs," and was obliged to inform his "kind tutor" of his "condition, who immediately sent for a physician to me." Falling ill and having "been groaning under an unspeakable pressure both of body and mind for above a twelve-month," he finally found that "God was pleased to set" him "free."[14]

About fifteen years later, after Whitefield had become the most eloquent and charismatic preacher of the message of the new birth to countless thousands of people throughout the American colonies, he preached to the inhabitants of Newport, Rhode Island, one of whom, Susanna Anthony, was profoundly affected by what she heard. After listening to Whitefield preach, fourteen-year-old Susanna found that she had gotten "more acquaintance with the work of God in the souls of his people," and she "resolved more diligently to labor after a life of holiness, and inward conformity to God." But immediately she found herself beset by Satan, who "roared after his prey" and tried, she said, "to persuade me my day of grace was over; that all my strivings would not signify any thing; that God had cast me off." Her case seemed hopeless, and she "felt the arrows of God within me. I roared, by reason of the disquietude of my soul; and was strongly beset to lay violent hands on myself, verily fearing, if I lived, I should be a most blasphemous wretch; being strongly and violently urged to utter some shocking imprecations on God, and my own soul, and every thing sacred." "O!," she added, "how many hours have I spent bewailing a lost God, and a lost Heaven; crying out, 'I am undone! I am undone! condemned already, and shall be damned!'" Soon she was "on the brink of despair," yet she told no one of her desperate situation. "I had cast off all regard for my body. One of my hands, I had so long neglected, only when I wrung it in distress, that it began to wither and perish. I had scarce any command or use of it."

A year later, in 1741, Susanna Anthony went to hear the Reverend Gilbert Tennant preach, and again her distress mounted. Her friends were concerned for her, but she "burst into tears, and told them they did not know what a dreadful creature I was; what dreadful thoughts I had." Her agonies continued for a long while to come: "I was ready to wish I never had been: and that I was any thing but a living soul. It is impossible for the tongue or pen of mortals to describe the agony of my soul; the amazing load that pressed on me. It seemed as though I should have twisted every bone out of its place: and have often since wondered that I never disjointed a bone, when, through the violence of my distress, I wrung my hands, twisted every joint, and strained every nerve; biting my flesh; gnashing my teeth; throwing myself on the floor." As her distress increased, she found that "the necessaries of life grew tasteless," and she began to "mortify and cross" her appetite; but, "though I took only enough to preserve life, yet every mouthful seemed to seal up my condemnation. And therefore I seemed ready to give up, and wholly abstain, rather than endure the distress of mind that every morsel I took filled me with." Her parents noticed her aversion to food and counseled her against it—her "temptation was discovered." Although she "could not see any conspiracy against my life," she noted, "my design was to mortify myself."[15]

Evangelicals usually found themselves in a constant battle with their own inescapable flesh and, like Edwards, felt most comfortable when mortifying themselves in greater or lesser degrees. The body was a source of unending temptation and distress, to be denied and bridled in every way possible. George Whitefield, too, was convinced that "mortification itself, when once practised, is the greatest pleasure in the world." As he noted, "there is really more pleasure in these formidable duties of self-denial and mortification, than in the highest indulgences of the greatest epicure upon earth." To take such pleasure in pain and self-denial required a special sensibility. But evangelicals experienced such intense alienation from their own bodies that they could not help feeling pleasure when suffering the afflictions which both God and they themselves inflicted.[16]

"That Monster, Self"

THROUGHOUT THEIR LIFETIMES, evangelicals were engaged in a constant battle not only against the flesh but even more encompassingly against everything within themselves that gave them a sense of self and self-worth. Self-denial meant nothing less than the denial of the *self*. Ideally, evangelicals had no self, for the self was the agent of sin and the source of discontent. Few, if any, were able to deny themselves altogether, for something within them resisted such annihilation. But the self was under constant attack from the conscience, as the wars within their psyches and souls waxed and waned in intensity throughout their lives. Their consciences never ceased to torment them so long as the self remained unsubdued. The chief sin was the sin of pride—and pride meant a high valuation of self. For evangelicals, therefore, life was nothing less than a constant battle with pride and self, and a constant seeking after humility, abasement, and impotency. The attack upon the self, in all its guises and manifestations, was one of the central themes of evangelical piety and temperament throughout the seventeenth and eighteenth centuries.[17]

Before being able to experience the new birth, evangelicals first had to discover the worthlessness of the self. It was essential that they feel and see the true nature of their innermost selves—the natural corruption and depravity which doomed them to eternal damnation. At the age of about eighteen, the Reverend Aaron Burr, like so many others, discovered that his pride and self-confidence rested upon a false perception of his own true nature. He recalled that while still a student in college, "it pleased God to open my Eyes and Shew me Something of what I was." He saw "my Self to be exceeding vile and odious in the Sight of an Holy God. . . . I beheld such a Foundation of Sin and Corruption, as I never imagin'd was in the Heart of any Man—I soon Chang'd My Thought of being better than others and conclud'd there was not such another Sinner on the Face of God's Earth. I was much inclined to despairing Thoughts of God's Mercy from a sense of my own Vileness. . . . I did then and do Still think there never was such a Bottomless Depth of Pride and Hypocrisy, Such an amazing Scene of the Most vile and abominable Thoughts indulged in the Heart of any Sinner as there was in mine."

Stephen Crisp, a nineteenth-century Quaker, recalled that his "general and constant cry was after the power by which I might overcome corruptions." He "knew that without the power of God I must perish, let them say what they would, and I could not reckon myself saved while I was captivated with a corrupt and rebellious nature, let them all say what they would." By the time he had reached the age of eighteen or so, "The rough and rebellious nature being now grown strong, and I in the prime and strength of my youth, and seeing how others spent their time in pleasure and vanity, a secret lust and desire kindled in me to partake of their cup." Although he still found that "for a time I was kept in as with a bit," nevertheless he knew that "all this while self stood uncrucified, and all that was gotten was but sacrificed and offered up for the obtaining a reputation to self, which should have been kept in the cross."[18]

Voicing the common theme of evangelical consciousness of the self before regeneration, John Greene, a New England Puritan of the mid-seventeenth century, acknowledged that God had let him "see much of the wretchedness" of his heart, and he "thought none so vile as I none so evil an heart so proud so stubborn so rebellious and I thought God would never show mercy to so vile a miserable wretch as I was." This vision of the inward self, a vision experienced in greater and lesser degree by most evangelicals, was the source of the despair and hopelessness that so often preceded conversions. In the end, every individual had to discover for himself and herself the truth embedded in Aaron Burr's personal experience, when he was finally driven to conclude that "I had been deceiving my Self with a false Hope and false Confidence—that Self had been at the Bottom of all." Not until individuals could bring themselves, or be brought by God, to reject their very selves as worthless, sinful, and justly damned creatures, could they ever hope to be born again.[19]

The denial of the self, indispensable for salvation, was nevertheless extraordinarily difficult to accomplish. Many evangelicals experienced a powerful impulse to resist the process of self-abasement and self-mortification that preceded their conversions. They could not accept the feelings of selflessness that were requisite for rebirth. Yet the savage attacks of conscience, which heightened their inner sense of corruption and depravity, and their physical actions, which inflicted pain and suffering upon their bodies, were all preparations for self-rejection—for the moment when they would come to feel utterly alienated from themselves and hostile to their innermost impulses toward pleasure, self-satisfaction, and self-regard. Before they could be born again, they must feel that they were totally deserving of nothing more than damnation. Self-righteousness and self-worth must be both denied and destroyed before being born again.

Whenever possible, evangelicals sought to give up the self entirely into the hands of God, so that they had no identity of their own, nothing they could perceive of as belonging to themselves. On Saturday morning, January 12, 1723, Jonathan Edwards "solemnly renewed" his "baptismal covenant and a self-dedication," made previously at the time of entering "into the communion of the church." "I have been before God," he said, "and have given myself, all that I am, and have, to God; so that I am not, in any respect, my own. I can challenge no right in this understanding, this will, these affections, which are in me. Neither have I any right to this body, or any of its members—no right to this tongue, these hands, these feet; no right to these senses, these eyes, these ears, this smell, or this taste. I have given myself clear away, and have not retained any thing, as my own. I gave myself to God, in my baptism, and I have been this morning to him, and told him, that I gave myself *wholly* to him. . . . Now, henceforth, I am not to act, in any respect, as my own." When Cotton Mather was almost twenty-three, early in 1686, he too gave himself completely to the Lord: "I then gave my *Self*, my whole *Self*, all my powers, Members, Interests, and Capacities, which, I owned, was the least that I owned, unto the Lord." In February 1757, Susanna Anthony also renewed her covenant with the Lord, trusting, she said, that "I was clear, fixed and hearty in the dedication and consecration of my whole self, body and soul, and every member, power or faculty; all I am, and all I have; every interest or concern, temporal, spiritual and eternal: yea, I think there was not the least reserve; not the least iota, but was solemnly given up to God."

Benjamin Lyon was not quite as certain as Susanna Anthony that he could give himself up entirely to the Lord, although that was his wish, as he noted in his diary in July 1762: "O that I might be Enabled to make a full and an intire Choice of the blessed god as my only lord and portion, forsaking all for him, for him only. O that I could from my heart fully Comply and close with the Religion of the blessed Jesus in all things, may I imbrace it in all its Dificulties. O that I could Even hate my Dearest Earthly Enjoyments and Even my own life also for Christ. O that I could give up my Self, all I have to him wholly and for ever without keeping back any thing, or making any Reserve." But the tone of his words hints strongly, as his whole diary confirms, that he was still keeping back something of himself from the Lord. That undoubtedly was why he also wished that he "could come up to the great Duty of Self Denial for Christ." "Lord," he prayed, "make me heartily willing to be nothing So that Christ may be all in all." Lyon's doubts reflected his own acute awareness of the persistence of self and of pride within him and in all his thoughts and actions. The same was true of other evangelicals, for pride and self were not so easily denied, even when the self had been dedicated solemnly to the service of the Lord.[20]

The preoccupation of evangelicals with the self and the perception of selfhood as the source of sin were evident throughout their lifetimes. Cotton Mather lectured himself about the mortification of the self in 1711. "The mysterious Nature and Working of *Pride* and *Self*, in my depraved Soul, must be my most exquisite Study; and I must be restless until I find the Dispositions thereof mortified in me by a superiour and

Coelestial Principle," he declared. "How else can I be meet for the *Inheritance of the Saints in Light?*" In 1708, when Alice Hayes was writing her memoirs and reflecting upon her life, she found that "I may say, in the bowedness of my spirit, that I have no might of my own, nor power, nor ability, but what" the Lord "shall be pleased to give me"; "and let nothing be attributed to that monster, self," she added. Similarly, Sarah Prince Gill, the daughter of the Reverend Thomas Prince (a leading New Light evangelical preacher in Boston and one of the most active proponents of the Great Awakening), wrote in her diary in 1757: "I found my latent Pride and self confidence catch'd at it and o how awfull it seem'd—I felt afraid of indulging self and cried to God to humble me and keep me low at his Foot . . . and so build up what can never be too low: Self." Hannah Heaton, too, was dismayed by the presence of her own self in all her actions and thoughts: "how my corruptions soon was in arms again o how selfish I felt I see my prayrs was Selfish I am now looking within me the more I serch the more I see. I find in my heart one abomination under another and another under that and I am a fighting against them but cant lay them. I am now just like a silly maid that sees her house defiled and goes to sweeping of it and the more she sweeps the more the dust flies and all because she forgot to sprincle it to lay the dust. Lord help me to look by faith to the blood of sprinkling to lay the dust and smudder [?] of sin. O is there a time a coming when I shall have a better heart, when I shall be as holy as god can make me altho now my soul is in anguish while I am writing because of sin. Self in myself I hate tis matter of my groan." The inescapable "self in myself" was the root of her anguish, as it was for so many other evangelicals as well.[21]

The actions that daily testified to the hateful presence of self were manifested most often in the sin of pride. "Remember," Jonathan Edwards wrote to a young woman in Connecticut in 1741, "that pride is the worst viper that is in the heart, the greatest disturber of the soul's peace, and of sweet communion with Christ: it was the first sin committed, and lies lowest in the foundation of Satan's whole building, and is with the greatest difficulty rooted out, and is the most hidden, secret, and deceitful of all lusts, and often creeps insensibly into the midst of religion"; "even, sometimes," he added, "under the disguise of humility itself."[22]

As Edwards said of himself, "The very thought of any joy arising in me, on any consideration of my own amiableness, performances, or experiences, or any goodness of heart or life, is nauseous and detestable to me." "And yet," he had to acknowledge, "I am greatly afflicted with a proud and selfrighteous spirit, much more sensibly than I used to be formerly. I see that serpent rising and putting forth its head continually, every where, all around me." Edwards's daughter, Esther Edwards Burr, also felt the workings of pride: "O! Sir," she wrote to her father, "what cause of deep humiliation and abasement of soul have I, on account of remaining corruption, which I see working, especially pride! Oh! how many shapes does pride cloak itself in." So, too, when the Reverend David Hall looked back over his own preaching at the end of December 1741, which had "been attended with great awakenings," he said that "I find that Cursed root of pride springing up in my heart and when I have been carried forth in preaching or discourse to begin to be pleased with my self: but O I am sure it becomes me to think most Humbly of my self and give God the praise which belongs only unto him." As he added prayerfully, "the Lord Check every degree of pride in me or sure I am undone." And when Benjamin Lyon spent a day of public fasting and prayer declared throughout the colony of Connecticut in April 1763, he reflected that "My Sins are many, and great. I have Committed a cloud of Sins the year past. Sins of thought, of word, and of Deed. Filled with pride, O how that Accursed Root of Bitterness Spreads it Self over my whole Soul. Appears in praying, Reading, Meditating, Conversation and Examination. Lamentable it is that I harbour this Enemy of god in my Boosom as I do." "Vengance, lord, vengance Upon my pride," he cried. "I do not Seriously Consider I have nothing that is good but what I have Received of the[e] my god, Even to good thoughts, or Desires. Lord, give me to See my Self, how Unlike I am to thee, and that will kill my pride." Michael Wigglesworth also was perpetually engaged in battles with his own pride. "Pride I feel still again and again abounding, self-admiration, though destroying my self daly." The enemy, the wily and dangerous serpent, had to be destroyed, for by the killing of pride evangelicals were killing the self as well. But the self, as Wigglesworth and others knew from experience, always rebounded to life and thus had to be destroyed "daly." The monster had to be slain. But how?[23]

The experiences of countless evangelicals who warred against the self confirmed Jonathan Edwards's conviction that "a great and most essential thing in true religion" was nothing less than "evangelical humiliation and its counterpart, self-denial." The "essence of evangelical humiliation consists," Edwards said, "in such humility, as becomes a creature, in itself exceeding sinful, under a dispensation of grace; consisting in a mean esteem of himself, as in himself nothing, and altogether contemptible and odious; attended with a mortification of a disposition to exalt himself, and a free renunciation of his own glory." And the duty of self-denial, he said, "consists in two things": "first, in a man's denying his worldly inclinations, and in forsaking and renouncing all worldly objects and enjoyments; and secondly, in denying his natural self-exaltation, and renouncing his own dignity and glory, and in being emptied of himself; so that he does freely and from his very heart, as it were renounce himself, and annihilate himself. Thus the Christian doth, in evangelical humiliation." As always, Edwards spoke from experience, his own and others. The denial, the humiliation, the renunciation, and the annihilation of self were central elements of evangelicalism. For all of these essential tasks, only the evangelical conscience sufficed.[24]

The conscience was omnipresent, unceasingly active, unrelentingly thorough in its searches and judgments, ferocious in its attacks, and never contented with its victories so long as the self survived. For evangelicals, the conscience within was the principal instrument for the attack upon the self that dominated their lives. The punishments and afflictions they felt within, as well as those suffered from outward causes, never sufficed to allay the need for further denial, more humiliation, total annihilation of the self. Evangelicals felt their consciences to be alien but welcome presences within themselves, the part of the self, however, which they sought to identify with and to placate. Cotton Mather demonstrated vividly the identification with conscience even when it was most punitive and destructive of the self: "I find in my soul a strange Experience. I meet with very breaking and killing Things, which are the Chastisements of the holy GOD upon me, for my manifold Miscarriages. In the sad Things that befall me, the glorious GOD is gratified: it pleases Him, to behold His Justice thus Inflicting Strokes upon me. Now such is my Love unto my God; and so united is my Soul unto Him, that I have a secret Pleasure in my Thoughts of the Gratification which is done unto Him, in the sad Things which tear me to Pieces before Him. I fly away from even my very self into Him, and I take part with Him against myself: and it pleases me, that He is pleased, tho' I myself am dreadfully torn to Peeces in what is done unto me." Since conscience was the voice of God within the self, there could be no question of a need to strive to "fly away from even my very self" and to "take part with Him against myself." But the conscience also was the voice of parents, magnified, amplified, distorted, yet still recognizable. By taking the side of their consciences against the wishes and needs of the self, evangelicals could satisfy the demands and expectations of both their God and the parents of their childhood.[25]

The imagery characteristically associated by evangelicals with self-denial suggests the unconscious restoration of the feelings of childhood, when individuals were small and low to the ground, while parents and other adults loomed big and tall above them. Self-denial was part of becoming a child again, for it meant being "low" and "nothing." Thus Edwards advised the young woman in Connecticut that the best signs she might discover of her Christian state would be those which had two effects: "those that make you least and lowest, and most like a child; and those that most engage and fix your heart, in a full and firm disposition to deny yourself for God, and to spend and be spent for him." "In all your course, walk with God, and follow Christ, as a little, poor helpless child, taking hold of Christ's hand," he urged. For Jonathan Edwards, who was unusually tall himself, height implied danger. "Lightning more commonly strikes high things," he noted, "such as high towers, spires, and pinnacles, and high trees, and is observed to be most terrible in mountainous places, which may signifie that heaven is an enemy to all proud persons and that [He] especially makes such the marks of His vengeance. . . . For the day of the Lord shall be upon every one that is proud and lofty, and upon every one that is lifted up, and he shall be brought low." Similarly, he observed that "If a building be built very high it must have its foundation laid answerably deep and low and must have its lower part answerably great and broad, or else it will be in danger of falling. So if a man be lifted up high in honour and prosperity, he will be in great danger of being overset unless his foundation be answerably strong and his heart be answerably established in knowledge and faith . . . and unless his lower parts, his humility, be answerably great and his foundation be laid answerably low and deep in self-abasement." To be proud thus was synonymous with being high and visible, and endangered by the wrath of God, whereas to be humble was to be low and out of sight, hidden from the wrath of God. "The soul of a true Christian," Edwards wrote in his meditations and repeated in his personal narrative, "appeared like such a little white flower as we see in the spring of the year; low and humble on the ground, opening its bosom to receive the pleasant beams of the sun's glory . . . standing peacefully and lovingly, in the midst of other flowers round about; all in like manner opening their bosoms, to drink in the light of the sun." The little flowers were like little children standing around their parents, passive, silent, receptive, with nothing of their own to give but ready to receive warmth and enlightenment from the sources of life themselves. Edwards himself suggested the analogy as he pursued the imagery. "There was no part of creature holiness, that I had so great a sense of its loveliness," he said, "as humility, brokenness of heart and poverty of spirit; and there was nothing that I so earnestly longed for. My heart panted after this, to lie low before God, as in the dust; that I might be nothing, and that God might be ALL, that I might become as a little child." The same experience of being little, low, and like a child also characterized Christian love generally, according to Edwards. "A truly Christian love, either to God or men, is a humble broken-hearted love," he said. "The desires of the saints, however earnest, are humble desires: their hope is an humble hope; and their joy, even when it is unspeakable, and full of glory, is a humble, brokenhearted joy, and leaves the Christian more poor in spirit, and more like a little child, and more disposed to an universal lowliness of behavior."[26]

To become a child again, though, also implied the necessity for becoming "nothing," of being virtually annihilated, and having no self at all. Sometimes during intense communions with his Saviour, Edwards felt "inward strugglings and breathings, and groanings that cannot be uttered, to be emptied of myself, and swallowed up in Christ." In 1737, he "had a view that for me was extraordinary, of the glory of the Son of God, as Mediator between God and man." During the course of an hour's rapturous immersion in his vision of Christ, who "appeared ineffably excellent with an excellency great enough to swallow up all thought and conception," Edwards found himself "in a flood of tears, and weeping aloud." "I felt an ardency of soul to be, what I know not otherwise how to express, emptied and annihilated," he recalled. So too Susanna Anthony, in March 1757, experienced a longing "to lie in the dust, and live on God for every mercy; to be nothing, and Christ all." Charles Jeffry Smith, a young Presbyterian minister who traveled and preached through Virginia and other colonies during the early 1760's, noted in his diary in June 1763 that "I feel my unworthiness of the ministerial Honour, and my unfitness for the Arduous Work, but yet I hant such a deep Sense thereof as I want to have; tho perhaps I have had for some days past meaner thoughts of myself than I ever had." "I long to be wholly emptied of self," he said, "and to have all my dependance upon Christ." As Benjamin Lyon also prayed, "lord make me heartily willing to be nothing So that Christ may be all in all." After a day of unsatisfactory preaching in Berwick, Maine, in September 1741, Daniel Rogers pleaded that "God would humble me, and Empty me of Self, and fill me with his fullness." David Brainerd often felt contented when he found himself conscious of being nothing. Late in May 1742, while in New Haven, Connecticut, he "scarce ever felt so calm in my Life; I rejoyced in Resignation, and giving my self up to God, to be wholly and intirely devoted to him forever." Early in June, he reported in his diary that he felt "much deserted: But all this teaches me my Nothingness and Vileness more than ever." Two days later, he "enjoyed one sweet and precious Season this Day: I never felt it so sweet to be nothing, and less than nothing, and to be accounted nothing." On July 4, he hoped "that my weary *Pilgrimage* in the World would be *short*, and that it would not be long before I was brought to my heavenly Home and Father's Houses: I was sweetly resigned to God's Will, to tarry his Time, to do his Work, and suffer his Pleasure. I felt *Thankfulness* to God for all my pressing *Desertions* of late"; "for I am perswaded," he added, "they have been made a Means of making me more humble, and much more resign'd. I felt pleased, to be *little*, to be *nothing*, and to *lie in the Dust*." As Francis Howgill, a Quaker minister in mid-seventeenth-century England, declared, "Self must be denied, and that you must deny if you will receive of him, that he may be all and you nothing."[27]

The powerful experiences of Isaac Penington, another ardent first-generation Quaker, demonstrated the sustained longings of many evangelicals for being little and nothing, without self altogether. As he observed of Christ's disciples, they "feel their own poverty and nothingness, as in themselves; and that their way to become strong in Christ is first to become weak in themselves; and so when they are strong in him, he who is their strength is glorified and admired, and self is of no reputation or value forever and ever; for that is cleaved to which brought self down; and that power and spirit being cleaved to, it still keeps it down." And he advised one Friend, "thou must become a child, thou must lose thy own will quite by degrees. Thou must wait for life to be measured out by the Father and be content with what proportion, and at what time, he shall please to measure." "Oh! be little, be little," he urged, "and then thou wilt be content with little." Like Howgill, Penington, and others, Nathan Cole found himself desirous of being nothing long after his own dramatic conversion, when, in 1760, "God sweetly humbled" him "down to his feet" and "gave me to see," he said, "my own unworthiness; and nothingness before him, he gave me to see the wretchedness and vileness of my own Nature in a great degree."[28]

For some evangelicals, the quest for nothingness occasionally verged upon actual suicide. Hannah Heaton recalled, "in years back I use[d] to be worried to make away with my self when sudden trouble come on me and when my little daughter dyed Satans tone was go hang your self, go hang your self, and when I saw a convenient place I could hardly tell how to keep from it sometimes." After her daughter's death, she said, "I thot I had murdered it as much as if I had cut of[f] its head for it was my sins that caused the lord to take it. . . . I remembered I was lamenting, roaring, and crying. I wondred in my heart why the authority did not com and take me to prison and put me to death for murder for I thot I deserved it as much as ever any did in this world. . . . Now I lay bound under this tryal about nine months till I thot I must have lost my sences." Her suicidal thoughts tormented her in silence, for there was no one around in whom she could confide: "I had none on earth I durst complain to with freedom and my godly parents now towards a hundred miles of[f] and the sea between." She was alone, though surrounded by children, husband, and neighbors, for they all rejected her piety and mocked her religion.[29]

Susanna Anthony almost succumbed to the temptation to kill herself, believing that "I was an outcast, rejected of God; that I had better put an end to my life, than live to treasure up wrath against the day of wrath." The "cruel instrument was present to accomplish the hellish design. This temptation rushed on me with such impetuous force, that I found it would be highly dangerous" to stay in the room. Rushing through the house, she happened to see a book of her sister's on "Advice to Sinners Under Conviction, &c. with some Scruples of the Tempted resolved," which spoke directly to her experience and prevented her from committing "that soul shuddering sin, self-murder." Suddenly, she recalled, "satan felt the force of these commissioned lines, and fled the field." "For now," she said, "I saw the power, wisdom and goodness of that Being, whom I was tempted to disbelieve. . . . The darkness and horror disappeared. This was the Lord's doing, and it was marvellous in mine eyes. There was no human contrivance in it. I saw the power and grace of

Christ. . . . O, how unutterable my joy! I sang of free and surprising grace; and, with the leper, was constrained, by gratitude and love, to return and give glory to God."[30]

Nathan Cole, too, found himself tormented with suicidal impulses early in 1745, several years after his conversion, when his "Sins seemed in some measure to reign which made me fear; and Satan was my Enemy and was permitted to tempt me, and he told me I was not converted; and I was afraid I was not." Soon he found he needed to be certain. "Well Satan comes upon me and says there is one way to know quick; destroy your self says he and you will soon know; for if you be converted you will certainly be saved; and if not you never will be converted, therefore destroy your self and you will know at once." Cole said: "I told him I will not on no account; but he followed me day after day and week after week for about three months with this horrible temptation." Satan was always at his elbow, telling him to use his knife "now, now," but he kept resisting the impulse. Finally, after talking with his wife and another "experienced Christian" after a church meeting, "A ray of divine light broke into my Soul," and "the Devil leav'd away ashamed, and I seemed to feel him go off as plain as I cou'd feel my Cloathes taken of[f] my back." Actual suicide was rare, in fact, although Jonathan Edwards's uncle, Joseph Hawley, who "had been for a Considerable Time Greatly Concern'd about the Condition of his soul" and fell "into deep melancholly," cut his own throat and died.[31]

For most evangelicals, daily life itself was a persistent experience of self-destruction. Cotton Mather constantly fasted and sought, as he noted in 1713, "to *Die Daily*, and become a Man dead unto this World; crucified unto all worldly Enjoyments and Impressions!" "I resolve exceedingly to study this Mystery and Attainment of practical Christianity," he said, "and live in the daily Practice of it, and be restless until I find a very sensible and powerful Mortification brought upon all my Inclinations for this World, and every Thing that is in it." Toward the end of his life, his preoccupation with self-abasement and humiliation grew increasingly intense, becoming a desire for martyrdom and death. In 1721, after finding himself under attack from many of his fellow townsmen in Boston for his support of the new methods of inoculation for smallpox, Mather's pleasure at the prospect of suffering as Christ had suffered, and being crucified as Christ was crucified, reveals the depths of his hostility toward his own body and inner self: "I am filled with unutterable Joy at the Prospect of my approaching Martyrdom. I know not what is the Meaning of it; I find, my Mouth strangely stop'd, my Heart strangely cold, if I go to ask for a Deliverance from it. But, when I think on my suffering Death for saving the Lives of dying People, it even ravishes me with a Joy unspeakable and full of Glory. I cannot help longing for the Hour, when it will be accomplished. I am even afraid almost of doing any thing for my praeservation. I have a Crown before me; and I now know by Feeling, what I formerly knew only by Reading, of the divine Consolations with which the Minds of Martyrs have been sometimes irradiated." Three years later, Mather saw himself not only as suffering but as being crucified daily. "I do most freely submitt and consent unto the Condition of a *crucified Man*," he noted, "and am willing to have my Crucifixion go on with a perpetual Succession of Pains and Pangs, without any Prospect of any Outgate, but at and by the dying Hour." His own close identification with Christ made his martyrdom bearable and meaningful: "It is to me a Thought full of Consolation; that if I have a Glorious CHRIST living in me, and have Him upon my Eye and my Cry unto Him to enter me, and possess me, and quicken me, for every Step of my Living unto GOD, I shall have Him, also suffering in me, and in all my Afflictions He will be afflicted." Such sufferings of the body and of the soul were vivid testimonies of the presence of Christ within, testimonies of experience that the self had been denied and crucified, had become nothing so that Christ and God might be all.[32]

The acute and sustained sufferings of many Quakers who sought to take up the Cross of Christ and to crucify the flesh and the self throughout the seventeenth century also suggest the joys which those who felt the presence of Christ within and who believed in the necessity for the subjection of the body could derive from the punishments inflicted upon their flesh. Like Francis Howgill, many early Quakers discovered for themselves that God "hath shed abroad his grace in my heart, which saves me from sin, and leads out of the works of condemnation into his habitation, where no unclean thing can enter." "And this grace," he continued, "has separated me from sin, and has constrained me to deny myself, and follow him through the death of the cross, and through the denial of all, both country and nation, kindred, and tongues, and people, and from wife and children and houses and lands, to publish his name abroad contrary to my own will, and to make known" to others "the riches of his grace, which all who wait in the light of Christ Jesus will come to see." For evangelicals such as Howgill, the denial of the self not only propelled them into the suffering ministry but also confirmed, by frequent martyrdom, the conviction that the self must be crucified and die to the world and the flesh altogether. Isaac Penington spoke for others when he wrote: "We were all made by him who is the great potter or former of all things . . . till it hath quite confounded and brought us to a perfect loss in all our own hopes, desires, and apprehensions; yea, till at last it hath quite swallowed us up in itself: Where, when we are dead, buried, and cease to be, know, or desire any more, that Life may at length spring up in us, which till then we are incapable of any distinct desiring or possessing. And the passage to this, though it be very dreadful to the flesh, being even through the Gates of Hell, death and destruction, yet it is in no small measure joyful to the eye of that Spirit which discerns it to be but a passage, and a necessary passage too." The self must die again and again. For many evangelicals, life remained an unceasing war with the self and an unending quest, fulfilled only by death itself, for selflessness. Only then could the monster self be slain at last, and the self become truly one with Christ.[33]

For some evangelicals, one of the most powerful desires of all was for oneness with Christ—a virtual fusing of the self with Divinity, so that there would be no separation or any distinctions between self and God. As Thomas Shepard reflected in 1643, "by faith the souls of the saints do melt into Christ: they destroy themselves and make Christ all; they have no righteousness but Christ's, no wills but melted into Christ's will and Christ's ends, no power but Christ's." The imagery of being "melted" and "swallowed" reflects the persistent wish to be incorporated into Christ's body and lose the self altogether. Sarah Edwards, Jonathan's intensely pious wife, experienced a rapturous communion with God early in January 1742, during which she found that "This lively sense of the beauty and excellency of divine things, continued during the morning, accompanied with peculiar sweetness and delight." "To my own imagination," she recalled, "my soul seemed to be gone out of me to God and Christ in heaven, and to have very little relation to my body. God and Christ were so present to me, and so near me, that I seemed removed from myself. The spiritual beauty of the Father and the Saviour, seemed to engross my whole mind; and it was the instinctive feeling of my heart, 'Thou art; and there is none beside thee.' I never felt such an entire emptiness of self-love, or any regard to any private, selfish interest of my own. It seemed to me, that I had entirely done with myself. . . . The glory of God seemed to be all, and in all, and to swallow up every wish and desire of my heart." That same afternoon, she went to hear a sermon which promised that "those, who have assurance, have a foretaste of heavenly glory," and found that she "knew the truth of it from what I then felt: I knew that I then tasted the clusters of the heavenly Canaan: My soul was filled and overwhelmed with light, and love, and joy in the Holy Ghost, and seemed just ready to go away from the body." "I could scarcely refrain from expressing my joy aloud, in the midst of the service," she noted. "I had in the mean time, an overwhelming sense of the glory of God, as the Great Eternal All, and of the happiness of having my own will entirely subdued to his will. I knew that the foretaste of glory, which I then had in my soul, came from him, that I certainly should go to him, and should, as it were, drop into the Divine Being, and be swallowed up in God." Her husband also thought "how happy I should be, if I might enjoy that God, and be rapt up to him in heaven, and be as it were swallowed up in him for ever!"[34]

Cotton Mather also speaks of the "*sacrificing-Stroke*, which with a Self annihilation will bring me on towards an Union with God, and an Acquiescence in Him, and in His Will; and when I feel in this way GOD becoming ALL in ALL unto me, I would be entirely swallowed up in Him." As Sarah Prince Gill prayed, in a paper entitled "God all, and in All":

> O though self-existent! self-sufficient Being! Let me know of *Thee*
> all that mortality is capable of knowing . . . let me know thee so as
> to love thee, so as to form me into a resemblance of thee in moral
> rectitude; knowing thy sovereignty will subdue me; knowing thy
> holiness will abase me; thy goodness will melt me; thy wisdom
> will astonish me; thy grace will allure me; therefore I beg to see
> thee as thou art in the face of Jesus the Mediator; a sight of thee,
> out of him, will consume me; but through him, attract me; and
> then I shall fly to and embrace him, and be for him, and my all
> shall be swallowed up in him who is the brightness of the Father's
> glory, and the express image of his person—Then, to the only liv-
> ing and true God, the Father, the Son, and the Holy Spirit, shall I
> devote my all, and spend an eternity, in the sublimest adorations,
> services, and praises, to him that sits on the throne, and to the
> Lamb, for ever and ever. Amen. Hallelujah!"

To be swallowed up and one with God was the ideal state, rarely fulfilled
in this life, but promised for the next. To have no self or to have one's self
melted into the being of Divinity—this was an ultimate aim of evangelical piety and one of the most urgent of the evangelical's innermost
desires.[35]

The fear of separation, of being left alone without the presence of
God in daily life, was a persistent torment to many evangelicals. After a
day of "Uneasiness in the family, Jangling, hard Speeches Unadvised
words," Benjamin Lyon felt that he and his family thereby "Dishonour
God, Crucify the Dear Redeemer, and grieve the blessed Spirit." Thus, he
added, "we Daily Dishonour god. Defile our own Souls and make up a
Seperating wall between god and our own Souls." Susanna Anthony also
knew from experience the anguish of feeling "a Separating wall between
god and our own souls," as her desire for "a closer union with God" and
her dismay and discomfort when she felt distant from God confirm.
"What! banishment from God! That I cannot bear. I am undone, I am
ruined, if separated from God. I cannot, I cannot! What! torn from my
centre: rent from my life! O hell of hells, beyond all conception," she
cried out in her diary in November 1762. To be left alone with the self
was intolerable, Hell itself on this earth. Only when close to God, preferably with the self not only denied but obliterated altogether, could evangelicals feel secure. Only then would they be nothing and God all.[36]

Broken Wills and Tender Hearts

BEFORE CONVERSION, evangelicals often felt themselves to be capable of bringing about their own salvation by the exercise of their own wills and by the power which they felt they had over their own actions and lives. Their sense of potency, of being able to act effectively and freely on their own behalf, their ability to shape their own lives, to control their own destinies both on earth and through eternity by the fulfillment of their own inner needs and goals, permitted them to be contented with the performance of religious duties—prayers, attendance at sermons, participation in the holy sacraments, even membership in churches at times—in the expectation of being able to recommend themselves to God by their actions and to achieve salvation by their own efforts.

In the terminology of the seventeenth and eighteenth centuries, the expectation of gaining salvation by the performance of religious duties, of good works, and by virtuous behavior generally was called Arminianism. The general notion of the term "Arminian" identified it with the freedom of the will. Before joining the congregation in Wenham, Massachusetts, in 1645, George Norton acknowledged that he previously "fell into Arminianism and held from free will"—notions which he subsequently rejected. Jane Holmes, who joined with Thomas Shepard's congregation in Cambridge, Massachusetts, recalled that while in England she had gone to the vicar of the local church, "an opposer of the truth," whom she said was "an Arminian, one that sought free will" and opposed the Puritans. For at least two centuries, Arminianism retained the same connotations—free will and good works as the means of achieving grace and salvation. Evangelicals consistently denounced these convictions, convinced instead that salvation depended entirely upon God's gift of free grace and not upon any merit or works by individuals; they were utterly certain, from the depths of their beings and undeniable personal experience, that the human will was not free. On the reception of free grace and the experience of unfree wills depended the central event of their lives—the new birth or conversion. But over and over again, evangelicals discovered from intense and painful personal experience that the new birth could not be achieved until their own wills had been conquered and annihilated. The rebreaking of the will, after so many years of willfulness and self-confidence, followed the systematic subjection of the self that preceded conversion. Most evangelicals, however, found themselves unable, of their own accord, to give up their own wills altogether in order to follow the will of God alone. But until they did so, the grace which they sought and the assurance of personal salvation which they longed for and needed, could not be felt or seen within themselves.[37]

Many evangelicals discovered that before their conversions they had been Arminians, whether knowingly or not, contenting themselves with the belief that they could bring about their own salvation through their own actions and by the exertion of their own free will. Nathan Cole, the Connecticut farmer who was converted in 1741, recalled that "When I was young I had very early Convictions; but after I grew up I was an Arminian untill I was near 30 years of age; I intended to be saved by my own works such as prayers and good deeds." John Wesley, too, found that he could not be converted and discover true faith, which he desired and sought, except "By absolutely renouncing all dependence, in whole or in part, upon my own works or righteousness, on which I had really grounded my hope of salvation, though I knew it not, from my youth up." Susanna Low, of Ipswich, Massachusetts, confessed that "I saw when I was a Child that there was a heaven and a Hell and was afraid I should go to hell and went about to build up a righteousness of my own: and so went on till the Earthquake in [17]55. When I was Shaken much and Set about making myself better, but Settled on the sandy foundation of my own Righteousness," which subsequently, at the time of her conversion, she discovered to be "a false foundation."[38]

Similarly, Nathaniel Sparhawk—a wealthy merchant and deacon in the church in Cambridge under Thomas Shepard's ministry—recalled that in his childhood, "his mother took much pain with him," and that in later years, he looked toward "the means appointed" for salvation and thereby "sought the Lord. And here he abode in his own strength, striving for a better condition, looking to means"; but he found nevertheless that "all could not help." Roger Haynes, a young gentleman who was the son of the governor of the new colony in Connecticut, confessed that he, too, "by the means I did find ease my carnal way in the very slubbering of duties over and, when my conscience was pacified, this was all I looked for." Daniel Sanders, who had been "religiously brought up," recalled that he had "resolved to walk in a Christian course, but did it in my own strength," soon thereafter "found the Lord forsaking" him. In neighboring Wenham, Anne Fiske declared that her own "particular sins were foolishness, vanity, and pride," and that before she heard her minister "pressing the necessity of believing in the Lord," she had "rested on performances."[39]

When Samuel Hopkins reached the age of eighteen or nineteen, he joined his parents' church. "I was serious, and was thought to be a pious youth . . . I was constant in reading the bible, and in attending on public and secret religion. And sometimes at night . . . when I thought of confessing the sins I had been guilty of that day, and asking pardon, I could not recollect that I had committed one sin that day." He found himself agreeing with several men "who were gross Arminians" that conversion consisted "chiefly in externals," much to the surprise and dismay of his mother, who overheard the conversation and warned him against that assumption. His fellow student at Yale, David Brainerd, also was greatly concerned about religion, praying, listening to sermons, and thinking of joining a church. "In short," he said, "I had a very good outside, and rested entirely on my Duties, tho' I was not sensible of it." Subsequently, it became utterly clear to him that he had "proceeded a considerable Length on a *self-righteous* Foundation; and should have been entirely lost and undone, had not the meer Mercy of God prevented." He continued to have "a secret latent Hope of *recommending* my self to God by my religious Duties," a hope shared by countless other evangelicals before their conversions.[40]

The experiences of the Reverend Aaron Burr, an early president of Princeton, encapsulate many of the central elements of evangelical experience prior to conversion which augmented the sense of power, of self, and of free will that were implied in Arminianism. As he wrote to Jonathan Edwards, his father-in-law, in March 1741, about his own religious experiences: "From my Childhood I used to be under Distress of mind," owing to "great Terrours and horrors from a guilty Conscience and the Fears of Hell; at these Times, as I remember, I used to get Relief by Promises and Resolutions," which implied that he could do something on his own behalf to gain the favor of God and ensure his own salvation. "I used (when my Distress was great) to Set my Self as twere in the Presence of God and Make over his Resolutions which would give Me ease and make Me more Strict in Secret Prayer for a Season," but "then Would all Wear off and I become as vain and careless as ever." "Thus I continued," he said, "under frequent Stiring of God's Spirit," which he "resisted and Stifled" until he became a student in college in 1734. "After this I reason'd my Self into a More thorough Reformation; forsook every thing But what the D[evi]l and my own deceitfull Heart flatered Me was right." He then "Set up the Practice of all outward Duties and soon began to be well pleas'd with my Self." By reading a number of books by non-evangelical writers, he "form'd Such a rational Religion (as I then Call'd it) as afforded Me no Small Delight Such as twas. I thought there were few Such Christians to be found. When I used to hear of Ministers Speaking against the Arminian Scheme, I used to pity their Ignorance."

Obviously, Burr himself was an Arminian in his youth, confident of himself and of his ability to be good and do good works toward his own salvation. He was very pleased with himself, and "never Imagin'd but that I was much better than the most of those among whom I conversed. And I secretly rejoiced that others were worse than I, for the Comparison used to afford Me peace and comfort." From the vantage point of subsequent experience and altered perspectives upon himself and his life, however, Burr could only look back upon this period of his youth and cry out, with dismay, "But O! the Pride that then reign'd in my Heart; It was the

Secret Spring of all my Actions; Whether I had to do with God or Man."
"All this time," he said, "I never saw the Badness of my own Heart." So
long as he remained proud, self-confident, self-willed, and so long as he
contented himself with outward duties and religious practices, so long,
in other words, as he was an Arminian like Nathan Cole and many
others, Burr was unable to be assured of his own salvation.[41]

In time, Burr was converted and discovered that he also underwent
"a very considerable Change in my Principals, from an Arminian; became a Calvinist," which meant, in effect, that he had given up his own
belief in the freedom of his will for a conviction of the freeness of grace
and the impotency of his will. The transformation, however, was not the
result of an intellectual persuasion, but rather was profoundly emotional
and intuitive—as he said at the time of his conversion: "I had not any
thing So clear a View of the Calvinistical Doctrines as I have had Since,"
and "used often to be puzzled with many Dificulties about them." But the
crucial fact was that despite his intellectual difficulties, he "Seemed to
have an inward Sense of these Truths; and thought they must be so
whether I could answer Objections made against them or not." Burr was
very much like Thomas Shepard, who had written a century earlier: "I
have met with all kinds of temptations but after my conversion was never
tempted to Arminianism, my own experience so sensibly confuting the
freedom of will." The rejection of Arminianism was a response to intense
personal experience, an inner certainty (independent of logic) that the
human will was not, and could not be, free.[42]

Joseph Pike discovered by experience that he, too, had no strength
of his own sufficient to bring about his own salvation. He saw that if he
"persisted in vanity and wildness, I was in the way of destruction"; "and
when the terrors of the Lord were upon me," he said, "I would take up
fresh resolutions to refrain from and avoid such conduct. But these resolutions came to nothing, being made in my own strength." As he discovered in due course, "I clearly saw, that I was not capable, by any ability
of my own, to preserve myself from the least evil, agreeably to the saying
of our blessed Lord, 'Without me ye can do nothing.' "[43]

Experience taught John Wesley the same lesson—that his own
efforts and works could never suffice to bring about his salvation. After
spending two years preaching in the newly established colony in Georgia,
Wesley returned to England in January 1738. Despite his own ministry to
the colonists, his American experience only taught him, as his journal
testifies, "that I who went to America to convert others, was never myself
converted to God." When he looked closely over his life and considered
his knowledge as well as his actions, he asked himself: "Does all this (be
it more or less, it matters not) make me acceptable to God? Does all I
ever did or can know, say, give, do, or suffer, justify me in his sight?
Yea, or the constant use of all the means of grace? (which nevertheless
is meet, right, and our bounden duty.). . . . Or, (to come closer yet,) the

having a rational conviction of all the truths of Christianity? Does all this give me a claim to the holy, heavenly, divine character of a Christian?" "By no means," he concluded. Without "faith in Christ," these things "are dung and dross, meet only to be purged away by the fire that never shall be quenched." He then added:

> This then have I learned in the ends of the earth: That I am fallen short of the glory of God; that my whole heart is altogether corrupt and abominable, and consequently my whole life; (seeing it cannot be, that an evil tree should bring forth good fruit;) that alienated as I am from the life of God, I am a child of wrath, an heir of hell; that my own works, my own sufferings, my own righteousness, are so far from reconciling me to an offended God, so far from making any atonement for the least of those sins, which are more in number than the hairs of my head, that the Most specious of them need an atonement themselves, or they cannot abide his righteous judgement, that having the sentence of death in my heart, and having nothing in or of myself to plead, I have no hope, but that of being justified freely, "through the redemption that is in Jesus:" I have no hope but that if I seek I shall find Christ, and "be found in him, not having my own righteousness, but that which is through the faith of Christ: the righteousness which is of God by faith."

He further observed that "The faith I want is, 'A sure trust and confidence in God, that through the merits of Christ my sins are forgiven, and I reconciled to the favour of God.'" And subsequently, in a footnote to his journal, he added revealingly that the faith he wanted was "The faith of a *son*."[44]

Late in May, Wesley wrote to a friend that he saw "that the whole law of God is holy, just, and good." "I know," he said, "every thought, every temper of my soul, ought to bear God's image and superscription. But how am I fallen from the glory of God! I feel that 'I am sold under sin.' I know that I, too, deserve nothing but wrath, being full of all abominations; and having no good thing in me, to atone for them, or to remove the wrath of God." "All my works, my righteousness, my prayers," he added, "need an atonement for themselves. So that my mouth is stopped. I have nothing to plead. God is holy; I am unholy. God is a consuming fire; I am altogether a sinner, meet to be consumed." Although Wesley had long sought to gain "inward holiness," and could say that "the image of God, was what I aimed at in all, by doing his will, not my own," he remained nevertheless "In this vile, abject state of bondage to sin," which he indeed was fighting continually, but not conquering. Only when he had acknowledged his own depravity, his total impotency, his utter inability to save himself by any works or merit in himself, could he gain assurance of the faith he sought. Wesley knew from personal experience the truth of his subsequent declaration, central to his religious doctrines, that "inasmuch as God works in you, you are now able to work out your own salvation. Since he worketh in you of his own good pleasure, without any merit of yours, both to will and to do, it is possible for you to fulfill all righteousness."[45]

When utter powerlessness was felt and acknowledged, conversion was possible at last. The experience of Isaac Backus captures the sense of total impotency well:

> On August the 29 1741 as I was mowing in the field alone—I was thinking of my case; and all my past Life seemed to be brought fresh to my view and it appeared indeed nothing but a life of Sin—I felt so that I left work and went and sat Down under a shadey tree, and I was brought to Look Particularly into my duties and striveings How I had tried to get help by awakening Preaching but found it fail:—had tried to Mend my Self by my Tears prayers and Promises of doing better but all in vain—my heart was Hard and full of corruption still and it Appeared clear to me then that I had tried Every way that Posibly I Could and if I perished Forever I could do no more—and the Justice of God Shined so clear Before my eyes in Condemning such a guilty Rebel that I could say no more—but fell at his feet [.] I see that I was in his hands and he had a right To do with me just as he Pleased And I lay like a Dead Vile Creature before him. I felt a calm in my mind—them tossings And tumults that I felt before seemed to be gone.

Only when Backus felt himself to be "a helpless Creature," only when he saw that he was in God's hands "and he had a right To do with me just as he Pleased," only then could the battle against God's sovereignty, power, and freedom of choice cease. Having come to the point where the savage and unrelenting attacks of conscience had made him intensely aware of his own inner corruption and sinfulness, and being acutely aware of his own inability to bring about his own salvation, Backus felt what so many other evangelicals also experienced during the course of their conversions: the inescapable necessity for giving up his own self and self-will into the hands of God. There could be no inner assurance of salvation, no consciousness of grace, until the inner battles with the self and the will were brought to an end by the acknowledgment of unconditional surrender. No other terms sufficed for salvation. The omnipotence of God required the total impotency of individuals. Only then could God's will be done by people on earth.[46]

The breaking of the sinner's will was the decisive culmination of the process of conversion. It was only after their wills had been broken that individuals could know they had experienced their new birth. The will was the focal point of all their inner battles, the inner citadel which had to be subdued and conquered, however well defended it might be on the peripheries by every possible action of the self, with its full panoply of pride, self-regard, and self-righteousness. Unless the will could be conquered, there could be no cessation of the hostilities, no abatement of the sustained enmity and the rebelliousness experienced by individuals in their relationships with God. As the Reverend Peter Thacher, minister to the first congregation in Middleborough, Massachusetts, observed in December 1741, after a powerful revival: "Those who have had such Joys, tell me they arrive to it in this Way; First awakened to see the many and horrible Acts of Sin thro' their Lives; then led to a View of their Original Sin, the Guiltiness and utter Helplessness of their Condition, of the Sufficiency of JESUS CHRIST: They beheld him in his Word, embrace and go out to the Promise, and CHRIST in the Promise; and this is the Foundation of their Comfort: They feel the Change in their Wills." This inner feeling was the crucial experience which brought about the conviction, indispensable for the new birth, that the will had been subdued.[47]

The necessity for the surrender of personal will to the absolute will of God was a constant theme in evangelical discussions of conversion. When the Reverend Francis Wayland pondered the implications of his own conquest of his infant son's will, he unhesitatingly asserted that God dealt with sinners in the same way. "To yield to the sinner's will, and save him without the unconditional surrender of his will," he said, "would be to make the sinner's will the centre of the moral universe." Nothing could be worse; but fortunately, God "only requires of him to surrender his own wilful and wicked opposition, and be happy." In conversion, Wayland said, "The sinner has only to submit himself to the righteous government of God, and accept of the Saviour's sacrifice, and the agony is over." "Once conversion is past," Wayland assured his readers, "You will be filled with love to God. . . . You will find that happiness can never be obtained by obeying your own will, but that it is obtained only by relinquishing it, and making God the centre of your affections, the eternal rest of your soul." His advice to all was: "*Submit yourself unto God.*" When this was done, they too would find that God "only asks you to be his dear child." Only by "renouncing our own will, and placing the will of God on the throne of our hearts," Wayland declared, could repentance and conversion be assured.[48]

Similar views had been set forth almost a century earlier by Susanna Wesley in her letter on the education of her children. For her, there could be no question of the fact that "self-will is the root of all sin and misery," nor that "religion is nothing else than doing the will of God and not our own: that the one grand impediment to our temporal and eternal happiness being this self-will, no indulgence of it can be trivial, no denial unprofitable. Heaven or hell depends on this alone." The conquest and submission of the will were indispensable for salvation. As Jonathan Edwards warned his congregation, "God has undertaken to deal with such men as you are. It is his manner commonly first to let men try their utmost strength . . . and when they have done what they can, and all fails, then God takes the matter into his own hands.—So it seems by your obstinacy, as if God intended to undertake to deal with you." Edwards declared with unhesitating conviction, "He will undertake to subdue you. . . . And You will be convinced; you will be subdued effectually: your hearts will be broken with a witness; your strength will be utterly broken, your courage and hope will sink. God will surely break those who will not bow." When Edwards thus spoke of "hearts" being broken, he was speaking of sinners' wills. The terms were synonymous.[49]

The inability of people to relinquish their own wills and to give up their personal will to the will of God sometimes caused extraordinary anguish and intense despair. Accounts of the experiences of people converted during revivals often speak of their inward struggles to submit their wills and to acknowledge the impotency of their exertions as they sought to be conquered by God. Daniel Rogers reported early in 1742, during a revival in Ipswich, that "Many New Converts were filled with the Holy Ghost in Sweet humble self abasing Frames—laying low in the Dust before God." He went to visit "Brother Samuel and found his Wife Powerfully wro't upon, her Will Sweetly bow'd in Submission to God." On another occasion, Rogers reported that "Peine's Daughter was now in the Pangs of the new Birth—Struggling with her Pride and Hardness of Heart, obstinacy of Will"; "I pray'd with her," he noted, "and God seem'd immediately to appear for her help—and to get the conquest— She said She was now heartily willing to accept of Christ and that She did close with him—the Love of God and Christ came into her soul—and she called upon us to praise God." Simultaneously, numerous others within the congregation also were being struck down, some crying out, fainting, and giving loud vocal expression to their inner anguish and fear. Rogers explained to his congregation that "the faulty Cause was in the Sinners Will—arising from Pride and other Lusts in the Heart." That evening, he observed, "God gave a most remarkable Testimony to his word—by his Spirit Convincing some persons of the Sin of Willfull Unbelief forcing 'em to Speak it out in an Amazing Manner particularly in one Instance—Ebenezer Harris— . . . the above said young man broke out in a most Surprising manner Roaring out the cursed Enmity of his Heart against Christ (Speaking directly to Him) Crying and Saying to Him—that he had shot an arrow which was sharp in his heart; that he wouldn't come to Him, at the Same Time—giveing Thanks that he was wounded—and praying that He might be conquered—presently after He seem'd to Submitt and received Hope in Christs mercy, and then some Comfort and Joy."[50]

The Reverend Josiah Crocker reported similar experiences in his congregation at Taunton, Massachusetts, in 1744, where many people "having wearied themselves with seeking rest in and from themselves, their duties, tears, repentings, et cetera, and being convinced of God's righteousness, though he should cast them off for ever," were finally "brought to submit to God's sovereignty." "Upon their submission," he noted, "they felt a calmness in their souls, having done quarrelling and disputing with the justice of God." Peter Thacher reported very similar experiences among the new converts in his parish in Middleborough, Massachusetts, in 1741. "How pleasantly affecting to hear them tell of their submission to God's righteousness," he said, "resigning to the hands of justice, and how sweetly and speedily in a moment they found themselves inclosed in the everlasting arms of mercy!" "Who would not be encouraged to come to this submission?" he asked. "Most of the new converts," he observed, "find they built on the sand, that they lived to themselves, rested in their duties, were mere hypocrites; and after a while, they joyfully tell me: 'I have found my feet on the rock. I never knew what it was to have my will subdued and heart changed and Christ there, till now.' " Only a totally broken will could bring assurance of grace and of the transformation of the new birth itself.[51]

The long and painful quest by Nathan Cole for assurance of his own salvation—a process which took more than two years of exquisite anguish and inner torment—was brought to a successful conclusion only when, after every effort on his own behalf had failed to bring comfort and assurance of grace, he finally felt that his heart or will was broken. "I went month after month mourning and begging for mercy," he recalled, "I tryed every way I could think to help my self but all ways failed:—Poor me it took away most all my Comfort of eating, drinking, Sleeping, or working. Hell fire was most always in my mind; and I have hundreds of times put my fingers into my pipe when I have been smoking to feel how fire felt: And to see how my Body could bear to lye in Hell fire for ever and ever."

Time passed until one day, looking into a fire burning near his bed, he found "these thoughts in my mind, Oh that I might creep into that fire and lye there and burn to death and die for ever Soul and Body; Oh that God would suffer it—Oh that God would suffer it.—Poor Soul—" "And while these thoughts were in my mind," he recalled, "God appeared unto me and made me Skringe: before whose face the heavens and the earth fled away; and I was Shrinked into nothing; I knew not whether I was in the body or out, I seemed to hang in open Air before God, and he seemed to Speak to me in an angry and Sovereign way what won't you trust your Soul with God; My heart answered O yes, yes, yes; before I could stir my tongue or lips." When the vision vanished, Cole found that "every thing was in its place again and I was on my Bed. My heart was broken; my burden was fallen of [f] my mind; I was set free, my distress was gone, and I was filled with a pineing desire to see Christs own words in the bible." Soon afterwards, he "saw that Darkness could as well be in the Clear light of the Sun, as well as Sin in the presence of God; who is so holy and Sovereign; now I saw that I must suffer as well as do for Christ, now I saw that I must for sake all and follow Christ; now I saw with new eyes; all things became new, A new God; new thoughts and a new heart"—all signs of the new birth itself.

Cole was still uncertain whether his experience had actually been a conversion experience, but he said, "Now I began to hope I should be converted some time or other, for I was sure that God had done some great thing for my soul; I knew that God had subdued my stubborn heart: I knew my heart would never rise so against God as it had done." His will had been conquered; his conversion, as he later realized, had been accomplished. Only when he had ceased to hope that he could save himself, when he had been forced by his own experience of impotency and sin to submit fully to God's saving and free grace, only when he felt his will to be broken and no longer free—only then could he be saved.[52]

The subjugation and unconditional surrender of the will, though so hard to achieve, was a common experience of evangelicals, as many of their accounts of conversion experiences attest. Some of Thomas Shepard's congregation in Cambridge also spoke about their own experiences with the subjection of their wills. John Sill's wife confessed that "She thought she was living but found it hard if the Lord should damn her." But she discovered that the "Lord in some measure subdued this cursed will to ly at [the] feet of mercy. Let Him do what He would." Mary Sparhawk recalled that "the Lord showed her sin more and more; but hearing what an enmity there was in the will against God, she saw it so clearly." She found, however, that she still "had a will to resist" Christ, despite hearing a sermon which "exhorted" her "to go to Him, to plead with God to subdue her will, which she did, yet saw her rebellion still exceedingly." For some time yet to come, she found it "hard to submit to the condemning will of God"; but in time, she came to say: "let Him do what He will, and thus the Lord gave her a contentedness of spirit." Mary Parish "sought the Lord to humble" her. She also heard "what a sin it was not to believe, yet," she recalled, "I heard affections might be wrought on and not the will. And I saw my heart opposite to the Lord and hence desire of Lord to change my will." Roger Haynes also remembered that he had "had many proud thoughts when [the] Lord made me sensible of yet subjecting my heart to His will and no sooner did I ever subject my heart to His will but had some answer of prayer."[53]

The subjection of John Green's will to the will of God formed one of the central themes of his relation of religious experiences before the Reverend Michael Wigglesworth's congregation in 1653. Green recalled "all my disobedience to parents," and other sins, which made him see that he "was far from God and God far from me." His sense of impotency to act on his own behalf distressed him, for he felt that he "had no power to think one good thought speak one good word," and he said, "I found nothing in myself, I saw my help must be only in going to the Lord Jesus Christ." Hearing the Reverend Mr. Mitchel preach made him think that "it were my happiness that I might fear and love" God "and sin no more," knowing that his "hope must be only from the Lord out of his free and abundant grace and mercy to me." He believed that he had "no power against the last temptation," and that "only the Lord could pardon my sins, subdue my lusts, remove my temptations." As he recalled, "I thought the Lord was able to subdue my proud heart rebellious will making me lay at his feet able to conquer all my sins and temptations." His "rebellious will" was the central issue, for it was the source of his enmity to God and God's law. When asked if he "had a dear love to God's will," he replied: "I have found my heart opposed to all that is good and that hath been my burden and a means to make me loathe myself the more." As he noted, "I see that the nub of all lay in my will." Only God could enable him to "part with sin," for "of myself," he said, "I could not leave them." As he observed toward the end of his narration, "I have searched to see whether I loved God's company or no and I have found indeed my opposition against it." "Yet," he added, "I have found in some poor measure that God hath helped me to take delight in his will."[54]

A century later, in 1764, a number of newly converted members of the Reverend John Cleaveland's parish in Ipswich, Massachusetts, spoke about their own experiences of having their wills subjected to the will of God at the time of their rebirth, and of surrendering themselves unconditionally to God. John Lendal confessed that he had "been not only a person void of Religion but of Morality, and a great opposer of the present work of God a-going on among us." But after hearing Cleaveland preach, he was brought "to See the Wrath of God was out against Me, and I was in immediate Danger of Stepping into the Flames of Hell." In due course, after hearing another preacher, he went home and found that "just as I got home I found my Will bow to Christ, which I was Sensible had Stood out against him, and I was willing to Give all up to Christ, and Christ appeared all Together lovely, that Justice was Satisfied by his alsufficient Righteousness and my Soul was filled with peace of Conscience and Joy in the holy Ghost." Elizabeth Marshall, too, "was bro't to see that" she "had a dreadful hard heart and Stubborn Will and was burdened with Guilt for a good many Weeks, and saw it would be just with God to cast" her "into hell." "I saw Christ was willing," she said, "but I had been unwilling but now found I was willing, my Burden went off and my Soul was filled with Love to Christ and hatred of all sin, and was Sensible that my heart was vile." Mary Story remembered that she had had "a Sense that God was Angry with me, and I wanted Something to reconcile God to me." When she thought that "Christ was not willing to save me and I must perish," she felt her "heart rise with Enmity against God, and I wished I had no Soul." In time, though, she became "sensible that Christ was willing but I was unwilling, and my Soul kept crying to the Lord all the way that he would bow my Stubborn Will and make me willing to accept of Christ." Her admission to the church on June 29, 1764, confirms her acceptance of Christ and the submission of her will.[55]

The subjection of the will and the necessity for absolute obedience to the will of God were central themes in the accounts of conversion experiences among early Quakers as well. Before Stephen Crisp was converted in 1655, about the age of twenty-seven, he had given himself up for lost, when suddenly he heard the Lord thunder "through me, saying, that which is weary must die." "So I turned in my seat," he recalled, "and waited in the belief of God, for the death of that part which was weary of the work of God, and grew more diligent in seeking death, that I might be baptized for the dead; and that I might know how to put off the old man with his deed and words, and imaginations, his fashions and customs, his friendship and wisdom, and all that appertained to him, and the cross of Christ was laid upon me, and I bore it." "As I came willingly to take it up," he noted, "I found it to be to me, that thing which I had sought from my childhood, even the power of God; for by it, I was crucified to the world, and it to me, which nothing else ever could do." He knew then that if he took "up the cross," he would "obtain victory, for that is the power of God through faith to salvation." Thereafter, he said, "it was my great care night and day, to keep so low and out of the workings of my own will, that I might discern the mind of God, and do it, though in never so great a cross to my own."[56]

The first conversion of Joseph Pike occurred in 1669, at the age of about twelve, when after months of intense anguish and sorrow, he "became obedient" to the Lord's "divine light and good Spirit in my soul, without which I could not perform anything that was acceptable to God." He found that "After the baptizing power of the Lord had thus seized upon me, I had dominion given me over those temptations, which had before so often prevailed upon me, and I grew easier in spirit, and had great sweetness and comfort." As the years passed, however, and he reached the age of eighteen, he discovered that he had lost the "state of purity" which he had achieved before. Once again he felt himself visited by the Lord, who showed him "a full and clear sight" of his "condition, and how I was estranged from him in spirit; and that if I continued therein, I should grow harder and harder, and in the end, be undone for ever." "The sense of this brought me into great horror and distress, with bitter lamentation," he recalled, "until the Lord was mercifully pleased to tender my spirit a little, and assist me to pray unto him for a repentant heart, on account of my past disobedience, in so ungratefully departing from him." He soon saw that "nothing could destroy this, but the axe, the sword, the hammer, and the fire of his Holy Spirit, and that I must be regenerated and born again, before I could ever attain to the condition I had lost. . . . Then, oh! the agony, the horror that seized my soul, I am not able to express it. I often thought no one's condition was ever like mine; when I turned my mind inward, my soul seemed like a habitation of dragons, which were ready to devour me."

For many months, Pike continued to be afflicted. In time, he said, "I came to know they were from the Lord, and that it was a time of the ministration of condemnation, in order to bring me nearer to the Lord, by breaking down and mortifying the natural and fleshly part in me, which had grown strong, and was not to inherit the kingdom of God." "Through these sore exercises and taking up the cross of Christ under them," he added, "my own natural will and affections became much broken, and I was, in measure, as a little child, depending upon the Lord for strength and ability to do his will." Only by becoming a child again, with no will of his own, could he at last be enabled to do the will of God.[57]

The experiences of earliest childhood had prepared many who were to be reborn as adults to deny their own wills altogether, to subdue the self, and to obey the word and will of God. Indeed, doing the will of God and not their own became the central motif in their lives, providing the indispensable evidence they needed to assure them that they truly had become children of God.

Authoritarian Temperaments: Evangelical Responses to Power

FOR EVANGELICALS, authority was synonymous with power, and power, in turn, was perceived in terms of absolute sovereignty. Power always meant *total* authority—authority which could not be compromised by the wishes or the personal needs of individuals. Parental power was absolute, of course, and the crushing of the child's will by the exertion of systematic efforts on the part of parents was justified by the conviction that parental power and authority were beyond question within the confines of the household. Children should never feel that they could deflect or alter the will of a parent to suit their own wishes. The conquest of the child's will meant the unqualified victory of parental will and authority.[58]

Divine authority, too, always was perceived by evangelicals in terms of sovereignty, and sovereignty, in turn, meant *total* power. Jonathan Edwards was preoccupied with the nature of Divine authority, certain that God's authority was absolute and sovereign. Among the attributes of God's sovereignty, he included "supreme, universal, and infinite *power*; whereby he is able to do what he pleases, without control, without any confinement of that power, without any subjection in the least measure to any other power; and so without any hindrance or restraint, that it should be either impossible, or at all difficult, for him to accomplish his will; and without any dependence of his power on any other power, from whence it should be derived, or which it should stand in any need of"; "so far from this," he noted, "that all other power is derived from him, and is absolutely dependent on him." Secondly, Edwards said, "he has supreme *authority*; absolute and most perfect right to do what he wills, without subjection to any superior authority, or any derivation of authority from any other, or limitation by any distinct independent authority," so that, third, "his *will* is supreme, underived, and independent on anything without himself; being in everything determined by his own counsel, having no other rule but his own wisdom; his will not being subject to, or restrained by the will of any other, and others' wills being perfectly subject to his." Fourth, Edwards said, "his *wisdom*, which determines his will, is supreme, perfect, underived, self-sufficient, and independent." Thus, finally, Edwards asserted, "There is no other divine sovereignty but this: and this is properly *absolute sovereignty*: no other is desirable; nor would any other be honorable, or happy: and indeed there is no other conceivable or possible."[59]

The absolutism of God's sovereignty was connected closely to the absolute authority of God's will, so that for Edwards, power, authority, will, and wisdom all combined to form a single complex of the attributes of Divinity, which provided no opening for the will or the wishes of humanity. Despite his assertion that "there is no other conceivable or possible"—something which many other nonevangelical Christians would dispute—there is no doubt about his own personal certainty of the necessity for his belief in Divine absolute sovereignty. As he said in his personal narrative, "The doctrines of God's absolute sovereignty, and free grace, in shewing mercy to whom he would shew mercy; and man's absolute dependence on the operations of god's Holy Spirit, have very often appeared to me as sweet and glorious doctrines. These doctrines have been much my delight." "It has often been my delight to approach God," he noted, "and adore him as a sovereign God, and ask sovereign mercy of him." The love of sovereignty and of absolute power possessed by God sprang from deep within Edwards's own psyche and self. These were not abstractions to him but daily experiences.[60]

For Edwards, as for other evangelicals, it was inconceivable that individuals could limit the power, authority, or will of God. There could be no boundaries established that would confine or limit God's sovereignty. The total power of God and the utter impotency of mankind formed persistent polarities which defined the relationship of God and mankind. The powerless could not negotiate with the powerful, nor could they find any way to establish any claims to the affection or the grace of God by virtue of anything in themselves. The conception of Divine sovereignty that shaped the evangelical mentality precluded the conception of covenants—binding agreements limiting the exercise of power and authority undertaken by two legally equal parties—since there could be no equality between God and man. That is why God's wrath seemed so frightening to individuals like Edwards, who warned his congregation in his sermon on the plight of "Sinners in the Hands of an Angry God" that "they have no refuge, nothing to take hold of; all that preserves them every moment is the mere arbitrary will, and uncovenanted, unobliged forbearance of an incensed God." Without God's will and grace, they would all be damned. Free grace was a gift, unmerited and undeserved, which alone could ensure salvation. But free grace was necessary for evangelicals precisely because of their conviction that God was sovereign, with total power and authority, while they were entirely without power or wills of their own. Total submission and surrender were the only terms acceptable to God.[61]

Many evangelicals, however, had fought hard against the annihilation of the self, against the impotency of their wills, and against the acknowledgment that they could do nothing to save themselves. Often they remembered periods in their childhood and youth when they hated the thought that God was sovereign, totally powerful and completely free to save or damn every person no matter what they might do. As Jonathan Edwards recalled, "From my childhood up, my mind had been full of objections against the doctrine of God's sovereignty, in choosing whom he would to eternal life, and rejecting whom he pleased; leaving them eternally to perish, and be everlastingly tormented in hell. It used to appear like a horrible doctrine to me." "But I remember the time very well," he said, "when I seemed to be convinced, and fully satisfied, as to this sovereignty of God, and his justice in thus eternally disposing of men, according to his sovereign pleasure." "But," Edwards added, "never could give an account, how, or by what means, I was thus convinced." Although as an adult he could say that "Absolute sovereignty is what I love to ascribe to God," he also had to acknowledge that "my first conviction was not so."

David Brainerd also remembered that he had had "a great inward Opposition to . . . the *Sovereignty* of God." "I could not bear," he said, "that it should be wholly at God's pleasure, to save or damn me, just as he would." And he often felt an "Enmity against the Sovereignty of God" which made him afraid. Susanna Anthony also remembered that she had "quarreled with the sovereignty of God." The same was true of Isaac Backus, who "found Dreadful Qurelings against God, especially Against his Sovereignty and the freeness of his Grace—that he was no ways obliged to give me His Grace, let me do as much as I would." Before his conversion, the Reverend Aaron Burr said that he saw that his "Heart was fill'd with an Opposition to every Thing that was good and knew it must be Changed by the Almighty Power of divine Grace or I cou'd never be saved. I think I had a Sense of being in the Hands of a Sovereign God. That if he sent Me to Hell and Saved others, I must pronounce him just with my last Breath. That it must be by free Sovereign Grace if I ever was

Saved." He also acknowledged, however, that he "used to meet with Many Objections against the Sovereignty of God—But I found Something within that acquiesced in it." Like Burr and like Edwards, virtually everyone who was to be born again "found Something within that acquiesced," an acquiescence that came from the acknowledgment, at last, of the total impotence of the self and the omnipotence of Divinity.[62]

Evangelicals felt the deep attractions of sovereign power and the need for total submission. When considering the attributes of "real, genuine Christianity," John Wesley noted that "A Christian cannot think of the Author of his Being, without abasing himself before him: without a deep sense of the distance between a worm of earth, and him that sitteth on the circle of the heavens. In his presence he sinks into the dust, knowing himself to be less than nothing in his eye: and being conscious, in a manner words cannot express, of his own littleness, ignorance, foolishness." The distance between God and individuals was immense; a gulf yawned between them. The imagery of childhood and of the parenthood of God shaped Wesley's statement about true Christians and conveyed the certainty, similar to Edwards's, of the utter submission of the child to the absolute authority and power of the parent: "He has a continual sense of his dependence on the Parent of Good, for his Being, and all the blessings that attend it. . . . And hence he acquiesces in whatsoever appears to be his will, not only with patience, but with thankfulness. He willingly resigns all he is, all he has, to his wise and gracious disposal. The ruling temper of his heart, is the most absolute submission, and the tenderest gratitude to his Sovereign Benefactor."[63]

The "most absolute submission" did not permit any qualifications to compromise the necessity for total obedience; and Wesley was certain, as might be expected, that "The Will of God is the supreme, unalterable rule for every intelligent creature; equally binding every angel in heaven, and every man upon earth." "Nor can it be otherwise," he added, since it is "the natural, necessary result of the relation between creatures and their Creator," just as it might also be from the relation to parents and children. "If the Will of God be our one rule of action, in every thing, great and small," said Wesley, "it follows, by undeniable consequence, that we are not to do our own will in any thing." By this, Wesley really meant having no personal will in any respect whatsoever. Christians were to give themselves entirely over to the will of God and to His every disposition for them. "Thus, we are to use our understanding, our imagination, our memory, wholly to the glory of him that gave them. Thus our will is to be wholly given up to him, and all our affections to be regulated as he directs. We are to love and hate, to rejoice and grieve, to desire and shun, to hope and fear, according to the rule which he prescribes whose we are, and whom we are to serve in all things." "Even our thoughts," added Wesley, "are not our own in this sense; they are not at our own disposal: but for every deliberate motion of our minds, we are accountable to our Master."

Thus self-denial and taking up the Cross of Christ were indispensable methods for submitting totally to the will of God. Only when the self was suppressed altogether could obedience be assured. Self-will was the surest sign for Wesley of the fact that one was not a real Christian. The presence of the self and of self-will constituted an ever-present threat to the ability of a Christian to obey the will of God without hesitation or questioning.[64]

Evangelicals were preoccupied with the necessity for obedience. After their conversions, their lives were devoted to the maintenance of as perfectly obedient and submissive a stance as they were capable of achieving, so that they could be certain that they were following the will of God and not their own in any respect. The denial of their own will became one of the central themes of their lives, the dominant motif of their writings, and the driving force behind their daily prayers, their daily actions, and the private and public works in which they were engaged. They felt themselves freest when most subjected to the will of God. The paradox of Christian liberty, as they defined it, was expressed eloquently by the Reverend Samuel Phillips, minister to the South Parish of Andover, Massachusetts, for many decades during the eighteenth century, who declared that "True liberty" consisted "in having the mind truly enlightened; and the power of sin and lust broken in the soul; and the appetites and passions under the government of right reason; and all the powers united to maintain good order in the Soul; and, every thought brought into captivity, to the obedience of Christ." "O blessed Captivity! no other than perfect liberty," he declared. "Such truly walk at liberty, who have no will of their own, but resign themselves to the commanding and disposing will of the only wise God." Evangelicals throughout the seventeenth and eighteenth centuries shared this definition of "True liberty," and found in obedience and submission to the will of God the only satisfactory evidence they possessed that they were truly children of God.[65]

In mid-January 1761, at the age of thirty-four, Susanna Anthony prayed in her diary, "O my God, my God, thine I am. O take me into thine own merciful and gracious hands. Subdue every lust. Conform me to thy blessed law. Resign me to thy sovereign will." As she acknowledged, "I know I am absolutely dependent on thee . . . it is thy own infinite dignity to be self-sufficient and independent. And it is my highest felicity to be dependent and insufficient. . . ." The following November, she continued to voice her vision of Divine sovereignty and her own intense need to be conquered and to surrender to the absolute power of God: "I long for nothing so much as entire conformity to thee; a cordial and absolute subjection to thy sovereign will. . . . I am thine; make me what thou wilt have me to be. Spare not the rod, to spoil thy child. Thou best knowest what is best for me. Father, I submit. Let me not reluct. It is right thou shouldest take thine own way. I glory in thine adorable sovereignty. I would not, for a thousand worlds, be left to my own choice. I had ruined myself eternally, long before now, if left to myself." As she declared, "I trust that I have a principle of real grace; but I cannot keep it; I cannot exercise it of myself. All my sufficiency is of thee. O omnipotent Redeemer, maintain thy conquest."[66]

In Susanna Anthony's mind, God's power and authority, the attributes of His government, were absolute and unbounded. There could be no limits placed upon His sovereignty or any of His actions toward mankind. In April 1774, she found that "the infinitely condescending Jehovah has set himself before me, as so infinitely fit to govern, and worthy to be submitted to, yea, rejoiced in, in every dispensation," and she asked, "O when shall my whole soul unite in the most perfect manner, strongest degree and universal extent, to every exhibition of the unbounded, infinite, glorious rectitude and perfection of Jehovah's nature and government!" She had been often professing her "hearty subjection to him, and his government." "I have been calling him Lord and King," she said, "owning his infinite right and fitness to govern; recounting his sovereign authority; exclaiming against every degree of opposition to him, and his government." Anthony exulted in the "unbounded" sovereignty and omnipotent power of Divine government, and was happiest when she was most submissive to the Divine will. Whenever she felt herself thinking that she was somebody, with wishes, desires, and needs of her own, she knew that she was imperiled and sought, again and again, to deny herself altogether. True liberty was synonymous with absolute conformity to the will of God. Nothing less sufficed.[67]

The dominant theme running through the diary of Sarah Prince Gill also was submission and conformity to the Divine will in every possible respect. Sarah Gill was constantly on guard against her own willfulness and her own sense of self, convinced, as were so many others, that both were ruinous for the soul. As she observed, "I love to serve my friends, but I delight vastly more in feeling my very will entirely subject to God— Yea I have found an unspeakable pleasure in having my [will?] crossed, and my carnal desires denied by him—and I do know that I never felt better pleased than when I surrendered my will, affections, and all my concerns [?] into his hands, and left it with him to do just what he pleased therewith—Is not this real religion?" she asked, just as John Wesley did. "I would have it the very breath of my heart daily, hourly, and in every moment of my life, 'Father, not as I will, but as thou wilt.' " "O my heavenly Father," she prayed, "give me this conformity to thee— Let my will be crossed, humbled, broken, till it is swallowed up in thine. Let thy will be the rule of mine; empty me of self and mould me into thine image, for Christ's sake." In the privacy of her diary, she admitted that "I dare not say I *am sure I surrendered My self to him*, but I tried to do it." She sometimes found that her heart was "often rising up in secret disatisfaction with the Providences of God—O My heart is hard—my will is Stubborn: Yea 'tis obstinately Stubborn." During a period of anxiety and inner conflict over a prospective suitor, she wrote: "I feel willing to have it ordered one way or the other just as it pleases him and resigning myself to him to dispose of absolutely. I now wait for the discovery of his Will. [I?] dare not decide my-self and dread nothing more than to be left to the Bent of my own heart."

Several months later, during a time in which she felt very close to God, she looked toward "a fixed determined Choice of him as my *Portion*—to a frequent surrender of my all to him—to ardent breathings after communion with him and Conformity to his *Nature* in Habitual Holiness and *Will* in an active uniform Steady Obedience"; "nothing do I long for so much," she said, "as to be *All for God* to have my Soul brought near to him and to lay in a holy subjection to him and to live and act entirely for him." But she found that she couldn't "rest till this is wrought till my Will is broken and God alone be Exalted in me—I delight in the thought of Sacrificing my All to him and to have him Possess and rule me entirely and I can't be Easy to be only so now and then but I want to be so Continually. I long to be allways Swallowed up in him!" She desired, she said, nothing so much "as to have sin rooted out of me, and the Image of the Holy God implanted in me and to be intirely subject to the Whole Preceptive Will of God and allso to resign to, and acquiesce in all his disposing will concerning me—I want to yield entirely to his Government without so much as one reservation, no not of the dearest Enjoyment but yield all to him." "Tis the Contrary to this," she acknowledged, "that is all my Unhappiness." Divine government, for Sarah Prince Gill, meant total power, which required "entire" subjection. Self-will was the persistent source of all her unhappiness because she was never able to deny her own self and self-will altogether for very long.[68]

The theme of obedience and the utter denial of self-will shaped the recollections of David Ferris, whose entire adult life was lived in terms of his need to do only the will of God, never his own. Ferris was born in Stratford, Connecticut, in 1707, the third of eight children in a family of pious Presbyterians. Early in his life, his father removed the family from Stratford to the newly settled town of New Milford. He recalled that his mother, "being a religious woman, and much concerned for the good of her offspring, both temporally and spiritually," often gave them "good advice and admonition." Ferris was deeply affected during the revival in 1727 and joined with the Presbyterian church in New Milford. While a student at Yale College, he found himself holding views considered by some of his friends and people in authority to be heretical, verging toward the Quakers, although he knew nothing about them at the time. In due course, however, he was drawn closer toward the Quakers, and eventually attended a yearly meeting on Long Island, whereupon, he said, "I rejoiced to find *that* which I had been seeking; and soon owned them to be the Lord's people; the true church of Christ," and he "also found they held and believed the same doctrines, the truth of which had been manifested to me immediately by the Holy Spirit." He decided then to leave Yale, and went home to confront his father, who refused at first even to speak to him. Having given up the prospect of entering the ministry and having "disobliged" his father, who refused to give him any financial support, he found himself at the age of twenty-five in need of a livelihood. He decided to move to Philadelphia, where he taught school for a while.[69]

Ferris had discovered that he could do nothing that was not directly consonant with the will of God, and was able to act only when certain that he knew God's will for him. He found that his mind was "humbled and made subject to the cross of Christ," and that he was "heartily willing to take it up, daily, and follow him, my kind leader, in the narrow way of self-denial. . . . He now became my director in all things; showing me clearly what my duties were; and enabling me to perform them in an acceptable manner." "But if, at any time, I acted in my own will," he observed, "I lost my strength, and found no acceptance nor benefit by my performances; by which I gradually learnt, that I could do nothing, acceptably, without the immediate assistance of the spirit of Christ the Redeemer."[70]

One series of memorable episodes in David Ferris's life exemplifies the necessity of submission to Divine guidance and the Divine will that continued to characterize his life. After residing in Philadelphia about six months, and having joined the Society of Friends, he "began to think of settling" himself, "and to marry, when the way would appear without obstruction; which was not then the case." He decided that marriage "was *honorable* to all who married from pure motives, to the right person, and in the proper way and time, as divine Providence should direct." He was convinced that it was "essential that all men should *seek for wisdom, and wait for it*, to guide them in this important undertaking; because, no man, without divine assistance, is able to discover who is the right person for him to marry; but the Creator of both can and will direct him." In due course, he discovered nearby "a comely young woman, of a good, reputable family; educated in plainness; favored with good natural talents; and in good circumstances." He thought he might be successful in a suit of marriage, but after getting encouragement from friends, he noted that "From inattention to my heavenly Guide, I took the hint from man; and following my own inclination, I moved without asking my divine Master's advice." He went to her house and spent an evening with the young woman and her mother. "But I think I had not chatted with them more than half an hour," he said, "before I heard something, like a still small voice, saying to me, 'Seekest thou great things for thyself?—seek them not.' This language pierced me like a sword to the heart. It so filled me with confusion that I was unfit for any further conversation." He left precipitously, and for several months thereafter felt "confused and benumbed." He did not "suddenly see" that his "error was acting without permission," but feared instead that he might never "be suffered to

marry." "At length," he said, "I was brought to submit, and say 'Amen.' "
Sometime later, "after I had been much mortified and humbled, under a
sense of my former misstep, I went, one day, to a Friend's house to dine."
He observed "a young woman sitting opposite to me," but "took very little
notice of her" until "a language very quietly, and very pleasantly, passed
through my mind, on this wise, 'If thou wilt marry that young woman,
thou shalt be happy with her.' " "There was such a degree of divine virtue
attending the intimation," he acknowledged, "that it removed all doubt
concerning its origin and Author." He quickly noticed, however, that the
unknown young woman was lame, and felt himself displeased "that I
should have a cripple allotted to me. It was clear to me, beyond all doubt,
that the language I had heard was from heaven; but I presumptuously
thought I would rather choose for myself."

For weeks Ferris resisted the thought of marriage to her. "At length
it pleased the Lord, once more, clearly to show me that if I would submit,
it should not only tend to my own happiness, but that a blessing should
rest on my posterity." In time, he found himself "fully resigned." He even
found that "after divine Goodness had prevailed over my rebellious
nature, all things relating to my marriage wore a pleasant aspect. The
young woman appeared beautiful; and I was prepared to receive her as a
gift from heaven; fully as good as I deserved." Having come at last to a
decision, he waited another six months "for my parent's consent, from
New England," and married finally in September 1735. Why, it might be
wondered, would a man twenty-eight years old who had been disinherited
by his father and removed himself a great distance from his parents and
family still feel bound to seek his parents' consent to a marriage designed
for him by God? He, of course, does not say, but evidently his parents'
authority was still felt despite the distance and the independence he had
gained. His patient waiting for his parents' consent suggests the early
sources of Ferris's intense and inescapable need for submission to the
will of his God.[71]

Obedience to authority was to be maintained whatever Ferris's own
wishes or desires or will might be. Only then could he be content. Subsequently, he found himself seeking to know the will of God again in order
to make a decision about removing his own family from Philadelphia to
Wilmington, which he did in 1737, and about changing his occupation
from teacher to storekeeper, which he also did, after being "convinced that
I ought to ask counsel of the great Counsellor" and certain that "I did not
run in my own will, and choose my own ways. I was satisfied, that, as we
were blessed with a divine Teacher, it was our duty to follow his directions, in temporal, as well as spiritual concerns; especially in movements
of importance." Only in one way—a call to Ferris to preach the Gospel—
did he resist doing the will of God, finding one excuse after another for
more than twenty years. At long last, in 1755 at the age of forty-eight, he

heeded the call. "My feelings," he said, "were like those of a prisoner who had been long in bonds and was set at liberty."[72]

A century earlier, other Quakers too had found their own lives devoted with passionate intensity and urgency to doing the will of God through the arduous and dangerous task of preaching the word throughout England and the newly established colonies in America. Boston—the Puritan citadel, founded and settled during the early 1630's—became the focal point for a series of efforts by Quakers to preach the Gospel, but they met with fierce hostility, which ultimately resulted in the banishment from the Massachusetts Bay colony of twenty-two Quakers, the deaths of three or four, physical mutilation of several, and brutal beatings of more than thirty others. To do the will of God in Boston, if one were a Quaker during the fifties and early sixties, was a dangerous if not always a fatal enterprise. Thus Marmaduke Stevenson, who had been a farmer in Yorkshire until he received the Light in 1655, found himself imprisoned in Boston late in 1659, awaiting death by sentence of the court. He recalled his visit to Rhode Island, where "the Word of the Lord came unto me, saying, 'Go to Boston with thy brother William Robinson.' And at his command I was obedient and gave up myself to do his will, that so his work and service may be accomplished; for he had said unto me that he had a great work for me to do, which is now come to pass. And for yielding obedience to and obeying the voice and command of the Everliving God, which created heaven and earth, and the fountains of waters, do I with my dear brother suffer outward bonds near unto death. And this is given forth to be upon record, that all people may know who hear it, that we came not in our own wills but in the will of God."

Stevenson's brother in Christ and traveling companion, William Robinson, was also imprisoned in Boston. Robinson wrote to the court that he had been traveling in Rhode Island early in 1659, when

> the Word of the Lord came expressly to me, which did fill me immediately with life and power and heavenly love, by which he constrained me and commanded me to pass to the town of Boston, my life to lay down in his will, for the accomplishing of his service that he had there to perform at the day appointed; to which heavenly voice I presently yielded obedience, not questioning the Lord how he would bring the thing to pass, being I was a child and obedience was demanded of me by the Lord. . . . And my life did say Amen to what the Lord required of me and had commanded me to do, and willingly was I given up from that time to this day, the will of the Lord to do, and perform, whatever becomes of my body. . . . I being a child, and durst not question the Lord in the least, but rather willing to lay down my life than to bring dishonor to the Lord; and as the Lord made me willing,

dealing gently and kindly with me, as a tender father towards a
faithful child whom he dearly loves, so the Lord did deal with me
in ministering of his life unto me, which gave and gives me
strength to perform what the Lord hath required of me.[73]

The necessity for obedience to the perceived will of God transcended
everything, including life itself, as the experiences of countless evangelicals during the mid-seventeenth century throughout the Anglo-American
world testified. The total submission and even annihilation of the flesh
itself, the torments of imprisonment and physical punishments inflicted
on many evangelicals through these centuries, demonstrate the consuming necessity for absolute obedience to the will of God which they
experienced throughout their lives, once their conversions had been accomplished. Being reborn meant being able, with the help of Divine grace,
to have no self-will, and to fulfill the will of God, whatever the consequences for the self or the body. As Richard Hubberthorne declared from
prison in Chester, England, in February 1654, having been "called to
forsake Father and Mother, lands and living to go in obedience to the
Lord," it was "for yielding obedience to the Lord and his commands, and
not giving obedience to the corrupt will of man, who commands me contrary to what the Lord hath commended" that "I suffer under the persecu-
tion of those who are set in the place of rulers and magistrates, professing
themselves to be ministers of the Law of England to act justice according
to that Law." Wherever they might be, evangelicals often found themselves in conflict with the "corrupt will of man," which stood opposed to
the will of God. They believed, as did Susanna Wesley and virtually every
evangelical throughout these centuries, "that religion is nothing else than
doing the will of God and not our own." The need for obedience was paramount, whatever became of the individual.[74]

Soldiers for Christ:
Anger, Aggression, and Enemies

THE EVANGELICAL PREOCCUPATION with obedience, submission, the denial
of self-will and of self—themes of constant significance over the period—
evoked a response from deep within individuals which, though often
deflected, could not be evaded. Feelings of anger and of rage, of resistance
and of rebellion surged inside them. Yet anger was an emotion virtually
forbidden to evangelicals. So much of their life was taken up with the

denial and the suppression of anger that it is easy to overlook the profound importance that anger had in their lives, and the powerful forces it released to shape and influence their temperaments and their pieties. Deeply buried within their own psyches, rage and rebellion constantly erupted, placing constant pressures upon them which, more often than not, they resisted and rejected. Few passed through childhood without accumulating a deep and unfathomable reservoir of hostility toward their parents and toward the exercise of parental power and authority, feelings of rage that continued to shape their responses to themselves, to their God, and to the world in which they lived.

Although the anger that evangelicals harbored within themselves sprang from their early resistance to being broken and conquered, to being made submissive and impotent, anger was an emotion that they rarely allowed themselves to express openly, either toward their own parents or toward their Divine parent in Heaven. How, then, were their feelings of anger and the consequent aggressiveness manifested in their lives? The answer was: in three paramount ways. The first was the intense and sustained hostility which they felt toward themselves, evident in their efforts to placate implacable consciences and in their systematic efforts to mortify and subdue the body and the self. The recurrent pattern of elation and depression, with its dominant moods of melancholy and anxiety, reflects the inner warfare with the self, the extraordinary aggressiveness of the conscience, the self-directed anger, and the unending efforts to feel at peace so characteristic of evangelicals. The second consisted in their active rebellion against the will of God, and the constant fear which haunted so many that they might be rebellious even if they did not seem to be. And the third was evident in their behavior toward other people and the outer world generally. Evangelicals often perceived the world as a dangerous and seductive place, and they often saw evidence of anger and hostility in other people which they denied within themselves.[75]

The persistent feeling expressed by many evangelicals that other people were dangerous and aggressive, were intent upon doing harm to either their bodies or their souls, could in extreme instances become a paranoid vision of the outer world—a vision undoubtedly rooted in the denial of anger and the projection of inadmissible feelings within the self upon other people outside and beyond the self. Wherever evangelicals looked, they saw people who seemed to them to be the enemies of God's will and ways—and thus the enemies of themselves as well. Consequently, by becoming soldiers for Christ and warring against the unregenerated people of the world, evangelicals often demonstrated a remarkable capacity for vigorous and sustained aggressiveness in the outer world and for verbal and theological battles with their enemies. As embodiments of God's will, evangelicals were able to vent their anger and aggression on people who were neither their parents nor their God but who, nevertheless, by symbolizing both sin and authority, provided legitimate outlets for the hostility and rage suppressed so long.

The expression of anger was denied by evangelicals from earliest childhood. An observer of Jonathan and Sarah Edwards's family noted that "Quarrelling and contention, which too frequently take place among children, were in her family wholly unknown." Sarah Edwards "carefully observed the first appearance of resentment and ill will in her young children, towards any person whatever, and did not connive at it, as many who have the care of children do, but was careful to show her displeasure, and suppress it to the utmost; yet, not by angry, wrathful words, which often provoke children to wrath, and stir up their irascible passions, rather than abate them." As a young man, Jonathan Edwards was determined to deny any feelings of anger, particularly toward his parents and other members of his own family. He resolved "To endeavour, to my utmost, to deny whatever is not most agreeable to a good and universally sweet and benevolent, quiet, peaceable, contented and easy, compassionate and generous, humble and meek, submissive and obliging, diligent and industrious, charitable and even, patient, moderate, forgiving and sincere, temper"; and on another occasion, "Not only to refrain from an air of dislike, fretfulness, and anger in conversation, but to exhibit an air of love, cheerfulness and benignity." And he vowed, too, "When I am most conscious of provocations to ill-nature and anger, that I will strive most to feel and act good-naturedly," indicating the effort he took to control his own feelings, and to deny those he found objectionable. Edwards was self-consciously seeking to present the appearance of good nature, even when inwardly he knew he felt intensely angry. The outward appearances of his behavior, then, were no guarantee of the absence of hostility and anger within. This he clearly understood from his own experience.[76]

Years later, in a sermon on the subject of men as the natural enemies of God, Edwards explored the relationship of anger, hatred, and appearances with a sensitivity and perceptiveness that grew out of his own self-knowledge. The explosive and frightening feelings of rebellious rage, which had constantly erupted during the battles over the child's will in early childhood but were always suppressed and denied, provided Edwards with a telling analogy for the relationship of man and God. Addressing his congregation of saints and sinners, Edwards noted, "You object against your having a mortal hatred against God; that you never felt any desire to dethrone him. But one reason has been that it has always been conceived so impossible by you. But if the throne of God were within your reach, and you knew it, it would not be safe one hour. Who knows what thoughts would presently arise in your heart by such an opportunity, and what disposition would be raised up in your heart?" Edwards knew, of course, that men would immediately say to themselves: " 'Now I have opportunity to set myself at liberty—that I need not be kept in continual slavery by the strict law of God—Then I may take my liberty to walk in that way I like best, and need not be continually in such slavish fear of God's displeasure.' "

Self-assertion and self-will were the principal desires that would be liberated by the dethronement of God. But, Edwards acknowledged, most men "are foolishly insensible of what is in their own hearts," and would not acknowledge such thoughts as likely to arise in themselves. The reason for their "having no more of the sensible exercises of hatred to God," however, "is owing to a being restrained by fear. You have always been taught what a dreadful thing it is to hate God, and how terrible his displeasure; that God sees the heart and knows all the thoughts; and that you are in his hands, and he can make you as miserable as he pleases, and as soon as he pleases. And these things have restrained you: it has kept down your enmity and made that serpent afraid to show its head, as otherwise it would do." "If a wrathful man were wholly under the power of an enemy," Edwards added, "he would be afraid to exercise his hatred in outward acts, unless it were with great disguise." Indeed, as Edwards also knew, "he would be afraid so much as to believe himself, that he hated his enemy: but there would be all manner of disguise and hypocrisy, and feigning even of thoughts and affections"—not unlike those Edwards had sought to create in himself earlier.

As a result of such fears and denials, he noted that "your enmity was been kept under *restraint*: and thus it has been from your infancy. You have grown up in it, so that it is become an *habitual* restraint. You dare not so much as think that you hate God. If you do exercise hatred, you have a disguise for it, whereby you endeavour even to hide it from your own conscience; and so have all along deceived yourself." From earliest childhood, then, Edwards perceived the pattern of self-deception and the denial of anger and hostility that underlay the hatred he saw people feeling toward God before they were regenerated. But it was so deeply hidden and transformed that they themselves scarcely knew what they really felt.

Their true emotions were thus buried beneath a façade of compliance and obedience, and even the respect which men show God "in their manner of speaking, their voice, gestures, and the like" is "done in mere hypocrisy. All this seeming respect is feigned, there is no sincerity in it: there is external respect, but none in the heart." The reason for this "seeming respect," Edwards said, "is owing to their education. They have been taught from their infancy that they ought to show great respect to God." Nevertheless, "That show of respect which you make is forced. You come to God, and make a great show of respect to him, and use very respectful terms, with a reverential tone and manner of speaking; and your countenance is grave and solemn"; but all this is done because "You are afraid that God will execute his wrath upon you, and so you feign a great deal of respect, that he may not be angry with you. . . . All that you do in religion is forced and feigned. Through the greatness of God's power, you yield feigned obedience. You are in God's power, and he is able to destroy you; and so you feign a great deal of respect to him, that he might not destroy you." Absolute obedience in the face of absolute power was therefore the result of fear alone. "Take away fear, and a regard to your own interest," Edwards noted, "and there would soon be an end to all those appearances of love, honour, and reverence, which now you make. All these things are not at all inconsistent with the most implacable enmity."[77]

What Edwards observed of individuals in relation to God could just as readily be said of children in relation to parents, for the central dynamic of relationships is identical. Evangelicals went through life, as Edwards realized, denying the anger and hostility that they felt deep within. Their depression, their rebelliousness, and their warfare with the world all testified to the perpetual presence within of the dangerous, vigorously denied feelings of anger and hostility.

The denial of anger is most evident in the efforts made by so many evangelicals to appear in their own eyes and the eyes of others as peaceful, humble, and controlled individuals. Anger upset them when they felt it, for it seemed to be very threatening to their own sense of inner security. Cotton Mather, often a very angry man whose invective poured like torrents against his enemies, nevertheless was uncomfortable when he felt angry, as in one instance in 1711 when he noted in his diary that "If any little Occasion for my Anger, do occur by any Neglect, or by something amiss, in my Family, I would with all possible Decency govern my Passion. My Anger shall not break out, into any froward, peevish, indecent Expressions." Hannah Heaton, too, felt distressed by her own anger, as her experience when she got up one morning reveals: "a wait was on my mind and a temptation took hold on me and I was angry and spoke rashly and wickedly but in a few moments I was sorely greived I went alone and confest it to god then I went and sat down by him that I spoke wickedly to. I told him I was sorry. I asked for forgiveness and my tears ran freely. I told him that god had said he would not forgive them that would not forgive others and he was mild and spoke lovingly to me. Ah I am ashamed to write what I said in anger I am ashamed to have it brought into judgment at the great day. Ah I cant forgive my Self altho I believe god has forgiven me." Despite having a husband and children who scoffed at her piety and religious convictions, she constantly sought to maintain peace within her own household. Yet in March 1775, she reported that "an angry contention arose in the family. Now I had a great sence of the sin. I went crying to one and to the other pleading for peace. With tears I begged them for Christ sake to leave of[f]. I told them to forgive each other," but "at first they seemed affended at me but I kept on crying to them to make peace. At last they began to come too and presently made up the matter [and] went about their work pleasantly." Anger was intolerable to her, and she could not stand for anyone to express their feelings of anger and hostility within her house.[78]

Benjamin Lyon, another Connecticut New Light and a separatist like Heaton, found himself disturbed by domestic gusts of anger. On February 12, 1763, he noted that "this Day hath been an Uncomfortable Day indeed. I Rebuked Eliakim and my wife was Exceedingly Affronted with me. We have been in a Jar, Contending, Uneasiness. Oh, Oh. The Unhappiness of a Contencious life, how we Dishonour god, wound the Dear Redeemer, and grieve the holy Spirit, Defile our own Souls, Seal up our own Condemnation." "Surely," he added, "I need to Examine whether I am not the Cause. Surely I am imprudent, Ungarded, Soon Angry, peevish, I am a man of froward lips. Unhappy man that I am. Lord pardon the Iniquity of thy Servant, for it is very great. I am a man of polluted lips. . . . O for grace; So as we may live in peace, in love, and Unity. . . . O lord, forsake not us Utterly, give us not over to bite and Devour one another. Let us not be Consumed one of another." Several months later, he wrote again, "Anger I am full of, how Soon Angry at the Smallest thing, what peevishness fretfulness, hard Speeches, Uncharitable Speeches hath proceeded from me. Lord pardon me, help me to do So no more, bring me into Sweet Subjection to thy blessed Self, and give me that meek, and Quiet Spirit which in thy Sight is of great price." When anger was felt and voiced, it evoked a swift denunciation of guilt, which was followed by renewed efforts to suppress anger and put a "meek, and Quiet Spirit" in its place.[79]

Quakers, too, learned to suppress their anger and hostility toward parents, brothers, and sisters early in life, so that the peace and unity which they valued so highly could become realities within their households. They, too, sought to deny every sign of anger and contentiousness within themselves and within their families. Their testimonies for peace, their constant quest for meekness, humility, and self-effacement all combined to make them highly sensitive to the expression of anger. John Banks, an early minister often imprisoned in England for his activities, wrote to his eldest son from prison in 1684 that he ought to "be careful that there be no strife between thee and thy sisters and brother upon any occasion, neither in words nor actions; but be tender and loving one to another." He urged his daughters to "be sure you speak no ill one of the other, nor do ill to any body," telling them to "be loving, kind, and respectful one to the other, and to your brethren, sister and servants; and help one another willingly in all things, but especially your dear mother; be dutiful and obedient unto her in all things, what she bids you do, I charge you, do it readily and willingly, without murmuring." To his youngest children he said, "be sure you love one another," concluding his letter with the prayer that the Lord would "bless and preserve you all, in love, unity, peace, and quietness"—the dominant motifs of Quaker households for many generations.[80]

The very intensity of the early Quaker testimony for peace suggests equally intense feelings of anger and aggression which, though denied, continued to propel them in their constant warfare with the self and the world. Total obedience to the will of God and the absolute denial of the self and self-will became the hallmarks of early Quaker experience and piety; but simultaneously Quakers, like so many other evangelicals, also found themselves most joyful and content when most actively engaged in the denunciation and conversion of the unregenerated people of the world around them. The imagery of warfare held a fascinating and important place in their thought, and the experiences of soldiering for Christ shaped many of their lives. By fulfilling the will of God and denying their own wills, they were able both to deny their inner anger and hostility and to vent it freely upon their numerous enemies who were not yet Friends.

In 1651, William Dewsbury evoked the imagery of Christian warfare, summoning "all saints and children of the most high God, whom he hath called and chosen out of the world, and all their customs, fashions, worships, forms, observations and traditions, which are set up by the will of man, to wait upon him in the light, the counsel of Jesus Christ, the Captain of our salvation; every one in your measure stand valiant soldiers, and be not discouraged, neither at the enemy within nor without, lift up your heads, and behold your King Jesus Christ, who is present with you, to dash in pieces and destroy all your enemies for you. Stand faithful in his counsel, and walk in his power, everyone in your measure; and be bold in the Lord, for you are the Army of the Lord God Almighty, his mighty Host, whom he hath chosen out of the world to make known his eternal power in, to sound out his eternal and powerful Word." The call to enlist in God's army was heeded by many Quakers, including the enthusiast James Nayler, who declared that *"The Lamb's War you must know* before you can witness his kingdom, and how you have been called into his war, and whether you have been faithful and chosen there or no. . . . Christ has a war with his enemies, to which he calls his subjects to serve him against all the powers of darkness of this world, and all things of this old world, the ways and fashions of it will he overturn, and all things will he make new, which the god of this world has polluted, and where his children have corrupted themselves, and do service to the lust, and devourer. This the Lamb wars against, in whomsoever he appears, and calls them to join with him herein in heart and mind, and with all their whole might."

As Alice Hayes (who became a minister late in the seventeenth century) urged readers of her memoirs: "Resolve, by the help of his grace, to follow on wherever he will lead you: for assuredly, he will give you power to tread on scorpions, and to keep under you every foul spirit. And in your obedience you will be watchful in the light, by which you may see every appearance of evil; resist it by the assistance of the Spirit, and not give it any entertainment." "Remember," she added, "that you are soldiers under the banner of the unconquered Captain, Christ Jesus, who always stood by his own in every age."[81]

Warfare was essential if the conquest of the sins of the world and the transformation of behavior and belief sought by early Quakers and other evangelicals was to be brought about. For those who valued meekness and peace, the role of soldier nevertheless was inescapable. As Jonathan Edwards acknowledged, "The whole Christian life is compared to a warfare, and fitly so. And the most eminent Christians are the best soldiers, endowed with the greatest degrees of Christian fortitude." But he also noted that Christian fortitude was very different "from a brutal fierceness, or the boldness of beasts of prey." To Edwards, "The strength of the good soldier of Jesus Christ, appears in nothing more, than in steadfastly maintaining the holy calm, meekness, sweetness, and benevolence of his mind, amidst all the storms, injuries, strange behavior, and surprising acts and events of this evil and unreasonable world. The Scripture seems to intimate that true fortitude consists chiefly in this, 'He that is slow to anger, is better than the mighty; and he that ruleth his spirit, than he that taketh a city' (Prov. 16:32)." Edwards was certain that "a good soldier of Jesus Christ" would be discerned by his ability to maintain "the humility, quietness, and gentleness of a lamb, and the harmlessness, and love, and sweetness of a dove." But he was also convinced that "When persons are fierce and violent, and exert their sharp and bitter passions, it shows weakness, instead of strength and fortitude." Not even Christ's soldiers could be angry or violent in their passions. Anger was too dangerous, too frightening an emotion to allow even Christian warfare to be propelled by it. Gentle, harmless soldiers were best; yet the corruptions and sins of the world and the self often demanded more from individuals, including Edwards himself. No one reading his sermons can miss his brilliant evocation and use of the theme of anger as a weapon in his extraordinary intellectual and emotional warfare as a soldier for Christ.

Yet the tensions and contradictions within evangelicals continued to shape ambivalent responses to the self, the world, and to the enemies they saw everywhere around them. However meek and mild their soldiering may have appeared to themselves, others often saw something else as they became the targets of the warfare waged so vigorously by evangelicals.[82] As soldiers in Christ's army, evangelicals felt themselves directly under the command of God and in direct communication with God's will and ways through His word. Their mentality was such that they could not escape the conviction that they were embattled with everyone who did not share their beliefs, accept their values, or wish to conform their lives to the patterns of simplicity, rigor, and asceticism essential to evangelicals. There were only two choices: to be a soldier for Christ, or an enemy of Christ. There could be no middle way. As Samuel Finley, an itinerant Presbyterian preacher in both the Middle colonies and New England during the 1740's, declared, "I look upon all Neutres, as Enemies, in

Affairs of Religion. Away with your carnal Prudence! And either follow *God* or *Baal. He that is not* actually *with us, is against us; and he that gathereth not with us, scattereth abroad."* The absolutist mentality thus fed upon liberated feelings of hostility, which were to be directed against the world and its wicked inhabitants in order to make them surrender and conform to the Divine will and to the ways of God's saints.[83]

Half a century earlier, the Reverend Samuel Parris delivered a sermon before his congregation in Salem-Village following the condemnation of six people for witchcraft, including a member in full communion from his congregation, declaring that "Here are but two parties in the world: the lamb and his followers, and the dragon and his followers. And these are contrary one to the other." Those who "are ag[a]inst the lamb, against the peace and prosperity of Zion, the interest of Christ," he told his listeners, "are for the devil. Here are no neuters." "Everyone," he insisted, "is on one side or the other." This polarity, central to evangelical experience throughout the centuries, was caught by the imagery of warfare and of soldiering in Christ's army. But it also undergirded the responses of many evangelicals to the world in which they lived as they sought continually to discover which side people were really on—Christ's or the devil's. They always feared, as Parris did, that they would not see "the vileness of our natures," and they knew, too, as Parris did, "that we should be ever praying that we not be left to our own lusts: for then we shall, by and by, fall in with devils, and with the dragon make war with the lamb and his followers." The wars within the self and the wars outside the self with the enemies of Christ and of God were part of the same experience and temperament. Witches were only one manifestation of an enduring battle with the devil and the world—a warfare that always fed upon liberated feelings of anger, of hostility, and of fear.[84]

The dominant enemies of evangelicals throughout the seventeenth and eighteenth centuries were those people whom they felt to be believers in nurture as opposed to the new birth; those who trusted in the efficacy of good works as a means of achieving salvation rather than total reliance upon free and undeserved grace; and those whom they perceived as Arminians, who threatened to subvert and corrupt the churches of the land and to lead countless souls to the destruction of eternal damnation. Confident that there was only one truth, one way, and one pattern set for the piety, beliefs, and behavior of true Christians, evangelicals could not tolerate the presence of more moderate, more catholic, less strict and pure modes of piety and character. As Charles Chauncy, one of the leading Old Light opponents of the evangelical revivals of the 1740's, put it: "a grand discriminating Mark" of the enthusiastic revivals of the period was "that it makes Men spiritually proud and conceited beyond Measure, infinitely censorious and uncharitable, to Neighbours, to Relations, even the nearest and dearest; to Ministers in an especial Manner; yea, to all Mankind, who are not as they are, and don't think and act as they do."[85]

In mid-January 1637, the Reverend John Wheelwright sounded the call to battle in Boston during a period of intense debate and contention over fundamental issues of piety and doctrine (known as the Antinomian crisis) that split the newly established colony apart and ultimately resulted in the banishment of Wheelwright, Anne Hutchinson, and many others. Wheelwright delivered a powerful fast-day sermon in which he proclaimed, "we must all prepare for a spirituall combate, we must put on the whole armour of God," and "all the children of God ought to shew themselves valient, they should have their swords redy, they must fight, and fight with spirituall weapons." The reason for this preparation for war in defense of the doctrine of the Covenant of grace was clear to Wheelwright: "if we would have the Lord Jesus Christ to be abundantly present with us, we must all of us prepare for battell and come out against the enimyes of the Lord, and If we do not strive, those under a covenant of works will prevaile." He was fighting for the conviction that individuals could do nothing whatsoever to bring about their own salvation, free grace alone sufficing, and against the notion that good works or actions could be part of the process leading toward the new birth. "It will be objected," he noted, "that divers of those who are oposite to the wayes of grace and free covenant of grace, they are wondrous holy people, therefore it should seeme to be a very uncharitable thing in the servants of God to condemne such, as if so be they were enimyes to the Lord and his truth, whilest they are so exceedingly holy and strict in their way." But his answer, given immediately, was: "Brethren, those under a covenant of works, [the] more holy they are, the greater enimyes they are to Christ." "We know (through the mercy of God)," he said, "as soone as Christ cometh into the soule, he maketh the creature nothing: therefore if men be so holy and so strict and zealous, and trust to themselves, and their righteousness, and knoweth not the wayes of grace, but oppose free grace; such as these, have not the Lord Jesus Christ"; "therefore," he urged, "set upon such with the sword of the Spiritt, the word of God." Yet, like evangelicals elsewhere and at other times, he also reminded his audience that "we must consider, that we cannot do any of this, by any strength that is in our selves, but we must consider that it is the Lord that must helpe us and act in us, and worke in us, and the Lord must do all . . . so in some measure, we must looke for the Spirit of the Lord to come upon us, and then we shall do mighty things through the Lord, it is the Lord himselfe that must effect and do all." Wheelwright was direct in his answer to the objection that his advice "will cause a combustion in the Church and comon wealth," stating: "I must confesse and acknowledge it will do so, but what then?"[86]

That was the true spirit of Christ's soldiers, compelled to fulfill their vision of the true way and Gospel, and utterly indifferent to the consequences. Wheelwright and the followers of Anne Hutchinson joined in their vociferous and sustained denunciations of ministers and doctrines to the point where they seemed to threaten the very survival of the colony itself. For them, there were only two choices—to accept the doctrines of free grace and the new birth, or to be considered an enemy of God.

The doctrines of free grace and the call for pure churches also became the battle cries for a subsequent generation, who rediscovered for themselves the powerful experience of the new birth and a sense of new light that came to be associated with the immense and profoundly consequential series of revivals known as the Great Awakening during the early 1740's. One of the most striking and significant facets of the complex character of the Great Awakening is the extraordinary ferocity of the attacks of the evangelicals upon the ministry and churches of the standing order, which seemed to them to be corrupted and impure, given over to the notion of the usefulness of works and either openly or latently Arminian. Again and again, in church after church, town after town, colony after colony, the same battles were joined. As Jonathan Edwards observed in 1742, in his essay on the great revival sweeping throughout the land, "This is the most important affair that ever New England was called to be concerned in. When a people are engaged in war with a powerful and crafty nation, it concerns them to manage an affair of such consequence with the utmost discretion." "Of what vast importance then must it be," he added, "that we should be vigilant and prudent in the management of this great war that New England now has, with so great a host of such subtle and cruel enemies, wherein we must either conquer or be conquered; and the consequence of victory, on one side, will be our eternal destruction in both soul and body in hell; and on the other side, our obtaining the kingdom of heaven and reigning in it in eternal glory?" If this war should be successful, Edwards hoped that it "would make New England a kind of heaven upon earth."[87]

Evangelicals spared no epithets in their verbal warfare with ministers who seemed to them to be preaching eternal death. No quarter was given, no concessions were made, no associations were possible as group after group split in two over the issues of piety and practice that set evangelicals apart from nonevangelicals. Evangelicals everywhere attacked their enemies mercilessly, supremely confident always that they alone possessed the truth and knew the will of God for people on earth. Throughout the literature of the period, private as well as public, there is a recurrent pattern of aggressiveness and hostility on the part of evangelicals, which reveals those powerful impulses toward purification of the world and the churches which provided legitimate outlets for feelings of rage and aggression that must otherwise have been denied.[88]

Contentiousness and "party spirit" were widespread, consequences in part at least of the liberation of anger in the cause of Christ. The Reverend Ebenezer Punderson, for instance, who was a minister for the Church of England in North Groton, Connecticut, wrote about his experiences in 1742 after preaching a sermon in Norwich, when "one of these enthusiasts came to me and demanded my experience; (which is very common;) his request being denied, he pronounced me unconverted, and, not only going myself, but leading all under my charge, down to hell." On another occasion, another "exhorter" came to his house, "declared me as upright and as exemplary a person as any he knew in the world, yet he knew I was unconverted, and leading my people down to hell; he affirmed that he was sent with a message from God, and felt the Spirit upon him," and "he seemed sincere." When subsequently Mr. Croswell, "the dissenting teacher in this parish, with two attendants, came singing to my house, pronounced me unconverted, yet, at the time, declared that he did not know me guilty of any crime," Punderson "assured him that, in my opinion, it was a greater crime for him thus to murder my soul, usefulness and reputation in the world, than for me to attempt his natural life; and that he certainly must be a worse man, thus, in cool blood and under a religious pretence, to pronounce damnation against me, than for a common swearer to say to another 'God damn you' "; "since this," he noted, "he is not so fierce as before." Punderson had a point, but not one that would persuade any evangelical who perceived men like Punderson as an enemy to God's word and ways. From Punderson's point of view, however, the denunciation of himself and innumerable others as men of damnable doctrines and damnable experience could be seen only as an act of aggression.[89]

The Reverend John Bass was minister to a congregation in Ashford, Connecticut, until forced to resign by the majority of the members of his church in 1750. He wrote an account of the experience, declaring that "I design not to injure or offend any Body," but also stating his confidence that "when I have wronged no Body, I am maligned and reviled as I have been, I matter it not as to any Hurt such snarling Bigots can do me." When he first began to preach at Ashford in 1743, he believed himself to be a Calvinist. But in time, after examining "anew the Foundation of my Faith," he found himself "obliged to recant some former sentiments," though he tried to keep his new convictions to himself, refraining from speaking about them in sermons because he thought his congregation "could not bear them as yet." But his new sentiments were "discovered by some of my eagle-eyed People," who whispered about their suspicions and swiftly broke out in a "flaming Contention." Then a group of offended members came to him to ask about his principles, declaring to him "that there is great Uneasiness among us on account of some Principles that you and some others hold, as we think, which appear to us very dangerous." As a result, Bass and six other men wrote a statement about their own principles, "being desirous to maintain Peace and Concord in the Church of Christ, and always ready to contribute, according to our Power, towards the Removing of such Difficulties as arise among us"—a declaration which said, among other things, that while they were "sensible there be different Sentiments among us about the Meaning of some Scripture-

Passages," they also believed that "different Sentiments we are apt to think there always will be among Men, while in the present State of Frailty and Imperfection." At the same time, "As we claim the Liberty of judging for our selves in Matters of Religion, so we are ready to grant the same Liberty to every Member in this Church, and to every Man in the World; and while we impose not upon any one, we hope none will be so unchristian-like as to impose upon us." After their statement had been read to the congregation, Bass found that "All this was not, as I could find, in the least Satisfactory. 'Twas hissed at." Immediately, a counter-statement was read, listing his "neglect to preach up the Doctrine of Original Sin, and the Necessity of the New-Birth," as well as other doctrines "plainly set forth in the Word of God, and necessary to be preached by every Minister of Christ, as fundamental Articles of the Christian Religion: In which we say you are very defective." They concluded by stating that "Now from all these Things we think neither your Preaching nor your Principles are good." In due course, after calling a council of ministers to consider the matter, Bass was dismissed.

Bass thus learned just how different his views were from those of the majority of his own congregation, and was forced to recognize "That the Scheme of Religion I espouse, as Things now go in the Country, has a Tendency to fling all that are known to fall in with it, out of the good Liking of the Generality of People, and to deprive such, if Clergymen, of their Livings," which his own experience amply confirmed. He found himself to be an enemy of his people. Unable to share his own professed readiness to live with sentiments and views different from his own, his congregation—many of whom were ardent believers in the doctrines of free grace and the new birth—saw no alternative to casting him out of their midst. John Bass was only one of the many individuals who learned, from bitter personal experience, what it was like to be accounted an enemy of Christ and of His army of Christian saints.[90]

The full measure of the aggressiveness and anger of evangelicals has never been taken by historians, even though the actions of evangelicals provide an unending record of their warfare with the unregenerate world in which they lived. Much of the time, their aggressiveness was confined to words rather than to deeds. Yet while these could not actually kill, and while they generally refrained from the use of physical violence, evangelicals knew that words could wound. Throughout the seventeenth and eighteenth centuries, words were indispensable weapons in the arsenal of evangelical soldiers arrayed together in Christ's advancing armies. The very violence of their language and the ferocity of their denunciations—both of individuals and of doctrines—revealed the powerful impulses of hostility that erupted from deep within these repressed individuals. Yet such anger emerged only under stress and only occasionally in the course of a lifetime. Revivals were a major outlet for such feelings, and the Great Awakening—like the Antinomian crisis a century earlier and other revivals elsewhere—elicited personal expressions of anger and hostility that were often startling and disturbing to individuals who hitherto had kept their feelings closely in check or suppressed altogether.

Some evangelicals, however, spent most of their lifetime engaged in a personal war with the enemies who surrounded them. Cotton Mather, for example, endured much of his life surrounded by enemies, and often felt himself under attack by nearly everyone he knew. Throughout his diaries, the theme of being surrounded by personal enemies who slandered, reviled, and sometimes threatened him with physical attacks recurs continually. Yet he in turn was renowned for his vitriolic tongue as he continually denounced the sins and errors of others. In September 1709, he noted that "The other Ministers of the Neighbourhood, are this Day feasting with our wicked Governour"; but, he acknowledged, "I have, by my provoking Plainness and Freedom, in telling this *Ahab* of his wickedness, procured myself to be left out of his Invitations. I rejoiced in my Liberty from the Temptations, with which they were encumbered, while they were *eating of his Dainties* and durst not *reprove* him." "And," he added, "considering the Power and Malice of my Enemies, I thought it proper for me, to be this day *Fasting*, in Secret, before the Lord."

Mather's growing sense of being surrounded by personal enemies was revealed with the utmost clarity in 1724, when he listed systematically all the sources of his discomfort and trials, including the following: "there is not a Man in the world, so Reviled, so slandered, so cursed, among the *Sailors*" as himself; "where is the Man, whom the *female Sex* have spitt more of their Venom at?"; "where is the Man, who has been tormented with such monstrous *Relatives?*"; "How little *Comfort*, yea, how much contrary to it, have I seen in my *Children?*"; "there is no Man whom the Countrey so loads with Disrespects, and with Calumnies and manifold Expressions of Aversion." Even the government had discountenanced him, "yea, the *Indecencies* and *Indignities* which it hath multiplied upon me, are such as no other Man has been treated withal"; worse still, perhaps, Harvard College "forever putts all possible Marks of Disesteem upon me"; "I have had more *Books* written against me; more Pamphlets to traduce me, and reproach me, and bely me, than any man that I know in the World"; not least was the fact that although "Indeed, I find *some* cordial Friends," he had to add, "But, how *few!*" Mather's sense of the lack of friends and supporters was only somewhat more extreme than the feelings of many evangelicals, who also perceived themselves to be living in a world inhabited mostly by dangerous, hostile, and seductive people. Feeling so vulnerable and endangered, they, like Cotton Mather, discovered that taking the offensive against their enemies was the best defense.[91]

For many evangelicals, the experience of rebirth liberated feelings of anger and hostility that could be expressed verbally. The Reverend Ebenezer Parkman reported several encounters with angry parishioners during the height of the Great Awakening which could have been repeated by other ministers elsewhere as well. In May 1744, for instance, he recorded a meeting with the wife of Stephen Fay, who "desir'd to Speak alone with me." The "Conversation" was "the most unaccountable and intolerable that ever I met with," he observed, "Making Exceptions against the most inexceptionable parts of my Sermon today; and declaring her great Dissatisfaction to my preaching in general, and to my Ministration, and yet in plain Terms said she could not give any Reason why." Clearly Mrs. Fay did not know why she felt as she did and was prepared to submit to the counsel offered to her by Parkman. On another occasion, Parkman sought reconciliation with another disaffected member of his congregation, who refused to say that he "was Sorry for his undutifull Conduct towards me in Time past" without also receiving in turn "an acknowledgment from Me also with regard to my Carriage towards him—which I could see no ground for." Parkman then reported that the man, Mr. Cook, had tried "his unaccountable ways of Softening his Several harsh allegations against me, and heavy Complaints of me from Time to Time," including the assertion that "I had abus'd him more than any Man in the world" and "That I was an Enemy of the Work of God." At the end of this interchange, Cook sent a "Strange Message" to Parkman, saying "that he felt So towards me and Sometimes that he could Bite Me." Thus both biting words and biting the minister expressed the hostility felt by a man who was unreconciled to a minister whose authority he ought to acknowledge and whose teachings he ought to accept. The wish to attack and hurt could not have been expressed more directly, although the feelings that prompted the wish remained hidden from Parkman himself.[92]

Remarkably similar experiences were evident half a century earlier in Salem-Village and surrounding communities in Essex County, Massachusetts, during the witchcraft crisis. The liberation of hostile feelings, of anger, hatred, and aggressiveness (which led in a number of instances to the deaths of individuals accused of being witches by people within the same or nearby communities), and the physical symptoms of attacks—biting, pinching, choking, and hitting—provide one of the most dramatic instances of the open expression of long-suppressed emotions in New England's history. Twelve-year-old Abigail Williams, one of the afflicted girls, had "several Sore Fits" during public worship, "which did something interrupt me in my First Prayer; being so unusual," reported the Reverend Deodat Lawson. But immediately "After Psalm was Sung, Abigail Williams said to me, 'Now stand up, and Name your Text': And after it was read, she said, 'It is a long Text.'" Then, Lawson observed, "In the beginning of Sermon, Mrs. Pope, a Woman afflicted, said to me, 'Now there is enough of that.'" In both instances, women had spoken out hostilely in public against their minister, just as others were to do during the revivals of the Great Awakening.[93]

By joining the ranks of Christ's armies, evangelicals often experienced a welcome release from such pent-up feelings of rage, repressed since childhood as a consequence of their lost battles of will with the sovereign authorities that governed their lives. Whatever the sources of their personal aggressiveness, the role of soldier provided a legitimate and valuable outlet for their feelings, with more enemies around than any single person could expect to conquer in a lifetime. The role of soldier seemed well suited to the temperaments of many evangelicals, since it both liberated and suppressed altogether their sense of individuality and of self. Having experienced the breaking of self-will several times during the course of their lives, and always seeking to ensure that their own wills had been replaced by the will of God, evangelicals could both deny and assert the self simultaneously. By doing only the will of God, and not their own, they could act the part of Christ's soldiers enthusiastically, feeling free to combat in others the sins which tormented them. As soldiers for Christ, evangelicals appeared to be extraordinarily self-confident and self-assertive, their aggressiveness and their anger channeled into the permanent warfare of the saints with the sins and corruptions of the world and its unregenerated inhabitants.

While soldiering was a role ordinarily reserved exclusively for men, evangelical women obviously joined the ranks of Christ's armies as readily as men did. When evangelical women stepped out of their proper places and dared (as Anne Hutchinson, Mary Dyer, Mrs. Fay, Mrs. Pope, and many others did) to address themselves directly, boldly, effectively, and critically to the men who dominated their lives—as husbands, magistrates, and ministers—they were also laying claim to a realm of experience and expression that ordinarily was reserved for men. As soldiers for Christ, both men and women felt brave and hardy, bold and aggressive in their warfare with the enemies of God's will and ways. By enlisting in this perpetual war with the world and most of its inhabitants, evangelicals of both sexes were able to achieve a sense of personal potency, efficacy, and fulfillment that normally was considered to be the prerogative of the male sex alone.[94]

Brides of Christ: Femininity, Masculinity, and Sexuality

WHILE THE AGGRESSIVE AND BOLD public behavior of evangelicals who saw themselves as soldiers in Christ's army provided many people with a sense of self-assertion and of manliness, the ideal evangelical, nevertheless, was self-less and feminine. Evangelicals believed that a truly gracious Christian was a person who was self-denying, will-less, subject and submissive, humble and meek, chaste and pure—all supposedly female attributes. Men, on the other hand, were thought to be naturally superior, willful, active, hardy, industrious, and rational. Yet most evangelicals spent much of their lives denying precisely these aspects of their own temperaments and experiences. In order to be saved, both men and women had to subdue those parts of their being that seemed to be "masculine," and to enhance and assert those aspects of their being that seemed to be "feminine." For many men, one of the central sources of resistance to the experience of being broken and submitting to the will of God that was necessary for the new birth was their reluctance to relinquish their sense of masculinity. Becoming children of God not only implied the re-breaking of their wills but also a return to the first years of life in which boys and girls were both perceived as feminine.[95]

As adults, evangelicals experienced lifelong difficulties with their sexual identities and their sexuality. For evangelical women, adult experience developed continuously from their earliest experiences in childhood, since they had been feminine since infancy, and trained and educated accordingly throughout the formative years of childhood and youth. But for men, the denial of their masculinity implied in evangelical religious experience and beliefs proved to be a source of persistent inner conflict as they sought to balance their masculine and feminine impulses, desires, and sensibilities. In addition, for both women and men, the intensity of the parent-child relationship in early life often provided the psychic matrix for inner conflicts over sexuality and sexual identity in adulthood. Although evangelicals who sought to deny their own sexuality and to limit their own enjoyment of sensual experience were often parents of many children, the large number of children born to many evangelical families were not testimony to the comfortable sexuality of their parents. Evangelicals were generally filled with guilt and shame over their bodies and their sexual desires, even when they acted upon them. For evangelical men, the persistent theme of guilt also seems to have been intimately connected to the inner conflicts experienced over their sexual identity. Sexuality was one of the aspects of their masculinity with which they felt least comfortable. By becoming brides of Christ, evangelicals were able to reconcile some of the conflicting elements at war within the self.[96]

Evangelical men found themselves able and willing to assume the passive role, and the symbolic identity of a woman, in relation to their Saviour, thus denying their own masculinity as the only means of being assured of salvation. As Isaac Penington testified in 1667, after recounting his own spiritual experiences, "these things I do not utter in a boasting way, but would rather be speaking of my nothingness, my emptiness, my weakness, my manifold infirmities, which I feel more than ever. The Lord has broken the man's part in me, and I am a worm and no man before him." Only when "the man's part" was "broken" could an evangelical

male rest assured of being truly subject to Christ's government. As John
Rogers exhorted his children in 1742, "be carefull not to make your Duties
and Reformations and Repentance your Righteousness, but resolve by the
Grace of God you will have Christ and his Righteousness whatever it cost
you, And see that you have this Evidence that you are in Christ, that you
are new Creatures." "Gird up therefore the Loyns of your Mind," he
pleaded, "act with a manly Vigour and Resolution, being sensible of your
own utter Impotency, depending only on the Strength of Christ and
the effectual Influences of his Spirit." To be *both* manly and impotent
was a contradiction to be resolved, for most evangelicals, in favor of
impotency.[97]

For a man to become the bride of Christ, even symbolically, required
the denial of many of his most masculine traits. Yet marriage to Christ
was often the way in which individuals expressed their desire for union
with Christ and for a life of subjection to his government. Early in 1741,
Joseph Bean, as a twenty-two-year-old in Boston, was locked in battle with
his own inner corruptions and lusts, "so Universally Corrupted in every
power and faculty" of his soul, subjected frequently to the burden of
"unchast and immodist thoughts," which "run through my head," and
often experiencing "filthy" dreams at night. In April, while a friend got
married in a room below, he went "up stars by my Self all alone and thare
pleded with God that this Night be the Weden Night betwen Christ and
my Soul." Shortly thereafter, he dreamed about a beautiful boy whom
Satan lay upon and crushed his bones while threatening him, "and the
young man look on me vary Stedely Smiling and his Countenance even
Shind in short he Lookt the butifulest that ever I saw any in all my Life
which made me Sum times for to think it was the Son of God." Finally, on
June 25, 1741, Bean wrote out a covenant in which, he said, he gave himself up to God, "an do hereby Solomly Joyn my Self in marige Covanant
to him. . . . But sence such is thine unparalleled love: I do here with all
my power accept the and do take the for my head husband for biter for
worse for richer for poorer for all tims and Conditions to love honour and
obay the before all others and this to the deth: I Imbrace the in all thy
offices. I Renounce my own worthyness and do here avow the to be the
Lord my Righteousness: I Renounce mine own wisdom and do here take
the for my only gide: I renounce mine own will and take thy will for my
Law."[98]

For the Reverend Thomas Shepard, too, the relation of a Christian
was like a marriage to Christ. While he knew that "union to Christ was
my greatest good," he also sometimes felt himself "estranged from the
life of God" and separated from the close union he sought with Christ.
As he noted in May 1641, "I saw with sadness my widow-like separation
and disunion from my Husband and my God, and that we two were now
parted that had been nearer together once." George Fox wrote to newly

convinced Friends in Germany in 1683, noting that "sufferings attends Friends in most places, and imprisonments very much, but the Lord with his power doth support his faithful people to stand for his glory," with many "precious Meetings in Wm. Penn's Country and in New Jersey," as well as elsewhere. He closed by saying, "the Lord keep and preserve all Friends chaste in his power, as virgins with oil in their lamps, that they may enter in with the Bridegroom, and not only so, but be married unto him, Christ Jesus, and keep in him the Sanctuary." Chastity, subjection, obedience—all were essential for the union with Christ as husband that these men sought.[99]

Marriage with Christ implied the willingness of everyone, including men, to accept the role of wife and woman. Yet within the context of daily experience, or at least the prescriptions for relationships of husbands and wives, the roles assigned to men and women differed significantly. As John Wesley stated, "It is the duty of a husband to govern his wife, and to maintain her," and a husband must "keep his authority" and "use it." When husbands "walk uprightly and religiously" in their households and "give a good example to all in the house," it seemed obvious to Wesley that "any reasonable woman will give him the better place, whom she sees to be the better person." Wesley insisted that a wife must "know herself the inferior, and behave as such." "Where the woman counts herself equal with her husband, (much more, if she counts herself better,) the root of all good carriage is withered, the fountain thereof dried up," he said. "Whoever, therefore, would be a good wife, let this sink into her inmost soul, 'My husband is my superior, my better: he has the right to rule over me. God has given it him, and I will not strive against God. He is my superior, my better.'" This fundamental pattern of dominance and submission, of authority in the male and subjection in the female, of superiority as the prerogative of masculinity and inferiority as the badge of femininity, continued to characterize marriages for many generations.[100]

Jonathan Edwards, also, believed in the natural superiority of husbands and the necessity for submissiveness in wives. He found the analogy of faith and marriage apt and powerful. "The soul is espoused and married unto Jesus Christ; the believing soul is the bride and spouse of the Son of God. The union between Christ and believers is very often represented to a marriage." "This similitude is much insisted on in Scripture," he noted, "how sweetly is it set forth in the Song of Songs! Now it is by faith that the soul is united unto Christ; faith is this bride's reception of Christ as a bridegroom." "Let us, following this similitude, that we may illustrate the nature of faith," he added, "a little consider what are those affections and motions of heart that are proper and suitable in a spouse toward her bridegroom, what are those conjugal motions of soul which are most agreeable to, and do most harmonize with, that relation that she bears as a spouse." Edwards continued his observations by articulating what he took to be common assumptions:

> Now it is easy to everyone to know that when marriage is according to nature and God's designation, when a woman is married to an husband she receives him as a guide, as a protector, a safeguard and defense, a shelter from harms and dangers, a reliever from distresses, a comforter in afflictions, a support in discouragements. God has so designed it, and therefore has made man of a more robust [nature], and strong in body and mind, with more wisdom, strength and courage, fit to protect and defend; but he has made woman weaker, more soft and tender, more fearful, and more affectionate, as a fit object of generous protection and defense. Hence it is, that it is natural in women to look most at valor and fortitude, wisdom, generosity and greatness of soul: these virtues do (or at least ought, according to nature) move most upon the affections of the woman. Hence, also it is that man naturally looks most at a soft and tender disposition of mind, and those virtues and affections which spring from it, such as humility, modesty, purity, chastity. And the affections which he most naturally looks at in her, are a sweet and entire confidence and trust, submission and resignation; for when he receives a woman as wife, he receives her as an object of his guardianship and protection, and therefore looks at those qualifications and dispositions which exert themselves in trust and confidence. Thus it's against nature for a man to love a woman as wife that is rugged, daring and presumptuous, and trusts to herself, and thinks she is able to protect herself and needs none of her husband's defense or guidance. And it is impossible a woman should love a man as her husband, except she can confide in him, and sweetly rest in him as a safeguard.

Edwards could not have been more explicit about the traits of character which he associated with the two sexes—activity, strength, combativeness, wisdom, and "greatness of soul" in men; passivity, weakness, dependency, emotionalism, and self-doubt in women. And it was altogether reasonable, according to these assumptions, to perceive the relationship of the faithful Christian to Christ in terms of femininity and marriage: "Thus also, when the believer receives Christ by faith, he receives him as a safeguard and shelter from the wrath of God and eternal torments, and defense from all the harms and dangers which he fears. . . . Wherefore, the dispositions of soul which Christ looks at in his spouse are a sweet reliance and confidence in him, a humble trust in him as her only rock of defense, whither she may flee. And Christ will not receive those as the objects of his salvation who trust to themselves, their own strength or worthiness, but those alone who entirely rely on him. The reason of this is very natural and easy." All Christians who had received saving faith thus became brides of Christ, men as well as women; and Edwards made clear the necessity for men as well as women to assume those traits of character and modes of behavior identified as being peculiarly feminine in early American culture. The implication clearly was that for men to be saved they had to cease being masculine.[101]

Not surprisingly, evangelical men found themselves profoundly uncomfortable not only with masculinity but also with sexuality in general, and with the parts of the body that were most closely connected to sexuality. The penis was subject to constant denial and hostility. Masturbation was forbidden, of course, although as many accounts of experiences by young men prior to their conversions acknowledge, it was a constant temptation and often a frequent indulgence. Edwards's injunction to himself in the privacy of his own notebooks is characteristic of evangelicals: "There is the tongue and another member of the body that have a natural bridle, which is to signify to us the peculiar need we have to bridle and restrain those two members." He could not bring himself to write a specific descriptive word for the penis which, having a foreskin, offered a constant reminder of the "peculiar need" of bridling and restraint.[102]

Again in the privacy of a notebook, young Nicholas Gilman, who later became an ardent New Light preacher in New Hampshire, wrote out a series of rules for his own conduct, which included "Rules for Right improving my Time," "Rules for right ordering my words and outward actions," "Rules for Temperance in Meat," considerations of the "Evill Consequents of Drunkenness," and "Signs of Drunkenness," as well as the following "Rules for Suppressing Voluptuousness":

1 Suppress your sensual Desires at the first approach.
2 Divert them with some Laudable Employment.
3 Look upon pleasure not on that side next to the Sun.
4 Often Consider and contemplate the Joys of Heaven.

He also considered the temptations toward masturbation and sexuality generally, and remedies for the vice. The "Evill Consequents of Uncleaness" include the following:

1 Uncleaness of all vices is most shamefull
2 The Appetites of uncleaness are full of cares and Trouble and its fruition is Sorrow and repentance
3 Most of its kinds involve the ruin of Two Souls
4 Tis that which the Devil Delights to imitate
5 It hath a professed enmity against the body. 1 Cor: 6.18
6 Tis Contrary to the Spirit of Governments

As for "Remedies against uncleaness," Gilman noted six methods:

1 When a Temptation assaults thee flee from it
2 Avoid Idleness
3 Give no entertainment to the begginnings of Lust
4 Fly all Occasions of Lust
5 When Assaulted alone Go into Company
6 Use frequent and earnest prayer to the King of Purities, the
  first of Virgins, the Eternall God that he would be pleased to
  reprove and cast out the unclean Spirit

Quite consistently, Gilman also included rules for himself about "Acts
of Chastity in Generall":

1 To Resist all unchast thoughts
2 To have a Chast Eye
3 To have a heart and mind Chast and Pure
4 To discourse chastly and purely[103]

Cotton Mather too had rules for himself about impure thoughts,
which he continued to invoke throughout his adulthood. In 1713—after
his wife had died and he found that his "glorious Lord" had "brought"
him "into a State of widowhood" and felt that he "must also look upon
myself as obliged unto a Continuance in that State, all the rest of my
little Time in this World"—he noted that he must "quicken, and most
religiously observe, a Rule heretofore practised with me, that if an impure
Thought start into my Mind, I must presently reject it, and rebuke it,
and make it a Provocation to form an holy Thought in Contradiction to
it," hoping to gain "the Grace of the most unspotted Purity" so that he
would "not grieve the holy Spirit of God, and provoke Him to be my
Enemy." Mather evidently considered sex mean and vile, despite the
children he produced with such regularity with his wives. In October
1711, while "continually crying to God, for His Favour to my Children,"
he felt that he "ought to bewayl some inexpressible Circumstances of
Meanness, relating to their Original, their Production and Conception."
"I ought to obtain a Pardon thro' the Blood of that Holy Thing, which
was Born of the Virgin," he said. "That so no Vileness of that Nature,"
alluding to the sexual act itself, "may have any Influence, to render
them abominable to Heaven, and cast them out of its favourable
Protection."[104]

The association of sex with abominations and vileness, and with
filthiness in general, is evident in George Fox's injunction to English
Friends in 1680: "Now let all Friends be careful to keep in the holy
chaste life over all lust and uncleanness of filthy fornication. . . . Now
those that profess the truth should know more virtue and dominion over

the filthy lusts, and keep their bodies clean till the day of their marriage and time of death, that all may be kept in chastness and purity to God's glory." But marriage did not erase the feeling that sex itself was "filthy" and something to be indulged in only for procreation, never for pleasure. Perhaps this is one of the reasons for the subliminal power of the imagery of the serpent—the emblem of the devil himself—always rising and threatening. The phallic associations of snakes and penises could only make the devil even more frightening and threatening than ever.[105]

The unceasing torments of sexuality and the impulse to masturbate are revealed with startling clarity in the shorthand notes kept in the diary of young Michael Wigglesworth while a tutor at Harvard during the early 1650's. Fearful of his own intense pride, he wrote in his regular script, "ah Lord I am vile, I desire to abhor my self (o that I could !) before the[e] for these things," following his exclamation with the secret shorthand notation: "I find such unresistable torments of carnal lusts or provocation unto the ejection of seed that I find my self unable to read any thing to inform me about my distemper because of the prevailing or rising of my lusts." The following month, he noted, "Some filthiness escaped me in a filthy dream. The Lord notwithstanding." In October, soon after learning of his own father's death, he again noted that "The last night some filthiness in a vile dream escaped me for which I loathe myself and desire to abase myself before my God." Sexuality, even in marriage, was filthy and sinful to Wigglesworth, as his words to God imply: "Behold I am vile, when thou showest me my face I abhor my self. Who can bring a clean thing out of filthiness, I was conceived bred brought up in sin." When he contemplated marriage for himself, he revealed his own deep-set fear that he might already have a dangerous venereal disease, possibly gonorrhea. Before actually marrying, he consulted a physician about his disease, but was told that "mine was not vera Gon." Even after the consummation of his marriage, undertaken in part as an unemotional solution to his sexual torments, he cried out in his diary, "O Lord! let my cry come up unto thee for all the blessing of a marryed estate, A heart suitable thereto, chastity especially thereby, and life and health if it be they will." So "chastity" could be commensurate with marriage, in Wigglesworth's opinion; yet he added, "I feel the stirrings and strongly of my former distemper even after the use of marriage the next day which makes me exceeding afraid." Soon thereafter, in July 1655, he was praying to the Lord again, this time noting "carnal lusts also exceeding prevailing. Lord forgive my intemperance in the use of marriage for thy sons sake." By September, he noted in his diary that he and his wife could not sleep apart "without obloquy and reproach," and yet "neither can we lay together without exposing me to the return of grievous disease." The next day, he noted that "some night pollution escaped me notwithstanding my earnest prayer to the contrary which brought to mind my old sins now too much forgotten."

After his wife died in 1659, he lived alone without another wife for twenty years, a constant invalid afflicted with what might have been essentially psychosomatic ailments. Sex, for Wigglesworth, was dangerous, and he could never escape the association of sexuality, filthiness, and sin. He was certainly not unique in his response to his own inner sexual impulses and needs.[106]

The profound discomfort that some evangelical males experienced with regard to sexuality, and the necessity they felt for the denial of many aspects of their own masculinity, suggest that they may have both identified with and felt intense hostility toward women, and their own mothers in particular. Their alienation from their bodies and rejection of their penises suggest an unconscious defense against erotic impulses and intimacy with their mothers. A number of eminent evangelicals recalled intimate relationships with their mothers, a sense of being very special, precious, and close—Thomas Shepard, Increase Mather, George Whitefield all remembered their mothers with unusual fondness. Both John Wesley and Jonathan Edwards grew up in households dominated by females. Wesley was the favorite child of Susanna Wesley, surrounded by sisters during much of his early life; Edwards grew up as the only male child, with four sisters older than himself and six sisters younger. The "feminization" of these young males began in infancy and early childhood, but the continued conflicts which persisted throughout their adulthood suggest strongly that they continued to be plagued with unresolved doubts about their own identity as males. Some sources make sense only if latent homosexuality is assumed. To become the bride of Christ certainly carries this as one of several possible meanings.[107]

Some of the imagery associated with women in the private notebook of Jonathan Edwards strongly suggests an unconscious association of women with danger and disappointment. Hell itself was sometimes associated in European tradition with the vagina, and the imagery of Hell could evoke images of devouring and dangerous vaginal cavities. As Edwards said, "The torrents and floods of liquid fire that sometimes are vomited out from the lower parts of the earth, the belly of hell, by the mouths of volcanos, indicate or shadow forth what is in hell, viz., as it were, a lake of fire and brimstone, deluges of fire and wrath to overwhelm wicked men." The earth also was associated with mothers by Edwards, but the image of motherhood is sometimes the image of destruction: "The earth or this earthly world does by men's persons as it does by their bodies: it devours men and eats them up. As we see this our mother that brought us forth and at whose breasts we are nourished is cruel to us, she is hungry for the flesh of her children, and swallows up mankind, one generation after another, in the grave, and is insatiable in her appetite. So she does mystically those that live by the breasts of the earth and depend on worldly things for happiness; the earth undoes and ruins them. It makes them miserable forever, it devours and eats up the inhabitants thereof according to the evil report that the spies brought up of the land of Canaan." Numbers 13 is not actually about the devouring earth-mother, but about only men. There is a power behind this image which suggests that Edwards, too, harbored an intense fear of women, and a sense of the powerful engulfment of women, which would not be too surprising, given his own experiences as the only son in a large family of girls. For Edwards, as for other evangelicals, religious convictions gained immeasurable power from the unconscious associations with oedipal feelings that threatened their innermost sexual identity.[108]

The power of unconscious oedipal conflicts as a factor shaping the "feminization" of young males is nowhere more clearly evident than in the diary of Michael Wigglesworth. Born in Yorkshire in 1631, Wigglesworth spent the first nine years of his life as an only child (his sister was not born until late 1640). By the time his diary began in 1653, Wigglesworth's constant preoccupation is with his own intense sense of distance, separation, and rebellion from God, his heavenly Father. The central themes of his life are expressed simultaneously in a single exhortation to God: "Therefore Lord hear my crys, my sighings, my groans bottle thou my tears wherewith I seek at the hands of a father pardon and power over my still prevailing lusts, principally pride and sensuality, want of love to thee and fervent desires after communion with thee." Wigglesworth felt that he did not love God enough. As he prayed, "Lord shed thy love abroad in my heart, inflame me with love to thee again, giving hope and assurance in beleeving, and patience in waiting thy pleasure for doing good either to me or mine. Harden not my heart from thy fear and love." "I am affraid," he confessed, "because I feel so little love to the[e]. . . . O restore to me the sence of thy favour which is better than life." "Verily," he acknowledged, "thou art my father. . . . Put the spirit of a child into me and constantly maintain it." Wigglesworth often acknowledged in his own diary his own "want of love and dutifulness to my parents," but it was his father especially whom he could not love. Shortly after learning of his father's death, he noted in shorthand his hope that he "might not be secretly glad that my father was gone." Later, he again acknowledged his "desert to be kickt out of this world because I have not had naturall affections to my natural father, but requited him and all my governours evil for good," as well as deserving "to be shut out of the world to come, because I have rebell'd against and dishonour'd and disregarded my heavenly father, been a viper in his bosom where he has nourished me." For Wigglesworth, God was not only his Father but also his husband and head. He feared on one occasion "that I wrong and griev my head and husband so by not loving and delighting in his presence; by my liking other loves more than him." Several days later, he noted that "It grieveth me for my whoarish departures of heart from the Lord. That I do not live upon him, to him, and walk with him in the world. And now methinks these sabbaths are blessed seasons wherein poor wandring harlots, may return to their husband again." For all of his hostility and lack of love for his own father, he could be comfortable only when reassured of the love of his Father in Heaven. Yet he did not love Him enough either.[109]

Who, then, did he love, besides himself when occasionally filled with pride and self-love? There is no evidence in his diary that he loved his wife, who was a cousin on his mother's side of the family sufficiently close to cause worry about incest; but there is evidence that he loved some of his Harvard students quite consciously. One day, he was disturbed by "much distracted thoughts I find arising from too much doting affection," directed (as he then immediately added in shorthand) "to some of my pupils one of whom went to Boston with me today." On another occasion, he noted that "I find my spirit so exceeding carried with love to my pupils that I cant tell how to take up my rest in God." Several weeks later, he was meditating and thought, "will the Lord now again return and embrace me in the arms of his dearest love? wil he fall upon my neck and kiss me? for he was pleased to give in some secret and silent evidence of his love." The thought of being embraced, kissed, and loved by the Lord might also have corresponded to some of his own inward desires, for on one occasion at least he reported feeling "such filthy lust also flowing from my fond affection to my pupils whiles in their presence on the third day after noon that I confess myself an object of God's loathing." There is little reason to doubt that Michael Wigglesworth was truly enamored of some of the young adolescent boys whom he taught, or that he felt profoundly uncomfortable with the "filthy lust" on his part that their presence evoked.[110]

For Wigglesworth, religious sensibilities, oedipal conflicts, and "feminization" were intimately interconnected, mirroring his persistent conflicts with his own masculinity and his need to see himself in the role of wife rather than husband. The inner conflicts that these tensions and needs produced may well account for his own extraordinary guilt and fear. They almost certainly underlay his need for punishment, articulated so powerfully later in his famous poem on the Day of Doom, one of the classics of the fire and brimstone tradition in New England.

For young women, too, unconscious oedipal ties to fathers had profound effects upon their personalities, their sexual identity and relationships, and upon the dynamics of their piety. The experiences of Sarah Prince Gill suggest the intricate interplay between a daughter's intense love for her earthly father and her devotion to her heavenly Father, while at the same time providing evidence of a powerful inhibition toward involvement with any males other than her father. Sarah Prince Gill's experience also indicates the vital importance for young women of the affection and friendship of other young women.

Sarah Prince grew up in the household of the Reverend Thomas

Prince, the leading evangelical preacher in mid-eighteenth-century Boston and one of the most ardent supporters of the revivals of the Great Awakening during the 1740's, the period in which Sarah was converted. Although she was one of five children, three of her siblings had died by late 1748. After her elder sister, Mercy, died in 1752, she became the only surviving child, living for some time with her father and mother. Thus she maintained an intimate relationship with her father throughout her twenties, while she was unmarried and uninvolved with marriageable men. On several occasions, she found herself being courted with the prospect of marriage opening up before her, yet she discovered one reason or another to remain single.[111]

Throughout the 1750's, Sarah Prince corresponded with Esther Edwards Burr. The two women established an extraordinarily close and intimate friendship, sustained by the journals they kept and sent to each other periodically. Sarah and Esther were as close as, if not even closer than, sisters. As Esther wrote to Sarah in 1754, "I esteem you one of the best, and in some respects nerer than any Sister I have. I have not one Sister I can write so freely to as to you the Sister of my heart." Sarah, in return, felt that Esther was "the Beloved of my heart, my dearest Friend," whose death in April 1758, as Sarah wrote in her diary, was "the heaviest affliction next to the Death of My dear sister *Mercy* I ever met with." "My whole Prospects in this World are now changed. My whole dependence for comfort in this World gone.—She was dear to me as the apple of my Eye—she knew and felt all my Griefs. She laid out herself for my good and was ever assiduously studying it. The God of Nature had furnished her with all that I desir'd in a Friend—her Natural Powers were Superior to most Women, her knowledge was extensive of Men and Things her Accomplishments fine—her Prudence forethought and Sagacity wonderfull—her Modesty rare—In Friendly Qualities none Exceeded her—She was made for a refin'd Friend. how Faithful? how Sincere? How Open hearted? how Tender how carefull how disinterested—" "And," she added with emphasis, "*she was mine!* O the tenderness which tied our hearts! O the comfort I have Enjoy'd in her for allmost 7 years." There could be no doubt whatsoever of her love for Esther Burr, nor of Esther's importance in her life. Sarah's love had been reciprocated fully, however. Esther wrote her in 1755: "As you Say, I believe tis true that I love you too much, that is I am too fond of you, but I cant esteem and vallue [you] too greatly, that is Sertain—Consider my friend how rare a thing tis to meet with Such a friend as I have in my *Fidelia*."[112]

Esther Burr nevertheless frequently chastised Sarah Prince as she evaded marriage to one man after another. As Esther wrote in 1756, after hearing about another escape, "I am almost two vext to write—I wonder in the name of honesty what business you had to run away time after time when you knew he was a coming—you may repent it when it is two late for I dont know of Such another Match on all accounts not on all our Share." But her injunctions were in vain, for Sarah could not bring herself to leave her father and her home to marry another man. Although she was nearly thirty years old, she did not seem to be able to marry until her father's death freed her.[113]

Sarah Prince was bound intimately to her father and found his death almost more than she could bear. Her diary records her constant preoccupation with her heavenly Father, and the need she felt to do His will utterly and entirely, without the least hesitation or assertion of self in any instance. On September 9, 1758, when her father was very ill, she wrote that "God is again holding his rod over me and it points at the very Dearest and Best of all my Finite Comforts—the los[s] of my Dearest *Father!*" "At times," she added, "I am allmost sunk with the Prospect and ready to think tis impossible to Live under such a Stroke.— can't feel willing—My Veins are inexpressibly horn'd—I want to be humbled at the Foot of Divine Absolute Sovereignty and Yield My all to God freely and chearfully as his due." "O," she cried, "that my Will may be broken and God have the Empire of my Will, Affections, and whole man intirely." Several weeks later, as her father sank deeper toward his death, she exclaimed: "Surely this is one of Natures tenderest ties, viz. the Bond which unites a Parent and child—Especially such a Parent . . . I thought when my Sister Died I felt all that could be felt but twas not Like this Union. Never was a harder struggle than I felt thro' the day." For many long and painful hours, she struggled with her own feelings toward her dying father, unable to give him up and let him go: "Un- speakably[?] distres'd was I for him and for myself—Satan was Suffered to fill me with horrid Fears. A Stubbor[n] will raged within. I felt an Enmity rise against God in this his Dispensation But I hope was burdened with it and help'd to wrastle with strong cries and tears and gronings not to be Uttered for full resignation and Subjection to God and I felt for about half an hour before he died a [won]drous change within," she noted, "my Will melted and brought to Comply and a happy Calm Ensued. He died in a Gentle Manner."[114]

Five months passed after her father's death without a single entry being made in her diary, which had previously been kept with great regularity. The next entry, March 25, 1759, was written "two days before Marriage." She had agreed to marry Moses Gill, a prominent merchant. Her father's death had released her, but marriage brought no lasting peace. For the remainder of her diary, she constantly mourns the loss of the intense and intimate closeness with God that she had almost always felt in her father's lifetime during the years of intimacy and daily contact. Now, she noted early in November 1760, after more than a year of marriage, "I have been endeavouring to look inward and seek to know my case godward and I find that I am Evidently under an awfull withdraw of Gracious Influences." Early in the spring of 1764, she still felt that her God was distant and making His presence felt rarely. Accordingly, she sought humiliation and prayer, "on account of My *own soul*, which is an awful state of distance and disafection to God and his Ways; to seek his Gracious Influences to make me holy, to Empty me of Sin, the World, Sensual Aims, Corrupt Affections, and determine me *for*, and fix me *on*, *himself*, so as that I may be for him, and his service intirely and forever." With her father gone, her life was saddened as well by the loss of the presence of her heavenly Father. Without a father, without her sisters, without her dearest and most intimate friend, she had no emotional sustenance. Though marriage brought responsibility, it did not seem to provide her with a sense of being loved. Perhaps no man other than her own father could have given her that.[115]

Marriage also posed problems for two leading English evangelists, George Whitefield and John Wesley. Wesley remained unmarried until 1751, when he wed Molly Vazeille at the age of forty-eight—entering into a marriage that brought neither comfort nor satisfaction but only many years of domestic strife. George Whitefield married at a younger age, taking a wife in 1741 at the age of twenty-six. His decision evidently was sudden and unexpected, for his experiences with the prospects of marriage in previous years gave no grounds for expecting him ever to marry. For Whitefield, as for so many other evangelicals, marriage to Christ was the role that gave the most comfort and that he felt described best the union of the regenerated Christian and the Saviour. As he said in a sermon preached in Philadelphia during the early 1740's, "My Lord, even the Lord *Jesus* . . . has made a Marriage Feast, and offers to espouse all Sinners to himself, and to make them Flesh of his Flesh, and Bone of his Bone. He is willing to be united to you by one Spirit." "Come then, my Brethren," he exhorted, "come to the Marriage.— Do not play the Harlot any longer.—Let this be the Day of your Espousals with *Jesus Christ*, he only is your lawful Husband." While Whitefield thus exhorted sinners to come to Christ and take Him "only" as their "lawful Husband," he also felt himself truly married only to Jesus. Sex ought to be denied and the lusts of the flesh mortified. As he proclaimed in a sermon on early piety: "we see mere striplings not only practising, but delighting in such religious duties, and in the days of their youth, when, if ever, they have a relish for sensual pleasures, subduing and despising the lust of the flesh, the lust of the eye and the pride of life. . . . He knows not what men mean by talking of mortification, self-denial and retirement as hard and rigorous duties, for he has so accustomed himself to them, that . . . they now become even natural."[116]

Although Whitefield had become involved with the Delamotte family and their daughter Elizabeth while in England, he was unable to propose marriage to her without at the same time ensuring that his proposal would prove unacceptable. While crossing the Atlantic in early 1740 from England to Georgia, he decided to propose marriage to Elizabeth. Yet his letter to her noted: "There is nothing I dread more than having my heart drawn away by earthly objects.—When that time comes, it will be over with me indeed; I must then bid adieu to zeal and fervency of spirit, and in effect bid the Lord Jesus to depart from me. For alas, what room can there be for God, when a rival hath taken possession of the heart?" He clearly felt unable to marry at this point, because his own intimacy with Christ would be broken. He could not admit affection for anyone else—though he could accept the fact that a wife might be useful to him. In a letter to another man, written during this period, he noted that "I often have great inward trials. . . . I believe it to be God's will that I should marry. One who may be looked upon as a superior, is absolutely necessary for the due management of affairs [at his orphanage in Georgia]." "However," he continued, "I pray God that I may not have a wife till I can live as though I had none." He then added, "You may communicate this to some of our intimates, for I would call Christ and His disciples to the marriage."[117]

The decision was now made to write a proposal of marriage to Elizabeth's parents first, and then, if they approved, to Elizabeth herself. But Whitefield's letters made abundantly clear his intention to have her come for the specific purpose of taking care of the orphanage he was establishing in Georgia. As he reassured her parents, "You need not be afraid of sending me a refusal. For, I bless God, if I know anything of my own heart, I am free from that foolish passion which the world calls *Love*. I write only because I believe it is the will of God that I should alter my state; but your denial will fully convince me, that your daughter is not the person appointed by God for me. He knows my heart; I would not marry but for Him, and in Him, for ten thousand worlds." He then wrote to Elizabeth, "I think I can call the God of Abraham, Isaac and Jacob, to be witness that I desire 'to take you my sister to wife, not for lust, but uprightly;' and therefore I hope He will mercifully ordain, if it be His blessed will we should be joined together, that we may walk as Zachary and Elizabeth did, in all the ordinances of the Lord blameless." And he noted in closing, "I trust, I love you only for God, and desire to be joined to you only by His command and for His sake." Not surprisingly, the suit was not successful. After four months, he finally heard from Elizabeth, and then wrote to another male friend, William Seward, that "I want a *gracious woman* that is dead to every thing but JESUS, and is qualified to govern children, and direct persons of her own sex. Such a one would help, but not retard me in my dear LORD's work. I wait upon the LORD every moment; I hang upon my JESUS: and he is so infinitely condescending, that he daily grants me fresh tokens of his love, and assures me that he will not permit me to fall by the hands of a woman."

A woman "dead to every thing" surely meant dead to sensuality and the pleasures of the body as well. Whitefield seemed relieved to think that he would not "fall by the hands of a woman." Both his actions and his words reveal a profound fear of women and of marriage, a fear that rested in part, at least, upon a rigorous alienation from his own sexuality and his own manliness. Love, or at least the love of women, was not for him.[118]

Whitefield's letters to friends, acquaintances, and fellow ministers, however, abound with expressions of love and affection, brotherly care, and close ties through their kinship in Christ. In July 1739, for instance, he wrote to a friend who had evidently fallen away from the Christian path, "has my familiar friend, who has been dear to me as my own soul, has he taken part with, and gone back to the enemy," calling upon him to "Return, return. My dear friend, I cannot part from you for ever." He signed himself, "Your most affectionate friend and servant in CHRIST." In November 1739, he wrote "Dear Brother J." that "Indeed I love you. Why? Because I hope you are an *Israelite;* and one of those babes to whom it has been our LORD's good pleasure to reveal the mysteries of the kingdom of GOD," signing himself, "Your affectionate friend, brother and servant." All of Whitefield's companions were male, his fellow ministers were male, and the acquaintances with whom he corresponded were predominantly male. This may account for the rumor of homosexuality that apparently followed him from Maryland to Pennsylvania during the early summer of 1740.[119]

Possibly some of the colonists were especially sensitive to any hint of love between men, as suggested by the observation of the Reverend Jonathan Parsons, of the West Parish in Lyme, Connecticut, about the behavior of two men in his church during a heated revival: "One thing complained of as an indecency was, that two men embraced each other in their arms before the blessing was given," a "fact" which he supposed "true," but not "so very indecent, as some would represent it." In any case, although the rumor about Whitefield was apparently groundless, it evidently seemed credible to enough people for one man to take special pains to deny it. Perhaps Whitefield's contemporaries observed or felt a special affinity toward other men in his character or behavior.[120] In any event, Whitefield decided to marry a year later after his return to England.

On November 14, 1741, he went to Wales and married Elizabeth James, a widow ten years his senior (she was thirty-six). He wrote of his wife that she was "Once gay, but for three years last past a despised follower of the Lamb of God, neither rich in fortune nor beautiful as to her person, but I believe a true child of God, and one who would not, I think, attempt to hinder me in His work for the world." And he added in a letter to the Reverend Gilbert Tennant, after a similar comment on his wife, "In that respect, I am just the same as before marriage." Perhaps he thought he had found, at last, a perfect woman to head his orphanage. Certainly, given his brief description of his wife, there is little reason to assume that passion had anything to do with his decision to marry. He remained as free to preach, travel, and maintain his devotion and duty to his Saviour as ever before. His own true marriage to Christ continued without the constant seductions of the passions and the flesh that bothered so many other evangelicals.[121]

The acute sensitivity of some evangelicals to any hint of effeminacy, any relationship or appearance that might endanger a precariously established sense of masculinity, could account for the persistent preference for short hair and an abhorrence or fear of wearing the hair too long. Within the context of the styles of the seventeenth and eighteenth centuries, length of hair was one aspect of appearance that varied considerably; Puritans and evangelicals were more notably drawn to shorter cuts than many of their contemporaries, who often wore their hair below the neck, as well as sporting wigs with long, flowing locks. Hair became a political as well as a religious badge during the English civil war in the mid-seventeenth century.[122]

The practice of wearing wigs also evoked a strong response. The Reverend Solomon Stoddard, for instance, acknowledged the tendency in past decades for men to wear their hair longer than during the civil war era in the mid-seventeenth century, but nevertheless declared that "it seems utterly Unlawful to wear their Hair long; It is a great Burden and Cumber; it is Effiminacy, and a vast Expence." As for "Periwigs," Stoddard stated that, among other vicious things, they made men proud: "It is from an Affectation of *Swaggering*; it is an Affecting of *Finery* that there is no just occasion for. They count it *Brave* to be in the Fashion; crave the honour of being counted as *Gallant* as others. It is too much *Flanting*." In addition, "It is *contrary to Gravity*. There is a Masculine Gravity that should appear in the Countenances of Men, discovering a Solemnity of Spirit. But this *Practice* is *Light*, and *Effeminat*." But what, in the context of the seventeenth and eighteenth centuries, did it mean for a man to be effeminate? The answer is difficult to pinpoint, but one source of concern about the appearance of effeminacy was the doubt about sexual identity among many males. For evangelicals, and for some others too, short hair was an outward, visible declaration of masculinity, a declaration made necessary, it seems, by inner insecurity. After all, although a man might consider himself to be a bride of Christ, he still needed some reassurance that he was a man as well. Short hair and simply styled clothing served this need. For many men, of course, long hair was a comfortable fashion that did not produce any inner insecurities about their own masculinity. But these were also men who would have found it difficult to deny their own masculinity sufficiently to become brides of Christ or even evangelicals at all.[123]

The Quest for Purity

EVANGELICALS WERE PURISTS; they sought a life of purity, churches that were pure, and communities bound together in unity, harmony, and purity. The wars that the evangelicals waged against the self, the Church, and the world bore witness to their constant preoccupation with absolute conformity to the rules set forth by God for the lives, thoughts, and feelings of His people. Over and over again, they sought to make themselves as perfect as possible and as pure as possible, and to deny or control their innermost feelings and thoughts—which seemed to reveal the persistence of the sinfulness, corruption, and depravity that was so much a part of their own experience and belief. In a profound way, their intense desire for purity was the counterpart to their equally intense awareness of defilement and sin. Both were experienced in extreme forms. The evangelicals could never be comfortable with an existence somewhere between these polarities of purity and corruption, although, in fact, most led lives that swung periodically between these poles. The impulse was always present to escape from sin and toward the achievement of purity in themselves, their churches, and the world of which they were a part. The purist impulse, so central to the evangelicals' temperament, was evident in every aspect of their life, their experience, and their piety.[124]

Pursuing a sense of inward purity, evangelicals not only sought to mortify the self and the flesh but also to adhere to a pattern of life that permitted no deviations from the path set forth for them in the rules laid down by their parents and their God. They often described themselves or were described by others as people notably "exact," "precise," or "strict" in their modes of living. When Richard Rogers, a seventeenth-century English Puritan, was told that his behavior was too "precise," he replied that he served "a precise God." In the summer of 1655, as Increase Mather experienced the "extremity of anguish and horror" of conscience which preceded his conversion, he recalled that "Some of my companions would deride me for my now preciseness and tender conscience." Almost a century later, Joseph Bean found himself similarly tormented before his own conversion, and discovered that "as I got acquainted moore with young pepel I found this Precise way of living as thay called it would not du for me so that I must leve this strickt way of living or Else my acquantance, for thay would not sute together." George Whitefield was described by a man who had lived in his household for several years in terms that reveal with the utmost clarity the obsessive quality of his exactitude: "He was very exact to the time appointed for his stated meals; a few minutes delay would be considered a great fault. He was irritable, but soon appeased. . . . Not a paper must have been out of place, or put up irregularly. Each part of the furniture must have been likewise in its place before [he retired at night]."[125]

Methodism itself was named because of the extraordinary strictness and discipline that shaped the lives of the first group of Oxford evangelicals who became the instigators of the great revivals of the mid-eighteenth century in England, including Whitefield and the Wesleys. The precise and methodical pattern of life inculcated in the Wesley children by their mother continued to shape their preoccupation with rules and discipline for the rest of their lives. For evangelicals, exactitude, precision, and the necessity for living by rule were indispensable as protections against those impulses and feelings that always threatened to overwhelm them with a sense of impurity and sin.

In 1760, Nathan Cole described the necessity for a life closely regulated by God's rules, which served to protect him against all the sins and corruptions of his own heart:

> . . . now God gave me to see many plagues that Mankind were plagued with; as pride and prejudice . . . anger . . . honour . . . pride; and . . . riches . . . Covetousness, Selfishness, malice, and envy. I saw such a hateful nature in these evil tempers, that I thought my heart and Soul did hate them perfectly; so that I was not willing they should live in my breast, but that I would immediately make war with them and cast them out with all my might; I will not lose my happiness of my mind for these evil tempers for I never can feel happy with them in me, I will conquer or die in the cause is my mind: I was talking with a Christian about these things, and he asked me how I lived now, are you not plagued with these evil tempers and with a rambling mind; I told him yes, but I have found out a new way to get rid of them for once I used to stand and fight them, and the more I fought the more they plagued me, but now I get rid of them by turning my mind into the ways of Gods Commands, and so walk as well as I can, and thus I leave them or they me, for they cannot walk in Gods Ways: therefore I find the best way to get rid of them is to live by rule, even the rule of Gods word, for they cannot harm any man in that way; but when a man is out of the Rule, they are after him at once. . . .[126]

By controlling their own behavior rigorously, evangelicals sought to suppress their unacceptable feelings and thoughts. Any deviation, any omission might threaten them with the emergence of inadmissible feelings and desires. They could not tolerate much personal freedom or flexibility. There was too much danger in not adhering to the rules that governed their lives. As a result, evangelicals were methodical and extremely self-disciplined. Threatened continually by enemies from both within and without, they found reassurance in following the will of God, knowing that their own wills had been conquered and had been surrendered altogether. Their preoccupation with precision and purity justified their own continuous self-repression. The vigorous efforts evangelicals made to mold themselves into disciplined soldiers for Christ reflected their deeply rooted desire for purity and perfection in every aspect of their character and behavior. The less freedom and deviation from the rules they allowed themselves, the more likely they were to be certain of achieving the goals they set for themselves. They always felt most at peace when least free to act, to think, to feel, or to will for themselves.[127]

Paradoxically, this active self-discipline and strict adherence to the will and rules set forth for them by God freed these evangelicals to participate with remarkable energy and confidence in the world in which they lived. Once they could be certain that they were no longer pursuing self-will or selfish ends, they could act freely and forcefully on behalf of the will they perceived designed for them by God. For these particular children of the Lord, the sense of freedom that always followed from total submission—a freedom shaped by the experiences of earliest childhood as well as by the subsequent traumas of the new birth—often provided them with extraordinary levels of energy and determination. They were able to serve their God in the world to the utmost limits of their physical and their emotional capacities: hence the paradox of seeing men and women actively fulfilling the will of God and not their own by preaching, traveling, and spending themselves entirely for the sake of a Divine master, while at the same time asserting the utter impotency and feebleness of humanity in general. Only when the energies that had been consumed by resistance and rebelliousness—both in childhood and in later life—were freed by the experience of total submission and the absolute surrender of self and self-will could evangelicals find the inner strength and vitality they needed for their permanent warfare with the world at large. By denying their own personal freedom (convinced that their own wills were unfree and dangerous), they appeared to be people who were intensely individualistic, self-assertive, and autonomous. But the intensity of their quest for the precise fulfillment of God's law and word, and their unending efforts to repress the self and self-will as thoroughly as possible, made it impossible for evangelicals ever to be truly comfortable with a sense of individual autonomy. Their personalities were too rigid, too defensive, too systematically repressive to enable them to tolerate much liberty for themselves. By leading lives of rigorous purity and precision, they provided themselves with the assurance, stemming from strict compliance to rules set by someone other than themselves, that they were fulfilling the expectations and commands set forth for them by God. Only then could they feel truly free.

Since evangelicals allowed themselves no freedom to follow their own wills and ways, they could not allow anyone else the freedom they were denied. Over and over again, the quest for purity and the need for absolute obedience to the rules of God prompted many of them to mount sustained attacks upon the customs, habits, and styles of life of the nonevangelical inhabitants of the world. The world, too, must be made to live in conformity to God's will and ways. No one was exempt from the insistent demand by evangelicals that the society around them should conform to their own inner vision of purity, simplicity, discipline, and grace. Evangelicals were always at war with the unregenerated part of humanity, always seeking both to convert others and to render them replicas of themselves. Such absolutist mentalities could not tolerate the varieties and complexities of character that characterized people who did not share their special modes of temperament and piety.

As a result, evangelicals throughout the seventeenth, eighteenth, and nineteenth centuries found themselves constantly battling against the sins of their contemporaries. In the middle of the seventeenth century, George Fox traveled throughout England denouncing the ways and pleasures of the people who scorned and opposed him. He sought to transform their lives as his own had been, to remake the very essence of their life styles, which seemed to him filled with every vice and sin known to mankind:

> About this time I was sorely exercised in going to their courts to cry for justice, and in speaking and writing to judges and justices to do justly, and in warning such as kept public houses for entertainment that they should not let people have more drink than would do them good, and in testifying against their wakes or feasts, their May-games, sports, plays, and shows, which trained up people to vanity and looseness, and led them from the fear of God, and the days they had set forth for holy-days were usually the times wherein they most dishonoured God by these things. In fairs also, and in markets, I was made to declare against their deceitful merchandise and cheating and cozening, warning all to deal justly, to speak the truth . . . and to do unto others as they would have others do unto them, and forewarning them of the great and terrible day of the Lord which would come upon them all. I was moved also to cry against all sorts of music, and against the mountebanks playing tricks on their stages, for they burdened the pure life and stirred up people's minds to vanity.
>
> I was much exercised too, with school-masters and school-mistresses, warning them to teach their children sobriety in the

fear of the Lord, that they might not be nursed and trained up in lightness, vanity, and wantonness. Likewise I was made to warn masters and mistresses, fathers and mothers in private families, to take care that their children and servants might be trained up in the fear of the Lord; and that they themselves should be therein examples and patterns of sobriety and virtue to them.

Nothing escaped Fox's scrutiny, nor his warnings (public and private), for he "was made" to speak by the Lord, and sought to transform people's entire lives in the name of "the pure life."[128]

George Whitefield, too, felt compelled to denounce the levity and sins of the people whom he visited, and sought to bring about their renunciation of the world and the self, just as he himself had done. Traveling through the colonies on his first visit, early in December 1739, he stopped in Annapolis, Maryland, where he met the governor and the minister of the parish. They welcomed him warmly, introduced him to some other gentlemen, and gathered at "a gentleman's house," where they had "some useful conversation":

Our conversation ran chiefly on the new birth, and the folly and sinfulness of those amusements, whereby the polite part of the world are so fatally diverted from the pursuit of the one thing needful. Some of the company, I believe, thought I was too strict, and were very strenuous in defence of what they called *innocent* diversions; but when I told them everything was sinful which was not done with a single eye to God's glory, and that such entertainments not only discovered a levity of mind, but were contrary to the whole tenor of the Gospel of Christ, they seemed somewhat convinced; at least, I trust it set them *doubting*, and I pray God they may *doubt* more and more, for cards, dancing, and such like, draw the soul from God, and lull it asleep as much as drunkenness and debauchery. Every minister of Christ ought, with the authority of an apostle, to declare and testify the dreadful snare of the devil, whereby he leads many captive at his will, by the falsely called *innocent* entertainments of the polite part of the world; for women are as much enslaved to their fashionable diversions, as men are to their bottle and their hounds. Self-pleasing, self-seeking is the *ruling principle* in both; and therefore, such things are to be spoken against, not only as so many trifling amusements, but as things which shew that the heart is wholly alienated from the life of God. If I may speak from my own, as well as others' experience, as soon as ever the soul is stirred up to seek after God, it cannot away with any such thing, and nothing but what leads toward God can delight it; and therefore, when in company, I love to lay the axe to the root of the tree, shew the necessity of a thorough change of heart, and then all things fall to the ground at once.[129]

King James I would have recognized George Whitefield and others like him as one of those " 'precise persons' who claimed that enjoyment and recreation were incompatible with true religion." They appeared both in England and in America as one generation of evangelicals after another sought to remake the world in the evangelical image. Because the image that they had of themselves was self-less, ascetic, repressive, always at odds with the feelings of sensuality, of desire and pleasure, their efforts to regenerate the world and transform the modes of life of everyone else generally took the form of an all-out attack rather than of persuasion. To make the world pure required more discipline, more self-denial, more repression of the senses than many people—not yet or never to be evangelicals—could accept or achieve. As a result, the quest for purity remained a constant theme in the response of evangelicals to the world. But only occasionally, in certain times and places, did it become the dominant pattern of behavior and values for the communities and societies in which they lived.[130]

Evangelicals were far more successful, on the whole, in their quest for purity within the churches to which they committed themselves. The recurrent motif of purity in worship and in church membership was exemplified in the persistent urge to separate themselves from institutions that seemed to be corrupted and worldly, and that appeared to contain both saints and sinners as members of the same church. The evangelical impulse always was toward the creation of "pure" churches, containing only those people who could demonstrate to others their own inner grace and the assurance of visible sainthood. Only those who had experienced the new birth qualified for membership, for the sacraments were to be limited to those who alone had evidence of being saved. Evangelicals could tolerate no halfway measures or states of grace. Individuals were either saved or damned, and churches ought to consist exclusively of those who had been born again. The quest for pure churches and the concomitant tendency among evangelicals to separate from the established churches (which usually incorporated both the saved and the damned as fully as possible) were the result, in part, of their own individual experiences of rebirth. Conversion made them the experimental witnesses of their own inner transformations, with the result that they wanted fellowship only with other true saints like themselves. But pure churches were also one more facet of the evangelical quest for self-annihilation, of the experience of submerging the self through unification with Christ.[131]

Ideally, all Christians were not only pure in their doctrines and practices but were also of one mind and one heart, following one way.

Purity implied uniformity—total agreement and absolute compliance with a single mode of piety and of belief. Ideally again, the hope of evangelicals was to make all mankind into a single, unified, purified whole, alike in their conformity to the rules and will of God as revealed in His written word. As Ebenezer Frothingham, a New Light separatist from Connecticut who was deeply engaged in the conflicts arising from the Great Awakening, said of Jonathan Edwards's essay on the qualifications for membership of saints in New England's churches, he hoped God would "make it Instrumental of bringing the Saints in *New-England* into the real order of the Gospel, that so we may be of one Heart, and brought [i]nto one Practice in attending the institutions of the Gospel of Jesus Christ." He acknowledged his desire for "a pure Church" and felt that others, including Edwards, shared his desire. Nathan Cole had a similar vision after dreaming one morning in 1758 of "going to a Meeting of the Saints," gathered together singing so melodiously "that it ravished my Soul," everyone present having "a cheerful voice and countenance." After he woke up, he said: "My heart and soul was in a sweet frame, and I seemed to hear their sound of praise for many days; when I was with them I seemed to feel perfectly their feeling, they felt all as one as if they had been made up all into one man, all drinked into one Spirit and oneness, and whatever trouble or affliction they went through in this world they had borne it patiently as Coming from the hand of God it turned into sound joy in their heart . . . and those Relations and friends of theirs that were dead and in hell was no grief to them, for they were so sweetly conformed to Gods will that his will was theirs and they rejoyced in it."[132]

Often the impulse for fusion and for purity contained in the vision of the union of Christian saints was part of a millennial vision of the distant—or not so distant—future, as in the case of Jonathan Parsons, whose vision captures the essence of the evangelical purist impulse: "O happy day, when the whole body shall be incorporated, and united in Christ their common head! Happy day, when all are stamped with the same image and superscription, and influenced by the same power. O when will that day come, that all shall be knit together in the bond of love and charity, all of one heart; one in their designs and aims; one in their desires and prayers; one in love and affection, and be perfect in one."[133]

The quest for union, for oneness, for merging together into a single pure church, often stemmed from the experience of utter aloneness and isolation that so many people felt in their lives. The individualism of evangelicals was vitally important, for they confronted their God and their fates directly and alone. As Ebenezer Frothingham declared, "if we rightly consider the Nature of Practice in Religion, on Obedience to God, we shall see an absolute Necessity for every Person to act singly, as in the Sight of God only; and this is the Way, under God, to bring the Saints all to worship God sociably, and yet have no Dependence one upon another." These were enduring polarities in evangelical experience: utter aloneness versus the unity and fusion of oneness. There did not seem to be a comfortable middle ground. But the quest for purity in the church could lead men and women in and out of churches over the course of their lifetimes, as they sought (but rarely found) the requisite degrees of perfection and unity which alone could assure them that they had joined in fellowship with the true saints. Both experiences— aloneness and union with others—were part of the same pattern of temperament and piety that formed the central configurations of evangelical experience and belief.[134]

Alienated from themselves, ill at ease with the world, they could never cease their quests for personal purification and for the purification of the world in which they lived. Purists at heart, they found themselves also striving to fulfill the will of God in themselves and in the world, whatever the consequences. Only then, when they felt their own wills subdued, their selves subjected, their desires curbed, could they begin to feel the sense of freedom and of ease that came from absolute obedience to the powers shaping and governing their lives. Having first destroyed themselves, they found that they could be saved; and in their own personal salvation lay hope for the transformation of the world in which they lived.

PART THREE

THE MODERATES:
The Self Controlled

~§ IV §~

Authoritative Families:
Moderate Modes
of Child-Rearing

THROUGHOUT THE SEVENTEENTH AND EIGHTEENTH CENTURIES, and indeed well into the nineteenth century, many people reared their children in ways that differed significantly from the aggressively repressive methods characteristic of evangelicals. Instead of being authoritarian, many families tried to be authoritative, respectful toward legitimate and essential authority within the family, yet aware of the need to limit the exercise of authority within certain established boundaries. Overall, the most significant aspect of these authoritative families was the moderation that manifested itself in most aspects of their lives and in the relationships of parents with their children. Moderates shared the conviction that legitimate authority, parental as well as other kinds, was limited, that human nature was sinful but not altogether corrupted, that reason ought to govern the passions, that a well-governed self was temperate and balanced, and that religious piety ought to be infused with a concern for good and virtuous behavior as well as for grace. They also agreed that children were to be obedient and loving, but they did not share the impulse to break their children's wills. As a result of such attitudes and convictions, the dominant theme that recurs in the lives and writings of these moderate and authoritative families over the centuries is one of "love and duty" rather than the "love and fear" which marked so many evangelical families.[1]

Although most moderates rejected the harsh and inflexible assertion of parental authority and absolute power over children that produced the fear so often felt by evangelicals, their methods of discipline and of nurture, though more temperate and subtler than those of evangelicals, were likewise designed to mold and shape the emerging personalities of their children. Moderates preferred to bend rather than to break their children's wills; but the process was no less effective for being less direct and explicit. The pressures upon their children were consistent, persistent, and profoundly influential. In the end, moderates were as intent as evangelicals upon ensuring the obedience of their children. Although the children of moderates grew to maturity with the sense that their own wills were free and within their own power to control, they also developed consciences which ensured that they, too, would prefer to choose the ways set forth for them rather than counter their parents' wills and wishes.

The Household Setting

THE MODERATE FAMILY flourished best when nurtured and sustained by the connections of kinship and by stability of residence. The more complex the relationships of individuals within households, the more extended the family network, the more likely were members of the immediate family to feel themselves part of an intricate set of human relationships extending beyond the household into the community and beyond the community to more distant places as well. Both in New England and elsewhere, many families rooted themselves rapidly and permanently in particular communities, remaining there generation after generation, growing ever larger in numbers and increasingly connected through proliferating kinship ties to more and more families in their own community and elsewhere. As a result, children often grew up in places that included one or two sets of grandparents, numerous uncles and aunts, cousins of various degrees, parents-in-law, and neighbors whose ties reached back over many years. Households, too, sometimes became more complicated by the residence of married children with their aging parents or, more often, the adjacent residences of parents and married children. Servants, whether indentured, hired, or enslaved, constituted another significant presence. Growing up in such households and such communities had a profound impact upon the development of temperament and piety in the children who were to be moderates.[2]

The complexities of kinship connections and the social world of individuals reared in established communities imbued these children from their earliest years with an awareness of the many degrees of relationship that can bind people together through birth and marriage. They also provided such children with a sense of attachment both to people and to places that would undergird their sense of self and the world for the rest of their lives. The moderates' children grew up with a knowledge of the connections and differences that bound people together or kept them apart, and an awareness of the status, rank, and social position of themselves and everyone else around them, which enabled them to locate themselves and others. They also knew that they had become part of their complex local worlds by virtue of being born into them. The worlds in which many early Americans thus grew up were marked by gradations and connections. It was almost impossible not to sense that one was part of a larger community and to be aware that the surrounding world was a complicated place. So long as they remained in the places where they were born and grew up, individuals nurtured in situations like these would not experience the pangs of isolation, the anxieties of uprooting, or the difficulties of recreating ties to others that marked the lives of so many people throughout these centuries. Connection, not separation, characterized the relationships of most people in these little communities.[3]

One of the most significant aspects of the experience of growing up within the extended families and communities that developed so rapidly throughout the colonies was the relationship between three generations of members of particular families. Unlike the evangelicals—who sought to isolate their children from the influences of grandparents and others in order to intensify the relationship of parents to their own children— moderates characteristically welcomed the influence and assistance of grandparents in the rearing of their children. John Winthrop, who became governor of the newly established colony in Massachusetts Bay and one of the most influential members of the colony until his death in 1649, grew up as an only son in the Groton, Lincolnshire, household of the Winthrops, and continued to reside with his mother and father after his marriage. After the deaths of his first and second wives, he remained in residence in Groton with his third wife, Margaret, until his departure for America in 1629. From the family correspondence, it is clear that his father and mother played an active role in his life and in the lives of his children. Shortly before John's marriage to Margaret, Adam Winthrop wrote to assure her that he was "already inflamed with a fatherly Love and affection towardes yow," and that he was happy to think that "in my olde age I shal injoye the familiar company of so virtuous and loving a daughter."

Samuel Sewall, a prominent merchant in Boston during the late seventeenth and early eighteenth centuries, chose to reside with his parents-in-law after marrying Hannah Hull early in 1676. His mother-in-law, Judith Hull, continued to play a significant role in the rearing of the Sewall children and remained an important presence within the household until her death in 1695. In 1686, for instance, Sewall noted that his son "Little Hull speaks *Apple* plainly in the hearing of his

Grand-Mother and Eliza Land; this the first word." In 1690, he noted
that "Little Joseph sucks his last as is design'd, his Grandmother taking
him into her Chamber in order to wean him." The Reverend Samuel
Johnson, born in 1696 in Guilford, Connecticut, the son and grandson
of deacons in the town's Congregational church, was deeply influenced
by his grandfather for the first six years of his life. He recalled that he
had been "early taught to read by the care of his grandfather, who was
very fond of him," and that his grandfather had often carried him
"about with him to visit the ancient people" and made him recite his
lessons from memory. Johnson, in turn, played a significant role in the
education of his own grandsons, with whom he lived for a number of
years after his son built "an elegant apartment" for his father in his
own house. Johnson noted in his autobiography that "No man could be
happier than he was in a most tender and dutiful son and daughter-in-
law whose affectionate tenderness together with the endearments and
caresses of his young grandchildren" helped console him after the death
of his wife.

John Adams, also the son of a Congregational deacon and the fourth
generation of Adamses to live in Braintree, Massachusetts, valued the
role of grandmothers highly in the rearing of his own children. After
the death of Abigail Adams's mother, Elizabeth Quincy Smith, in 1775,
John wrote to his wife that he grieved "for nobody more than my
Children, and Brothers Smiths and Mr. Cranch's [his brothers-in-law]. Her
most amiable, and discreet Example, as well as her Kind Skill and Care
I have ever relyed upon in my own Mind, for the Education of these
little Swarms." "Not that I have not a proper Esteem for the Capacity
and Disposition of the Mothers," he hastened to add, "but I know that
the Efforts of the Grandmother, are of great Importance, when they
second those of the Parent. And I am sure that my Children are the
better for the forming Hand of their Grandmother." Abigail Adams, too,
also was sure that "The instructions of my own Grandmamma are as
fresh upon my mind this day [October 25, 1775] as any I ever received
from my own parents and made as lasting and powerful impressions."
Her sentiment was shared by many moderates who concurred that
grandparents could have an important and beneficial influence over
grandchildren.[4]

During the summer of 1772, after her marriage to Elisha Hutchinson, Mary Watson Hutchinson wrote to her grandmother, Mary Oliver,
from the Hutchinson family's elegant country house in Milton to tell
her of her gratitude "for the Love which you have ever Shown to me.
When I was early deprived of my Mamma, you took me home, treated
me in the tenderest manner, and became another Mamma to me, took
Care of, and wisely instructed me at an age when I most wanted it, was
a guide to me in my Younger Years, and I hope, my Dear Mamma, you

will still favour me with your advise, and direction, which I have ever found necessary for my happiness to follow." She could not help acknowledging, too, that her grandmother, her "Dear Grandpapa, and the rest of my Friends which I have left behind, engrosses the greatest part of my thoughts." She recalled "With pleasure . . . those happy hours which I have spent with you. I can't help sometimes imagining myself one of the happy number, setting in the Hall listening attentively to the entertaining, and instructing Conversation of my Grandpapa [Peter Oliver]; at other times, I place myself at his right hand at the Table; either viewing the Maps, or hearing him read, and with the greatest pleasure attending to the remarks, and improving Observations which he makes." "Oh my Mamma," she asked, "is it not wrong thus to indulge myself? tho' I am very happy now, and think that I am blessed far above the Common Lot, in having Friends that treat me in so kind and Affectionate manner as they do here Yet, I cannot wholly wean myself from those, who from my infancy have shown such parental Love and unabated Affection for me. I have the highest Veneration for my New Papa, who treats me with all the Affection of a Father. Never one received greater kindness, Love and Friendship, from a Sister then I do from my Peggy," the youngest of the Hutchinson daughters, and the devoted companion of her father. In closing, she sent her duty to her grandfather and "the truest filial Affection" for her grandmother.[5]

The presence of grandparents within the household or sufficiently nearby to play a significant role provided children with contact with important adults other than their own parents, and also with constant alternative sources of authority and guidance. The deep affection felt and expressed by many grandparents for their grandchildren left permanent memories and had an enduring influence upon the development of their children's children. Perhaps most important, however, was the simple fact that their presence complicated the lines of authority within the family and provided children with options that did not exist in evangelical families.

Parental power in moderate families was rarely total because of the presence of other influential adults within the household. One of the central axioms of authoritarianism—total power wielded by parents, total impotency and powerlessness of children—was transformed under these more complicated circumstances into a series of graduated authorities and competing powers within the family, for parents still owed some degree of deference and obedience to the grandparents, just as children owed deference and obedience to the parents. And grandparents could and did interfere with and influence the rearing of grandchildren. The complexities both of the relationships of individuals within specific households and of the relationships of kindred throughout the community ensured that the experiences of such children would establish a consciousness of degrees of authority, of connections, and of obligations to superiors, inferiors, and equals that would remain imprinted upon their characters for a lifetime. Authority within such households could never be absolute.[6]

Innocent Infants

MODERATES EXPERIENCED none of the ambivalence that so often marked the responses of evangelicals to their newborn children, nor did they perceive their infants as depraved or dangerous creatures. They welcomed their children into the world with pleasure, affection, and happy anticipation of the years to come, during which their children would grow to maturity and become responsible and virtuous members of the community. As the Reverend Samuel Willard, one of the leading moderates among the New England clergy during the late seventeenth and early eighteenth centuries, noted, "the Love of Parents to their Children is such as admits not of suitable words to express it, it being so intense and infiuential, so that God himself is pleased to resemble His Love to His Children by this, there being no Comparison that better resembleth it."[7]

Most moderates took for granted the belief that their infant children were innocent of sin at birth, and that they would be welcomed in Heaven should they die before reaching the age of reason. The imagery associated with infancy was loving and positive: children were sweet, tender, promising, pretty little birds rather than frightening birds of prey. The joy and hopes associated with the birth of a child were expressed about 1620 by Adam Winthrop's verses celebrating the arrival of the Lady Mildmay's first son:

> *My soule doth praise the Lord and magnifie his name,*
> *For this sweete babe which in your wombe he did most finely frame.*
> *And on a blessed day hath made him to be borne,*
> *That with his giftes of heavenly grace his soule he might adorne.*
> *God graunt him happie days in joye and peace to lyve,*
> *And more of this most blessed fruite hereafter to you give.*

In another verse, he wrote: "Welcome sweete babe thou art unto thy parents deare,/Whose hartes thou hast filled with joy, as well that doth appeare." In 1714, Adam Winthrop's great-grandson Wait Winthrop, wrote to his son John to inform him that the "great and good God," "This wonderful Jehovah, who gave you and us the sweet babe that came to smile upon us, has been pleased to take it to himselfe again to those eternall mantions of glory which eye hath not seen nor ear heard"— his five-month-old granddaughter was now in Heaven. Two years later, after learning of the birth of another grandson, Wait prayed that "the God of Abraham, the God of Isaac, and the God of Jacob, yea, the God of our Fathers . . . bless the lad with all the blessings of heven and earth, but espetially with the blessings of the new and everlasting covenant, that he may grow up to do worthily in his generation and promote the kingdom of the Lord Jesus Christ, and serve him in sincerity." Shortly afterwards, however, the infant died, whereupon his son wrote that his grandson had been "A sensible, quiet, meek, yet cheerly-tempered child, strong-natured, hearty, fatt. How often have we pleasd ourselves with the thoughts of your seeing this your pretty grandson, who had so manly, beautiful and gracefull a look; but Providence has ordered otherwise." Like the Winthrops, Samuel Sewall also took for granted the belief that his own infant son would go directly to Heaven after his premature death in 1685, noting that "he fell asleep, I hope in Jesus, and that a Mansion was ready for him in the Father's House." In 1696, Sewall mourned the stillbirth of a son while he was away visiting his parents and relatives. "I was grievously stung to find a sweet desirable Son dead, who had none of my help to succour him and save his life."[8]

Throughout the eighteenth and early nineteenth centuries, too, moderates took for granted the innocent nature of their infant children. As Isaac Norris, an eminent gentleman and leader of Philadelphia society, noted in 1746, "My little Babes have yet no Characteristick but their innocence." When Eliza Clitherall's four-year-old son, James, died in North Carolina of yellow fever in 1812, she observed that her "darling," "sweet Boy" died after three days of delirium and pain, whereupon "his little angel soul took its flight to Heaven." She remembered him as "an uncommon child—so good, so loving, so gentle," adding that "he was a bud, too excellent to bloom on Earth but is a blooming plant in Paradise." Similarly, Sarah Pemberton Rhoads, a Quaker, wrote after the death of her four-year-old grandson: "precious Innocent! Thou art happily released from a world of Sorrow and Care! before thy pure mind could be sensible of either Trouble, or disappointment." She added a few lines of a poem that began: "Death gently call'd him from his guiltless play/ . . . Let grief Submit to power all good and wise,/ And yield the Spotless Victim, to the Skies." For more than two centuries, the theme of the innocence of infancy had been voiced by moderates of various persuasions, indicating the affection and hopes with which parents first received their offspring. Love began in the cradle, and was to be sustained for the rest of their lives, binding parents and children together into close-knit, affectionate families.[9]

The intense love felt by John Saffin of Boston for his children (five of whom died between 1661 and 1678) shaped the pleasure he derived from his offspring. In 1660, he ended a loving poem to his wife with these lines for his firstborn year-old son:

> Meanwhile my Johnny-Boy is not forgott
> Him I Remember tho he heeds it not;
> Sweet Babe! how doe I mind thy perking Smiles
> And pretty Toys thou usest other whiles.

In another poem, probably written after an infant son's death in 1661, Saffin addresses his infant child in terms that reveal his sense of the tenderness, innocence, and promise of his offspring:

> Thy harmless quarrells, which so long Remaine
> Untill a Teat, doe make thee friends againe;
> I likewise feel those paines that have opprest,
> Thy tender Body with whole Nights unrest:
> . . .
> Thy Mothers teares dry'd with her Sighs so deep:
> (Enough to make a Marble Heart to weep;)
> And such like Symptomes as these Ever are
> The Marks of Love, and of Paternall Care;
> Me thinks I hear thy Mother to the prate
> Like to thy Self, that thou mayest imitate
> And then againe to joy that other while,
> Thy wonton Innocence should laugh, and smile
> And notice take of what may seem to high
> For thy Juviniller, Capacity.
> Thy promising perfection every way:
> Seems to bespeake thee faine another Day.
> And so Adieu my Dove, Heavens grant that wee
> May with our Wonted Joy, Each other see.

Saffin described his seven-year-old son, who died of "a fflux," as "A Brave Comely And Every way Beautifull, and as witty and towardly a Child as one Shall See Amongst A thousand." His grief at the loss of such promising and lovely children was almost more than he could bear, despite the comfort of his hopes for their eternal salvation.[10]

The Adamses, more controlled in their responses to their offspring than Saffin, nevertheless were delighted by their infants. Abigail wrote to a friend after the birth of her daughter in 1765 that she had "become a Mamma . . . Bless'd with a charming Girl whose pretty Smiles already delight my Heart, who is the Dear Image of her still Dearer Pappa." "You my Friend are well acquainted with all the tender feelings of a parent," she added, "therefore I need not apologise for the present overflow." Two years later, writing to her sister, she asked about her little niece, noting "How every word and action of these little creatures, twines round ones heart," and acknowledging that "All their little pranks which would seem ridiculous to relate, are pleasing to a parent." Yet she felt self-conscious about her own devotion to her children, and had to admit that previously she had been "vex'd" with other parents re-counting "the chit chat of little Miss, and Master said or did such and such a queer thing," a "weakness" which she "can now more easily forgive." Too much affection, she evidently felt, was unbecoming a parent; yet she and her husband loved their children deeply from infancy. John Adams acknowledged "that Affection which we feel for our lovely Babes," in 1774, and longed for the time "when My Dear Wife and my Charming little Prattlers will embrace me." Their "Little flock" constituted their "treasure of children."[11]

Similarly, in March 1777, Timothy Pickering of Salem hailed his wife, Rebecca, as "the happy mother of a lovely boy," and clearly was pleased to hear that "my boy is *a very handsome child*—and that he is *the image of his father*." The following December, he wrote again, saying, "O how happy should I be ever to be present with you, to lesson your cares, to add to your pleasures, to share the pleasing task of rearing our offspring, early to teach him useful knowledge and lead him in the paths of virtue." "By the way," he added, "I have had such accounts of our dear little boy, that no one can conceive my anxiety to see him. All agree that he grows finely, and Doctor Orne says he is a *Treasure*." By August 1778, Pickering was planning to have his wife and son join him in Philadelphia. He longed for their presence. "What satisfaction to see you contented and happy," he wrote, as he envisaged their company. "How delightful to see the childish amusements of our sweet boy to hear his fond prattle and view his little wanton tricks? What joy and wonder to observe his growing mind? and what pleasure to communicate instruction?"[12]

Bending the Will: Moderate Discipline and Voluntary Obedience

THE PERSISTENT EVANGELICAL PREOCCUPATION with breaking children's wills at a very early age in order to establish a permanent pattern of submission and obedience both to parents and to God did not shape the attitudes of moderates toward the disciplining of their children. Whereas evangelicals perceived the child's will as rigid and obstinate, so strong and powerful that nothing less than total conquest could subdue it, moderates saw it as more pliable and yielding. There was no necessity to break the child's will when it could be bent and shaped by parents whose goal was to form characters of piety and virtue in their offspring.[13]

Moderates were as concerned about obedience and dutiful behavior in children as evangelicals, but their responses to the issues of discipline were more temperate and flexible. From their lack of concern with discipline and the nature of their children's wills—reflected in their general disinterest in the issue of discipline in their diaries, correspondence, and public writings—moderates seem to have been more confident than evangelicals that their methods of discipline and careful oversight of their children's behavior from infancy to adulthood would be successful. The evidence from their family papers generally indicates that they did indeed nurture children who would become remarkably obedient, as well as deeply affectionate toward their parents, combining their expressions of love with an equally important declaration of dutifulness. The theme of obedience was profoundly important in the lives and the attitudes of moderates, but it was never forced. The necessary degree of obedience by children was the result of the influence of parental example and reasoning rather than of early conquest.*

Moderates from the seventeenth century through the mid-nineteenth century agreed that parental authority and power were limited, that parents could have an "Authoritative influence" over their children's lives but never an authoritarian power. As the Reverend Samuel Willard, one of the most influential moderates in late seventeenth- and early eighteenth-century New England, declared in 1703: "It is the Duty of Parents to exercise a Parental Government over their Children," but he also noted "That this Government is not Despotical or Arbitrary is certain; for tho' they are more left at liberty to exercise their Prudence in the Administration of it; yet there are Limits set to it in the word of God, and Rules laid down, which prescribe the Duties of it, in the Compass whereof they are to contain themselves." As he stated, without qualification, *"the Authority of Parents over their Children is Limited*. It is so by the Com-

---

* Although, on balance, John Locke can be put into the category of "moderate," his views on early child-rearing, expounded in *Some Thoughts Concerning Education* (1690), were almost as repressive as those of evangelicals such as Susanna Wesley. Locke insisted that "children, when little, should look upon their parents as their lords, their absolute governors," and noted that "the less reason they have of their own, the more are they to be under the absolute power and restraint of those, in whose hands they are." By the time children became conscious of having wills of their own, they already had been made compliant with their parents' commands. (Philip J. Greven, Jr., ed., *Child-Rearing Concepts, 1628–1861: Historical Sources* [Itasca, Ill., 1973], pp. 26, 25.) For an analysis of the Calvinist sources and implications of Locke's thought, see John Dunn, *The Political Thought of John Locke: An Historical Account of the Argument of the 'Two Treatises of Government'* (Cambridge, Eng., 1969), especially pp. 18, 256–61.

mand of God who hath not left them a boundless Authority; but hath told them how they shall, and how they shall not exercise their power over them." The absolutism of evangelical parents thus was denied by moderates like Willard. A century and a half later, the Reverend Horace Bushnell, a Congregationalist, still felt impelled by the practices of many evangelicals during the 1840's to declare that "it should never be forgotten, in this due assertion of authority and restrictive law, that there is a great difference between the imperative and the dictatorial; between the exact and the exacting. . . . No parent has a right to put oppression on a child, in the name of authority. And if he uses authority in that way, to annoy the child's peace, and even to forbid his possession of himself, he should not complain, if the impatience he creates grows into a bitter animosity, and finally a stiff rebellion." Moderate parents sought conscientiously to ensure that their own children would not feel the need for rebelliousness by limiting the nature of their own parental authority and setting bounds to their own power.[14]

The Reverend Samuel Willard observed in 1703 that parents "ought to maintain their Authority, by avoiding the extreams of Rigour and Indulgence. As Children are not to be treated either as Brutes or Slaves, so neither with over fondness, and letting them enjoy their Wills in every thing." Parents, he believed, "are so to Love" their children "as to let them know their Place; and so also to Rule them, as to let them know their Paternal Affection to them. They must be neither too Familiar with them, lest they despise their Authority, and wrest it from them; nor too much Estrange themselves from them, lest they be discouraged; and think themselves Disregarded." "And great Discretion is here to be used," he added, "according to their divers Tempers and Dispositions." Balancing discipline between the extremes of repressiveness and indulgence, moderates constantly felt the tensions inherent in the intense devotion to their children which always accompanied the equally intense desire to have their children behave obediently and dutifully. But there was never any question about the crucial assumption by moderate parents that their authority over their children was limited, and that the obedience of children to the wills and commands of parents was to be voluntary. Since parents did not possess absolute power and authority, they also felt no need to conquer or crush the emerging wills of their children. To impose unlimited power upon tender and helpless infants and young children, as evangelicals did in order to break their wills, would seem to moderates an abuse of authority, not a proper exercise of family government. Obedience must be given to authority willingly, not because of force. As Samuel Willard commented, when the commands of parents "are according to the Word of God," children ought not to obey their parents "as of constraint, but with a willing Mind, and with all Alacrity. For no Obedience but what is voluntary, is acceptable to God."[15]

The theme of voluntary and affectionate obedience also dominated the views of the Reverend Joseph Fish, of Stonington, Connecticut, as to the proper methods of disciplining children. After the death of his daughter Rebecca, in 1766, Fish delivered a sermon which included a remarkable passage on his own attitudes toward his daughter's early disciplining and her subsequent character:

> She was never treated with *Severity* of Discipline, nor *made* obedient by the Force of austere parental Commands: but governed by the gentle Reins of *Love* and *Tenderness*, accompanying the Light of *Counsel* and *advice*. And her Returns were answerably Tender and Yielding.—When, at any time, her *Fancy*, (amidst of Youth) unhappily took a Turn, that did not well comport with her Parents Sentiments, Her tender Make would discover the *Cross* She felt therein, by *Tears*, or Such like Softness: but so far from resolving upon her *own* way, that She would Say and often repeat it, "I am determined to be Dutifull." Indeed, She had such a Settled Regard and Steady Flow of Affection, for her *parents*, together with the Fear of God, that she *Could* not be *otherwise*.

Clearly, Fish was profoundly opposed to "severity of Discipline," preferring gentler methods, with advice and parental counseling taking the place of "the Force of austere Parental Commands" characteristic, as he well knew, of evangelicals. He noted of his daughter's behavior:

> And how penitently do[e]s She Reflect on her Self, upon discovering any mistake—how sweetly bless her God and the Guides of her Youth, when happily Extricated from Such Perplexing Snares— These Severe Exercises of her Mind, issuing thus happily, to her Self and Friends, under the Influence of the most kind and gentle measures, on the one hand, Answered by the most tender filial Affection and dutifull Behaviour, on the other; and So, attended with the daily Exchange of mutual Endearments, through the whole, May Serve to correct the (too common) *Severity* of Parents, in Such Cases, and put us upon a Serious Enquiry, Whether it is not the most natural and likely Method, containing the most powerfull Argument to gain a worthy point, for Parents to treat their Children with Tenderness and Patience? Thereby nourishing the *Principle*, and keeping alive the true *Spirit of Obedience* in them, while we counsel and advise them.

The issue thus was set forth clearly by Fish—the nature of obedience that resulted from gentle methods of discipline rather than the harsher methods common to so many families. Fish was convinced that moderation was more effective in establishing "tender filial Affection and dutifull Behaviour" in his own children than severity. His daughter's life of piety and affectionate obedience to her parents amply confirmed his convictions. As he noted, "if *Children* are of a tender *Make*, they neither *need*, nor can they *bear*, nor, even be supposed to, *deserve*, Severity." "And if they are of a more hardy and Stubborn *Make*," he added, "What So likely, as *Goodness*, Moderation and Patience, to work them into a humane Shape, and Mould them into a Gospel Temper? Thus *Our* heavenly Father behaves towards *us*. *With Loving kindness have I drawn them*. And Reproves the Contrary Behaviour in Parents." Seven years later, another of Fish's daughters, Mary Fish Dickinson, considered the necessary qualifications of a husband, and stated that "above all a husband must take care to cultivate" the children's minds, "instructing them in the grand principles of religion, and see to it that his example corresponds with the precepts of the same." She also insisted that he "be kind and tender, which will bind them to obedience, when the severe treatment would excite in them not a fillial, but slavish fear." Her father's precepts for gentle, moderate, and tender government of children were hers as well.[16]

Timothy Pickering, too, was confident that he could gain the respectful obedience of his children without being harsh or severe in either his discipline or his attitudes toward them. As he wrote to Rebecca in 1783 about their six-year-old son, "it is doubtless far better to apply to the *natural ambition* than to the *fears* of a child: the latter will only make hardened rogues of the bold, and confound the tender hearted: while nothing is more animating than just applause." Twelve years later, while John was a student at Harvard College, Pickering wrote to him to voice virtually the same sentiments with respect to the methods of government of students by college officials: "For my own part, I should suppose it very practicible for the governors of such an institution to make their pupils perfectly easy in their company, and the advantages to the latter would be immense: but when we see so many parants unsociable and stern, can we wonder that others uninfluenced by allurements of affection, should be *distant?*" "My manners, you know are just the reverse," he reminded his son. "My greatest happiness with my children consists in my familiarity, and their consequent affection, freedom and confidence. Your brothers always accept me with the same ease that they converse with one another (unless they are making some request the propriety of which they doubt) and yet they are never wanting in respect. Were the governors and teachers at every place of instruction to adopt the same measure, instead of *fear only*, they would meet with the pleasing returns of *respect, esteem* and *affection*." These were the perennial tokens of filial duty and love, and they resulted, as Pickering observed, from methods of government that eschewed the evocation of fear. Moderates knew how to obtain the obedience of their children without either breaking their wills or forcing their compliance with parental wishes. But they insisted, nevertheless, upon a dutiful bearing. As Pickering noted of his son's letters in 1792, "I observe you conclude your letters with *dutiful* and *obedient:*—quere the difference?" The terms were synonymous insofar as duty always implied obedience.[17]

The tenderness and moderation of Joseph Fish and Timothy Pickering might very well have struck the Reverend Samuel Johnson as excessive, although he, too, would have agreed upon the importance of obedience in shaping the character of children. Although Johnson never advocated breaking children's wills, he was afraid of too much indulgence and tenderness in their rearing—a fear shared by other moderates who also sought a balance between their love for and their authority over their offspring. Johnson, like most moderates, was intensely concerned with the obedience of children and their dutifulness, their readiness to accept the authority and the wishes of parents, and their desire to lead orderly, virtuous lives. In a remarkable pamphlet called *Raphael, or the Genius of the English America*, written sometime after 1763 but not published, Samuel Johnson set forth his mature views on education and the proper methods of rearing children—views that reveal much about the tensions between authority and liberty, between tenderness and love and prompt and ready obedience. Johnson observed that "it is a foolish fondness of seeming tenderness that is usually the occasion of most of the miscarriages attending" the education of youth. "Necessary therefore it is that parents should have a very jealous eye over that weak fondness of theirs and obstinately resist it as a violent temptation to them to yield indulgence to the little perverse humors of their tender offspring, which if they do not they will be in danger of proving in effect rather their destroyers and murderers than their kind nurses and guardians; and let them consider what a terrible account they will have to give of the important charge they are betrusted with if through their own foolish indulgence and mismanagement their dearest offspring are ruined."

The theme of excessive indulgence and fondness persisted in the private and public writings of moderates, who not only felt intense affection for their children but also were convinced that too much love without commensurate measures to establish their authority could ruin their children for life. In these views, Johnson was speaking for many parents besides himself. He was persuaded that the chief foundations "of all that is virtuous, good and orderly among mankind" were "obedience to laws and authority, self-denial and industry"—three characteristics of the temperament of many moderates. In order to achieve these goals, Johnson believed that

> The first and principal care in the education of a child should be to establish your authority over him by inflexibly insisting on reverence and obedience and therefore it is best never to require any-

thing of him but when you intend to be peremptorily obeyed, for
if you are lax and negligent in some things and at some times, he
will soon expect you should be so on other occasions and always,
and this will in a little time grow into an habit of disobedience.
You should therefore take care to command nothing rashly and
unadvisedly, nothing but what is reasonable, fit, and just, but
when you have declared your will see that it be ever immediately
and punctually obeyed, and let him always feel the comfort, the
pleasure and advantage of an orderly, regular and obedient behavior, and let pain, shame and disgrace ever attend the contrary.
And if he be thus always habitually inured by a steady conduct
from the beginning to an invariable obedience and submission to
government this will render all your other endeavors to promote
his good the more easy and successful and withal prepare him
when he goes from under your care to act for himself, to be an
orderly, obedient and well behaved member of the community.[18]

Like Johnson, other moderate parents were deeply concerned with
securing obedience from their children. John Adams, for instance, enjoined his three-year-old son to "Be always dutiful and obedient to your
Mamma and mind your Books—for it is only from your Books and the
kind Instructions of your Parents that you can expect to be usefull in the
World." Charles Chauncy extolled the character of seventeen-year-old
Elisabeth Price in a funeral sermon preached after her death in 1731,
observing that her bearing toward her parents had been full of "love,
tenderness, honor, and reverence," and that "She chearfully obey'd their
commands, attended their instruction; hearkened to their advice, and
follow'd their counsels. And as she did not allow of the least unseemly
disobedient behavior towards them in her self, so neither could she bear
it in her brethren and sisters." She always was grieved by any "disrespect,
irreverence, or undutifulness" toward her parents.

During the early nineteenth century, Eliza Clitherall declared in her
memoir of her life that "Our children were all gifted with good, amiable,
and affectionate dispositions. From the cradle they were taught obedience
and obedience, was *the Mother of loving habits*." She also noted, however,
that her children had "obey'd, respected, lov'd, valued—but never *fear'd*
their Father." Similarly, Timothy Pickering wrote to his wife after the
birth of their first child, enjoining her "*not to spoil our little son by too
much fondness*. An only child, an only son, is oftener injured by the ill-
judged indulgence, than the severity of a parent.—Let him be taught
obedience and *modesty*, at the same time that he is treated with the
affection which becomes a mother." Obedience and affection were both
essential, but affection should never overwhelm the necessity for obtaining a child's obedience to parental wishes and commands.[19]

The same concern for dutiful obedience, and wariness of excessive

affection or indulgence of children, was evident in Henry Drinker's injunction to his wife while he was imprisoned for being a Quaker pacifist
in 1778. By looking forward to the time when their children would come
"to the Foot-stool of Jesus, that he may lay his hands on them and bless
them," Drinker felt that he and his wife could "look beyond the natural
and immediate connection of parent and child," so that "it will not be our
study to indulge every froward humour and indolent habit, rather watching to cherish promote the growth of such evil and destructive weeds—
which too many sadly mistaken and fond parents are in the practice of—
Instead of bringing their Children up in the early part of their lives under
the Discipline of the Cross—in a respectful deportment towards their
parents and Elders, and a watchful care to oblige and serve them and
render every tender and Affectionate Office." Similarly, George Churchman, also a Quaker, recalled that his mother had been "a careful Mother"
to her only child, "yet was as clear as most women of indulging improperly: I believe she endeavor'd to discharge a parental duty, by suitable
checks and restraint in my minority, as well as by prudent counsel and
advice afterwards, whenever she saw occasion." David Cooper, another
Quaker moderate, counseled his daughter Martha, who had just married
and become a stepmother to her new husband's children, that "Wisdom
ever teaches that in fixing rules of life, as also in perticular Actions, we
should look forward to Consiquences"—which indicated to him that
although her "Husbands Children appear of dispositions not hard to govern," she must not let this lead her "into an indulgence that will not bear
to be continued at a future day, now is the time to fix the habit of being
Obeyed." He warned her also to "Cherish and fix their Love" so as to prevent mean gossip; but cautioned that "by an unlimitted indulgence now,
every restraint hereafter however reasonable will be ascribed to a Step-
Mothers Severity." In Cooper's view, the "exacting a strict Obedience is so
important, that no head of a family can support their station with any
degree of peace and satisfaction without [it], and by a timely and steady
care is easely maintained, whereby a deal of Jarring, Scoulding, and
Correcting is avoided"; John Locke, whose advice he cites, would have
agreed.[20]

The importance of the early establishment of limited but effective
parental authority, and of due obedience from children by means of bending their wills at an early age, was set forth clearly by the London yearly
meeting of Quakers in 1822:

> Much of the undue liberty indulged in by the youth, is often occa-
> sioned by the early indulgence granted to them by the parent:
> wherefore this meeting tenderly, affectionately, yet earnestly, in-
> treats such as are parents, or have the care of children, that they
> be very early and firm in endeavouring to habituate them to a due

subjection of their will; that, having maturely weighed the injunctions which they find necessary to impose, they suffer them not
to be disregarded and disobeyed. The habit of obedience, which
may thus be induced, will render the relation of parent and child
additionally endearing; and as it will prepare the infant mind for
a more ready reception of the necessary restraints of the cross, it
may be considered, in part, as preparing the way of the Lord:
whilst those who neglect to bend the tender minds of their children to parental authority, and connive at their early tendencies
to hurtful gratifications, are, more or less, making way for the
enemy and destroyer.

The imagery of limitations—"undue liberty," "due subjection," "necessary
restraints"—and the establishment of habits of obedience show the moderation inherent in their advocacy of bending "the tender minds of their
children"; but obedience remained an issue of paramount importance to
Quakers, as to most other moderates over the centuries.[21]

Late in the eighteenth century, the Reverend Enos Hitchcock, a Congregationalist of Connecticut, published a fictional account of the Bloomsgrove family which articulated similar principles, including the notion
of childhood as an age of impressions and the necessity for loving obedience of children:

As parents are to be the models, upon which children are to form
their temper and manners, so they should understand what they
would have their children acquainted with; and be themselves
what they wish their children to be. In their parents, Osander and
Rozella [the Bloomsgrove children] saw the fair form of virtue in
its most pleasing attitude: their example acted in concert with
their counsel, and seldom failed of its proper effect. They were
careful to acquire an entire authority over their children, which
they continued to exercise without severity, or having recourse to
any violence. The propriety of this step will appear, if we consider
that reason, in children, is feeble even after it begins to exert
itself, and that parental authority is the substitute which nature
has provided for the period of impressions: —and, as no work of
God is left imperfect, children are directed by instinct to obey
their parents; and if they be not unkindly treated, their obedience
is not only voluntary, but affectionate.

Implicitly, Hitchcock assumed that the wills of the Bloomsgrove children
were being bent according to their parents' goals by a process of loving
but firm discipline, which eventually would be confirmed by the children's willing compliance with their parents' wishes and commands. Yet

Hitchcock, like most moderates during the seventeenth and eighteenth centuries, did not address himself explicitly or systematically to the central issue of evangelical writings on childhood: the necessity for breaking the will early in life.[22]

By the early nineteenth century, the appearance in print of apologias in defense of the practice of breaking children's wills (such as the one published anonymously by the Reverend Francis Wayland in 1831) marked the beginning of the public discussion of the issue that persistently divided evangelicals from moderates. As the Reverend Theodore Parker, an eminent Unitarian of Boston, noted sometime during the late 1840's or early 1850's, "Men often speak of breaking the will of a child"; but, he added, "it seems to me they had better break the neck. The will needs regulation, not destroying. I should as soon think of breaking the legs of a horse in training him, as a child's will." Parker preferred to "discipline and develop" the will "into harmonious proportions. I never yet heard of a will in itself too strong, more than of an arm too mighty, or a mind too comprehensive in its grasp, too powerful in its hold." Like so many nonevangelicals of centuries past, Parker believed that "The instruction of children should be such as to animate, inspire, and train, but not to hew, cut, and carve; for I would always treat a child as a live tree, which was to be helped to grow, never as a dry, dead timber, to be carved into this or that shape, and to have certain mouldings grooved upon it."[23]

The most notable attack upon the evangelical preoccupation with breaking the will was launched by the Reverend Horace Bushnell, in his *Christian Nurture* (1847), about the time that Parker was expressing his dismay at the long-established and still-current practice. For Bushnell, the age of impressions in infancy was the period of life in which the child lived most under the influence and "the will of the parents, having no will developed for responsible action." But, like many evangelicals, Bushnell found some of the expressions of the infant's will "sometimes even frightful." This was the very reason why "the age of impressions, the age prior to language and responsible choice," was "most profoundly critical in its importance. It is the age in which the will-power of the soul is to be tamed or subordinated to a higher control; that of obedience to parents, that of duty and religion." At this point, early in life, the child "is now given, will and all, as wax, to the wise molding-power of control," Bushnell said. The critical difference between Bushnell's viewpoint and that of the evangelicals was contained in his description of the process of bending and molding the child's will to the will of the parents:

> Beginning, then, to lift his will in mutiny, and swell in self-asserting obstinacy, refusing to go or come, or stand, or withhold in this or that, let there be no fight begun, or issue made with him, as if it were the true thing now to break his will, or drive him out

of it by mere terrors and pains. This willfulness, or obstinacy, is not so purely bad, or evil, as it seems. It is partly his feeling of himself and you, in which he is getting hold of the conditions of authority, and feeling out his limitations. No, this breaking of a child's will to which many well-meaning parents set themselves, with such instant, almost passionate resolution, is the way they take to make him a coward, or a thief, or a hypocrite, or a mean-spirited and driveling sycophant—nothing in fact is more dreadful to thought than this breaking of a will, when it breaks, as it often does, the personality itself, and all highest, noblest firmness of manhood. The true problem is different; it is not to break, but to bend rather, to draw the will down, or away from self-assertion toward self-devotion, to teach it the way of submitting to wise limitations, to raise it into the great and glorious liberties of a state of loyalty to God.

Bushnell obviously is just as concerned about the establishment of parental authority and the obedience of children as any evangelical; but his conception of the nature of authority and obedience is different, as his insistence upon the child's submitting to "wise limitations" indicates. Parental authority was lawful and necessary, but not absolute; and by bending rather than breaking the child's will, parents were acting to confirm both their authority and their willingness to abide by the limitations of their own power over their children. The child was to obey willingly, not involuntarily. Bushnell made his point clear in his explicit directions to parents for bending a child's will:

See then how it is to be done. The child has no force, however stout he is in his will. Take him up then, when the fit is upon him, carry him, stand him on his feet, set him here or there, do just that in him which he refuses to do in himself—all this gently and kindly as if he were capable of maintaining no issue at all. Do it again and again, as often as may be necessary. By-and-bye, he will begin to perceive that his obstinacy is but the fussing of his weakness; till finally, as the sense of limitation comes up into a sense of law and duty, he will be found to have learned, even beforehand, the folly of mere self-assertion. And when he has reached this point of felt obligation to obedience it will even exalt into greater dignity and capacity, that sublime power of self-government, by which his manhood is to be most distinguished.

Bushnell never underestimated the powerful influence of parents, or their ultimate success in the process of bending the wills of their children, but his central concern was to have the child obey parents *voluntarily* rather than as the result of fear and force. "Let the child be brought to do right because it is right, and not because it is unsafe, or appears badly, to do wrong. In every case of discipline for ill-nature, wrong, willfulness, disobedience, be it understood, that the real point is carried never till the child is gentled into love and duty; sorry, in all heartiness, for the past, with a glad mind set to the choice of doing right and pleasing God."[24]

"Planting the Seeds of Virtue"
in Childhood and Youth

IN STRIKING CONTRAST to the evangelicals, who insisted upon the decisive conquest of a child's will and the unconditional surrender of the child to the will of the parent, the moderates were concerned with the *process* of growth and development in their children from infancy to adulthood. Their goal from the outset was to mold the temperaments and values of their children gradually, so that the commitment to reason, virtue, and piety that shaped their own lives would also, in due course, shape the lives of their children. The persistent emphasis by moderates on the "tenderness" of children implied a degree of malleability and susceptibility to influence and external impressions that would make unnecessary the confrontations and battles of wills which so often characterized the relationships of evangelical parents with their children. The imagery of growth and the perception of children as tender young plants or twigs that needed to be shaped by careful and conscientious pruning and guidance often provided useful analogies for parental experience. As Charles Chauncy, one of the leading moderates in mid-eighteenth-century Massachusetts, observed, "the law of growth from infancy and childhood, to a state of maturity with respect to both mind and body" is what "makes way for thousands of kind offices in parents towards children" and "also for the trial and improvement of many important vitrues."[25]

The Reverend Joseph Fish, the Old Light Congregationalist minister to a parish in Stonington, Connecticut, who shared many views in common with Chauncy, responded to his own children much as Chauncy did to children in general. In 1754, he sent his children to visit Mrs. Sarah Osborn, and then wrote to tell her that "in nothing do Friends more Ingratiate themselves with Such as are *Parents*, Than by Acts of Love and Tenderness to their *Children*." "Our whole little Crop is under your Eye," he said, "Small Indeed, but precious to *us*, whose Children They are: And more especially as they are Candidates for Eternal Glory.—Your Generous

Love for Them . . . will, we doubt not, Incline you to assist us, in Cultivating their young and Tender Years; By Leading of them to esteem and Relish whatsoever Things are *True*, whatsoever Things are *Honest, Just, Pure, Lovely*, and of *Good Report*." "You wont Fail to Check them for any thing that Appears Indecent, Light or Vain, especially at the House and worship of God," he urged, but added, "Tho' I hope they will be Carefull to give no Occasion."²⁶

Thirteen years later, Fish and his wife, Rebecca, wrote to their son-in-law to express their hopes and views about the rearing of grandchildren—a letter that epitomizes the preoccupation with nurture and growth characteristic of most moderates. They hoped that the Lord would "Grant *You*, their Parents, all that *Wisdom, Prudence, Meekness, Moderation, Patience* and *Gentleness* which is necessary to Govern their tender Age and to guide their heedless Steps, in the Way of Safety, Truth, and Duty." "Always View them as *Children*," they urged, "Flowers just opening.— Reason, and all their Faculties, but in the Bud; to be tenderly and Discreetly handled: And wait patiently, in the Way of *repeated* Instructions, (giving Line upon Line &c:) hoping and looking for full ripe Fruit; but not *before the Season*." The Fishes were acutely aware of the process of development in children, as the imagery of budding, ripening, and seasons reveals, just as they were aware of the process of the gradual emergence of reasonableness in their children. Their hopes for their grandchildren were evident from Fish's observation that "One great end of my Desiring to live a little longer in the World" was so that he might "have Opportunity and Grace to assist you in the Education of your dear, lovely Offspring." Grandparents knew how important their own contributions to the education and development of grandchildren could be, just as many parents welcomed their involvement with grandchildren. They prayed that "God would bestow his Early Grace" upon their grandchildren, "that they may live to his Glory here, And that you and We may with them rejoyce eternally together here after!" They concluded, "We are one in the dearest Affection for our beloved *Sons* and precious *Daughter*, for Jose and the other dear [grand-]Children . . . who have justly merritted the Esteem and Love, of your most tender Parents."²⁷

The correspondence between Abigail Adams and Mercy Otis Warren during the summer of 1773 further amplifies the themes of nurturance and cultivation of children. Abigail's own family then consisted of four children, ranging in age from less than one year to eight years. "I am sensible," she wrote, "I have an important trust committed to me; and tho I feel my-self very uneaquel to it, tis still incumbent upon me to discharge it in the best manner I am capable of. I was really so well pleased with your little offspring," whom she had met recently during a visit to the Warrens' house in Plymouth, "that I must beg the favour of you to communicate to me the happy Art of 'rearing the tender thought, teaching the young Idea how to shoot, and pouring fresh instruction o'er the

Mind.' May the Natural Benevolence of your Heart, prompt you to assist a young and almost inexperienced Mother in this Arduous Business, that the tender twigs alloted to my care, may be so cultivated as to do honour to their parents and prove blessing[s] to the riseing generation." She added that when she "saw the happy fruits of your attention in your well ordered family," she "felt a Sort of Emulation glowing" in her "Bosom" to imitate the " 'Parent who vast pleasure find's/In forming her childrens minds.' " In reply, Mercy Warren wrote to Abigail that "you ask assistance and advice in the mighty task of cultivating the minds and planting the seeds of Virtue in the infant Bosom, from one who is yet looking abroad for Every foreign aid to Enable her to the discharge of a duty that is of the utmost importance to society though for a Number of Years it is almost wholly left to our uninstructed sex."[28]

A decade later, the Reverend Enos Hitchcock was voicing similar views about the early cultivation of virtue, calling upon "affectionate parents and trusty guardians" of children, "by the love you bear to your tender charges; watch the first dawn of reason, beaming forth its immortal rays, and pour religious instruction into the opening genius; follow it through the several stages of its growth, with due cultivation, to its mature state." Aware as he was of the long process of growth, much as Charles Chauncy had been earlier, Hitchcock urged parents to "Take the helpless creature by the hand, and lead it 'in the way it should go.' " There was the "strongest probability," he felt, "that, 'when it is old it will not depart from it.' Let the mind be early formed to virtue—Let the principles of it be deeply rooted, before the habits of vice get possession there. Be more solicitous to see" children "distinguished by the unaffected goodness of their hearts, and the unsullied purity of their manners, than by the brilliancy of their wit, or their beauty."[29]

Nonevangelical Quakers throughout the eighteenth century showed the same preoccupation with molding and nurturing the tender characters of infants and young children, and forming habits of virtue and good behavior. As Thomas Chalkley observed in 1730: "From the breast, and the arms, to the seventh year of our age, who can relate the world of trouble our parents have with us, to keep us out of harm's way, to keep us from bad company, to keep us in health as much as lays in their power; to clothe us and keep us whole and clean, and take care that we learn no ill words or manners; for about this time little youths are very apt to learn good or evil; and the careful, virtuous parents, would do well to endeavour to cultivate their tender minds, and to plant things good and profitable in them betimes."[30]

The epistles of advice and cautions from the yearly meetings of Friends in London often contained admonitions to parents about the rearing and education of their children which expressed Quaker assumptions about the nature of infants and very young children. The meeting of 1731, for instance, declared that "it hath been found by experience, that good impressions, made early on the tender minds of children, have proved lasting means of preserving them in a religious life and conversation." The meeting of 1766 urged parents to attend carefully to the religious education of their children, "and to be more solicitous that their tender minds may be impressed with virtuous principles, and early directed into the path of purity, by which they may obtain the pearl of great price." The general concern of parents for their offspring, which involved the oversight of every aspect of their life and development, was justified by the conviction that parental influence could shape the character and piety of their children and thus affect their chances for salvation in the future. The meeting of 1767 recommended "that the most early opportunities may be taken, in their tender years," to impress upon children "a sense of the Divine Being, his wisdom, power, and omnipresence, so as to beget a reverent awe and fear of him in their hearts; and, as their capacities enlarge, to acquaint them with the Holy Scriptures, by frequent and diligent reading therein; instructing them in the great love of God to mankind through Jesus Christ, the work of salvation by him, and sanctification through his blessed Spirit." The meeting noted, however: "For though virtue descendeth not by lineal succession, nor piety by inheritance, yet we trust, the Almighty doth graciously regard the sincere endeavors of those parents, whose early and constant care is over their offspring, for their good; who labour to instruct them in the fear of the Lord, and in an humble waiting for, and feeling after those secret and tender visitations of divine love, which are afforded for the help and direction of all. Be ye therefore excited to a faithful discharge of your duty." Early nurture and the influence of parents on their young children were indispensable for the development of piety and virtue in later years, and throughout the eighteenth and into the nineteenth century, Quaker moderates emphasized the importance of early childhood: early impressions left lasting imprints.[31]

When Horace Bushnell published *Christian Nurture*, he built upon views that had persisted among moderates for many generations. Bushnell denied the necessity for the emotional struggles and anguish of the new birth, arguing instead that grace was infused gradually from infancy, and that "family government should be a converting ordinance, as truly as preaching." The first three years of life were crucially important in shaping the Christian's character, and the "age of impressions"—as Bushnell called infancy and early childhood—was the key to the establishment of Christian piety and virtue in later life. He was convinced that "more, as a general fact, is done, or lost by neglect of doing, on a child's immortality, in the first three years of his life, than in all his years of discipline afterwards." "Let every Christian father and mother understand," he said, "when their child is three years old, that they have done more than half of all they will ever do for his character."

Echoing the views of families like the Fishes and the Adamses,

Bushnell stressed that "Infancy and childhood are the ages most pliant to good. And who can think it necessary that the plastic nature of childhood must first be hardened into stone, and stiffened into enmity towards God and all duty, before it can become a candidate for Christian character!" The question was rhetorical, for Bushnell was fully aware of the traditional evangelical insistence upon the rigidly formed character of infancy and early childhood. He not only assumed that the nature of young children was pliable, but that initially infants had no innate character at all. From birth, children were open to impressions from their parents and the world around them, so that their characters would be formed by their nurture and by the nature of the impressions that came from the people who cared for them. "For a considerable time after birth, the child has no capacity of will and choice developed, and therefore is not a subject of influence, in the common sense of that term. He is not as yet a complete individual; he has only powers and capacities that prepare him to be, when they are unfolded." "Meantime," he said, the child "is open to *impressions* from every thing he sees. His character is forming, under a principle, not of choice, but of nurture."

Because of the early plasticity of the infant's character and the openness of the young child to external impressions, Bushnell noted the importance of "the handling of infancy. If it is unchristian, it will beget unchristian states, or impressions. If it is gentle, even patient and loving, it prepares a mood and temper like its own." "There is scarcely room to doubt," he declared, "that all most crabbed, hateful, resentful, passionate, ill-natured characters; all most even, lovely, firm and true, are prepared, in a great degree, by the handling of the nursery. To these and all such modes of feeling and treatment as make up the element of the infant's life, it is passive as wax to the seal." What the parent did to the child thus became a matter of decisive importance; future salvation, as well as the ability to lead a life of virtue and good repute in this world, depended upon "Early Culture," as Mercy Warren also knew. This was the reason for Bushnell's conviction that "the very idea of Christian education" is "that it begins with nurture or cultivation."[32]

For moderates, however, Christian education and the nurturing of virtue and industry did not cease after childhood, but continued unabated through the stage of life known to them as youth.[33] Since the development of temperament and of piety was part of a sustained process of parental molding and guidance, the influence of parents could still be effective when their children had become youths. "By Virtue of that stimulating Passion or Principle of *Imitation*, so deeply radicated in human Nature, *Example* has usually a very attractive Force and Government over Mankind," observed the Reverend Thomas Foxcroft in 1732 in Boston, "and a distinguishing Efficacy on *young* People in particular," he noted. Foxcroft declared that "we find by constant Experience" that "it strikes very powerfully on their tender and ductile Minds; is more engaging than the strongest and most persuasive Reasonings, or the most solemn Precepts of Superiors; and has the earliest Influence, to bias their Thoughts and Inclinations, and to form their Deportment." "Thus 'tis in Morality and Civils," he added, "and thus in Christianity and Spirituals." Given these assumptions of the tenderness of young minds and their susceptibility to early bias and shaping, Foxcroft asserted: "It's of great Importance therefore, *what Precedents* young People have set before them, in the Family and Place of their Education." Charles Chauncy, too, believed that the "age of life" commonly known as youth was when "we are *now* most free from a wrong bias; and lie most open to the impressions of religious principles. . . . For this age of life is easily wrought upon, and moulded almost into any form." As he asked his audience, "what likelihood is there of our being recovered to God and duty, after we are grown old in sin, when we could not be prevailed with in our young and tender years? While young our hearts are soft; our wills pliable and yielding; our consciences easily awaken'd, affections mov'd, and minds impressed with a sense of religion." Tender, soft, pliable, yielding, impressionable—his images connote the possibility of shaping character to desirable forms and to achieve desirable ends. As Chauncy declared, "when once the seeds of virtue have taken root in our young and tender minds, they will grow up into nature and fit us to live in the world: setting us in a good measure free from the power of lust, preserving us from the infection of evil example, and guarding us against the force of those numberless temptations we shall meet with."[34]

Mercy Otis Warren felt that she would "Esteem it a happiness indeed if I can acquit myself of the important Charge (by providence devolved on Every Mother), to the approbation of the judicious Observer of Life, but," she added, "a much more noble pleasure is the Conscious satisfaction of having Exerted our utmost Efforts to rear the tender plant and Early impress the youthful mind, with such sentiments that if properly Cultivated when they go out of our hands they may become useful in their several departments on the present theatre of action, and happy forever when the immortal mind shall be introduced into more Enlarged and Glorious scenes." Most important of all for the shaping of children's character was "an invariable Attachment to truth. I have ever thought a careful Attention to fix a sacred regard to Veracity in the Bosom of Youth the surest Guard to Virtue, and the most powerful Barrier against the sallies of Vice through Every future period of life. I cannot but think it is of much the most importance of any single principle in the Early Culture, for when it has taken deep root it usually produces not only Generosity of mind but a train of other Exelent qualities." Once this was established, she believed, the child would follow the "path of Rectitude" without deviations.[35]

Mercy Otis Warren also relied upon her eldest son's confidence in her love and, presumably, his need for her love and approval in order to ensure that he would adhere to her precepts and follow her unceasing guidance. Just after James Warren, Jr., entered college in 1772, she wrote to assure him that "if my dear son was not sensible her affection was so great that she never could forget him, while she remembered anything," her recent "unusual silence" might be a cause for concern; but she assured him that "I do not much fear that I shall ever be subjected to much disappointment or pain, for any deviations in a son like yourself," whom she believed to be "well disposed, against the snares of vice, and the contagion of bad example, which like an army of scorpions, lie in wait to destroy." In another letter, written the following year, she urged her son "to persevere in the path of duty, diligently striving to mend the heart and to improve your morals at the same time that you are improving the means to cultivate your understanding." She was confident, however, that "to a well disposed mind, the least hint will be treasured up and usefully improved, especially when impressed from the lip of a fond mother whose peace the remainder of her life depends on the behaviour and well being of her children." She assured him: "I am not apprehensive that you will wilfully cause the painful disappointment to yours that some unhappy parents feel,—who if their sons do not fall into gross errors, they yet have the mortification to see them more attentive to external appearance than to the due improvement of reason;—squandering the precious moments in idle amusements—more solicitous for outward decorations of person than the cultivation of their understanding or the governments of their hearts." By June 1776, she seemed confident that "From your own reflection—from your sensibility and regard to character you stand in as little need of frequent admonitions against the insinuations of criminal pleasure as any one of your age"; but, she added, "who can pronounce himself safe?"[36]

Abigail Adams observed to her husband: "Every virtuous example has powerfull impressions in early youth. Many years of vice and vicious examples do not erase from the mind seeds sown in early life. They take a deep root, and tho often crop'd will spring again." She was of one mind with her husband, who declared in 1774 that "above all Cares of this Life let our ardent Anxiety be, to mould the Minds and Manners of our Children." In 1778, after young John Quincy Adams had crossed the Atlantic Ocean with his father to France, Abigail wrote to tell him that although it was "a very difficult task my dear son for a tender parent to bring their mind to part with a child of your years into a distant land," she was reassured because "the most Excellent parent and Guardian"—his father—had gone with him. She enjoined him "to attend constantly and steadfastly to the precepts and instructions of your Father as you value the happiness of your Mother and your own welfare. His care and attention to you render many things unnecessary for me to write which I might otherways do, but the inadvertency and Heedlessness of youth, requires line upon line and precept upon precept, and when inforced by the joint efforts of both parents will I hope have a due influence upon your Conduct, for dear as you are to me, I had much rather you should have found your Grave in the ocean you have crossd, or any untimely death crop you in your Infant years, rather than see you an immoral profligate or a Graceless child." In the case of this particular eldest son, there was no cause to worry. He never deviated from the paths set forth so assiduously and consistently by his loving but authoritative parents.[37]

Abigail's concern for her son's behavior and growth in virtue did not abate as he grew up, however, but continued to shape her injunctions to him. In 1783, after he had gone abroad with his father, she acknowledged that her anxieties had been "and still are great, lest the numerous temptations and snares of vice should vitiate your early habits of virtue, and destroy those principles, which you are now capable of reasoning upon, and discerning the beauty and utility of, as the only rational source of happiness here, or foundation of felicity hereafter." As she asked rhetorically, "What is it, that affectionate parents require of their children, for all their care, anxiety, and toil on their account? Only that they would be wise and virtuous, benevolent and kind." She added, as Timothy Pickering also did, that her son should "Ever keep in mind . . . that your parents are your disinterested friends, and that if, at any time, their advice militates with your own opinion or the advice of others, you ought always to be diffident of your own judgement; because you may rest assured, that their opinion is founded on experience and long observation, and that they would not direct you but to promote your happiness." "Be thankful to a kind Providence," she urged, "who has hitherto preserved the lives of your parents, the natural guardians of your youthful years," and she adduced her own thankfulness for the long lives of her parents and her "regret" at the "loss of them" because of feeling "daily" the "want of their advice and assistance."

In due course, Abigail's anxieties over John Quincy's ability to eschew vice and to follow the paths of virtue diminished, and she recognized her own success at implanting the seeds of duty and obedience in her eldest son. She wrote to her sister from London in 1786: "I think I may with justice say, that a due sense of moral obligation, integrity, and honor, are the predominant traits of his character; and these are good foundations, upon which one may reasonably build hopes of future usefulness. The longer I live in the world, and the more I see of mankind, the more deeply I am impressed with the importance and necessity of good principles and virtuous examples being placed before youth, in the most amiable and engaging manner, whilst the mind is uncontaminated, and open to impressions." No son could possibly have fulfilled his mother's hopes more completely than John Quincy Adams, who had become as dutiful, virtuous, useful, and eminent a citizen as any in the country.[38]

Love and Duty:
The Obligations of Connection

THROUGHOUT THE CENTURIES, love and domestic affection were the bonds that united parents and children in the families of moderates; and often the feelings of tenderness and love were so intense that they threatened to become excessive. Indeed, "unbounded" love was a constant source of concern to moderates, for whom even love ought to be moderated and kept within due bounds. Love provided the foundation for the obedience and dutifulness of children, and shaped the consciences that sustained the commitment of so many moderates to the paths of duty and virtue set forth for them by their affectionate parents. But love was still not—as in some families—the dominant theme. Duty was of even greater significance as a motif of the moderate temperament and religious experience.

Although children in the families of moderates grew up feeling that their own wills were free and that their compliance with the wills of their parents was voluntary, they also grew up with an equally intense sense of limits upon their freedom expressed by the term "duty." "Duty"—which almost always balanced "love"—was a word that implied subordination, deference, and respect, the obligations of inferior persons to superior persons both within the family and within the community at large. As the Reverend Samuel Willard declared, "The Fifth Commandment requireth, the preserving the Honour, and performing the Duties belonging to every one in their several Places and Relations, As Superiors, Inferiors, or Equals." Growing up in households that sometimes contained elderly grandparents as well as young servants, and in communities that often contained numerous relatives as well as friends and neighbors, the children of moderates were imbued with a sense of their relationships with a wide variety of people of different degrees of closeness in terms of both kinship and friendship. As Willard said, the fifth commandment "hath a proper respect to the Order which God hath placed among Mankind; and the Relative Duties which do flow from the Nature of the Order." For "it is a Truth," he noted, "that every Duty hath it's Duty founded in some Relation, which we bear to the Object of it."[39]

Duty epitomized the sense of connection and of relationship that shaped the moderate consciousness, and the sense of obligation that bound members of families and of communities together. "Duty" implied mutual obligations, mutual ties, mutual respect, as well as a certain degree of formality and of constraint in relationships. "Duty" was the term that expressed the obligations of obedience of the governed to their gov-

ernors—whether children to parents, wives to husbands, parents to grandparents, or servants to masters. By maintaining the prerogatives of age
and status, the obligations of familial duty established and sustained a
sense of proper distance between family members, and provided individuals with a formal relationship to balance the affection and love that always threatened to diminish proper distances. Duty thus was essential for
the definition of family relationships, since it ensured that each set of relationships would be governed by rules of decorum and obedience while also
sustaining a sense of reciprocity. Duty symbolized the maintenance of
position and place within the familial order, by asserting both the obligations of obedience and the limitations upon the exercise of authority and
power.

Children grew up with an awareness of gradations and degrees of
relationship that sustained the general conception of "human society" as
"a network of dual relationships . . . in which one party was usually subordinate to the other"—as Edmund Morgan has observed of New Englanders in the seventeenth century. He notes that the "final significance of the
fact that Puritans conceived social order in terms of dual relationships"
was that "no man could be a servant or a minister or a king in any general
or absolute sense but only in relation to another man or group of men."
Wives and husbands as well as children and parents were bound together
in these dual relationships; but individuals also had significant relationships with people other than their spouses, children, and parents. In some,
a person would be the inferior party, while in others the superior party.
No relationship was absolute or exclusive; instead, all were part of a
network connecting individuals to other members of their families and
to people outside as well.[40]

These complex relationships thus limited the exercise of authority
and the obligations of obedience, and they helped to sustain the sense,
rooted in these moderate families, of the limitations upon power that
could or should be exercised within any set of relationships between two
people. As Willard put it, "It is certain, that from all the Relations that
Men bear each to other, there are reciprocal Duties incumbent on them. . . .
So that as the Duties to Superiours is in the first place pointed nextly to,
which is to be paid them by Inferiours; so there is to be considered under
this Precept, the Duties which Superiours do owe to Inferiours; for they
are not more left by the Word of God to be *despotical*, than the others to
be *disobliged*." Duties meant the obligations of *both* parties to each
other—parents to children as well as children to parents.[41]

The letters that passed between Governor John Winthrop—leader of
the Massachusetts Bay colony during the 1630's and 1640's—and his sons
combined an extraordinary degree of affection and openness with an
equally strong sense of duty and the obligations of filial obedience. When
the eldest Winthrop son, John, Jr., went to Trinity College in Dublin, his
father wrote to say that "I cannot passe by an opportunitye, without some

testimonye of my fatherly affection, and care of your welfare." Five years later, Winthrop wrote, "My Good Sonne, As I have allwayes observed your lovinge and dutyful respectes towardes me, so must I needes allso now" (owing to his son's concern over his infected finger) and "that care and paynes you have taken to procure my ease; which, besides the confirminge of my fatherly affection towardes you, wilbe layd up in store with the righteous Lorde, for length of dayes and blessing upon you in tyme to come." Three days later, his son wrote, addressing his letter: "To the wor[shipfu]ll his very loving father John Winthrop Esq[uir]e in Groton," and concluding: "Thus my duty remembered to your selfe my mother and grandmother, with my love to my brothers, and sister; and the rest of our friendes I commend you to godes protection and rest Your obedient sonne."

Similarly, as befitted the sense of the subordinate relationship of a wife to her husband, Margaret Winthrop frequently acknowledged her own dutifulness and respect to her husband, as in her letter to "hir very louinge Husban," in which she sent him "my best love and all due respect," signing herself "Your faythful and obedient wife." The Winthrops' pious and dutiful son, Forth, wrote to his "Most Lovinge Father" in 1629 to say that he "would be loath soe far to violate the lawes of Nature or infringe the praecepts of nurture, and education, as to undertake any enterprize of moment without your leave, knowledg[e], consent, and licence," hoping that his father would give him permission to marry his cousin. But he added that he had "made noe mention of any such thing, nor till I shall knowe your will, pleasure and advice here in will I." To his father's "wisdome" he "most humblye" submitted himself, awaiting the "expectation of your councell, instruction, and direction, what best you in your wisdoem shall see most fittinge for me to be done or left undone, and soe committing this to you and you to the protection of the allmighty with my most humble duty remembred to your self" and others, he remained his "obedient sonne." Forth's brother, Henry, however, was not so dutiful and compliant, choosing to marry his cousin without tarrying for the consent of his elders. As his uncle wrote plaintively to his father, "my Nephew says plainly if he cannot have my good will to have my daughter he will have her without [it]." And he did. Yet the family did not cast Henry out for his misdeeds, but continued to love and forgive him throughout his errant life. For the Winthrops, love and duty combined to form a dominant theme in their lives, reflecting their sensitive response to the obligations of relationships and the degrees of deference and obedience inherent in their different relations as parents and as children. John Winthrop himself was no less loving and dutiful with his own parents, with whom he continued to live until his departure for America.[42]

The next generation of Winthrops continued the loving and dutiful relationships of parents and children, as the letters of Fitz-John Winthrop to his parents reveal. At the age of nearly twenty-three, he was in London, having previously been commissioned in the Parliamentary army. In a

letter addressed to "his Honored Mother, Madam Elizabeth Winthrop, att
Heartford in New England," he said that "as I am rendered [incapable] to
tender any thing more then an humble acknowledgment of your greate
love and affection to me, soe I will never forget to shew my grateful remembrance. My greatest trouble which I have met with, since my being
in these parts of the earth, is my absence from you, which, though
hetherto I have bin deprived of the hapiness of being with you, yet I hope
Providence will shortly order my returne to you," signing himself "Your
obedient son and servant." In a subsequent letter to his father, John
Winthrop, Jr., Fitz-John discussed the perennial problem of money,
noting for his "Honored" father's sake that "What I have spent since my
foure yeare travell may easily be knowne, and whether I could have sayled
nerer the winde than I have don I refer myself to your owne consure. I
allwaies kept a just decorum betwene those extremes, and, as I did never
prodigally spend, soe I did never basely spaire, which is most hateful to
my naturall inclination." His worries over his future and his finances
expressed, he concluded by saying: "Sir, I shall not farther trouble you
at present but the tender of my humble duty to yourself and affectionat[e]
love to my deare brother, earnestly beging your prayers for a blessing
upon, honored father, Your obedient son."

Four days later, Fitz-John wrote to his father again, declaring that
"I can never suffitiently express the tender and fatherly care you are
pleased to continue of me. My dew and strict observiance of such com-
[m]ands and directions as you shall please to order me to observe shall be
punctually obayed. I have soe perfictly learnt the obedience of a child that
I dare not in the least scruple that ready performance of any imposition
you shall please to laye upon me." He continued:

> Sir, what you shall please to direct for my waye of settlement I
> shall redily comply with your pleasure theirin, though if my owne
> inclination should have any share in the disposall of myself, I
> would not as yet accept the profer of a maried life, in which theire
> is soe many restless and inavoydiable cares and inconveniances
> attending that the very thought theirof forbids me attempting it.
> [True to his own wishes, he never formally married, but lived with
> the mother of his child in the 1670's despite public and familial
> disapproval.] I am yet young enough to spend som few yeares
> more in travell, in which the cheife end of my adventure should
> be the attainment of much experience, which might hapily proove
> more advantagious than what I could otherwise undertake. My
> owne inclination leades to that designe. However, my owne will
> and desires shall be subordinate to your pleasure and intensions
> concerning me, and shall not act anything theirin without your
> free and willing approbation in a case of such importance. Sir, I
> shall not farther trouble your more serious occasions at present,

but the tender of my humble duty to yourself and affectionat love
to my deare bro[ther] and remain, honored father, Your most
obedient son and humble servant, J. Winthrop.

Thus dutiful and obedient, Fitz-John expressed his willing subordination
to the superior will of his father, yet also was a man who would lead a life
of self-fulfillment as an American gentleman. Having "tender" and loving
parents, his sense of obligation was always buttressed by his knowledge
of their affection, so that the pattern of love and duty was sustained in
the Winthrop family through successive generations.[43]
    The sense of both duty and deep affection characteristic of so many
moderates is evident in the correspondence that took place during the
early eighteenth century between Isaac Norris, Jr., and his father, Isaac
Norris, Sr., eminent Quaker merchant and politician in early Pennsylvania. Early in 1721, for instance, young Isaac wrote to his "Dear Father,"
observing at the outset that "The easy life I live with Such Parents and
the reciprocal pleasure of oblidging and being oblidged, one would think
could leave few Endearments equivalent." He now looked forward to the
future, hoping that "a wellgrounded Sence of Religion and Morality shall
be my Guides," and hoping that "I am not even now too Young to be
beneficial to my Self and friends As it may fall in my way—" However, he
added, "when I propose any thing to thee of my Entr'ing into the World.
It is always with a suitable defference to thy Judgment and Experience."
Hearing of a voyage from Philadelphia to Newfoundland and London,
young Isaac desired his father's "consent to Such a Voyage—And, tho I
might write my thought here I will be more pleasing If thyne Antidate
them and believe it my advantage." As he then noted, "I So entirely confide in thy Affection and Care of my Welfare: That as I do not rashly propose, so neither Shall I too Strenuously prosecute it: But leave it to Thy
Candour and Leasure. I hope however, thou mayst determine This always
to Approve my Self Thy Dutiful Son." The following May, parental consent obviously having been granted, young Isaac wrote again to his father
from St. John, Newfoundland; he closed this letter by saying: "Dear
father I continue to begg thy Advice and prayers which I doubt not will be
Effectual and which I Am resolved to be careful to deserve. I write to no
Body else by this Vessell therefore Desire thou wouldst remember me
affectionately to Brother Griffitts and family, Sister Harrison and Uncle
and Aunt Hill. Coz Betty and all who may enquire of me, and thy Self and
those I continually think of receive the Duty and affection of—Thy Dutifull and Affectionate Son." By late summer, he was in London, again
writing his "Honour'd father" about various unsuccessful efforts to sell
oil, seal skins, and other goods in Newfoundland, and adding that "I hope
and believe my Dear Mother will be easy in any thing relating to me, and
Assure herself I Shall endeavour to maintain a clear Character here as

well as elsewhere, and give you no Occasion of trouble or complaint for I cannot be vicious enough (I am well assur'd) to wrong So much tenderness as you have always Shown." Obedient and dutiful under the most trying temptations, he seemed confident that the love and obligations inherent in his filial relationship with his tender parents would guard him in the paths of duty and virtue even in London. As he concluded his letter, "Dear father I have nothing to ask but thy blessing and Remembrance of me, for which I Shall endeavour to approve my Self Thy dutiful and affectionate Son."[44]

By 1734, young Isaac could write to his father that "I am in this Stage of Life not only to consider thee as a parent but a kind friend, and one who will think most favourably of errors in Judgement or conduct." He was confident that he had "no View or Interest Seperate" from his father's, and that if he had "made a wrong step" during his absence from home in the conduct of his father's business, "I believe I need only ask it, to be excus'd." The son's complete confidence in the affection, obligation, and friendship of his father could not be more evident than in this particular letter.[45]

The Norrises were a deeply affectionate family, yet duty always played a major role in their relationships. As Isaac Norris, Sr., observed in 1746, his "little Babes have yet no Charracteristick but their innocence" and "the World is new and glittering to their view," although he held himself "obliged to rectify their understanding on that head and as their years increase to inculcate the duties which may become them in the several stations they may have occasion to act in." The sense both of duty and of closeness that bound the family together was also evident from the letter Debby Norris wrote to her brother, Isaac, Jr., in 1734, while he was away again on a business trip. Hearing that he might return with a wife, she was pleased, but added that "father is dull at times when he Reflects he is now in his 64th year and his Son at Such a distance from him." She then observed for her brother's consideration: "when I consider how good and Gracious a God we have in granting the lives of our parents to Such an Age, I cant but think its our Duty not only in Obaying them, but Contributing as much as is in our power to Make the Latter part of Life as easy and agreeable as possible, Which I am sure can never be to ours While a Child of theirs is at such a distance."[46]

The same deep concern and affection were evident in the families of other Quaker moderates also. While Samuel Emlen was away from Pennsylvania on a trip to England, he wrote to his wife, Sarah, in 1772, asking her to kiss their daughter "affectionately in my name and give my Love to Samy," adding that he was hopeful from her letter "that he is orderly, tell him it will be of a great Comfort to me to know he is dutiful to Thee doing all he can for thy ease and help in my absence." Subsequently, he desired that his son might "be restrain'd from undue Liberty of running in the

Street with wild Boys. Tell him I love him, and I very much wish him to be quite dutiful and loving to Thee, minding what thou sayest to him, not daring to be cross or rebellious. If he behaves well to thee, it will mightily recommend him to me but if he is naughty and undutiful to Thee, it will afflict and trouble me," adding, "if he would make me glad and comfortable he must be a Good, sober Boy." Similarly, Henry Drinker hoped that "It would . . . be difficult and painful" for his children "to manifest any unbecoming and undutiful conduct" to their "tender Mother and Aunt" during his absence. Three months later, Henry wrote again, acknowledging that "The Relation my dear Son gives of his orderly regular deportment and the earnest desire he expressed to be exemplary and steady in his Religious and Filial Duty (the latter being also a very serious and important Religious Duty) is very comfortable and acceptable to his Affectionate Father"; and, he added, "I hope his Sisters, more advanced in Age and experience then he is, are daily and hourly showing him the Beauty and excellency of such a deportment, as well as by a watchful circumspect conduct manifesting that they are anxiously thoughtful and truly desirous of Divine protection and regard." The combination of intense and fulsomely expressed affection from parents with an equally strong wish to see sober, dutiful, and obedient behavior of children was as fully characteristic of moderates who were Quakers as it was of moderates in other denominations.[47]

The Clarke family of Salem, Massachusetts, corresponded with two distant sons whose careers took them to the Caribbean and eventually to England, and the letters on both sides manifested once again a familial preoccupation with the dutifulness of children toward parents. In 1764, William Clarke, then about eighteen years old, wrote to his "Honour'd Mother" from Barbados to tell her that he was "afraid that by your maternal fondness you will spoil Frank," his nine-year-old brother, whom he thought should "be put to School in Boston." His elder brother, John, was with him on the island but evidently had been ill. William hoped that "it will be in John's power one of these days to help you and all the family. He bids me tell you he thinks you one of the best of mothers, and tho' He has been so long from you yet he retains a great sence of Duty and hopes it may shortly be in his power to help us all." He signed himself "your most Dutyf[ull] Son." In 1768, one of the Clarke sons wrote his seventeen-year-old sister, Hannah, from Dominique to tell her that their brother, Samuel, had praised her highly, saying "you are the finest Girl in Salem and that your Conduct gains you a great many Friends." "As no Brother has a greater affection for their Brothers and Sisters than I have," he said, "permit me to offer you my advice. Lay a good foundation and form your mind to noble Principals by a strict observance of Religion. Be obedient in a most particular manner to your mother for she is a most excellent Parent and gave you Being, revere her and make her happy in her old Age never thwart her." He added: "If I find on my coming to New England which I hope I shall very soon that you dont treat your Mother well, I shall dispise you and will not look on you as any way connected with me. So you may see what my sentiments are on it."

In 1769, John Clarke wrote to his mother to inform her of his marriage, hoping that it would be "agreeable" to her, since "it gives me an ample fortune to Support my self." The following month, her new daughter-in-law, Ann Jones Clarke, wrote her "Honoured Mother" to express her hope for a visit to Salem so that she would have the "Inexpresable Happyness of Seeing you, my Dear Mother and the Rest of the family and In trying to do Everything to Shew my Duty and to Gain the Esteem of So Amiable a parent as you are." She added: "I will answer for your Son that he will do Everything to Make you happy as on your Happiness depends ours." In 1771, John and his family were still in Barbados, when he wrote to tell his mother that brother William was going to England, having been appointed comptroller of customs at Tobago; he concluded by saying that his wife "Joyns me in Duty and Great Affection to You," signing himself "Your Dutifull Son."[48]

The Adamses also stressed both love and duty in their relationships with their children, but felt that the obligations of duty were central to the shaping of character and a life of private as well as public virtue. While John Adams was in Philadelphia in 1774, he wrote to his daughter Abigail, then nine, to acknowledge receipt of her "pretty Letter" which, he said, "has given me a great deal of Pleasure, both as it is a Token of your Duty and Affection to me and as it is a Proof of your Improvement in your hand Writing and in the faculties of the Mind." He also wanted his daughter to tell her three younger brothers that "they must be good Children and mind their Books, and listen to the Advice of their excellent Mamma, whose Instructions will do them good as long as they live, and after they shall be no more in this World." "Tell them," he went on, that "they must all strive to qualify themselves to be good and usefull Men—that so they may be Blessings to the Parents, and to Mankind, as well as qualified to be Blessings to those who shall come after them." A month later, seven-year-old John Quincy Adams wrote to his father, having "been trying ever since you went away to learn to write you a Letter," but reassured by the fact that "Mamma says you will accept my endeavours, and that my Duty to you may be expressed in poor writing as well as good." He added: "I hope I grow a better Boy and that you will have no occasion to be ashamed of me when you return," and concluded by saying, "I am Sir your Dutiful Son." John Adams, too, continually acknowledged both his love and his duty to his parents, kin, and friends. In April 1775, for instance, he sent "My Love to the Children and all the Family. My Duty to my Mother, and Love to my two Brothers. My Duty to your Father. . . . My Duty to your Mother, and a thousand thanks for her Cake. Love to Brother Cranch and sister, and to sister Betcy."[49]

In 1780, Abigail Adams wrote to her son John Quincy to set forth in more ample detail the obligations of duty that he ought to fulfill in every sphere of life. The preservation of his life by "that Being who streached out the Heavens as a span, who holdeth the ocean in the hollow of his hand, and rideth upon the wings of the wind" ought to make him consider "for what purpose you are continued in Life?—It is not to rove from clime to clime, to gratify an Idle curiosity," she said, "but every new Mercy you receive is a New Debt upon you, a new obligation to a diligent discharge of the various relations in which you stand connected; in the first place to your Great Preserver, in the next to Society in General, in particular to your Country, to your parents and to yourself." No individual was utterly alone and private; instead, each was always obligated by a series of relationships and connections that bound him to an everwidening circle of people, from the most intimate and domestic ties to the ties of public life and religious duty.

Abigail went on to say that the "attainment" of future happiness necessitated being "bound to the performance of certain duties which all tend to the happiness and welfare of Society and are comprised in one short sentance expressive of universal Benevolence, 'Thou shalt Love thy Neighbour as thyself.'" She was certain that "the Supreme Being made the good will of Man towards his fellow creatures an Evidence of his regard to him, and to this purpose has constituted him a Dependant Being, and made his happiness to consist in Society." As a result, she declared, "Justice, humanity and Benevolence are the duties you owe to society in General." "To your Country," she added, "the same duties are incumbent upon you with the additional obligation of sacrificeing ease, pleasure, wealth and life itself for its defence and security." After the duties owed to his country, "To your parents you owe Love, reverence and obedience to all just and Equitable commands." As "To yourself— here indeed is a wide Field to expatiate upon," she declared. "To become what you ought to be and, what a fond Mother wishes to see you" (*not* what he himself might wish to be or hope to be but what he *ought* to be), she had even more advice and instructions to offer. But duty broadly construed formed the matrix of his life.[50]

The obligations of obedience and dutifulness which John Dickinson felt toward his parents mirrored those felt by John Quincy Adams. So intense and binding were the bonds of affection and duty uniting young Dickinson to his parents that he would never be entirely free from the problems connected with his own independence and separation from parents. Born in 1732 in Maryland, and growing up in Delaware, Dickinson went to London early in 1754 to pursue the study of law. The letters he wrote from England to his "Honoured Father" and "Honoured Mother" reveal with startling clarity the intensity of the bonds which relationships imposed upon this young man, and which continued to be part of his personality for decades to come. Immediately on landing in England, he wrote to tell his parents: "It is with the greatest happiness that I can acquaint you with my arrival in England, a happiness which arises infinitely less from a sense of my own safety than from the ease and delight which I am certain it will give to the best and tendrest of parents." He begged his father to "believe that all the care in my power shall be taken in every step, that I always shall preserve the warmest, the gratefullest remembrance of the innumerable blessings your unequald goodness has bestowd." "I pray you to be assiord [assured] that no distance can obliterate my sense of my duty," he declared, "no temptations damp my earnest endeavours to answer your expectations. That pleasing prospect can afford me comfort even here, gives new life to my industry, and makes London agreable." But, he added, "never shall I feel that calm, delightful happiness I have enjoyd till I see you again." Fully conscious that "Virtuous company is the strongest guard to a person's morals," he was intent upon returning to his father "not only pure in my morals, but improved in every thing you desire, especially in my business." He concluded his first letter by assuring his father of his hope that "in whatever part of the world I may be, I shall always approve myself your most dutiful and most affectionate son John Dickinson." Three months later, he told his father again that "nothing can contribute more to my comfort . . . than frequently hearing of your health, and that nothing can enforce my duty so much as your admonitions. The very thoughts of my parents, their expectations, their desires, engrave it anew in my heart: this is the anchor that keeps the giddiness of youth from shipwreck."

He was insistent upon reassuring his parents of his scrupulous adherence to the paths of virtue obviously set forth for him by them. "As to the vicious pleasures of London," he told them, "I know not what they are; I never hear of them, and never think of them." He was confident that "what little reputation I have been so happy as to acquire in my native country" would always serve "as a pledge of my good behaviour," particularly since he was "resolved to return with credit." By May, the matter of money came up, but he hastened to reassure his parents of their generosity in sending him the sum of £230, "especially when I consider the care and trouble it costs the best, the dearest of parents." But "tho I endeavour to comfort myself that I spend it innocently," he added, "and, as I flatter myself, prudently, yet I shall never be easy or contented unless you think so too." Since his parents supplied the money and he knew "what returns you expect, I am filld," he said, "with concern and care."

Dickinson had a finely developed sense of family connections. As he wrote to his mother in May 1754, "notwithstanding all the diversions of England, I shall return to America with rapture. . . . America is, to be sure, a wilderness and [yet?] that wilderness to me is more pleasing than this charming garden." "I dont know how," he added, "but I dont seem to have any connections with this country," whereas America brought to mind images of "my Honoured Parents, my dear relations, my friends and every thing that makes life valuable." Yet still he desired to remain longer in

England, and was pleased in January 1755 to receive his father's approbation for a longer sojourn there. "My mind was before so filld with a
sense of your great favours," he wrote to his father, "that it is not possible
to give it my additional impulse to enforce my duty, and such a profusion
of tenderness must certainly make me a bankrupt in gratitude." Subsequently, when the prospect of marriage arose, he hastened to write that
"I am very glad I think so much like my Honourd Parents with respect to
marriage. I never shall think I am at liberty to dispose of myself without
their consent who gave me being, and if I shoud ever be so mad as to do
it, tho you shoud forgive me, I shoud never forgive myself." So important
was his parents' approval of his every action that he wrote to them in June
1756, observing that anyone who might happen to read his letters might
"think it a little odd to talk so much to you about the method of studying
law, but they woud excuse it if they knew the tenderness with which you
regard everything that concerns me, and how little pleasure I take in any
thing unless sweetened by a consciousness of your knowledge and approbation of it." He flattered himself "with the most agreable hopes of returning to my native country with some share of reputation, that is, with
proofs of not having mispent my time . . . and I hope my friends and myself will find sufficient satisfaction in my having dischargd my duty
according to my abilities, if not according to our wishes."[51]

There could be little reason to doubt that Dickinson had pursued the
paths of virtue and duty throughout his stay in the mother country, since
he continued to be concerned with deserving the love and approval of his
parents years after his return to America. In March 1764, he wrote his
mother to tell her that he had been chosen to "a new office" as "a Director
of the Library Company." She would be pleased to know that "the Choice
is made by Men of Sense and Virtue—whose approbation You have always
taught Me to esteem a Blessing—" "I will always endeavour to practice
all your Precepts," he assured her, although now a man of thirty-one years
himself, so that "whatever you hear about Me from the worthy may afford
you Delight—and that I may enjoy the inexpressible Happiness of thinking that You receive Pleasure from the Conduct of your Most dutiful and
most affectionate Son." By the following fall, she was planning to move to
Philadelphia to be with her son, whose conscientious fulfillment of her
wishes and scrupulous adherence to her values had never abated in the
least from his youth nor in all likelihood from earliest childhood. For John
Dickinson, the obligations of filial duty ceased only with the death of his
parents; but the obligations born of connections and relationships to
kindred and others were no less binding, and these continued throughout
a lifetime.[52]

Peter Oliver, an eminent gentleman and Chief Justice of the Superior
Court in Massachusetts, was another moderate who insisted on the necessity for dutiful behavior stemming from both the love and the respect

children felt for their parents. In a letter to Polly Watson, his granddaughter, written from his country estate at Middleborough, Massachusetts, on January 1, 1767, Oliver set forth for her benefit the principles that should govern her "future Conduct." He began with her "duty" to her "Creator," for, as he said to her with emphasis, "Virtue is the only Foundation of Happiness; and it is Virtue, to reverence, obey and delight in Him." But he also wanted to stress the duties owed "to your fellow Creation, Mankind," since she was "placed here, in a State, ordained by the God of Nature, surrounded with your Species of various Orders, Degrees and Relations: Parents, other Relations, Friends, and let me add Enemies," he said, since he believed everyone had at least one. "Here are the high and the low, the rich and the poor, they all meet together, and you are to remember that *the Lord is the Maker of them all.*" "Amidst this Variety," he added, "you see, that there is a different Behaviour respectively required, for there is something peculiarly belonging to every Circumstance of Life." Her first and principal duty in life, after her duty to God, was to her parents; he wanted her to pause and "reflect upon the strong Obligations that you are under to these Parents, to perform every Duty of Respect, Obedience and Love which they have the justest Claim to from You." "And let me remind You here," he went on, "that your future Happiness in Life, if it is continued to You for any Length of Time, depends much upon your right Performance of this Duty." He was confident that Polly would never be undutiful toward her parents, which would cause her, he said, to "Degrade your self below a Brute, especially not to Love those who are the Objects of all others Esteem." "But I recommend it to You," he added, "to convince your self and them also, that your Love to them is sincere, *by chearfully* obeying their Commands and expressing the highest Respect to them: I say, *chearfully*, for whatever good Action you do, there is no Virtue in it unless it is done with a willing Mind; for, otherwise, it shews that you had rather not do it, if it was not through Fear of some ill Consequence, and when there is a great Proportion of Fear there is a small Degree of Love"; "therefore," he concluded, "you may depend upon it, that Love is not well founded that doth not dispose a Person in a *most chearfull* Manner to oblige the Object beloved."

A sense of obligation thus arose from love and duty—and not from fear—according to Oliver, who urged Polly always to defer to the judgment of her parents, and never to "express any Uneasiness (at doing what either of them require of You) in Word or Action," for it would only be "a great Discredit and Uneasiness to You," he warned, adding that "I assure You that the good Opinion of the World, if it is founded upon your good Behaviour, will be of very great Service to You in Life." Finally, "as to *Respect*," he said, "I hardly know how to distinguish it from a true Love and Affection; for if your Love is well founded, Respect will arise upon it; but it chiefly consists in having a high Regard for them in your own

Mind and expressing that Regard with Decency and good Manners in their Presence; and in their absence to express your self relating to them in Terms of Honour and Esteem." "Keep these Rules fixed in your Mind," he urged, and promised that "I will answer for not only theirs but for the Love of all who know your good Behaviour." "Remember," he told her in closing, "your Reputation depends much upon your Conduct *now*."[53]

The preoccupation of moderate parents with dutiful obedience by their children could not always disguise the dominant theme of control that emerges from so many moderate families. Occasionally, children refused to be controlled beyond a certain point, although parents rarely ceased to exercise their prerogatives. Even the Adamses produced a son whose life was to be a series of distressing failures of self-control brought about by alcoholism. In the home of Landon Carter of Sabine Hall in Virginia, the daily exertion of parental control over the entire household long after childhood had passed for most of its members reveals with stark and vivid clarity the obsessive desire on the part of some moderates, at least, to sustain their earlier controls—even after their children had married and become parents themselves.[54]

Landon Carter, like other parents elsewhere, constantly resorted to his control over his land and personal estate as a means to keep his errant children in line, often threatening to alter his will if their behavior did not suit him. Since his eldest son and namesake also lived with his wife and children in the same household, Carter constantly found opportunities to exert his own desire for dominion over the lives of those around him. He was continually displeased by his grandchildren's table manners, by his daughter-in-law's moods, by his son's drinking and gambling, and even by the way in which his son ran his plantations. Carter could never escape his consciousness of "the ingratitude in a man who knows every Shilling of all that he has got almost everywhere came from me." He also found his grandson to be "incontrolable." In 1776, Carter, then in his mid-sixties, was particularly annoyed by the gaming, drinking, and indolence of his son and friends, which continued unabated for several days, after which he "modestly protested against it and removed the table and cards." This led to "Sulkiness" on the part of his son and others, whereupon, Carter noted, "I laughed and wished them better tempers and Perhaps a few years could convince them they had treated me ill. I was told by the 40 year old man [his son] he was not a child to be controuled; but I answered 40 ought to hear reasons." So it went in the Carter family; but the theme of control was revealed dramatically through the persistent efforts by the father to govern what he continued to see as "his" household. In this instance, as in others, the price of economic dependence was persistent control. The fact that Carter perceived his son as an undutiful, ungrateful, and dissipated antagonist only adds to the evidence that he himself could not cease his efforts to keep everyone around him under his own personal control. From the sons' point of view, such control was for children only. But the father demonstrated almost daily by his words and actions that his children, at least, would never be freed entirely from such bonds.[55]

Throughout childhood and youth, most moderates nevertheless proved themselves to be the dutiful, affectionate, and conscientious off-spring their parents had sought to nurture and to guide in the proper paths of piety, industry, and virtue. The combination of love and duty provided a powerful method of domestic education for children, which left its imprint upon their temperaments and their piety for the remainder of their lives. For the most part, moderates found it difficult to resist com-plying with the authoritative influence of parents, feeling increasingly obligated to fulfill the wishes of their parents as they grew to maturity. As a result, they rarely experienced the great emotional crises which so often wracked evangelicals, and their youth passed without great stress or strain. The sense of rebelliousness felt by so many youthful evangelicals is usually absent from the documents that pertain to moderates—unless it was simply more diffuse and temperate. Although they grew up without having experienced the early conquest of the self that was characteristic of evangelicals, they nevertheless had had their wills bent to conform to the wills of their parents and other significant adults.

Obedience thus became a persistent theme in the lives of moder-ates; but the emphasis upon dutifulness implied always that the obedi-ence of children and youths to parents would seem to be voluntary, the result of their love both of themselves and of their parents. Since their sense of self had not been crushed altogether early in life, they grew up feeling more at ease within themselves than most evangelicals and were better prepared, in their maturity, to be more independent and self-willed than most evangelicals ever could be. Yet the experiences of child-hood and youth also left moderates with an enduring sense of the limits of the self and of their autonomy, and with a persistent need to check, to limit, and thus to govern the self. Having grown up in families that pro-vided clear limits and boundaries to their liberty of action, expression, and of feeling, moderates subsequently found that their own consciences provided the inner boundaries that were to be so visible and influential in their temperaments, piety, and thought.

Sober, Virtuous, and Pious People: Themes of Moderate Temperaments and Piety

FOR MORE THAN TWO CENTURIES, moderates felt and discerned the difference in temperament, attitudes, beliefs, and values that distinguished them from evangelicals, who, by their vociferous rejection of moderation and all that it implied, frequently made the lines separating purists from moderates seem sharp and clear. Evangelicals felt the total corruption and depravity of human nature rooted deeply within themselves; moderates perceived the frailties and imperfections in human nature but felt that their own innermost nature retained some good despite their proclivity to sin and vice. Evangelicals felt the self to be the source of sin, alienation, and perpetual discontent, whereas moderates felt the self to be something valued and nurtured while also being closely watched and governed. Evangelicals often sought to annihilate the self, whereas moderates sought to control the self, to provide effective boundaries around the passions while acknowledging their necessity. Evangelicals sought to annihilate their own wills and rejoiced when they felt these being broken and subjected; moderates valued their wills and sensed that they were free while also being prepared, under certain circumstances, to yield voluntarily to superior wills. Evangelicals were convinced that only the new birth and an intense conversion experience could provide evidence of regeneration and thus of salvation, while moderates denied the need for total transformation implicit in the new birth, and insisted instead upon the process of gradual growth in grace and the development of habits of virtue that would eventuate in salvation. Evangelicals believed in a God of immense and unbounded power and authority, whose gift of grace to mankind was utterly free and unmerited by any human actions, whereas moderates were persuaded that God's power, while awesome, was bounded and contained through either a series of covenants or a series of natural laws, providing regular methods of achieving grace more dependent upon human actions and merit than evangelicals could ever allow. Instead of believing in a God of wrath and caprice, they believed in a God of love and order, a God who abided by certain established and knowable rules and limits. Evangelicals sought isolation from the corruptions and sins of the world, while moderates preferred to contend with the world and to accept, as inevitable and unavoidable, the mixture of vice and virtue in humanity, while seeking always to foster virtue and diminish vice. And finally, whereas evangelicals sought purity by excluding from their own ranks the imperfect as well as the unregenerate, moderates were content to live with imperfection. In these and other ways, evangelicals and moderates exemplified distinctive patterns of temperament, religious experience, and belief that formed surprisingly consistent clusters of attitudes, feelings, and perceptions of the self and the world over a very long period of time.

Nonetheless, moderation was often a precarious emotional and intellectual achievement, a complex balance of feelings and thoughts which revealed more clearly than one might imagine possible just how much many moderates shared with evangelicals. Subtle differences in attitude could have profound consequences for the shaping of differences in character and belief, yet they could also provide an undercurrent of affinity that reflected the similarities of formative experiences. One of the most telling clues to the precarious balance between the intellect and the feelings characteristic of so many moderates was the controlled passion which dominated their personalities. If their passions had been less intense, less powerful, less threatening, their preoccupations with control and order and their fears of loss of control and of disorder might have been less intense and less persistent. But they were always concerned lest their own feelings and proclivities to vice would overwhelm them. The outer world often became a mirror for their inner tensions, and their responses to the issues of their times in turn were always shaped by their own inner ambivalences and sustained tensions. Moderation rarely meant freedom from inner tension. Many moderates, like their evangelical counterparts, were often people of intense feelings and convictions. But these moderates sought to live with their own inner ambivalence, whereas evangelicals sought to deny it altogether. The differences between an authoritarian character and an authoritative character are often subtle, but they are also profoundly significant.

The inner tensions and persistent ambivalence characteristic of moderates were tempered sufficiently in many individuals so that they appeared to be far less tightly controlled and passionate people, more at ease with themselves and with the world in which they lived. For such moderates, the gulf between themselves and the evangelicals was far wider. Their temperaments were less rigid, and they allowed themselves more leeway in their self-fulfillment. The spectrum within the moderate configuration was relatively wide, including people very close in temperament to evangelicals and people very close in temperament to the genteel—a spectrum that might run from John Winthrop to John Adams to Benjamin Franklin to Thomas Jefferson, to cite only the most famous individuals whose temperaments locate them within the moderate mode. But moderates generally shared far more in common with each other than they did with the evangelicals or the genteel, despite the affinities particular people might have felt toward either of these other modes.

A Sense of Connections:
Organicism and the Chain of Being

OVER THE CENTURIES, two interconnected assumptions shaped the thought and perceptions of moderates and sustained their commitments to moderation: "organicism"—the belief that human society and institutions form a complex, interconnected whole, analogous to the human body, made up of indispensable but distinctive parts—and "the chain of being"— the belief that the entire universe, both inanimate and animate, was arranged by God hierarchically in subtly tiered ranks of being, function, and virtue. Both assumptions were ancient and commonplace, but they remained vital to the feelings and thoughts of moderates in America for several centuries.*

For moderates, the imagery of the body that formed the recurrent motif of organicism, and the imagery of the chain of being with its im-

* While the theme of hierarchy is familiar (from studies such as Arthur O. Lovejoy, *The Great Chain of Being: A Study of the History of an Idea* [Cambridge, Mass., 1936], and E. M. W. Tillyard, *The Elizabethan World Picture* [New York, n.d.]), the theme of organicism has been relatively neglected. Edmund S. Morgan does not include organicism among the distinctive ideas of Puritan political thought in his introduction to the sources that he edited, *Puritan Political Ideas, 1558–1794* (Indianapolis, 1965), even though the concept is readily apparent from the sources themselves. However, both Michael Walzer, in *The Revolution of the Saints: A Study in the Origins of Radical Politics* (Cambridge, Mass., 1965), and Daniel Walker Howe, in *The Unitarian Conscience: Harvard Moral Philosophy, 1805–1861* (Cambridge, Mass., 1970), provide illuminating and suggestive analyses of both these themes. The theme of organicism merits further attention since it continued to shape the thought of some Americans from the seventeenth century to the mid-nineteenth century. And as Lewis H. Lapham's fascinating analysis "Military Theology," *Harper's Magazine* (July 1971), vol. 243, pp. 73–85, demonstrates, the organicist and hierarchical ideas of the early American moderates from John Winthrop onward continue to appeal to at least some officers in the present military establishment of the United States.

mensely complex series of gradations of rank and purpose, provided powerful paradigms for the relationships that bound individuals together in families, communities, churches, and political states generally, as well as linking individuals to the natural world in which they lived. Their sense of connection and of relationship, rooted in their daily lives and feelings for people and places, could best be expressed through the interconnected imagery of hierarchy, ranks, and the inescapable ties of parts to the whole.[1]

For Governor John Winthrop, the chain of being was evident in all creation, and the due subordination of every part of the hierarchy formed a recurrent theme in his thought and writings. In the remarkable sermon which he delivered on board the ship *Arbella* in 1630, as he and his fellow passengers were crossing the Atlantic to America, Winthrop declared that "God almightie in his most holy and wise providence hath soe disposed of the Condicion of mankinde, as in all times some must be rich some poore, some highe and eminent in power and dignitie; others meane and in subjeccion." The reason for this evident ranking of mankind, he said, was manifest in God's delight "to shew forthe the glory of his wisdome in the variety and differance of the Creatures and the glory of his power, in ordering all these differences for the preservacion and good of the whole." Winthrop was utterly confident that a properly ordered commonwealth would require everyone who belonged to the community to be "members of the same body," who would be "knitt together in this worke as one man." He was certain, too, that in their new community "the care of the publique must oversway all private respects" because, he asserted, "it is a true rule that perticuler estates cannot subsist in the ruine of the publique."[2]

From the outset, the theme of the community as a body with interdependent but hierarchically ranked parts was to be a powerful motif in the thought and actions of many Americans. In 1676, the Reverend William Hubbard, another moderate, voiced similar views in one of his election day sermons examining the "Happiness of the People." The themes of order and of rank pervaded his sermon as he asked "what Order is?" His answer, a commonplace one, was: "Such a disposition of things in themselves equall and unequall, as gives to every one their due and proper place." "It suited the wisdom of the infinite and omnipotent Creator," he observed, "to make the world of differing parts, which necessarily supposes that there must be differing places, for those differing things to be disposed into, which is Order." These designs of the Creator were evident, he said, in both the political and the natural worlds. God, "who assumes to him self the title of being the God of Glory, is the God of peace, o[f] Order and not of confusion. . . . He is so in his Palace of the world, as well as in his temple of his Church: in both may be observed a sweet subordination of persons and things, each unto other."[3]

Hubbard's assumptions remained virtually unchanged in the writings of the Reverend Samuel Johnson in the mid-eighteenth century. Johnson was convinced that a person who knew what truth was also would know that truth "apprehends things as being what they are, their beings and relations, connections, and dependencies as they stand variously situated one to another. And things are said to be good as they answer their several ends according to their several situations and relations one to another, and as conspiring to the harmony, order, beauty and advantage of the whole, and particularly to the well-being and happiness of the rational human nature." The reason for this harmony, according to Johnson, was "manifest that the great Author of your beings, by all these common sentiments, necessities, and interests, affections, relations and dependencies, has evidently designed to tie you together and lay you under a necessity of considering yourselves as a system or whole made up of a vast number and diversity of members, connected together in such a manner, that no one with any pretense to true wisdom can propose his own real interest, his own good and happiness, without being at the same time solicitous for the weal and advantage of every other person that is at all useful in any kind of business whatsoever." When these relationships and obligations were fulfilled, the result would be "to make the whole a beautiful, orderly and well-connected system."[4]

Both Joseph Fish and Charles Chauncy—Old Light moderates during and after the great revivals of the 1740's—shared the characteristic assumptions about the chain of being and about organicism. As Fish observed in 1755, "Look over the whole Creation here below, and we may plainly see a beautiful Gradation, or an easy Transition from one Species, or Sort of Creatures, to another, observed by the great Creator of all Things: one is a little Step above the others; that is most below. The Highest of a lower Kind of Creatures, approaches very near the lowest of a higher." The same hierarchy pervaded the social order as well: "from the Head of a Nation or Province, down to the master of a Family, our concern for the Public Good should rise according to the place we Occupy." The chain of being was of immense importance in Chauncy's thought, too, providing him with an enduring pattern of relationships arranged into orderly hierarchies of duties and obligations as well as functions. We find that "individuals in every kind are wisely and variously related to each other; and not only so, but the kinds themselves are; in like manner, related to one another, so as to be parts properly fitted to fill up this system; and constitute it a good particular whole." The hierarchical arrangement of the whole system of nature also corresponded to the degrees of moral capacities and attainments. "In a creation inconceivably diversified," Chauncy noted, "it may be proper there should be as great a variety of moral beings, as of meerly animal ones; and that there should be a similar gradation from the highest to the lowest order of them." The chain of being and the consequent interconnection of every individual with every other, according to their proper ranks and stations in life, provided

Chauncy with a central perspective upon all human relationships and with an enduring model of connections and dependencies that he applied to every aspect of the world in which he lived.[5]

John Adams, too, took the chain of being for granted. As a young man of twenty-one in 1756, he contemplated the possibility of comprehending "the Whole created Universe, with all its inhabitants, their various Relations, Dependencies, Duties and necessities," and decided that "a Being of such great Capacity, indowed with sufficient Power, would be an accomplished Judge of all rational Beings." He was fascinated by the "infinite Magnificence of Nature," with all its beauties and wonders, and felt certain that "God whose almighty Fiat first produced this amazing Universe, had the whole Plan in View from all Eternity, intimately and perfectly knew the Nature and all the Properties of all these his Creatures." There was no doubt in his mind that the entire universe had been arranged according to the principles of the chain of being. "We observe, in the animate and in the inanimate Creation," he noted in his diary, "a surprizing Diversity, and a surprizing Uniformity. Of inanimate Substances, there is a great variety, from the Pebble in the Streets, quite up to the Vegetables in the Forrest. Of animals there is no less a Variety of Species from the Animalculs that escape our naked sight, quite through the intermediate Kinds up to Elephants, Horses, men." Yet, he said, "notwithstanding this Variety, there is, from the highest Species of animals upon this Globe which is generally thought to be Man, a regular and uniform Subordination of one Tribe to another down to the apparently insignificant animalcules in pepper Water, and the same Subordination continues quite through the Vegetable Kingdom." "And it is worth observing," he added, "that each Species regularly and uniformly preserve all their essential and peculiar properties, without partaking of the peculiar Properties of others." Only the "continual and vigilant Providence of God" could "preserve this prodigious Variety of Species's and this inflexible Uniformity among the Individuals," he believed.[6]

The themes of the hierarchy of the chain of being, and of the organicism that subordinated parts to the whole, continued to shape the thought of moderates during the late eighteenth and early nineteenth centuries. Daniel Howe noted that Unitarian moralists favored the "theme of social interdependence" throughout the first half of the nineteenth century, and believed that "The ideal commonwealth was an organic unit, composed, like a living body, of interrelated parts, each contributing its essential function." Hierarchies and organicism were profoundly important dimensions of Unitarian thought; they found expression in innumerable aspects of their views of self, the family, society, and the world generally. The Unitarians were as preoccupied with connections, subordination, and duties of the various members of society as their predecessors had been.[7]

Organicism also dominated the assumptions governing Horace

Bushnell's development of the notion of Christian nurture, for he, like his Unitarian contemporaries, was dismayed by the "bent toward individualism" that dominated all "modern notions and speculations," and was deeply concerned by the loss of "the idea of organic powers and relations." He admitted that "We have gained immense advantages, in modern times, as regards society, government, and character, by liberating and exalting the individual man," but was also convinced that "we are never, at any age, so completely individual as to be clear of organic connections that affect our character. To a certain extent and for certain purposes, we are individuals, acting each from his own will. Then to a certain extent and for certain other purposes, we are parts or members of a common body, as truly as the limbs of a tree." The family, as both Bushnell and the Unitarian moralists agreed, was of central importance for shaping an awareness of the organic connections of individuals to each other and to society as a whole. According to Bushnell, the organic nature of family relations and the subtle process within the family of instilling values into the temperaments—creating the character—of children were an inherent part of the organicism he valued, indispensable to Christian nurture as a whole. The fundamental assumptions underlying the thought of these nineteenth-century moderates differed little from the assumptions about the chain of being and organicism that had shaped the thought and attitudes of earlier generations of moderates. The continuities are remarkable.[8]

"This Contrariety in Man": The Frailties of Human Nature

THE UTTER CERTAINTY shared by evangelicals, whose daily experience confirmed their belief in original sin, that human nature was totally corrupted prior to regeneration and that the human body was the source of sin and suffering, which must be mortified and denied as fully as possible, did not conform to the experiences and beliefs of moderates. Their responses to human nature were more complex and less bleak. While usually acknowledging the persistence of sin and evil in the world, which they saw as the result of some degree of depravity in human nature, they also felt confident that human nature contained much good and promise as well. Their emphasis was upon the frailties and contrarities of human nature, rather than upon total depravity. As a result, moderates responded to their own selves and bodies with less fear and more optimism than their evangelical counterparts.

For many moderates, the imagery of the "great chain of being" linking God with His entire creation in an ascending hierarchy from the least consequential inanimate objects to a series of minutely graduated animate beings—the highest and noblest of whom are human beings, who rank below the celestial beings but high in the universal hierarchy of being—provided a satisfying perspective upon human nature. As the Reverend John Wise declared in 1717, waiving "the Consideration of Mans Moral Turpitude," man could be viewed "Physically as a Creature which God has made and furnished essentially with many Enobling Immunities, which render him the most August Animal in the World"; and still, "whatever has happened since his Creation," he added, "he remains at the upper-end of Nature, and as such is a Creature of a very Noble Character." Similarly, the Reverend Samuel Willard, who also believed intently in a hierarchically ordered universe, could exclaim exultantly, "See what an excellent being man was as he came out of the hands of his Creator. . . . God made all things in wondrous wisdom but here was a result of all God's creating wisdom gathered together in one. There were many beams of his wisdom, power and goodness scattered among other creatures; here they are all contracted in this little model." Human nature thus was poised between animals and angels, partaking both of the nature of the former and the promise of the latter.[9]

William Livingston put it thus in 1753: "Man, considered in different Lights, is of all Creatures the most base and abject, the most noble and august. As in one View he has the Mortification to call Corruption his Father; he may, in another, claim Kindred with Angels, and triumph in the Immortality of his Being. . . . He is endowed with Reason, and surrounded with Darkness. His Grandeur and Wretchedness are alike conspicuous. He may without Vanity reflect on himself, as capable of a Participation of the Divinity; and without Error rank himself with the meanest Reptile." As a result of this complex and contradictory nature, Livingston believed that " 'Tis the Inattention to this Contrariety in Man to which we are to ascribe all the false and imperfect Representations of human Nature." On the one hand, some "have only considered it in the bright Part of its Character, have exaggerated its Dignity, and declaim'd on its Perfection and Glory, without the least Notice of its Infirmity and Vileness. Others on the Contrary, strangers to its Excellence, but conscious of its Meaness, have degraded and vilified the Species; and represented Man as utterly abominable, and the Object of Horror." For Livingston, as for most moderates, "Revelation alone" provided answers to the enigmas of human nature's contradictions: "It represents Man as originally happy and innocent, and still retaining, amidst all his adventitious Impurity, some of the shattered Rays and pompous Ruins of his primitive Lustre. It reveals the Origin of his double Nature, in unfolding his Desertion from God, by aiming at Independence; and presuming to make himself the Centre of his own Happiness." "And hence," he noted, "his present Degredation and Abasement."[10]

The theme of the double nature of mankind, poised uneasily above the animals and below the angels, emerges over and over again in the private and public writings of moderates, who retained a vivid sense of sin while also experiencing an equally firm confidence in the potentialities of human nature for happiness and for virtue. The Reverend Samuel Willard, summing up the views of many seventeenth-century moderates in the ministry of New England, asserted that "Man consists of two essential constituting parts, viz. a body, and a reasonable soul. Neither of these alone is the man, but both in conjunction . . . both go together to his specifications and personality." For Willard, the place of humanity on the chain of being accounted for its affinities with both animals and angels; but while he believed that "everything ingredient to the nature of brute animals is an essential dimension of man's natural endowment," he was also convinced that "That which opens the peculiarly human arena . . . is 'the reasonable soul' added to the inconstant nature man receives from the lower echelons in the great chain of being. This higher power carries man into the invisible, constant world, the abode of angels." The instincts and passions reflected the animal nature of mankind, while reason and the soul declared mankind's potential connections with the angels.[11]

Later in the eighteenth century, the same assumptions continued to shape the thought of Charles Chauncy, who believed, like Willard, that human nature was of a "compound make; in consequence of which we are partly animal, and partly rational, being allied both to the highest, and the lowest orders of beings in the universe." Unhappiness resulted from the "consequence of the imperfection that is natural to us as creatures," Chauncy believed, when individuals "from free choice, act below" their "character as men." "If we would be happy," he said, "as beings of our rank in the scale of existence, we must act up to our character, and not as if we had no understanding, and there were no difference between us and the beast that perishes." He agreed with others that humanity was "in a corrupt state." "The fall has introduc'd great weakness into your reasonable nature," he told his congregation in 1742, but "great weakness" was a vastly different thing from total and ineradicable depravity.[12]

Similar views on human nature and the position of humanity within the chain of being were voiced by Samuel Johnson, who observed in 1748: "He who is sole and sovereign Lord of his favors, and delights in variety in all his works, may bestow or withhold what degrees of perfection he pleases; and as he at first made man a little lower than the angels, so now he sees fit in consequence of the punishment of Adam's sin, to make him, perhaps, a great deal lower than he made him at first." Yet Johnson also noted that "man with all his frailties, has even now a condition of being that is desirable, and (if he uses it well) capable of high improvements and great happiness." A comparable view appeared in Johnson's essay on Raphael, written sometime after 1763, in response to the assertion that "human kind" was a "miserable species of animals": "Weak, low and untoward as they are, they are rational and immortal spirits, and as such they are natures of very great dignity, and ought to be dearly loved and their weal solicitously sought and tendered." As Raphael urged, voicing Johnson's views, "Let every one know himself, his own darkness and weakness, and then learn how much allowance it becomes him to make for others. Let the frailty of human nature be considered with great compassion"—a sentiment shared by many other moderates as well.[13]

The contrarities of human nature are dominant motifs underpinning the emotional and intellectual lives of John and Abigail Adams, who perceived human nature as continually pressured by the passions and restrained by the dictates of reason, oscillating continuously between the perils and temptations of vice and the necessity for virtue. But, as Adams observed in 1760 at the age of twenty-six, "Vice and folly are so interwoven in all human Affairs that they could not possibly be wholly separated from them without tearing and rending the whole system of human Nature, and state. Nothing would remain as it is." Again, in 1772, he commented: "Human Nature, depraved as it is, has interwoven in its very Frame, a Love of Truth, Sincerity, and Integrity," which can be overcome only with difficulty. The Adamses shared a relatively dark view of human nature, as John's comment to Abigail in 1764 before their marriage suggests: "Intimacy with the most of People, will bring you acquainted with Vices and Errors, and Follies enough to make you despize them. Nay Intimacy with the most celebrated will very much diminish our Reverence and Admiration." Several months later, after a long separation, John wrote that "My soul and Body have both been thrown into Disorder, by your Absence, and a Month of [sic] two more would make me the most insufferable Cynick in the World. I see nothing but Faults, Follies, Frailties and Defects in any Body, lately. People have lost all their good Properties or I my Justice, or Discernment." But Adams also believed, as he observed in 1775, that "Human nature with all its infirmities and depravation is still capable of great things. It is capable of attaining to degrees of wisdom and of goodness, which, we have reason to believe, appear respectable in the estimation of superior intelligences."

Abigail, who like John was convinced that "Humane Nature is the same in all ages and Countrys," tended to be more pessimistic in her views of human vices. She wrote to John in late 1775: "I am more and more convinced that Man is a dangerous creature," and although her husband told her "of degrees of perfection to which Humane Nature is capable of arriving, and I believe it," nevertheless "at the same time," she lamented "that our admiration should arise from the scarcity of the instances." The following year, Abigail again wrote that "When I reflect upon Humane Nature, the various passions and appetites to which it is subject, I am ready to cry out with the Psalmist Lord what is Man?" The passions and the appetites—legacies of humanity's kinship with the animal world—were powerful and often dangerous unless governed and controlled by reason and the will, the faculties that alone distinguished men from the beasts and allied humanity with those higher on the universal scale of being.[14]

James Logan, of Philadelphia, viewed the passions and appetites of human nature more positively and approvingly than Abigail Adams, although he entirely agreed with her insistence upon the need to govern them properly. In his discourse on "The Duties of Man as they may be deduced from Nature," written sometime during the 1730's but never published, Logan insisted that "a man without Passions or Affections is only a Creature of the Brain, and we m[ay] as well imagine a man acting without any Senses: for both the o[ne] and the other are constituent parts or powers of our frame, and absolutely necessary to our being humane Creatures." Logan, like most moderates, believed that "All our Appetites Sensations Affections and Passions have manifestly been given us for Ends directly tending to our Support, Pleasure or Happiness." He included "our bodily Appetites and Gratifications of our Senses," among them both hunger and thirst, as well as sexual desire, observing that "the Continuation of the Species being of the greatest importance in the established course of Nature; because many Reflections might damp or retard our care in that Article, there is the Strongest Provision made by most powerful Inclinations, and these also are attended with Gratifications proportionable." For Logan, the needs and desires of the body, and the feelings and emotions of the heart, were implanted for the good and the pleasure of humanity; thus they were not to be considered the ineradicable sources of sin and corruption that evangelicals always felt within themselves.[15]

Self-Approbation and Self-Love

IN STRIKING CONTRAST to the evangelicals, for whom life required constant warfare against the self, the moderates accepted the self as worthy of love, respect, and nurture, as the fundamental source of their own happiness in this world, and as the means for securing happiness in the world to come. Self-love rather than self-hate characterized their responses to their own bodies, feelings, thoughts, desires, and actions—the pivotal passion that shaped their entire personalities and attitudes. Only when self-love grew excessive, transcending its proper bounds, did it become dangerous or vicious. Like all passions, self-love had limits. But when properly regulated, self-love was indispensable in order to live as a virtuous and happy human being. For all the imperfections and frailties inherent in human nature, for all the wickedness humanity was capable of doing, moderates always retained a deeply grounded sense of respect for their own selfhood, confident that a proper regard for one's self was the basis for a proper regard for the selves of others.

Although Giles Firman immigrated to the newly established colony in Massachusetts Bay during the early 1630's, settling in Ipswich, where he practiced medicine, he returned to England in the late 1640's and remained there to fight on the king's side of the civil war. In 1670, he published *The Real Christian*, which set forth his anti-evangelical views for the enlightenment of his former fellow colonists who remained in New England. He was confident that self-love was necessary and was the source of happiness in both this world and the next. As he declared, "Never did God declare against self, or call a man to deny himself in that which hinders his own salvation and happiness." Similarly, Samuel Willard, the spokesman for several generations of New England Covenant theologians, also believed that self-love, properly conceived and regulated, was essential for mankind's happiness and salvation. For Willard, there was both a "sinful self-love" and a "regular self-love," the former being an excessive and exclusive form of love, the latter a regulated and proportionate form of love. "This regular self-love," Willard said, "is the rule of our loving our neighbor. As our love ought not to center in our selves, but to extend to others, so in our application of it, we ought to take our measure from our self-love, to regulate us in our love to others." As Willard's biographer observed, "To fail to love oneself as God intends is to undermine one's affective relationship to the world. Self-haters, Willard emphatically maintains, are disobedient to the laws of nature and nature's God: 'there is a love which is due to a man's self, without which he cannot perform the duties of the law which belong to himself.'" But love itself, like every other affection, was to be expressed according to the gradations of relationship binding individuals to others, gradations that were strongest for the self, family, and friends, and weaker as relationships increased in distance and decreased in their intensity. As Willard noted, "Every man owes the first and principal of this love to himself. Every man is his own next neighbor. . . . I owe charity to others, but it must begin at home." Only by loving one's self could one possibly be able to love others as well. But too much self-love would interfere with the love of others, and thus was to be condemned as selfishness.[16]

When Charles Chauncy considered the "variety of affections and passions" that were "implanted" in man, he was confident that "they are all designed to promote his good, not his hurt." As he observed, "Was he destitute of self-love, how feeble and languid would be his endeavors, if he endeavoured at all, to preserve life, or render it so comfortable as it might be?" Far from feeling, as so many evangelicals did, that self-love was sinful and evil, and that life itself was only a hindrance to be escaped as rapidly as possible, Chauncy, like most moderates, believed that self-love or "self-approbation" was the source of the "noblest-kind of pleasure we are capable of"—the pleasures of the mind and of reason. "It is by knowing the constitution of man, that he is formed with a capacity to receive pleasure; with a state of mind inclining him to pursue it, both for his own private good, and the good of others" that it is possible to know "what is fit and reasonable conduct in him." Chauncy believed that "the two grand principles in human nature, self-love and benevolence, the former determining us to private, the latter to public, good, are accompanied, each of them, with particular appetites and passions, severally adapted to promote the more effectual prosecution of these ends, as occasion may require." "Self-love," he noted, "is a general, calm, dispassionate principle."

Happiness in this life as well as in the life to come was one of the central themes of Chauncy's writings; and self-love was of the utmost importance, together with the social affections of benevolence, for establishing the happiness which God had designed as an integral part of human nature. The "Supreme Being himself" had "made us men with intellectual and moral powers, after the similitude of his own, though in a low degree, he has planted a capacity in our nature of being happy with the like kind of happiness, he himself exists in the enjoyment of." "Benignity of heart, probity of mind, conscious integrity, self-approbation, and a good hope of the approbation of our Maker, evidenced to us by an habitual, steady course of freely chusing and practising the things that are comly, 'just, pure, lovely, and of good report,' are the true source of the moral happiness we are formed capable of."[17]

The Reverend Samuel Cooper, one of Chauncy's fellow ministers in Boston and a moderate Old Light Congregationalist, also believed that "were it possible for a rational Creature, to extinguish the Principle of Self-Love, far from being any Vertue or Perfection, this would at once appear as a gross and monstrous Defect in his Constitution." Like other moderates, Cooper was convinced that self-love "had to be regulated"; but once done, "a regular self-love is the foundation of all virtue and religion, the cement of all society, the life of faith and hope, and the spring of all moral and rational action." For Cooper, both "self-interest and social concern" were essential—what Chauncy would call self-approbation and benevolence—while it also was evident that "the Perfection of Virtue lies, in maintaining them in a due Ballance, and allowing of each it's proper Energy and Scope."[18]

Samuel Johnson agreed with both Chauncy and Cooper on the importance of self-love in shaping the obligations and commitments of individuals to society as a whole. Since "every man feels a great delight in being well respected, duly valued, well-spoken of and kindly treated by others," it was obvious that "Our love of our selves becomes the foundation of our love of others, and of all the social passions by which we are so readily carried to yield to each one his due, to have mutual pleasure in each other's enjoyments, and mutual sympathy and fellow-feeling in each other's calamities . . . and hence spring all the social virtues of justice, truth, faithfulness, kindness and benevolence, mercy and charity, all which are in the nature of things necessary to public peace and order." Clearly, without self-regard and self-respect, there could be no regard, respect, or love for others.[19]

Writing to his recently married daughter, David Cooper, a Pennsylvania Quaker, noted for her benefit in 1772 that "However Contemptible a Conceited disposition appears, he who does not shew a proper regard for himself, will receive but little from others"; nor, he hastened to add, "do I consider this at all incompatible with Humility that great Christian Virtue,—" "With regard to Religion, and in reference to our Creator," he added, "we can hardly estimate ourselves too low, but with regard to our fellow Men, if we do not support our own Station and Rank, we give up our claim to their Respect and Esteem, and in exchange shall receive their Slight and Contempt." "Reverence thy self," he urged, and then "The Worlds Reverence will follow." Similarly, although Elizabeth Willing, of Philadelphia, admitted to herself in 1768 "what selfish Creatures we are," since "there is scarsely a single act of our lives that has not a View to self," she added: "however we must not be displeased at this as it is Natural and what ever is realy so, cannot be blameworthy."[20]

For James Logan, too, self-love was both natural and necessary. He observed "the first and principal" of the affections and passions, which "manifestly appear to have been implanted in Infants or Children, before they are capable of Reflection or at least of making any free Use of Reason exclusive of those effects of bodily Pain or Pleasure, Fear grief or Joy" to be nothing other than "Self-Love,"—a word, he noted, "that Seems to have a very disadvantageous Sound to some peoples ears, yet which in the thing it Self is So highly consistent with the Same divine Wisdom, by which any other excellency was formed that it must be confessed primarily necessary, and that a Creature without it must have been absolutely imperfect and defective, and in the present Order of things could not have Subsisted." Self-love, Logan believed, was essential as the basis for the love of others; and he was convinced that "Families Should commence and be continued by the Strongest Ties of Affection in Conjugal Parental, Filial and Fraternal Love," which self-love ultimately made possible.[21]

Benjamin Franklin also recognized that self-love, or vanity, was disapproved of by many people. "Most people dislike vanity in others," he observed, "whatever share they have of it themselves; but I give it fair quarter wherever I meet with it, being persuaded that it is often productive of good to the possessor, and to others that are within his

sphere of action"; and therefore, he added, "in many cases, it would
not be altogether absurd if a man were to thank God for his vanity
among the other comforts of life." Self-love was evident in Franklin
throughout his long and happy life. As he observed of his youth in
Philadelphia, "I had therefore a tolerable character to begin the world
with; I valued it properly, and determin'd to preserve it." No evangelical
could ever have been so self-approving. Even John Adams, as an old
man whose readings and observations of human nature during the
course of a long lifetime sometimes "sickened" him in his "very Soul,"
could say, nevertheless: "Yet I never can be a Misanthrope. Homo Sum
["I am a man"]. I must hate myself before I can hate my Fellow Men:
and that I cannot and will not do."[22]

Moderates did not war against the self as evangelicals did. Over
the centuries, they responded both to their physical selves and to the
self as a whole in ways which differed profoundly from the intense
mistrust and hostility felt by evangelicals. Instead of feeling a need to
reject the appetites of the body and the passions of the self, instead of
waging constant and total warfare against the impulses and desires
of their natures, moderates accepted the appetites and passions that
allied them with the animal world as essential aspects of their humanity,
indispensable for the preservation and pleasures of the self. The sense
of self-approval which shaped their temperaments had enduring consequences for their responses to the self, to others, and to the world at
large; it provided them with a sense of inner security and self-confidence
that they never felt compelled to deny. But for many moderates, this
sense of self-approval was conditional, dependent upon the conscientious
pursuit of certain personal goals, and requiring persistent effort to
sustain. Self-approval demanded self-government, once the government
of parents had been outgrown.

"The Due Government of the Passions": Self-Control and Temperate Self-Denial

THE PERSISTENT GOAL OF MODERATES was self-control rather than self-
annihilation. As a result, they were preoccupied with limitations, boundaries, and balance—the imagery of containment and of control, of
harmony and of order. The passions and appetites inherent in human
nature were to be subordinated to the dictates of reason and the will,
but they were not to be eradicated or denied altogether. The self was
a composite of indispensable elements, feelings as well as intellect, and

neither alone sufficed to make a person fully human. In order to achieve the desired degree of moderation in life, many people felt themselves to be under constant pressures arising from the uneasy balance between their impulses and their beliefs. The achievement of a sense of well-ordered balance and harmony within the self depended upon the ability of an individual to govern the unruly passions effectively while still allowing them their proper roles in his or her life. Self-government was to be an exercise in limits and in boundaries, in the due subordination of the various elements which together comprise human nature, just as the elements of the universe as a whole were arranged within the great chain of being.

Moderates were preoccupied with self-established and self-maintained inner boundaries over their own passions and appetites. As one seventeenth-century Puritan declared, "When the Passions and Affections of the Soul are broken loose, having shaken off the reins of government . . . they fill his Ears with clamour and importunity. . . . This is the State of the Unregenerate. . . . Care then should be taken to Quell this unhappy Tumult, to reduce every affection within its proper bounds." And the Reverend Richard Rogers, an early Puritan whose late-sixteenth-century diary exemplifies the temperament of a man preoccupied with self-control and with boundaries, felt that "the Lord hath hedged me in on every side." He observed that he did "not so much complaine of the great evil" that he did "as of the little good." Even when he set himself "to moderate diet and regard of good ordre evry way" so that he "felt and found my hart as well contented in such a sober course and in subduinge all inordinate affec[tions] evry way as I can wish," he felt himself tempted by "deceivable alurementes," which sometimes caused him to be carried away with an "inordinate passion" that dimmed his sense of spiritual things. Experience taught him that "it is a most hard thing to keepe our lives and hartes in good order any longe time togither."[23]

John Winthrop, too, knew from experience how difficult it was to keep himself in good order, for the desires of the flesh constantly impelled him to watch and exercise strong control over his own passions and feelings, and to restrain his love of the world, which interfered continually with his sense of love for God and his own soul. Yet Winthrop, unlike evangelicals, never sought to deny his appetites or passions altogether, choosing instead to aim for a life of moderation in all things. He recalled once that early in his youth he had been "still very wild, and dissolute, and as years came on my lusts grew stronger, but yet," he noted, "under some restraint of my naturall reason." Throughout his life, he felt himself to be subject to "continuall conflicts between the flesh and the spirit," always discovering that "When the flesh prevayles the spirit withdrawes." But while he sought always to check and to control the desires of the flesh, he also felt that they were a worthy part of his own nature so long as they kept within their own due bounds. Occasionally the impulses and desires of his flesh were so strong that he felt they were his bitter enemies, as in 1616, when he observed that the "fleshe is eagerly inclined to pride, and wantonnesse, by which it playes the tirant over the poore soule, makinge it a verye slave." But more often he found, "by ofte and evident experience," that when "I hould under the fleshe by temperate diet, and not sufferinge the minde or outward senses to have everye thinge that they desire, and weane it from the love of the worlde," he could then "praye without wearinesse, or ordinary wanderinge of heart," and was "farre more fitt and cheerefull to the duties of my callinge and other duties" than at other times. Once, feeling out of sorts because of his worldly inclinations, he prayed for assistance from God, and soon, "I renounced my beloved pleasures, and was willinge to denye my selfe." His experience showed him that "that usuall cause of the heavinesse and uncomfortable life of many Christians is not their religion, or the want of outward comforts . . . but because their consciences enforce them to leave somme beloved unlawfull libertie before their hearts are resolved willingly to forsake it."

On another occasion, Winthrop noted that after "Remittinge my care and watche, and givinge libertie to the fleshe, I was againe unsettled," whereupon he resolved "to keepe a better watche, and to holde under the fleshe by temperate diet, and diligence" in his calling. "It wounded my heart in the eveninge when I looked backe and sawe the daye misspent in the service of the worlde, and in fulfillinge the will of my fleshe," he observed. Experience taught him that "when I have suffered my heart to take too much joye in any earthly thinge, I have been sure (for the most parte) in the turninge, to meet with a fitt of melancollike discontent," so that he concluded that it was "good wisdome for me to keep to a meane in my joyes, especially in worldly things; moderate comforts being constant and sweeter, or saufer [safer], then suche as beinge exceedinge in measure faile as much in their continuance." Neither the flesh nor the world were to be denied altogether, but both must be kept within the limits of moderation through the self-discipline of constant self-government. The pressures of the passions and the desires of the flesh were continuous, requiring constant watchfulness and control. But as Perry Miller so aptly observed, in a statement that applies to Winthrop and to countless other moderates as well, "Puritanism condemned not natural passions but inordinate passions, not man's desires but his enslavement to them, not the pleasures found in the satisfaction of appetites, but the tricks devised to prod satiated appetites into further concupiscence." Only by subordinating the passions and appetites to the dictates of reason and the control of the will could the moderation and sobriety of life valued so highly by Winthrop and others be achieved.[24]

The qualified acceptance of the appetites and passions inherent in human nature was of central importance to the moderates' view of themselves and to their attitudes generally. As Charles Chauncy declared: "The plain truth is, there is no appetite, affection, or passion, as planted in our nature by the God who made us, but what was intended, and wisely adapted, to answer some valuable purpose or other; insomuch, that it would have been greatly disadvantageous to us, had we not been furnished with them." All of the "variety of affections and passions" that are "implanted" in a man are "all designed to promote his good, not his hurt." Self-love, resentment, ambition, and every other affection and passion were necessary and useful; but Chauncy, like other moderates, also was certain that "they are capable of abuse." As he noted, "men's appetites and passions, by being indulged beyond what is fit and right, may be heightened in their impetus, and quite altered from their natural state." The appetites and passions were part of humanity's lower nature, which was shared with the animals below mankind on the chain of being. They provided "only that lower sort of happiness we are furnished for, by means of our animal make," said Chauncy, adding: "This, it is true, is very considerable: And mankind have such an opinion of it, if we may guess at their thoughts by their practice. For sensual pleasures are the great object of their pursuit. Too many indulge them, as though they were designed for no higher happiness." Our fault, he went on, is "not that we have no value for animal gratifications, but that we value them too highly, and place too much of our happiness in them; as they contain only the lowest sort of good we are fitted for the enjoyment of, by means of our animal part." Proper though these bodily pleasures were when kept within their due limits, Chauncy nevertheless was convinced that "the great thing aimed at, by the Deity" was to "lay the best foundation for those intellectual and moral exercises, and the noble pleasures resulting therefrom, which so highly exalt our natures."

Chauncy knew that it was imperative that the appetites and passions be "kept under due government," by means of "a wise improvement of that reason, conscience, moral discernment, and other powers which our Maker has implanted in our constitution, on purpose to check the undue influence of our appetites and passions, and to keep them within their proper sphere." As he asked, confident of the right answer: "Will any man, not having darkened his heart, declare, speaking the truth, that he does not see it to be right, that he should govern his passions and keep his sensual appetites within the restraints of reason; and wrong, evidently wrong, to give way to anger, wrath, malice, and to take an unbounded liberty in gratifying his animal nature?" To allow the passions primacy would be "to invert their Frame" and to "place the Dominion in those Powers, which were made to be kept in Subjection." Chauncy characteristically observed, "The plain Truth is, an enlightened Mind, and not raised Affections, ought always to be the Guide of those who call themselves Men; and this, in the Affairs of Religion, as well as other Things." The main object was to hold men's "Powers" in "a State of due Subordination," by keeping "the Passions within their proper

Bounds, restraining them from usurping Dominion over the reasonable Nature." For Charles Chauncy, as for other moderates, the central need was to establish and to maintain "proper Bounds" within which their animal nature could function, proving both useful and a source of happiness.[25]

Other moderates such as James Logan shared Chauncy's desire for "proper Bounds" in order to keep the passions firmly in control. Logan agreed that "our Affections and Passions" are "the true Springs of our Actions," and that "therefore on the regulation and adjustment of their Motions principally depends all our Happiness in Life." Like Chauncy and others, Logan believed that human passions were "commendable" when "kept Strictly within bounds, and directed only" to their "proper End." Even a passion such as anger had its uses for self-preservation and the maintenance of authority in families, civil governments, and society generally. But anger, like several other passions, "is extreamly apt" to "exceed the bounds, within which, to render it truly useful," Logan said, so that "it ought to be carefully restrained." With the guidance of reason and the conscience, he was confident that such self-control would succeed, and that the desired balance in the expression of the appetites and passions would be maintained.[26]

Abigail Adams also believed in the primacy of reason and the imperative necessity to control and limit the passions and appetites of humanity. "Ungoverned passions have been aptly compaired to the Boisterous ocean," she wrote to her twelve-year-old son, John Quincy, in 1780, "which is known to produce the most terible Effects." " 'Passions are the Elements of Life' but elements," she added, "which are subject to the controul of Reason. Who ever will candidly examine themselves will find some degree of passion, peevishness or obstinacy in their Natural tempers." The "uncontroulable indulgence" of any of these "is sufficient to render the possessor unhappy in himself and dissagreable to all who are so unhappy as to be wittnesses of it, or suffer from its Effects." As she noted for John Quincy's edification, "you my dear son are formed with a constitution feelingly alive, your passions are strong and impetuous and tho I have sometimes seen them hurry you into excesses, yet with pleasure I have observed a frankness and Generosity accompany your Efforts to govern and subdue them." "Few persons," she observed, "are so subject to passion but that they can command themselves when they have a motive sufficiently strong, and those who are most apt to transgress will restrain themselves through respect and Reverence to Superiours, and even where they wish to recommend themselves to their equals." "The due Government of the passions has been considered in all ages as a most valuable acquisition," she noted. She hoped that her young son would "learn betimes from your own observation and experience to govern and controul yourself. Having once obtained this self government you will find a foundation laid for happiness to yourself and usefullness to Mankind." Even love itself could be excessive and out of control, as she noted the next year in a letter to her husband, in which she wrote that "My two dear Boys cannot immagine how ardently I long to fold them to my Bosom, or the still dearer parent conceive the flood of tenderness which Breaks the prescribed Bounds and overflows the Heart," when she thought of the past and the future. Self-government meant keeping everything within "the prescribed Bounds," so that all passions, even love itself, would be contained, limited, and under the constant control of superior reason.[27]

The themes of self-government and of the subjection of the passions to the superior control of reason recur throughout the private writings of John Adams, who was preoccupied all through his lifetime with balance, control, and limits upon the appetites and passions inherent in human nature. In 1758, three years after graduating from Harvard College, he wrote playfully to a friend that "The only Thing I fear is, that all my Passions, which you know are the Gales of Life, as Reason is the Pilot, will go down into an everlasting Calm." "And what will a Pilot signify," he asked, "if there is no Wind." Both were essential—neither alone sufficed to make a person whole—but reason, clearly, was meant to be superior to the passions. Confident that "Habits of Temperance, Recollection and self Government will afford us a real and substantial Pleasure," Adams also believed that "He is not a wise man and is unfit to fill any important Station in Society, that has left one Passion in his Soul unsubdued." "These Passions should be bound fast and brought under the Yoke," he wrote in 1756. "Untame they are lawless Bulls, they roar and bluster, defy all Controul, and some times murder their proper owner. But properly inured to Obedience, they take their Places under the Yoke without Noise and labour vigorously in their masters Service."[28]

Although Adams believed that when human nature was "carefully observed and studied," man "will be found, a rational, sensible and social Animal, in all," he was certain that the passions were strong and in need of constant watch and government. Ambition especially, he felt, was "one of the more ungovernable Passions of the human Heart," while the "Love of Power, is insatiable and uncontroulable." As a young man just beginning to embark upon his career in law, Adams observed: "I begin to feel the Passions of the World. Ambition, Avarice, Intrigue, Party, all must be guarded." He never ceased to experience these passions, and he never ceased his efforts to guard against them and to keep them within secure boundaries, for he was well aware that sometimes "appetite and Passions" could be "too violent for the Government of Reason."[29]

Being an Adams, he was more fearful of the excessive appetites and passions of other people than of himself; but he knew from close self-examination and self-knowledge that he too had an ample share of intense and potentially violent passions which needed his constant attention. Ambition, avarice, and the love of power—central passions and appetites of human nature—formed the leitmotifs of John Adams's thoughts; while the need to check, to limit, to control the passions, to bind them within the generous confines of a well-governed and rational self, formed the counterpoint to the theme of unbounded passions throughout his life. As Adams observed in his *Discourses of Davila*, published in 1791, Nature "has wrought the passions into the texture and essence of the soul, and has not left it in the power of art to destroy them. To regulate and not to eradicate them is the province of policy," voicing the sentiments of countless moderates as well. "It is of the highest importance to education, to life, and to society, not only that they should not be destroyed, but that they should be gratified, encouraged, and arranged on the side of virtue."[30]

For Adams, balance was the central pivot upon which his understanding of human nature and of human politics turned, for a proper balance between the passions and reason was indispensable to the establishment and maintenance of moderation, and of liberty in general. In response to some of Mary Wollstonecraft's observations on the French Revolution, Adams noted in the margin of his copy of her book that he wanted her to "Allow the truth that all men are ferocious monsters when their passions are unrestrained." "Prepare bridles for them," he urged. When Mary Wollstonecraft wrote hopefully that "The improvement of the understanding will prevent those baneful excesses of passion which poison the heart," Adams responded by observing, "The understanding will only make rivalries more subtle and scientific, but the passions will never be prevented, they can only be balanced." As he noted of Wollstonecraft's book as a whole, "The improvement, the exaltation of the human character, the perfectibility of man, and the perfection of the human faculties are the divine objects which her enthusiasm beholds in beatific vision." "Alass," he added, "how airy and baseless a fabric! Yet she will not admit of the only means that can accomplish any part of her ardent prophecies: forms of government, so mixed, combined and balanced, as to restrain the passions of all orders of men." Adams believed that human liberty was constantly endangered by various enemies, which arose "from the strength of human passions, imaginations and prejudices, the imperfection of human knowledge, and the weakness of reason." But he never lost faith, as the evangelicals so often did, in the possibility that reason could and would prevail over the passions if they could be regulated and balanced properly.[31]

Samuel Johnson shared Adams's fear of "the tyranny of ungoverned lusts and passions which will not fail to produce all manner of trouble, mischief, confusion and every evil work." He, too, took for granted the belief that "whoever reflects and compares his senses, appetites and affections, which he has in common with inferior animals, with the vastly more noble powers of thinking and reasoning, can't but be sensible that his reason is designed to be the governing power in him"—an assumption that dominated the beliefs of moderates at all times. Since "reason" was "evidently given him to be the governing power, to preside over and direct all his senses, appetites, affections and actions, it is therefore his duty," Johnson said, speaking through Raphael, "to govern himself according to its dictates," so that "if he would consult his true happiness, his reason must not be thwarted by actions repugnant to the dictates of it." If this were to be done, he would find that from hence "would spring all the virtues of temperance, moderation, patience, and meekness, all which virtues have a natural tendency not only to the tranquility of each mind, but also of society, forasmuch as ungoverned lusts and passions tend to public mischief"—again, other moderates would have concurred readily. Like Chauncy, Johnson also felt that the "wild enthusiasm" of the revivals during the 1740's caused many people, whose affections and passions were excessive, to break "through all order and rule"; this would not have been the case had their reason prevailed over their passions, as it ought to have done. But powerful passions were part of human nature, and only constant self-discipline and self-denial within due limits could provide the restraints needed to establish the temperate, well-governed self valued so highly by Johnson and others.[32]

The nineteenth-century New England Unitarians also believed that reason ought to govern the passions so that a well-regulated, balanced, harmonious, and temperate character would be formed. Like many of their ancestors, they felt that "The function of prudence was 'to provide for our good on the whole, by the regulation, balancing, and use of the primary appetites, desires and affections.' " As Daniel Howe noted, Unitarians were persuaded that "Sin represented a failure to regulate impulses that were not in themselves evil," while "Virtue, conversely, could be identified with *'universal moderation.'* " Above all, Unitarians valued "harmony," with the consequence that "The Unitarian conscience was not a repressive, but an expressive faculty: not to crush, but to harmonize, regulate, and balance, was the task of the ruling power." The Reverend Henry Ware declared in his book on *The Formation of the Christian Character:* "The complete man is . . . wise, watchful, self-governed, self-sustaining; every part of him is in its right place, and of its right proportion, and every faculty is obedient to his will." In striking contrast to evangelicals, Unitarians like the Reverend John Emery Abbot were certain that Christianity "calls us not to annihilate our feelings, but only to regulate them." Clearly, Howe's observation about nineteenth-century Unitarians—that "In thought, as in feeling, *moderation* was their goal"—applies with equal force to moderates of all persuasions and periods.[33]

One of the most effective methods of regulating and governing the powerful passions and appetites inherent in human nature was by practicing temperate self-denial in every aspect of daily life—in diet, dress, furnishings—virtually all facets of an individual's response to the world.

Unlike many evangelicals, for whom self-denial meant an all-encompassing and self-mortifying asceticism, moderates were confident that temperance rather than total abstinence or severe restrictions would suffice to keep them within proper bounds. Like the Quaker Robert Barclay, moderates believed it was "beyond question, that whatever thing the creation affords is for the use of man, and the moderate use of them is lawful." Nonevangelical Quakers throughout the eighteenth century epitomized the ideal of temperance in all outward aspects of life, with their stress on simplicity, sobriety, and moderation. Like David Cooper, they were persuaded that "real Religion" was "a Religion that reforms the Creature, regulates the Passions, Appetites, and desires, shines forth in a steady uniform consistant conduct in every act of Life, teaches us to be more careful to please God than Men, restrains from doing an ill thing however secret, as much as if the whole World were Witnesses." The epistle for 1731 from the yearly meeting of Friends in London urged: "Let us walk wisely towards those that are without, as well as those within. Let our moderation and prudence, as well as truth and justice, appear unto all men, and in all things; in trading and commerce, in speech and communication, in eating and drinking, in habit and furniture; and, through all, in a meek, lowly, quiet spirit; that, as we profess to be a spiritually minded people, we may appear to be such, as being bounded by the cross of Christ, shew forth the power of that divine principle we make profession of, by a conversation every way agreeable thereunto." Moderation, regulation, and the maintenance of proper boundaries around the appetites, affections, and passions of humanity formed constant themes, enabling Friends to accept themselves in their entirety— partly animal, partly rational—while also keeping strict watch over themselves and strengthening their rational faculties and wills by the use of moderate self-denial in every aspect of life.[34]

Temperate self-denial was woven into the innermost sensibilities of moderates, as their attitudes toward dress, diet, and above all wealth and luxury revealed. One of the most revealing themes in John Adams's writings is his perception of the role of taste in shaping character, and the necessity for moderation in all aspects of one's outward life. Wealth and luxury were not necessarily evil, but he was certain that "An immoderate thirst of them is a vice, and is not honorable." He always was fascinated by wealth and the genteel life style that usually accompanied riches, but he also felt a constant need to guard against his own inclinations for luxury and elegance. As he wrote to his daughter Abigail from The Hague in 1782, "Your happiness is very near to me. But depend upon it, it is simplicity, not refinement nor elegance [that] can obtain it. By conquering your taste, (for taste is to be conquered, like unruly appetites and passions, or the mind is undone,) you will save yourself many perplexities and mortifications."[35]

Sufficiency but not excess, necessities but not superfluities, satisfaction but not surfeiting; these were the persistent goals of moderates of all persuasions, who sought to limit their own inner propensities to indulge their appetites or passions too much. Simple tastes—in food, clothing, housing, and life styles generally—were the expression of the inner equilibrium sought by moderates between too severe restriction and too great indulgence. Simplicity thus became a governing mode of being, for it allowed the appetites to be acted upon without rendering them excessive. But the balance was always a delicate one, constantly subject to disruption and disequilibrium.

John Adams led a life shaped by temperance and moderate self-denial. Although he was a man of intense appetites and passions, he felt compelled to keep them tightly reined. Even relaxation was difficult, as he discovered during the early 1770's after his solitary travels through New England undertaken to restore his health. He noted in his diary: "I hope I shall not take another Journey merely for my Health very soon. I feel sometimes sick of this—I feel guilty—I feel as if I ought not to saunter and loyter and trifle away this Time—I feel as if I ought to be employed, for the Benefit of my fellow Men, in some Way or other." For Adams, a life in public employments or in politics was actually a form of self-denial, for it kept him from his beloved wife and children and his house and farm in Braintree for months and years at a time. Both John and Abigail felt most comfortable when denying themselves something they desired or enjoyed. John said he thought himself "well rewarded, if my private Pleasure and Interest are sacrificed as they ever have been and will be, to the Happiness of others." Abigail, too, often felt "as if she was left alone in the world, unsupported and defenceless, with the important weight of Education upon her hands at a time of life when the young charge stand most in need of the joint Efforts and assistance of both parents." "I have sacrificed my own personal happiness," she declared, "and must look for my Sati[s]faction in the consciousness of having discharged my duty to the publick." For the Adamses, temperate self-denial was interwoven into the very fabric of their lives, an indispensable duty and attribute of their personalities, and an essential component of their commitment to the public good they valued so highly.[36]

Self-denial became an integral part of the temperaments of most moderates, many of whom found that the regulation of their appetites and passions and the maintenance of a temperate course of life were best accomplished by an unremitting industriousness. Industry thus provided one of the principal means of self-control. Work, activity, public life, the constant engagement in commerce, politics, and the law, afforded many moderates a life that left little time for leisure or excessive pleasure. Benjamin Rush, for instance, recalled that "From the time of my settlement in Philadelphia in 1769 'till 1775 I led a life of constant labor and self-denial." As a young doctor, he found himself constantly

attending crowds of poor people, both in his shop and in "nearly every
street and alley in the city," which he visited every day. Rush looked
upon his care for the city's poor as "acts of duty," which also had the
benefit of increasing his knowledge of diseases. Throughout his career,
he was remarkably busy and energetic, using every moment of time purposefully and frugally, a man proud of his "self-command." Similarly,
Benjamin Franklin recalled making plans early in life "for regulating
my future conduct in life," and the theme of self-regulation pervades his
writings. As a young man in Philadelphia, he educated himself, "by
constant study" and reading daily, observing that "Reading was the only
amusement I allow'd myself. I spent no time in taverns, games, or
frolicks of any kind; and my industry in my business continu'd as
indefatigable as it was necessary." Although his "original habits of
frugality" continued, Franklin nevertheless "considered industry as a
means of obtaining wealth and distinction," both of which, in due course,
he acquired. Yet the industriousness of his temperament never diminished, urging him constantly toward new experiments and inventions.

Thomas Jefferson, again, was a remarkably industrious man, leading him, as Fawn Brodie has observed, "to an astonishing regimen of
self-discipline which came close to being obsessive." Brodie adds that
"One of Jefferson's friends stated that 'when young he adopted a system,
perhaps an entire plan of life from which neither the exigencies of
business nor the allurements of pleasure could drive or seduce him.
Much of his success is to be ascribed to methodical industry.' " In 1787,
Jefferson made his views on industriousness very clear for the sake of
his young daughter Martha. "It is your future happiness which interests
me," he wrote, "and nothing can contribute more to it (moral rectitude
always excepted) than the contracting a habit of industry and activity.
Of all the cankers of human happiness, none corrodes it with so silent,
yet so baneful a tooth, as indolence. . . . Exercise and application produce
order in our affairs, health of body, chearfulness of mind, and these make
us precious to our friends." "It is while we are young that the habit of
industry is formed," he insisted, adding, "If not then, it never is afterwards."[37]

By being industrious, by practicing temperate self-denial, by living
lives of relative simplicity and frugality, moderates expressed their need
for self-control. In restraining their appetites and passions within due
bounds, they sought to provide themselves with a sense of inner harmony
and security which depended, however, upon the establishment of visible
and discernible limits on their feelings and actions. The inner boundaries
that regulated their lives varied in circumference, with some allowing
themselves more space for the expression of their appetites and passions
than others were able to tolerate. Yet most moderates felt comfortable
only when they operated within known and visible parameters and kept
themselves closely in check. By setting the limits themselves, they were

able to experience the sense of self-approval that distinguished them from evangelicals; and by allowing themselves to express all their appetites and passions in moderation, they were also able to avoid the need to deny the self as a whole, as evangelicals so often had to do. Yet the preoccupation with self-control which shaped the temperaments of moderates also suggests that they, too, were comfortable only with certain kinds of feelings and thoughts, and that their inner sense of freedom depended upon their willingness to keep themselves securely within the bounds set by their consciences.

"The Liberty of the Human Will"

ALTHOUGH MODERATES were often acutely conscious of the need for boundaries and limits upon their feelings and actions, their preoccupation with self-control always implied the ability of the self to control itself. Thus moderates took for granted the freedom of their own wills which most evangelicals denied. But the very fact that they took the liberty of the human will for granted meant that they rarely discussed the issue either in private or in public. They seemed to be convinced of their inner freedom, and of their ability to make choices and to direct the course of their own lives according to their own beliefs and desires by virtue of personal feelings and experiences, even when they found it difficult, if not impossible, to justify these feelings. As Charles Chauncy said, "It is readily allowed, liberty in man, in opposition to necessity, is one of the great wonders of God. The power in our nature that constitutes us free agents is an amazing contrivance of infinite wisdom. The modus of its existence and operation is too gre[at] for us to fathom. It has tried, and puzzled the greatest geniusses in all ages, and in all parts of the world. And, perhaps, we shall never be able, at least on this side of mortality, to take in a comprehensive idea of it." "But is this a good reason," he then asked, "why we should deny, or dispute, the real being of such a power in our constitution?" And he added, "We feel it to be a truth, in consequence of which we are, in a reasonable sense, masters of ourselves. Our daily experience, if attended to, will indubitably assure us, that the exertions of our minds and bodies are under our own dominion." Similarly, the Reverend Samuel Johnson believed that everyone was "intuitively conscious of our free agency." Confident that God had given humanity a "voluntary, self-exerting nature," with a free will to act and to choose, Johnson could only say that "if any one will yet doubt and quibble, I can only refer him to his own conscience for conviction, and if he will but reflect and think, I am astonished if what

I contend for be not self-evident." Nineteenth-century Unitarians, too, took the freedom of the human will for granted without offering any systematic defense of their assumption. As Levi Hedge declared, "The moral freedom of man is not a question of speculation, to be settled by abstract reasoning. . . . It is a question of fact to be decided by feeling. . . . We believe we are free, because we feel that we are so." This feeling, which emerged from the experiences of childhood, was to be of enormous significance in shaping the consciousness and the temperaments of moderates over the centuries.[38]

The arguments about the nature of the will often are complex and confusing, with ambiguities and paradoxes that betray the inner uncertainties felt by many over the extent to which their own and other wills were free. But the main thrust among moderates—including those most closely associated in New England with the tradition of the Covenant—was toward an expansion of the notion of the freedom of the human will and an insistence that morality itself demanded this freedom. As the Reverend Samuel Willard declared, "freedom of will properly consists in a spontaneity, or liberty of choosing or refusing. It is the privilege of a cause by counsel, and it supposeth an understanding to direct, and a will to elect or reject accordingly." "Such a freedom," he went on, "God did at first put into the angels and man; although it must always be considered in the subordination of a creature in the concourse or co-operation of God." And this freedom, he insisted, as other moderates were to do, "is the foundation of all moral transaction with such creatures." As he declared, "there is no obedience but what is voluntary. If the heart and will be not in it, but it be a forced thing, it cannot truly be called obedience." Since Willard believed that "absolutely nothing ever takes away 'the natural freedom of his will,' " not even Adam's fall could have been accomplished by Satan had not his will been tempted to evil and succumbed voluntarily to the temptations. Willard noted, "The tempter could only tempt. He could not compel. All his strength lay in his subtlety. Man's free will is incapable of compulsion."[39]

In the mid-eighteenth century, William Livingston, who became one of the most articulate exponents of the moderate viewpoint in the Middle colonies, declared that "The Study of human Nature will teach us, that Man in his original Structure and Constitution, was designed to act in a natural and moral Dependence on his Maker alone, and created solely for the Enjoyment of his own Happiness. His being a rational Creature necessarily implies in him a Freedom of Action, determinable by the Dictates of his own Reason, the self-resolving Exertions of his own Volition, and a Reverence to the Laws prescribed to him by his omnipotent Creator." "This Liberty of Action," he continued, "however modified by human Policy, cannot in the Nature of Things be separated from his Existence. For by admitting the Rationality of Man, you necessarily suppose him a free Agent." As he declared, "The Liberty of the human Will, and a Power of acting in Conformity thereto, are not only his indisputable Right, but also constitute his very Essence as a rational Creature; and cannot therefore, by any Means whatever, be alienated from him in a social State." Without free wills, there could be no other kinds of freedom or liberties, for voluntary choices were an indispensable part of being truly free.[40]

For Charles Chauncy, also, freedom of the human will was crucial to the establishment and maintenance of morality and of virtue. He took for granted the assumption that "As Men are rational, free Agents, they can't be religious but with the free Consent of their Wills; and this can be gain'd in no Way, but that of Reason and Persuasion." And he was utterly certain—indeed, he made this certainty the basis for his entire theology—that only by the ability to make free choices could humanity attain happiness and behave morally.[41]

Yet the freedom of the will and the necessity inherent in human nature to make choices voluntarily and independently of even the will of God meant that persons might choose evil as well as good, might "abuse their liberty" as well as "making a good use of it." But as Chauncy asked, "Will any say, it is better there should be no free agency, than that beings should be liable to abuse it?" For moderates like him, the answer was clear: the risks of being free were worth the gains to be obtained from liberty. As he asked, "can it be thought right, that so glorious a capacity for happiness as free agency, should be totally withheld from all beings, because it might possibly have been perverted in its tendency? What though some should abuse it, might not others make a wise improvement of it? And why should this be prevented? Why put [this] out of their power, by the non-bestowment of freedom of choice?"[42]

For Chauncy as for most moderates, however, human freedom and the liberty to make choices was never an absolute freedom, for only some choices were considered to be morally justified and virtuous. Because Chauncy became convinced that God ultimately planned to make all of mankind "finally happy" and thus in the end to offer salvation to everyone, he had to confront the problem of how the Divine will could be accomplished without compromising the liberty of the wills of people, who manifestly chose misery as often as happiness for themselves. After all, "such free agents as men are may oppose all methods that can be used with them, in consistency with liberty, and persist in wrong determinations, to the rendering themselves finally unhappy." But Chauncy was confident that such would not be the case finally because God did have ways of influencing and shaping the choices being made by mankind. "Who will undertake to make it evident, that infinite wisdom, excited by infinite benevolence, is incapable of devising expedients, whereby moral agents, without any violence offered to their liberty, may certainly be led, if not at first, yet after various repeated trials, into such determinations, and consequent actions, as would finally prepare them for happiness?" he wondered. "It would be hard to suppose," he declared, "that infinite wisdom should finally be outdone by the obstinacy and folly of any free agents whatsoever."[43]

God, like moderate parents, knew how to bend and shape the wills of His children so that their choices, though made freely according to their own wishes and desires, nevertheless would coincide in the end with His will also. Moderates thus often harbored an inner awareness of the necessity of choosing *only* those things that would bring about their personal happiness and the happiness of others, both in this world and in the world to come. Although their experiences and feelings from early childhood had nurtured their inner sense of freedom and had provided them with an enduring sense of self-worth and self-approval, many moderates found their sense of personal choice to be a persistent source of anxiety and concern. Indeed, for moderates generally the freedom of the human will often was burdensome, since it left them with no alternative to an enduring consciousness of personal responsibility for their own success or failure to live a virtuous and dutiful life.

"Habits of Piety and Virtue"

BOTH THE SENSE OF PERSONAL RESPONSIBILITY, which grew out of the persuasion that the will was free, and the belief that the achievement of grace and future salvation was a gradual process, which continued throughout life from early childhood to old age, provided the basis for the belief of most moderates that piety and virtue were indispensable for human happiness. Characteristically, moderates were preoccupied with the duties of life and the fostering of habits that would sustain their sense of compliance with their consciences. From childhood, the obligations of duty and the necessity for a life of virtue had been inculcated. As adults, most moderates continued to be deeply concerned with their ability to live a life that accorded with the expectations of their parents and their God, as well as, ultimately, of themselves.

A life of virtue and the importance of duty were central themes in the writings and actions of the Reverend Samuel Johnson, who was convinced that "Without counsel, design and free choice there can be no such thing as virtue, for herein does the very essence of virtue consist," observing that "in spite of every temptation to the contrary from private views, we sincerely and freely design to do our duty in all that we do by a power of such actions and behavior as tends to promote the true weal and happiness of ourselves in conjunction with that of others" while simultaneously doing "honor to that almighty Being on whom we all depend." Johnson was certain that it was "our bounden duty to yield obedience" to all "the laws of God," whether "they be discovered by our own reason or dictated by God himself, and in a free and voluntary conformity to these laws from a sense of duty to Him, consists moral good, and the contrary is moral evil."

A deeply rooted sense of duty thus shaped Johnson's views of the obligations that a life of virtue placed upon mankind to fulfill the laws and to obey the will of God. He was convinced, too, that the fulfillment of these duties of piety and virtue in this life was to be the basis for the dispositions of individual fates in the life to come. Since this present world "is but a temporary and probationary state," Johnson said, it was evident that God had resolved "to treat all men" in the "future state" of being "according to the use they shall have made of his several allotments to them in this world: *i.e.*, to render the good happy and the wicked miserable; in various proportions, according to their behavior." Even future happiness or misery was to be graduated according to a scale of virtue in this life. As he said, God "lays you under no necessity of being finally miserable, but leaves it possible for you to be happy in proportion to your powers and advantages, so that it will be your own fault alone if you miscarry."

On his thirty-third birthday in 1729, Johnson wrote in his diary to acknowledge that "my circumstances of life are entirely to my wishes, and I am as happy as I can desire to be in this state of probation. God is good to me in every respect." "All my grief," he added, "is that I do not make returns answerable to my obligations, but am often ungrateful, forgetting and provoking him by my misdeeds, and that I am under no better advantage to do good and so little success attends my feeble endeavors." He hoped that as he got "along nearer and nearer to the future and eternal state of my existence," God would enable him "to be more and more fitted for it, by mortifying the powers of sin, and improving myself in the love and practice of all those graces and virtues that may qualify me for the everlasting enjoyment of thee my God for thy dear Son's sake."[44]

Timothy Pickering, too, valued a sanctified heart and a life of active virtue. He was confident, as he wrote to his wife soon after their marriage in 1776, that God's Providence was good, and that "to those who by patient continuance in well doing, seek for glory, honour and immortality, no event can be unhappy," adding that "to such our kind, heavenly parent will grant a life above the stars, where the tumult and din of war approach not; where there will be uninterrupted harmony and love." "Into this blest place, when we quit this earthly stage, let us, my dearest, by the path of virtue, pray and strive to enter: and Oh: All-Gracious God!" he prayed, "grant free admittance to thy humble suppliants!" The following summer, he wrote to her from Philadelphia, acknowledging that "perhaps we never know the value of domestic sweets, till taught by absence," but also noting that they ought not to "fix our expectation of happiness on aught below the skies: because all is fleeting and unstable. At the same time, with cheerful hearts let us enjoy the indulgent bounties of our kind Heavenly Parent—("to enjoy is to obey")—without boding future ills, to make our lives unhappy. . . . And yet we should believe afflictions possible; knowing that we are in the hands of him who gave us being, who is infinitely wise, just and good." "For which reason," he added, "conscious of uniform endeavours to practice every duty of piety and virtue we ought not to be anxious about future events."

For Pickering—as for Samuel Johnson—duty loomed large as a recurrent theme in his thoughts. He wrote to Rebecca in May 1778, "How important then" is it "that our conduct here be such as we may look back upon with pleasure. How greatly will it contribute to our happiness, if we shall be able to reflect with truth, that we faithfully and with affection discharged all the duties which our connection required? Still further, that we practiced every duty towards our neighbour; and every act of piety towards the great supreme?—Let us then ever strive to act this noble part." Several years later, he stated that he and Rebecca could "anticipate our departure hence" with pleasure, after they had fulfilled God's "wise purposes" and "performed the various offices in life which our stations and connections require."[45]

In 1788, Pickering wrote to his son John, who was being educated with relatives in Salem, enjoining him: "Above all, my dear child, remember your creator in the days of your youth. Piety, or constant reverence to God, and benevolence to your neighbours and to all mankind, are the great duties which will demand your daily and uniform attention. The good examples which will constantly be set before you in your uncle's family, joined with the natural goodness of your disposition will I doubt not preserve you in the way of virtue, and that is the only road to happiness in this world and the next. May God preserve you, my dear child, and make you eminently useful." Five and a half years later, Pickering wrote to tell John to "continue to write me frequently: for nothing can be more grateful than to receive continual manifestations of your proficiency in useful knowledge and perseverance in the paths of virtue, order and religion. These make you truly estimable, and daily more endear you to your affectionate father." In May 1796, after the death of his young son Charles, Pickering wrote again to two absent sons to inform them of their brother's death, acknowledging his own grief and disappointment. But he added that "we do not grieve as those who have no hopes beyond the grave. We look forward to a glorious resurrection to a life immortal," confident that Divine revelation not only "opens to us immortal life" but also "shows us the way to obtain it." "Thus our various duties to God, our creator and benefactor, to our neighbour, and to ourselves, are clearly delineated," he said, "and they are all concentrated in *love* or the exercise of *kind affection*. How happy would be the world, if we were 'kindly affectioned towards another?'" He never doubted that "by lives of piety and virtue" it was possible to "insure at least tranquillity in the world, and prepare for endless happiness in the next." By fulfilling all the duties of life according to one's rank and place, and by actively seeking to lead a life of virtue and piety, Pickering was confident that humanity would earn the everlasting approbation of God, as well as of its own conscience, and the reward due such earthly behavior in the life to come.[46]

John Adams also believed firmly in the rewards due to individuals whose lives had been shaped by the fulfillment of the duties of piety and virtue, which varied according to the ranks and abilities of individuals. As he mused in his diary in late April 1756, "Our proper Business in this Life is, not to accumulate large Fortunes, not to gain high Honours and important offices in the State, not to waste our Health and Spirits in Pursuit of the Sciences, but constantly to improve our selves in Habits of Piety and Virtue." Consequently, he added, "the meanest Mechanick, who endeavours in proportion to his Ability, to promote the happiness of his fellow men, deserves better of Society"—and of God as well, presumably—"and should be held in higher Esteem than the Greatest Magistrate, who uses his power for his own Pleasures or Avarice or Ambition."

For Adams, the "sure prospect of a happy immortality" was in fact a conditional prospect—something to be earned and merited by good and proper behavior, by making a life of piety and virtue habitual. "Our observing that the State of minority was designed to be an Education for mature Life, and that our good or ill Success in a mature Life, depends upon our good or ill improvement of our Advantages in Minority," he said, "renders it credible that this Life was designed to be an Education, for a future one, and that our Happiness or Misery in a future life will be alloted us, according as our Characters shall be virtuous or vicious." And he noted on another occasion in 1756, "God has told us, by the general Constitution of the World, by the Nature of all terrestial Enjoyments, and by the Constitution of our own Bodies, that This World was not designed for a lasting and a happy State, but rather for a State of moral Discipline, that we might have a fair Opportunity and continual Excitements to labour after a cheerful Resignation to all the Events of Providence, after Habits of Virtue, Self Government, and Piety." "And this Temper of mind," he noted, "is in our Power to acquire, and this alone can secure us against all the Adversities of Fortune, against all the Malice of men, against all the Opperations of Nature." "If I could but conform my Life and Conversation to my Speculations," he added, "I should be happy."

These speculations continued to shape Adams's piety and views for many years, since virtue and vice, rewards and punishments were themes of constant interest to him throughout his life. In 1770, for instance, he was still writing that "The Government of the Supream and alperfect Mind, over all his intellectual Creation, is by proportioning Rewards to Piety and Virtue, and Punishments to Disobedience and Vice. Virtue, by the Constitution of Nature carries in general its own Reward, and Vice its own Punishment, even in this World." But since there were so many exceptions to this rule on earth, Adams said, "the Joys of Heaven are prepared, and the Horrors of Hell in a future State to render the moral Government of the Universe, perfect and compleat."[47]

Abigail Adams, too, was certain that "The only sure and permanant foundation of virtue is Religion." She strongly urged her young son, John Quincy, in 1780 to "Let this important truth be engraven upon your Heart," as well as the conviction that "the foundation of Religion is the Belief of the one only God, and a just sense of his attributes as a Being infinately wise, just, and good, to whom you owe the highest reverence, Gratitude and Adoration, who superintends and Governs all Nature, even to Cloathing the lilies of the Field and hearing the young Ravens when they cry, but more particularly regards Man whom he created after his own Image and Breathed into him an immortal Spirit capable of a happiness beyond the Grave, to the attainment of which he is bound to the performance of certain duties which all tend to the happiness and welfare of Society and are comprised in one short sentence expressive of universal Benevolence, 'Thou shalt Love thy Neighbour as thyself.'" She was persuaded that "the Supreme Being made the good will of Man towards his fellow creatures an Evidence of his regard to him, and to this purpose has constituted him a Dependant Being, and made his happiness to consist in Society." But he also had the great duty of self-government set forth in order to become virtuous. As she told John Quincy, "'Virtue alone is happiness below,' and consists in cultivating and improveing every good inclination and in checking and subduing every propensity to Evil."[48]

In 1783, after two anguishing years of silence from her distant son, Abigail wrote to him again, acknowledging that her "anxieties have been and still are great, lest the numerous temptations and snares of vice should vitiate your early habits of virtue, and destroy those principles, which you are now capable of reasoning upon, and discerning the beauty and utility of, as the only rational s[o]urce of happiness here, or foundation of felicity hereafter." "Placed as we are in a transitory scene of probation," she wrote, and "drawing nigher and still nigher day after day to that important crisis which must introduce us into a new system of things, it ought certainly to be our principal concern to become qualified for our expected dignity." In order to be "qualified" and thus to merit future happiness, Abigail urged her son in a subsequent letter to be sure to see to it that his "mind be thoroughly impressed with the absolute necessity of universal virtue and goodness, as the only sure road to happiness, and may you walk therein with undeviating steps." As her husband had told their twelve-year-old daughter in 1777, "To be good, and to do good, is all We have to do."[49]

Eliza Lucas Pinckney of South Carolina shared Abigail Adams's confidence in the outcome of a life of piety and virtue. Born in the West Indies, educated for several years in England, raised an Anglican, young Eliza came to South Carolina with her family at about the age of fifteen in 1738. She remained there for most of the rest of her life, both before and after her marriage in 1744 to Charles Pinckney, a wealthy and prominent Charlestonian. In 1741, just as her brother was about to enter the army to follow his father's profession, she wrote to recommend that he "be particularly careful of his duty to his Creator, for nothing but an early piety and steady Virtue can make him happy." The following year, she wrote to him again to urge that he pursue the Christian "scheme," which meant "To live agreeably to the dictates of reason and religion, to keep a strict guard over not only our actions but our very thoughts before they ripen into action," adding that "to be active in every good word and work must produce a peace and calmness of mind beyond expression." She was fearful "least you should be infected with the fashonable but shameful vice too common among the young and gay of your sex," she told her brother; "I mean pretending a disbelief of and ridiculeing of religion; to do which," she declared, "they must first Enslave their reason." And then, she asked, "where is the rule of life?" She was confident that he, too, upon calm examination and reflection would believe in revelation, just as she did; and that "if we lead a life of piety here, 'tis a life of all others the most pleasing and agreeable." As she observed in 1759, she had long seen "how closely connected piety and happiness are together and so far as we transgress the one we lose the other."

Following the death of her husband in 1758, after fourteen years of a marriage remarkable for its harmony and affection, Eliza Lucas Pinckney observed that her two sons and one daughter were "all the remains of the best and most valuable of husbands to whose memmory I owe all the gratitude, duty and affection that can be due to Virtue, the most steady, uniform and unshaken that could possess the heart of man." She fully supported her husband's earlier decision to place his sons in a private school in England, his primary concern having been "The care of their morals and forming their tender minds to early habits of Virtue and piety," as she wrote in 1760. Her husband seemed to her to epitomize a life of piety and virtue, thus ensuring his continuing role beyond death as an exemplary model for her children. Her husband's life, she said, "was one continued course of active Virtue," which made it even more anguishing when she considered the loss her children experienced in their father's death: "Their Example, the protector and guide of their youth and the best and tenderest parent that Ever existed is taken from them."

Several years later, she herself warned her distant son "to be very careful of what acquaintances you make and what friendships you contract, for much depends on the example and advice of those we are fond of, and deviations from Virtue," even small ones, she insisted, "are extreamly hard to recover." Some months afterward, she wrote again to her eldest son: "From you, my dear Child, I hope better things, for though you are very young, you must know the welfair of a whole family depends in a great measure on the progress you make in moral Virtue, Religion, and learning, and I dont doubt but the Almighty will give you grace and enable you to answer all our hopes, if you do your part," just as she believed her children's father had always done. Her husband's religion, like her own, "was true religion free from sourness and superstition," and she was confident that they would be joined together again in Heaven, where she hoped to find "a Union of Virtuous souls where there is no more death, no more separation, but virtuous love and friendship to endure to Eternity!" Convinced that God gave grace to those who sought it and who sought also to lead lives of active virtue and piety, Eliza Pinckney suffered intensely over the loss of her husband, but took comfort from the prospect of having children as virtuous and dutiful as her husband had been. By sustaining the habits of piety first implanted in childhood and constantly reinforced throughout their lifetimes, moderates could fulfill the high expectations set forth for them by their parents.[50]

The Renovation of Nature and the Growth of Grace

FOR MOST MODERATES over the centuries, salvation was considered to be the likely reward for a life of piety and virtue. Unlike evangelicals—for whom the traumas of the new birth marked both the transformation from a state of sin to a state of grace and a radical alteration in their perceptions of themselves, as well as in their relationships to others and to God—moderates rarely experienced an abrupt crisis in their lives or sensed the need for dramatic alterations in their own characters or modes of being. Instead of abrupt conversions, moderates usually passed from infancy through the successive stages of childhood, youth, adulthood, and old age to the final dissolution of their bodies at death in an unbroken process of development and growth. They rarely knew what it felt like to be reborn, nor did they feel compelled to have their own wills broken in order to be assured of being in a state of grace. But they often spoke of conversion and the need for regeneration in order to be saved—

though by these terms they meant very different things from their evangelical counterparts.

For moderates, conversion was a gradual process rather than an abrupt transforming crisis; the imagery of growth, nurturance, and development was associated with the gradual infusion of grace, which encouraged the development of habits of piety and fostered the fulfillment of the duties inherent in a life of virtue. Never feeling themselves to be totally depraved, they never felt the need for total regeneration. Never utterly impotent and without wills of their own, they always felt confident that their own wills were free and that they therefore could be responsible for their own choices and actions. Salvation thus was to be the result of their own choice and behavior rather than, as evangelicals believed, the result of free but unmerited grace. For most moderates, salvation was to be the reward for the good life of piety that every person who kept the passions and appetites under proper restraints and exercised the rational faculties for the purpose of self-fulfillment and the benefit of society could reasonably expect.

As a result of these persuasions, moderates rarely felt torn apart the way evangelicals so often did, rarely felt the acute anguish and terror that so often preceded the new birth. Even their conversions were to be experienced as gradual, temperate, and relatively reassuring developments —though for some this very process could bring about nagging doubts and uncertainties. Without the transforming experience of the new birth, the infusion of grace might never be felt with sufficient certainty to provide complete assurance of future salvation. Consequently, running through the lives of many moderates was a sense of ambivalence about their own capacities to lead lives of sufficient piety and virtue to provide evidence of the grace they still believed necessary for eternal life. But at least they knew where to look for the evidence they desired: in their outward lives and in their actual behavior, with respect both to themselves and to others. By being responsible for their own fates, they carried an onerous burden of duty and obligation, which they could never escape. But by fulfilling the various duties incumbent upon each individual by virtue of his or her station and rank, moderates could hope to gain both the approbation and the rewards that always had been granted to them in fulfilling the expectations of their superiors—parental and others.

Since moderates did not hate themselves and always believed that a properly bounded self-love was a source of happiness rather than the basis of damnation, they never felt the need to transform human nature altogether, preferring instead to think of the gradual development and fulfillment of human nature. Since human depravity and sinfulness were not total, human nature could be renovated and improved, so that the distinctions between unregenerated human nature and regenerated or gracious human nature were never sharp or distinct. As Perry Miller noted, "One of the most pronounced and widespread characteristics of

Puritan thought in the seventeenth century is the constantly increasing emphasis put upon the remains of God's image in fallen men. It made what seems a concerted effort to salvage as much as possible from the rubbish heap." Thus John Preston, a seventeenth-century Puritan, did not hesitate to declare: "There is in naturall men not onely a light to know that this is good, or not good, and a Conscience to dictate; this you must doe, or not doe, but there is even an Inclination in the will and affections, whereby men are provoked to doe good, and to oppose the Evill. And therefore the proposition is true, that naturall men have some truths, because they have this Inclination remaining, even in the worst of them." Speaking of the Covenant theologians of the seventeenth century, Perry Miller aptly observed: "They did not forget that grace is an influx from the supernatural, but they preferred to concentrate upon its practical operations in the individual, and to conceive of it, not as a flash of supernal light that blinded the recipient, but as a reinvigoration of slumbering capacities already existing in the unregenerate soul." "As in the ruins of a palace, so runs one of their favorite metaphors," Miller goes on, "the materials still exist, but the 'order' is taken away; grace reestablishes the order by rebuilding with the same materials."

Thus there was no abrupt or sharp break between the state of nature and the state of grace, but rather a gradual process of rebuilding and reconstructing human nature to conform to reason and to virtue. As the Reverend Ebenezer Gay, a Bostonian of the mid-eighteenth century, said in words that differed hardly at all from those written a century earlier by other moderates, "The Grace of God . . . doth not destroy a reasonable nature . . . but sublimate and refine it. It does not obliterate but exceedingly brighten, what remains of the natural image of God, since the fall. It restores reason to its government over human passions, and directs it to its proper exercise."[51]

The nineteenth-century Unitarians were convinced that "The aim of man's being . . . can be nothing less than to arrive at the full perfection of the nature with which God has endowed him. To stop short of this, is to leave the divine work incomplete." Their central preoccupation was with the development of character, and as Daniel Howe notes, " 'Regeneration' was the inward transformation of the personality which was the aim of Unitarian self-development." He also points out that "The doctrine that man's salvation lay in 'a progressive purification of the personality,' during which the faculties were gradually brought into their proper relations"—a process indistinguishable from that of rebuilding and of restoration discussed by previous generations—"was not invented in the nineteenth century, nor original with Harvard Unitarians. Its origins go back at least as far as the seventeenth century."[52]

For over two centuries, then, a major element in the religious sensibilities and convictions of moderates was the belief that the transforming process by which human nature was to be regenerated was gradual, almost imperceptible, yet vitally important—a process that enabled people to fulfill their potentialities for good in this life to some degree, and to anticipate the completion of this process in the life to come. In Charleston, South Carolina, the experiences that Alexander Garden, an Anglican, had with George Whitefield and other evangelicals convinced him of the necessity of stating publicly the grounds for his personal opposition to the doctrines of the new birth and to the notion of an instantaneous transformation of human nature at the time of conversion. He thought of conversion as a gradual process, which employed reason rather than exploiting the passions. Whereas the enthusiastic evangelicals "conceive and insist upon Regeneration, to be an immediate, instantaneous Work of the Holy Spirit, wrought inwardly on the Hearts or Souls of Men, critically at some certain Time, in some certain Place, and on some certain Occasion; and by which the whole Interiour is at once, in a Moment, illuminated and reformed; the Understanding open'd, the Will over-ruled, and all the Inclinations, Appetites and Passions, quite alter'd and turn'd from Evil to Good, from being corrupt and vicious, to being pure, virtuous and holy," Garden believed that regeneration was "not the absolute, sole, or instantaneous, but the gradual co-operative Work of God's Holy Spirit, for Mankind, in them, and with them as moral agents." For him, conversion was not an event but a process, a gradual unfolding and growth, which first began with God "Breathing, as 'twere, on their corrupt, stony, dead Hearts, a Breath of new Life, preparing them to receive the good Seed of the Word;—then, watering the good Seed sown, that it may take Root downward, and bear Fruit upward, may spring and gradually grow up, first the Blade, then the Ear, then the full Corn in the Ear"; "in a Word," he said, "gently Co-operating, assisting, striving together with them, throughout the whole Course of their Lives, that they may grow in Grace; advance from Strength to Strength, from lower to higher Degrees of Knowledge, of Faith, of Renovation of their Minds, of Virtue, of Righteousness and true Holiness towards that Perfection which is attainable in this present State, of becoming the Children of God, by Adoption, regenerate or new born." So that his point would not be lost on his readers, he added: "Thus, my Brethren, the Work of Regeneration is not the Work of a Moment, a sudden instantaneous Work, like the miraculous Conversion of St. Paul . . . but a gradual and co-operative Work of the Holy Spirit, joining in with our Understandings, and leading us on by Reason and Persuasion, from one Degree to another, of Faith, good Dispositions, Acts, and Habits of Piety."[53]

When Joseph Fish looked back over the life of his pious and dutiful daughter, Rebecca Fish Douglas, after her death in 1766, he remarked upon "her tender Affection and Duty to Parents, Reverence for God and respectful Notice of his Providences towards her Self and others, Patience in Tribulation and quiet Submission to Crosses, Forgiving Injuries and returning good for evil, Sympathy towards the afflicted and Loving kindness to every Creature"—all of which were the "Common Fruits of a true Christian Spirit." "May we not (I say, from hence) be induced to think, That Christ was formed in her, while very young, as the true Cause and Spring of Such a Sweet and tender Spirit, as Appeared in her, through the general Course of her Life? Had She never discovered any higher Evidences of a Special Work of Grace, than what we have seen already, Should we not be very rash," he asked, "in concluding that She was Lost! Amidst all the Vanities of youth and Imperfections of Life, We know not of any, that could be judged inconsistent with the Being of Grace." Similarly, Charles Chauncy observed in 1732 after the death of another young woman: "I don't remember she was able to fix upon the particular time, in which she tho't she might pass under a work of sanctifying grace. Nor is it at all to be wondered at: When it was never observed, that the principles of corruption were habitually predominant in her, in any part of her life." From "the first appearances of reason, and all along till the time of her death," he said, "her general temper and behaviour were such as gave grounds to hope, that from a child she was savingly converted to God." In the 1840's, Horace Bushnell summed up the persuasions of moderates over the past centuries when he declared that "the child is to grow up a Christian, and never know himself as being otherwise." "In other words," he said, "the aim, effort, and expectation should be, not, as is commonly assumed, that the child is to grow up in sin, to be converted after he comes to a mature age; but that he is to open on the world as one that is spiritually renewed, not remembering the time when he went through a technical experience, but seeming rather to have loved what is good from his earliest years."[54]

Moderates of most persuasions believed that gradual conversion was a cooperative effort between God and individuals, in which people chose to act according to God's will for them, in which there were various degrees of ability, of compliance, and of fulfillment of the expectations and hopes set forth by God for humanity. God usually chose to cooperate with people through the means of grace He had provided—the Bible, the sacraments, baptism, sermons, and prayer—the central methods of piety offered, in various ways, by most churches to their members. Cooperation was essential to most moderates, who usually insisted that grace was still a gift of God, but a gift that individuals came to merit by their actions and their participation in the process which culminated in their inward renewal.

The convictions that the human will was free and that reason was the dominant faculty of human nature were of enduring importance to moderates as the grounds for their assurance that regeneration was a gradual process in which people could and must participate in cooperation with the influence of Divinity itself. Moderates always believed that individuals *chose* to be gracious. The development of grace was thus an active process, not a passively receptive stance. Salvation came only by conscious, rational, and voluntary choice—a choice that was always influenced by God's will but never coerced or forced by Him. God gave people the means necessary for achieving grace, and thus of ensuring salvation; but the imperfections and frailties of human nature were such that a state of perfect assurance of grace was rarely possible on this earth. What counted most was the effort, not the perfection of its expression. As Perry Miller said, describing seventeenth-century New England Puritans, "As long as we are in the flesh, we can never wholly be rid of sin, and regenerate faculties will many times slip back into depravity." Nevertheless, it still was possible to believe "that in regeneration God deals with men as rational creatures, converts them by an influence of grace and yet also by a rational enlightenment. . . . God dispenses grace to us in a manner suitable to 'intelligent creatures, made after the image of God, capable of judging and discerning the Reason and Equity of things, and of arguing one thing from another, and choosing and preferring one thing before another.' We come to faith voluntarily, 'Our Understanding must be eyes to our Will, and entertain the reason for our so doing.' Though the Holy Ghost is 'the author or efficient of this work, yet he makes use of us in the working of it.' Because grace does not destroy but rectifies nature, conversion must come through the reason." As Miller so aptly and suggestively went on to note, "In orthodox Puritan theory, grace is not thrust upon the soul unexpectedly and abruptly, but is insinuated according to the laws of psychology through means." The implantation of grace thus became an almost imperceptible and nearly always slow process in which individuals were to be active participants through the act of self-preparation for the receipt of the gift of grace.[55]

Again, Samuel Willard pointed out that "the habits of grace come in undiscerned." Since people were rational, with free wills, he believed that in the process of infusing grace, the will "must not be forced, but led." Ernest Lowrie describes Willard's conception of the process of insinuating grace through the active and willing cooperation of the person involved:

> The descent of the Spirit into the whole man begins with a persuasion of the mind. Slowly but surely the Spirit "applies himself" through the means of grace so that the understanding is informed of the truth. By "insinuating himself into their minds," the Spirit "works them up to make a deliberate choice, which is not wont to be instantaneous." It takes time to comtemplate, to deliberate; it takes courage to undergo self-examination. . . .
>
> After the understanding grasps thoroughly "the force of those arguments used by the Spirit" and can "see and approve" through

"a rational conviction" the grounds of God's acceptance of a
sinner, then the will "willingly" or "voluntarily" reaches out "to
embrace the object."

As a result of this slow process, it is evident, as Lowrie notes, that "The
recipient of God's grace chooses freely the gift." Without the voluntary
choice made possible by free will, no person would be considered truly
gracious. This was what Richard Sibbes, a leading Puritan theologian,
meant when he declared that "Though God's grace do all . . . yet we must
give our consent."[56]

Moderates, rejecting the notion of determination that shaped the
convictions of most evangelicals, also rejected the necessity for breaking
the will in order to be saved. Throughout the seventeenth and eighteenth
centuries, moderates thought not in terms of breaking but of bending
the will to conform to the will of God. As Richard Greenham—a late-
sixteenth-century English Puritan who spoke for the doctrines of the
Covenant—said, "God is not pleased but with voluntary offering," so
that, as Norman Petit noted, "man must yield to the covenant of his
own accord." Greenham insisted that the will must not be forced or
broken but yielded to God voluntarily: "I mean not that yielding which
the Lord by his threatening or judgments as by strong hand getteth of
us, which is no voluntary submission but a violent subjection and con-
straineth us rather than allureth us to obey the will of the Lord: but I
mean that willing humbling of ourselves before the face of God which
cometh from an heart bleeding at the conscience of its own unworthiness." And Richard Sibbes commented: "It is not enough to have the heart
broken," for "a pot may be broken in pieces, and yet be good for nothing;
so may a heart be, through terrors and sense of judgment, and yet be not
like wax, pliable." The heart or will thus ought to be "like wax, pliable,"
able to accept the imprinting of grace and virtuous principles, flexible
and open to influence and molding, but still free to choose or to reject.[57]

In the mid-1740's, William Livingston observed to a friend in
Connecticut that he could not "boast that extraordinary divine illumina-
tion so common to your Country men, and so seemingly interfering, by
its irresistibleness, to our free agency, and the notion of our being subjects of moral government." "Not that I would pretend to deny," he
hastened to add, as so many other moderates also would, "(What is
beyond all contradiction,) that the Father of Spirits may nea often does,
influence the minds of men. For that the Supreme and Infinite Being
may have an immediate and easy access to the humane mind, whenever
he pleases, is beyond all reasonable question"—an assumption common
to most moderates. He then observed that

As he originally formed it, he must be perfectly acquainted with
its internal frame, and all the different ways in which it is capable

of being impressed, and with what variety and degree of force impressions may be excited in it, but this I say must certainly be consistent, at least in his generall method, with the natural and regular exercise of our moral powers, and not with that irresistible energy contended for by some late Enthusiasts, who by stretching a metaphor to the utter Confusion of all reason and morality, would from thence, argumentatively conclude, that mankind are purely passive in their reformation from vice to virtue; that it is in the Spiritual birth as in the natural, and that the Conversion of Sinners is *wholly* performed by a superior and irresistible agency. Thus upon the single authority of a metaphor, Men are reduced to meer Machines, void of intelligence and free volition within themselves, and totally directed by inward incitation and impulse, which is impudently contemptuous of the reason of Mankind, subversive of all Religion, and an open defiance to good Philosophy.

Yet for all these objections to the evangelical doctrines of the impotent will and passive receipt of grace, Livingston still felt constrained to add: "Not that I would be understood to mean, my Candid friend, that a man by the most exalted pitch of morality can merit immortal felicity, or that he can arrive to any perfection in holiness without the co-operation of Gods Spirit. But there is an exertion of our own powers indispensibly necessary, a previous preparation to give a suitable reception to the divine guest who will not visit the temple of our hearts . . . till the money-changers of evil dispositions be banished, and an activity that we are Capable of Exerting to subdue our wicked hearts." As Jonathan Mayhew observed, echoing Livingston's privately expressed views, "However free the grace of God is, it is manifest that he has required something of us in order to our salvation."[58]

By preparing themselves carefully over the course of time, people participated in the process of the infusion of grace; ultimately, they would be able to yield themselves freely to take part in the Covenant of grace being offered to them by God for their salvation. As Sibbes said, "we are God's by 'voluntary acceptance of the covenant of grace.' " John Winthrop, too, was "perswaded (notwithstandinge callinge for a diligent and faithful use of all good meanes) that a Christian cannot too boldly relye upon God whilst he yieldes him selfe in obedience to his will: for it dothe so fittly agree to the nature of a yonge Childe, whereunto we must be like, if ever we shall come in heaven." The imagery of yielding the will implies the ability to give up one's own will freely, without being coerced or forced; rather, one was persuaded, through reason and love, of the necessity for obeying the will of God. Though moderates wished to be obedient to the will of God, their obedience, unlike that of evangelicals, was voluntary.[59]

"The Bewitching Charms of Despotic Sovereignty": The Boundaries of Power

MODERATES KNEW FROM EXPERIENCE, beginning in earliest childhood, how powerful even the most limited authorities could be under certain circumstances, for they had grown up under a parental guidance that had shaped their characters persistently and effectively. From infancy, they had felt the pressures of parental expectations and sensed the manipulativeness of benevolent authority as they were gradually, almost insensibly, formed into dutiful, loving children and thence into temperate, virtuous adults. Authority, they knew from experience, need not be absolute or tyrannical in order to be powerfully coercive; but, to justify the exercise of such authority, it had to be perceived as being benevolent, exercised for the happiness and good of its subjects. As children, moderates complied with the wills of their parents cheerfully and willingly, freely choosing to submit themselves to such guidance. But in doing so, they became aware, even if not consciously, of the power of the authority that governed them. Unlike evangelicals—who felt overwhelmed and unwillingly subjected to parental power, and thus in need later of a sense of total submission to authority in order to be comfortable—moderates felt that parental power was more benign and left more room for their own desires and the fulfillment of their own inner needs and wishes. But they also felt under constant pressure, experiencing an unending source of tension that arose from the exacting expectations voiced by parents for the development of their children's characters. No wonder, then, that so many moderates grew to maturity with a deeply rooted ambivalence about the nature and the exercise of power, and a desire to ensure that all power, Divine as well as human, be limited and contained.

Self-control was a dominant motif of their temperaments, of course; but the need to feel that power in general was both under control and benign shaped their attitudes toward authority wherever it might be visible—in parents, in magistrates, in ministers, or in God. Absolute sovereignty, so central to the feelings and the thought of evangelicals, was abhorrent to most moderates, for it implied total power and unlimited authority over persons and things in this world. For evangelicals, absolute power in God and perfect obedience by individuals were dominant persuasions. The moderates always recognized that power and authority could be absolute, but they feared too that all forms of sovereignty, wherever they might appear, would be destructive of their own carefully nurtured sense of self and of liberty. As a result, moderates over the centuries sought and found various ways of ensuring that power in all its manifestations would be controlled, kept within bounds, and never allowed to become excessive.

For many moderates throughout the seventeenth century and well into the eighteenth century, the imagery of the Covenant provided the central paradigm by which they could express both their awe of absolute power and sovereignty and their assurance that, in practice, such absolute authority would be restrained. In striking contrast to the evangelical insistence upon the absolute sovereignty of God—whose power and authority could never be limited, contained, or bounded by anyone or anything, who was under no conceivable obligation to give the indispensable gift of grace to anyone—moderates of the Federal or Covenant persuasion (analyzed with such brilliance in the writings of Perry Miller and others) insisted that God willingly and freely chose to relinquish His unbounded sovereignty by entering into an unbreakable Covenant with people, in order to provide them with the means for their salvation. Once God entered into a Covenant with an individual, thus establishing a contractual relationship between two unequal but now related parties, salvation was assured through the compliance of the person with the terms of the agreement that bound the two parties together. In return for voluntary fulfillment of the obligations of the Covenant, which was simply the requirement of faith, salvation was assured. But a Covenant was invalid unless entered into freely and voluntarily, for, as Samuel Willard observed, "a covenant is a voluntary obligation between persons about things wherein they enjoy a freedom of will, and have a power to choose or refuse. It is a deliberate thing wherein there is a counsel and a consent between rational and free agents."[60]

One of the main virtues of the Covenant was that it allowed for reliable, trustworthy relationships to be established freely between parties of inherently unequal rank or power—not least between God and humanity. As John Preston noted happily, the fact that "the Creator" would be "wiling to enter into Covenant" with his "creatures" implied "a kinde of equality between us." No evangelical would have dared assert such a possibility, which would have seemed utterly blasphemous and sinfully proud. But the moderates of the Covenant tradition not only felt themselves to be at least potentially almost equals to God, but also were confident that the very fact that God would bind Himself to them through a Covenant revealed His benevolence and love for mankind. Most important of all, however, was their certainty that, as Perry Miller observed, "He has transformed Himself in the covenant into a God vastly different from the inscrutable Divinity of pure Calvinism. He has become a God chained—by His own consent, it is true, but nevertheless a God restricted and circumscribed—a God who can be counted upon, a God who can be lived with." John Preston imagined God telling mankind that He was willing to enter into a Covenant with individuals, which meant, God supposedly said, that "I will [b]inde my selfe, I will ingage my selfe, I will enter into bond, as it were, I will not bee at liberty any more, but I am willing even to make a Covenant, a compact and agreement with thee." This would provide all the certainty of ultimate salvation anyone could need or want, so long as they, in turn, fulfilled their part of the agreement. By virtue of the Covenant, moderates of the Federalist persuasion were able to acknowledge the ultimately absolute power of God while resting assured that, in practice, even His power was limited.[61]

Like moderate parents, God chose freely to deal with His children as rational, free agents, close but subordinate, dutiful, obedient, and respectful but never truly fearful. The presence of the Covenant ensured the reciprocity of the bonds uniting God's children with Him, for they had the comfort of knowing that "If we be hemm'd in within this Covenant, wee cannot break out." They were assured that, as Peter Bulkley declared, "God conveys his salvation by way of covenant, and he doth it to those onely that are in covenant with him . . . this covenant must every soule enter into, every particular soul must enter into a particular covenant with God; out of this way there is no life."[62]

By entering into Covenant with God, individuals acknowledged their obligations to lead a life of piety and virtue to the fullest extent of their imperfect capacities, and to fulfill all the duties which their subordinate but intimate relationship with God required. As Charles Chauncy put it, during a funeral sermon preached at the death of a prominent Bostonian, "He had upon his Mind an habitual Awe of God; not such an one as drove him from his Presence"; "not such an one as made his Life uncomfortable to him," he noted, "But his Reverence of the divine Majesty was mixed with Love to him, and a Child-like confidence in him. And it had a powerful Tendency to keep him from every Thing disrespectful towards GOD, either in Thought, Speech or Behaviour." "As in Children who have in their Minds a true Fear of their Parents," he added, "the Influence of this Passion is not to fill them with a slavish uneasy Dread, but it tends rather to engage their Care to behave towards them with all dutiful Submission." Chauncy, like other moderates, was convinced that "submission even to the Deity ought always to be exercised under the conduct of reason and good sense."[63]

The Covenant provided dependable grounds for fulfilling the obligations of obedience inherent in humanity's inferior rank in relation to God. Jonathan Mayhew exhorted his congregation, "Let us consider of the relation which God stands in to us, and of our obligations to him; and give him the glory that is due unto his name." As he observed, "the whole of religion, in the largest sense of the word, ought to be considered as the service of God, the supreme Governor of the universe," which required everyone "to form just sentiments concerning the Being whom we serve; to be suitably affected towards him; to cultivate those regards of esteem, love, reverence, &c. which the perfections of his nature, and his relation to us, demand." Since "Piety, or the love of God, is the first and principle thing in religion," Mayhew said, "as much as loyalty to our earthly sovereign, is the first and principal thing in the character of a good subject," this doubtless is "the reason why the decalogue, that summary of man's duty, begins with our immediate duty to our Creator." For Mayhew and others, "substantial religion" consisted "in the practice of these sublime and heavenly duties." After all, he was confident that "Christianity is principally an institution of life and manners; designed to teach us how to be good men, and to show us the necessity of becoming so."

In religion as in life, duty was the inescapable obligation of every person toward superiors, as it also was a powerful limitation upon the abuse of authority and power on the part of superiors—whether human or Divine. Moderates like Mayhew were confident, ultimately, that their relationship to God would protect them from absolute and tyrannical power, for in the world of finely gradated ranks and obligations, there could be no such thing as absolute authority or total power exercised by one person over another.

God, by His own free choice, acted like an earthly moderate parent— omnipotent yet bounded by the obligations inherent in His relationship to His dutiful and obedient children. Since God "is the father of all, so his government is paternal," Mayhew said, "free from all unnecessary rigor;— uniform and steady, in opposition to all capriciousness and arbitrary proceedings; and . . . in the words of the Psalmist, That he is good to all, and his tender mercies, over all his works." For Mayhew, "The consideration of an universal kind providence presiding over the world, is, to them that will give themselves time to attend to it, a ground of continual peace, and composure of soul. All we need concern ourselves about is to do our own duty; the rest belongs to God; and he will doubtless do his part well." He added, "He that is conscious of the integrity of his own heart, may have confidence towards God; and exult . . . in hope of happiness both here and hereafter." God thus seemed not only benevolent and kind, but also dependable and trustworthy to those who abided by their duties and fulfilled the obligations their dependent relationship placed upon them in this life, confident that their rewards would be forthcoming.

→ A benevolent, reliable, and trustworthy God, who governed His universe ordinarily by uniform laws accessible to human reason, seemed—to Mayhew and others—to be a most plausible and satisfying notion of Divinity. The absolute sovereignty and uncontrollable power, the unfathomable and inexplicable choices and actions, the immense distance that separated the uncovenanted God of evangelicals from humanity—all these seemed abhorrent notions to Mayhew. As he declared, speaking for countless others as well:

The superintendency of divine providence, if conceived of in a right manner, is one of the most pleasurable and delightful considerations that can enter into the mind of a reasonable creature, sensible of his own weakness and various imperfections. Indeed, if instead of a wise and infinitely gracious Being, one whose kind regards are extended to all his intellectual creatures; and one who governs the world with a view at promoting the moral rectitude, and so of advancing the happiness of his creatures and offspring; I say, if instead of such a Being as this, we, in our imaginations, place, at the head of the universe, a capricious, humoursome and tyrannical Being; one who loves and hates at random, and has no uniform, consistent, and benevolent design; we form a scheme of principles, more destructive of rational happiness than that of Atheism itself. For any man had rather be left to the mercy of atoms, and fate, and chance, or any other chimerical Deity, than be subjected to the pleasure of such a monster, as an all-knowing, infinitely powerful Being, destitute of a steady, uniform principle of justice and goodness; delighting himself in the exercise of a wanton, licentious omnipotence—

The very thought of such an "infinitely powerful Being," who did not abide by "a steady, uniform principle of justice and goodness" but instead preferred to exercise a "licentious omnipotence," was truly horrifying. Moderates could not imagine being in the hands of such an unbounded, all-powerful, unpredictable God.

Whether through the Covenant, or through the use of natural law, which governed the universe with steady, uniform, and rational principles, moderates believed that God voluntarily limited His omnipotence in order to bring about the happiness and the salvation of mankind. While the principles of nature and of religion both taught "us to look upon God as transcending all his creatures in mercy and goodness," Mayhew said, "no less than in power and greatness," it was "our relation to him" that was the source of the ability to "always think of him with inward joy and pleasure."

What can be more unreasonable than for those who in God have a Father and Friend and Patron; one who is tenderly concerned for their welfare, and does what he can consistently with the rules of wisdom, to promote their best interests; what is more unreasonable than for such, to entertain gloomy and melancholy thoughts; and indulge superstitious fears, and groundless suspicions? Were God a malevolent Being; were he an unreasonable Tyrant; were he an hard Master; were he an implacable and revengeful Being; instead of a merciful and faithful Creator; a compassionate Parent; a gentle Master; a righteous Judge; we might well think of him with horror and dread; and even wish a period put to his existence. For whilst such a Being sways the scepter of the universe, no one can be secure a moment; but had better, were it possible, vanish into nothing, than have his future welfare depend upon the precarious pleasure of such a Sovereign. Such a Being were unworthy of any love, trust, confidence or reverence; and would be the proper object of dread and horror, and hatred to every rational creature. But God forbid that we should conceive of him in this manner.[64]

Samuel Johnson agreed fully with Jonathan Mayhew on the assumption that absolute, unlimited power and authority, even in God, was contrary to the true nature of God's being and action. As he said, "I cannot think of a greater dishonor that can be done to Almighty God, than to represent him as arbitrary, considered as a governor and a judge, when he has taken abundant care throughout the whole Scripture . . . to represent himself, not as an arbitrary, but as a moral governor of the world; proceeding upon stipulations with his reasonable creatures; treating them, not as machines or stocks and stones, but as rational and moral agents, such as he hath made them; bestowing means and assistances, and using arguments, motives and persuasions with them, such as promises, threatenings, examples, and the like; and rewarding or punishing them according as they shall be found to have conducted themselves. Such is the notion or conception that I am obliged to entertain of Almighty God, and with which everything in the Scriptures, I think, is clearly consistent." Johnson was certain that the doctrine of election, held by many evangelicals, which supposed "a mere sovereign, absolute and arbitrary decision of the eternal fate of mankind, antecedent to, or without any consideration of, their personal behavior," would "destroy the very being of the New Covenant, and by consequence, the whole design and purport of all revealed religion."

Although Johnson was willing to admit that God "is not accountable to his creatures for any of his proceedings," he nevertheless also believed "that his own infinite wisdom, holiness, justice, and goodness must be a law to him from which he cannot vary." By such laws, even God was bound. In the end, Johnson thought that the "good and merciful God" would find ways "to justify his own conduct, and that the judge of all the earth will do nothing but what is right, and that every mouth should be stopped in the Great Day," not, he noted, "by dint of sovereign arbitrary and uncontrollable power, but, by an inward conviction of the equity, fitness and reasonableness of all his proceedings, with regard to the condition of every individual of his creatures." This certainty of the ultimate "equity, fitness and reasonableness" of all that God chose to do was the source of Johnson's sense of trust and confidence in the fulfillment of the rewards due a virtuous life on earth. Since God was subject to laws and limits, He could be expected to fulfill His part of the Covenant with His people, and to award them with life eternal as the result of their good life on earth.[65]

Just as God permitted Himself to be bound by secure and dependable limits, which hedged in his ultimate power and sovereignty, so too was it imperative, moderates believed, to place secure and dependable boundaries about the exercise of power by human beings in every aspect of their public political authority. As William Livingston observed in 1752, "Power of all Kinds is intoxicating; but boundless Power, is insupportable by the giddy and arrogant Mind of MAN." Power, like vice, tempted everyone, but particularly men, who generally wielded authority and power in the world; and Livingston knew well that "The frail and delicate Structure of the human Eye, is not more incapable of enduring the dazzling Lustre of the Sun, than the Heart of Man, the bewitching Charms of despotic Sovereignty."[66]

Moderates who sought to set boundaries and to create limits upon power would have concurred with William Livingston's opinion that "a King, who pursues the true Glory and real Greatness, will never aim at absolute Dominion." "Lawless Power," he declared, "is a Power over Slaves, and void of every Thing sublime and generous. Obedience by Compulsion, is the Obedience of Vassals, who without Compulsion would disobey. The Affection of the People is the only Source of a chearful and rational Obedience." Livingston insisted that monarchical power, like other power, was and ought to be limited, "check'd and restrained," thus acting within the proper boundaries of the Constitution. As John Dickinson observed, in response to the question what constitutes a free people: "Not those, over whom government is reasonable and equitably exercised, but those, who live under a government so constitutionally checked and controlled, that proper provision is made against its being otherwise exercised." These assumptions were to shape the consciousness and the thought of moderates throughout the eighteenth century, as historians have been demonstrating in a series of brilliant examinations of political ideology; but they were also intimately connected to the need for control, for balance, and for temperance that marked the moderate temperament. The controls, however, were often precarious; the balance could teeter, and temperance become excess.[67]

Power was seductive and dangerous, a passion that constantly threatened to become excessive; yet, duly controlled and limited, power was also essential. As John Trenchard and Thomas Gordon noted in *Cato's Letters*—written in England during the early 1720's, and destined to become the most influential expression of the ideology of radical whiggery both in England and the colonies during the eighteenth century—"Power is like Fire; it warms, scorches, or destroys, according as it is watched, provoked, or increased. It is as dangerous as useful." They were convinced that "It is the Nature of Power to be ever encroaching, and converting every extraordinary Power, granted at particular Times, and upon particular Occasions, into an ordinary Power, to be used at all Times, and when there is no Occasion; nor does it ever part willingly with any Advantage." Experience taught that "Unlimited Power is so wild and monstrous a Thing, that however natural it be to desire it, it is as natural to oppose it"; "nor ought it to be trusted with any mortal Man," they added, "be his Intentions ever so upright."

The radical Whigs like Trenchard and Gordon were constantly afraid of the encroaching nature of power because "Power is naturally active, vigilant, and distrustful; which Qualities in it push it upon all Means and Expedients to fortify itself," they said, "and upon destroying all Opposition, and even all Seeds of Opposition, and make it restless as long as any Thing stands in its Way. It would do what it pleases, and have no Check." Power thus posed an enduring and endless threat to liberty—which, they observed, "is the Parent of Virtue, Pleasure, Plenty, and Security; and 'tis innocent, as well as lovely." Power was always identified with masculinity, while liberty was perceived as feminine. Not surprisingly, then, Trenchard and Gordon believed that "In all Contentions between Liberty and Power, the latter has almost constantly been the Aggressor." But liberty could never exist without power, which though dangerous was essential: "whereas Power can, and for the most part does, subsist where Liberty is not, Liberty cannot subsist without Power; so that she has, as it were the Enemy always at her Gates." Liberty thus was perceived as being both innocent and passive—in need of defenses against the active, intrusive, masculine aggressiveness of power. The problem, then, was not to abolish power but to contain and limit it, to place secure and reliable boundaries around the exercise of power so that liberty could be secured and protected.[68]

The association of boundless power with men was evident to Abigail Adams, who wrote in March 1776 asking her husband to "Remember the Ladies" in "the new Code of Laws" that he and his fellow legislators might make, and to "be more generous and favourable to them than your ancestors. Do not put such unlimited power into the hands of the Husbands." "Remember," she said, "all Men would be tyrants if they could." She added unhesitatingly, for her husband's benefit: "That your Sex are Naturally Tyrannical is a Truth so thoroughly established as to admit of no dispute, but such of you as wish to be happy, willingly give up the harsh title of Master for the more tender and endearing one of Friend. Why then, not put it out of the power of the vicious and the Lawless to use us with cruelty and indignity with impunity. Men of Sense in all Ages abhor those customs which treat us only as the vassals of your Sex." "Regard us then," she urged, "as Beings placed by providence under your protection and in immitation of the Supreem Being make use of that power only for our happiness."

Abigail Adams thus envisaged the relationships of wives and husbands in terms of the subordination and duty that had always combined to ensure the practical limitation of power and of authority within the moderate family. She did not envisage equality between wives and husbands, for the dependency and passivity associated with femininity made it seem unreasonable to expect women to take an active role in public affairs. John Adams's reply evoked the traditional limitations taken for granted by generations of moderates as practical boundaries upon masculine power and authority; nevertheless, it also revealed clearly the unexamined anxiety about masculine dominance that lay behind the need for such rigid male authority within the family as Abigail deplored: "As to your extraordinary Code of Laws, I cannot but laugh. We have been told that our Struggle has loosened the bands of Government every where. That Children and Apprentices were disobedient—that schools and Colledges were grown turbulent—that Indians slighted their Guardians and Negroes grew insolent to their Masters. But your Letter was the first Intimation that another Tribe more numerous and powerfull than all the rest were grown discontented." John Adams declared that his wife should "Depend upon it, We know better than to repeal our Masculine systems." "Altho they are in full Force," he acknowledged, "you know they are little more than Theory. We dare not exert our Power in its full Latitude"— thus inadvertently admitting the accuracy of her charge of "unlimited power" in the "hands of the Husbands." "We are obliged to go fair, and softly, and in Practice you know We are the subjects. We have only the Name of Masters, and rather than give up this, which would compleatly subject Us to the Despotism of the Peticoat, I hope General Washington and all our brave Heros would fight."* But power—as Abigail knew, and John too, in different, less personally threatening contexts—without reliable and established limits always could become excessive, and thus tyrannical. Her point made, she still felt the need to tell her friend Mercy Otis Warren about the exchange with her husband, observing that "as all Men of Delicacy and Sentiment are averse to Excercising the power they possess, yet as there is a natural propensity in Humane Nature to domination, I thought the most generous plan was to put it out of the power of the Abitrary and tyranick to injure us with impunity by Establishing some Laws in our favour upon just and Liberal principals."69

Abigail's desire to establish laws as permanent and effective limitations upon the abuse of power—so important to her husband and to other moderates in the area of political thought and institutions—met with resistance when translated into the touchy relationships that bound men and women together as husbands and wives. There men evidently felt the

---

* The subconscious power of Adam's phrase—"the Depotism of the Peticoat"—is suggested by the knowledge that he, too, had worn petticoats in his early childhood. As he noted in 1817 with respect to John Hancock: "We were at the same school together, as soon as we were out of petticoats" (Charles Francis Adams, ed., *The Works of John Adams, Second President of the United States*, 10 vols. [Boston, 1854], X, p. 259).

need to shore up and augment their own authority in order to preserve their sense of superiority. Yet they also knew, as Benjamin Franklin observed, that "It is the Man and Woman united that make the compleat human Being. Separate, she wants his Force of Body and Strength of Reason; he, her softness, Sensibility and acute Discernment. Together they are more likely to succeed in the World." As with power and liberty, both the masculine and the feminine traits of temperament were indispensable for a sense of wholeness and of balance, though the chain of being always justified the superiority of the masculine over the feminine. But excess of any kind was undesirable to moderates; so they always lived with an uneasy balance between the masculine and the feminine components of the self, just as they also lived with an awareness of the uneasy balance between power and liberty in the world. Only by keeping each in proper order and within proper limits could their security be assured.[70]

"The Choice of Hercules":
Manliness or Effeminacy?

THE PREOCCUPATIONS WITH POWER AND LIBERTY were only two facets of a general theme that underlies many aspects of the moderate experience and thought, although often hidden and disguised. The theme is manliness, and its counterpart, effeminacy. As we have seen, the concern for self-control, for keeping tight reins upon the appetites and passions, and for ensuring the supremacy of reason and the intellect as the governors of the self, burdened many moderates with an unceasing sense of tension, evident in both their life and thought. The preoccupation with self-government, with setting limits upon feelings as well as behavior, with constantly striking a balance between desire and duty, as well as the awareness of being always surrounded by temptations to move beyond the self-set boundaries—all these aspects of the moderate temperament revolved around a central pivot, the point which connected so many of the dualities shaping their consciousness. The pivot was their sexual identity, the point of balance between their masculine and feminine impulses, sensibilities, and feelings. Moderate men, however, always weighed the balance in favor of masculinity; and their preoccupation with self-control reflected their concern to ensure that the masculine components of the self would dominate the feminine components.

Moderates often liked to think of their piety as "manly," and the emphasis they placed upon reason in religion was an oblique way of asserting the superiority of those qualities of temperament that were perceived as masculine over those associated with the passions, which were perceived as feminine. While still a young man thinking of following a career in the ministry, John Adams fantasized about the nature of a Christian "Eutopa," in which a nation took "the Bible for their only law Book, and every member" regulated "his conduct by the precepts there exhibited." He imagined that "Every member" of the nation "would be obliged in Conscience to temperance and frugality and industry, to justice and kindness and Charity towards his fellow men, and to Piety and Love, and reverence towards almighty God," a place, in other words, where Adams believed "a rational and manly, a sincere and unaffected Piety and devotion, would reign in all Hearts." For Charles Chauncy, too, piety was manly and rational. He could not believe that it was "reasonable to think, that the Divine SPIRIT, in dealing with Men in a Way of Grace, and in Order to make them good Christians, would give their Passions the chief Sway over them." "Would not this be to invert their Frame?" he asked, "To place the Dominion in those Powers, which were made to be kept in Subjection?" Chauncy obviously believed, as moderates generally did, that "Reasonable Beings are not to be guided by Passion or Affection," and that they always needed "a due Ballance of Light and Knowledge in their Minds." As he said, "The plain Truth is, an enlightened Mind, and not raised Affections, ought always to be the Guide of those who call themselves Men; and this, in the Affairs of Religion, as well as other Things."[71]

For many moderates, however, the balance between reason and the passions, between an enlightened mind and the affections, between masculine and feminine impulses and sensibilities, proved to be a difficult one to maintain. Precisely because moderates desired to incorporate *both* parts of these dualities within the self, they often found themselves anxious about their ability to maintain their self-control. For all their intense desire to become virtuous, to ensure the governance of reason, to balance and moderate their temperaments, and to establish a habitual preference for a life of piety, moderates also felt the lure of excess and the possibility of succumbing to the temptations of the world. The world could be a seductive place, with many possibilities for exceeding the permissible limits they constantly set for themselves. The masculine elements of the self thus always seemed to be at risk, susceptible to domination by the feminine elements of the self, which provided a constant source of temptation for moderate men. Virtue stood ever endangered by vice, and moderation always could be overwhelmed by excess.

Thus the lures of the world required constant vigilance on the part of moderates—a sense of guarded involvement and an awareness of the ever-present dangers represented by the passions and appetites of the self. As Eliza Lucas Pinckney wrote to her son, Charles, during his stay in England in 1761, "you will be in a City surrounded with temptations with every youthful passion about you. It will therefore require your utmost vigilance to watch over your passions as well as your constant attendance at the Throne of Grace."[72]

Mercy Otis Warren, too, warned her son: "What vigilance is necessary, when the solicitations of thoughtless companions on the one side, and the clamour of youthful passions on the other, plead for deviations; and even stand ready to excuse the highest instances of indulgence to depraved appetite!" "If you escape uncontaminated," she noted, "it must be in some measure by learning early to discriminate between the unoffending mirth of the generous and open hearted, and the designed flighty vagaries of the virulent and narrow minded man." And the following year, she observed that "The knowledge of the world teaches to shun the snares thrown out to the unwary and unsuspecting and qualifies to become more amiable companions than if confined wholly to books. But the knowledge of ourselves my son is a science of higher importance;— this teaches to resist the impulse of appetite, to check the sallies of passion, at the same time it leads to certain permanent happiness, and renders us useful to society." From Mercy Otis Warren's perspective, there was no doubt whatsoever that "the great business of life is the regulation of the passions and the subjugating those appetites which tend to inflame them and to weaken the powers of the mind until it forgets the law of reason."[73]

In 1781, John Adams prayed for his distant son, hopeful that God would "bless" his "dear Son, and preserve his Health and his Manners, from the numberless dangers, that surround Us, wherever We go in this World." And Abigail Adams observed, after her eldest son had departed for Europe with his father, "There are many snares and temptations," which "may stain his morals even at this early period of life." But "to exclude him from temptation," she said, "would be to exclude him from the World in which he is to live, and the only method which can be persued with advantage is to fix the padlock upon the mind." Yet even when safely under lock and key, the minds of moderates remained conscious of the seductiveness of the world in which they lived. Experience taught them that the freedom of choice they valued so highly could be immensely burdensome, a source of unending anxiety over their ability to choose virtue and ignore the temptations of vice, and thus to assert the primacy of the masculine reason over feminine passion and feeling.[74]

John Adams exemplifies the anxieties and ambivalence characteristic of many moderates who were individuals of intense passions but nevertheless sought to govern themselves as reasonable, temperate people. For Adams, the classical fable of Hercules and the choice that he faced provided an endless fascination; it seemed to epitomize the ambivalence that lay at the center of Adams's own character. As early as 1759, he recorded in his diary: "The other night, the Choice of Hercules came into my mind, and left Impressions there which I hope will never be effaced nor long unheeded." He decided to write a fable suited to his "own Case," which began with Virtue addressing him with the question: "Which, dear Youth, will you prefer? a Life of Effeminacy, Indolence and obscurity, or a Life of Industry, Temperance, and Honour?" Virtue's advice, which Adams felt compelled to give to himself, was to "return to your Study, and bend your whole soul to the Institutes of the Law, and the Reports of Cases. . . . Let no trifling Diversion or amuzement or Company decoy you from your Books, i.e. let no Girl, no Gun, no Cards, no flutes, no Violins, no Dress, no Tobacco, no Laziness, decoy you from your Books." After two nights "and one day and an half, spent in a softening, enervating, dissipating, series of hustling, pratling, Poetry, Love, Courtship, Marriage," he thought that "During all this Time, I was seduced into the Course of unmanly Pleasures, that Vice describes to Hercules, forgetful of the glorious Promises of Fame, Immortality, and a good Conscience, which Virtue, makes to the same Hero, as Rewards of a hardy, toilsome, watchful Life, in the service of Man kind." All of the themes that were to continue to fascinate and haunt Adams for years to come are present in this fantasy: seduction, temptation, effeminacy, manliness, industry, fame, and watchfulness.[75]

So central was this imagery to Adams that he proposed that Hercules should be imprinted on the seal being designed for the newly confederated states in August 1776. He imagined "The Hero resting on his Clubb. Virtue pointing to her rugged Mountain, on one Hand, and perswading him to ascend. Sloth, glancing at her flowery Paths of Pleasure, wantonly reclining on the Ground, displaying the Charms of her Eloquence and Person, to seduce him into Vice." Again in 1780, Adams wrote to Abigail from Paris, acknowledging that "There is every Thing here that can inform the Understanding, or refine the Taste, and indeed one would think that could purify the Heart." "Yet it must be remembered," he added, "there is every thing here too, which can seduce, betray, deceive, deprave, corrupt and debauch it. Hercules marches here in full View of the Steeps of Virtue on one hand, and the flowerly Paths of Pleasure on the other—" and there were few, he noted regretfully, "who make the Choice of Hercules." "That my Children may follow his Example, is my earnest Prayer: but I sometimes tremble," he acknowledged, "when I hear the syren songs of sloth, least they should be captivated with her bewitching Charms and her soft, insinuating Musick."[76]

The imagery that surrounds the choice of Hercules in Adams's successive versions of the fable is that of masculinity and of femininity—hard versus soft, rugged versus indolent, manly versus effeminate. Like Adams in his own youth, Hercules is always in danger of being "seduced into the Course of unmanly Pleasures." Adams was afraid of being thought soft, indolent, passionate, and of being weak or subordinate; the choice confronting him, like Hercules, was to assert the predominance of the traits he perceived as masculine. In effect, despite all the great seductiveness of his feminine impulses and desires, the arduous and unpleasant impulses of masculine virtue must be preferred. Fear came from temptation—from an ever-present lure to deny the hardiness, rigor, and rationality associated with manhood for the soft, light, pleasant impulses of feminine vice. Men were supposed to be rational, women more passionate. And men above all, perhaps, were meant to be superior. To succumb to the lures of feminine seductiveness would be to relinquish the sense of superiority inherent in being a man. And that neither John Adams nor any other moderate male was prepared to do. But the preoccupation with the fable of Hercules revealed just how difficult the role of masculinity seemed to some people. The fact that there was a *choice* to be made at all was sufficient to provide men, at least, with a constant source of inner anxiety.

A similar set of choices confronted Thomas Jefferson in 1786 after the departure from Paris of Maria Cosway, a married woman whom he loved with uncharacteristic passion. In a letter to her, he fantasized about a dialogue between the Head and the Heart, the enduring dialogue that always preoccupied moderates between reason and the passions, between the intellect and their feelings. The Head observed that "Everything in this world is a matter of calculation. Advance then with caution, the balance in your hand. Put into one scale the pleasures which any object may offer; but put fairly into the other, the pains which are to follow, and see which preponderates. . . . Do not bite at the bait of pleasure, till you know there is no hook beneath it." "The art of life," Jefferson observed, speaking still as the Head, "is the art of avoiding pain; and he is the best pilot, who steers clearest of the rocks and shoals with which it is beset." The imagery of being guided through life, cautiously steering clear of the dangers that lay on either side, captures the sense (so characteristic of moderates) of always balancing between dangerous extremes. Although "Pleasure is always before us," the Head also noted that "misfortune is at our side: while running after that, this arrests us." The Head's advice, under the circumstances, was "to retire within ourselves, and to suffice for our own happiness . . . for nothing is ours, which another may deprive us of." Hence, Jefferson adds, "the inestimable value of intellectual pleasures."

The response of the Heart was altogether opposed to the proposal "to wrap ourselves in the mantle of self-sufficiency." It insisted instead that "friendship is precious, not only in the shade, but in the sunshine of life," and was confident that "thanks to a benevolent arrangement of things, the greater part of life is sunshine." The Heart insisted that control of the Head be contained within "the proper limits of your office. When nature assigned us the same habitation, she gave us over it a divided empire. To you, she allotted the field of science; to me [the Heart], that of morals. . . . Morals were too essential to the happiness of man, to be risked on the uncertain combinations of the Head. She laid their foundation, therefore, in sentiment, not in science." Nevertheless, even the Heart had to acknowledge to the Head that "you pretend authority to the sovereign control of our conduct, in all its parts; and a respect for your grave saws and maxims, a desire to do what is right, has sometimes induced me to conform to your counsels." And while the Heart recognized that "We have no rose without its thorn; no pleasure without alloy," Jefferson acknowledged openly that "when I look back on the pleasures of which it is the consequence, I am conscious they were worth the price I am paying." Therein lay one of the principal differences between the temperament of Jefferson and that of his friend Adams, for Jefferson, at least occasionally, was willing to pay the price for pleasures, while Adams never could.[77]

Perhaps Jefferson was more at ease with both his masculine *and* his feminine sensibilities than Adams, who always felt more endangered and threatened by the passions and appetites both within and without. But both men were agreed upon the persistent dialogue between the Head and the Heart, which, as moderates, they could not escape. Yet even Jefferson ordinarily concurred that the inner balance they desired and felt to be necessary in order to achieve a sense of inner equilibrium was to be weighted in favor of reason (the Head) and the masculine side of the self, rather than in favor of the passions (the Heart) and the feminine side of the self.[78]

Among the most compelling passions moderates felt within themselves was that of their own sexuality. The fact that Jefferson wrote a dialogue between the Head and the Heart to one of the few women he appears to have loved was not accidental, but surely a response to his own sexual passion (if not its fulfillment) for Maria Cosway. The evidence is sparse, yet suggestive always of the desire to balance sexual desire with temperance and self-control. John Adams noted with pride in his autobiography that although he "was of an amorous disposition and very early from ten or eleven Years of Age, was very fond of the Society of females," nevertheless "No Virgin or Matron ever had cause to blush at the sight of me, or to regret her Acquaintance with me. No Father, Brother, Son or Friend ever had cause of Grief or Resentment for any Intercourse between me and any Daughter, Sister, Mother, or any other Relation of the female Sex." "My Children," he added, "may be assured that no illegitimate Brother or Sister exists or ever existed." Adams believed that he owed "this blessing to my Education." "My Parents," he recalled, "held every Species of Libertinage in such Contempt and horror, and held up constantly to view such pictures of disgrace, of baseness and of Ruin, that my natural temperament was always overawed by my Principles and Sense of decorum." "This Blessing," he added, "has been rendered the more prescious to me, as I have seen enough of the Effects of a different practice."

Since Adams, like Jefferson, did not marry until nearly thirty, his life of continence except within the bounds of marriage provided notable evidence of the governance of reason over the passions. Benjamin Franklin, of course, seems to have been the exception among the well-known figures in mid-eighteenth-century America, since he acknowledged in his autobiography that "that hard-to-be governed passion of youth hurried me frequently into intrigues with low women that fell in my way." Yet during the subsequent years of his life, after his marriage, there is remarkably little evidence suggesting that his sexual life was one "either of promiscuity or its opposite." Franklin obviously enjoyed the company of women while abroad, yet his prolonged absence from his wife might suggest, among other things, an uneasiness with his sexuality. Indeed, one might well wonder about the prolonged absences of such men from their wives in the light of their feelings about their own sexuality. Public life could have been a way to evade sexual passions, as well as to gratify the obligations of duty and political service so essential to many moderate men.[79]

Unlike evangelicals, however, who warred against their sexual passions even when succumbing to them, moderates felt comfortable with sexuality within proper bounds. As Abigail Adams observed in 1785, "The human mind is an active principle, always in search of some gratification," and thus she favored "those writings which tend to elevate it to the contemplation of truth and virtue, and to teach it that it is capable of rising to higher degrees of excellence than the mere gratification of sensual appetites and passions" (which implies that they are thus to be enjoyed within bounds). Similarly, John Adams noted that "Love, that divine Passion, which Nature has implanted for the Renovation of the species, and the greatest solace of our Lives: virtuous Love, I mean, from whence the greatest Part of human Happiness originates," was intended by God to be "both a Duty of our Nature and the greatest source of our Bliss." But he was dismayed by "these modern seminaries"—local taverns—which "have almost extinguished or at least changed into filthiness and brutal Debauch" this great and virtuous passion. The proper path was one of moderation and temperate enjoyment of sensual pleasures, not the guilt and shame that prompted the denial of the flesh by so many evangelicals. Still, moderates usually were most comfortable when the passions were weak and reason strong, for then they enjoyed the pleasures of nature without feeling endangered by vice. So long as they felt themselves to be under control, they could enjoy the reasonable desires of both the body and the passions, and thus combine properly their masculine and their feminine impulses. But the temptations to transcend these boundaries were always present, and vice never ceased to be alluring.[80]

The temptations extended to other pleasures as well, which could also exceed their proper bounds and make a person too effeminate. Eliza Lucas Pinckney observed to a friend, "That there is any real hurt in a pack of Cards or going a suet [sweet] figure round the room [while dancing], etc., no body I believe are obsurd enough to think, but tis the use we make of them." "The danger," she went on, "arises from the too frequent indulging our selves in them which tends to effaminate the mind as it takes it of[f] of the pleasures of a superior and more exalted Nature as well as waists our time." As she noted, "where these airry pleasures have taken intire possession of the mind the rational faculties are more and more unactive," which convinced her that "'tis not playing a game at Cards or going to a ball now and then to relax the mind—but the immoderate love of them is sinful." That was always the issue, just as moderation was always the goal. Unlike evangelicals—for whom even such pleasures were dangerous, sinful, to be forbidden altogether—moderates could enjoy the temperate pastimes of cards and dancing, but not their excessive indulgence. For that, of course, would make them feel "effeminate," and would compromise the dominance of manly reason even in the lives of women such as Mrs. Pinckney. John Dickinson summed up the position best, observing that "Moderation in everything is a Source of Happiness—Too much writing—too much reading—too much eating—too much Drinking—too much Exercise—too much Idleness—too much loving—too much Continence—too much Law—Physics—or Religion—all equally throw us from the Balance of real Pleasure." But the temptations to excess were always to be guarded against and warded off, so that the needed balance could be maintained.[81]

Unbounded Passions: Ambition, Avarice, and Anger

IN A LESS VISIBLE but not less significant way, the interest of moderates in the issues of masculinity and femininity extended to other central and enduring passions as well. The need for self-control, for balance, and for regulation applied with particular force to three passions that preoccupied many moderates: ambition, which involved the assertion of the self and thus was considered to be a masculine prerogative; avarice, which led to the indulgence of the self through wealth and luxury and indolence, and was thus considered to be a feminine inclination; and anger, which involved the failure of self-control and excessive passions, and thus seemed unmanly. None of these passions was thought to be unworthy of human nature if kept within the proper bounds. But the fear of losing control, of ceasing to be within bounds, of being subject to excessive and unreasonable passions, provided one of the enduring themes of moderate experience and thought.

"How unbounded is ambition and what ravages has it made among the human Species," Abigail Adams observed to her friend Mercy Otis Warren. Yet she also added a significant qualification: "This passion of

Ambition when it centers in an honest mind possess'd of great Abilities may and often has done imminent Service to the World. There are but few minds if any wholy destitute of it, and tho in itself it is Laudible yet there is nothing in Nature so amiable but the passions and intrest of Men will pervert to very base purposes." Her association of ambition with men was not accidental, nor was her belief in the perversion of an otherwise natural and worthy passion unusual.[82]

For her husband, two things especially at once fascinated and repelled him throughout his life—fame and fortune, or, in the coupled terms that recur so repetitively in his private and public writings as to become one of the central themes of his life, ambition and avarice. These were to be the enduring temptations and the most seductive passions of John Adams's life, posing the most difficult choices that he, like Hercules, constantly confronted. They reflected the uneasy balance within Adams of his masculine and his feminine impulses, and always seemed to threaten him by escaping the bounds he placed around both.

When Virtue offered Adams the choice in 1759 between "a Life of Effeminacy, Indolence and obscurity"—distinguishing traits of femininity—and "a Life of Industry, Temperance, and Honour"—the active and ambitious traits of manliness—Adams responded with a renewed vigor in asserting his own eager desire and preference for "Activity, Boldness, Forwardness," which he knew "will draw attention." He was unwilling to "confine" himself "to a Chamber for nothing," studying the law. "Ile have some Boon, in Return," he declared, "Exchange, fame, fortune, or something." Three months later, he noted in the privacy of his diary that "Reputation ought to be the perpetual subject of my Thoughts, and Aim of my Behaviour. How shall I gain a Reputation! How shall I Spread an Opinion of myself as a lawyer of distinguished Genius, Learning, and Virtue." The same ideas were still on his mind four days later. As he thought about the pleasure associated with "a gradual ascent to fame and fortune," he imagined that "the Pleasure that they give will be imperceptible"; but, he told himself, "by a bold, sudden rise, I shall feel all the Joys of each at once." "Have I Genius and Resolution and Health enough for such an attchievement?" he wondered. The previous year, when Adams had asked himself, "What are the Motives, that ought to urge me to hard study?" his answer included "The Desire of Fame, Fortune and personal Pleasure." On another occasion, however, Adams noted in his diary: "I begin to feel the Passions of the World. Ambition, Avarice, Intrigue, Party," adding, of course, that "all must be guarded." Unguarded and unbounded, these passions posed a constant threat to his sense of inner security and propriety. Yet his early desire to assert himself, to be esteemed, honored, and recognized, to assert his masculine sense of superiority and accomplishment in the world at large, never could be quelled, even when it threatened to get out of control and thus to make him exceedingly anxious.[83]

John Adams knew that he was an intensely ambitious man. Thomas Hutchinson, drawing upon observations over many years, observed that Adams's "ambition was without bounds," and, Hutchinson added, "he has acknowledged to his acquaintance that he could not look with complacency upon any man who was in possession of more wealth, more honours, or more knowledge than himself." Though neither Hutchinson nor Adams knew then that he was destined to become President of the new Republic, the intense ambitiousness which Hutchinson and others discerned, and which Adams both recognized and sought to keep within bounds, would dominate his life and thought for more than half a century. As a result, Adams constantly deplored excessive ambition in others as he tried to guard against the powerful passion that continually sought to dominate him too.[84]

Along with the unslakable thirst for fame and distinction that shaped Adams's temperament went a persistent fascination with wealth and all that usually goes with fortunes. As the son of a modest farmer, Adams never forgot that he had had to make his own way in the world and to gather his worldly wealth by his own industrious labors in the law. Hutchinson was correct about Adams not being able to "look with complacency" upon men of greater wealth than himself, for his diary reflects a constant sensitivity and hostility toward people of greater wealth and elegance. It was not an accident that Adams presented Hercules' choice in 1772 as the choice between "the Ascent of Virtue"—which involved climbing "a Mountain quite inaccessible, a Path beset with Serpents, and Beasts of Prey, as well as Thorns and Briars," with precipices, gulfs, and the sword of Damocles all threatening those who sought to climb up—and the prospect of "Pleasures, of every Kind, Honours, such as the World calls by that Name, and showers of Gold and Silver." Six months earlier, Adams had noted: "It has been my Fate, to be acquainted, in the Way of my Business, with a Number of very rich men." "But there is not one of all these," he asserted, "who derives more Pleasure from his Property than I do from mine. My little Farm, and Stock, and Cash, affords me as much Satisfaction, as all their immense Tracts, extensive Navigation, sumptuous Buildings, their vast Sums at Interest, and Stocks in Trade yield to them. The Pleasures of Property, arise from Acquis[it]ion more than Possession, for what is to come rather than from what is." "These Men feel their Fortunes," he noted disapprovingly. "They feel the Strength and Importance, which their Riches give them in the World. Their Courage and Spirits are bouyed up, their Imaginations are inflated by them. The rich are seldom remarkable for Modesty, Ingenuity, or Humanity. Their Wealth has rather a Tendency to make them penurious and selfish." Several months later, he sat down to take stock of himself at the age of thirty-seven, aware of how little money and property he had accumulated for himself and his family, and "determined" that "my own Life, and the Welfare of my whole Family, which is much dearer to me, are too great Sacrifices for me to make. I have served my Country, and her professed Friends, at an immense Expense, to me, of Time, Peace, Health, Money, and Preferment, both of which last [i.e., avarice and ambition] have courted my Acceptance, and been inexorably refused, least I should be laid under a Temptation to forsake the Sentiments of the Friends of this Country."[85]

The choice of Hercules always involved temptations and seductions—especially those of ambition and fortune—for virtue always resulted from the active choice of individuals to keep themselves within proper bounds, to watch and guard themselves against the allurements of vice and passion that surrounded them. While Adams might hope, by devoting himself "wholly to my private Business, my Office and my farm," to be able to "lay a Foundation for better Fortune to my Children, and an happier life than has fallen to my Share," he also knew, as the intensity of his preoccupation with the seductions of wealth and fame testify, that excess in anything was dangerous. He comforted himself subsequently with the thought that, as he said, "I was not sent into this World to spend my days in Sports, Diversions and Pleasures. I was born for Business; for both Activity and Study. I have little Appetite, or Relish for any Thing else." He could never forget that although some of his contemporaries, mostly lawyers and merchants, had grown rich, like John Lowell of Newbury port, who built himself "an House, like the Palace of a Nobleman, and lives in great Splendor," he was still "Poor in Comparison of others." But the temptations were always there, always requiring the utmost care to resist the lures of avarice. The constant linkage in Adams's writings of avarice with ambition was not accidental, for they formed two of the major passions that moderates must watch and control. They were very tempting—and very dangerous.[86]

Benjamin Franklin as a youth also experienced the tempting passions that preoccupied Adams. Among his articles of belief, which he wrote out for himself in 1728, Franklin expressed his hope "That I may avoid Avarice, Ambition, and Intemperance, Luxury and Lasciviousness," a list that corresponds remarkably well with Adams's concerns, though Franklin managed in the course of his long lifetime to give himself considerably more leeway than Adams. But the preoccupation with simplicity and industry that runs throughout his writings also suggests the constant concern with being seduced by the passions of ambition and of avarice, and thus disrupting the balance needed for self-approbation.[87]

The loss of self-control was perhaps most evident in the passion of anger, which seemed to be too intense, too excessive, too frightening a passion to be expressed freely and directly by most moderates. Indeed, the inner goal of moderation and temperance in all things made anger seem unwarranted. Moderates often contained their anger effectively, thus producing at least the appearance of tempers that were equitable, calm, and reasonable—the manly and self-controlled temperaments they prized so highly.

Many moderates felt sufficiently at ease within themselves to have remained peaceable and tolerant of others even under the most provoking circumstances, indicating the absence of repressed anger within their temperaments. The Reverend John Lowell, for instance, found himself at odds with some of the ardent evangelical members of his church in Newbury, Massachusetts, who, during the Great Awakening, separated from his congregation and set up a new purified church of their own. Replying to a letter from a committee of the separates early in January 1744, Lowell said that "I know Brethren it is the language of the day with some People, that the Churches of our Lord Jesus Christ (walking in the faith and order of the Gospel, being of one mind, and living in Peace,) are in a dead state, but I believe that they are never more likely, than when in this state, to have the God of Love and Peace with them." He reminded his former church members that he had devoted himself to the ministry for eighteen years, and preached the doctrines of the Gospel as he understood them; yet "to be called Pharisee, blind and represented as wanting a sense of the great and important things of religion, or their not being imprest upon my own soul, Unskilfulness, Unfaithfullness and all other things that can be said against me are no more than have in these times, been said of the greatest and best of men among us." He could not think his "Company would be acceptable to such as preferred the advice, and sat under the teaching of one who has made it his constant Practice to revile me, and publickly as well as privately inculcated the Danger of hearkening to me, representing me as unconverted, blind, and leading Souls to hell, who has shamefully entreated my Fathers and Brethren in the Ministry, declaring he saw the mark of the Beast in the face of one of the Ministers of this Town."

Lowell then addressed himself directly to the charge by the separates of his being angry himself in his discussions with them:

Brethren when you mention my being in a Passion or angry when you have been discoursing with me, I must say that I am not conscious of my having treated any of my People, when they came to me upon Spiritual accounts, with any desire of my help, but with the utmost Tenderness and many are my witnesses how much I have born the Indiscretions and follies of many without any Emotion of Spirit, nay astonishing to multitudes has been the Temper which I have exprest under the most insulting and provoking Carriage—In my own house I have been to an unheard of degree abused—I have been threatened, I have had the foot stamp'd, and the Fist shook at me, when I have been calm by reasoning upon the Disorders of the times, was this intreating me like a Father? When in express words the lie was given me in my own house by one of you, did I not with the utmost calmness shew him how he was mistaken in a matter of fact? and when he was made sensible of his mistake, did I any other than gently reprove him for his being so abusive?

Lowell's self-defense suggests that he valued self-control and the immediate expression of anger rather than the hostile language and bottled-up anger that had erupted in the words and actions of some of his parishioners.[88]

Similarly, the Reverend John Barnard, minister of a church in Marblehead, Massachusetts, could look back over a long life and observe that "My church and congregation have once or twice been in danger of being thrown into a controversy; but a good and wise God has been pleased so to direct me, in the management of the affairs, that the fire has been quenched before it broke out into a flame; though I had some of the chief and stubbornest spirits to deal with; and now for more than one and fifty years we have enjoyed great peace and unity among us, as any church in the country." Many of these qualities were captured in a portrait penned by the Reverend Isaac Stiles, of Newport, describing an elderly Connecticut man, Dr. Joshua Babcock, who died at the age of seventy-six. He had been "educated a Sabbatarian Baptist, and was always a man of strict morals," "no Deist but a firm Believer of Revelation," who read "the arminian polite Divines" and "liked what is called a sensible rational polite Religion." He was a man who was "much for Moral Virtue," Stiles noted, and "was really generous and catholic in his Charity and Benevolence towards all Christian Sects—and never spake of or treated any of them with Acrimony and unkindness." Quaker moderates, of course, were noted for their calmness, temperance, and their peaceable ways; but other moderates also often felt themselves sufficiently at ease with their consciences and the world to avoid the feelings of anger and hostility that beset evangelicals with such remarkable ferocity. When their tempers were in balance and their self-control assured, moderates indeed could be what they hoped to be, and thus were able to be more charitable and benevolent toward others than most evangelicals usually felt capable of being.[89]

Yet precisely because self-control was so difficult to achieve for some moderates, anger posed a continuous threat to their inner equilibrium. Many moderates seemed to others to be more acerbic, passionate, and contentious than they themselves would have wished to be. John Adams, Charles Chauncy, and Jonathan Mayhew, for instance, each possessed a temperament that valued self-control while also being extremely volatile and passionate. Similarly, Landon Carter noted after "another domestick storm," which "began with a Joke," that "our tempers are such that both Mr. Carter [his son] and myself forgot the bounds of our convixions." However, he hastily added, "though I don't record it as an excuse or Justification I must be persuaded I am not the aggressor." That, of course, was a commonly shared desire.[90]

The presence of anxiety in some moderate temperaments often provided the emotional source for the expression of anger and hostility. The theme of temptation and seduction which shaped the consciousness of many moderates, such as the Adamses, elicited anger as well as anxiety, which was directed toward the sources of temptation wherever they might be found in the world at large. For moderates such as these, the inner balance and self-control so essential to their sense of well-being and inner security were difficult to sustain. Their passions were too intense to permit an easy accommodation to the governance of reason. Moderation for such people thus was always an achievement, not something to be taken for granted. The fear of losing control always lay behind the feelings of anger, even if the latter were sometimes both experienced and expressed.

Diversity and Order
in Church and Community

IN STRIKING CONTRAST to evangelicals, whose temperaments propelled them on an urgent quest for purity in both their churches and the world at large, moderates over the centuries were able to accept the imperfections of the self and the world and to live with more diversity of belief and behavior than evangelicals could tolerate. Yet moderates also were preoccupied with order, since a sense of order both within the self and in the outer world was essential to their confidence that they lived in a rational, balanced, and free manner in their families, communities, and churches. As Charles Chauncy said, "Good Order is the Strength and Beauty of the World.—The prosperity both of *Church* and *State* depends very much upon it." But evangelicals and moderates differed profoundly in their perceptions of what constituted "good order" in both communities and churches. Evangelicals insisted that order always necessitated uniformity in the beliefs and behavior of the individuals who constituted any truly pure and gracious group, so that every person's private will was to be submitted wholly to the will of God, who alone provided the rules of conduct and of piety that ought to govern life. Moderates, however, insisted that order implied diversity in the beliefs and behavior of individuals, who had free wills and might choose different personal paths to a life of virtue, duty, and piety. Moderates cherished unity, but they did not believe that it was disconsonant with diversity. Indeed, they usually valued differences of belief and of behavior so long as they seemed reasonable, prizing them as indispensable elements of the balance they desired and as necessary elements for the preservation of liberty itself.[91]

By denying the necessity for purity and uniformity, moderates were able to envisage and to foster churches and communities that contained a diverse and varied population—which, ideally, included nearly everyone. As a result, the radically sharp division between saints and sinners, between the regenerate and the unregenerate, between the saved and the damned, between the pure church and the sinful and corrupt world, which evangelicals sought, seemed both unnecessary and undesirable to moderates. Instead of being exclusive in their responses to others, moderates generally were inclusive—seeking to incorporate within a single body all those people who might wish to be a part, yet assuring each of the right to liberty of conscience and freedom of choice within the various institutions (familial, religious, communal, and political) that formed the community as a whole. Their inner consciousness of the freedom of their own wills led them to value the freedom of choice for others as well, just as their sense of self-love often enabled them to trust the benevolence and love of others. Yet their intense sense of duty and of place, which assured them space to be themselves, also linked them inextricably to others.[92]

Moderates generally would have agreed with the opinion of the Reverend Richard Baxter, an eminent English Anglican preacher, who declared in the seventeenth century that "I would not be a Member of a Church gathered out of many Parishes, in such a Place as London: Cohabitation is in Nature and Scripture Example, made the necessary Disposition of the Materials of a Church." Baxter, like most moderates, could not understand the urgent desire on the part of so many of his contemporaries to separate from the standing churches and to form pure churches of their own. Separatists persistently rejected the traditional notion, still powerfully persuasive to Baxter and to other moderates, that church membership was synonymous with residence, with "Co-habitation," and came with the simple act of being born within the religiously defined community. Evangelicals rejected this definition of a church, insisting instead upon membership consisting exclusively of those who had experienced the new birth—a membership both voluntary and pure. Residence was inconsequential to evangelicals, for their church members stood apart from the world rather than being indistinguishable from the residents of the secular community.[93]

The emphasis placed by moderates of various persuasions upon nurture and growth in grace, the whole conception of regeneration as a gradual, almost imperceptible process of renovation that was never to be fully completed or fulfilled in this life, fostered their desire for churches which encompassed the whole community—sinners as well as saints, everyone whatever their degree of grace and piety. Ebenezer Frothingham was basically right in 1750 when he charged, with horror and dismay arising from his own thirst for purity and righteousness: "The Churches that we have separated from generally hold, that external Morality is the Door into the Church, and that the Lord's Supper is a converting Ordinance; or that all have a Right to join with the Church, that will make an outward public Profession of Christianity, altho' they be unconverted."[94]

Throughout the seventeenth and eighteenth centuries, moderates of all persuasions sought to extend rather than to contract the boundaries of church membership, to incorporate as many people as possible under the watch and government of churches. The evangelicals, on the other hand, sought always to exclude the unregenerate, to ferret out and banish the hypocrites from among the saints within the pure churches they had supposedly established as islands of Christian grace surrounded by the threatening seas of vice and damnation.

In New England, the moderate tendency to extend the boundaries of church membership was evident within the first generation. But it became pronounced with the maturing of the second and third generations, not all of whom experienced the new birth or were able to meet the established requirements of grace for membership in the churches. By the early 1660's, the development of the practice that came to be known as the Half-way Covenant created within many New England congregations a new category of membership for the as yet unregenerated children of saints. The children of regenerate saints thus could be accepted as members of the churches (without the privileges of voting or taking the sacraments) by acknowledging their baptismal covenants and agreeing to place themselves under the discipline of the church, in anticipation of eventually receiving the grace they hoped for and sought. Over the course of time, many churches opened even the sacraments themselves to the unregenerated, arguing that participation in the celebration of the sacraments could be part of the process of conversion itself, a means provided by God for the transmission of grace to His children. But the ferocious controversies that often erupted in New England congregations over the degree to which membership would be opened and extended signaled the persistent purism of many of the evangelicals within the congregations.[95]

The issue of the nature of church membership never ceased to cause contention and friction. Although some churches retained a form of purity by including only the certifiably gracious as voting members, others moved to include virtually the entire body of inhabitants who might wish to join the church. The process of identifying the church with the entire parish or community, rather than with only a small group of regenerated saints, has been traced by many historians; but it is essential to note that moderates nearly always preferred their churches to be as inclusive as possible. They could tolerate the uneasy and confusing mixture of saints and sinners within the same body, for they felt increasingly certain that membership itself was one of the major means for communicating and nurturing the growth of grace. If habits of piety and virtue were to be instilled and sustained in the people, churches must seek to include as many as possible within their boundaries. In effect, the equation of residence within a parish with membership in the community church—for moderates often still cherished the ancient ideal of a single church in each separate parish—became a major theme in moderate thought and writings.

When evangelicals challenged the conception of inclusive membership, and sought to separate from the standing churches to form pure churches of their own—thus dividing themselves visibly from the rest of the inhabitants of the community, declaring the members of the standing churches to be corrupted and unregenerate and thus enemies of God— moderates found their own moderation and tolerance subjected to intense pressure and strain. When moderates rose in defense of the standing churches, insisting upon the maintenance of the bonds and covenants that bound people together, they believed that they were defending their churches, their communities, and their society as a whole against the seemingly corrosive individualism which they perceived at the core of the evangelical spirit. As moderates, they were not hostile to individualism— indeed, they valued their own uniqueness and prized themselves highly— but they were convinced that individualism always needed to be balanced by the duties and obligations incumbent upon individuals as members of the larger community.

The relationship of individuals to the public political community was explored during the early 1720's by John Trenchard and Thomas Gordon, whose political assumptions (articulated in the pages of *The Independent Whig* and *Cato's Letters*) appealed to moderates on both sides of the Atlantic. When Cato asked, "What is the Publick?" he answered: "the collective Body of private Men, as every private Man is a Member of the Publick." He added the observation that "as the Whole ought to be concerned for the Preservation of every private Individual, it is the Duty of every Individual to be concerned for the Whole, in which himself is included." Cato was confident that "True and impartial Liberty" was "the Right of every Man to pursue the natural, reasonable, and religious Dictates of his own Mind; to think what he will, and act as he thinks, provided he acts not to the Prejudice of another." Cato admired religion when informed by the principles of reason and subject to the controlled expression of the passions and the fulfillment of the duties of piety; but he deplored the "mad Freaks of an Enthusiast," who seemed to epitomize bigotry and unreason from his perspective.[96]

Cato was insistent upon liberty of conscience in religious as well as political matters, being aware of the persistent tendency toward the suppression of differences by ardent religious zealots, and convinced that "Bigotry, standing upon the Ruins of Reason, and being conducted by no Light but that of an inflamed Imagination, and a sour, bitter, and narrow Spirit" was capable of every form of "Violence" and "Barbarity." Whether in religion or in politics, he believed that liberty required the preservation of individual opinions and differences, while at the same time demanding that individuals subordinate their own private interests to the interests of the public whenever necessary—but without denying their individuality altogether. In considering the nature of "Publick Spirit," Cato noted, "I will readily own, that every Man has a Right and a Call to provide for himself, to attend upon his own Affairs, and to study his own Happiness. All that I contend for is, that this Duty of a Man to himself be performed subsequently to the general Welfare, and consistently with it. The Affairs of All should be minded preferably to the Affairs of One."[97]

But Cato also knew from experience that men differed over the meaning of public spirit, and over the degrees of subordination of individual interests and happiness that were necessary for the good of the community as a whole. "There is a Sort of Men found almost every where," he noted, "who having got a Set of gainful and favourite Speculations, are always ready to spread and enforce them, and call their doing so *Publick Spirit*, though it often turns the World topsy-turvy." The crux of Cato's argument rested upon his conviction that "Opinions, bare Opinions, signify no more to the World, than do the several Tastes of Men; and all Mankind must be made of one Complexion, of one Size, and of one Age, before they can be all made of the same Mind. Those Patrons therefore of dry Dreams, who do Mischief to the World to make it better, are the Pests and Distressers of Mankind, and shut themselves out from all Pretence to the Love of their Country: S[t]range Men! They would force all Men into an absolute Certainty about absolute Uncertainties and Contradictions; they would ascertain Ambiguities, without removing them; and plague and punish Men for having but five Senses." Cato thus was adamantly against the possibility that unity and harmony within the community could be achieved by imposing uniformity of opinion upon all members of the public. Unity and happiness did not imply absolute agreement on principles or practices, but resulted from every individual pursuing the interests best suited to his or her own particular tastes and opinions. Uniformity of opinion could never signify the presence of liberty, but only its opposite—tyranny.[98]

William Livingston—whose essays in *The Independent Reflector*, published in New York during the early 1750's, were profoundly influenced by the writings of Trenchard and Gordon published three decades earlier in England—also shared Cato's sense of the due subordination of individuals to the public community, while also valuing diversity and private conscience highly. "If we trace the Wisdom of Providence in the Harmony of the Creation; the mutual Dependence of human Nature, renders it demonstrably certain," he wrote, "that Man was not designed solely for his own Happiness, but also to promote the Felicity of his Fellow-Creatures. . . . Every Person born within the Verge of Society, immediately becomes a Subject of that Community in which he first breathes the vital Element; and is so far a Part of the political Whole, that the Rules of Justice inhibit those Actions which, tho' tending to his own

Advantage, are injurious to the public Weal." Like Cato, Livingston was certain that the very presence of differences of opinion and of interests within the political community would ensure the preservation of liberty; by balancing one opinion against another, and by each guarding against excessive power, authority, or encroachments from others, the liberty of the public as a whole would be protected. When considering the establishment of a new college in New York, he argued vigorously against the proposal to make it a denominational college, run and controlled by a single religious group. He was confident that "as we are split into so great a Variety of Opinions and Professions; had each Individual his Share in the Government of the Academy, the Jealousy of all Parties combating each other, would inevitably produce a perfect Freedom for each particular Party." Livingston thus argued early in the 1750's that public liberty was best preserved through the constant contention of different groups or parties—religious or political—within the community as a whole, an argument that depended in large measure upon the assumption, common to most moderates, that the body politic was constituted of graduated ranks, with distinctive callings, interests, and opinions.[99]

In many ways, moderates often proved themselves to be conservative people—respectful of the past, committed to the institutions of the present, and eager to ensure the future commitment of subsequent generations to the same values and institutions. Their temperaments fostered their conservativism, with their desire for order, balance, harmony, and temperance, their sense of self-approval and self-respect, of duty and obligations, their willingness to live with imperfection yet also to strive for a life of virtue and piety. Their desire for self-control also fostered the desire for a world that was similarly under control, providing them with the sense of security that came from familiarity and reliability. Unlike evangelicals, whose temperaments and piety so often made them intensely discontented with themselves and with the institutions that impinged upon their lives, so that they were eager to regenerate and thus transform the world in which they lived, moderates usually preferred to maintain the status quo and to live with the institutions with which they were familiar. Nevertheless, many moderates also felt uncomfortable with institutions and with the world generally whenever they suspected that the balance, order, and controls they valued might be altered or undermined, or changed significantly. As a result, the stance of moderates also could be visibly ambivalent, and thus subject to change as the world about them changed. So long as the proper degrees of order, balance, and control were evident in the religious and secular worlds, they could sustain their preferred self-image of moderation, reason, and virtue, leading lives designed to secure happiness both for themselves and others. Sometimes this was possible; at other times it was not. Depending upon circumstances, therefore, the ambivalent moderate would either find self-fulfillment or experience an anxious discontent.

PART FOUR

THE GENTEEL:
The Self Asserted

❧ VI ❧

Affectionate Families:
Genteel Modes of Child-Rearing

THE EMERGENCE OF A NATIVE AMERICAN GENTRY throughout the colonies, which began in the mid-seventeenth century and continued unabated throughout the eighteenth century, coincided with the development of distinctive patterns of family life that set many families of wealth, eminence, and power apart from their contemporaries of both evangelical and moderate persuasions. Many of these gentry families had much in common with the attitudes and sensibilities of the moderates, and they continued to shape the relationships of parents and children according to the attitudes and assumptions characteristic of the moderate temperament. In many ways, the genteel style of child-rearing and of family life which emerged particularly in New England and in the Middle colonies continued to bear the imprint of the values and attitudes of moderation. Yet by the middle of the eighteenth century, if not before, some families had begun to rear their children in ways that would have seemed sinfully and dangerously indulgent to most moderates. These families of ease and elegance, whose material circumstances seemed secure and whose life style often conformed to the models for gentility developed in England and eagerly emulated throughout the colonies if never copied with exactitude, were notable for the intensity of their affection and love for the members of the family. Fond affection rather than conscientious discipline shaped the relationships between the generations. Yet simultaneously these families also emphasized the necessity for correct and proper behavior within the family context. They thus combined an extraordinarily intense and binding affection with an equally intense awareness of decorum and distance. As a result, the dominant theme that marked many gentry families was "love and reverence." Fear was inconceivable, duty was taken for granted, so that reverence—a sense of awe, respect, and intimate distance—and unbounded love distinguished these families from most of their contemporaries.[1]

"Our Family Circle"

TO AN EXTRAORDINARY DEGREE, genteel families cherished and fostered a sense of domesticity and intimacy within the family group. There is an intensity about their preoccupation with their families that is quite remarkable, and the imagery of the "family circle," which appears in the correspondence of some families in the second half of the eighteenth century, captures the essence of the sense of an enclosed and geographically bounded group, cohesive and harmonious, intimate and contained, but separate from the world surrounding it. The imagery of a circle was apt, for it captured dimensions of family experience and family values that seemed to mark the members of these genteel families both with a devotion to each other within the household—parents, children, and grandparents—and with a sense of separation or at least of far less involvement with more distant kin and neighbors. Unlike moderates, whose sense of kinship and of connection with more distant members of their families and their neighbors was often immensely complex and influential, members of many gentry families seemed to be more self-consciously set apart from the world in which they lived. These genteel families had a sense of profound obligation toward and connection with their kindred. Yet what mattered most to them was not the distant but the close members of their families—their own children above all, but their parents, brothers, sisters, and in-laws as well. The household thus became the focal point for a pleasurable and valued intimacy between the generations, the one secure place where peace, harmony, and love reigned and everyone could feel secure in the affection and respect of all.

The family of Governor Thomas Hutchinson, the most eminent and admired as well as the most ardently hated defender of British authority in colonial Massachusetts, epitomized the sense of intimacy and domesticity characteristic of genteel families in the mid-eighteenth century. As Bernard Bailyn has noted, "The family group was extraordinarily close: the force of cohesion that bound them fits no ordinary description. It was not merely that they lived together harmoniously until the older children married . . . nor that their family letters over a period of almost fifty years express continuing affection, intimacy, and trust. More than that: they could not bear to break away, and sought to keep the group intact, to tighten the bonds, even in the centrifuge of marriage." Kinship ties played a powerful role in shaping the lives of the Hutchinsons, since a series of marriages bound them together with the Sanfords and the Olivers.

Mary Hutchinson's memories of her years in the Oliver household corresponded to the experiences of her Hutchinson in-laws in their own family circle, for they preferred to live together or close at hand so as never to lose touch. About a decade later, after the anguishing exile from their beloved estate at Milton and all their friends and connections in Massachusetts, Mary Hutchinson wrote to someone—perhaps her father— in America from England to observe that independence "is not [an] Affliction to me . . . I only regret my separation from those I so dearly love." But she was contented in England, because she had "the Best of Husbands—one whose aim and endeavour is to soften the cares of Life, and make me happy." "Whilst Heaven spares me this invaluable blessing I shall be rich indeed," she added. "I have four children who in dividing my time and attention are a constant source of employment and pleasure— Mr. H[utchinson] sometimes calls them his Fortune—his Family Estate and boasts of his Riches." Having lost everything else—fortune, estate, business, and country—the Hutchinsons remained secure in their attachment and devotion to one another. The family circle remained the one thing that continued unabated until death disrupted it.[2]

The sense of family cohesiveness and affection that bound the Hutchinsons together also shaped the sensibilities of the Allen family of Pennsylvania. James Allen was the son of one of the wealthiest and most prominent men in the colony—Chief Justice William Allen—and in time became a lawyer of wealth and standing too. He continued to have close relationships with his three brothers and two sisters. In 1777, after the family scattered about owing to the war, Allen retired to his country estate, keeping himself "very busy in gardening, planting &c," and longing "most ardently to see my brothers, whose society would at this time be peculiarly desireable." "There are few families," he noted in his diary, "who live on terms of purer love and friendship than ours; which is owing not only to natural affection, but the conviction of each others integrity and disinterestedness."

These convictions obviously were of the utmost importance to Allen's concept of a gentleman's family such as his. In February 1778, the death of his brother John "was to me the most afflicting in my whole life," he said, after learning "of the death of the most affectionate of brothers and best of men. As I loved him, with the warmest and purest affection, my distress was infinite." His brother had been "the most dutiful and affectionate son, the fondest husband and parent, the most disinterested and kindest brother and the most indulgent master that ever lived. . . . He was distinguished for his courtesy, affability, modesty, humility and good-breeding. . . . His good nature, chearfulness and condescension, were uniform and unaffected and made him the delight of all who knew him." Significantly, Allen added, "What shall I say of the sentiments of his own family where his vast worth was fully known! He never had a thought or design in which his own interest was seperate from theirs; to advance which he would have sacrificed every pleasure and advantage. With us," his family, "he ever lived on terms of the purest love and disinterested friendship." By the summer of 1778, several of Allen's brothers had been forced to take refuge with the British troops, thus irretrievably casting their lots with the loyalists, while Allen himself remained uneasily behind on his country estate, appalled by independence yet unwilling to depart with his brothers. "Our family, linked together by the purest and most disinterested affection is totally unhinged," he noted sadly.[3]

But even under the most trying circumstances, which unhinged many families through uprooting and exile during the 1770's and 1780's, the sense of family affection and intimacy fostered an intense and sustaining feeling of happiness in the midst of suffering. In 1799, long after the traumas of the revolution were over, Marianne Belcher, the wife of Andrew Belcher, wrote to her sister-in-law in New England from Halifax, Nova Scotia, to give her "an account of our little ones—I never saw four finer healthier Children—and their minds keep pace with their bodily strength." Two of the children were in school, and two still at home. "My little Edward," the youngest child, "is the flower of the flock," she wrote. "I never Saw a lovelier little Creature—your Brother is very fond of them all." "I wish you could Sometimes peep into our family Circle," she added; "it would be difficult to find a happier Group."[4]

For families such as these among the affluent, educated, and socially eminent ranks of the American gentry, the domestic group formed a cohesive and intensely affectionate group of parents and children together, occasionally, with some of their other kindred. The family circle was felt to be the most secure place in the entire world—happy, embracing, forgiving, reliable, and free from selfishness. The members not only felt an extraordinarily strong sense of love for one another, they also felt an equally intense sense of obligation and of interest in one another. The family thus became something larger and more important than any single member, with an interest which incorporated the separate and private interests of each member into a familial identity that transcended but never seemed to be contrary to the interests of each individual bound into the group. The group which formed the family was narrow in scope and limited in size, contained virtually within the walls of the household itself, or at most within the walls of several interconnected households. Within these genteel households, however, were nurtured both the affection and the respect between the generations and between relations that were to become characteristic of the genteel family. Children were cherished and adored—a source of constant delight and pleasure to parents, whose affection for their offspring knew no bounds.*

---

* The impression one gets from the letters and family papers of genteel families is that most families had relatively few children being born or growing to maturity. Only careful demographic analysis will confirm or refute this impression, but two studies do suggest the possibility of fewer children in nonevangelical families than in evangelical families, or at least indicate the possibility of such differences occurring.[5]

"*Children Much Indulged*"

TO MANY OUTSIDERS, the most striking characteristic of genteel families was their unbounded indulgence of their children. By the standards of discipline and obedience that shaped the households of evangelicals and moderates, the children of genteel families too often seemed undisciplined, too free in their behavior, spoiled in their clothes and diet, vain, arrogant, and unchecked.

In Philadelphia, Ann Head Warder deplored the indulgence of children by many of her relatives and friends, some of whose children seemed to her to be "like tyrants. My heart inwardly mourned," she said, "at the mistaken kindness of parents who [unwisely?] indulge their children in this country, to an excess which I doubt not terminates in many a ones ruin. I have many times warmly expressed my disapprobation of their unjustifiable treatment—suffering them to range at freedom, intermixing with just such companions as best suit their inclinations." "Oh what a detestable and much to be despised custom," she declared in the privacy of her diary. Several months later, she observed that young "Tommy Fisher is all attention, or Sally," his mother, "would not be happy, as she seems of a rather fretful disposition." "Don't manage her children to my mind," she declared. "Overlooking them very improperly and at other times indulging them as much"—a method that she believed "will destroy the best tempers." A week later, she noted contentedly in her diary that her friend Sally Parker was "exceedingly fond" of her son, as "indeed all" were, adding the pleasing observation that "But tho my own boy, I know not who can help it, his conduct differs so greatly from all here, which is the remark and admiration of every one, though they will not summon courage to pursue the road" and thus follow her own paths of parental discipline. "For from foolish indulgence to every wish," she believed, "they know not what to want and so are always fretting." "Anthony Morris is a living witness," she declared. "His inclinations must never be crossed. So he is a torment to every one who has to do with him." His parents, in all likelihood, thought differently, for many genteel Philadelphians believed that children ought to be indulged, their wishes and wills fulfilled rather than denied.[6]

Genteel Virginians, too, were known "to countenance indulgence to children," as a young Presbyterian tutor from New Jersey, Philip Fithian, observed disapprovingly while in residence in the household of Robert Carter of Nomini Hall in 1773.[7] No doubt with just such families in mind, the *Virginia Gazette* reprinted a report in 1767 from an English paper about the visit of a gentleman to "a friend's house in the country," where he promised himself "much satisfaction." "I have, however, been greatly disappointed in my expectations," he noted,

> for on my arrival here I found a house full of children, who are *humoured* beyond measure, and indeed absolutely spoiled by the ridiculous indulgence of a fond mother. . . . The second day of my visit, in the midst of dinner, the eldest boy, who is eight years old, whipped off my periwig with great dexterity, and received the applause of the table for his humor and spirit. . . . Six of the children are permitted to sit at the table, who entirely monopolize the wings of fowls; and the most delicate morsels of every dish because the mother has discovered that her children has not *strong* stomachs. In the morning, before my friend is up, I generally take a turn upon the gravel walk, where I could wish to enjoy my own thoughts without interruption; but I am here instantly attended by my little tormentors, who follow me backwards and forwards, and play at what they call *Running after the Gentleman*. My whip, which was a present from an old friend, has been lashed to pieces by one of the boys, who is fond of horses; and the handle is turned into a hobby horse. . . . The mother's attention to the children entirely destroys all conversation; and once as an amusement for the evenings, we attempted to begin reading *Tom Jones*, but were interrupted, in the second page, by little *Sammy*, who is suffered to whip his top in the parlour . . . and a little miss, at breakfast, is allowed to drink up all the cream, and put her fingers into the sugar dish, because she was once *sickly*. . . . It is whispered in the family that I am a mighty good sort of a man, but that I cannot *talk to children*.

In concluding, he acknowledged that while he revered his hostess "as the mother," he wished he "could recommend her as the manager of children," hoping that she would be able by chance to read his letter in order "to convince her how absurd it is to suppose that others can be as much interested in her own children as herself. I would teach her that what I complain of as matter of inconvenience may, one day, prove to her a severe trial; and that early licentiousness will, at last, mock that paternal affection from whose mistaken indulgence it arose." This gentleman's experience in a genteel English country house undoubtedly could have been duplicated at many of the Virginia gentry's houses, if Fithian's assumption about their proclivity for indulgence was correct.[8]

Above all else, genteel parents adored their children from infancy on through adulthood. Their letters are filled with demonstrations of their intense affection for their children, their sense of devotion to them, and the pleasure they derived from having them nearby. In part, no doubt, the intensity of their devotion resulted from the likelihood of having few children survive to adulthood—whether as a result of early death or by virtue of never having had many children to begin with. These families were rarely notably large in size, so that each child became very precious to the parents; yet the delight that parents characteristically experienced was always felt from the beginning with the birth of the first child. Early in January 1763, the Reverend Mather Byles, Jr., who converted from the Congregational faith to the Church of England and eventually was driven into exile with his family from New England, wrote to his father in Boston that "My daughter grows remarkably fast; and is universally allowed to be a fine baby. She is in charming health and spirits; this instant crowing in her mamma's lap, and using every little artifice to interrup[t] me and attract my attention. (I wish Sir you could see what a beauty she is)."

The letters written by the Reverend Penuel Bowen, an Anglican from Boston who traveled to South Carolina during the mid-1780's in hopes of finding a parish for himself, reveal a very similar devotion to his wife and a deeply felt affection for his children. In 1786, he wrote to one of his daughters from Charleston: "You surely know that Papa loves you dearly and Papa thinks you love him. Do you not wish to see me again to come between my knees if not sit in my lap and mix a little pleasing chit chat." The following year, he wrote from Savannah to assure his wife and "the dear flock" that they "have my warmest embraces"; "What a void in the affections of the mind—this separation makes," he said sadly. "Do my dear be happy yourself: Charge the young (Petts) (a word peculiar to this Country for children much indulged) to be still very good." When Mrs. Sarah Gibbes of Charleston sat down to write to her beloved son at college at Princeton in 1784, she told him: "Our little blessings are well. Willmott has grown an amazing fine fellow, and full as sensible as Mercy Ladson was at her age: he is quite the pet of the house, can just step about and understands every word you say to him."[9]

The pleasures of parenthood are evident again in the correspondence of Andrew Belcher, a former New Englander in residence in Halifax, Nova Scotia, during the 1790's, who wrote to his sister in Cambridge, Massachusetts, to offer his "congratulations on the birth of an Heir—May yours in all time to come enjoy ten fold the good wishes you have express'd for *my little Alexander* and may they both ever prove the happiness and pride of their parents and friends." Four years later, he wrote to his sister to tell her that "We have now three Sons and One Daughter," promising that his wife would write her soon "and tell you all the wonderful perfections of our Children. They are indeed very fine and very good Children."

Edward and Anne Chandler, formerly from the colony of New York but separated from their American kindred by the war and their removal to England in the mid-1780's, also found an intense pleasure in their only daughter, who at seven months of age was "allowed by every person to be as beautiful a Child as ever was Created, and as saucy as ever the Mother was," as Edward observed to his American brother-in-law. Several months later, he wrote again: "Hear is the Mother and daughter along side me and they make such a noise that it is impossible for me to proceed any farther at present—" "Wherefore must drop my pen," he added, "and take my dear baby to play with." "Oh Samy," he declared, "she is the loveliest Child that ever god Created. There is nothing in this world half so dear to me as my Child. And a beautiful babe she is—and every body is fond of her. I wish you was hear to see her. I am Confident you would almost eat her up." Seven months later, his "little saucy Impertinent beauty" was at last weaned by her mother at the age of seventeen months, owing to "the perswasion of her friends." As he told his brother-in-law, "Samy if you was but to see her you would be astonished to see what a lively sensible dear dear little Child she is. I love her better than I do my self." Shortly before his daughter's third birthday, however, Anne Chandler died, to the utter despair of her adoring husband. But he acknowledged that his daughter was "the Idol of my soul and the only remains of a woman whom I loved admired and adored above anything in this world." His love for them knew no bounds.[10]

Thanks to the financial straits of Tench Francis, a prominent Philadelphia Anglican, the intense affection binding parents and children together in their small family circle is reflected in the letters which Tench and Anne Francis wrote across the Atlantic for two years, beginning in 1767. Anne acknowledged that only the prospect of her husband's successful quest in London could "reconcile" her "to the Cruel Separation I have suffered from the friend of my bosom. I shall not look forward with eagerness till the happy period arrives that will once more unite me to the Man my Soul Adores. Farewell thou dearest best of Husbands and be assured I am as much Yours as you can wish me to be." The previous day, she had written to say that "Dame Fortune has been Cross to us this Last Season indeed," but hoped "she will soon turn the Wheel Again in our favor." She assured her distant husband that "our dear Son is as Affectionate as ever and gives me great pleasure. He sometimes breaks out and Complains heavily of your long Absence which rouses all my tenderness and in a moment unfits me for any Argument that can Appease him." "Johnny interrupts me," she noted, "reminding me of a promise I have made him of going today to visit your Mother at the Falls"; "you know his impatient temper and can guess how tedious the moments pass till we set out. His spirits are ten times greater than ever and I begin to doubt of my Abilities to keep them under proper regulations." Her husband replied: "There is no one thing under Heaven I more Ardently desire than that Happiness of Clasping you and my dear little Boy once more in my fond Arms, and until that blessd Moment there can be no peace for the Breast of your most Affectionate Husband." Several months later, he wrote again, hoping still to "be able [to] repair my

Injured Fortune" and telling Anne to "Kiss my little Son for me, I dont know which I want most to See, you or him."

In November 1767, Tench wrote to say that "The News of the Birth of our fourth Son gave me more Satisfaction and Joy than those of all his other Brothers together"—only one of whom survived—adding that "he is welcome doubly so since the Life and Health of his Mother is Secure." He wanted her not to nurse her baby, observing that "I know your Ambition in this point" but praying that she would not go "beyond the bounds of Prudence." He acknowledged that " 'tis very hard for a Tender Mother to part with her dear Babe from her Breast"—something many mothers were doing eagerly both in Philadelphia and elsewhere—"yet remember you owe a great deal to yourself," as well as to her other son and husband. His advice went unheeded, however, for the following February she wrote to remind him of their sixth wedding anniversary and to assure him that she was "in perfect good health, nursing our dear Baby, who is as lovely as a Babe can be—Johnny and he, both perfectly well." "Johnny is just come up to me all over snow and Mad," she added, "with a long story of a frolick he has had with Jeremy and somebody throwing snowballs. He takes his Book well and I am sure will please you, tho indeed he wants your care," admitting to her husband that "I cant help spoiling him by granting him a double portion of love and indulgence."[11]

The children of Deborah Norris Logan and her husband, the eminent Dr. George Logan, who resided in the elegant house known as Stenton, near Philadelphia, also received ample portions of "love and indulgence" from their devoted parents. After the birth of her first son, Albanus, in November 1783, Deborah Logan continued to nurse him for eighteen months. In August 1784, she wrote to her brother, Isaac Norris, then traveling in Europe, to tell him "about my dear little Boy," who "is prodigiously grown and I am told he is a most lovely Child; takes a great deal of Notice and is excessively engaging, he was just now here playing on the table and wanting much to have the Ink Stand in his possession—his little form is so pleasing that I would not wish it mended," and adding, "I am sure thee would love him." In a subsequent letter to her beloved brother, written the following summer, she observed that she was "alone at Stenton . . . the day has been very gloomy and I have spent it in reading and caressing my Child." "My little Alban improved finely," she noted, "he is a most lovly Boy. Quite of the *Equestrian* order for he makes every thing serve for a horse and rides about continually." In a letter written in April 1785, Mary Norris, her mother, observed that her "Son is a Charming boy, has had the Small-pox, and runs about, and begins to talk," adding that "his Papa doats on him."[12]

For the loving and proud parents of such endearing and precious children, the issue of spoiling or indulgence simply did not arise—or at least it is notably absent from their correspondence and private writings.

Their children grew up from infancy immersed in an atmosphere of affection and of devotion to their needs and wishes, the center of their parents' attention and care, so that their affection for their parents grew equally intense and important to them. There never was any sense of being purposely thwarted or denied in their wishes. Their wills were never broken, nor were the pressures felt for bending their wills, as moderate parents would have insisted was necessary. The few descriptions that are to be found of their early behavior suggest an exuberance, a joyfulness, a delight in unbounded play which seems to have characterized the first five or six years of life for the children of genteel parents.

As a result, the children who grew up in these families began their lives with a sense of self-worth, self-love, and self-confidence that set them apart from those reared in different ways. They also began their lives with a sense of inner security that was missing from many of their contemporaries, a security which would be manifested in countless aspects of their life and thought throughout adulthood. By beginning their lives with an abundance of love and relatively few restraints, they developed a self fully as loving and approving of itself as their parents had been of them in their childhood.

Surrogate Parents: Nurses and Servants in the Genteel Household

IN MANY GENTEEL FAMILIES, parenthood was shared with members of the household who were not kindred; and much of the actual work associated with the care, feeding, and discipline of children was done by people employed for the purpose: nurses, servants, or slaves. Their presence within the genteel household is rarely noted in the letters and occasional diaries that were written by genteel women and men, but their significance both for the rearing of children and for the functioning of the household was immense. In genteel households in the Northern and Middle colonies, nurses and servants often would be free, white, and employed for the specific purpose of caring for children. In genteel households throughout the South, however, nurses usually were black and enslaved, thus adding another dimension to the influence shaping the characters of genteel children. But in either case, the most significant factor was simply that people who were not the children's parents were responsible for most of their daily care and oversight from infancy.[13]

The presence of nurses in the household is noted occasionally by parents. In 1785, for instance, Debby Norris's mother observed that "Debby is so engaged with her Son She could not write," a duty which could not be fulfilled owing to the fact that "the Maid who takes care of the Child is absent." While the Reverend Penuel Bowen was absent from his family in Boston on a trip to South Carolina, he wrote to ask if his youngest daughter, who was then about two and a half years old, was minding her mother and her nurse. Sometimes nurses remained in the household many years, as the letters from the Hutchinson family occasionally reveal. Early in 1774, prior to departing for England, Governor Thomas Hutchinson wrote to his son to dissuade him from going with him, and observed in passing that "Nurse said nothing to me" about a message concerning "the Doctor's wine until this minute," which indicates that she was still a member of the Hutchinson household long after the children had grown up beyond infancy and childhood. Subsequently, after the Hutchinsons arrived in London, Peggy Hutchinson wrote to her sister to tell about their recent experiences, adding in a postscript that "Papa sends his love to you: mine to Nurse if she is with you: tell her I wanted her to hold my head," no doubt while being seasick during their long voyage. Though brief, her message was obviously a testament to her love and reliance upon the nurse who undoubtedly had reared her for many years.[14]

In genteel Southern households, slaves were responsible for children from infancy and were in constant attendance upon their young charges. In December 1773, young Philip Fithian noted in his diary: "The conversation at supper was on Nursing Children; I find it is common here for people of Fortune to have their young Children suckled by the Negroes!" After infancy, children ordinarily were attended by personal slaves. In the Carter household, Fithian believed that "the children are more kind and complaisant to the servants who constantly attend them than we are to our superiors in age and condition."[15]

In the households of the genteel, both South and North, children occupied a space between parents and servants, a special niche, as it were, that probably accounts in part for the remarkably indulgent attitudes of so many genteel parents. The unqualified love and devotion of genteel parents for their infants and young children was possible, often, because their feelings were unqualified by the daily confrontations of so many parents with children. The children could become the amusing companions of parents who saw little of them during the day or night. When they ceased to be amusing or pleasing, parents always had someone else present to whom they could turn over the responsibilities of caring for them—whether their nurses or the servants or slaves whose job it was to clothe, feed, watch, and discipline the adored offspring.

The use of surrogate parents by the genteel also fostered the development of manners and of respectfulness, for children often saw their parents only in formal circumstances. Perhaps this was responsible for the development of the sense of awe and distance that characterized the perception of parents by so many genteel children. These parents were obviously deeply devoted and loving, yet they were also often at a distance from their children. Seeing their parents only occasionally, in situations that might be quite formal, children could develop a sense of them as benign but distant beings, very affectionate but also powerful and awesome, while simultaneously perceiving their nurses as the sources of sustenance, care, and discipline. If so—the evidence is so inadequate concerning these matters—then it is possible to perceive the sources for the sense of harmony and of benevolence characteristic of so many genteel families. If parents often seemed distant or remote, the signs of love and concern they might feel for their children could become indispensable to the inner security and contentment of their offspring.

"To Curb Their Children Is to Spoil Their Genius"

THE PLEASURE AND AMUSEMENT that children provided for parents suggest parental tolerance toward the willfulness and demands of their young offspring and a reluctance, except under the most provocative circumstances, to restrain or punish them. Indeed, "indulgence" always connoted a lack of discipline to evangelicals and to moderates, who feared that they themselves might not be sufficiently vigorous in either breaking or bending the emerging wills of their young children, and who knew, from observation and experience, the likely consequences of inadequate early discipline. Yet for the genteel throughout the colonies, the issue of discipline is notably absent from letters or diaries. They always seemed comfortable and pleased by evidence of self-will in their children's temperaments and behavior. But moderates often noted that the genteel spoiled their children and failed to discipline them properly. As Landon Carter, of Sabine Hall, Virginia (a man of moderate temperament although himself a gentleman), noted in 1776, nothing was "so common as to hear Parents say, 'to curb their children is to spoil their genius,'" a view he personally deplored. Carter had found that "through this part of the world . . . even children just cloathing are instructing their Parents; and what is worse those Parents who practiced this when Children themselves, know not how to curb their children now they attempt it."[16]

The contrast between the evangelicals' insistence upon breaking children's wills and the gentry's unwillingness to curb their children's wills had profound significance for the shaping of two opposite modes of temperament and of piety. Yet in the South, at least, where slavery was a daily reality shaping the consciousness of genteel children from infancy, the breaking of the will could often be observed even when it was not experienced personally. The genteel treated their black slaves the way evangelicals treated their own children—both sought to conquer and to subdue willfulness and the sense of self as soon as possible. Thus, ironically, genteel Southerners and others who owned slaves and evangelicals everywhere shared a crucial experience, though with a fundamental difference: what the evangelicals did to their own children, the genteel Southerners did only to their slaves. The children of the genteel grew up free from the experience of having their wills conquered, yet also conscious of the fact that slaves had no free will of their own and, in a very special way, no self of their own. Hence it was possible, in the course of maturing, for both evangelicals and many genteel Southerners to share a special concern with the whole issue of enslavement and of having the will and self rendered submissive.[17]

Thomas Jefferson was struck by the tendency of children to imitate the behavior of adults toward slaves, and by the psychological impact upon children of the power they might exercise over the slaves who ostensibly were responsible for their care and government. As he observed, "The whole commerce between master and slave is a perpetual exercise of the most boisterous passions, the most unremitting despotism on the one part, and degrading submissions on the other. Our children see this, and learn to imitate it; for man is an imitative animal. . . . From his cradle to his grave he is learning to do what he sees others do." Jefferson knew from experience the likelihood of children learning to be tyrannical from watching parents with slaves. "The parent storms, the child looks on, catches the lineaments of wrath, puts on the same airs in the circle of smaller slaves, gives a loose to his worst passions, and thus nursed, educated, and daily exercised in tyranny, cannot but be stamped by it with odious peculiarities." No doubt Jefferson was right. But the presence of slaves in the genteel household also had another effect, subtler but no less significant for the development of character: the slaves could bear the brunt of the discipline that otherwise might have been focused upon the children themselves. In effect, many genteel Southerners could indulge their children and permit them to grow up with little if any consistent discipline because such discipline was reserved principally for their slaves.[18]

Another Southerner, born in Maryland and growing up in Delaware in a Quaker family, observed similar consequences from the experiences of children who grew up in households surrounded by slaves. While in London, young John Dickinson wrote to his father in 1754, offering some observations upon his own and others' educations. He noted that when many "young fellows from America" came to London, they began "to see the difference between themselves and the polite part of the world," which made them "miserable." In trying to emulate their English betters, these young Americans often ended by "tottring on the side of a jail," which Dickinson traced "to their childhood." As he declared, "What a nest of vices shall we find in the education of a gentleman's son in America? The little mortal can no sooner talk than he is exercising his commands over the black children about him; no sooner walks, but he is beating them for executing his orders too slowly or wrong." "What passions spring up from hence," he asked, knowing well that "crops of pride, selfishness, peevishness, violence, anger, mean[n]ess, revenge and cruelty" were the ones to be expected. Dickinson believed that "By governing slaves from his infancy," the child later "becomes a slave himself; from amongst them, he is out of his element: he dreads the sight of an equal; he is cowardly and sheepish before persons of any fashion, barbrous and tyrannical amongst inferiors." He was convinced that "in a great measure is this the case in the colonies: by conversing constantly with slaves, they acquire a mean, groveling way of thinking, with the utmost pride and conceit." The ambivalence inherent in the temperament of such persons, oscillating between groveling and conceit, was not far from the mark in some instances, at least, although groveling was the very last thing a true gentleman could ever tolerate in himself. His pride was too great and his desire for superiority too dominant. Yet the fear that he could be perceived as one who might grovel nevertheless may have haunted him, and prompted many of the displays of manly prowess so valued by Southerners. Ultimately, however, the fact that their own self-will was never broken in childhood remained an enduring source for their ability, as mature men, to assert their wills without a sense of inner conflict.[19]

Of equal importance in the subsequent ability of genteel Southerners (and probably others as well) to express themselves freely without a sense of guilt was the fact that the method of discipline favored by parents, however rarely employed, was whipping. Often physical punishments were left to people other than the parents to inflict—nurses, governesses, tutors, or household servants and slaves, who had primary responsibility for the behavior of the children. By having other people impose whatever discipline was necessary, genteel parents could remain the loving, tender, and indulgent sources of affection and objects of respect within the family. Since so much of the actual care of children was being done by other people, parents were not responsible for the constant supervision and disciplining of children. They could devote themselves fully to the pleasures of being parents and playing fondly with their offspring, secure in the knowledge that other people within their households would provide the essential care and oversight—and most of the discipline—of their children. Still, occasions might arise that called for more stringent responses, either from parents or those people responsible for caring for their children, and the method of discipline preferred evidently was physical punishment. For the Virginia gentry, at least, the limited evidence points directly to whipping as the chief method of discipline among the unruly and indulged children of genteel families.

In Landon Carter's extended household at Sabine Hall, where he lived with his married son, daughter-in-law, and grandchildren, as well as with two unmarried daughters of his own, surrounded and cared for by numerous black slaves, the effects of early and sustained indulgence upon children's characters were manifested to their distressed grandfather time and again. Carter was a man of moderate tastes and temperament, similar in many ways to his New England contemporary John Adams; but he also shared the proclivity of many Virginia gentlemen for physical responses to people or things that frustrated or annoyed him. Unlike his son and daughter-in-law, he believed in some discipline being imposed upon his grandchildren, usually whippings, as his own instinctive reactions to being angered indicate. One incident in the Carter household remained indelibly impressed upon Landon Carter's memory, a scene that reveals with the utmost clarity the variety of reactions toward the impudent behavior of his young grandson. In late June 1766, Landon noted in his diary:

> We had this day a domestic gust. My daughters, Lucy and Judy, mentioned a piece of impudent behaviour of little Landon [his grandson] to his mother; telling her when she said she would whip him, that he did not care if she did. His father heard this unmoved. The child denied it. I bid him come and tell me what he did say for I could not bear a child should be sawsy to his Mother. He would not come and I got up and took him by the arm. He would not speak. I then shook him but his outrageous father says I struck him. At Breakfast the Young Gent. would not come in though twice called by his father and once Sent for by him and twice by me. I then got up, and gave him one cut over the left arm with the lash of my whip and the other over the banister by him. Madame then rose like a bedlamite [someone insane] that her child should be struck with a whip and up came her Knight Errant to his father with some heavy God damning's, but he prudently did not touch me. Otherwise my whip handle should have settled him if I could. Madam pretended to rave like a Mad-woman. I shewed the child's arm was but commonly red with the stroke; but all would not do. . . . As this child is thus encouraged to insult me, I have been at great expence hitherto in maintaining him but I will be at no more. And so I shall give notice.

Carter's threat proved idle, but the memory of this incident continued to rankle as he saw his grandchildren continue in their unruly
and saucy ways. In January 1772, he observed that his daughter-in-law,
whom he blamed most for allowing the children to grow up this way,
had "ruined" her son "entirely" "by storming at me whenever I would
have corrected him [as] a child," while her daughter, at the age of
thirteen, "has already got to be as sawsy a Minx as ever sat at my table.
She can't eat brown bread, not bread without toasting; She cannot drink
Coffee, etc." Like so many Virginian children, the Carters often suffered
from fevers; but young Landon refused to take any medication for his
recurrent fevers, since "anything that he fancys Physick," his grandfather noted, "he will not take for father, mother, nor for me. This has
these fools brought their son to by taking him both of them from me who
was only going to give him a gentle Correction when a child." The
following June, as his grandson prepared to depart for college in Williamsburg, which his grandfather expected "to make him the most out-
rageous scoundrel that ever appeared in human Shape," Carter noted:
"I this day saw an instance of filial behaviour to his mother that would
have shocked me, had I not most sensibly known that this woman together with his father has contributed to ruin one of the most orderly boys
of his time, by bellowing out to take him from under a very Just correction I was many years ago going to give him, for even an insult to that
very woman." The very fact that Landon Carter could not forget this
incident is suggestive, for it indicates both the unwillingness of his son
and daughter-in-law to discipline his grandson and the instinctive resort
by Carter himself to physical punishment for behavior that met with his
disapproval. Whipping seemed to him to be the appropriate response by
parents or adults to the impudence and disobedience of children.[20]

Robert Carter of Nomini Hall, Landon's nephew, also shared the
conviction that whippings were the best means of disciplining children, as
the remarkable diary kept by the young Presbyterian tutor Philip Fithian
reveals with striking details. Robert Carter often punished his sons himself, as well as asking others, such as their tutors, to act on his behalf.
Not long after arriving in the Carter household. Fithian noted that two
of the Carter children—Bob, the second son, who was then sixteen years
old, and Nancy, who was thirteen—"had a quarrel—Bob called Nancy
a Lyar; Nancy upbraided Bob, on the other Hand, with being flog'd by
their Pappa; often by the Masters in College; that he had stol'n Rum,
and had got drunk; and that he used to run away," accusations which
"so violently exasperated *Bob* that he struck her in his Rage." Immediately after breakfast, Fithian received "a Message from Mr *Carter*, that
he desired me to correct *Bob* severely immediately," which he reluctantly
but necessarily undertook to do, "it being the first attempt of the kind
I have ever made." After being whipped and promising "peace among
the children, and Good Behaviour in general," Fithian observed that Bob

"conducts himself through this day with great Humility, and unusual diligence," adding hopefully that "it will be fine if it continues." The following June, he noted in his diary "a long and useful conversation" he had had with Mrs. Carter, who told him "openly and candidly the Several failings of her children, and indeed She knows them perfectly— In particular she knows not what to do with her perverse Son *Bob*—He abuses his Mama, Miss Sally [the housekeeper], the children, Family, and is much given to slander." "Poor unhappy youth," he observed, "I fear he will come to an unhappy end!" He added immediately: "This afternoon I found it necessary to correct Bob Severely for impertinence in School." In the Carter family, young Bob obviously was the major source of contention and conflict, and the one punished most often. But he never ceased to act in ways that caused both his tutor and his father to inflict severe and repeated whippings. Like his cousin, he did pretty much what he wanted, whatever the consequences.[21]

The use of physical punishment as a principal means of discipline seems to have been more characteristic of Southern genteel families than those in the Northern and Middle colonies, but the evidence that survives is too spare to be entirely conclusive. What matters most, however, is the implication of this choice for the emerging characters of their children—especially their sons, who seem to have been the major recipients of the whippings. The most important consequence, and the most striking difference in character from an evangelical or a moderate, is the evident lack of conscience among the youthful members of these genteel families. The genteel simply did not have consciences as active, as punitive, or as constrictive as those evident among both evangelicals and moderates. The choice of whipping as the main method of disciplining children was almost certain *not* to produce characters that were obsessed with guilt and self-denial. The whipping served to resolve their guilt— Bob "confess'd himself guilty" to his tutor on that first occasion of being whipped by him—and left them freed from the inner burdens of conscience.*

---

* The frequent use of physical punishments by genteel Southerners also may have fostered the general tendency toward physical violence and combativeness among both youthful and mature gentlemen, who preferred to express their anger openly and to engage in various forms of personal aggressiveness rather than trying to deny or suppress their feelings. As Ben Carter, the eldest of Robert Carter's sons, who was then about eighteen years old, told his tutor "after a long dispute on the practice of fighting—He thinks it best for two persons who have any dispute to go out in good-humor and fight manfully, and says they will be sooner and longer friends than to brood and harbour malice."[22] Fighting both expressed anger and resolved guilt, for the conscience was clear thereafter.

From Feminine to Masculine:
The Emergence of a Young Gentleman

SINCE MOST OF THE PORTRAITS of children painted in America throughout the seventeenth and eighteenth centuries were commissioned by families of "the better sort," the argument about the feminization of young children applies with the greatest assurance to the offspring of genteel families throughout this period. The combination of intense and unbounded affection, a sense of the preciousness and individuality of each child, and a desire to record the images of infancy, childhood, and youth for future years fostered the portraiture that became so significant for the genteel. As historical evidence, these portraits are notable both for their revelation of the remarkable continuity of the practice of dressing children of both sexes in feminine clothing and for the degree of elegance in the actual clothing worn by so many of the children portrayed. The wealth and social aspirations of the parents were manifested in the clothing they chose for their children, just as their desire to assure the association of childhood with femininity also was apparent decade after decade, in virtually all the colonies and states. The choice of clothing for male children from infancy to about the age of six was so much a part of tradition that it was never discussed. Among the genteel, at least, it simply was the way children were to be dressed. All children began life clothed in the image of femininity.

Infant clothing did not vary much, being essentially long gowns that went right over the child's feet, and had differing degrees of ornamentation. The portrait of six-month-old Mary Freake, painted in Boston in 1674, shows her in clothing very similar in style to the gowns of older children, except for the leading strings that trail behind her dress, and the close-fitting lace cap, characteristic of infants through the years. Her clothing is almost identical in style to that of Henry Gibbs, the son of Robert Gibbs, a wealthy Boston merchant. Henry Gibbs was painted at the age of one and a half years, inscribed precisely on his portrait with the date, 1670. He, too, wears a close-fitting cap with lace, with a long apron over his gown, as well as what appears to be a bead necklace. Mrs. Daniel Rea's daughter, painted about 1757, is portrayed barefooted, with a loosely fitting soft and simply cut gown; while the portrait of Francis O. Watts, dated 1805, shows a young boy, perhaps a year or two old since he is standing alone, with a low-cut, loose gown that covers his petticoats and reaches to his-ankles. Mrs. William Taylor's two-year-old son, Daniel Boardman, who was born in 1788 and painted in 1790, also has on a low-cut long gown that covers his feet. Mrs. Aphia Salisbury Rich's baby Edward, painted in 1833, depicts a child in a puffed-sleeved, long gown, wearing a necklace and holding a flower; without the accompanying description, the child's gender would be impossible to determine. Again, the twin children of Mrs. Paul Smith Palmer, Charles and Emma, are dressed exactly alike. Only their mother knew which one sat upon her lap, for the cut of their hair and the objects they hold in their hands fail to distinguish the daughter from the son. For the first few years, at least, it was evidently very difficult to tell girls and boys apart in terms of clothing and physical appearance.[23]

The same visual identification of both sexes continued from the age of two to about the age of six. Boys were dressed in long gowns that reached to the floor, wore long hair during the seventeenth and eighteenth centuries similar to girls (in the 1840's, both boys and girls wore very short hair, together with their usual dresses, which added a new dimension to the affinities of the sexes as well as to the complexities of gender identification), and continued to be marked by the appearance of an essentially feminine style. Robert Gibbs, Henry Gibbs's brother, was painted at the age of four and a half years in 1670, wearing a long gown very similar to his younger brothers' but without a cap covering his below-shoulder-length hair. Three-year-old James Badger was painted by his father in 1760, wearing a low-cut gown that reached to his ankles, his neck ornamented with a bow, his hair long but pulled back. An unknown boy painted about 1700 combines an ankle-length, gorgeously flowered gown with a coat of equal length that resembles the coats of adult men of the period. The lovely portrait of Thomas Aston Coffin, painted by John Singleton Copley between 1757 and 1759, also depicts a boy in a simple, low-cut satin gown, ornamented with a single large ribbon tied in a bow at the side and buttons down the front to the waist. His costume is similar to that of the brother of Christopher Gore painted by Copley about 1755, which, except for the buttons, resembles the dresses of his younger sisters.[24]

The similarities of dress for young boys and girls continued to be apparent through the first part of the nineteenth century as well, as a comparison of the unidentified portrait of a boy with a hammer and two girls, painted about 1845, demonstrates. All three have on dresses that are virtually indistinguishable in style, with rounded necks, closely fitted waists, and bloomers underneath. All three have short-cut hair, making it impossible to be certain of their gender without the assistance of the clues supplied by the hammer and flowers they hold. Similarly, the double portrait of Charles Eaton and his sister, painted in 1848, reveals the same style clothing and the same closely cut hair. The feminization of boys in terms of clothing and physical appearance thus continued unabated until at least the middle of the nineteenth century. This accounts for the difficulties of identification experienced by experts on early American paintings and portraits, who so often are forced to label paintings of children as simply "child." But the significant fact was that boys were dressed like girls and women for the first five or six years of their lives.[25]

After the age of about six, however, the visible signs of gender became sharply distinguished, as boys were taken out of gowns and put into breeches. Being breeched was an event of major importance in the lives of most boys. The sudden transformation of the six-year-old boy from a child in gowns, petticoats, and other feminine clothing into a boy in trousers and jacket must have been a marked experience for most male children over more than two centuries. The portraits of boys after the age of six always depict them in clothing similar to the clothes worn by adult men. Jonathan Mountfort, who was born in 1746, is portrayed in adult male clothing at about the age of seven in Copley's early painting. The elder Gore son is depicted in the jacket and breeches of an adult male in the mid-1750's. The styles changed, but the fundamental identification of young males with the visual appearance of adult males remained the same. One remarkably revealing portrait of the four sons of the Knapp family of New York City during the early 1850's demonstrates the gradations of style for boys from the long gowns of the earlier years to the adult styles of older boys. The youngest son is in a long, fancily embroidered dress, while the next to youngest wears a coat and ruffled shirt. The third son, standing to the right, also has on a ruffled shirt but wears a short fitted jacket. The eldest son, standing and holding the youngest, is dressed in the clothes of an adult, without the ruffles, jackets, or coats of his younger brothers. In a single painting, four different styles of clothing set apart the young males by age.[26]

The clothing of girls of six years and older did not change significantly from the styles of their earlier years. They continued to wear long gowns and to dress essentially as their mothers did, indicating an unbroken visual identity in their lives from infancy to old age. The outward form of their appearance was maintained, while their brothers and other young males were being set off from the female sex by their abrupt transformation in appearance. The clothing of the two Gore daughters painted about 1755 by Copley is similar, being simply cut gowns not dissimilar from those of adult women of the same period and rank. For girls, the transition from infancy to childhood, youth, and thence adulthood would be accomplished without sharp or drastic alterations of appearance to provide visual confirmation of a change in age or status. Their fate was to remain female all their lives. Only their brothers would experience a dramatic change in the outward signs of gender in childhood as they donned the clothing appropriate to young males.

Although the transition from feminine clothing to masculine styles similar to those worn by adult men is evident in period portraits, the literary evidence is extremely rare. One marvelously revealing exception, however, is to be found in the correspondence of the Reverend Mather Byles, Jr., who was driven out of Connecticut during the revolution and forced to resettle, reluctantly and uncomfortably, in Halifax, Nova Scotia. In October 1786, he wrote to his two sisters, who had remained in Boston throughout the revolution to care for their elderly father, the famous wit and satirist Mather Byles, Sr.—who shared his son's dislike of the Whig patriots but preferred to remain in the town that had always been his home—to describe to them the following domestic scene:

> Belcher [his son] finishing his sixth Year, makes his first Appearance in Jacket and Trowsers: and I assure you he struts, and swells, and puffs, and looks as important as a Boston Committee-Man. It was an affecting and interesting Sight, when with Calmness, Deliberation, and Solemnity, he collected, of his own Accord, all his Tunicks, Petticoats, and Linen, folded them up very carefully in the exactest Order, and presented them to Louisa for Doll-rags. He next proceeded into the Kitchen, took up the Cat, whom he is to hug no longer, and gave her the last affectionate Embrace. He then went up Stairs, stripped himself of the Cloaths he had on, assumed his new Garb, returned with his Eyes sparkling, and very politely paid his Compliments to the Family. In short, the whole Scene was vastly pathetic and sentimental.[27]

The rite of passage had been completed. Henceforth, young Belcher Byles was to behave according to the rational and ceremonious fashion associated with gentlemen, giving up, for all time to come, the pleasures of hugging the cat. No longer would he allow himself the feelings, affections, or passions of childhood—feelings, affections, and passions that his sisters, however, would still be allowed to experience and express. Putting on jacket and trousers was a symbolic act of the utmost significance, for it meant that the boy had become a male—not yet a man, but no longer to be thought of as associated with women. His delight and pride at this moment were evident to his moved and pleased father. What his mother and sisters thought of this scene will never be known.

Although the transition for the sons of genteel families from early childhood to later childhood and youth marked the assumption of masculine attitudes and modes of behavior, it was less complete than one might imagine. Indeed, young gentlemen, unlike the sons of evangelicals and moderates, always maintained their feminine past as a visible and important facet both of their temperaments and their way of life. They were trained to behave in ways that always emphasized good manners, decorum, and politeness, which enabled them to relate to the ladies in their lives with the genteel behavior considered proper in such families. In addition, the elegance of their clothing, the readiness with which they wore their hair long, either naturally or in wigs, and the grace with which they danced—all reflected the ease with which they accepted expressions of feminine styles and sensibilities in their own selves. Young gentlemen did not feel any need to reject or to deny the experiences of their first six years of life; thus they often found themselves able to express *both* their masculine and their feminine impulses more readily, freely, and openly than either evangelicals or moderates usually were able to do. As a result of being freed from the burden of guilt and repression, or the tensions of anxiety that might arise from submerging the feminine side of the self, such young gentlemen often became far more self-confident and self-assured than most moderates and all evangelicals were ever likely to become.

*"The Great School of the World":
Educating Young Gentlemen*

SINCE THE SOCIAL LIFE of genteel youth was part of the process of shaping them for their future entry into the world of polite, mannerly, and genteel adults, the education of young gentlemen also was designed to prepare them for the worldliness of adulthood: lives to be led in commerce or trade, in managing landed estates of considerable size, value, and complexity, in politics and roles of leadership both within their local communities and often in their colonies as well. To be worldly was to be prepared to deal effectively with the tasks associated with gentility in the seventeenth and eighteenth centuries. For many genteel youths, education more often was acquired through informal channels of limited effectiveness in terms of scholarly knowledge than through a rigorous classical education that might end with a college degree. Some youths, of course, experienced both forms of education—Thomas Hutchinson, for instance —but most were content to become gentlemen of the world rather than scholars. The experiences of young John Parke Custis probably were not atypical, for they reflect the central concerns of the genteel for practical, secular, and limited education—an education that would prepare sons for the world of public activities and accomplishments.

When the Reverend Jonathan Boucher heard that George Washington was considering sending his fourteen-year-old stepson, John Parke Custis, to him for an education, he obviously was pleased. Although he had had "Youths, whose Fortunes, Inclinations and Capacities all gave" him "Room for the most pleasing Hopes," he discovered that "no sooner do They arrive at that Period of Life when They might be expected more successfully to apply to their Studies, than They either marry, or are remov'd from School on some, perhaps even still, less justifiable Motive." Boucher recognized that in the case of Custis, "His Education hitherto may be call'd a private one," to which he attributed "that peculiar Innocence and *Sanctity of Manners* which are so amiable in Him." He also wondered if his young pupil was not "more artless, more unskill'd in a necessary Address, than He ought to be, 'ere He is turned out into a World like This?" As an educator, Boucher was aware that "In a private Seminary his Passions cou'd be seldom aroused: He had few or no Competitors, and therefore cou'd not so advantageously, as in a more public Place, be inured to combat those little oppositions and Collisions of Interest, which resemble in Miniature the Contests that happen in the great School of the World."[28]

Boucher knew very well that "There is a Deal of Difference to be observed in the Educating a Gentleman, and a mere Scholar." One of the best methods of education, he believed, was the grand tour, the travels— preferably abroad in England or on the European continent—so often recommended as the proper completion of an education in worldliness for young gentlemen. In August 1770, Boucher proposed to accompany his pupil on just such a trip, and wrote to Washington to justify and explain the proposal. While acknowledging that "The light, giddy, fantastical frothy and frivolous Characters amongst Us, would only be made worse, and rendered incurable" by such travels, he hastened to add that "to Me it is beyond a Dispute, that to an observant Mind . . . there is not another so eligible a System to be taken to form and polish the manners of a liberal Youth, and to fit Him for the Business and Conversation of the World." Boucher noted that "The peculiar Advantages which result to Youth from Travel, are said to be first, an Easy Address, the wearing off national Prejudices, and the finding nothing ridiculous in national Peculiarities; and above all, that supreme Accomplishment which we call a *Knowledge of the World.*" By this he meant "that easy that elegant that useful Knowledge which results from an enlarged observation of Men and Things, from an Acquaintance with the Customs . . . Politics, Government, Religion, and Manners, in a Word, from the Study and Contemplation of Men, as They present Themselves on the great stage of the World, in various Forms, and under Different Appearances. This is that Master Science, which every G-man [gentleman] should know, and which yet no school nor College can teach Him."[29]

Although nothing came of this proposal for a grand tour with young Custis, Boucher never varied from his convictions about the purpose of education for young gentlemen. He was untroubled by his awareness of Custis's scholarly deficiencies after being under his tutelage for several years, deficiencies pointed out to George Washington by the Reverend

John Witherspoon, president of the College at Princeton in New Jersey. Boucher observed that "Had Dr. Witherspoon been pleased candidly and fully to have examined this young Gentleman, I shou'd have had nothing to fear. He would not, indeed, have found Him possess'd of much of that dry, useless, and disgusting School-boy kind of Learning fit only for a Pedant; but I trust, He would have found Him not illy accomplished, considering his manners, Temper, and Years, in that liberal, manly, and necessary Knowledge befitting a Gentleman." Boucher declared his personal "abhorrence" of "that servile System of teaching Boys Words rather than Things; and of getting a parcel of Lumber by Rote, which may be useful and necessary to a School-master, but can never be so to a Man of the World." And that, of course, was precisely the point of his methods of education: to ensure the polishing of young men of the world. Thus he could assure Custis's guardian that he did not doubt, "in due Time, to deliver Him up to you a *good* Man, if not a very *learned* one."[30]

At Boucher's suggestion, the Washingtons decided to send John Parke Custis to New York to attend King's College (later Columbia). In Boucher's opinion, New York was preferable to Philadelphia as a town, since "It is inhabited by some People of the most considerable Rank and Fortune: it is a Place of the greatest Resort for Strangers of Distinction; it is the Head-Quarters of the Military; and, on all these Accounts, is, I am told, generally reckon'd the most fashionable and polite Place on the Continent. As a Situation, therefore, for a young Gentleman, who is to be Educated a little in the World, as well as in Books, it wou'd seem, that it deserves the Preference." From John Parke Custis's point of view, the choice of King's College was indeed a happy one, for he immediately discovered upon arriving at the college that he was "settled in every respect according to my Satisfaction." "There has Nothing been omitted by the Professors, which could be in any means conducive to my Happiness, and contentment," he told his "dear Mama," adding, "I believe I may say without vanity that I am Look'd upon in a particular Light by them all," conscious as he was of the fact that "there is as much Distinction made between me, and the other Students as can be expected." As a result of the attentions of his professors, "I have reason to form the most pleasing Hope of Pleasure, and Satisfaction"—a word which he crossed out and substituted, revealingly, "entertainment"—"in the pursuit of my Studies." So even at college the young gentleman found what he most sought: pleasure, satisfaction, and entertainment. Having his personal servant always at hand to prepare his meals and care for his rooms probably augmented his daily satisfactions, but at least his studies did not interfere with his pleasures. Like so many other young gentlemen, however, Custis never completed his college education, choosing instead to marry and enter the world on his own, secure in his youth, fortune, and family. With his marriage, in his twentieth year, the young gentleman entered the world of adults for which he had been preparing for many years.[31]

To Become "a Notable Housewife" and "Mother": Educating Young Ladies

WHILE YOUNG GENTLEMEN were being educated to take their places in the public world of men and affairs as well as the private world of polite society, young ladies were being educated for different and far more restricted purposes: to become wives, mothers, and household managers. From their earliest years, girls in genteel families were prepared for a life of subordination and domesticity. As Benedict Calvert observed to George Washington in 1773, with respect to the prospective engagement of his daughter Nelly to John Parke Custis, "it has ever been the Endeavour of her Mother and me, to bring her up in such a manner, as to ensure the happiness of her future Husband, in which, I think, we have not been unsuccessfull"; "if we have," he added, "we shall be greatly disappointed." Her husband's happiness—not her own—was the central purpose of her previous education, and the plan of education followed by many genteel families served similar purposes. To become accomplished in all the arts and skills associated both with domesticity and gentility—cooking, sewing, music, dancing—as well as being literate and knowledgeable to a limited degree were the goals of education for young ladies.[32]

Other Virginians, including Thomas Jefferson, shared the same assumptions about the proper training for genteel young ladies. In 1783, after leaving his daughter Martha in Philadelphia, under the care and tutelage of Mrs. Thomas Hopkinson, Jefferson wrote to his daughter, telling her, among other things, how to distribute her time in order to meet with his approval. His instructions reflect the concerns of a gentleman for his daughter's education:

> from 8. to 10 o'clock practise music.
> from 10. to 1. dance one day and draw another.
> from 1. to 2. draw on the day you dance, and write a letter the next day.
> from 3. to 4. read French.
> from 4. to 5. exercise yourself in music.
> from 5. till bedtime read English, write &c.

He also urged her to "Take care that you never spell a word wrong," observing that "It produces great praise to a lady to spell well." Jefferson did not hesitate to stress to his daughter that he had placed his happiness on seeing her "good and accomplished," the central purposes that underlay his design for her education. These were the objectives for genteel ladies everywhere—to be virtuous and to be adept in the arts of sociability and domesticity. Several months later, Jefferson reiterated the point, telling Martha that "I rest the happiness of my life on seeing you beloved by all the world, which you will be sure to be if to a good heart you join those accomplishments so peculiarly pleasing in your sex." These peculiarly feminine accomplishments were also implicit in the questions Jefferson addressed to his younger daughter, Mary, in the spring of 1790: "How many pages a day you read in Don Quixot? How far you are advanced in him? Whether you repeat a Grammar lesson every day? What else you read? How many hours a day you sew? Whether you have an opportunity of continuing your music? Whether you know how to make a pudding yet, to cut out a beef stake, to sow spinach or to set a hen?" While Jefferson thus desired his daughters to be well read and literate, he was also intent upon ensuring that they were prepared to assume the roles of married ladies in due course. As he said in February 1791 to Martha, who had married the previous year, her "two last letters are those which have given me the greatest pleasure of any I ever received from you. The one announced that you were become a notable housewife, the other a mother."[33]

For young genteel girls everywhere, the purpose of education was the same: to prepare them for their roles as wives, mothers, and household managers, while at the same time providing them with all the accomplishments deemed essential to polite society—music, dancing, conversation— the indispensable means of the sociability so essential to the life styles of the genteel. Philip Fithian, the Carter children's tutor, noted that he was responsible for five girls "between five and fourteen years Old. The Girls all dress in White, and are remarkably genteel. They have been educated in the City Williamsburg in this Colony—The two eldest are now learning Music, one to play the Harpsichord; the other the Guittar, in the practice of which they spend three Days in the Week." As he observed of Miss Priscilla, the eldest daughter (who was then about sixteen), she "is steady, studious, docile, quick of apprehension, and makes good progress in what She undertakes"—all indicative of the fact that she was a good pupil. In addition, however, "She is small of her age, has a mild winning Presence, a sweet obliging Temper, never swears, which is here a distinguished virtue, dances finely, plays well on key'd Instruments, and is upon the whole in the first Class of the female Sex." The results of a proper education for a young lady were evident to Fithian in the person of Miss Betsey Lee, who visited the Carters in July 1774. He noted that "She wore a light Chintz Gown, very fine, with a blue stamp; elegantly made, and which set well upon her. . . . In one word Her Dress was rich and fashionable—Her Behaviour such as I should expect to find in a Lady whose education had been conducted with some care and skill; and her person, abstracted from the embelishments of Dress and good Breeding, not much handsomer than the generality of Women." There could be no doubt that Miss Lee was indeed a Lady. Her family, wealth, good breeding, and education ensured the appearance as well as the manner of gentility; and the fact that she was present at the Carter plantation on a social occasion was simply part of the larger pattern of sociability and entertainment that dominated the lives of so many of those among the ranks of the genteel.[34]

"One Continued Scene of Idleness and Dissipation": The Pleasures of Genteel Youth

THE CONTRASTS BETWEEN the experiences of the youthful members of genteel families and those of evangelical or even moderate families epitomize some of the most significant differences of temperament and of piety that distinguished these genteel youths from so many of their contemporaries. Their correspondence and the rare diaries and journals kept are startlingly secular, almost innocent of concern with piety or with religious issues, devoid of the constant guilt and self-lacerations of evangelical diaries and letters, devoid, too, of the self-conscious restraints imposed by so many moderates. Genteel youths of both sexes seemed to derive immense pleasure from their lives, filled as they were with dancing, music, friends, outings, visits, and courting. What they noted—both in the privacy of their infrequent diaries and more often in their correspondence—were the events of their daily lives and the people with whom they had friendly relationships. Rarely were they concerned with their own inner feelings or thoughts, and never were they conscious of the self-examining so characteristic of evangelicals and moderates. Their writings—most notable for what they do not contain, for the very absence of self-analysis and guilt, of an ever-active conscience perpetually preventing them from taking pleasure in their lives—mark these genteel youths as being profoundly different from their anxious, morose, and guilty contemporaries. They were too busy and too contented to take time to record their innermost feelings or thoughts. And when they did take time, they usually preferred to note, for their own or others' enjoyment, what they had done rather than what they thought. Pleasure—whether in the form of clothing, eating, dancing, travel, or friendship—was not to be denied but enjoyed and indulged. Genteel youths simply did not feel guilty over the actions of their own lives. Their inner monitors were silent, content to let them do as they wished and to enjoy themselves to the utmost.

The correspondence between three young friends—Susan Kitteridge of Andover, Eliza Waite of Salem, and Mary Green of Boston—written between 1786 and 1791 is characteristic of the preoccupations and attitudes of many genteel young people. Their letters are filled with gossip, descriptions of dances and of boys, declarations of devotion to friendship signified by their pet names for each other—the concerns of girls whose entire lives were shaped by their social engagements and their friendships. As a group, they are remarkably unconcerned with religious matters or doctrines, reflecting at most a lightly felt piety.

One particular letter written from Augusta (Mary Green) to Julia (Eliza Waite), possibly in 1786, on a Sunday afternoon captures the tone and character of their correspondence generally. Augusta began her letter by telling Julia that "Health, happiness, and the sincerest congratulations attend my Dear Julia and her safe arrival: realy your absenting yourself from town has made such depression on my spirits as to render me incapable of writing or any thing else." It being a Sunday, she told Julia, "I dedicated one half of the day to the supreme-being, and am determined to dedicate the other part of it to you my friend; indeed I think I shall employ my time better in writing to you, than I could possibly in doing any thing else, for I shall reap from your epistles both pleasure and profit." "The motives are selfish," she acknowledged, "but you must allow they are just." She continued: "Just after I was seated at the window who should I see but the Beautiful Mr. H--l, riding by with too other Gentlemen, he looked out and cri'd I shall call here in a few moments, accordingly, he came accompany'd with the other too," telling her friend, "I think Julia it possible our Beauty look'd Handsomer than ever." After recounting the delightful visit from her handsome gentleman, she added, "well now to return to my cute evening for I have spent a very agreeable one considering all things." Judging by this and other letters, Augusta and her friends often spent "cute" evenings that were indeed "very agreeable," just as many other such genteel people were to do in the course of their lives. Their social circles shaped their pleasure and gave substance to their lives.[35]

Even under the difficult circumstances of war, the preoccupations of a young Quaker girl taking refuge with her family from the British army in the countryside beyond Philadelphia in 1778 still reflect the pleasures of gossip, adventures, and handsome young men characteristic of so many genteel young ladies. Fifteen-year-old Sally Wister kept a journal for her friend, Deborah Norris, recounting her adventures with the company of officers and soldiers who were frequently camped at her house in the Montgomery County countryside. One day, for instance, two "genteel men of the military order rode up to the door" and requested quarters in the house for General Smallwood, which her aunt agreed to provide; and after one of the officers had ridden away, she recalled, "When we were alone, our dress and lips were put in order for conquest, and the hopes of adven-

ture gave brightness to each before passive countenance." She was fascinated by the handsome and genteel young officers who passed through
the house, constantly describing them and their actions to her friend, such
as one adventure that began with "two dragoons" riding up to their door
while their cousin was visiting. "The junior sisters, Liddy and Betsey,
join'd by me," she told Debby, "ventur'd to send our compliments to the
Captain and Watts. Prissa insists that it is vastly indelicate, and that she
has done with us. Hey day! What prudish notions are those, Priscilla? I
banish prudery." "Suppose," she said, "we had sent our *love* to him, where
has been the impropriety? for really he had a person that was love-
inspiring, tho' I escap'd, and may say, *Io triumphe.* I answer not for the
other girls, but am apt to conclude that Cupid shot his arrows, and that
maybe they had effect." "A fine evening this," she concluded, very pleased
with herself.[36]

Eliza Southgate, too, led a happy and busy social life, as her letters
indicate. In February 1800, at the age of sixteen and a half, she wrote to
her sister from Boston "to relate the manner in which I have spent my
time. I have been continually engaged in parties, plays, balls, &c. &c.,"
adding that "Since the first week I came to town, I have attended all the
balls and assemblies, one one week and one the next. . . . They are very
brilliant, and I have formed a number of pleasing acquaintances there,"
dancing "until 1 o'clock," delighting in the fact that "they have charming
suppers, table laid entirely with china," and pleased that she "had charming partners always." In closing, she asked her sister to "Give my best
respects to Pappa and Mamma, and tell them I shall soon be tired of this
dissipated life and almost want to go home already." In a postscript, she
asked her mother for a wig, telling her that "I must either cut my hair or
have one, I cannot dress it at all *stylish*" since no one else had long hair.
Two years later, Eliza wrote to her mother from Ballston Springs, New
York, on a visit to the Derby family. She had been at Ballston for two
weeks, where, she said, "It has been one continued scene of idleness and
dissipation—have a ball every other night, ride, walk, stroll about the
piazzas, dress,—indeed we do nothing that seems like improvement"; but,
she added as justification, "still I think there is no place where one may
study the different characters and dispositions to greater advantage. You
meet here the most genteel people from every part of the country,—ceremony is thrown off and you are acquainted very soon. You may select
those you please for intimates, and among so many you certainly will find
some agreeable, amiable companions."[37]

For most genteel young people, "agreeable, amiable companions"
were always the principal source of pleasure and amusement in the
midst of the busy social life they led. As Julia Stockton Rush (a daughter
of Richard Stockton, an eminent and wealthy gentleman in Princeton)
wrote to her sister from Philadelphia in March 1798, "I have lived in a
continual whirl of company since the first of the year," adding, "that kind

of life was never agreeable to me, it is less so that it ever was, but we must make sacrifices of our own likings to the pleasures of our children— Emely has gone much more into company this winter," in order to "make Marias visit as agreeable as possible, and I think she has had her fill of disipated pleasure—they have been to twelve dances this winter, besides tea parties innumerable." But the "dissipation" that she and others observed obviously was immensely pleasurable to her daughter, as it was to so many others. Nothing, it seemed, could keep children at home, and "the pleasures of our children" always came first.[38]

Shortly after arriving at Nomini Hall in 1773, Philip Fithian discovered how important dancing and other genteel entertainments were to the children and parents alike in the Carter household. In mid-December, the dancing teacher came to the plantation to give lessons to the Carters and their neighbors. Fithian, who had never learned to dance, watched as they danced "several Minuets" with "great ease and propriety; after which the whole company Joined in country-dances, and it was indeed beautiful to admiration, to see such a number of young persons, set off by dress to the best Advantage, moving easily, to the sound of well performed Music, and with perfect regularity, tho' apparently in the utmost Disorder." Later, "When it grew too dark to dance," the young gentlemen walked over to Fithian's room, where they "conversed til half after six." "Nothing is now to be heard of in conversation," he observed, "but the *Balls*, the *Fox-hunts*, the fine *entertainments*, and the *good fellowship*, which are to be exhibited at the approaching *Christmas*."

With considerable frequency and obvious pleasure, the Carter children were invited to attend balls and entertainments at neighboring plantations as well as their own. In mid-January, Fithian noted that "Mrs *Carter*, Miss *Prissy*, and *Nancy* dressed splendidly" and set out to attend a ball, their brothers having been allowed by their father to go and "to stay all this Night." They returned telling of the large assembly of ladies and gentlemen, nearly seventy in all, and pleased "that the company was genteel." After returning to Nomini Hall, Mrs. Carter insisted that Fithian too come to the ball, which he agreed to do with great reluctance, as one might expect from a young Presbyterian moderate. When he got to the house, he saw, for the first time, gentlemen playing cards, "drinking for Pleasure," and dancing—the usual activities at any such gathering. But since he neither danced nor played cards, he was relieved to be able to depart in company of Mrs. Carter, and to be safely home in his own room by "half after twelve." The young Carter boys, however, spent the night in their revels. The next day, they were "yet at the Dance," though Bob returned "Home about six, but so sleepy that he is actually stupified!", exclaimed Fithian. The pleasures of unceasing amusement had taken their toll, but it is doubtful if anyone at Nomini Hall other than Fithian would have noticed.[39]

The experiences of young John Parke Custis in Annapolis under the tutelage of Jonathan Boucher as at home in Virginia confirm the emphasis on pleasure. "He has many Invitations to Visits, Balls, and other Scenes of Pleasure, to which neither You or I can refuse his going." Boucher realized that Custis "seldom or never goes abroad without learning Something I cou'd have wish'd Him not to have learn'd," for it was evident that "somehow or other He has contriv'd to learn a great deal of Idleness and Dissipation amongst Them. One inspires Him with a Passion for Dress—Another for Racing, Foxhunting &c," and others encouraged him "to talk of Guns and Rifles, with much more Satisfaction than I can persuade Him to talk of Books, or literary Subjects."[40]

Everywhere the pattern of pleasure was much the same among the youth of such genteel families. Dancing, music, games, drinking, hunting, and sports—all were an integral part of their lives as they grew to maturity. Pleasure was important and formed a significant part of their activities. There was nothing sinful about such pursuits—they were part of the normal experience of young ladies and gentlemen, who unquestionably would have shared the sense of dismay voiced by a gentleman who resided near the Carter plantation and informed Fithian in March 1774 that "the *Anabaptists* in *Louden County* are growing very numerous; and seem to be increasing in afluence [influence?]; and as he thinks quite destroying pleasure in the Country; for they encourage ardent Pray'r; strong and constant faith, and an intire Banishment of *Gaming, Dancing,* and Sabbath-Day Diversions." Among the genteel youth of the various colonies and states, however, there was little prospect of their pleasures being destroyed. They knew how to play and to enjoy themselves without feeling guilty.[41]

❧ VII ❧

"A Polite and Hospitable People": Themes of Genteel Temperaments and Piety

---

TOWARD THE END OF THE EIGHTEENTH CENTURY, when the Reverend Devereux Jarratt recalled his childhood in Virginia during the 1730's and 1740's, he remembered the simplicity of his family's existence. He had been reared by parents who were simple, industrious, and pious people, and who kept both the clothing and the food for their family very plain. Jarratt recalled that neither tea nor coffee was ever used in his family, since they were considered luxuries which only the "richer sort" might afford and use. But, as Jarratt recollected, "to such people I had no access. We were accustomed to look upon, what were called gentle folks, as beings of a superior order." "For my part," he added, "I was quite shy of them, and kept off at a humble distance. A periwig, in those days, was a distinguishing badge of gentle folk—and when I saw a man riding the road, near our house, with a wig on, it would so alarm my fears, and give me such a disagreeable feeling, that, I dare say, I would run off, as for my life." Such experiences left indelible memories, for the distinctions of social life were felt realities and not mere abstractions. As Jarratt cogently pointed out, "Such ideas of the difference between gentle and simple, were I believe, universal among all of my rank and age." Jarratt himself never erased these ideas from his own mind, for he always believed in the necessity for "a proper distinction, between the various orders of the people," despite the alterations in social relationships and attitudes in the new American Republic.[1]

For more than two centuries, social assumptions such as these had shaped the consciousness of the Anglo-American world. The conviction that the world in which people lived and functioned was divided into two visibly distinct ranks—the gentry and the nongentry—mirrored the realities of economic and social existence throughout most of the American colonies, evident in some as early as the middle of the seventeenth century and in all by the early decades of the eighteenth century. Everywhere—in the Northern, Middle, and Southern colonies—the genteel were distinguished by countless visible signs that set them apart from ordinary people. Taken together, these signs accumulated to form a style of life that was markedly different from the relatively simple and unostentatious modes of living characteristic of the great majority of people everywhere. The proliferation of elegant houses both in towns and in the surrounding countryside, the purchasing of costly and beautiful furniture and furnishings, the use of carriages, an abundance of servants or slaves to provide the essential services to run these households—all these were obvious manifestations of wealth and gentility. Many of the objects that the genteel of these centuries bought and used, and many of the houses that they built and lived in, survive today, mute but visible testaments to the elegance and formality of life style of these early Americans.[2]

Throughout the Northern and Middle colonies, the genteel often shared many traits of character, values, and sensibilities common to moderates. Like so many moderates, the genteel in these regions took for granted the organicism of the social as well as the natural world, and accepted the imagery of the great chain of being as an appropriate symbol for both nature and society. Like the moderates, they believed in the dominance of reason over the passions, and in the necessity for the close regulation of the passions in order to ensure virtue. And, like the moderates, they also believed in the necessity for the fulfillment of duties and obligations—within the family, the community, and in the world at large generally.[3]

Some of these themes were evident in the letter that Elizabeth Powel, the daughter of one wealthy and prominent Philadelphia gentleman and the wife of another, addressed to her nephew while he was abroad in Europe in 1809, in an effort to retrieve "the four preceding Years" of his life, which his aunt felt had been "so unavailingly and painfully thrown away." Her hope, however, was that he would return to Pennsylvania an educated and refined gentleman, and she left him with a clear sense of what she meant by the notion of a gentleman. She wanted him to return with his "Mind well stored with useful and ornamental knowledge," with his manners "polished by an intercourse with the best breed, and best informed Characters in Europe," and with his "native innocence" and "purity of Heart;—and indeed all" of his "virtues so strengthened, and confirmed" that she could be proud to see him become a "worthy and accomplished Gentleman." As his aunt, however, she warned him against "fashionable dissipation," instructing him "That to be noble and independent a Man must be completely the Master of his passions." In her mind, it was evident that "Physical strength, and vehement passions are the characteristicks of a Savage—regulated passions, improved intellect,

cultivated taste, a love of Science—the fine arts, and indeed all the em-
bellishments of polished Society,—are the Characteristicks of a Gentleman who wishes to be pre-eminently wise, and virtuous."⁴

But gentlemen also had other characteristics that were not usually
shared by moderates. As Jonathan Sewall observed of John Adams, after
they met once more during the 1780's in London, where Sewall had fled
into exile and Adams had come as ambassador for the newly formed
Republic, he was not "qualifyed by nature or education to shine in Courts."
John Adams, he pointed out, "cant dance, drink, game, flatter, promise,
dress, swear with the gentlemen, and talk small talk and flirt with the
Ladys"—"in short," Sewall observed, "he has none of the essential *Arts*
or *ornaments* which constitute a Courtier." Yet as both men knew from
experience, these arts and ornaments were precisely the attributes that
set the genteel off most visibly from so many of their contemporaries—
moderates and evangelicals alike. Such marks of gentility were evident
throughout the colonies, in Southern as well as Northern climates.⁵

To be able to do all the things Jonathan Sewall thought characteristic
of gentlemen and courtiers required a temperament free from the inner
anxieties and ambivalences characteristic of so many moderates. As we
have seen, the genteel rarely suffered from the wracking and continuous
inner torments that plagued so many evangelicals. The genteel were far
more self-assured, more secure, and more at ease with themselves and
their world than either moderates or evangelicals generally were able to
be. They were rarely disturbed by a sense of mistrust either of themselves
or of others—a mistrust that often grew into a pervasive sense of paranoia
in the minds of so many of their contemporaries. Their characters seemed
to be relatively impervious to such inner threats and anxieties. In their
piety as in their temperaments, the genteel were remarkably comfortable
and contented. Characteristically, they were preoccupied with the outward manifestations of piety rather than with the inner world of feelings
and of personal experience. Consequently, they were concerned primarily
with religious experience as an external ritual—with the ceremonialism
and formality of worship and with the church as a social institution. The
appeal of the Church of England for many of the genteel throughout the
colonies during the seventeenth and eighteenth centuries—even for many
who had been reared in other denominations—derived as much from its
ceremonies and ritual as from its doctrines. While the genteel seemed to
take the freedom of their own wills for granted and were comfortable
with an Arminian or non-Calvinist theology, they also seemed confident
that a life of piety and virtue would be rewarded in the life to come without requiring any undue concern on earth. The genteel everywhere took
their piety lightly, transforming their own religious experiences into
active sociability, always confident that they would be among the people
rewarded with eternal life by a benevolent deity.⁶

The confidence which the genteel felt toward the life to come mirrored the remarkable self-confidence that shaped their entire lives, and manifested itself in virtually every aspect of their worldly experience. In striking contrast to evangelicals, who always sought to suppress the self, and to moderates, who always sought to control the self, the genteel always sought to assert the self. To be eminent, high, and visible, to be proud and self-assured, to be powerful and self-assertive—these were the prerogatives of gentility throughout the Anglo-American world. The display, ornamentation, and indulgence of the self were all interconnected facets of the same temperament. The genteel were no less preoccupied with the self than were evangelicals or moderates, yet their sense of self was perceptibly different. Thus Devereux Jarratt's experience mirrored the reality of the gulf that divided the genteel from the rest of the world, and set them at opposite ends of the spectrum from evangelicals.

Unexamined Selves: The Outward Turning of Consciousness

THE GENTEEL were as consistent in avoiding their feelings and emotions as evangelicals were in probing and assessing theirs. The contrast between the evangelical and the genteel mind is immediately evident in the diaries they kept: evangelicals are ever preoccupied with their inner states of being, weighing and evaluating sin and grace, probing the sources of their guilt and discontent, searching always for the signs of grace and assurance of Divine love, constantly and repetitively surveying their inner life—and usually ignoring altogether the outer life they were also leading. Evangelical diaries usually are concerned exclusively with the inward self, actions being of interest only insofar as they reveal something of significance about the state of sin or grace within. Genteel diaries, conversely, are concerned with the self in action, the outward experiences of daily life rather than the inner responses to the events themselves. The experiences count for more than the feelings that might have accompanied them. They are almost invariably records of what people did rather than what they thought or felt. Nothing could be more revealing of their outwardly turned consciousness than the diaries they kept. They are barren of personal insight or self-reflection, purposefully avoiding the confrontations with the self that were the daily experience of evangelicals.

The preoccupation with outward happenings, the details of daily experience from morning to night, the faithful recording of what was

done without noting what was felt or thought about events as they trans-
pired, are characteristic of the diaries kept so assiduously in shorthand by
William Byrd II, a man of immense wealth, eminence, and gentility in
Virginia. For all the voluminousness of these private diaries, Byrd remains mostly hidden behind his record of his personal life. His outward
life is preserved in exhaustive detail; but his character, his temperament,
elude the reader as he recounts his daily activities year in and year out,
both in London and in Virginia. Virtually any daily entry will serve as an
example of his preoccupations and his method of writing:

> [London, August 14, 1719] I rose about 6 o'clock and read a chap-
> ter in Hebrew and some Greek. I said my prayers, and had milk
> for breakfast. The weather was cold and cloudy, and it rained
> pretty much. Then I danced my dance and read some Latin till
> eleven and then went to church. After church I went upon the
> Walk where I played at lottery ticket and won a little. About 2
> o'clock I went to dine with Jack Sambrooke and ate some chicken
> and bacon. After dinner I drank some coffee and about four we
> went to the Walk, from whence I went to my lodging and read some
> Latin till six and then returned to the Walk where I went one half
> with Mrs. C-m-t-n and we won twenty shillings apiece. About 8
> o'clock we went to our private ball where I danced with Lady Jane
> Hamilton. There was a fine supper and I ate some tongue. We
> danced till 2 o'clock and then I went home in the chair and
> neglected my prayers, for which God forgive me.

The active verbs dominate: he rose, read, said, had, went, played, ate,
drank, went, read, went, ate, danced—but what he felt or thought about
these various activities is rarely revealed. What mattered most was what
he had done—for the specificity of the details about his food, for example,
or the weather, or the naming of the people whom he saw are the essence
of his inner experience, a faithful record, it seems, of his inner as well as
his outer life. The same pattern continued after his return to Virginia.

For Byrd, the self was ever in action—eating, drinking, seeing,
doing—rarely pausing to look inward. Only occasionally, and almost
inadvertently, does Byrd provide insights into his emotional life and his
inner experiences. On January 2, 1721, for instance, he recorded having
"dreamed I was very dear to the King and he made me Secretary of State
and I advised with my Lord Oxford how to manage that great office." Yet
even in his dreams, Byrd was actively pursuing outward interests, pressing his political ambitions to the very source of power and patronage itself—the king and his advisers. His subliminal concern was "how to
manage," but not how to respond to the eminence or power that he envisaged. The dream obviously pleased him.[7]

The diaries kept by three genteel New Englanders are remarkably similar to Byrd's, despite the obvious differences in time and place. All share his preoccupation with action and other people, while remaining opaque in terms of the individual's feelings and attitudes toward the experiences or people being catalogued. The diary kept by John Rowe, a wealthy Boston merchant, during the mid-eighteenth century is a laconic account of his daily activities, as the following entries made in June 1768 typify:

> June 4. King's Birthday. Guns Firing, Drinking Healths etc.
> June 6. Dine at the Coffee House with the Governour and Council, the Officers of the Artillery and many other Gentlemen—Mr Clark of Lexington preached a Sensible Discourse on the Occasion.
> June 7. My New Store Raised this Day.
> June 8. Wednesday. A fine morning WNW. Capt Freeman arrived from Bristol in whom came Passengers Lady Frankland and Henry Cromwell. Dined at Mr Inman's with him, the Reverend Mr Brown of Portsmouth the Reverend Doctor Cooper President at New York, The Reverend Mr Troutbeck and wife, Mr Robert Temple and wife, The Reverend Mr Sargent of Cambridge, Mrs Rowe and Sucky [her daughter] came home and spent the evening with Mrs Rowe and Sucky.[8]

Governor Thomas Hutchinson's diary was similarly filled with explicit details of the people in London with whom he conversed or whom he had met, the things he did, political matters, but almost nothing that might be considered intimate or personal. On May 30, 1775, for instance, he noted:

> I called this morning upon Mr Cornwall, Jenkinson, Lord Suffolk, Lord Loudoun, Lord George Germaine, Lady Gage; found them all at home: and upon Lord Hillsborough, who was in the country; and upon Mr Keene.
> The alarm of yesterday much abated. Great expectation of Gage's account.
> Drank tea at the Bishop of London's Palace at Fulham, my sons and daughter: no other company besides the Bishop and his lady.

Hutchinson was most interested in the people he met and talked with, and while he recorded some of his political conversations in considerable detail, he rarely commented on his own attitudes or feelings.[9]

The same was true of the lengthy journal kept in exile by Samuel Curwen, who noted on Monday, April 1, 1776, that he

Walkt up to London to pay my respects to Gov. H[utchinson] whom I found alone reading a new pamphlet entitled "An Enquiry wether Great Britain or America is most in fault." He invited me to dine on a pudding and a bit of roast mutton, which I accepted; taking leave for the present I departed, walking through the palace and park to Mr. Bliss's lodgings, when soon after arrived Judge Sewall, Mr. Oxnard and Smith, with whom I went to Exeter Exchange, to have a view of the Modell of the City of Paris. . . . From thence separating I returned to the Governor with whom only young Oliver and myself dined. From thence in my return passing through Leicester Square I called in at Mr. Copely's to see Mr. Clarke and the family, who kindly pressed my staying to tea, and in the meantime was amused by seeing his performances in painting. . . . Returned with Mr. Clarke, who was going to see his son, sick, as far as Temple barr, where by good fortune I got into a full coach, taking a very agreeable young Lady in my lap, who was obliging enough to accept it rather than turn me out of the Coach, she having taken a place first. It proved a most fine Evening which closed a fine day. Arrived at home at 8 o'clock after the pleasantest passage up I ever experienced.

Curwen's fascination with the world surrounding him—the buildings, the people, the customs—made him an acute observer of the outward appearances of the English towns and countryside that he constantly toured and enjoyed. But his diary, once again, tells us very little about his inner feelings or attitudes toward the external world in which he was so entirely caught up. His lack of introspection is typical of the outwardly directed sensibilities of the genteel generally.[10]

Thomas Hutchinson, an exemplary New England gentleman, "felt no elemental discontent, no romantic aspirations." He was a man whose personality was remarkably elusive, whose prose too was abstract, bland, "still," who was cautious, prudent, carefully controlled. " 'My temper,' he said, 'does not incline to enthusiasm.' " Hutchinson was a man deeply committed to restraint and caution; but, as Bernard Bailyn so perceptively notes, "None of this rationality and circumspection was a strenuous achievement for him. There is no evidence, as there is for John Adams, of a struggle between nature and nurture, between powerful erratic impulses and the constraints of culture. . . . He maintained without a struggle a correct and honorable code of conduct." And it is this particular aspect of Hutchinson's character—maintaining the correct code of conduct throughout life "without a struggle"—that sets him and others like him apart from most of their contemporaries.[11]

The genteel diaries reflect people at ease with themselves, devoid of guilt, free from the pangs of remorse for thoughts and feelings that they sought to deny or suppress, and free, too, to enjoy themselves to the limits of their ability. The absence of anguish, of guilt, of a sense of inner depravity, of self-loathing and dislike, of elation as well as despair (the oscillating moods so characteristic of evangelicals), combined with the even, calm, temperate, routine responses of these individuals to the daily experiences of their lives—these are the characteristics that set them apart from most of their contemporaries, and mark them at once as possessors of the temperaments of comfortable gentility. They felt no need to look within, no desire to examine their feelings or thoughts, no urge to be self-conscious. On the contrary, their diaries suggest precisely the opposite desires—to avoid self-awareness as much as possible, to deflect their scrutiny toward the world in which they lived so avidly and successfully, toward the people they knew and with whom they were connected or involved. No matter how varied their temperaments, they were of one mind in their indifference to the *inner* self.

The Self Indulged

THE GENTEEL, nevertheless, were preoccupied with the *outer* self. Everything about their lives was designed to please and to enhance the self, and self-indulgence shaped their entire existence. The genteel loved the self and set out to display, ornament, and gratify it as fully as possible in this world. In their clothing, their food, their housing, their styles of life generally, the genteel demonstrated their preoccupation with the self.

Clothing, of course, provided one of the most visible signs of self-indulgence, and the preoccupation of the genteel with beautiful and luxurious clothes from childhood through youth to maturity reflects their concern with self-display and self-ornamentation generally. Governor Jonathan Belcher of Massachusetts, for instance, always encouraged his son and namesake to "be always handsomely drest (your hair especially)" when he appeared "before persons of rank and distinction." He had sent his second son and the youngest of his three children, whom he adored and indulged for many years, to England to learn law, after his graduation from Harvard College in 1728. In 1734, he wrote to confirm his son's annual expense account of £200 a year—more than many New England farmers ever possessed—observing that "I expect it shou'd always make you appear pretty and handsome." At the same time, he ordered his son, then twenty-four years old, to "get on a handsome fair long wigg." On another occasion, Belcher advised him to "take care to be genteely drest to make a handsome appearance before" Lord Townsend, one of his patrons. By 1739, he was dismayed to find his son spending "more than four times" what he himself spent a year on clothing, and warned that this was excessive. By the time his son was nearly thirty-two and still living in London at his expense, Belcher wrote to ask, "After a succession of my loud warning letters for many years past, how is it possible you should bring yourself into such straits, with such large supplies as you have had from me? To indulge yourself in your vast, extravagant expence you had need had a silver mine." Other parents might have said similar things in response to the self-indulgence of their children, yet they would never have wavered from their belief that such display and ornamentation were indispensable signs of gentility.[12]

Clothing, of course, was only a small aspect of the entire life style of the genteel, which was designed to enhance and display the self as well as to indulge it. John Adams, the quintessential moderate, could not help observing the luxuriousness of the life styles of the genteel wherever he visited them. In May 1761, for instance, he drew upon his knowledge for a satirical essay intended for publication in the Boston *Gazette*, which caught many of the most obvious facts of the genteel life:

> Our Gentry has given frequent Invitations, to the Country Repre-
> sentatives [in the Provincial Assembly at Boston], and to other
> Country Gentlemen, who had Acquaintance here, to Entertain-
> ments. The Productions of every Element and Climate were as-
> sembled, and the nicest Art and Cookery employed to regale them.
> The furniture of our Houses and Tables were proportionably rich
> and gay. Our Persons were cloathed in silks and Laces and Velvet,
> and our Daughters especially blazed in the rich vestments of
> Princesses. At the same Time the poor Gentlemen were scarcely
> able to walk the streets, for the Multitude of Chariots, or to hear
> themselves speak for the rapid Rattling of Hoofs and Wheels. . . .
> These Appearances at the Churches, assemblies, Concerts, Private
> Houses and streets, gave the Country an opinion, either that Bos-
> ton was vastly rich or vastly extravagant, and they dared not, by
> any public speech or Conduct suppose the latter least they should
> give offence to us, who had treated them even with assiduous
> Complaisance and Hospitality.

Personal experience only confirmed the observations expressed in his satire. In mid-January 1766, for instance, Adams dined with Nicholas Boylston, a wealthy merchant, and reported in his diary: "An elegant Dinner indeed! Went over the House to view the Furniture, which alone cost a thousand Pounds sterling. A Seat it is for a noble Man, a Prince.

The Turkey Carpets, the painted Hangings, the Marble Tables, the rich Beds with crimson Damask Curtains and Counterpins, the beautiful Chimny Clock, the Spacious Garden, are the most magnificent of any Thing I have ever seen."[13]

The elegance and self-indulgence characteristic of the genteel life style in New England were also abundantly evident to Adams during his first visit to the Middle colonies in 1774 as a delegate to the first Continental Congress. On a Monday morning in late August, while visiting New York, Adams and several friends

> rode three Miles out of Town, to Mr. Morine Scotts to break fast. A very pleasant Ride! Mr. Scott has an elegant Seat there, with Hudsons River just behind his House, and a rural Prospect all round him. Mr. Scott, his Lady and Daughter, and her Husband Mr. Litchfield were dressed to receive Us. We satt in a fine Airy Entry, till called into a front Room to break fast. A more elegant Breakfast, I never saw—rich Plate—a very large Silver Coffee Pott, a very large Silver Tea Pott—Napkins of the very finest Materials, and toast and bread and butter in great Perfection. After breakfast, a Plate of beautifull Peaches, another of Pairs and another of Plumbs and a Muskmellen were placed on the Table.[14]

Adams occasionally commented on the richness and elegance of the furnishings and housing of the genteel families that he visited both in New York and in Pennsylvania, obviously impressed by surroundings the genteel seemed to take for granted. While in Philadelphia the following September, for instance, he "visited Mr. Cadwallader a Gentleman of large Fortune, a grand and elegant House And Furniture. We then visited Mr. Powell, another splendid Seat." The following week, after a busy day in committee, he dined with a large company "at Mr. Powells," where he experienced "A most sinfull Feast again! Every Thing which could delight the Eye, or allure the Taste"—precisely the temptations most enticing to a moderate such as Adams—including an immense array of "Curds and Creams, Jellies, Sweet meats of various sorts, 20 sorts of Tarts, fools, Trifles, floating Islands, whipped Sillabubs &c. &c.—Parmesan Cheese, Punch, Wine, Porter, Beer &c. &c." The sheer abundance signified by the repeated et ceteras undoubtedly constituted part of the sinfulness of the feast; but, to the genteel, such delights to the eyes and allures to the taste were a matter of course and in no way considered sinful. The genteel could indulge themselves with food as readily as they could enjoy their elegant surroundings, at ease with the pleasures their wealth could bestow and their desires fulfill. Ladies and gentlemen took such indulgence in stride, confident that they were worthy and deserving of these pleasures and satisfactions, both aesthetic and visceral. Only John Adams felt guilty for such indulgence of his appetites. Self-denial, however, was not part of the ordinary vocabulary of gentility.[15] *

Contented Selves:
Pleasure and Sociability

PERHAPS IN NO OTHER WAY did the genteel differ more from their evangelical and moderate contemporaries than in their capacity for enjoyment of life and for contentment with themselves and the world in which they lived. In their easy acceptance of themselves and their place in society, in their ability to gratify their physical, emotional, and aesthetic needs and desires, the genteel found it possible to preoccupy themselves with other people and with the circumstances of their daily lives, filling their days with activity and with pleasure, and thus avoiding the daily scrutiny of self that dominated the lives of so many evangelicals and moderates. The records of their outward experience—eating, drinking, entertaining family and friends, meeting and talking with people, going to dances and plays, listening to music, playing cards—reveal not only what they did but what they *enjoyed* doing, for their pleasure in the events of their days usually was evident. The very fact that they seemed to be able to enjoy

---

* Self-indulgence carried to excess, as done by some of the genteel, could become self-destructive. Alcoholism and gambling constituted two common forms of overindulgence among the genteel (although not limited to them, of course), and both topics deserve more analysis. My guess is that alcoholism was linked closely to "indulgence" in childhood, forming the negative side of development open to genteel children. Gambling, which became a chronic passion of many gentlemen, especially Southerners, seems to have expressed a circuitous form of rebelliousness by children fated to be rich: persistent gambling was a reliable method of destroying family wealth and ensuring the impoverishment (at least relatively) of a man's own children.

Gaming was a persistent theme in the lives of Landon Carter's sons. From Carter's point of view, "the Gaming table" was a place "where self and gain alone Govern, at the Sacrifice of every duty, whether Moral or religious" (Jack P. Greene, ed., *The Diary of Colonel Landon Carter of Sabine Hall, 1752–1778*, 2 vols. [Charlottesville, Va., 1965], II, p. 1122). Few aspects of his sons' lives upset him more than their incessant gambling. In this instance, it seems clear that gambling provided the Carter sons with their only legitimate means of resisting their father's determined control over their lives. Since virtually their entire estates had been given to them by him, they could hurt him most by dissipating their inheritances through gambling. See also T. H. Breen's fascinating study "Horses and Gentlemen: The Cultural Significance of Gambling Among the Gentry of Virginia," *William and Mary Quarterly* XXXIV (1977), pp. 239–57.

themselves distinguished them from their evangelical counterparts—for whom life itself was a burden to be escaped as rapidly as possible for the future joys of eternal life hereafter—and from the anxious moderates— who often did things that brought pleasure, but rarely without subsequent guilt and moral discomfort. The sociability of the genteel was a reflection not simply of wealth but of easy consciences, for they could allow themselves to enjoy their lives without feeling guilty. Pleasure was not a sin.

As early as 1744, the genteel members of Boston's upper ranks were busily enjoying themselves, as revealed by the observations of Dr. Alexander Hamilton, a Scottish gentleman who had emigrated several years before to Maryland. He found that "the better sort are polite, mannerly, and hospitable to strangers," and noted that "Assemblys of the gayer sort are frequent here; the gentlemen and ladys meeting almost every week att consorts of musick and balls." "I was present att two or three such," he said, "and saw as fine a ring of ladys, as good dancing, and heard musick as elegant as I had been witness to any where." "I must take notice," he added, "that this place abounds with pritty women who appear rather more abroad than they do att York and dress elegantly. They are, for the most part, free and affable as well as pritty. I saw not one prude while I was here."[16]

A few decades later, the life of another wealthy and prominent Bostonian, John Rowe, merchant and gentleman, also was often gratifying and pleasurable. His diary faithfully records the names of the innumerable people with whom he visited or dined. In February 1770, his wife "to please Sucky made a Dance and entertainment which was a Genteel One," he observed. On Christmas Day, 1770, he dined at home with his wife and daughter and five friends, who "staid and spent the afternoon and evening and wee were very Cheerfull." The following day, he "Spent the evening at Mr Lewis Deblois with him and his new wife and a very Large Company too many to enumerate—a very Genteel Entertainment," as he noted approvingly. Early in January 1771, he described going to a number of concerts and dances, including the celebration of the queen's birthday, which involved spending the evening "at Concert Hall with a very Grand Assembly, Gouvernour, Lieutenant Governour, Commodore, Colonel, Captains of the Navy and Army, Commissioners, all the Best People in town—A General Coalition so that Harmony Peace and Friendship will once more be Established in Boston—Very Good Dancing and Good Musick, but very Bad Wine and Punch." In March, he was pleased to observe that "the Company that waited on the Governour were Gentlemen of Reputation and the Best Fortunes—I spent the evening at the Assembly which was very Brilliant." The pinnacle of Rowe's social career was experienced on July 16, 1772, when Ralph Inman, an immensely wealthy resident of Cambridge (who was soon to be driven into exile), "made the Genteelest Entertainment I ever saw" on behalf of his son, newly graduated from Harvard. Rowe noted that Inman "had Three hundred forty seven Gentlemen and Ladies dined," including "The Governour and Family, The Lieutenant Governour and Family, The Admiral and Family and all the Remainder, Gentlemen and Ladies of Character and Reputation. The whole was conducted with much Ease and Pleasure and all Joyned in making each other Happy—"; "such an Entertainment has not been made in New England before on any Occasion," Rowe observed, adding that he also "went to the Ball at the Town House, where most of the Company went to Dance—they were all very happy and Cheerful and the whole was conducted to the General Satisfaction of all present." Ease, pleasure, happiness, and satisfaction with life—these were hallmarks of gentility.[17]

Indeed, the same life style was evident elsewhere throughout the colonies—more subdued or more extravagant, depending upon the time and place, but always preoccupied with an unending round of social activities and diversions. Early in September 1769, a gentleman from Philadelphia, John Hughes, traveled north by land through New England to Portsmouth, New Hampshire, where he had been given the job of Collector of Customs. Upon his arrival in Portsmouth, he reported to his son that he "was received in the most Obliging Manner by all Ranks of People, And particularly so by his Excellency the Governor who is of the first family in this place who by their Wealth, Marriages, And Great Offices, Are Strictly Connected with most of the best families in the province— And are not only a Gay and Genteel, But a polite and Hospitable people." Hughes thus was pleased to discover that the genteel even in distant Portsmouth were very much like those familiar to him in Philadelphia. Other Philadelphians also discovered the similarities of the genteel in both the Middle and the Southern colonies.[18]

The sociability and hospitality of genteel Southerners were always visible to strangers and to themselves, forming one of the dominant motifs in both their life styles and their temperaments. Genteel Southerners enjoyed the constant dining, dancing, and celebrating that drew people together from miles around; and the gatherings at the large, opulent houses of the gentry often lasted for days and many nights of feasting— satiating the appetites and the passions of those who participated. The descriptions of the balls, dinners, and festivities among Southern genteel families are interchangeable with those from genteel families elsewhere.[19]

Gentle Men and Gentle Women:
Masculine and Feminine

THE EXTERIOR WORLD that surrounded the genteel almost everywhere suggests an inner balance between the masculine and feminine components of their characters, the harmonious fusing of a life style profoundly feminine in its aesthetic sensibilities with a ready engagement on the part of gentlemen in the active public life of agriculture, commerce, and politics, the exclusive prerogatives of men. Gentlemen were comfortable with their feminine impulses and sensibilities, their self-assurance providing an unconscious testament to their inner security over their own masculinity. Gentlemen were comfortable with elegance, with politeness and good manners, and the ceremony of genteel society; they were responsive and sensitive to beauty and to the aesthetics of the objects with which they surrounded themselves. The feminization of gentility did not threaten gentlemen who could express their feminine impulses as freely and openly as their masculine impulses. They felt no inner need to repress or deny the feminine side of their temperaments; consequently, they rarely experienced a sense of anxiety or ambivalence.*

The absence of inner repressiveness characteristic of the genteel was manifested in every aspect of their outer lives—in their clothing and personal adornment, in the furnishings of their houses, in their dwellings and the surrounding landscapes, in everything they either wore or used. From the early seventeenth century to at least the last quarter of the eighteenth century, from New Hampshire to South Carolina, the genteel set themselves apart from the common ranks by the visible badges of wealth and social distinctions. The objects they purchased and used: magnificent chairs, chests, tables, beautiful crystal, china, and silver; the paintings they commissioned: most of the portraits for the period represent the genteel of all ages and both sexes; the houses they constructed and lived in, both in towns and in the countryside—all provide enduring evidence of their wealth and their taste, visible testaments to the aesthetic sensibilities of successive genteel generations in every colony. In every aspect of their lives, the genteel sought to create and sustain a private world of beauty and of elegance, pleasing to the eye, the touch, the

---

* Rhys Isaac has pointed out to me the transformation of the meaning of the word "gentle" from its earlier association with "genteel" or "wellborn," which implies economic and social distinctions, to "soft," "docile," or "moderate," implying qualities of temperament that were always associated with femininity and thus with the attributes of gender rather than social rank.

taste, a world of objects and people that would always enhance their sense of pleasure and self-satisfaction.

Genteel males were able, as adults, to incorporate rather than to repress the experiences of childhood that had identified them so closely and so visibly with femininity. Having been clothed as children in long dresses and gowns, these men continued to dress in styles that, to many of their contemporaries, would have appeared feminine: luxurious fabrics in satins, silks, velvets of gorgeous hues and colors, embellished often with embroidery and lace—the elegant and beautiful clothing that immediately set them off as genteel. Even more strikingly, of course, genteel men often wore their hair long, either in great flowing wigs or naturally. Long hair and gentility were synonymous—but long hair also was symbolic of their enduring capacity to accept a close identification with femininity. The portraits of gentlemen in the seventeenth and eighteenth centuries are striking evidence of the ease with which genteel men were able to appear in clothing which bore a close affinity to that of genteel women—they seem to be exuberantly flaunting their hair and clothes, confident of remaining entirely masculine while looking quite feminine.

The ease with which genteel men balanced their feminine and their masculine sensibilities is evident in a brief anecdote recounted by young Sally Wister—the Quaker girl from Philadelphia who had taken refuge with her family in the countryside during the revolutionary war—in the journal she kept for the amusement of her friend Deborah Norris. Her observations reveal several different attitudes toward hair and suggest the significance of powdering and caring for hair by many genteel young men while in the Continental army. When she first encountered a young Virginian captain, she discovered that his name was "not Dyer, but Alexander Spotswood Dandridge, which certainly gives a genteel idea of the man," she thought. She added, "His person is more elegantly form'd than any I ever saw; tall and commanding," thus making him "the handsomest man I ever beheld." After chatting with him that evening, she observed that he "is sensible, and (divested of some freedoms, which might be call'd gallant in the fashionable world) he is polite and agreeable." She was disturbed by his "propensity to swearing," to which comment he replied after being asked why he did so, "It is a favorite vice, Miss Sally." Dandridge, in the course of their conversation, said that he had "no patience with those officers who, every morn, before they went on detachments, would wait to be dress'd and powder'd. 'I am,'" she said, "'excessively fond of powder, and think it very becoming.'" He answered that he was "'very careless'" about such matters, but the next morning, she reported, "He was powder'd very white, a (pretty colored) brown coat, lapell'd with green, and white waistcoat," all of which meant that "He made a truly elegant figure." On seeing him, she said, "'Oh, dear, I see thee is powder'd,'" to which he replyed, "'Yes ma'am. I have dress'd myself off for you.'"

Dandridge could afford to powder his hair and dress elegantly, despite his preference against it—at least while compaigning. His sense of being manly was in no way disturbed by his elegant appearance. For many of his contemporaries, however, particularly among the more radical revolutionaries, powdered hair and elegant clothing were too effeminate to be tolerated. They preferred their hair short and unpowdered and their clothing simple. That way they could be certain of appearing manly. Dandridge and other genteel young men evidently did not share such sensibilities nor feel such needs.[20]

Being "polite and agreeable," as Dandridge and other gentlemen were, was part of the preoccupation with good manners and the ceremony of "the fashionable world" of the genteel everywhere. The inculcation of manners and of polite behavior on the part of both sexes had begun early in childhood and continued unabated throughout their lives. Yet the grace and ease with which gentlemen and ladies conversed, courted, and conducted themselves on all social occasions were also part of the fusing of feminine and masculine sensibilities inherent in gentility—a persistent reflection of the affinities that bound gentle men and gentle women together within the carefully defined social etiquette that shaped so many aspects of their public life and social activities.

The genteel also sought to create settings for their sociability which would ensure that they would be protected against unpleasantness, discomfort, anger, and intimacy. The physical appearance of their houses— with the spacious dimensions of Georgian and Federalist buildings providing room for entertainment as well as elegance and formality of design and decoration—emphasized the cool restraint and balance of sensibilities that dominated both their architecture and their furnishings. Within these surroundings, the genteel pursued a pattern of polite formality which dominated their relationships with other people and provided them with secure foundations for maintaining reliable spaces between people— spaces that inhibited intimacy with outsiders and ensured the privacy of their own feelings and thoughts. Politeness was the best protection the genteel had against feelings that made them uncomfortable. Thus good manners were indispensable to the maintenance of their personal equanimity.

Good manners were apparently of the utmost importance to Martha Jefferson Randolph, who hoped that her youthful son would learn by keeping company with the "virtuous and well bred . . . that it is not customary for genteel society to indulge mean and little passions." "Good manners," she observed in a letter to her father, "are I believe more important in forming the character than good sense and reflection because called in to action before our habits are formed and before that period at which the understanding is sufficiently matured to be of much importance in preventing bad one's." Having just read "a very sensible little book" by a French author, "in which the author proves that the various little rules of etiquette which though scrupulously observed have been thought lightly of as *ceremonies* are really derived from the most amiable and virtuous feelings of the heart," she acknowledged never having been "fully aware of the influence of good manner upon the morals." Good manners also concerned Governor Jonathan Belcher as he sought to offer helpful advice to his son studying law in London. "You must really, Jonathan, learn to be the gentleman, to be mannerly and gratefull, or who will serve you?" he asked in 1734. Obviously, good manners and polished behavior were taken for granted by the genteel, and inculcated from early childhood.[21]

The ceremonies of polite society provided a sense of security which arose from the knowledge that a proper distance could always be maintained between individuals while still allowing them to be close. In a sense, good manners enabled gentlemen and ladies to express their feminine impulses of sentiment, tenderness, and involvement with others, while also guarding them against feelings of excess or passion that might make them uncomfortable. As much as possible, the genteel preferred to avoid discussing subjects that were controversial—politics, religion, or intimate matters—being content to talk about the details of their daily experiences, gossip about the people in their lives, share their interests in the events that gave them pleasure, but avoiding anything that might cause disagreements or unpleasantness. The ceremonies associated with tea in genteel households in pre-revolutionary America epitomized the restraint that unspoken agreement placed upon their conversations and their feelings. Women gossiped, as Alexander Hamilton observed while in Boston. After an afternoon spent in the company of "a very agreeable lady," he noted that "The conversation was lively, entertaining, and solid, neither tainted with false or triffling wit nor ill natured satire or reflexion, of late so much the topic of tea tables. I was glad to find that in most of the politer caballs of ladys in this town the odious theme of scandal and detraction over their tea had become quite unfashionable and unpolite and was banished intirely to the assemblies of the meaner sort." In many respects, the formality associated with the "polite part of the world"—as George Whitefield designated genteel Marylanders—was the best assurance of protection from the confrontations with the self and with the world that distinguished evangelicals and moderates.[22]

"Nature Had Intended Him for Some Asiatic Prince": Sensuality and Sexuality

THE ABILITY OF THE GENTEEL to gratify the senses of taste, sight, and feeling also extended to their ability, often, to gratify the sensual desires of the flesh as well. The whole issue of sexuality and sensuality among the genteel is problematic, since so few sources remain to describe either their feelings or their behavior. Yet the few that do survive suggest that the genteel were far more expressive of their sexual impulses and desires both before and after marriage than were most evangelicals or moderates.

The issue is not simply fornication, but attitudes toward sexuality and the fulfillment of sexual desires generally. Evangelicals often produced many children, yet their sexual repressiveness remained a potent source of inner anxiety, a deeply buried root of their profound hostility toward the body and the senses. The genteel, on the other hand, were far more at ease with their sensuality and with sexual experience. By their acceptance of their inner desires and of the dual components of their temperaments, genteel men were often able to express their sexual impulses more readily and freely than other men. Even aesthetically, the genteel were far more responsive to the sensual qualities of their immediate environment—to the pleasures of feeling the fabrics that clothed them and adorned their houses, to the tactile and visual delight of the beautiful objects they used and surrounded themselves with. Their entire environment provided a constant source of subtly sensual pleasure, a constant gratification to the senses. Each chair, each table, each chest or highboy was a form of mobile sculpture, to be used and enjoyed without conscious thought. Their employment of color, of embellishment in both architecture and furnishings augmented their aesthetic sensibilities and gave to their surroundings a sensuous quality missing from the lives of so many of their contemporaries. But this aesthetic sensuality—controlled, balanced, harmonized though it so often was by the classicism of the mid-eighteenth century— also extended to the pleasures of the body, to sexuality itself. Pleasure was not to be restricted solely to the public dimensions of daily life but should reach into the most private, and thus the most obscure, dimensions of experience as well.[23]

Thanks to an occasional diary, it is possible to get a rare glimpse into the sexual experiences of genteel men such as William Byrd, the remarkable Virginia gentleman who possessed powerful sexual appetites and was almost always able to gratify them. Byrd's London diary, for instance, provides an ample and precise record of his sexual life—should anyone care to catalogue his orgasms—and reveals the importance of sexuality as a source both of pleasure and of activity. In addition to mistresses, he constantly availed himself of the women on the London streets for fleeting sexual encounters. In June 1718, for instance, he went with a friend "to the park, where we had appointed to meet some ladies but they failed. Then we went to Spring Gardens where we picked up two women and carried them into the arbor and ate some cold veal and about 10 o'clock we carried them to the bagnio, where we bathed and lay with them all night and I rogered mine twice and slept pretty well, but neglected my prayers."

After returning to Virginia as a widower, Byrd's maid, Annie, usually served to gratify his sexual needs, for he constantly noted that he "committed uncleanness with Annie, for which God forgive me," as he prayed ritualistically and without guilt. While his wife, Lucy Parkes Byrd, was alive, he would note that "I gave my wife a flourish in which she had a great deal of pleasure," or "I gave my wife a flourish, notwithstanding she was indisposed," or, "I gave my wife a powerful flourish and gave her great ecstasy and refreshment." On another day, Byrd and his wife "had a little quarrel which I reconciled with a flourish," adding that "it is to be observed that the flourish was performed on the billiard table."[24]

Byrd's constant fulfillment of his own sexual desires may well have been characteristic of many genteel Southern men with ready, if illicit, access to sexual relationships with their slaves. The rumors and surmises reported by Philip Fithian about young Ben Carter, eighteen years old and the eldest of Robert Carter's sons, suggest the readiness with which sexual relationships between young white youths and their black servants were envisaged. In late March 1774, Ben's younger brother Bob enraged him by intimating that he had heard rumors in the neighborhood about him: "it is reported that two Sundays ago you took Sukey (a young likely Negro Girl maid to Mrs Carters youngest Son) into your stable, and there for a considerable time lock'd yourselves together!" But before his brother could reply, the bell rang and they were sent off.

The following September, the household was disturbed by the intrusion of someone into the nursery about one o'clock in the morning, whose "design," Fithian said, "was either to rob the House, or commit fornication with *Sukey*, (a plump, sleek, likely Negro Girl about sixteen)." While some said the apparition was "a Ghost because it would not speak," Fithian thought that "more probably it was one of the warm-blooded, well fed young Negroes, trying for the company of buxom *Sukey*." By the next day, Fithian wrote: "It is whispered to Day that B. . . . is the Ghost that walk'd in the Nursery the other night," but, he added, "I think the report is false, and arises from calumny." Several days later, Fithian recounted, with no apparent surprise at the easy openness about sexual matters among the members of the family, that Ben "with great Humour either out of a *Bravado* or for Revenge gave out in the Family to day that it is the opinion of a certain *Female*, of considerable Note in the family, that all the male Children which shall be born in this unlucky year, tho' they may be fair to the Sight, will be yet unable, from a Debility of Constitution, to do their Duty, with respect to Women, either married or," he added suggestively, "single." Fithian added his opinion that *"Ben*, by this stratagem, whether it be real or otherwise, is levil with the invidious Vixen which suspected him of entering the Nursery to visit black-faced Sukey." Soon even Fithian began to think that perhaps Ben had been guilty of this attempted liaison after all. "I begin to suspect him of being actually engaged in what several alledge against him—But I will keep off so long as I possibly can, so unwelcome, so unwelcome and so Base a thought of its Reality." Fithian's response, characteristic of a young moderate Presbyterian, was thus preserved; Ben's was not. What matters most is not the actuality but the presumption—so readily made within the Carter household—that Ben had tried. Within such households, sexuality was a part of the consciousness and, no doubt, of the experience of many genteel men, before marriage as well as afterwards.[25]

The visible passions of young Jack Custis were a source of considerable uneasiness both to his stepfather, George Washington, and to his tutor, the Reverend Jonathan Boucher. In mid-December 1770, Washington sent Jack back to Annapolis from Mount Vernon, acknowledging to Boucher that his stepson's mind was "a good deal released from Study, and more than ever turned to Dogs Horses and Guns," as well as to "Dress and equipage." Washington recognized that "The time of Life he is now advancing into requires the most friendly aid and Council (especially in such a place as Annapolis)"; otherwise, he added, "the warmth of his own Passions, assisted by the bad example of other Youth, may prompt him to actions derogatory of Virtue, and that Innocence of Manners which one could wish to preserve him in." Washington requested that Boucher keep Jack under his own roof as much as possible, and not to "allow him to be rambling about of Nights in Company with those, who do not care how debauched and viceous his Conduct may be." Boucher was well aware of his young student's temperament. As early as August 1770, he had acknowledged to Washington that the chief failings of Jack's character were "that He is constitutionally somewhat too warm, indolent, and voluptuous." Although Boucher was confident that "As yet these propensities are but in Embrio," he realized that "Ere long, however, They will discover Themselves, and if not duly and carefully regulated, it is Easy to see to what They will lead."

More specifically, Boucher anticipated that young Jack would "soon lose all Relish for mental Excellence," and that he would become "Sunk in unmanly Sloth," with his estate "left to the Management of some worthless Overseer." Finally, he foresaw that his student would "Himself soon be entangled in some matrimonial Adventure, in which as Passion will have much to say, it is not very likely Reason will be much listened to." Boucher's fears proved accurate in due course. By December, in response to Washington's concerned letter, Boucher acknowledged having "observ'd his growing Passions taking this unpleasing Cast, without the Power of preventing it." He was most alarmed by young Custis's "Love of Ease, and Love of Pleasure—Pleasure of a Kind exceedingly uncommon at his Years"—an allusion to his emerging sexuality. "I must confess to You," Boucher added, "I never did in my Life know a Youth so exceedingly indolent, or so surprisingly voluptuous: one would suppose Nature had intended Him for some Asiatic Prince."

He also realized that "It could not be but that at one Time or other Mr. Custis must have been introduc'd into Life, as 'tis call'd"—a euphemism for sexual experience which suggests the ready acceptance of sexuality by the genteel. Young Custis obviously had a "Propensity" for the female sex that left his tutor at a loss "to judge" or "to describe." By the spring of 1773, Jack Custis had acted upon his impulses and precipitously engaged himself, without parental consent, to marry Nelly Calvert, the daughter of a prominent and wealthy Marylander. All that Boucher could say to Washington was that he had never had "the most distant Suspicion of any such Thing's being in Agitation." Yet he could foresee that the engagement would cause Jack to "consider Himself as not less bound in Honour, to avoid all those sordid and less noble Pursuits, which wou'd debase, and render Him unworthy of Her." In due course, parental consent to the marriage was forthcoming and the marriage consummated, thus providing a legitimate outlet for the voluptuousness that had been evident for so many years. Jack Custis saw to this on his own.[26]

Southerners were not unique in their easy sexuality, however, as the experience of Dr. Hamilton in New York suggests. He reported having gone out to a coffeehouse in the evening with a friend, "expecting to sup and have some chat snugly by ourselves, but we were interrupted by three young rakes who bounced in upon us, and then the conversation turned from a grave to a wanton strain." "There was nothing talked of but ladys and lovers," he recalled, "and a good deal of polite smutt. We drank two remarkable toasts which I never before heard mentioned: the first was to our dear selves, and the tenour of the other was my own health. I told them that if such rediculous toasts should be heard of out of doors, we should procure the name of the Selfish Club. We supped and dismissed att 9 o'clock." "Mr. Bourdillion and I went home like two philosophers," he noted, but "the others went a whoreing like three rakes."[27]

Not every genteel male chose to avail himself even of readily offered opportunities, however, and many undoubtedly must have been more like their moderate contemporaries, who would have been responsive but inhibited by the temptations of sexual pleasures. Samuel Curwen, in his early sixties, looked with uneasy fascination upon the opportunities offered by many women in London. In July 1775, while visiting Vauxhall Gardens with some friends, he was "not a little mortifyed at the sight of so many pitiable votaries to Venus as appeared before our eyes in the walks, some solitary, some in company of persons of pleasure Whose mistaken happiness consists," as he insisted, "in lustful gratification; many of these devoted roulakes appeared in as genteel dresses as any of the Company and of as agreeable an aspect." "Very polite company frequent this resort," he noted, "I seeing coronets on some of the Coaches." Several months later, Curwen and his friends spent the evening "in drinking 2 bowls punch, supping on Mutton chop and smoaking" at the "Turks head." Afterwards, "we traversed the purlieus of Lewdness and debauchery and were pretty grossly addressed in Grosvenor Square, making no reply, hastened to the Strand but my companions being full of spirits, and disposed to merriment one of them seeing a solitary Girl of which this part of the Town is overspread and addressing her in the customary stile threw her into my arms, and invited her to accompany me, assuring her I was in quest of game. Notwithstanding my denial the girl was unwilling to believe me though I endeavoured to persuade that the Young Gentleman whom she first met was more for her purpose." Finally, with great difficulty disengaging himself from the girl, Curwen found that his companions had "enjoyed the scene that furnished them with much mirth and me with very serious reflections on the contemptible situation vice reduces its miserable slaves to"—and yet he had thought that his younger companion might be interested in his pursuer. What he himself might have done at a younger age under similar circumstances can only be imagined.[28]

The vocabulary of corruption and of sin so characteristic of evangelicals had no place in the writings of the genteel. They were at ease with their physical bodies just as they were at ease with the world outside, and this inner ease provided them with feelings of self-assurance and self-approval that far exceeded the experiences of most evangelicals and many moderates. Sexuality was only part, and often no doubt a small part, of the experiences of the genteel; but it symbolized their most basic responses to the self—acceptance, approval, and fulfillment. Self-love was not a sin, nor self-gratification a vice.

Acceptable Passions:
Anger, Ambition, and Pride

THE GENTEEL WERE ABLE TO ACCEPT the passions that most preoccupied both evangelicals and moderates: anger, ambition, pride. Their wealth made avarice unnecessary in most instances, although undoubtedly it had played a notable role in the initial acquisition of family wealth at some prior point. The genteel seemed to be unusually free to express their emotions, just as they felt able to accept their sexuality. When they felt ambitious, they acted upon their feelings. When they felt proud, they displayed their feelings, though they also took care to contain their passions within the bounds of propriety in many social situations. But for many of the genteel, particularly Southerners, the expression of feelings was often immediate, voluble, and direct. Their self-assurance permitted them to express themselves rather than to repress such feelings or keep them tightly under control.

William Byrd's life ordinarily was calm and contented, but he also records faithfully his expression of anger and outrage toward his servants and his family. Byrd quarreled frequently with his wife, Lucy Parkes, but was just as readily reconciled. Anger was sudden and vociferous and equally swiftly forgotten. Being so freely expressed, there was little chance of having the feelings of discontent and disapproval associated with anger smoldering away beneath the placid surface, as so often was the case with others. On the last day of December 1711, for instance, he reported that "My wife and I had a terrible quarrel about whipping Eugene [one of the house slaves] while Mr. Mumford was there but she had a mind to show her authority before company but I would not suffer it, which she took very ill; however for peace sake I made the first advance toward a reconciliation which I obtained with some difficulty and after abundance of crying. However it spoiled the mirth of the evening, but I was not conscious that I was to blame in that quarrel." The next morning, he "lay abed till 9 o'clock this morning to bring my wife into temper again and rogered her by way of reconciliation." From experiences such as this, it is apparent that William Byrd could accept himself as he was, at ease with most of his feelings, desires, and inclinations, and able to express his emotions quite openly. There is little that seems to have been held back by Byrd, little that was being consciously repressed. He did not feel threatened by his anger. His feelings were familiar and acceptable, on the whole, to him. Thus even in his rages or angry moods, he seemed to be fundamentally easy and contented with himself.[29]

For many genteel Southerners, the volatility of their feelings and their ready expression of anger provided an undercurrent of strong and excitable feelings, which were contained within the perimeters of polite social relationships. The excessive politeness and ceremonialism of Southerners may well have been a response to the intensity of their feelings of love and of hostility, to inner states of feeling that belied the courtliness of their formal relationships. There is so little direct evidence about such feelings that the relationship between the ready expression of anger (which often flared and died away with equal rapidity, instead of smoldering or being denied altogether) and the emphasis upon politeness and formality in social relationships can only be surmised. But from the little evidence that survives, genteel Southerners often seem to be notably open and at ease with their feelings, whatever their nature. Their passions were expressed, not denied; yet their expression was contained within an elaborately developed set of ceremonies and social rules, which sustained their sense of being polite, courteous, mannerly, and genteel.

The genteel in more northerly regions seem to have been more equable in their temperaments. Their passions seemed to be less volatile, perhaps less strong; and they seemed less prone to feel or to express a sense of anger. For many ladies and gentlemen, anger was not a serious problem, since they rarely felt the impulse within themselves; and when they did, they were able to command their passion and sustain their sense of themselves as polite, decorous, and respectable people. Being comfortable within themselves, they could deal with their occasional feelings of anger without feeling unduly stressed or threatened.

Ambition, too, was a passion that the genteel could express freely if they felt it. Governor Jonathan Belcher constantly encouraged his son to be ambitious, confident that gentlemen ought to be eminent and wealthy and worthy of respect. He wanted his son to pursue his legal studies diligently so that "no labour shall be wanting in you to shine in your profession, and to merit the favour of mankind, and that the present opportunity of young gentlemen's rising in the law shall be a spur to your ambition." "These are laudable resolutions," the father observed, "and render you worthy of my best future care." Belcher looked forward eagerly to seeing his son, as a lawyer, "shining with a greater lustre in all futurity." He wanted nothing more than "to stimulate" his son's "ambition."[30]

Yet ambition actually was a passion that the genteel often did not feel as intensely as many moderates did. There was little need, when they already possessed everything that others so eagerly desired and sought—wealth, offices, and power. Nevertheless, gentlemen could express their personal ambitiousness through their play—in gambling, horse racing, and hunting. The ambition clearly was to win or to be first among equals. As Rhys Isaac has observed, "the gentry style . . . is best understood in relation to the concept of honor—the proving of prowess. A formality of manners barely concealed adversary relationships" among

Virginia gentlemen, so that "the essence of social exchange was overt self-assertion."[31]

The preoccupation with displays of personal prowess and success was a ritualization of ambition while simultaneously declaring disdain for ambitiousness. To win at cards, to be the best dancer, to have one's horse come first in a race were pleasing, since they enhanced the reputation, respect, and honor bestowed upon the men who were successful; yet gentlemen could also feel that their feats were only part of a game.

Perhaps the deeper significance of these feats for many of the genteel derived from the obvious association of such games and pastimes with manliness—and the proving of prowess thus was actually a vital complement to the polite and mannerly behavior required of them in other settings. In effect, the preoccupation of many gentlemen with gambling, drinking, and horses were expressive of their masculinity, as bold and as visible as their expression of their femininity within the formal, decorous, and elegant settings of sociability, both private and public, that also constituted so important a part of their life and temperament. Self-assertion and ambition thus became important aspects of the gentleman's sense of his manliness, a major element in the public displays that always placed gentlemen at the center of attention.

The passion which dominated the genteel temperament was pride. Only rarely did the genteel express their sense of pride and self-worth in words, since their actions always made their statements for them. Everything about their style of life emphasized their inner sense of self-regard, the high valuation they placed upon themselves; and everything they possessed was designed to display their sense of pride to the world at large. The genteel respected themselves and expected the world at large to respect them also. When Governor Belcher's son reached the age of twenty-four, the indulgent and proud father noted to a friend that "for the future . . . we must give him his due honour, and not say, He is a pretty youth, but that Mr. Belcher of the Temple is a gentleman of good sense, &ca. Such a way of mentioning him in conversation will give him respect among mankind." When James Allen, a wealthy gentleman from Philadelphia, heard of the death of his brother, he described him as the perfect gentleman: "He was distinguished for his courtesy, affability, modesty, humility and good-breeding; for his courage, frankness, candour, zeal and attachment to his friends, without one selfish Idea. His good nature, chearfulness and condescension, were uniform and unaffected and made him the delight of all who knew him." "With all these," Allen added, "he had the pride and spirit of a Gentleman and no man carried his notions of Honor, and integrity higher." For the Allens as for other genteel families, such pride and spirit were indispensable elements of gentility. Everything about their lives confirmed their inner sense of pride, the pleasure that they took from their feelings of self-love, self-respect, and self-assertion.[32]

"A Fondness for Superiority":
Eminence, Power, and Institutions

"THERE IS A CERTAIN SOMETHING in human Nature, let it be called Pride, a Fondness for Superiority, or any more moderate Term, as may strike the Fancy best," observed Peter Oliver—a member of the Governor's Council and a man of great wealth and eminence in Massachusetts prior to the revolution—"which stimulates the Mind to act as a Bell Weather to a Flock, to hand our Names down to Posterity as Leaders, either in Religion, Politicks, or some other System, as may suit our Genius best." "This something," he added, "discovers itself in its earliest Infancy, and continues to our latest Dotage." Though he wrote these words in exile, Oliver could not escape the presumption of superiority and of leadership that had characterized the genteel in Anglo-America for generations. Whether gentility was inherited or acquired, the presumption of superiority was the quintessence of being genteel. In wealth, in social rank, in political authority, the genteel took eminence for granted, confident that they were worthy of their positions and their prerogatives, proud of themselves and their families for their positions in their communities and in society, eager to ensure the perpetuation of their superiority from one generation to the next.[33]

Just as the creation of a distinctive style of life characteristic of the genteel throughout the colonies set off the "polite part of the world" from the "meaner sort," so too the language of the genteel often conveyed their personal sense of distance from and superiority to the common people. The "best people," the "better sort," the "polite part," "men of sense"—these were terms appropriate for the genteel, whereas others might be designated as the "common people," "inferior orders," and, at the lowest levels of the social hierarchy, the "rabble." The words conveyed attitudes of social arrogance and even, at times, of contempt for persons who were not genteel themselves. The genteel could not tolerate any infringement upon their sense of superiority. They took their right to leadership and to eminence for granted. And so long as others also shared their assumptions and deferred to their claims to social and political preeminence, they could sustain their sense of being more genteel, more mannerly, more polite, and more worthy than most of their contemporaries.*

Throughout the Anglo-American world, authority and power were the perquisites of wealth and superiority. Gentlemen ordinarily expected

---

* The separation between the genteel and the rest of the world became increasingly evident during the middle of the eighteenth century and was symbolized, appropriately, by two visible shelters: the country houses that sprang up throughout the colonies, and the carriages that provided transporta-

to govern at all levels of society, from the parish to the provincial councils and governorships. The genteel exercised power unself-consciously, taking their eminence and their authority as much for granted as they took the rest of their worldly possessions. Their sense of self-confidence, and the ease with which they assumed roles of leadership in both private and public spheres of action, reflected their unconscious sense of security with respect to the exercise of authority and of power—both their own and others'. They were confident, from earliest childhood, that authorities were benign, designed to sustain and support them rather than being hostile to their own personal interests. Their self-confidence and inner security enabled them to be deferential to those in authority above them while remaining free to govern those beneath them. Deference was possible because of the belief that authority was legitimate, trustworthy, and necessary. The genteel respected power, whether exercised by men in positions superior to themselves or exercised by themselves over others. Power, as such, did not threaten them as it did so many evangelicals and moderates.[34]

One of the most important sources for the confidence that the genteel felt in their authority and power stemmed from their respect and admiration for institutions of all kinds—political, religious, and domestic. They were men deeply involved in virtually every institution of consequence in their societies, and they knew from their own personal experience that these institutions provided reliable channels for the expression of their own and others' needs and desires. Institutions of government were not abstractions but known realities to gentlemen throughout the colonies. They provided the settings and the contexts for the exercise of authority that were indispensable to their sense of superiority and eminence.*

tion for many of the genteel. Both their houses (which also tended increasingly to be clustered more closely together into discrete residential areas of the major towns as well as being isolated in the country at a distance from the towns) and their carriages served the purpose of separating the genteel from the ordinary ranks of the people. In Cambridge, Massachusetts, for instance, Brattle Street, which came to be known as Tory Row, provided the focal point for a network of rich, eminent, and prominent families. The process is covered in Carol Berkin, *Jonathan Sewall: Odyssey of an American Loyalist* (New York, 1974), p. 94; Bernard Bailyn, *The Ordeal of Thomas Hutchinson* (Cambridge, Mass., 1974); Frederick B. Tolles, *Meeting House and Counting House: The Quaker Merchants of Colonial Philadelphia, 1682–1763* (New York, 1963), pp. 132–5; and Carl Bridenbaugh, *Cities in Revolt: Urban Life in America, 1743–1776* (New York, 1964), pp. 337–42.

The reactions of Grace Growden Galloway of Philadelphia to the sudden reverses of rank and fortune during the revolution are illuminating examples of genteel attitudes under stress. See Raymond C. Werner, ed., "Diary of Grace Growden Galloway," *PMHB*, LV (1931), pp. 32–94; LVIII (1934), pp. 152–89.

* Recently, historians have begun to recognize the importance of the distinction between the "court" and the "country" parties that appeared throughout the colonies, beginning in the late seventeenth century, as they had appeared several generations earlier in England. The genteel, on the whole, associated themselves with the "court" parties in New England.[35]

The sense of superiority, both conscious and unconscious, that marked so many aspects of the lives of the genteel reflected the remarkable involvement of many in the affairs of their world—in agriculture, commerce, manufacturing, and politics—an involvement which often extended from their local communities to the level of provincial affairs and even, frequently, to the most distant parts of the empire and beyond. Gentlemen traditionally were used to running things in this world rather than concerning themselves overly much with the world to come. Their love of this world, and the pleasure their engagement with the world gave them, made the experience of daily life, both private and public, far more important to them than anything more abstract or theoretical. Their preoccupations were worldly, and they cared far more about the realities of their complex social and political relationships and the problems confronting them in the management of their businesses or political offices than they did about the possibility that the world they knew so well and in which they functioned so successfully would be altered in any substantial way.

Wealth, social rank, and political prominence usually combined to make the genteel profoundly conservative people. They took their positions of prominence for granted, confident that they were both deserving and worthy of their wealth and eminence. The genteel ordinarily preferred to maintain their world rather than transform it. More often than not, they simply took the world in which they lived with such obvious success and pleasure entirely for granted, rarely pausing to question themselves or anything about their lives. They were too content with themselves and with their lives to wonder why others did not always share their presumptions.

"Religious Without Feeling": Public Piety and Inner Assurance

THE CONFIDENCE that the genteel felt about themselves in this world extended to the world to come as well. They felt secure about God's love and benevolence and comfortable with their relationships with Him. The haunting thought that they might not be worthy of His love or His grace did not disturb them as it did so many moderates, and the possibility that they might be excluded altogether from His grace was unthinkable, however much it might torment evangelicals. The piety of the genteel thus became an extension of the self-love, self-assurance, and self-assertiveness that shaped their temperaments and their involvement with the world in which they lived, forming a continuum between the known world of daily experience and the anticipated world that awaited them after death. For the genteel, the act of worship was the central expression of their sense of continuity and of self-confidence—a ritual that served both to display their personal worth to the people who observed them and to confirm their sense of worthiness for salvation when this life had come to an end. The piety of the genteel became a public act, not an inner preoccupation. Their religious experience thus was profoundly different from that of both evangelicals and moderates, but no less significant as an expression of self both in this world and the world to come.[36]

The pervasive preoccupation of evangelicals with sin, corruption, grace, and the new birth, and their constant concern with the state of their inner being, are notably absent from both the public and the private writings of the genteel. Their correspondence, as we have seen, is preoccupied with secular matters, rarely alluding to religious issues or being concerned with religious sentiments. Their diaries, too, almost always record outer experiences, with at most hasty and indifferent references to religious thoughts or activities. Consider the following day in the life of William Byrd:

> [December 25, 1709] I rose at 7 o'clock and ate milk for breakfast. I neglected to say my prayers because of my company. . . . About 11 o'clock the rest of the company ate some broiled turkey for their breakfast. Then we went to church, notwithstanding it rained a little, where Mr. Anderson preached a good sermon for the occasion. I received the Sacrament with great devoutness. After church the same company went to dine with me and I ate roast beef for dinner. . . . Then we took a walk about the plantation, but a great fog soon drove us into the house again. In the evening we were merry with nonsense and so were my servants. I said my prayers shortly and had good health, good thoughts, and good humor, thanks be to God Almighty.

A pleasant, sociable, utterly predictable and comfortable day was passed by this Virginia gentleman, just as countless others had been and were yet to be before he passed out of this life, confident to the end, no doubt, of his own worthiness. He recorded all of this faithfully, fortunately; but what he had thought about anything he had done during the day he never bothered to say. What mattered most was what he had done, not what he had felt. His religious experience was synonymous with his activities.[37]

John Rowe, who served as a vestryman at Trinity Church in Boston, would not have felt too out of place among the Virginians of his own social rank, for he, too, liked to worship without being discomforted or provoked into thought or feelings that he preferred remain unnoticed.

On Sunday, September 21, 1766, he noted that both the sermons he had heard that day "were good and sensible Discourses but a little Metaphisical." For him, even a little metaphysics was obviously too much. In mid-June 1767, he observed that it had been "Convention Day with the Episcopal Clergy. I went to church this morning, Mr Troutbeck read prayers and Mr Gilchrist of Salem preached," adding, "twas a Sensible Sermon." That, obviously, was what he enjoyed most. Late in January 1767, he wrote that "Mr Walter read prayers and preached. A most charming Discourse." Other entries were similar, indicative of his frequent enjoyment of the sermons he heard, so long as they were "sensible" and not enthusiastic.[38]

The genteel did not wish to have their feelings touched deeply, preferring always to hear discourses from the pulpit that were rational, sensible, and moral, the polite and genteel modes of discourse, which would distinguish their sermons immediately from those of their evangelical contemporaries. The genteel preferred "practical religion" to "speculative" religion, which they associated with evangelicals. The observations penned by the Reverend Penuel Bowen, after traveling through South Carolina and Georgia in search of a parish for himself in the mid-1780's, capture the essence of the genteel mode of piety not only in the South, as he believed, but elsewhere as well. "In Charleston," he said, "the inhabitants seem to be easy and toler[a]ble polite without cultervating the principle—religious without feeling—In a word this appears to me the grand Criterion of difference between South and North—That there [the North] everything is contrived, felt and agitated deep—here [in the South] the deep parts of animation are not disturbed—People will be easy—will not give themselves carping cares, or seek deep for pleasures. Their religion is not affected but it is unmeaning."[39]

In George Washington, Bowen might have found the epitome of the religious sensibilities he observed—for Washington most assuredly was "religious without feeling." Indeed, his piety and his religious convictions were so muted, so elusive, so infrequently expressed that only by the closest scutiny of his writings was it possible to discern, as Paul Boller has done, the fundamental themes of his piety and his responses to religious worship. An Anglican by birth and conviction, Washington served as a vestryman of his parish church for many years, attending services; but never once, so far as is known, did he choose to take communion. His correspondence and diary are almost barren of references to the Bible, and utterly devoid of references to Christ. As Boller notes, "the name of Christ, in any connection whatsoever, does not appear anywhere in his many letters to friends and associates throughout his life." There is not even any direct evidence that he "ever pronounced a blessing at meals in his own household." "In the main," Boller observes, "Washington's God was an impersonal force with whose decrees the efforts of human beings (whose freedom to choose was presumably part of the providential plan) somehow always balanced out in the end. It cannot be said that Washington ever experienced any feeling of personal intimacy or communion with his God; nor does the aesthetic side of religion—the poetic beauty of scriptural passages or the liturgy of the Angelican church— seem to have had any great appeal for him. His allusions to religion are almost totally lacking in depths of feeling." Washington was at ease with himself and his God. He was unafraid of life and unafraid of death. The equanimity with which he approached everything he did, the confidence he had in himself, the assurance he felt about his place in the world—all combined to infuse Washington's piety with a sense of calm and contentment. Like John Rowe and others among the genteel, Washington felt no need for metaphysics and no desire to be reborn. He was content to be himself and to live out his life without reflection on the past or anxious concern for the future.[40]

In part, the sense of contentment felt by the genteel sprang from deep within their own temperaments, for being at ease within, they also felt at ease with themselves in the world at large. Their contentment, however, was also sustained by their conviction of the goodness and benevolence of God and His desire to see His people happy. Elisha Hutchinson, the governor's son, already much in love with Polly Watson, asked her on her birthday: "What shall we say then to seventeen years full of goodness? It is not only the reflection on the favours which we ourselves are the subjects of that fills us with gratitude, the mercies which those experience, who are near and dear to us, do oftentimes equally affect us." He added that he scarcely knew "whether most to admire or adore, the goodness of Providence," adding his wish, "May the same kind hand, still confirm your health, and long preserve that life, in which I seem to be so much interested, and before another Anniversary, may we be happy—very happy in each other." The following year, after her marriage to Elisha, Mary (or Polly), wrote to tell her "Dear Mamma" that "I acknowledge myself under infinite Obligations to the kind giver of all things. When I consider the m[a]ny unmerited favours which he has bestow'd upon me, I am lost in the most gratefull Admiration, and hope so to live, as to show that I am not wholly insensible of the goodness which I have received from his hand." George Washington, too, was confident of the benevolence of Providence, whom he thought to be "a 'benign' and 'beneficent Being.'" As Boller observes, Washington called Providence "the 'Supreme Author of all Good,' a 'Gracious and all kind Providence,' the 'Supreme Dispenser of every Good,' the 'author of all care and good,'" whose "ultimate goal, he once said, was 'to bring round the greatest degree of happiness to the greatest number of his people.'" This optimism about the world and its inhabitants was evident both in the lives and in the piety of the genteel, whose experience so often confirmed their confidence in the benevolence of Providence.[41]

For the genteel, God often seemed to be not only benign and intent upon the happiness of His people but also distant and abstract. He was thought of frequently as a powerful being, who governed His world rationally and in an orderly fashion. Occasionally, under duress and afflictions, the genteel voiced a sense of their being wisely governed—even controlled—by God. Governor Hutchinson, for example, wrote to his son from London in July 1775, after learning about the anguishing events transpiring across the sea in Massachusetts, acknowledging that "The change in our condition has been great, sudden, and unexpected; and however adverse it is ordered by the infinitely Wise Governor of the World, and we not only ought not to murmur and repine, but to fortify ourselves against a depression of spirits. We have cause to be thankful that we have yet the necessaries, though we are deprived of many of the comforts of life." Under very similar circumstances, Samuel Curwen, also in London in exile, wrote on the last day of December 1775: "May the afflictions through the past year which I have suffered and am now suffering in an unhappy banishment from my Country, family, friends and acquaintances be the means of increasing my reliance on and sub- mission to the all disposing hand of the wise and righteous Governor of the universe." Earlier in the year, he had observed that "God is the Supreme director of man and natural causes. To him I commend myself, and may he dispose of us in what way and manner soever, and at ever period seems fitting to his infinite wisdom, and the great purposes of his Providence, and may I without murmuring submit to all the allotment of the wise and righteous Governor of the world." For George Washington, too, God was the "great governor of the Universe," and also "the great Ruler of events." He felt comfortable with his sense of Providence working in mysterious ways to govern the world, confident of the ultimate wisdom and order with which Providence directed events. Because of His benev- olence and His wisdom, because He always acted to increase human happiness and to minimize human suffering, God's power and government seemed to the genteel to be a source of comfort and of confidence. However distant He might seem at times, He was always deserving of admiration and respect. His power was never feared. [42]

This sense of confidence, ease, and contentment with both the self and the world often made it possible for the genteel to be tolerant of other points of view and other religious convictions. As Governor Hutch- inson said, "the longer I live the less stress I lay upon modes and forms in religion, and do not love a good man the less because he and I are not just of the same way of thinking." For George Washington, too, an easy tolerance for diverse religious opinions formed a continuous theme in his responses to religious controversies. "Of all the animosities which have existed among mankind," he wrote in 1792, "those which are caused by a difference of sentiments in religion appear to me the most inveterate and distressing, and ought most to be deprecated." "I was in hopes," he added, "that the enlightened and liberal policy, which has marked the

present age, would at least have reconciled *Christians* of every denomination so far, that we should never again see their religious disputes carried
to such a pitch as to endanger the peace of Society." What he most dis-
liked was contentiousness and conflict among religious groups; yet he
was convinced that "The mind is so formed in different persons as to
contemplate the same objects in different points of view." "Hence originates the difference on questions of the greatest import, human and
divine," he acknowledged, at ease with the differences which he knew to
be inevitable. For Washington, as for others, the necessity for complete
liberty of conscience and freedom from civil interference was self-evident.
In 1790, he addressed himself to Roman Catholics in the United States
and expressed his belief that "As mankind become more liberal, they will
be more apt to allow, that all who conduct themselves as worthy members
of the community, are equally entitled to the protection of civil government. I hope ever to see America among the foremost nations in examples
of justice and liberality."[43]

The genteel shared a dislike of bigotry in all its manifestations and
were always profoundly uncomfortable with the intensity of feelings
that propelled pious evangelicals in their quest for purity. Absolute
adherence to modes of belief and of being seemed always dangerously
"enthusiastic" to the sensibilities of the genteel. Intellectual and religious
tolerance were part of their temperaments, rooted in their carefully nurtured and sustained sense of inner assurance and self-confidence, maintained by their sense of propriety and good manners, and confirmed as
well by their religious convictions and experiences.

But tolerance also was an expression of the deeply embedded conviction shared by the genteel that religious experience and religious
worship were public expressions of the harmonious gathering of the
whole community, joined together in the institutions, and the rituals and
ceremonies, which symbolized the essential unity of both this world and
the next. Their piety was synonymous with the act of worship, and thus
was always directed outwardly by visible signs of communion with both
worlds. Their public actions and public worship therefore became the
principal means of expression for their piety. Contrary to the Reverend
Bowen's observation that such religion was "unmeaning," it was most
meaningful to those who shared the sense of the continuum between this
world and the next, and who felt that their personal position at the
apex of the social, economic, and political ranks in this world gave them
a particularly significant role as mediators between the two worlds. The
genteel saw to it that their worshipping was visible to the rest of the
community—thus asserting both their confidence in their personal worthiness in this life and their assurance of worthiness for eternal life in the
world to come. Their presence in church was a necessary statement, a
recurrent testament to their conviction that the church was an integral
part of their world and that they were an indispensable part of the

church. Their churches *were* the world, not set apart from the world. The genteel thus incorporated piety and worship into their lives as completely as did evangelicals, yet experienced something altogether different by doing so.

The seeming worldliness of the worship in churches dominated by the genteel was expressed often by the appearance of sociability, which indeed was one of the principal purposes of gathering together for religious services. Philip Fithian observed these modes of worship and of sociability among the families surrounding the Carter plantation at Nomini Hall in Virginia. Even before he had left New Jersey, he "was told often . . . that coming into Virginia would bring me into the midst of many dangerous Temptations: Gay Company, frequent entertainments, little practical devotion, no remote pretention to Heart religion, daily examples in Men of the highest quality, of Luxury, intemperance, and impiety," and his experience subsequently confirmed much that he had anticipated. In mid-April 1774, he returned home to New Jersey for a brief visit, which made him acutely conscious of the differences separating his own modes of worship from those he encountered in Virginia. After attending church, he observed: "How unlike *Virginia*, no rings of Beaux chatting before and after Sermon on Gallantry; no assembling in crowds after Service to dine and bargain; no cool, spiritless harangue from the Pulpit; Minister and people here seem in some small measure to reverence the Day, there neither do the one or the other."

The next month, back at the Carters', he observed that "A Sunday in Virginia dont seem to wear the same Dress as our Sundays to the Northward—Generally here by five o-Clock on Saturday every Face (especially the Negroes) looks festive and cheerful—All the lower class of People, and the Servants, and the Slaves, consider it as a Day of Pleasure and amusement, and spend it in such Diversions as they severally choose—The Gentlemen go to Church to be sure, but they make that itself a matter of convenience, and account the Church a useful weekly resort to do Business." Fithian's observations capture the fusing of the two worlds that marked the religious experience of the genteel, for there seemed little to distinguish the Sabbath from any other day apart from attendance at church. Yet the attendance of the genteel and other members of the surrounding community in the parish church was an important public statement, made so by the very act of being present together and worshipping together.[44]

The ancient notion of the self and the world, which sought to bring both together into a relatively harmonious relationship, also allowed the genteel to experience the world without guilt and to accept the self without shame. The genteel gathered to celebrate the self, the world, and God; to confirm their sense of security and of self-confidence through the ancient prayers and rituals, the age-old ceremonies, which continued to appeal to those people who felt at ease with themselves and their world, and comfortable with the prospects for the world to come. Their sociability and their self-display—seated at the center of the church in all their elegant finery, the gentlemen having waited until the last possible moment before the service began to march in as a group of superior beings—were symbolic of their ability to feel no sense of inner discontinuity between the self and the world, or between this world and the next. Such feelings made self-scrutiny and self-awareness unnecessary. Their actions could always speak more directly and visibly than words. They found the formal prayers and reliable rituals sufficient to express their feelings and their needs, and they were comforted by being placed at the center of one of the most durable institutions ever known.

The genteel were often drawn toward the Church of England as the embodiment of their religious sensibilities and as the most visible expression of their preference for ritual, ceremony, and stable institutions. In Boston, the genteel had begun to worship in the Church of England during the last quarter of the seventeenth century, and many shifted their membership from Congregational or Presbyterian churches to the Church of England during the course of the eighteenth century. Even when, as in the case of Governor Hutchinson, they chose to remain attached to the Congregational form of worship, they still felt drawn toward the Church of England. By the middle of the eighteenth century, genteel Quakers also began to shift their attachments from the meeting to the church, while in the South, the church had always been the dominant institution, even though it often functioned erratically and feebly. Yet even when the church seemed weakest at the parish level, it remained part of an ancient, complex, and traditional religious order, which reached backwards in time many centuries. The church thus stood as the antithesis of the evangelical gathering of saints, whose quest for purity impelled them to withdraw from the corruptions of this world.[45]

The genteel were too caught up in their world to imagine that anyone would wish to transform it. To war against the self and the world was inconceivable, just as the necessity to be reborn in order to be saved was unthinkable, utterly foreign to their own personal experience and absent from their religious experience. The genteel preferred the world to stay as they found it, enjoying themselves in their various capacities and roles. Ideally, they would have liked to have their eminence and worthiness displayed before the public, while also fulfilling the duties and obligations inherent in their exalted rank as leaders, superiors, and masters. In order to do this, however, the genteel required both the acceptance of their rank and leadership by the people whom they led— the deference due to gentility by those who themselves were not genteel— and also the maintenance of the appropriate public and private contexts within which to display themselves and to assert their superiority. They needed institutions just as much as they needed inferiors; both were essential to the self-image that gentility fostered. Their public was indispensable to them, for without public displays of eminence, authority, and power the genteel would not be able to feel entirely at ease, since they needed to sense their connectedness with the outer world in order to be assured that the self and the world were united and at peace.

For long periods of time in many different places throughout the Anglo-American world, the stability and connectedness of the world at large made it possible for the genteel to live a life of self-fulfillment, self-indulgence, and self-assertion, while also fulfilling their roles as people of the highest rank who were the visible leaders of their communities, churches, and provinces. Yet they also knew, even if only subliminally, that their temperaments, their life style, and their modes of piety were antithetical to those of many other people around them. Though they themselves preferred to enjoy the world, others insisted upon warring against the world. Though they felt proud of themselves and self-confident, others hated pride and self-confidence and sought to extinguish the sense of self altogether. Though they were content to live lives unbroken by intense feelings of inner sin and guilt, others constantly lived with the knowledge of sin and guilt. Though they never felt any need or desire to be reborn, others insisted that the new birth was the only way to be assured of salvation. In these and other ways, the genteel always were at odds with evangelicals. Being virtually poles apart in their temperaments, their piety, and their experiences, the genteel and the evangelicals had entirely different senses of self and of the world. Although they often shared the same landscape, they always inhabited different worlds, both inwardly and outwardly.

PART FIVE

EPILOGUE

❧ VIII ❧

The Clash of Temperaments:
Some Reflections on the
First American Civil War

THE GREAT ANGLO-AMERICAN CRISIS of the 1760's and 1770's was like a powerful earthquake which shook the world of the colonists and transformed the political landscape in America for centuries to come. Yet like other earthquakes, the revolutionary crisis erupted along the lines of the deep faults that had existed within colonial society for generations, even when they went unobserved and remained inactive. The Great Awakening of the 1730's and 1740's had made many of the deepest faults visible through the sudden conflicts over religious beliefs and practices, dividing churches and communities throughout the colonies along lines of temperament and of piety that could be traced backwards through time to the mid-seventeenth century. In many localities, the intense revivals separated ardent evangelicals from moderates and the genteel. A generation later, the crisis of the 1760's and 1770's followed the fault lines opened to view during the 1730's and 1740's, but intensified the pressures upon the social and political worlds of the British-Americans to the point of total rupture, symbolized by the Declaration of Independence in 1776, which marked the divide between two worlds.

"An American Monarchy or Republic?"

ON JULY 3, 1776, one day after "the greatest Question was decided, which ever was debated in America," even John Adams felt compelled, looking back over the events of the previous fifteen years, to declare to

Abigail that he was "surprised at the Suddenness, as well as the Greatness of this Revolution." A month later, he still found "the Change We have seen astonishing," and wondered "Would any Man, two Years ago have believed it possible, to accomplish such an Alteration in the Prejudices, Passions, Sentiments, and Principles of these thirteen little States as to make every one of them completely republican, and to make them own it?" "Idolatry to Monarchs, and servility to Aristocratical Pride," he noted, "was never so totally eradicated, from so many Minds in so short a Time." Adams's sense of surprise and wonder at the sudden transformation from a monarchy to a Republic was warranted, yet he himself had been one of those most instrumental in bringing about this transformation.[1]

Why did Adams, and so many others, find it imperative by 1776 to repudiate their allegiance to monarchy and to create a Republic? Early in January of 1776, John Adams made his personal answer to such a question clear. "Pray Madam," he asked his good friend and correspondent Mercy Otis Warren, "are you for an American Monarchy or Republic?" Monarchy, he noted, "is the genteelest and most fashionable Government, and I dont know why the Ladies ought not to consult Elegance and the Fashion as well in Government as Gowns, Bureaus or Chariots." According to Adams, "A Monarchy would probably, somehow or other make me rich, but it would produce so much Taste and Politeness so much elegance in Dress, Furniture, Equipage, so much Musick and Dancing, so much Fencing and Skaiting, so much Cards and Backgammon; so much Horse Racing and Cockfighting, so many Balls and Assemblies, so many Plays and Concerts that the very Imagination of them makes me feel vain, light, frivolous," and, he admitted, "insignificant." A monarchy, in short, would make John Adams into a gentleman—and an insignificant gentleman at that. Yet Adams knew that he was not genteel, and for years had been conscious of the differences that distinguished his temperament, values, and style of life from those of the ladies and gentlemen whom he knew and observed throughout the colonies. In July 1774, for instance, he noted the "universal Spirit of Debauchery, Dissipation, Luxury, Effeminancy and Gaming" which had begun to spread through the land, and observed to Abigail that "There is not a Sin which prevails more universally and has prevailed longer, than Prodigality, in Furniture, Equipage, Apparell and Diet." But these were the most visible forms of display of gentility throughout the colonies—and the signs, to Adams as to others, of a monarchical style of life.[2]

Adams, however, assured Mercy Otis Warren that "For my own part I am so tasteless as to prefer a Republic, if We must erect an independent Government in America, which you know is utterly against my Inclination," he hastily added. He was convinced that "a Republic, altho it will infallibly beggar me and my Children, will produce Strength. Hardiness Activity, Courage, Fortitude and Enterprise; the manly noble and Sublime Qualities in human Nature, in Abundance." He was per-

suaded, too, that "Under a well regulated Commonwealth, the People
must be wise virtuous and cannot be otherwise," and was certain as well
that "Virtue and Simplicity of Manners are indispensably necessary in a
Republic among all orders and Degrees of Men." What he was not certain
about, however, was "whether there is public Virtue enough" in America
"to Support a Republic." Nevertheless, there was no longer any doubt in
Adams's mind about the option to be preferred: a Republic, rather than
the monarchy under which he and every other British-American had lived
generation after generation for more than a century and a half.[3]

The choice posed by John Adams to Mercy Otis Warren was one
that soon confronted every British-American, leading people throughout
the colonies toward the bitter anguish and suffering of a civil war. The
events that led to this choice are so well known as to need little comment
—the Stamp Act crisis of 1765, the Townsend Acts of 1767, the "mas-
sacre" of 1770, the Tea Act and the tea party in Boston in 1773, the
coercive acts of 1774, and the battles in Lexington and Concord in the
spring of 1775, which culminated in independence in mid-1776—yet
Adams did not stress these familiar or soon-to-be-familiar acts and events.
What Adams offered his friend and fellow republican was not simply a
choice of political allegiances but a choice of life styles, of sensibilities,
of taste. The choice between being a monarchist or becoming a republican
thus involved the entire way of life of every person throughout the
colonies. But the choice also, above all else, involved the entire self, and
thus became a matter of temperament. The political choices and the
ideological commitments that accompanied them rested, in the last analysis, upon intensely personal inclinations.[4]

The centrality of temperament in the political confrontations of the
revolutionary era was evident to people on both sides of the divide. Jonathan Boucher, a monarchist and a loyalist, observed after taking refuge
in England that the "principles and ways of thinking of Whigs and
Tories, or of Republicans and Loyalists, are hardly more different than
are their tempers." Similarly, Thomas Jefferson, a republican and a
Whig, observed to his friend John Adams in 1813 that "The same
political parties which now agitate the U.S. have existed thro' all time."
"And in fact," he noted, "the terms of whig and tory belong to natural,
as well as to civil history. They denote the temper and constitution
of mind of different individuals."[5]

If temperament provides a key to the choices which individuals
made between monarchy and republicanism in 1776, it is evident that
different temperaments encouraged different choices. No one has ever
been able to ascertain with certainty how many chose to be American
and republicans, but John Adams's barber's assumption in April 1776 still
seems appropriate: "One sett are staunch Americans, another staunch
Britons I suppose, and a Third half Way Men, Neutral Beings, moderate
Men, prudent Folks—for such is the Division among Men upon all

Occasions and every Question." Two extremes and a middle thus provided a three-way split among the people with respect to the central question of allegiance—a tripartite division which is also suggested by the persistent presence within the colonies of the three distinctive patterns of temperament and piety explored in previous chapters.[6]

To become a republican proved to be entirely consonant with the evangelical temperament, and republicanism in 1776 was to be virtually indistinguishable from evangelicalism as a political ideology. To become a republican also was possible for many moderates, although the persistent ambivalence of moderates on so many issues and in so many ways also made it unlikely that all moderates would be able to cast off their allegiance to monarchy and to cast their lot with the republicans. To become a republican was almost impossible, however, for many of the genteel, who, as a group, had always been most closely associated with royal authority throughout the colonies and committed to a style of life appropriate, as Adams said, to monarchies. In reality, the choices between monarchy and republicanism arrayed people throughout the colonies along a spectrum of opinion between the two extremes. Thus moderates who inclined toward evangelicalism would be far more likely to become republicans than would moderates whose inclinations were toward gentility, just as those among the genteel who were drawn toward the moderate position would be less likely to remain loyal to the monarchy than would those who were the most quintessentially genteel. Over and over again, on a series of issues, it is possible to discern the presence of three distinctive modes of temperament, thought, belief, and response to the common issues and events that shaped the political consciousness of the people throughout the 1760's and 1770's.*

* I am persuaded that, instead of a single unified tradition of radical Whig ideology, recent studies reveal the presence by the mid-eighteenth century of at least *three* distinctive patterns of ideology. The dominant mode, associated with the leadership of the revolutionary movement and explored by Bernard Bailyn, I would call "moderate"; while the second mode, less visible and less well understood (but obvious from the studies by Gordon S. Wood, Alan Heimert, and Cushing Strout), I would call "evangelical." Thus there were, in reality, two basic forms of radical Whig ideology present simultaneously rather than the single form assumed by most historians. In addition, however, a third ideological mode existed, which was not really part of the radical Whig tradition. Perhaps it ought to be called "non-Whig" or "Walpolean Whig" to distinguish it from radical whiggery. But whatever the term, the ideology was most closely associated with the "genteel" mode of temperament discussed in this book. The best analysis of this non-Whig ideology is to be found in Bailyn's study of Thomas Hutchinson. The ideological patterns of American political life in the mid-eighteenth century thus were closely associated with the three distinctive forms of temperament.[7]

Mother Country, Father-King:
Perceptions of Power and Authority

THE NATURE OF POWER and the nature of authority were two of the most divisive and important issues of the revolutionary era. Both issues pre-occupied people and shaped the public debates that dominated the political controversies of the period. Yet both issues also evoked associations that drew upon memories from childhood and from experiences in adult-hood. Politics no less than piety mirrored themes associated with child-hood in the minds of people of all political persuasions. The imagery and rhetoric of political controversies constantly evoked these associations, thus linking public political issues with the most intimate personal issues, which still survived in the psyches of every individual. To perceive Eng-land as the mother country and King George III as the father of his people made it difficult for people to escape either the unconscious associations of their own childhood experiences or, perhaps even more immediately, their experiences as parents of children of their own. But childhood had differed significantly for different people, providing at least three distinc-tive modes of experience that had shaped the psyches and sensibilities of adults, and resulted in three distinctive modes of response to the issues of power and of authority.[8]

Tyranny was not an abstraction to evangelicals: many whose wills had been broken in early childhood knew from personal experience how powerful, how coercive, how aggressive, and how dangerous sovereign authorities could be when dealing with willful but powerless people. Power was absolute and unlimited, political and parental alike; and gov-ernment, properly established, consisted of obedience by the governed and of authority by the governors. Evangelical parents believed that their power over their children was absolute, and believed too that their obedi-ence to their own parents was and remained complete and unswerving. The authoritarianism of their temperaments permitted no deviations from their inner sense of compliance and submission to the powers that domi-nated their lives—both secular and Divine. Evangelicals rarely acknowl-edged any feelings of resistance or hostility toward the sovereign powers that had shaped their personal lives from earliest childhood through adulthood. They were too close, too present, too powerful to permit much open response. Yet evangelicals also could be extraordinarily vocal and active in expressing their hostilities and fears in public and in less inti-mate contexts. Politics provided many with an outlet for their buried feelings that was not only safe but satisfying. For evangelicals, the mother country and the father-king became symbolic representations of the dangerous, seductive, and powerful tyrants of their childhood—and images, too, of themselves as parents. Powerful men were tyrannical since their power was absolute and unlimited, while powerful women were seductive, out to entice people into voluptuousness and vice. Thus it was not surprising for evangelicals to associate the monarch and the mother country with tyranny and vice and to resist, with the passion of the once-impotent and crushed, the designs upon their liberty that seemed evident in everything these sovereigns did.

Moderates perceived power and responded to authority quite differently from evangelicals, for they had little personal experience with tyranny. Childhood had prepared moderates to accept legitimate and limited authorities—parental and political alike—and given them a life-long preoccupation with balancing the liberties of the governed with the prerogatives of the governors. The English constitution, with its classic mixture of three distinct forms of government (monarchy, aristocracy, and democracy), which were always in harmonious balance, seemed to provide moderates with the perfect paradigm for political authority. Obedience was voluntary but also necessary. Authority was limited but effective. Yet moderates also were constantly afraid that this ideally balanced and limited form of government would tip, would become unbalanced in the direction not of liberty but of power. Moderates always felt the pressures of the passions with their accompanying tendency toward excess; and the desire for power, perhaps more than any other passion, was the most persistent and the most dangerous. The experiences of childhood played a significant part in sensitizing many moderates to the relative weakness of liberty and the relative strength of power. So long as both were maintained in balance, as the English constitution was designed to ensure, moderates felt secure. But experience had taught that power, in the persons of parents, actually had the upper hand. Liberty, therefore, always had to be defended.

For many of the genteel, struggles with authority were unimaginable, since they perceived both parental and political authority as essentially benign and indulgent. The genteel family often provided a matrix of experience that mirrored, with astonishing faithfulness, the patterns of authority and of allegiance within the empire as a whole. From the point of view of genteel children, parents appeared as distant, loving, indulgent, and awesome, powerful, and respected domestic monarchs whose authority was delegated to others, to intermediaries and surrogates who actually administered the household and governed the children on a day-to-day basis—the servants, nurses, governesses, and tutors whose presence was so much a part of genteel households. If these individuals seemed harsh or unfair, children nevertheless could maintain their convictions about the affection and benign authority of their sovereign parents. Yet parents were distant from their children and thus inaccessible to them much of the time, so that children grew to maturity with a sense of awesome respect for the authority and power of their parents. But they were seldom afraid, nor were they anxious. They knew that their parents loved them intensely, for affection had infused the genteel family's relationships from infancy. But they also felt themselves to be unable to separate from these authorities who were so benign and so worthy of their respect and dutiful allegiance.

In due course, genteel children grew to see themselves as intimately connected to the interests of their parents and to the family as a whole, a sense fostered by the intensity of their domestic feelings. Never having felt tyrannized, the genteel often found themselves unable to imagine that tyranny either at home or abroad could be the reality so many others felt and perceived. Experience seemed to the genteel to demonstrate something quite different from the experiences of evangelicals and many moderates: that power was not dangerous, nor was it invariably in conflict with liberty. For the genteel, both power and authority were necessary in any well-governed family and in any well-ordered state. They were simply not afraid of power the way so many others were.

The Nature of Liberty

THE CONTROVERSIES OF THE 1760's AND 1770's involved efforts on the part of some Americans to define the limits of power and of authority, and to defend the liberties of the people against the encroachments, as they perceived them, of power. Yet others, equally knowledgeable and perceptive, felt no such need to defend liberty against power, but rather saw a compelling reason to strengthen power and authority against what they perceived as licentiousness and anarchy. Both sides, however, were convinced that liberty was at issue, though their analyses and their actions more often than not were opposite to each other. The question thus arises as to what different groups of Americans meant by the word "liberty."*
No one wished to be unfree, though many were quite prepared to deprive others of their personal liberties for the duration of their lives; but the

---

* As Alan Heimert observed: "Almost any reading of the literature of pre-Revolutionary America soon yields the conclusion that many of the ideas apparently held in common by all American Protestants were not in fact shared. By virtue of the disparate intellectual universes out of which the utterances of Calvinism and Liberalism emerged, the same word as employed by each often contained and communicated a quite different meaning" (Alan Heimert, *Religion and the American Mind from the Great Awakening to the Revolution* [Cambridge, Mass., 1966], p. 12). This insight continues to be profoundly important.

political debates that shaped the consciousness of many Americans during the 1760's and 1770's reflected at least three distinctive conceptions of the meaning of liberty.[9]

Liberty for the genteel was not something to be defined so much as it was to be preserved and enjoyed, by maintaining the institutions of government and sustaining the effectiveness of the law as the medium through which conflicts were to be resolved and disorders prevented. These gentlemen shared a profound sense of loyalty and esteem for the institutions of their communities and the empire—local, provincial, and imperial; religious, social, and political. Individual liberty was to be assured by the maintenance of these institutions and by the subordination of private interests to the interests of the public without, however, denying individual interest or preventing the fulfillment of individual ambitions for success or happiness. Above all else, perhaps, they believed themselves to be, as Daniel Leonard, a wealthy lawyer and prominent Massachusetts gentleman, said, "friends of the English constitution, equally tenacious of the privileges of the people, and of the prerogative of the crown," confident that the ties of duty and affection that bound them to the mother country also guaranteed the preservation of liberty throughout the colonies. They proved themselves to be government men, on the whole, and thus became defenders of British dominion in America. As conservatives, they could do nothing less, for the weight of experience over more than a century and a half had created the institutions and the forms of government that seemed, to most of the genteel, to be worthy of preservation as the surest means of preserving their own and others' liberties.[10]

Temperamentally, the genteel were disinclined to speculate about abstract political issues, and their general response to the issues of the decade that preceded independence seems to have been one of relative silence. They did not feel the anxieties or the fears, they did not perceive the threats or the dangers to liberty from abroad. Many gentlemen, of course, were actively engaged in the political life of their own provinces at various levels and were more concerned with practical matters than with ideology. Indeed, they seemed to be indifferent to the ideological currents swirling all about them, for they were intent upon sustaining their own positions in the world which they had known since childhood and in which they had learned to operate with such success. To conserve rather than to reconstruct or transform the world that they inherited was their choice, for they had no taste for the lurid rhetoric of radical whiggery, nor any desire to make themselves or others more virtuous and perfect than they already were. Their response to political issues thus was to be essentially pragmatic, reacting to the actualities rather than the potentialities of the political processes and institutions that engaged their attention and efforts.[11]

For the genteel, liberty was never thought of as an absolute but as an integral part of the social and political fabric of a well-ordered community, a state of relative liberty rather than one of absolute liberty. In exchanging a state of nature for a civil society, there must always be "a great restraint of natural liberty," as Governor Thomas Hutchinson said. Individuals "must part with some Priviledges, real or imaginary," which were enjoyed in the state of nature "in order to obtain greater Advantages," as Peter Oliver pointed out, in "a State of *civil* Liberty." For the genteel, the confidence that authority and power were benign and necessary for the maintenance of order and of liberty made it possible for them to accept the limitations upon personal liberty which, in actuality, were always present. They would have concurred with Edmund Burke, too, in his belief that "Abstract liberty, like other mere abstractions, is not to be found." As Burke said at a subsequent time, "Far from any resemblance to those propositions in geometry and metaphysics, which admit no medium, but must be true or false in all their latitude, social and civil freedom, like all other things in common life, are variously mixed and modified, enjoyed in very different degrees, and shaped into an infinite diversity of forms, according to the temper and circumstances of every community. The *extreme* of liberty (which is its abstract perfection, but its real fault) obtains nowhere, nor ought to obtain anywhere. . . . Liberty too must be limited in order to be possessed." The same theme runs throughout both the public and private writings of Thomas Hutchinson, the most articulate and sensitive exponent of the genteel position in America. As he observed in a private letter, which was stolen and then published by his political enemies, "the measures necessary for the peace and good order of the colonies" made it clear that there must be "an abridgment of what is called English liberty." Hutchinson added his doubts about the possibility of projecting "a system of government in which a colony 3,000 miles distant from the parent state shall enjoy all the liberties of the parent state. . . . I wish to see the good of the colony when I wish to see some restraint of liberty rather than [that] the connection with the parent state should be broken, for I am sure such a breach must prove the ruin of the colony." In this instance, what seemed both necessary and desirable to one gentleman proved to be anathema to many others.[12]

The genteel who remained loyal were cognizant of the fragility of the political authority of governmental institutions throughout the colonies— a perception amply confirmed by the virtual collapse of royal authority during the crises of the 1760's and early 1770's. Experience confirmed the erosion of the institutional context so essential to the preservation of liberty, as these conservatives perceived it. For they felt that the established institutional order must be maintained in order to preserve the liberty of all people rather than to ensure the liberty of only some of the people. Like Daniel Leonard, they were prepared to acknowledge that "No government, however perfect in theory, is administered in perfection; the frailty of man does not admit of it." But when "A small mistake, in point of policy," is used to "persuade the people that their rulers are tyrants, and the whole government a system of oppression," then, as Leonard knew from bitter experience, "the seeds of sedition are usually sown, and the people are led to sacrifice real liberty to licentiousness, which gradually ripens into rebellion and civil war."[13]

Moderates, too, could be conservatives, but their form of conservatism was quite distinct from that of the genteel. Moderates rarely were Burkeans since they thought of liberty as something much more specific and concrete, and also more abstract and ideal, than the genteel, and they added connotations to the word that would have dismayed many genteel loyalists. Moderates drew some of their theoretical perspectives upon the nature of liberty from the writings of the English radical Whig authors of the late seventeenth and early eighteenth centuries, especially John Trenchard and Thomas Gordon, whose *Cato's Letters* proved to be a perennial favorite among educated American moderates throughout the eighteenth century. "By Liberty," Cato wrote early in 1721, "I understand the Power which every Man has over his own Actions, and his Right to enjoy the Fruit of his Labour, Art, and Industry, as far as by it he hurts not the Society, or any Members of it, by taking from any Member, or by hindering him from enjoying what he himself enjoys."

Cato was utterly clear as to the limitations that ought to be placed upon government or power in relation to the private affairs of individuals. "Government," he said, is "intended to protect Men from the Injuries of one another, and not to direct them in their own Affairs, in which no one is interested but themselves." He believed that "It is plain, that such busy Care and officious Intrusion into the personal Affairs, or private Actions, Thoughts, and Imaginations of Men, has in it more Craft than Kindness; and is only a Device to mislead People, and pick their Pockets, under the false Pretence of the publick and their private Go[o]d." As he noted, speaking for subsequent generations of moderates as well, "True and impartial Liberty is therefore the Right of every Man to pursue the natural, reasonable, and religious Dictates of his own Mind; to think what he will, and act as he thinks, provided he acts not to the prejudice of another," which made it clear to Cato, as it did to others, "that Civil Government is only a partial Restraint put by the Laws of Agreement and Society upon natural and absolute Liberty, which might otherwise grow licentious." Finally, Cato pointed out to his readers for generations to come both in England and in America that "Free Government is the protecting the People in their Liberties by stated Rules: Tyranny is a brutish Struggle for unlimited Liberty to one or a few, who would rob all others of their Liberty, and act by no Rule but lawless Lust." The rule of law thus was the guarantor of liberty for Englishmen; but Cato, like many American moderates, could not conceive of any limits being placed upon individual liberty without simultaneously fearing that the lure of power would overwhelm the desire for liberty, thus bringing about the tyranny that he and others dreaded.[14]

For many American moderates, the preservation of liberty became a source of endless anxiety. Their perceptions of the nature of liberty made it imperative that no change whatsoever should occur in the relationship of liberty to power, since any change was most likely to tip the balance in favor of power, thus preparing the way for tyranny. As John Dickinson noted, "A perpetual *jealousy*, respecting liberty, is absolutely requisite in all free states. The very texture of their constitution, in *mixed* governments, demands it. For the *cautions* with which power is distributed among the several orders, *imply*, that *each* has that share which is proper for the general welfare, and therefore that any further acquisition must be pernicious." And John Adams declared in an oration at Braintree, Massachusetts, in 1772, "Liberty, under every conceivable Form of Government is always in Danger," owing to the "more ungovernable Passions of the human Heart," two of which—ambition and the love of power—were ever present. As Adams warned, "There is Danger from all Men. The only Maxim of a free Government, ought to be to trust no Man living, with Power to endanger the public Liberty." For Adams, as for many moderates, it was abundantly clear from both historical experience and personal conviction that "Liberty depends upon an exact Ballance, a nice Counterpoise of all the Powers of the state." For moderates such as these, there could be no alliance between liberty and power, no degrees of liberty that would allow for accptable restraints upon individual liberties and public liberties as well as for powerful government and strong political institutions. The balance was too delicate, too easily tipped and overturned.[15]

By conceiving of liberty in this manner, moderates lost the flexibility of response to changing political circumstances and to alterations in political institutions that could be accommodated more easily by the pragmatic perceptions of the Burkean conservatism of many of the genteel. Moderates thus were unable to adjust themselves to change, always fearful that any change would be for the worse and that their liberty would be endangered by any alteration in the status quo.

By 1776, many moderates actually were no longer defending the status quo as it existed at that point in time, but defending the status quo ante—as it had existed at some prior period. They were not conserving their social or political order, for the direction of change that they observed everywhere, and especially those changes most closely associated with the visible life style and sensibilities of gentility, was ominous. Always ambivalent, always anxious, these moderates felt that the liberty they cherished was slipping away, being subverted and eroded. They had ceased to be desirous of preserving the world as it was, preferring to re-

turn it to a world more in keeping with the temperate, moderate, balanced, virtuous, and self-restraining modes of being and of behavior that
seemed most in keeping with their own temperaments.[16]

The moderates' characteristic preoccupation with virtue added a
distinctive element to their conception of liberty by 1776, which not only
set them apart from the genteel but also from the position etched so
clearly by Trenchard and Gordon in *Cato's Letters*. In April 1776, John
Adams wrote again to Mercy Otis Warren, observing that when the "Principles" of a republic "are pure," it is "admirable" and "productive of every
Thing, which is great and excellent among Men." "But its Principles are
as easily destroyed," he reminded her, "as human Nature is corrupted."
"Such a Government is only to be supported," he noted, "by pure Religion
or Austere Morals. Public Virtue cannot exist in a Nation without private,
and public Virtue is the only Foundation of Republics. There must be a
positive Passion for the public good, the public Interest, Honour, Power
and Glory, established in the Minds of the People, or there can be no
Republican Government, *nor any real Liberty*"; "and this public Passion,"
he insisted, "must be Superiour to all private Passions. Men must be
ready, they must pride themselves, and be happy to sacrifice their private
Pleasures, Passions and Interests, nay, their private Friendships and
dearest Connections, when they stand in Competition with the Rights of
Society." He meant nothing less than the sacrifice of his own children if
need be, for he had written another letter the previous day to Abigail in
which he observed: "I believe my Children will think I might as well have
thought and laboured, a little, night and Day for their Benefit. . . . But I
will not bear the Reproaches of my Children. I will tell them that I studied
and laboured to procure a free Constitution of Government for them to
solace themselves under, and if they do not prefer this to ample Fortune,
to Ease and Elegance, they are not my Children, and I care not what becomes of them." His denials must become theirs as well, lest they, too, be
tempted. But he offered them no choice: "They shall live upon thin Diet,
wear mean Cloaths, and work hard, with Chearfull Hearts and free Spirits
or they may be the Children of the Earth or of no one, for me." As for his
sons, he told Abigail to "Let them revere nothing but Religion, Morality
and Liberty." Yet the liberty of which he spoke at that moment was
the liberty only to be a republican. No other choice would have been
permitted.[17]

For Adams to link republicanism with "pure Religion or Austere
Morals" as he did early in 1776 was to reveal with startling clarity the
extent of the emotional and intellectual alliance between some moderates
and most evangelicals. For a brief moment in time, moderates like Adams
ceased to be moderate—for they had accepted the necessity for a dramatic
transformation of values and sensibilities among the American people as
the indispensable prerequisite for virtuous republicanism.[18]

For evangelicals, liberty meant the total denial of the self and the obliteration of self-interest by the creation of a pure and perfectly united political community. Liberty thus was not thought of in terms of individuals but of the public collectively. For evangelical republicans, political liberty became synonymous with piety and true virtue, for only the moral reformation of the entire people could make possible the regeneration of the political world as well. Liberty thus became the freedom to be pure and virtuous, free from corruption and from sin. Evangelicals were never comfortable with personal freedom, since the authoritarianism of their temperaments made liberty meaningful only when it assured the denial of individual freedom to sin. Only when the self was suppressed could they feel free. In 1753, an anonymous writer in *The Independent Reflector* expressed this spirit vividly, in language that anticipated the views of evangelicals two decades later as he set out to "prove, that ever[y] Member of the Community, who is not actuated by a Public Spirit, or a Patriot Disposition, may and ought to be deemed an Enemy to his Country." He was convinced, as Cato was not, that "Family Affection and private Friendship, if they so engross our Hearts as to render us insensible of the general Welfare, are not only mean and unworthy Passions, but naturally hurry us into the basest, the vilest, and most immoral Conduct." He believed that "it is surely not less absurd than wicked, to give the Preference to the Blind Dictates of Passion, or the narrow Ties of personal Attachment," and warned that "to coil ourselves up within the dirty Shell of our own private Interest and Conveniency, careless of the common Good; is denying our Title to Humanity, and forfeiting the Character of rational Beings."[19]

Ordinarily, evangelicals were concerned far more with the state of their souls and with the world to come than they were with the present world and practical politics. Yet from the outset of the controversies in the mid-1760's, the alliance of evangelicals with the most ardent and most radical political opposition to royal authority had been obvious to observers throughout the colonies. The spirit of enthusiasm was evident in the drive to identify and to drive out those who seemed intent upon self-interest rather than the common good. By 1776, the belief that true liberty required the total suppression of the self, and that a republic required the regeneration of the body politic to create a state of true piety and virtue throughout the land, made it clear that the evangelical quest for liberty required nothing less than the total transformation of the social and political worlds of the colonists. Experience was to demonstrate that the evangelical impulse was not conservative in any sense but truly radical, not moderate but extremist.[20]

Effeminate or Manly?:
Seduction, Temptation,
and Political Paranoia

ANXIETY AND FEAR shaped the consciousness of the men and women who chose to become republicans in 1776. Many people began to believe that a conscious conspiracy against their liberties had been set into action among politicians both at home and in England and throughout the colonies as well. The fear of conspiracy, as Bernard Bailyn has argued so persuasively, proved to be the decisive propellant toward independence and toward the preservation of liberty through the establishment of a new Republic in America. Yet these fears and anxieties, which manifested themselves in the persistent and ever-increasing political paranoia among future republicans, were not felt by all people everywhere. Indeed, many were persuaded on the basis of the same evidence that no such conspiracy against liberty existed or even was being contemplated. As Peter Van Schaack, a gentleman from New York, observed, "taking the whole of the acts complained of together, they do not, I think, manifest a system of slavery, but may fairly be imputed to human frailty and the difficulty of the subject. Most of them seem to have sprung out of particular occasions, and are unconnected with each other." In short, he said, "I think those acts may have been passed without a preconcerted plan of enslaving us, and it appears to me that the more favorable construction ought ever to be put on the conduct of our rulers."

John Adams, on the other hand, was intent upon showing his fellow citizens "the wicked policy of the tories—trace their plan from its first rude sketches to its present complete draught," as he perceived it early in 1775. Adams wanted to "Shew that it has been much longer in contemplation, than is generally known,—who were the first in it—their views, motives and secret springs of action—and the means they have employed." Indeed, according to Adams, "some of the most intrigueing and powerful citizens have conceived the design of enslaving their country, and building their own greatness on its ruins." In view of such designs, he did not hesitate to tell his audience that such "a settled plan . . . will justify a revolution."[21]

While it is clear, as Bernard Bailyn has suggested, that the fear of conspiracy had "roots elaborately embedded in Anglo-American political culture," and while it is clear, too, as Gordon Wood has suggested, that the particular mode of thought characteristic of radical Whig ideology legitimized and rationalized such fears, the fear of conspiracy also had roots buried deeply in the innermost recesses of the psyches of numerous Americans. If we are to understand the persistent theme of political paranoia which runs throughout early American history—and later history as well, of course, to the present day—we must begin to acknowledge that the fear of conspiracy also drew upon nonrational sources of emotion (anxiety and fear especially), as well as upon the rational sources more familiar to most historians. Here, too, temperament and sensibilities played a powerful role in shaping the sensitivity of some people to possible conspiracies and designs against their liberties, their bodies, and their wills, while leaving others relatively indifferent or immune to such anxieties. But it was the interplay between both nonrational and unconscious anxieties and rational and conscious fears that provided the explosive amalgam which propelled people toward independence and a new Republic in 1776.[22]

On the level of rational consciousness, the most obvious fear and the most consequential source of anxiety was the sense that the monarchy and all it symbolized was gaining ground rather than losing. The people who were to become republicans came to share the conviction voiced in 1774 by Joseph Hawley, of Northampton, Massachusetts, once a member of Jonathan Edwards's congregation, that "It is *now* or never, that we must assert our liberty. Twenty years will make the number of tories on this continent equal to the number of whigs." Despite all that had occurred during the past ten years, Hawley and others felt that the supporters of royal government and their officials were increasingly successful in their efforts to strengthen royal authority over the colonies. In June 1771, John Adams, for instance, observed in the privacy of his diary (itself one of the most remarkably revealing sources extant for the connections between the rational and the nonrational preoccupations of future republicans) that "Caesar, by destroying the Roman Republic, made himself perpetual Dictator," while in Massachusetts, Thomas "Hutchinson, by countenancing and supporting a System of Corruption and all Tyranny, has made himself Governor—and the mad Idolatry of the People, always the surest Instruments of their own Servitude, laid prostrate at the Feet of both." Despite the fact that Adams had "for 10 Years together invariably opposed this System, and its fautors," and indeed had done so with "great Anxiety, and Hazard, with continual Application to Business, with loss of Health, Reputation, Profit, and as fair Prospects and Opportunities of Advancement, as others who have greedily embraced them," he also recognized that "It has prevailed in some Measure, and the People are now worshipping the Authors and Abetters of it, and despizing, insulting, and abusing, the Opposers of it." By December 1772, he acknowledged that "The Prospect before me . . . is very gloomy. My Country is in deep Distress, and has very little Ground of Hope, that She will soon, if ever get out of it. The System of a mean, and a merciless Administration, is

gaining Ground upon our Patriots every Day." "The Body of the People,"
he observed, "seem to be worn out, by struggling, and Venality, Servility
and Prostitution, eat and spread like a Cancer." The anxieties of men like
Adams clearly were a response to their fears that they were losing their
fight against the lures of the court—the administration of royal officials,
their policies, and their seductive appeal to the people throughout the
colonies. Time seemed to be running on the side of monarchy in the early
1770's. Every day, the American provinces seemed to be becoming more
and more like England.[23]

Unconsciously, many Americans were afraid of seduction, of being
tempted by "the genteelest and most fashionable" form of government,
with all the self-indulgent modes of life and self-enhancing modes of
being that ordinarily accompanied gentility and monarchies. The theme
of the seductiveness of vice was ever present in the writings of John
Adams, of course (who proposed the choice of Hercules as the appropriate
image to be inscribed on the seal of the newly confederated states in
August 1776), always sensitive to the presence of wealth, elegance, and
ease, always denying his own desires for "money and preferment" which
ever seemed to be courting him, always visible in the persons of both his
genteel friends and his bitter enemies, Governor Hutchinson in particular. In July 1772, he decided "to meddle not with public Affairs of Town
or Province," but determined instead to advance his private interests and
to "lay a Foundation for better Fortune to my Children, and an happier
Life than has fallen to my Share." For years past, Adams noted, "I have
served my Country, and her professed Friends, at an immense Expense,
to me, of Time, Peace, Health, Money, and Preferment, both of which last
have courted my Acceptance, and been inexorably refused, least I should
be laid under a Temptation to forsake the Sentiments of the Friends of
this Country." No wonder, then, that he believed that "A Tempter and
Tormentor, is the Character of the Devil," adding immediately that
"Hutchinson, Oliver, and others of their Circle, who for their own Ends
of Ambition and Avarice, have procured, promoted, encouraged, coun-
cilled, aided and abetted the Taxation of America, have been the Real
Tempters of their Countrymen and Women, into all the Vices, sins,
Crimes and follies which that Taxation has occasioned." No one can read
Adams's diary without being acutely aware of the centrality of this
temptation in his inner response to the seductiveness of the court and all
that it symbolized throughout the 1760's and 1770's. His ambivalence on
this, as on so many other matters, again made it seem possible that he,
too, might succumb one day.*

---

* John Adams also observed the seduction of Daniel Leonard, one of his
"cordial, confidential, and bosom friends," and one of the three men of whom
he recalled that "I never, in the whole course of my life" had lived "in more
perfect intimacy." Thus when he observed that Governor Hutchinson "courted"
Leonard "with the ardor of a lover," he acknowledged the analogy of a

John Adams might have felt the impact of John Hancock's warning to Bostonians in March 1774; "Suffer not yourselves to be betrayed by the soft arts of luxury and effeminancy, into the pit digged for your destruction. Despise the glare of wealth. That people who pay greater respect to a wealthy villain, than to an honest upright man in poverty, almost deserve to be enslaved; they plainly shew that wealth, however it may be acquired, is in their esteem, to be preferred to virtue." Hancock, too, was fearful of the seductiveness of the monarchical style of life—fearful that "all the arts which idleness and luxury could invest, were used to betray our youth of one sex into extravagance and effeminancy, and of the other to infamy and ruin," fearful, too, that the temptation had succeeded "but too well." As he asked his audience, "did not our youth forget they were Americans, and regardless of the admonitions of the wise and aged, servilely copy from their tyrants those vices which finally must overthrow the empire of Great Britain?"[25]

The fear of effeminacy—so striking among many of those who were to become republicans—was one of the most powerful inner sources for the encircling paranoia that dominated their political consciousness throughout the 1760's and 1770's. Psychologists and others have often observed the close association of paranoia with unconscious fears and anxieties over masculine and feminine impulses and feelings. The fear of effeminacy thus suggests a source for some of the inner anxieties of many Americans, and provides a useful clue to the psychological roots of the paranoid vision of the political world that dominated the politics of the period. Indeed, the political choices that faced British-Americans in 1776 involved nothing less than a choice between being or becoming effeminate and being or becoming manly—for monarchies and monarchical styles of life evoked the imagery of femininity, while republics and republican styles of life evoked the imagery of manliness.[26]

Thus the attraction of one form of government or the other was never simply a matter of political conviction, but reached directly into the unconscious associations of sexual identity that shaped the temperaments of many Americans in very different ways. For evangelical men, the conflict over masculine and feminine impulses was most intense, since it pervaded their psyches as they constantly sought the total submission of self and self-will that they associated with women and children, yet also felt the powerful assertiveness of the self and self-will that they associated with being men. Moderates, too, felt an inner ambivalence over their

---

courtship between two men and the seductiveness of the court party and its leader in Massachusetts. The fact that Leonard also "wore a broad gold lace round the brim of his hat" and "had made his cloak glitter with laces still broader," thus revealing "a heart that delighted in so much finery" to be an easy mark for seduction by another man, makes one wonder if Adams also perceived the intimate friend who became a political enemy as an "effeminate" person.[24]

feminine and masculine impulses as they sought to keep them in balance. Yet they always feared the power of the seductive passions, which they associated with femininity, and feared that the control of reason, which they associated with masculinity, would be overcome. As a result, both evangelicals and moderates experienced an inner tension and anxiety over their masculine and feminine feelings and impulses that may very well have shaped their public fears and fostered their sense of conspiracies endangering them. The inner dangers were always present; the outer world simply provided the temptations and the lures that could cause them to succumb to impulses they sought to keep under control. Only the genteel, on the whole, seemed to be at ease with both their feminine and their masculine feelings and impulses, and thus only they were able to be comfortable with the appearance of what republicans described as "effeminacy." The relative immunity of many of the genteel to the paranoid vision of politics which gripped so many evangelicals and moderates suggests that their inner security over both components of their sexual identities may have made a decisive difference to their perceptions of the political process, as well as to their temperaments.

The desire of future republicans to be manly rather than effeminate also evoked other, closely related associations which became central to their pervasive fear of a conspiracy against their liberties. Perhaps the most obvious, and also the most important, was simply their fear of being enslaved. The point of the conspiracy that so many people believed to be directed against themselves was nothing less than the deprivation for individuals of their own liberty and their personal enslavement—that is, the prospect that they would be placed in a state of being without wills of their own. The central issue thus became the issue of personal autonomy or the freedom of a person's self and self-will. For evangelicals, of course, these issues were perhaps the central issues of their life, rooted in personal experience from earliest childhood. For moderates, the freedom of the self and of self-will was taken for granted, but only under certain circumstances and within certain boundaries. The possibility also was always present that excess could lead to the destruction of the balance and moderation required for their sense of inner autonomy and freedom. People with these temperaments could feel a sense of anxiety and fear about the possibility that their own selves and self-will would be rendered powerless by dangerous and powerful forces outside the self; and their proclivity to political paranoia thus expressed their inner sensitivity to the whole issue of selfhood and self-will. But the desire to appear manly also rested upon the common assumption that only men were capable of being self-assertive and self-willed in public, while both women and children ordinarily were to have no wills of their own. To become enslaved and to be deprived of self-will thus also was to become effeminate, thereby interweaving two of the central themes of the conspiracy against their liberties.[27]

For many of the colonists, the fear of enslavement also evoked other personal associations, however, especially in the South, where the enslavement of almost the entire black population made slavery a daily reality. Perhaps this, more than anything else, accounts for the alliance of both moderate and genteel Southerners against royal authority, and their prominent role in the republican movement. The assertion of the self and of self-will that was so characteristic of the genteel temperament everywhere was particularly dramatic among genteel Southerners, who were surrounded constantly by people without legal selves and without the ability to assert their own wills. The preoccupation of many Virginians and other Southerners with enslavement from abroad mirrored their own daily assertion of almost unlimited power over their own enslaved people, a form of domesticated tyranny that could not be escaped.[28]

The fear of conspiracy, which gripped so many minds so tightly and persuasively during these decades, also gained much of its psychic power over the minds of evangelicals and many moderates from the immediacy of their personal experience. When we realize that many of the very people most anxious about the existence of a powerful conspiracy that threatened to enslave them, to deprive them of their own wills, to reduce them to a state of effeminacy, and thus to tyrannize them also were among the people who were most actively seeking either to suppress or to control the self and self-will, both in themselves and in their children, it becomes clear that the external threat reverberated inwardly as well. Without such an inner resonance, it is almost impossible to account for the extraordinary passion, hatred, and hostility that the presumed conspirators and their secret designs evoked from so many future republicans. The wars of the self against the self became transformed into attacks of others upon the self—and external enemies and dangers were easier to confront than inner enemies, as evangelicals knew from much personal experience.

For evangelicals, who became the most ardent republicans of all, and the most ferocious in the attack upon the monarchy and all that it symbolized, the belief that actual persons existed both in England and in the colonies who could be identified as conspirators against their liberties and as tyrants in disguise made it possible for them to attack the authorities that had threatened them all of their lives. Yet the most powerful authorities of all—parents—could never be attacked nor their authority denied. Obedience of children never ceased, and so long as the authorities that had shaped their temperaments and beliefs were present—in life or in their consciences—evangelicals could neither escape nor repudiate their sovereignty over their lives. Politics liberated feelings of anger and of hostility, however, in ways that were impossible ordinarily, and the belief in a conspiracy against their liberties fueled their public struggles to protect the self and their wills from enslavement. Ironically, not even the successful struggle against the alleged conspirators could make evangelicals comfortable with personal autonomy and self-will, for the republic they were to create in place of the monarchy was designed to suppress the self altogether.

A Revolution of Saints

REPUBLICANISM IN 1776 involved nothing less than the attempt by many Americans to bring about the regeneration of American society and politics. Evangelicalism provided one of the central impulses for republicanism, and the modalities of evangelical piety and temperament shaped the political practices of those who were to be the most ardent republicans.* Republicanism was seen as the new birth of politics, intended to bring about a secular and collective transformation as swift, as dramatic, and as consequential as the conversions that had transformed the lives of untold thousands of individuals throughout the colonies for generations past. The central dynamics of the revolutionary experience constantly reveal the presence of the evangelical impulse as the confrontations between republicans and monarchists, between Whigs and Tories, shaped the destinies of Americans everywhere. For a brief moment in 1776, evangelicals found themselves in alliance with many moderates, whose ambivalence momentarily was resolved in favor of piety, virtue, and public liberty. But this alliance against both monarchy and gentility, which had been growing increasingly evident, also required the total transformation of American life and thought. Nothing less seemed sufficient, given the overwhelming dangers of being seduced and tempted by the sinful pleasures and indulgent lives of so many British-Americans.

---

 * For comparisons, see Michael Walzer's impressive study of seventeenth-century English Puritans: *The Revolution of the Saints: A Study in the Origins of Radical Politics* (Cambridge, Mass., 1965).
 The most extensive and illuminating analysis of the relationship of evangelicalism to the revolution is to be found in Alan Heimert's *Religion and the American Mind from the Great Awakening to the Revolution* (Cambridge, Mass., 1966). While I cannot share Heimert's conviction that Calvinist evangelicals were "preparing to make America safe for democracy" (p. 516), I find his arguments (pp. 514–19) about the Rousseauean elements of Calvinist political thought to be entirely persuasive. As he demonstrates, evangelicals were not Lockeans, although the "rationalists" or "Liberals" often were. This crucial difference of outlook and assumption was to have a profound impact upon the nature of the revolutionary crisis. The key to Heimert's argument is to be found in his observation that "The evangelical Revolutionary impulse, like that of the Great Awakening, represented a counterthrust to the seeming tendency of American history. . . . The Calvinist Revolutionary crusade had many particular goals, but at its center was the hope of nipping in the bud, as it were, an ethos which, if allowed to thrive, would produce in America all manner of unvirtuous fruits" (p. 481).

Faced with such sin and corruption, only regeneration could save the people from themselves. The desire for political regeneration and the total annihilation of self-interest and selfishness, the hope for a new birth that so often transformed a life of sin and of corruption into a life of grace, selflessness, and purity, were visible in the actions of many American Whigs in the mid-1770's as they sought to separate the virtuous members of the new republican community from the corrupt and unregenerated adherents of the ancient monarchical order.[29]

The intrusion of evangelicalism into local political controversies often made the implications of the new republicanism vividly clear. At some point in 1776, a New Jersey "Mechanic" sent an anonymous warning to a fellow citizen, Mr. Bernardus Legrange, to inform him, in case he had not already realized, that "You are looked upon by all the Virtuous inhabitants of this City to be a most inveterate enemy to your Country, as such you justly deserve to be despised by every good man. You are esteemed as a man but of very little Sense, and a disturber of the Community, as such, you deserve punishment." After noting the efforts on the part of "a corrupted, and venal ministry together with a deluded King" to make "a number of Acts tending to enslave the inhabitants of North America," and offering details of successive instances of their "impious practices" and "black designs," the mechanic observed that "at a time when every true friend to Liberty is roused with an honest indignation of avenging his Country's wrongs," Legrange had "from the beginning of the present contest for Liberty" always agreed "with the distructive measures persued against us." "Have we not then Sufficient reason to pronounce you an Enemy to your Country," the anonymous writer asked, "nay to brand you with the odious name of Traitor?"

It was clear to Legrange's fellow citizen that he had tended "to disunite the people" and had "of late become an avowed enemy to Liberty, and true Virtue." The mechanic, however, still believed that even Legrange might be transformed from an enemy into a patriot: "Be advised for once, change your wicked heart, become a friend to your Country, hearken not to the unwholesome advice of your wicked wife. . . . Let me intreat you to imitate the man of true virtue, and lover of his Country." Then, in an eloquent and enthusiastic vision, the mechanic offered Legrange a glimpse of what this conversion might bring about:

> Lay aside (for one minute) your Prejudices, and view the man who is a true friend to the rights of mankind, and I think your guilty Soul will be struck with Conviction, and you will be persuaded to follow his example. To behold the noblest disposition of the Christian and Patriot united; an overflowing benevolence, generosity, and candour of heart, joined to an intimate persuasion that on it depends the happiness and glory both of King and People, to see these shining out in publick is a prospect that can

not but inspire a general Sentiment of Satisfaction and gladness more easy to be felt than expressed. The Patriot stands undaunted when the storms of mingling war rage around him; firm as himself, his bolder heart clad with awful justice spurns every danger; all his united efforts seek the publick good: *he* is a friend to trampled worth, and suffering right, corruption and bribery durst not attempt his virtue joined to publick zeal, and honour of adamantine proof; his heart is pure, and detached from sordid pleasures; a soul panting after perfection; striving to imitate the goodness of Heaven and devoted to the service of mankind, he is roused by the first pang of his Suffering Country; gives his whole illustrious spirit to her relief, rises above all human allurements, never remits his zeal; fears nothing; regards nothing; but the Sentiments which Virtue and magnanimity inspire; the Sacred flame thus enkindled is not fed by the fuel of faction, or party spirit, But by pure Benevolence and love of the Publick, and when he leaves this tabernacle of clay, Methinks I see his mounting Spirit, freed from the tangling earth, regain the realms of day, it's native Country. Behold! *he* is approved by the tremendous judge of Heaven, and Earth, and joined to the presence of the *Almighty Father* he takes his rank in glory and in bliss.

Perhaps even Legrange thus might be converted from an enemy of liberty to a true patriot. But "if neither reason, justice, or humanity are able to change your Sentiments, and daily practice," the mechanic warned, "be assured there is a fatal day approaching which will bring *ruin* to your devoted head." For those who persisted in sin, damnation was the only prospect in their future; and as thousands of native-born Americans were to discover during the years preceding and following independence, the inability to renounce their allegiance to the monarchy and all that it symbolized made them into enemies of the republicans.[30]

Even before independence was declared, the bitter implications of the "political Enthusiasm" which prompted the assault upon everyone considered to be seducers, traitors, and enemies of American liberties thus grew perplexingly evident to many of the people who became victims of the "Christian *Liberty Men*," who thought in turn that "they did *God* good Service in persecuting and destroying all those who dared to be of different Opinions from them." Daniel Leonard, who was the epitome of gentility in New England and knew the political scene from close observation, observed with dismay in 1775 that "so many respectable persons have been abused, and forced to sign recantations and resignations; that so many persons, to avoid such reiterated insults as are more to be deprecated by a man of sentiment than death itself, have been obliged to quit their houses, families, and businesses, and fly to the army for protection; that husband has been separated from wife, father from son, brother from brother, the sweet intercourse of conjugal and natural affection interrupted, and the unfortunate refugee forced to abandon all the comforts of domestic life." "My countrymen," he went on, "I beg you to pause and reflect on this conduct. Have not these people, that are thus insulted, as good a right to think and act for themselves in matters of the last importance, as the Whigs? Are they not as closely connected with the interest of their country, as the Whigs?" "Do not their former lives and conversations appear to have been regulated by principle," he asked, "as much as those of the Whigs? You must answer—yes! Why, then," he wondered, "do you suffer them to be cruelly treated, for differing in sentiment from you? Is it consistent with that liberty you profess?"[31]

As many thousands of people were driven from their homes, banished from their country, and forced into exile elsewhere within the British Empire during the 1770's and 1780's, the answer to Leonard's question became clear to all. Those who were unwilling or unable to be converted to republicanism were faced with no choice but to leave in order to remain faithful to the monarchy that always had governed their land. The evangelical vision of a perfected polity, virtuous, pure, and unanimous, and the belief that real liberty required the total suppression of the self for the good of the whole, justified the repressiveness evident throughout the colonies. Yet the experiences of the thousands of people who found themselves identified with the monarchy and declared to be public enemies—subject to constant personal harassment, abuse, and intimidation, as well as physical danger—made it clear that the republican vision was a partial vision, shared only by some of the people some of the time. Their suffering and their exile served to demonstrate the aptness of Governor Thomas Hutchinson's comment, drawn from his own ample experience, that "Nothing is more frequent, than for men, in the height of their struggles for liberty for themselves, to deny it to others."[32]

What Thomas Hutchinson and others who had felt the fury of the "political Enthusiasts" during the 1760's and 1770's might not have realized, however, was the extent to which the denial of liberty to others was possible and indeed necessary for evangelical Whigs because they also denied themselves the same liberties. Their temperaments shaped their perceptions of the self and the world in vastly different ways from the perceptions of both the moderates and the genteel. The evangelical vision of a republic of virtue and a regenerated social and political order emerged directly from the innermost recesses of their psyches and their souls. Their anxieties and their fears, their preoccupation with a conspiracy against their liberties, and their conviction that monarchy and gentility were corrupting the world to an intolerable and dangerous degree—all propelled them in their quest for a new republican order. But the temperaments of the moderates had always set them apart from evangelicals even when they shared certain basic concerns, such as the case with virtue. The republican vision of the mid-1770's obviously brought both temperaments together into a powerful, if temporary, alliance which sought to destroy the old monarchical order while creating a new republican order. Nevertheless, the moderate temperament always was uncomfortable with the extremism of the evangelical temperament—and thus could not accept the total suppression of the self and of self-will, nor the ascetic and repressive conception of virtue that appealed to evangelicals. However, they did share a sense of danger and an awareness that time was growing short if their worst fears were not to become realities.

Independence and republicanism in 1776 seemed to provide the answers to their needs, and they embarked together upon the creation of a "Christian Sparta" not only in Boston but elsewhere throughout the colonies. The choice of Sparta was apt, for Sparta had always symbolized the closely knit, self-less, ascetic, and repressive polity which stood in almost permanent opposition to the more open, self-expressive, self-regarding, and democratic polity of Athens. And the evangelical temperament, always at war with the self and the world, transformed the abstract and highly theoretical issues that shaped the constitutional debates of the 1760's and 1770's into a moral reformation which would bring into being nothing less than a new republic of virtue in America.[33]

The Republic of Virtue Rejected

THE REVOLUTION of the American saints failed. By 1780, Samuel Adams, the arch-revolutionary of the country, had begun to despair even of Boston, since all the vices and sins of the pre-revolutionary years had reappeared. As James Warren observed, "Boston society was 'more suitable to the effeminacy and ridiculous manners of Asiatic slavery, than to the hardy and sober manners of a New-England republic.' " The state of Massachusetts as a whole seemed to Adams and others to be "possessed by such 'a rage for Ease, Luxurious Living, and Expensive Diversions' that they got only jeers for their pains and were ridiculed 'in polite assemblies as *rigid republicans*, men of contracted minds, only because they will not conform to gaming, sabbath breaking, drinking and every other vice practiced by persons of (What is called) the bon ton.' " Even in the new Republic, the old ways of the genteel reappeared, as seductive and as enticing as ever. Moreover, the preoccupation of many republicans with virtue, both private and public, also had ceased to appeal to many Americans, and the identification of republicanism with purity and with virtue no longer seemed self-evident.[34]

Out of the experiences of the mid- to late 1770's came a resurgence of moderation, as well as the reappearance of seemingly suppressed modes of gentility. The experiences of creating new constitutions and new forms of government both in the various states and in the United States also transformed the meaning of liberty, and ensured the ultimate rejection by 1787 of the evangelical vision of true virtue and republican purity. Instead of seeking a regenerated people, many American politicians began to turn their attention to the establishment of new forms of government, new institutions, and new ways of arranging the exercise of authority and power in order to ensure the preservation of liberty. But the rejection of the politics of virtue, which had provided so much of the emotional propulsion behind the events of the civil war of the mid-seventies meant that the temperamental and intellectual preferences of moderates would take precedence in the political speculations of the decade that resulted in the establishment of a new Constitution for the United States and the formation of a new federal form of government. By 1790, even John Adams had come to realize that "all projects of government founded in the supposition or expectation of extraordinary degrees of virtue are evidently chimerical." He had also come to think that "knowledge and benevolence ought to be promoted as much as possible"; but, "despairing of ever seeing them sufficiently general for the security of society," he said, "I am for seeking institutions which may supply in some degree the defect." [35]

The rejection of the republic of virtue that had been the goal of evangelical republicans and their moderate allies in 1776 also meant the rejection of the evangelical vision of the public good obliterating individual self-interest and desires. Rather than suppressing individual liberties by ensuring that the whole community would be entirely of one mind, of one heart, and of one point of view, the Federalists of 1787 sought to balance the interests of individuals and the public so as to ensure the preservation of the good both of the parts and of the whole polity. The incipient totalitarianism of the evangelical mentality, evident in the sustained drive throughout the colonies to coerce and to convert everyone to the republican side and to banish all degrees of dissent, was repudiated by the Federal Constitution of 1787. Daniel Leonard had observed in 1775 that "Party is inseparable from a free state. The several distributions of power, as they are limited by, so they create perpetual dissentions between each other, about their respective boundaries"—a view that was to be explored with brilliant and persuasive eloquence by James Madison again in 1787 in *The Federalist*, Number 10.[36]

Madison recognized that "As long as the reason of man continues fallible, and he is at liberty to exercise it, different opinions will be formed," just as he recognized that "different degrees and kinds of property" also created divisions within society. Experience and human nature

combined to demonstrate to Madison and others that the earlier hopes of
a republic of virtue and of harmony and unity in the name of the public
good were unrealistic; indeed, they were detrimental to a properly constructed government if liberty was to be protected effectively. As he
pointed out, "It is in vain to say that enlightened statesmen will be able
to adjust these clashing interests, and render them all subservient to the
public good." The central problem thus became evident: "To secure the
public good and private rights" against the dangers of both minority factions and majority factions, and "at the same time to preserve the spirit
and form of popular government."

In *The Federalist*, Number 51, James Madison addressed an issue
that had been central to the republicanism of 1776—the belief that the
political community must be unified and entirely agreed, that the body
politic must have a will of its own superior to the will of any individuals
or groups within it, a belief which justified the expulsion and the intimidation of everyone who disagreed or dissented. The experiences of Americans during the mid-1770's made majority tyranny a reality felt by thousands and feared by countless others. As James Madison recognized, "It
is of great importance in a republic not only to guard the society against
the oppression of its rulers, but to guard one part of the society against the
injustices of the other part." "Different interests necessarily exist in different classes of citizens," he noted again, so that "If a majority be united
by a common interest, the rights of the minority will be insecure"—as
every supporter of royal authority in America had discovered through
personal experience. According to Madison, "There are but two methods
of providing against this evil: the one by creating a will in the community
independent of the majority—that is, of the society itself," which, in
essence, was the goal of evangelical republicans in 1776; while "the
other, by comprehending in the society so many separate descriptions of
citizens as will render an unjust combination of a majority of the whole
very improbable, if not impracticable." To the latter method Madison
looked in order to preserve the liberties of minorities in America. "In a
free government," he observed, "the security for civil rights must be the
same as that for religious rights. It consists in the one case in the multiplicity of interests, and in the other in the multiplicity of sects." Thus
Madison believed that diversity and variety, rather than uniformity and
homogeneity, were to be the guarantors of both personal and public liberty
for both minorities and majorities in the new Federal Republic he and
others had created. In setting forth this vision of liberty, Madison and his
fellow Federalists rejected the concept of liberty based upon virtue, purity,
and unanimity that had been set forth by many republicans a decade
earlier. Henceforth, the American Republic was to be a republic of law
and of institutions rather than a republic of virtue.[37]

The creation of the new Federal Republic of the United States of
America may have symbolized the rejection of the evangelical vision of a

pure, virtuous, and unanimous polity; but it did not and could not signify the disappearance of the evangelical temperament that had sustained that vision. By the early nineteenth century, the evangelical temperament had reemerged, and it continued for decades to shape the consciousness as well as the politics of Americans as they moved, once more, toward the abyss of internal conflict and civil war. Periodically, the dominance of one particular mode of temperament—which seemed to provide a relatively coherent ethos and ideology to most people in particular localities, regions, or even the nation as a whole—was challenged by other modes of temperament. The clash of temperaments that shaped the Anglo-American crisis of the mid-eighteenth century was only one of many such clashes. But the conflicts were episodic, whereas the temperaments themselves persisted continuously over a very long course of time. Indeed, the three temperaments which had shaped the history of early America so significantly were to continue to be visible for generations to come in the newly formed nation, with enduring consequences for the historical development of the United States.

ABBREVIATIONS

NOTES

PERMISSIONS

SOURCES

INDEX

ᴥᔰ ABBREVIATIONS ᔰᴥ

AHR	*American Historical Review*
AQ	*American Quarterly*
BPL	Department of Rare Books and Manuscripts, Boston Public Library
CHS	Connecticut Historical Society
EIHC	*Essex Institute Historical Collections*
HSP	Historical Society of Pennsylvania
JAH	*Journal of American History*
JIH	*Journal of Interdisciplinary History*
JSH	*Journal of Social History*
MHS	Massachusetts Historical Society
NEHGR	*New England Historical and Genealogical Register*
NEQ	*New England Quarterly*
NHHS	New Hampshire Historical Society
NYHS	New-York Historical Society
NYPL	Manuscripts and Archives Division, The New York Public Library, Astor, Lenox and Tilden Foundations
PMHB	*Pennsylvania Magazine of History and Biography*
SCHS	South Carolina Historical Society
WMQ	*William and Mary Quarterly*, Third Series
YCB	The Beinecke Rare Book and Manuscript Library, Yale University
YCS	Yale University Library

⊸§ NOTES §⊱

THROUGHOUT THE TEXT AND NOTES, I have spelled out contractions and altered both spelling and punctuation occasionally for the sake of clarity. I also have omitted italics except when necessary for emphasis. In general, however, I have retained the often idiosyncratic spelling and punctuation characteristic of so many sources in the seventeenth and eighteenth centuries.

I
Patterns for the Past

1 Perry Miller, *The New England Mind: The Seventeenth Century* (Cambridge, Mass., 1954; orig. ed., 1939), p. vii; Perry Miller, *The New England Mind: From Colony to Province* (Cambridge, Mass., 1953), p. x.

2 Perry Miller, *Errand into the Wilderness* (Cambridge, Mass., 1956), p. ix; Miller, *Seventeenth Century*, pp. 14, 22, 69.

3 Miller, "The Marrow of Puritan Divinity," *Errand*, p. 89. For the development of this argument, see Miller, *Seventeenth Century*.

4 Miller, *Seventeenth Century*, pp. 396, 400; Miller, *From Colony to Province*, pp. 484–5.

5 Miller, "Marrow of Puritan Divinity," *Errand*, p. 98. See also Miller's study *Jonathan Edwards* (n.p., 1949). For Miller's views on nineteenth-century evangelicalism, see *Nature's Nation* (Cambridge, Mass., 1967) and *The Life of the Mind in America: From the Revolution to the Civil War* (New York, 1965).

6 Among the numerous monographs on Puritanism and religion in Anglo-America, see: John F. H. New, *Anglican and Puritan: The Basis of Their Opposition, 1558–1640* (Stanford, Calif., 1964); Lazar Ziff, *The Career of John Cotton: Puritanism and the American Experience* (Princeton, N.J., 1962); Christopher Hill, *The World Turned Upside Down: Radical Ideas During the English Revolution* (New York, 1972); Edmund S. Morgan, *Visible Saints: The History of a Puritan Idea* (New York, 1963), and *The Gentle Puritan: A Life of Ezra Stiles, 1727–1795* (New Haven, Conn., 1962); Sacvan Bercovitch, *The Puritan Origins of the American Self* (New Haven, Conn., 1976); Robert G. Pope, *The Half-Way Covenant: Church Membership in Puritan New England* (Princeton, N.J., 1969); Melvin B. Endy, Jr., *William Penn and Early Quakerism* (Princeton, N.J., 1973); Emory Elliott, *Power and the Pulpit in Puritan New England* (Princeton, N.J., 1975); James W. Jones, *The Shattered Synthesis: New England Puritanism before the Great Awakening* (New Haven, Conn., 1973); Joseph J. Ellis, *The New England Mind in Transition: Samuel Johnson of Connecticut, 1696–1772* (New

Haven, Conn., 1973); C. C. Goen, *Revivalism and Separatism in New England, 1740–1800: Strict Congregationalists and Separate Baptists in the Great Awakening* (New Haven, Conn., 1962); William G. McLoughlin, *Isaac Backus and the American Pietistic Tradition* (Boston, Mass., 1967); Daniel Walker Howe, *The Unitarian Conscience: Harvard Moral Philosophy, 1805–1861* (Cambridge, Mass., 1970).

7 Norman Pettit, *The Heart Prepared: Grace and Conversion in Puritan Spiritual Life* (New Haven, Conn., 1966).

8 Norman S. Fiering, "Will and Intellect in the New England Mind," *WMQ,* XXIX (1972), pp. 523, 529, 531, 551.

9 David D. Hall, *The Faithful Shepherd: A History of the New England Ministry in the Seventeenth Century* (Chapel Hill, N.C., 1972), especially pp. 55, 61–2, 196, 202, 228, 236, 257, 262.

10 Ernest Benson Lowrie, *The Shape of the Puritan Mind: The Thought of Samuel Willard* (New Haven, Conn., 1974), and Robert Middlekauff, *The Mathers: Three Generations of Puritan Intellectuals, 1596–1728* (New York, 1971). See also my review of Middlekauff's *Mathers* in NYHS *Quarterly,* LVI (1972), pp. 86–8.

11 Pettit, *Heart Prepared,* pp. 189–90; Fiering, "Will and Intellect," pp. 552, 556.

12 Alan Heimert, *Religion and the American Mind from the Great Awakening to the Revolution* (Cambridge, Mass., 1966), pp. 3, 8, 22.

13 Bernard Bailyn, *The Ideological Origins of the American Revolution* (Cambridge, Mass., 1967), p. xi; Gordon S. Wood, *The Creation of the American Republic, 1776–1787* (Chapel Hill, N.C., 1969), p. 59. See also Bernard Bailyn, *The Origins of American Politics* (New York, 1968); T. H. Breen, *The Character of the Good Ruler: A Study of Puritan Political Ideas in New England, 1630–1730* (New Haven, Conn., 1970); Stephen E. Patterson, *Political Parties in Revolutionary Massachusetts* (Madison, Wisc., 1973).

14 John Locke, "Some Thoughts Concerning Education" (1690), and Horace Bushnell, "Christian Nurture (1847–1861)," in Philip J. Greven, Jr., ed., *Child-Rearing Concepts, 1628–1861: Historical Sources* (Itasca, Ill., 1973), pp. 28, 172. For Locke, see James Axtell, ed., *The Educational Writings of John Locke* (Cambridge, Eng., 1968), and John Dunn, *The Political Thought of John Locke: An Historical Account of the Argument of the "Two Treatises of Government"* (Cambridge, Eng., 1969).

The history of childhood in early America has been explored by historians from the late nineteenth century to the present. See, for instance, Alice Morse Earle, *Child-Life in Colonial Days* (New York, 1946; orig. ed. 1899); Arthur W. Calhoun, *A Social History of the American Family,* 3 vols. (New York, 1960; orig. ed. 1917); Sanford Fleming, *Children and Puritanism: The Place of Children in the Life and Thought of the New England Churches, 1620–1847* (New Haven, Conn., 1933); Edmund S. Morgan, *The Puritan Family: Religion and Domestic Relations in Seventeenth-Century New England,* rev. ed. (New York, 1966); Jane Carson, *Colonial Virginians at Play* (Williamsburg, Va., 1965); John Demos, *A Little Commonwealth: Family Life in Plymouth Colony* (New York, 1970); J. William Frost, *The Quaker Family in Colonial America: A Portrait of the Society of Friends* (New York, 1973); James Axtell, *The School upon the Hill: Education and Society in Colonial New England* (New Haven, Conn., 1974); Daniel Cal-

houn, *The Intelligence of a People* (Princeton, N.J., 1973). The study of childhood has gained increasing attention, evident in the numerous articles and even in the *Journal of the History of Childhood* (now transformed into the *Journal of Psychohistory*).
15 Miller, *Edwards*, p. xi.

II
Authoritarian Families: Modes of Evangelical Child-Rearing

1 John Wesley, "A Letter to Dr. Middleton," *The Works of the Rev. John Wesley*, 16 vols. (London, 1809–1812), XIII, pp. 246–7. For a collection of sources, see Philip J. Greven, Jr., ed., *Child-Rearing Concepts, 1628–1861: Historical Sources* (Itasca, Ill., 1973), and William G. McLoughlin, "Evangelical Child-Rearing in the Age of Jackson: Francis Wayland's View on When and How to Subdue the Willfulness of Children," *JSH*, 9 (1975), pp. 21–43. See also Monica Kiefer, *American Children through Their Books, 1700–1835* (Philadelphia, 1948), and Bernard Wishy, *The Child and the Republic: The Dawn of Modern American Child Nurture* (Philadelphia, 1968).
2 Samuel Hopkins, *Sketches of the Life of the Late, Rev. Samuel Hopkins . . . Written by Himself* (Hartford, Conn., 1805), pp. 23–4 (reprinted in part in Stephen Nissenbaum, ed., *The Great Awakening at Yale College* [Belmont, Calif., 1972], pp. 13–21). In addition, see Owen C. Watkins, *The Puritan Experience: Studies in Spiritual Autobiography* (New York, 1972); Daniel B. Shea, Jr., *Spiritual Autobiography in Early America* (Princeton, N.J., 1968); Robert C. Monk, *John Wesley: His Puritan Heritage* (Nashville, Tenn., 1966); John A. Newton, *Susanna Wesley and the Puritan Tradition in Methodism* (London, 1968); Howard H. Brinton, *Quaker Journals: Varieties of Religious Experience among Friends* (Wallingford, Pa., 1972).
3 Bruce Chapman Woolley, "Reverend Thomas Shepard's Cambridge Church Members 1636–1649; A Socio-Economic Analysis" (Ph.D. thesis, The University of Rochester, 1973), pp. 99, 113, 121, 146, 190; Robert G. Pope, ed., *The Notebook of the Reverend John Fiske, 1644–1675*, The Colonial Society of Massachusetts *Collections*, XLVII (Boston, 1974), pp. 146, 148, 89.
4 "Life of Elizabeth Stirredge," in *The Friends' Library: Comprising Journals, Doctrinal Treatises, and Other Writings of Members of the Religious Society of Friends*, II (Philadelphia, 1838), p. 187; Rufus M. Jones, ed.,*The Journal of George Fox*, paper ed. (New York, 1963), pp. 65–6; "Life of William Caton," *Friends' Library*, IX (1845), p. 435.
5 Michael McGiffert, ed., *God's Plot: The Paradoxes of Puritan Piety Being the Autobiography and Journal of Thomas Shepard* (Amherst, Mass., 1972), p. 38; M. G. Hall, ed., *The Autobiography of Increase Mather* (Worcester, Mass., 1962), p. 278; John Cleaveland, Ms. autobiographical fragment in John Cleaveland Mss., II, Essex Institute; David S. Lovejoy, ed., *Religious Enthusiasm and the Great Awakening* (Englewood Cliffs, N.J., 1969), p. 42; Samuel Hopkins, ed., *The Life and Character of Miss Susanna Anthony . . .*,

2nd ed. (Portland, Maine, 1810), pp. 13–14; *George Whitefield's Journals* (n.p., 1960), p. 37.

6 "Life of Joseph Pike," *Friends' Library*, II (1838), pp. 351–8.

7 In a subsequent study, I intend to explore the implications of migration for religious experience in considerable detail. For some suggestive evidence, see Philip J. Greven, Jr., *Four Generations: Population, Land, and Family in Colonial Andover, Massachusetts* (Ithaca, N.Y., 1970); Richard L. Bushman, *From Puritan to Yankee: Character and the Social Order in Connecticut, 1690–1765* (Cambridge, Mass., 1967), ch. IV, V; Richard T. Vann, *The Social Development of English Quakerism 1655–1755* (Cambridge, Mass., 1969), and "Nurture and Conversion in the Early Quaker Family," *Journal of Marriage and the Family*, 31 (1969), pp. 639–43; Gerald Francis Moran, "The Puritan Saint: Religious Experience, Church Membership, and Piety in Connecticut, 1636–1776" (Ph.D. thesis, Rutgers University, 1973); and Michael Walzer, *The Revolution of the Saints: A Study in the Origins of Radical Politics* (Cambridge, Mass., 1965), especially pp. 142–4, 200–4, 312–16. See also Emilio Willems, *Followers of the New Faith: Culture Change and the Rise of Protestantism in Brazil and Chile* (Nashville, 1967), and Bryan R. Roberts, "Protestant Groups and Coping with Urban Life in Guatemala City," *Journal of American Sociology*, 73 (1968), pp. 753–67. For the theme of exile and pilgrimage among English Puritans, see Walzer, *Revolution of the Saints*, pp. 130–5, 200–4, 312–16; Peter Laslett, *The World We Have Lost: England Before the Industrial Age* (New York, 1965).

8 John Dane ["A Declaration of Remarkabell Provedenses in the Corse of My Lyfe,"], "John Dane's Narrative, 1682," *NEHGR*, VIII (1854), pp. 149, 152.

9 Hannah Heaton, Spiritual Exercises, entry 102, in Calvin Eaton's Book, CHS, photocopy; Vann, *Social Development of English Quakerism*, p. 199.

10 Greven, *Child-Rearing Concepts*, pp. 64, 86. See also Walzer, *Revolution of the Saints*, pp. 188–90.

11 Greven, *Child-Rearing Concepts*, pp. 13, 64.

12 Greven, *Child-Rearing Concepts*, p. 11; "On the Birth of John Rogers Davies, The Author's Third Son," in Richard Beale Davis, ed., *Collected Poems of Samuel Davies, 1723–1761* (Gainesville, Fla., 1968), pp. 199–200. See also George William Pilcher, *Samuel Davies: Apostle of Dissent in Colonial Virginia* (Knoxville, Tenn., 1971), p. 41; Erik H. Erikson, *Childhood and Society*, 2nd ed. (New York, 1963), pp. 72–85, 247–54, and John Demos, *A Little Commonwealth: Family Life in Plymouth Colony* (New York, 1970).

13 John Harvard Ellis, ed., *The Works of Anne Bradstreet in Prose and Poetry* (New York, 1932), p. 151; Greven, *Child-Rearing Concepts*, pp. 101–2. See also H. Shelton Smith, *Changing Conceptions of Original Sin: A Study in American Theology Since 1750* (New York, 1955), and Peter Gregg Slater, "Views of Children and of Child Rearing During the Early National Period: A Study in the New England Intellect" (Ph.D. thesis, University of California at Berkeley, 1970). I am also grateful to Peter Slater for permitting me to read the manuscript for his forthcoming book: *Children in the New England Mind: From the Puritans to Bushnell*.

14 Ellis, *Works of Anne Bradstreet*, pp. 404, 406.

15 McGiffert, *God's Plot*, pp. 61, 69–70.

16 [Worthington Chauncey Ford, ed.], *Diary of Cotton Mather*, 2 vols. (New York, n.d.), I, pp. 218, 307, 336, 375, 574; II, p. 187; I, pp. 163–4; II, p. 7. See also Elizabeth Bancroft Schlesinger, "Cotton Mather and His Children," *WMQ*, X (1953), pp. 181–9.

17 Jonathan Edwards, *The Great Awakening*, C. C. Goen, ed. (New Haven, Conn., 1972), p. 394. Italics added.

18 For sources, see Greven, *Child-Rearing Concepts*, and McLoughlin, "Evangelical Child-Rearing." See also Robert L. Moore, "Justification without Joy: Psychohistorical Reflections on John Wesley's Childhood and Conversion," *History of Childhood Quarterly*, 2 (1974), pp. 31–52; Demos, *Little Commonwealth*; Daniel Walker Howe, "The Decline of Calvinism: An Approach to Its Study," *Comparative Studies in Society and History*, 14 (1972), p. 325. See also David Hunt, *Parents and Children in History: The Psychology of Family Life in Early Modern France* (New York, 1970); T. W. Adorno, *et al.*, *The Authoritarian Personality* (New York, 1969); David Mark Mantell, "Doves vs. Hawks: Guess Who Had the Authoritarian Parents?", *Psychology Today*, 8 (1974), pp. 56–62; Goodwin Watson, "Some Personality Differences in Children Related to Strict or Permissive Parental Discipline," *The Journal of Psychology*, 44 (1957), pp. 227–49; Diana Baumrind, "Effects of Authoritative Parental Control on Child Behavior," *Child Development*, 37 (1966), pp. 887–907; William H. Lyle and Eugene E. Levitt, "Punitiveness, Authoritarianism and Parental Discipline of Grade School Children," *Journal of Abnormal Social Psychology*, 51 (1955), pp. 42–6.

19 Greven, *Child-Rearing Concepts*, p. 72.

20 Greven, *Child-Rearing Concepts*, pp. 77–8.

21 Greven, *Child-Rearing Concepts*, pp. 105–6.

22 Clarence H. Faust and Thomas H. Johnson, eds., *Jonathan Edwards: Representative Selections* (New York, 1935), p. 198.

23 Hampshire Association of Ministers. A.(1) Records 1731–1747, April 18, 1738, F.25, Forbes Library, Northampton, Mass. I am indebted to Professor Mary Maples Dunn for this quotation.

24 Greven, *Child-Rearing Concepts*, pp. 81, 89.

25 John Wesley, "On Obedience to Parents," *Works*, VII, p. 103; *George Whitefield's Journal*, p. 146. The entire incident is revealing.

26 Esther Edwards Burr, Journal Addressed to Miss Prince, Oct. 1, 1754–Sept. 2, 1757, YCB, p. 67.

27 Greven, *Child-Rearing Concepts*, pp. 46–7. See also Newton, *Susanna Wesley and the Puritan Tradition*; Maldwyn Edwards, *Family Circle: A Study of the Epworth Household in Relation to John and Charles Wesley* (London, 1949); V. H. H. Green, *The Young Mr. Wesley: A Study of John Wesley and Oxford* (London, 1961), and *John Wesley* (London, 1964).

28 Greven, *Child-Rearing Concepts*, p. 90.

29 Greven, *Child-Rearing Concepts*, pp. 59–60.

30 Greven, *Child-Rearing Concepts*, pp. 13–14.

31 Greven, *Child-Rearing Concepts*, pp. 47–8.

32 McLoughlin, "Evangelical Child-Rearing," pp. 20–2.

33 "A Case of Conviction," *The American Baptist Magazine*, XI (1831), pp. 299–300.

34 Wesley, *Works*, X, p. 223.

35 Greven, *Child-Rearing Concepts*, pp. 15, 47, 62.
36 Wesley, *Works*, X, pp. 228–9; Richard L. Bushman, ed., *The Great Awakening: Documents on the Revival of Religion, 1740–1745* (New York, 1970), p. 32.
37 See Philippe Ariès, *Centuries of Childhood: A Social History of Family Life* (New York, 1962), p. 58, for a similar observation about European children; and Demos, *Little Commonwealth*, p. 140, and Alice Morse Earle, *Two Centuries of Costume in America*, 2 vols. (New York, 1968), I, ch. X. Although the fact of similar dress has been observed, no one as yet has pursued the implications very far.
38 Greven, *Child-Rearing Concepts*, pp. 78, 71–3.
39 "Life of Elizabeth Stirredge," p. 187; "Life of William Caton," *Friends' Library*, IX (1845), p. 435; "Journal of Charles Marshall," *Friends' Library*, IV (1840), p. 127.
40 Greven, *Child-Rearing Concepts*, p. 49.
41 Greven, *Child-Rearing Concepts*, pp. 49–50. For an analysis of the sustained control by parents over their grown children, see Greven, *Four Generations*.
42 Ellis, *Works of Anne Bradstreet*, pp. 7, 65, 50; Greven, *Child-Rearing Concepts*, p. 13.
43 Greven, *Child-Rearing Concepts*, p. 89.
44 For recent studies of conscience, see Wesley Allinsmith, "Conscience and Conflict: The Moral Force in Personality," *Child Development*, 28 (1957), pp. 469–76; Justin Aronfreed, *Conduct and Conscience: The Socialization of Internalized Overt Behavior* (New York, 1968); Leonore Boehm, "The Development of Conscience: A Comparison of American Children of Different Mental and Socioeconomic Levels," *Child Development*, 33 (1962), pp. 575–90; Leonore Boehm and Martin L. Nass, "Social Class Differences in Conscience Development," *Child Development*, 33 (1962), pp. 565–74; Roger V. Burton, Eleanor E. Macoby, and Wesley Allinsmith, "Antecedents of Resistance to Temptation in Four-Year-Old Children," *Child Development*, 32 (1961), pp. 689–710; Martin L. Hoffman, "Childrearing Practices and Moral Development: Generalizations from Empirical Research," *Child Development*, 34 (1963) pp. 295–318; Martin L. Hoffman, *Early Processes in Moral Development* (Chicago, 1968); M. L. Hoffman, *et al.*, "Parent Discipline and the Child's Moral Development," *Journal of Personality and Social Psychology*, 5 (1967), pp. 45–57; Lawrence Kohlberg, "Development of Moral Character and Moral Ideology," in M. L. Hoffman and L. W. Hoffman, eds., *Review of Child Development Research* (New York, 1964), pp. 383–432; Watson, "Some Personality Differences in Children"; John W. M. Whiting and Irvin L. Child, *Child Training and Personality: A Cross-Cultural Study* (New Haven, Conn., 1953).
45 Dane, "Narrative," p. 149.
46 "Life of Thomas Story," *Friends' Library*, X (1846), p. 7.
47 Greven, *Child-Rearing Concepts*, p. 44.
48 Rev. Timothy Edwards's Notices of his Father, Rich[ard] Edwards, Esq., Ms. notebook *ca.* 1718, in Edwards Mss., Andover Newton; Samuel G. Drake, *Some Memoirs of the Life and Writings of the Rev. Thomas Prince . . .* (Boston, 1851), p. 7; Cotton Mather, *Bonifacius: An Essay upon the Good*, David Levin, ed. (Cambridge, Mass., 1966), p. 47.

49 Greven, *Child-Rearing Concepts*, pp. 126–7.
50 Mather, *Bonifacius*, p. 47.
51 "Life of Joseph Pike," p. 356.
52 Whitefield, *Journal*, pp. 37–8. Brackets omitted.
53 McGiffert, *God's Plot*, pp. 41, 72.
54 "Life of Joseph Pike," p. 358; "Journal of John Banks," *Friends' Library*, II
     (1838), p. 9; "Life of John Gratton," *Friends' Library*, IX (1845), pp. 294–5.
     "A Short Account of Alice Hayes," *Friends' Library*, II (1838), p. 68.
55 Nissenbaum, *Great Awakening*, pp. 14, 37–8; Woolley, "Thomas Shepard's
     Cambridge Church Members," p. 99.
56 Samuel Gray to the Reverend Mr. Eleazer Wheelock, Boston, July 5, 1762,
     Ms. in Wheelock Coll., Dartmouth College.
57 The Spiritual Diary of Joseph Bean, February 1741–January 1744, Ms.
     Bryn Mawr College Library; "Memoirs of James Gough," *Friends' Library*, IX
     (1845), p. 6; Jonathan Edwards to Timothy Edwards, New Haven, July 24,
     1719, Edwards Mss., Andover-Newton; Faust and Johnson, *Edwards*, p. 42;
     Sereno E. Dwight, ed., *The Works of President Edwards: With a Memoir of
     His Life* (New York, 1829), I, pp. 86, 93.
58 Edmund S. Morgan, ed., *The Diary of Michael Wigglesworth, 1653–1657:
     The Conscience of a Puritan* (New York, 1965), pp. 107, 110, 114. Italics
     omitted.
59 Nissenbaum, *Great Awakening*, p. 14; "Life of Joseph Pike," p. 360.

III

"A Habitation of Dragons":
Themes of Evangelical Temperaments and Piety

1 Michael J. Crawford, ed., "The Spiritual Travels of Nathan Cole," *WMQ*,
     XXXIII (1976), p. 92, and the Ms., CHS; "Life of John Gratton," *Friends'
     Library*, IX (1845), p. 304; Richard L. Bushman, ed., *The Great Awakening:
     Documents on the Revival of Religion 1740–1745* (New York, 1970), p. 12;
     Jonathan Edwards, *Religious Affections*, John E. Smith, ed. (New Haven,
     Conn., 1959), p. 391; Hugh Barbour, *The Quakers in Puritan England* (New
     Haven, Conn., 1964), p. 98.
     For the analysis of conversion, see R. A. Knox, *Enthusiasm: A Chapter
     in the History of Religion with Special Reference to the XVII and XVIII
     Centuries* (Oxford, 1950); William James, *The Varieties of Religious Ex-
     perience: A Study in Human Nature* (New York, 1929); Edwin Diller Star-
     buck, *The Psychology of Religion: An Empirical Study of the Growth of
     Religious Consciousness* (New York, n.d.). See also Joel Allison, "Religious
     Conversion: Regression and Progression in an Adolescent Experience,"
     Journal for the Scientific Study of Religion, VIII (1969), pp. 23–38; Barbour,
     Quakers in Puritan England; F. W. B. Bullock, *Evangelical Conversion in
     Great Britain, 1696–1845* (St. Leonards-on-Sea, Eng., 1959); Richard L.
     Bushman, "Jonathan Edwards as Great Man: Identity, Conversion, and
     Leadership in the Great Awakening," *Soundings, An Interdisciplinary
     Journal*, LII (1969), pp. 15–46; Carl W. Christensen, "Religious Conversion

in Adolescence," *Pastoral Psychology*, 16 (1965), pp. 17–28; Bernhard Citron, *New Birth: A Study of the Evangelical Doctrine of Conversion in the Protestant Fathers* (Edinburgh, 1951); Elmer T. Clark, *The Psychology of Religious Awakening* (New York, 1929); Melvin B. Endy, Jr., *William Penn and Early Quakerism* (Princeton, N.J., 1975); Howard M. Feinstein, "The Prepared Heart: A Comparative Study of Puritan Theology and Psychoanalysis," *AQ*, XXII (1970), pp. 166–76; Robert L. Moore, "Justification Without Joy: Psychohistorical Reflections on John Wesley's Childhood and Conversion," *History of Childhood Quarterly*, 2 (1974), pp. 31–52; Gerald Francis Moran, "The Puritan Saint: Religious Experience, Church Membership, and Piety in Connecticut, 1636–1776" (Ph.D. thesis, Rutgers University, 1973); Norman Pettit, *The Heart Prepared: Grace and Conversion in Puritan Spiritual Life* (New Haven, Conn., 1966); Leon Salzman, "The Psychology of Religious and Ideological Conversion," *Psychiatry*, 16 (1953), pp. 177–87, and "Types of Religious Conversion," *Pastoral Psychology*, 17 (1969), pp. 8–20; Alan Simpson, *Puritanism in Old and New England* (Chicago, 1955); and Joseph Tracy, *The Great Awakening: A History of the Revival of Religion in the Time of Edwards and Whitefield* (Boston, 1842). In addition, see Geoffrey Nuttall, *The Holy Spirit in Puritan Faith and Experience* (Oxford, 1946); James F. Maclear, " 'The Heart of New England Rent': The Mystical Element in Early Puritan History," *Mississippi Valley Historical Review*, 42 (1956); and J. Rodney Fulcher, "Puritans and the Passions: The Faculty Psychology in American Puritanism," *Journal of the History of the Behavioral Sciences*, IX (1973), pp. 123–39.

2 John Wesley, "On the New Birth," *The Works of the Rev. John Wesley*, 16 vols. (London, 1809–1812), VII, pp. 299–300.

3 Clarence H. Faust and Thomas H. Johnson, eds., *Jonathan Edwards: Representative Selections* (New York, 1935), pp. 160, 164.

4 Wesley, "New Birth," *Works*, VII, p. 295.

5 Faust and Johnson, *Edwards*, p. 116; John Wesley, "On Self-Denial," *Works*, VIII, p. 359; John Wesley, "On Original Sin," *Works*, VII, p. 289.

6 [Worthington Chauncey Ford, ed.], *Diary of Cotton Mather*, 2 vols. (New York, n.d.), II, pp. 1–2; I, pp. 30–2, 357; II, p. 69.

7 Jonathan Edwards, *Images or Shadows of Divine Things*, Perry Miller, ed. (New Haven, Conn., 1948), pp. 91–4, 128–9. For studies of Edwards, see Alfred Owen Aldridge, *Jonathan Edwards* (New York, 1966); Richard L. Bushman, "Jonathan Edwards and Puritan Consciousness," *Journal for the Scientific Study of Religion*, V (1966), pp. 383–96; James Carse, *Jonathan Edwards and the Visibility of God* (New York, 1967); Conrad Cherry, *The Theology of Jonathan Edwards; A Reappraisal* (Gloucester, Mass., 1974); Perry Miller, *Jonathan Edwards* (n.p., 1949), perhaps the least satisfactory analysis of all, since Miller refused to concern himself with Edwards's life or psyche, intent only upon the analysis of his mind; Ola Elizabeth Winslow, *Jonathan Edwards, 1703–1758* (New York, 1961).

8 Samuel Hopkins, ed., *The Life and Character of Miss Susanna Anthony . . .*, 2nd ed. (Portland, Maine, 1810), pp. 67, 69, 151–2, 123–4.

9 Joseph Bean, The Spiritual Diary, typed copy, Bryn Mawr College Library; Daniel Rogers, Diary, 1740–1753, Ms. in Rogers Papers, Box 7, NYHS; Nicholas Gilman, Diary, March 3, 1742/3, Ms. NHHS; Benjamin Lyon, Diary,

1763–1767, 2 vols., CHS; Hannah Heaton, *Experiences or Spiritual Exercises of Hannah Heaton*, in Calvin Eaton's Book, photocopy of Ms., CHS.

10 Edmund S. Morgan, ed., *The Diary of Michael Wigglesworth 1653–1657: The Conscience of a Puritan* (New York, 1965), p. 53; Jonathan Edwards, *An Account of the Life of the late Reverend Mr. David Brainerd . . .* (Boston, 1749), pp. 100, 134–5. For studies of Wigglesworth, see Morgan's introduction to the *Diary* and Richard Crowder, *No Featherbed to Heaven: A Biography of Michael Wigglesworth 1631–1705* (n.p., 1962).

11 Daniel Rogers, Diary #1; Edwards, *Religious Affections*, p. 350.

12 Sereno E. Dwight, ed., *The Works of President Edwards: With a Memoir of His Life* (New York, 1829), I, pp. 77–8, 80–1, 90.

13 Philip J. Greven, Jr., ed., *Child-Rearing Concepts, 1628–1861: Historical Sources* (Itasca, Ill., 1973), pp. 68–9.

14 *George Whitefield's Journals* (n.p., 1960), pp. 50–8. For Whitefield, see Albert D. Belden, *George Whitefield—The Awakener: A Modern Study of the Evangelical Revival*, rev. ed. (London, 1953); Arnold A. Dallimore, *George Whitefield: The Life and Times of the Great Evangelist of the Eighteenth-Century Revival* (London, 1970); Stuart C. Henry, *George Whitefield: Wayfaring Witness* (Nashville, Tenn., 1957); William Howland Kenney, 3rd, "George Whitefield and Colonial Revivalism: The Social Sources of Charismatic Authority, 1737–1770" (Ph.D. thesis, University of Pennsylvania, 1967), and "George Whitefield, Dissenter Priest of the Great Awakening, 1739–1741," *WMQ*, XXVI (1969), pp. 75–93.

15 Hopkins, *Life of Susanna Anthony*, pp. 18–27.

16 George Whitefield to Mr. H., Dec. 4, 1734, and Whitefield to Mr. H., March 6, 1735, *The Works of the Reverend George Whitefield . . . Containing All his Sermons and Tracts . . . with a Select Collection of Letters . . .*, 6 vols. (London, 1751–1752), I, pp. 5, 8.

17 See Sigmund Freud's perceptive essay "Mourning and Melancholia," *Collected Papers*, Ernest Jones, ed. (New York, 1959), vol. 4, pp. 152–70. See also the remarkable analysis of early-nineteenth-century working-class Methodism in England by E. P. Thompson: "The Transforming Power of the Cross," *The Making of the English Working Class* (New York, 1963), ch. 11.

18 Aaron Burr to Jonathan Edwards, Newark, March 1741, Edwards Mss., Andover-Newton; "Life of Stephen Crisp," *Friends' Library*, XIV (1850), pp. 139–42.

19 Morgan, *Diary of Michael Wigglesworth*, p. 114; Burr to Edwards, March 1741.

20 Dwight, *Works of Edwards*, I, pp. 78–9; Ford, *Diary of Cotton Mather*, I, p. 112; Hopkins, *Life of Susanna Anthony*, p. 128; Lyon, Diary, July 31, 1762.

21 Ford, *Diary of Cotton Mather*, II, p. 45; "A Short Account of Alice Hayes," *Friends' Library*, II (1838), p. 78; Sarah [Prince] Gill, Journal, February 20, 1757, Ms. BPL; Heaton, Diary, p. 100.

22 Dwight, *Works of Edwards*, I, p. 151.

23 Faust and Johnson, *Edwards*, p. 71; Esther Burr to Jonathan Edwards, Princeton, Nov. 2, 1757, copy of Ms., Burr Family Papers, YCS; David Hall,

Diary, Jan. 1, 1741/2, Ms., MHS; Lyon, Diary, April 6, 1763; Morgan, *Diary of Michael Wigglesworth*, p. 4.

24 Edwards, *Religious Affections*, pp. 312, 315.

25 Ford, *Diary of Cotton Mather*, May 10, 1718, II, p. 533.

26 Dwight, *Works of Edwards*, I, pp. 151–2; Edwards, *Images or Shadows*, pp. 71, 90; Faust and Johnson, *Edwards*, pp. 63–4; Edwards, *Religious Affections*, pp. 339–40.

27 Faust and Johnson, *Edwards*, pp. 68–9; Hopkins, *Life of Susanna Anthony*, p. 130; Charles Jeffry Smith, Diary, June 1763, Ms., YCB; Lyon, Diary, July 31, 1762; Rogers, Diary, September 6, 1741; Edwards, *Account of Life of David Brainerd*, pp. 33, 37; Francis Howgill, "The Inheritance of Jacob Discovered," in Hugh Barbour and Arthur O. Roberts, eds., *Early Quaker Writings 1650–1700* (Grand Rapids, Mich., 1973), p. 175.

28 Barbour and Roberts, *Early Quaker Writings*, pp. 236, 239–40; Cole, "Spiritual Travels."

29 Heaton, Experiences.

30 Hopkins, *Life of Susanna Anthony*, pp. 25–7.

31 Cole, "Spiritual Travels," pp. 21–3; and Crawford, "Spiritual Travels of Cole," pp. 101–2; Faust and Johnson, *Edwards*, p. 83. See also Thompson, *Making of the English Working Class*, pp. 373–4.

32 Ford, *Diary of Cotton Mather*, II, pp. 264, 659–60, 708, 711.

33 Barbour and Roberts, *Early Quaker Writings*, pp. 175, 230.

34 Michael McGiffert, ed., *God's Plot: The Paradoxes of Puritan Piety. Being the Autobiography and Journal of Thomas Shepard* (n.p., 1972), p. 224; Dwight, *Works of Edwards*, I, pp. 179–80; Faust and Johnson, *Edwards*, p. 59. For the theme of fusion, see Helfaer, *Psychology of Religious Doubt*, pp. 72–3.

35 Ford, *Diary of Cotton Mather*, II, p. 337; Thomas Prince, *Dying Exercises of Mrs. Deborah Prince and Devout Meditations of Mrs. Sarah Gill . . .* (Newburyport, Mass., 1789), p. 35.

36 Lyon, Diary, March 14, 1763; Hopkins, *Life of Susanna Anthony*, pp. 148–9.

37 Robert G. Pope, ed., *The Notebook of the Reverend John Fiske*, Colonial Society of Massachusetts *Collections*, XLVII (1974), p. 36; Bruce Chapman Woolley, "Reverend Thomas Shepard's Cambridge Church Members 1636–1649: A Socio-Economic Analysis" (Ph.D. thesis, University of Rochester, 1973), p. 116. See also Jonathan Edwards, *Freedom of the Will*, Paul Ramsey, ed. (New Haven, Conn., 1957), and Conrad Wright, *The Beginnings of Unitarianism in America* (Boston, 1955), ch. 4, for discussion of free will; Gerald J. Goodwin, "The Myth of Arminian-Calvinism in Eighteenth-Century New England," *NEQ*, XLI (1968), pp. 213–37; John F. H. New, *Anglican and Puritan: The Basis of Their Opposition 1558–1640* (Stanford, Calif., 1964). See also Norman S. Fiering, "Will and Intellect in the New England Mind," *WMQ*, XXIX (1972), pp. 515–58.

38 Crawford, "Spiritual Travels of Cole," p. 92, italics omitted; *The Journal of the Rev. John Wesley A.M.*, 4 vols. (New York, 1913), I, p. 101; "Relations of Persons Joining the Church at Chebacco, 1764," in John Cleaveland Mss., Essex Institute.

39 Woolley, "Reverend Shepard's Church Members," pp. 106, 182, 113; Pope, *Notebook of John Fiske*, p. 6.

40 Stephen Nissenbaum, ed., *The Great Awakening at Yale College* (Belmont, Calif., 1972), pp. 15, 39.

41 Aaron Burr to Jonathan Edwards, March 1741, Edwards Mss., Andover Newton.

42 Burr to Edwards, March 1741; McGiffert, *God's Plot*, p. 73.

43 "Life of Joseph Pike," *Friends' Library*, II (1838), p. 358.

44 *Journal of John Wesley*, I, pp. 75–7.

45 *Journal of John Wesley*, I, pp. 95–8.

46 David S. Lovejoy, ed., *Religious Enthusiasm and the Great Awakening* (Englewood Cliffs, N.J., 1969), pp. 44–5. See William G. McLoughlin, *Isaac Backus and the American Pietistic Tradition* (Boston, 1967).

47 [Thomas Prince, ed.], *The Christian History, Containing Accounts of the Revival and Propagation of Religion in Great Britain and America for the Year 1743*, pp. 414–15.

48 William G. McLoughlin, "Evangelical Child-Rearing in the Age of Jackson: Francis Wayland's Views on When and How to Subdue the Willfulness of Children," *JSH*, 9 (1975), pp. 38–9.

49 Greven, *Child-Rearing Concepts*, pp. 48–9; Faust and Johnson, *Edwards*, p. 153; Jonathan Edwards, *The Great Awakening*, C. C. Goen, ed. (New Haven, Conn., 1972), p. 298, which makes the equation of "heart" and "will" clear.

50 Rogers, Diary, Jan. 6, 8, and March 1, 3, 14, 1741/2.

51 Tracy, *Great Awakening*, pp. 170, 174–5.

52 Cole, "Spiritual Travels." See also Bushman, *Great Awakening*, pp. 68–70.

53 Woolley, "Thomas Shepard's Cambridge Church Members," pp. 98, 111–12, 162–3, 185. See also Pope, *Notebook of John Fiske*, pp. 100–1.

54 Morgan, *Diary of Michael Wigglesworth*, pp. 114–21.

55 Cleaveland, "Relations of Persons Joining the Church."

56 "Life of Stephen Crisp," pp. 142–3.

57 "Life of Joseph Pike," pp. 359–62. See also "Life of Thomas Story," *Friends' Library*, X (1846), pp. 7–11, for a similar experience.

58 See T. W. Adorno, *et al.*, *The Authoritarian Personality* (New York, 1969); Ronald V. Sampson, *The Psychology of Power* (New York, 1968); David Mark Mantell, "Doves vs. Hawks: Guess Who Had the Authoritarian Parents?", *Psychology Today*, 8 (1974), pp. 56–62; and Diana Baumrind, "Effects of Authoritative Parental Control on Child Behavior," *Child Development*, 37 (1966), pp. 887–907, for a comparison of authoritarian, authoritative, and permissive modes of child-rearing and their effects upon personality.

59 Jonathan Edwards, *Freedom of the Will*, Paul Ramsey, ed. (New Haven, Conn., 1957), pp. 378–80.

60 Faust and Johnson, *Edwards*, p. 67.

61 Faust and Johnson, *Edwards*, p. 161. See also Robert Middlekauff, *The Mathers: Three Generations of Puritan Intelectuals, 1596–1728* (New York, 1971), pp. 61, 164–5, 235–7, which demonstrates that even the Covenant meant surrender for evangelicals.

62 Faust and Johnson, *Edwards*, pp. 58–9; Nissenbaum, *Great Awakening*, p. 44; Hopkins, *Life of Susanna Anthony*, p. 14; Lovejoy, *Religious Enthusiasm*, p. 44; Aaron Burr to Edwards, 1741.

63 Wesley, "Letters to Dr. Middleton," *Works*, XIII, pp. 246–7.

64 Wesley, *Works*, VIII, pp. 359, 288.

65 Samuel Phillips, *A Word in Season. Or, The Duty of People to Take and Keep the Oath of Allegiance to the Glorious God* . . . (Boston, 1727).

66 Hopkins, *Life of Susanna Anthony*, pp. 136, 141–2.

67 Hopkins, *Life of Susanna Anthony*, pp. 172–3. For the assault upon the great chain of being, characteristic of evangelicals, see the analysis of "The Attack upon the Traditional Political World" by Michael Walzer, *Revolution of the Saints*, especially pp. 149–71. For further discussion, see pp. 194–7.

68 Prince, *Dying Exercises of Deborah Prince*, pp. 41–2; Sarah Gill, Journal, Jan. 10, Sept. 12, Sept. 19, 1756; Jan. 19, Feb. 17, 1757.

69 David Ferris, *Memoirs of the Life of David Ferris, an Approved Minister of the Society of Friends* . . . *Written by Himself* (Philadelphia, 1855), pp. 16, 40–1.

70 Ferris, *Memoirs*, p. 22.

71 Ferris, *Memoirs*, pp. 48–52.

72 Ferris, *Memoirs*, pp. 56, 69.

73 Barbour and Roberts, *Early Quaker Writings*, pp. 137, 124, 129–30.

74 Barbour and Roberts, *Early Quaker Writings*, pp. 159–60; Greven, *Child-Rearing Concepts*, p. 48.

75 See, for instance, John Demos, "Underlying Themes in the Witchcraft of Seventeenth-Century New England," *AHR*, LXV (1970), pp. 1311–26; Paul Boyer and Stephen Nissenbaum, *Salem Possessed: The Social Origins of Witchcraft* (Cambridge, Mass., 1974); Middlekauff, *The Mathers*, pp. 326–30.

76 Greven, *Child-Rearing Concepts*, p. 78; Faust and Johnson, *Edwards*, pp. 42–3.

77 Jonathan Edwards, "Men Naturally God's Enemies," in Dwight, *Works of President Edwards*, VII, pp. 46–52.

78 Ford, *Diary of Cotton Mather*, II, p. 127; Heaton, Experiences, entry 90, 391 (March 7, 1775).

79 Lyon, Diary, Feb. 12, 1763, April 6, 1763.

80 "Journal of John Banks," *Friends' Library*, II (1838), pp. 35–6.

81 Barbour and Roberts, *Early Quaker Writings*, pp. 101–2, 114; "A Short Account of Alice Hayes," *Friends' Library*, II (1838), p. 79.

82 Edwards, *Religious Affections*, pp. 350–1. For the theme of warfare in seventeenth-century English Puritanism, see William Haller, *The Rise of Puritanism* (New York, 1938), pp. 142–72, and Walzer, *Revolution of the Saints*, pp. 64–5, 268–99 ("Politics and War"), for a brilliant analysis.

83 Alan Heimert and Perry Miller, eds., *The Great Awakening: Documents Illustrating the Crisis and Its Consequences* (Indianapolis, Ind., 1967), p. 166.

84 Paul Boyer and Stephen Nissenbaum, eds., *Salem-Village Witchcraft: A Documentary Record of Local Conflict in Colonial New England* (Belmont, Calif., 1972), p. 134. See also Boyer and Nissenbaum, *Salem Possessed*, pp. 153–78, for a perceptive analysis of the Reverend Parris.

85 Lovejoy, *Religious Enthusiasm*, p. 79.

86 David D. Hall, ed., *The Antinomian Controversy, 1636–1638: A Documentary History* (Middletown, Conn., 1968), pp. 158, 164–6. See also Emery Battis,

Saints and Sectaries: Anne Hutchinson and the Antinomian Controversy in the Massachusetts Bay Colony (Chapel Hill, N.C., 1962).

87 Edwards, *Great Awakening*, pp. 384–5.

88 See, for instance, Walzer, *Revolution of the Saints*, and two fascinating and important essays by Rhys Isaac: "Evangelical Revolt: The Nature of the Baptists' Challenge to the Traditional Order in Virgina, 1765 to 1775," *WMQ*, XXXI (1974), pp. 345–68, and "Preachers and Patriots: Popular Culture and the Revolution in Virginia," in Alfred A. Young, ed., *The American Revolution: Explorations in the History of Radicalism* (Dekalb, Ill., 1976), pp. 125–56. See also Barbour, *Quakers in Puritan England*, pp. 207–10; Christopher Hill, *The World Turned Upside Down: Radical Ideas during the English Revolution* (New York, 1972).

89 Heimert and Miller, *Great Awakening*, pp. 394–5.

90 Heimert and Miller, *Great Awakening*, pp. 466–7, 469–71, 479.

91 Ford, *Diary of Cotton Mather*, II, pp. 15, 706–7. Middlekauff, *The Mathers*, pp. 327–8, 362.

92 Francis G. Walett, ed., "The Diary of Ebenezer Parkman 1739–1744," in *American Antiquarian Society Proceedings* (1962), pp. 183, 414–15. The theme of oral aggression has also been explored by John Demos in "Underlying Themes in Witchcraft," pp. 1311–26.

93 Boyer and Nissenbaum, *Salem-Village Witchcraft*, p. 112.

94 See Lyle Koehler, "The Case of the American Jezebels: Anne Hutchinson and Female Agitation during the Years of Antinomian Turmoil, 1636–1640," *WMQ*, XXXI (1974), pp. 55–78.

95 See, for example, Julia Cherry Spruill, *Women's Life and Work in the Southern Colonies* (New York, 1972; orig. ed. 1938); Mary P. Ryan, *Womanhood in America: From Colonial Times to the Present* (New York, 1975); Koehler, "The Case of the American Jezebels"; Mary Beth Norton, "Eighteenth-Century American Women in Peace and War: The Case of the Loyalists," *WMQ*, XXXIII (1976), pp. 386–409; Randolph Shipley Klein, *Portrait of an Early American Family: The Shippens of Pennsylvania* (Philadelphia, 1975); Linda Grant DePauw, *Four Traditions: Women of New York during the American Revolution* (Albany, N.Y., 1974). For the nineteenth century, see Barbara Welter, "The Cult of True Womanhood, 1820–1860," *AQ*, XVII (1966), pp. 151–74; Carroll Smith-Rosenberg, "The Hysterical Woman: Sex Roles and Role Conflict in Nineteenth-Century America," *Social Research*, XXXIX (1972), pp. 652–78; John S. Haller, Jr., and Robin M. Haller, *The Physician and Sexuality in Victorian America* (Urbana, Ill., 1974); Nancy F. Cott, "Young Women in the Second Great Awakening in New England," *Feminist Studies*, 3 (1975), pp. 15–29; Kathryn Kish Sklar, *Catherine Beecher: A Study in American Domesticity* (New Haven, Conn., 1973). See also Peter Gabriel Filene, *Him/Her/Self: Sex Roles in Modern America* (New York, 1976). The most sensitive study so far of the themes of femininity and masculinity in eighteenth-century piety is Mary Maples Dunn's unpublished essay, "Women and Religion in Colonial America" (lecture given at Princeton University, Feb. 12, 1976).

96 See also Edmund S. Morgan's discussion of the theme of brides of Christ in *The Puritan Family: Religion and Domestic Relations in Seventeenth-Century New England*, rev. ed. (New York, 1966), pp. 161–8.

97 Barbour and Roberts, *Early Quaker Writings*, p. 234; John Rogers to his children, 1742, Ms., Rogers Papers, Box 7, NYHS.
98 Bean, Spiritual Diary. See also Lyon, Diary, July 13, 1765.
99 McGiffert, *God's Plot*, pp. 97–8; Barbour and Roberts, *Early Quaker Writings*, p. 497.
100 John Wesley, "The Duties of Husbands and Wives," *Works*, IX, pp. 74–5, 82.
101 Jonathan Edwards, "Miscellanies," No. 37 on "Faith," typed Ms., pp. 169–71, YCB.
102 Edwards, *Images or Shadows*, p. 90. For a different perspective upon attitudes toward sexuality in early America, see Edmund S. Morgan, "The Puritans and Sex," *New England Quarterly*, 15 (1942), pp. 591–607. Morgan's portrait is more consonant with the moderate's response to sexuality than with the evangelical's. See also Thompson, *Making of the English Working Class*, pp. 370–3, for a tantalizing analysis of Methodist imagery and sexuality.
103 Nicholas Gilman, "Spiritualia" (1724?–1736), Ms., MHS.
104 Ford, *Diary of Cotton Mather*, II, pp. 261, 118.
105 Barbour and Roberts, *Early Quaker Writings*, p. 509.
106 Morgan, *Diary of Michael Wigglesworth*, pp. 4, 6, 50, 53, 86 (note 42), 87–8, 92, 93.
107 The oedipal themes in Edwards have been explored in Richard Bushman's perceptive analysis, "Jonathan Edwards and Puritan Consciousness"; see also V. H. H. Green's *The Young Mr. Wesley: A Study of John Wesley and Oxford* (London, 1961) for an analysis of the feminine household in which the Wesley sons grew up. As Green notes, Wesley's "formative years were spent in the midst of a sisterhood in a household dominated by a matriarch." In addition, Green observes that "There was a decisive streak of femininity in John's character (and to some extent in that of Charles also)" (pp. 51–2), which subsequently had psychological repercussions. See also Halfaer, *Psychology of Religious Doubt*, pp. 72–6, 217–19, 314–16.
108 Edwards, *Images or Shadows*, pp. 83, 109. I am indebted to Louis Kern, who pointed out the European associations of the vagina and Hell in some of the paintings and etchings of the era of the Reformation.
109 Morgan, *Diary of Michael Wigglesworth*, pp. 19, 9–10, 50, 57, 82.
110 Morgan, *Diary of Michael Wigglesworth*, pp. 9, 11, 13, 31.
111 Samuel G. Drake, *Some Memoirs of the Life and Writings of the Rev. Thomas Prince . . .* (Boston, 1851), p. 11.
112 Sarah [Prince] Gill, Journal, April 21, 1756; Esther [Edwards] Burr, Journal Addressed to Miss Prince, Oct. 1, 1754–Sept. 2, 1757, Ms., p. 100, YCB.
113 Burr, Journal, p. 113.
114 Gill, Journal, Sept. 9, 1758, Oct. 21, 1758.
115 Gill, Journal, March 25, 1759, Nov. 2, 1760, March 9, 1764.
116 For Whitefield, see Henry, *George Whitefield*; Bushman, *Great Awakening*, p. 33; Dallimore, *George Whitefield*, I, p. 366.
117 Dallimore, *George Whitefield*, I, pp. 468–9.
118 Dallimore, *George Whitefield*, I, pp. 471–2; George Whitefield to William S. . . ., Whitefield, *Works*, I, p. 194.
119 Whitefield, *Works*, I, pp. 56–7, 123–4. See also Richard Hockley to Mr. Bernard Hannington, Philadelphia, June 8, 1740, and Richard Hockley to

Mr. Jno. Watson, Phiadelphia, Nov. 29, 1740, in Richard Hockley, Letter-book, 1737–1742, Ms. Haverford College. I am indebted to William Howland Kenney, 3rd's study "George Whitefield and Colonial Revivalism" for pointing out this rumor and the source (p. 65).

120 For Parsons, see Tracy, *Great Awakening*, p. 143. In addition, see Helfaer, *Psychology of Religious Doubt*, p. 132.

121 Belden, George Whitefield, p. 126; Whitefield, *Works*, I, p. 363. For details on his marriage and his wife, see Henry, *George Whitefield*, pp. 72–7.

122 See, for example, Lucy Hutchinson, *Memoirs of the Life of Colonel Hutchinson*, James Sutherland, ed. (London, 1973), pp. 62–3.

123 Perry Miller and Thomas Johnson, eds., *The Puritans* (New York, 1938), pp. 456–7. See also James Axtell, *The School upon a Hill: Education and Society in Colonial New England* (New Haven, Conn., 1974), pp. 161–5, for a discussion of wigs.

124 See Christopher Hill, *Society and Puritanism in Pre-Revolutionary England*, 2nd ed. (New York, 1967); Hill, *The World Turned Upside Down*; Simpson, *Puritanism*; B. R. White, *The English Separatist Tradition from the Marian Martyrs to the Pilgrim Fathers* (Oxford, 1971); Walzer, *Revolution of the Saints*; Umphrey Lee, *The Historical Background of Early Methodist Enthusiasm* (New York, 1931); Battis, *Saints and Sectaries*; Edmund S. Morgan, *Visible Saints: The History of a Puritan Idea* (New York, 1963); C. C. Goen, *Revivalism and Separatism in New England, 1740–1800: Strict Congregationalists and Separate Baptists in the Great Awakening* (New Haven, Conn., 1962); Melvin B. Endy, Jr., *William Penn and Early Quakerism* (Princeton, N.J., 1975); J. M. Bumsted and John E. Van de Wetering, *What Must I Do to Be Saved? The Great Awakening in Colonial America* (Hinsdale, Ill., 1976); Edwin Scott Gaustad, *The Great Awakening in New England* (New York, 1957); Alan Heimert, *Religion and the American Mind from the Great Awakening to the Revolution* (Cambridge, Mass., 1966); Rhys Isaac, "Evangelical Revolt: The Nature of the Baptists' Challenge to the Traditional Order in Virginia, 1765 to 1775," *WMQ*, XXXI (1974), pp. 345–68; Whitney R. Cross, *The Burned-Over District: The Social and Intellectual History of Enthusiastic Religion in Western New York* (Ithaca, N.Y., 1950). See also Alex Haley, ed., *The Autobiography of Malcolm X* (New York, 1966), for an extraordinary contemporary account.

125 David D. Hall, *The Faithful Shepherd: A History of the New England Ministry in the Seventeenth Century* (Chapel Hill, N.C., 1972), p. 65; M. G. Hall, ed., *The Autobiography of Increase Mather* (Worcester, Mass., 1962), p. 279; Bean, Spiritual Diary, typed copy; Henry, *George Whitefield*, p. 75.

126 Cole, Spiritual Travels, pp. 44–5.

127 See Walzer, *Revolution of the Saints*, for an analysis of self-discipline in seventeenth-century English Puritanism.

128 Jessamyn West, ed., *The Quaker Reader* (New York, 1962), p. 55.

129 *George Whitefield's Journals* (London, 1960), pp. 366–7, entry for Dec. 6, 1739.

130 New, *Anglican and Puritan*, p. 22. See also Walzer, *Revolution of the Saints*.

131 See, for instance, Goen, *Revivalism and Separatism in New England*; Barbour, *Quakers in Puritan England*; Geoffrey F. Nuttall, *Studies in Christian*

Enthusiasm Illustrated from Early Quakerism (Wallingford, Pa., 1948); and Isaac, "Evangelical Revolt," pp. 345–68.

132 Heimert and Miller, *Great Awakening*, pp. 444–5; Cole, Spiritual Travels, pp. 37–8.

133 Heimert, *Religion and the American Mind*, p. 117. For his discussion of millennialism, see pp. 59–70, 410–12, and *passim*.

134 Heimert and Miller, *Great Awakening*, p. 457.

IV
Authoritative Families: Moderate Modes of Child-Rearing

1 See Samuel Willard, *A Complete Body of Divinity in Two Hundred and Fifty Expository Lectures on the Assembly's Shorter Catechism* . . . (Boston, 1726), p. 607, and Diana Baumrind, "Effects of Authoritative Parental Control on Child Behavior," *Child Development*, 37 (1966), pp. 887–907, for observations on "authoritative" methods. For studies of "moderate" families, see Edmund S. Morgan, *The Puritan Family: Religion and Domestic Relations in Seventeenth-Century New England*, rev. ed. (New York, 1966); J. William Frost, *The Quaker Family in Colonial America: A Portrait of the Society of Friends* (New York, 1973); Alan MacFarlane, *The Family Life of Ralph Josselin, a Seventeenth-Century Clergyman: An Essay in Historical Anthropology* (Cambridge, Eng., 1970); Bernard Wishy, *The Child and the Republic: The Dawn of Modern American Child Nurture* (Philadelphia, 1968); Anne L. Kuhn, *The Mother's Role in Childhood Education: New England Concepts 1830–1860* (New Haven, Conn., 1947); Kirk Jeffrey, Jr., "Family History: The Middle-Class American Family in the Urban Context 1830–1870" (Ph.D. thesis, Stanford University, 1971); Mary Patricia Ryan, "American Society and the Cult of Domesticity, 1830–1860" (Ph.D. thesis, University of California, Santa Barbara, 1971); William R. Hutchison, "Cultural Strain and Protestant Liberalism," *AHR*, 76 (1971), especially pp. 400–5. See also Emory Elliott, *Power and the Pulpit in Puritan New England* (Princeton, N.J., 1975), especially ch. 2.

2 See Philip J. Greven, Jr., *Four Generations: Population, Land, and Family in Colonial Andover, Massachusetts* (Ithaca, N.Y., 1970).

3 See Morgan, *Puritan Family*, pp. 150–60.

4 Adam Winthrop to Margaret Tyndal, March 1618, *Winthrop Papers 1498–1649*, MHS *Collections*, 5 vols. (Boston, 1929–1947), I, pp. 220–1; Halsey M. Thomas, ed., *The Diary of Samuel Sewall 1674–1729*, 2 vols. (New York, 1973), I, pp. 96, 250; Herbert and Carol Schneider, eds., *Samuel Johnson: His Career and Writings*, 4 vols. (New York, 1929), I, pp. 3–4, 42; L. H. Butterfield, *et al.*, eds., *Adams Family Correspondence* (Cambridge, Mass., 1963–   ), I, pp. 300, 313. For the Winthrops, see Edmund S. Morgan, *The Puritan Dilemma: The Story of John Winthrop* (Boston, 1958); Richard S. Dunn, *Puritans and Yankees: The Winthrop Dynasty of New England* (Princeton, N.J., 1962); Robert C. Black, III, *The Younger John Winthrop* (New York, 1966). For Johnson, see Joseph J. Ellis, *The New England Mind*

in Transition: Samuel Johnson of Connecticut, 1696–1772 (New Haven, Conn., 1973).

5 Mary Hutchinson to Mrs. Oliver, Milton, July 24, 1772, Hutchinson-Watson Papers, MHS.

6 See Morgan, *Puritan Family*, pp. 25–8, 106–8.

7 Willard, *Compleat Body of Divinity*, p. 601.

8 *Winthrop Papers*, I, pp. 241–2; "Correspondence of Wait Winthrop," MHS *Collections*, 6th Series, V (1892), pp. 299–300, 315, 337n; Thomas, *Diary of Samuel Sewall*, I, pp. 89 (see also p. 266), 350.

9 Isaac Norris to Susy Wright, Fairhill, July 22, 1746, Norris of Fairhill Family Correspondence, II, HSP (see also Frost, *The Quaker Family*, pp. 66–7); Autobiography and Diary of Mrs. Eliza Clitherall, 1751–1860, 17 vols., typed copy, VI, p. 5, Southern Historical Collection, University of North Carolina, Chapel Hill; Sarah Pemberton Rhoads, Notebook, I, Samuel W. Fisher Mss., HSP.

10 Caroline Hazard, ed., *John Saffin his Book (1665–1708)* . . . (New York, 1928), pp. 184–5, 10–11.

11 Butterfield, *Adams Family Correspondence*, I, pp. 51, 57–8, 114, 135; II, p. 116.

12 Timothy Pickering, Letters to Rebecca, March 2, 1777, Dec. 13, 1777, Aug. 1, 1778, typed copies, Essex Institute.

13 See, for example, Charles Strickland, "A Transcendentalist Father: The Child-Rearing Practices of Bronson Alcott," *Perspectives in American History*, III (1969), pp. 5–73; Hutchison, "Cultural Strain"; Bruce Mazlish, *James and John Stuart Mill: Father and Son in the Nineteenth Century* (New York, 1975).

14 Willard, *Compleat Body of Divinity*, pp. 607, 603, 605 (this quotation was brought to my attention by Emory Elliott's *Power and Pulpit in Puritan New England* [Princeton, N.J., 1975] [italics omitted]); Philip J. Greven, Jr., ed., *Child-Rearing Concepts, 1628–1861: Historical Sources* (Itasca, Ill., 1973), pp. 180–1.

15 Willard, *Compleat Body of Divinity*, pp. 603, 606.

16 Joseph Fish, Sermon, "On the Death of my Dear Daughter, Rebecca Douglas," Dec. 14 and 21, 1766, Ms. Silliman Family Papers, Box 35, pp. 53–5, YCS; Mary Fish Dickinson, Qualities of a Husband, Aug. 3, 1773, YCS.

17 Pickering, Letters to Rebecca, Aug. 25, 1783; Pickering, Letters to Son John, Sept. 28, 1795, Sept. 29, 1792, typed copies, Essex Instiute.

18 Samuel Johnson, "Raphael, or the Genius of the English America," in Schneider, *Samuel Johnson*, II, pp. 555–6.

19 Butterfield, *Adams Family Correspondence*, I, p. 305; Charles Chauncy, *Early Piety Recommended and exemplify'd. A Sermon Occasioned by the Death of Elisabeth Price* . . . (Boston, 1732), p. 16; Autobiography and Diary of Eliza Clitherall, VI, p. 51; VII, p. 29; Pickering, Letters to Rebecca, June 14, 1777.

20 Henry Drinker to Eliza Drinker, Winchester, 1 mo. 25, 1778, Drinker Letters, Haverford College; George Churchman, Journal, vol. II, 1770, Haverford College; David Cooper, Letter to Martha, 1772, in Diary, Ms., Haverford College, and Diary, 1767.

21 *Rules of Discipline of the Religious Society of Friends, with Advices: Being Extracts from the Minutes and Epistles of Their Yearly Meeting, Held in London, from its First Institution* (London, 1834), p. 202.

22 Enos Hitchcock, *Memoirs of the Bloomsgrove Family. In a Series of Letters to a Respectable Citizen of Philadelphia* . . . (Boston, 1790), pp. 55–6. I am indebted to Peter Slater's "Views of Children and of Child Rearing During the Early National Period: A Study in the New England Intellect" (Ph.D. thesis, University of California at Berkeley, 1970), for bringing this source to my attention.

23 Theodore Parker, "Phases of Domestic Life," in Rufus Leighton, ed., *Lessons from the World of Matter and the World of Man* (Boston, n.d.), pp. 194–5.

24 Greven, *Child-Rearing Concepts*, pp. 169–70, 179. For Bushnell, see Barbara M. Cross, *Horace Bushnell: Minister to a Changing America* (Chicago, 1958); Jeffrey, "Family History," pp. 203–9; Hutchison, "Cultural Strain."

25 Charles Chauncy, *The Benevolence of the Deity, Fairly and Impartially Considered* (Boston, 1784), p. 276. For his views of the stages of growth from infancy to adulthood, see p. 115.

26 Joseph Fish to Mrs. Sarah Osborn, Stonington, July 3, 1754, YCS.

27 Joseph and Rebecca Fish to Mr. John Noyes of New Haven, Stonington, Sept. 29, 1767, YCS.

28 Butterfield, *Adams Family Correspondence*, I, pp. 85–7.

29 Enos Hitchcock, *A Discourse on Education* . . . (Providence, R.I., 1785), p. 14.

30 Frost, *Quaker Family*, p. 74.

31 *Epistles from the Yearly Meeting of Friends, Held in London* . . . (London, 1818), pp. 205–6, 368, 375.

32 Greven, *Child-Rearing Concepts*, pp. 178, 173, 143, 158, 167, 149. This assumption also can be traced at least as far back as the late seventeenth century to the writings of John Locke. See James Axtell, ed., *The Educational Writings of John Locke* (Cambridge, Eng., 1966), and Greven, *Child-Rearing Concepts*, pp. 18–41. See also John Dunn, *The Political Thought of John Locke: An Historical Account of the Argument of the "Two Treatises of Government"* (Cambridge, Eng., 1969).

33 For studies of youth, see Greven, *Four Generations*, and "Youth, Maturity, and Religious Conversion: A Note on the Ages of Converts in Andover, Massachusetts, 1711–1749," *EIHC*, CVIII (1972), pp. 119–34; N. Ray Hiner, "Adolescence in Eighteenth-Century America," *History of Childhood Quarterly*, 3 (1975), pp. 253–80; Ross Worn Beales, Jr., "Cares for the Rising Generation: Youth and Religion in Colonial New England" (Ph.D. thesis, University of California at Davis, 1971); John Demos and Virginia Demos, "Adolescence in Historical Perspective," *Journal of Marriage and the Family*, XXXI (1969), pp. 632–8; Joseph Kett, "Adolescence and Youth in Nineteenth Century America," *JIH*, 2 (1971), pp. 283–98; John R. Gillis, *Youth and History: Tradition and Change in European Age Relations 1770–Present* (New York, 1974).

34 Chauncy, *Early Piety*, pp. i, 3, 9–10.

35 Butterfield, *Adams Family Correspondence*, I, pp. 86–7.

36 Mercy Warren to James Warren, Jr., Plymouth, 1772, 1773, and June 1776, in Mercy [Otis] Warren, Letterbook, 1770–1800, pp. 213–18, MHS.

[37] Butterfield, *Adams Family Correspondence*, I, pp. 313, 114; III, p. 37.

[38] Charles Francis Adams, ed., *The Letters of Mrs. Adams, the Wife of John Adams*, 2 vols. (Boston, 1840), I, pp. 189–90; II, pp. 127–8.

[39] Willard, *Compleat Body of Divinity*, p. 598.

[40] Morgan, *The Puritan Family*, pp. 25, 28. Morgan's portrayal of the "Puritans" locates them consistently within the moderate rather than the evangelical mode.

[41] Willard, *Compleat Body of Divinity*, p. 600. For an analysis of Willard's thought, see Ernest Benson Lowrie, *The Shape of the Puritan Mind: The Thought of Samuel Willard* (New Haven, Conn., 1974).

[42] *Winthrop Papers*, I, p. 271, 282–3, 389, 390–1; II, pp. 98, 170–1, 79.

[43] "Correspondence of Fitz-John Winthrop," MHS *Collections* Fifth Series, VIII (1892), pp. 267–8, 269–70, 270–1. See Richard Dunn's fascinating portraits of Fitz-John and Wait Winthrop in *Puritans and Yankees*.

[44] Isaac Norris, Jr., to Isaac Norris, Philadelphia, January 1721; St. John, May 28, 1722; London, 30th 5th month, 1722, in Norris of Fairhill Family Correspondence, I, HSP.

[45] Isaac Norris, Jr., to Isaac Norris, Bristoll, Aug. 9, 1734, Norris of Fairhill Family Correspondence, I.

[46] Isaac Norris to Susy Wright, Fairhill, July 22, 1746, Family Correpsondence, II; Debby Norris to Isaac Norris, Jr., Aug. 4, 1734, Family Correspondence, I.

[47] Samuel Emlen to Sarah, London, 18th of 7th month, 1772, Letters of Samuel Emlen, HSP; Henry Drinker to Elizabeth Drinker, 9 month, 16, 1777; Winchester, 12 month, 27, 1777, Drinker Letters, Haverford College.

[48] William Clarke to Anne Clarke of Salem, Barbados, Jan. 16, 1764; William Clarke [?] to Hannah, Dominique, 1768; John Clarke to Mrs. Anne Clarke of Salem, Barbados, June 4, 1769; Ann Jones Clarke to Mrs. Anne Clarke of Salem, Barbados, July 1, 1769; John Clarke to Mrs. Anne Clarke, Barbados, Aug. 30, 1771. Clarke Family of Salem Letters, Essex Institute.

[49] Butterfield, *Adams Family Correspondence*, I, p. 160, 167, 189.

[50] Butterfield, *Adams Family Correspondence*, III, pp. 310–13. See also David F. Musto's perceptive analysis of "The Youth of John Quincy Adams," American Philosophical Society *Proceedings*, 113 (1969), pp. 269–82.

[51] H. Trevor Colbourn, "A Pennsylvania Farmer at the Court of King George: John Dickinson's London Letters, 1754–1756," *PMHB*, 86 (1962), pp. 248, 252, 253, 260, 262, 263, 269, 274, 275, 420, 434, 447, 448.

[52] John Dickinson to Mother, Philadelphia, March 7, 1763, Maria Dickinson Logan Family Papers, Box 1, HSP.

[53] Peter Oliver to Polly Watson, Middleborough, Jan. 1, 1767, Hutchinson-Watson Papers, MHS.

[54] See Jack P. Greene, ed., *The Diary of Colonel Landon Carter of Sabine Hall, 1752–1778*, 2 vols. (Charlottesville, Va., 1965), I, pp. 3–61, for an analysis of Carter's character and life. As Greene observes, "The ideal of moderation had traditionally been regarded as one of man's most useful devices for curbing his passions, and Carter made it his constant concern to live up to that ideal," being "thoroughly persuaded . . . that 'Extremes in any thing are bad'" (p. 16).

[55] Greene, *Diary of Landon Carter*, II, pp. 856, 900, 1002. See also Greven, *Four Generations*, for a discussion of the themes of control and independence.

V
Sober, Virtuous, and Pious People: Themes
of Moderate Temperaments and Piety

1 See Arthur O. Lovejoy, *The Great Chain of Being: A Study of the History of an Idea* (New York, 1960), and Michael Walzer, *The Revolution of the Saints: A Study in the Origins of Radical Politics* (Cambridge, Mass., 1965).

2 Perry Miller and Thomas H. Johnson, eds., *The Puritans* (New York, 1938), pp. 195–8.

3 Miller and Johnson, *The Puritans*, pp. 247–9.

4 Herbert Schneider and Carol Schneider, eds., *Samuel Johnson: His Career and Writings*, 4 vols. (New York, 1929), II, pp. 531, 545, 550–1.

5 Joseph Fish, *Angels Ministering to the People of God* . . . (Newport, R.I., 1755), pp. 4–5; Joseph Fish, *Christ Jesus the Physician* . . . (New London, Conn., 1760), p. 33; Charles Chauncy, *Benevolence of the Deity, Fairly and Impartially Considered* (Boston, 1784), pp. 58, 221–2.

6 L. H. Butterfield, *et al.*, eds., *Diary and Autobiography of John Adams*, 4 vols. (Cambridge, Mass., 1962), I, pp. 18, 30, 39.

7 Daniel Walker Howe, *The Unitarian Conscience: Harvard Moral Philosophy, 1805–1861* (Cambridge, Mass., 1970), p. 126; see also pp. 71, 125–31, 138–9.

8 Horace Bushnell, *Christian Nurture*, Luther A. Weigle, ed. (New Haven, Conn., 1967), pp. 74–5, 78.

9 Edmund S. Morgan, ed., *Puritan Political Ideas 1558–1794* (Indianapolis, 1965), p. 256; Ernest Benson Lowrie, *The Shape of the Puritan Mind: The Thought of Samuel Willard* (New Haven, Conn., 1974), p. 75 (italics omitted).

10 Milton M. Klein, ed., *The Independent Reflector or Weekly Essays on Sundry Important Subjects More Particularly Adapted to the Province of New York, by William Livingston and Others* (Cambridge, Mass., 1963), pp. 412–13. For similar notions in the seventeenth century, see Perry Miller, *The New England Mind: The Seventeenth Century* (Cambridge, Mass., 1954), pp. 184–7.

11 Lowrie, *Shape of the Puritan Mind*, pp. 77, 79.

12 Charles Chauncy, *The Benevolence of the Deity*, pp. 86, 49; Charles Chauncy, *Enthusiasm described and Caution'd against. A Sermon* . . . (Boston, 1742), p. 18. For Chauncy, see Edward M. Griffin, "A Biography of Charles Chauncy, 1705–1787" (Ph.D. thesis, Stanford University, 1967); James W. Jones, *The Shattered Synthesis: New England Puritanism before the Great Awakening* (New Haven, Conn., 1973), pp. 165–97.

13 Schneider, *Samuel Johnson*, III, p. 211; II, pp. 526, 582.

14 Butterfield, *Diary and Autobiography*, I, p. 184; II, p. 53; L. H. Butterfield, *et al.*, eds., *Adams Family Correspondence* (Cambridge, Mass., 1963–), I, pp. 25, 49, 317, 321, 329; II, p. 79.

15 James Logan, "The Duties of Man as they may be deduced from Nature." [*ca.* 1736], Ms., Logan Papers—Alverthorpe, HSP, pp. 22, 25. See Frederick Tolles, *James Logan and the Culture of Provincial America* (Boston, 1957).

16 Jones, *Shattered Synthesis*, p. 46; Lowrie, *Shape of the Puritan Mind*, pp. 106–7, 108.

17 Chauncy, *The Benevolence of the Deity*, pp. 223, 118, 23, 19, 48–9.
18 John G. Buchanan, "The Pursuit of Happiness: A Study of the Rev. Dr. Samuel Cooper, 1725–1783" (Ph.D. thesis, Duke University, 1971), pp. 133, 163, 165. See also Bernard Bailyn's superb analysis of the Reverend Andrew Eliot of Boston, in "Religion and Revolution: Three Biographical Studies," *Perspectives in American History*, IV (1970), pp. 87–110.
19 Schneider, *Samuel Johnson*, II, pp. 542–3.
20 David Cooper, Diary, 1772, Haverford College; Elizabeth Willing to Miss Lessly, Philadelphia, Aug. 3, 1768, Powel Collection, Elizabeth Powel, Duplicates of Letters, 1768–1820, HSP.
21 Logan, "Duties of Man," pp. 6, 8.
22 Henry Steele Commager, ed., *The Autobiography of Benjamin Franklin and Selections from His Other Writings* (New York, 1950), pp. 7, 66; Lester J. Cappon, ed., *The Adams-Jefferson Letters: The Complete Correspondence between Thomas Jefferson and Abigail and John Adams*, 2 vols. (Chapel Hill, N.C., 1959), II, p. 509.
23 Miller, *Seventeenth Century*, p. 261; M. M. Knappen, ed., *Two Elizabethan Puritan Diaries by Richard Rogers and Samuel Ward* (Gloucester, Mass., 1966), p. 89.
24 Allyn B. Forbes, ed., *Winthrop Papers, 1498–1649*, MHS Collections, 5 vols. (Boston, 1929–1947), I, pp. 154, 160, 193, 197, 200, 206, 208; Miller, *Seventeenth Century*, p. 42. See also Edmund S. Morgan, *The Puritan Dilemma: The Story of John Winthrop* (Boston, 1958).
25 Chauncy, *Benevolence of the Deity*, pp. 223–8, 91, 93, 226, 123; Charles Chauncy, *Seasonable Thoughts on the State of Religion in New-England* (Boston, 1743), pp. 324, 326–7, 328.
26 Logan, "Duties of Man," pp. 22, 30, 31.
27 Butterfield, *Adams Family Correspondence*, III, pp. 311–12; IV, p. 103.
28 L. H. Butterfield, *et al.*, eds., *The Earliest Diary of John Adams* (Cambridge, Mass., 1966), p. 64; Butterfield, *Diary and Autobiography*, I, pp. 31, 33–4.
29 Butterfield, *Diary and Autobiography*, II, pp. 56–7, 59; I, pp. 217, 190.
30 Andrienne Koch and William Peden, eds., *The Selected Writings of John and John Quincy Adams* (New York, 1946), pp. 130–1.
31 Zoltan Haraszti, *John Adams and the Prophets of Progress* (Cambridge, Mass., 1952), pp. 198, 229, 187, 151. For Adams, see John R. Howe, Jr., *The Changing Political Thought of John Adams* (Princeton, N.J., 1966); Gordon S. Wood, *The Creation of the American Republic 1776–1787* (Chapel Hill, N.C., 1969), ch. XIV; Peter Shaw, *The Character of John Adams* (Chapel Hill, N.C., 1976).
32 Schneider, *Samuel Johnson*, II, pp. 538, 539, 540; I, p. 28.
33 Howe, *Unitarian Conscience*, pp. 59, 61, 60, 119, 153, 157.
34 J. William Frost, *The Quaker Family in Colonial America: A Portrait of the Society of Friends* (New York, 1973), p. 188; Cooper, Letter to Martha in Diary, 1772; *Epistles from the Yearly Meeting of Friends, Held in London . . .* (London, 1818), pp. 206–7.
35 Haraszti, *Prophets of Progress*, p. 126; Butterfield, *Adams Family Correspondence*, IV, p. 384.
36 Butterfield, *Diary and Autobiography*, II, pp. 29–30; Butterfield, *Adams Family Correspondence*, I, p. 399; II, p. 398.

37 George W. Corner, ed., *The Autobiography of Benjamin Rush: His "Travels Through Life" Together with His Commonplace Book for 1789–1813* (Westport, Conn., 1970), pp. 83–4, 90–1, 107; Commager, *Autobiography of Benjamin Franklin*, pp. 58, 89, 90; Fawn M. Brodie, *Thomas Jefferson: An Intimate History* (New York, 1974), p. 63; Edwin Morris Betts and James Adam Bear, Jr., eds., *The Family Letters of Thomas Jefferson* (Columbia, Mo., 1966), p. 34.

38 Chauncy, *Benevolence of the Deity*, pp. 135–6; Schneider, *Samuel Johnson*, III, pp. 189–90, 209; Howe, *Unitarian Conscience*, p. 68. For discussions of the will in the seventeenth century, see Perry Miller, "The Marrow of Puritan Divinity," *Errand into the Wilderness* (Cambridge, Mass., 1956), and *Seventeenth Century*, especially pp. 249–51. Norman S. Fiering, "Will and Intellect in the New England Mind," *WMQ*, XXIX (1972), pp. 515–58, perceives two fundamentally opposed traditions concerning the will—the "intellectualist" and the "voluntarist"—and suggests that the "deep-running debate concerning psychological models" which "existed in seventeenth-century New England" can "be assessed as a debate based ultimately on temperamental preferences" (p. 549).

39 Lowrie, *Shape of the Puritan Mind*, pp. 25, 161–2, 124, 150. See also David D. Hall, *The Faithful Shepherd: A History of the New England Ministry in the Seventeenth Century* (Chapel Hill, N.C., 1972), pp. 56–8, for a discussion of free will.

40 Klein, *Independent Reflector*, pp. 330–1.

41 Conrad Wright, *The Beginnings of Unitarianism in America* (Boston, 1966), p. 94 (italics omitted). See also the chapter "The Freedom of the Will: 1754–1773," pp. 91–114, for a discussion of the issue during the mid-eighteenth century.

42 Chauncy, *Benevolence of the Deity*, p. 211.

43 Charles Chauncy, *The Mystery Hid from Ages and Generations* (New York, 1969), pp. 1–2.

44 Schneider, *Samuel Johnson*, II, pp. 538–9, 532; III, p. 168; II, pp. 594–5; I, p. 70.

45 Timothy Pickering, Letters to Rebecca, Providence, Dec. 28, 1776, Philadelphia, Aug. 1, 1777, York Town, May 19, 1778, Newburgh, Jan. 12, 1783, typed copies, Essex Institute.

46 Timothy Pickering, Letters to Son John, Wyoming, Aug. 4, 1788, Philadelphia, Jan. 17, 1794, Germantown, May 12, 1796, typed copies, Essex Institute; Pickering, Letters to Rebecca, Philadelphia, Aug. 3, 1778.

47 Butterfield, *Diary and Autobiography*, I, pp. 23, 25, 41–2, 365.

48 Butterfield, *Adams Family Correspondence*, III, pp. 310–11, 311–12.

49 Charles Francis Adams, ed., *The Letters of Mrs. Adams, the Wife of John Adams*, 2 vols. (Boston, 1840), II, pp. 189–90; I, p. 199; Butterfield, *Adams Family Correspondence*, II, p. 179.

50 Elise Pinckney and Marvin R. Zahniser, eds., *The Letterbook of Eliza Lucas Pinckney 1739–1762* (Chapel Hill, N.C., 1972), pp. 17, 51–2, 116, 156–7, 100, 159, 167, 101.

51 Miller, *Seventeenth Century*, p. 186; Miller, *Errand into the Wilderness*, pp. 75, 79; Jones, *Shattered Synthesis*, p. 141.

52 Howe, *Unitarian Conscience*, pp. 116, 118, 116.

[53] Alan Heimert and Perry Miller, eds., *The Great Awakening: Documents Illustrating the Crisis and Its Consequences* (Indianapolis, 1967), pp. 50, 55, 56.

[54] Joseph Fish, Sermon "On the Death of my Dear Daughter, Rebecca Douglas," Dec. 14 and 21, 1766, Ms., Silliman Family Papers, YCS; Charles Chauncy, *Early Piety Recommended and exemplify'd. A Sermon Occasioned by the Death of Elisabeth Price, An eminently pious Young Woman* . . . (Boston, 1732), p. 17; Horace Bushnell, "Christian Nurture," in Philip J. Greven, Jr., ed., *Child-Rearing Concepts, 1628–1861: Historical Sources* (Itasca, Ill., 1973), p. 139.

[55] Miller, *Seventeenth Century*, pp. 288–9.

[56] Lowrie, *Shape of the Puritan Mind*, pp. 190–2; Miller, *Errand into the Wilderness*, p. 84.

[57] Norman Pettit, *The Heart Prepared: Grace and Conversion in Puritan Spiritual Life* (New Haven, Conn., 1966), pp. 49, 69–70.

[58] William Livingston to Noah Welles, New York, Jan. 13, 1745/6, Johnson Family Papers, YCS; Charles W. Akers, *Called unto Liberty: A Life of Jonathan Mayhew, 1720–1766* (Cambridge, Mass., 1964), p. 123.

[59] Pettit, *Heart Prepared*, p. 73; *Winthrop Papers*, I, p. 224.

[60] Lowrie, *Shape of the Puritan Mind*, p. 135.

[61] Miller, *Errand into the Wilderness*, pp. 64, 63.

[62] Miller, *Seventeenth Century*, p. 389; Miller, *Errand into the Wilderness*, p. 62.

[63] Charles Chauncy, *Cornelius's Character. A Sermon Preach'd the Lord's Day after the Funeral of Mr. Cornelius Thayer* . . . (Boston, 1745), p. 10; Chauncy, *Benevolence of the Deity*, p. 180.

[64] Jonathan Mayhew, *Seven Sermons* (New York, 1969), pp. 97, 106, 109–10, 113, 137, 138, 156.

[65] Schneider, *Samuel Johnson*, III, pp. 167, 176–7, 204–5.

[66] Klein, *Independent Reflector*, p. 76.

[67] Klein, *Independent Reflector*, pp. 76, 81; Forrest McDonald, ed., *Empire and Nation*: Letters from a Farmer in Pennsylvania, *John Dickinson*; Letters from the Federal Farmer, *Richard Henry Lee* (Englewood Cliffs, N.J., 1962), p. 43.

[68] David L. Jacobson, ed., *The English Libertarian Heritage from the Writings of John Trenchard and Thomas Gordon in* The Independent Whig *and* Cato's Letters (Indianapolis, 1965), pp. 71, 257, 256, 70, 85–6. For analyses of these themes in the political ideology of eighteenth-century radical whiggery, see Bernard Bailyn, *The Ideological Origins of the American Revolution* (Cambridge, Mass., 1967), and Wood, *Creation of the American Republic*.

[69] Butterfield, *Adams Family Correspondence*, I, pp. 370, 382, 397.

[70] Leonard Labaree, *et al.*, eds., *The Papers of Benjamin Franklin* (New Haven, Conn., 1959–　　　), III, p. 30.

[71] Butterfield, *Diary and Autobiography*, I, p. 9; Chauncy, *Seasonable Thoughts on the State of Religion*, pp. 324–7.

[72] Pinckney, *Letterbook of Eliza Lucas Pinckney*, p. 159.

[73] Mercy Warren to James Warren, Jr., Plymouth, 1772, 1773, and June 1776, Mercy [Otis] Warren Letterbook, 1770–1800, pp. 213–14, 217, 218, MHS.

74 Butterfield, *Adams Family Correspondence*, IV, p. 264; II, pp. 390–1.
75 Butterfield, *Diary and Autobiography*, I, pp. 72–3. For a different perspective on the significance of this theme, see James McLachlan's superb essay: "The *Choice of Hercules*: American Student Societies in the Early 19th Century," in Lawrence Stone, ed., *The University in Society*, 2 vols. (Princeton, N.J., 1974), pp. 449–94.
76 Butterfield, *Adams Family Correspondence*, II, pp. 96–7; III, p. 333. For a perceptive analysis of Adams, see Shaw, *Character of John Adams*, which I read after completing my own manuscript.
77 Saul K. Padover, ed., *The Complete Jefferson: Containing His Major Writings, Published and Unpublished, except His Letters* (New York, 1943), pp. 827–30. See also Brodie, *Thomas Jefferson*, pp. 73–4, 185–6, 196–7, 199–245, for a discussion of these issues.
78 See Carl Binger, *Thomas Jefferson: A Well-Tempered Mind* (New York, 1970), for a discussion of the masculine and feminine components of his temperament.
79 Butterfield, *Diary and Autobiography*, III, pp. 260–1; Commager, *Autobiography of Benjamin Franklin*, p. 78; see also Claude-Anne Lopez and Eugenia W. Herbert, *The Private Franklin: The Man and His Family* (New York, 1975), pp. 26–7.
80 Adams, *Letters of Mrs. Adams*, II, p. 111; Butterfield, *Diary and Autobiography*, I, p. 192.
81 Pinckney, *Letterbook of Eliza Lucas Pinckney*, p. 48; David L. Jacobson, *John Dickinson and the Revolution in Pennsylvania 1764–1776* (Berkeley and Los Angeles, Calif., 1965), p. 5.
82 Butterfield, *Adams Family Correspondence*, I, pp. 97–8.
83 Butterfield, *Diary and Autobiography*, I, pp. 72, 73, 78, 80, 77, 217; Butterfield, *Earliest Diary*, p. 77; Butterfield, *Diary and Autobiography*, p. 217.
84 Thomas Hutchinson, *The History of the Colony of the Province of Massachusetts-Bay*, Lawrence Shaw Mayo, ed., 3 vols. (Cambridge, Mass., 1936), III, p. 214. See also Douglass Adair and John A. Schutz, eds., *Peter Oliver's Origin and Progress of the American Rebellion: A Tory View* (Stanford, Calif., 1961), p. 83, for a similar view of Adams, and Shaw, *Character of John Adams, passim.*
85 Butterfield, *Diary and Autobiography*, II, pp. 75, 61–2, 63.
86 Butterfield, *Diary and Autobiography*, II, pp. 63, 82; Butterfield, *Adams Family Correspondence*, I, p. 114.
87 Labaree, *Franklin Papers*, I, p. 108; see also Commager, *Autobiography of Benjamin Franklin*, p. 90.
88 The Rev. John Lowell to Mr. Timothy Toppan and Mr. Enoch Titcomb, Members of the 3rd Church of Christ in Newbury, Newbury, Jan. 3, 1743/4, Newbury Separate Papers, 1743–1746, Congregational Library, Boston.
89 "Autobiography of the Rev. John Barnard," MHS *Collections*, Third Series, V (1836), p. 232; Franklin Bowditch Dexter, ed., *The Literary Diary of Ezra Stiles, D.D., LL.D. President of Yale College*, 3 vols. (New York, 1901), III, pp. 67–8.
90 Jack P. Greene, ed., *The Diary of Colonel Landon Carter of Sabine Hall, 1752–1778*, 2 vols. (Charlottesville, Va., 1965), I, pp. 314–15. See also

Bailyn's portrait of Jonathan Mayhew in "Religion and Revolution," pp. 111–24; Akers, *Called unto Liberty.*

91 Heimert and Miller, *Great Awakening,* p. 298.

92 See, for instance, Morgan, *Puritan Family;* Hall, *Faithful Shepherd,* pp. 225 ff.; Richard T. Vann, *The Social Development of English Quakerism, 1655–1755* (Cambridge, Mass., 1969); Jones, *Shattered Synthesis;* Frost, *The Quaker Family.*

93 Geoffrey F. Nuttall, *Visible Saints: The Congregational Way, 1640–1660* (Oxford, 1957), p. 108.

94 Richard L. Bushman, ed., *The Great Awakening: Documents on the Revival of Religion, 1740–1745* (New York, 1970), p. 107.

95 See, for instance, Edmund S. Morgan, *The Visible Saints: The History of a Puritan Idea* (New York, 1963); Robert G. Pope, *The Half-Way Covenant: Church Membership in Puritan New England* (Princeton, N.J., 1969); Gerald Francis Moran, "The Puritan Saint: Religious Experience, Church Membership, and Piety in Connecticut, 1636–1776" (Ph.D. thesis, Rutgers University, 1973). See also the documents relating to the religious controversies of the 1730's and 1740's in Bushman, *Great Awakening,* and Heimert and Miller, *Great Awakening.*

96 Jacobson, *English Libertarian Heritage,* pp. 99, 30, 163. For interpretations of the radical Whig tradition, see Caroline Robbins, *The Eighteenth-Century Commonwealthman: Studies in the Transmission, Development and Circumstance of English Liberal Thought from the Restoration of Charles II Until the War with the Thirteen Colonies* (Cambridge, Mass., 1959); Bernard Bailyn, *Ideological Origins,* and *The Ordeal of Thomas Hutchinson* (Cambridge, Mass., 1974); Wood, *Creation of the American Republic;* and Mary Beth Norton, "The Loyalist Critique of the Revolution," *The Development of a Revolutionary Mentality* (Washington, D.C., 1972).

97 Jacobson, *English Libertarian Heritage,* pp. 168, 89–90.

98 Jacobson, *English Libertarian Heritage,* pp. 90, 91.

99 Klein, *Independent Reflector,* pp. 191, 195. See also Ezra Stiles's observations in Heimert and Miller, *Great Awakening,* p. 604.

VI
Affectionate Families: Genteel Modes of Child-Rearing

1 For some suggestive studies of the genteel, see E. P. Thompson, "Patrician Society, Plebian Culture," *JSH,* vol. 7 (1974), pp. 382–405; Richard S. Dunn, *Puritans and Yankees: The Winthrop Dynasty of New England 1630–1717* (Princeton, N.J., 1962), especially the studies of Fitz and Wait Winthrop; Carol Berkin, *Jonathan Sewall: Odyssey of an American Loyalist* (New York, 1974); Frederick B. Tolles, *Meeting House and Counting House: The Quaker Merchants of Colonial Philadelphia, 1682–1763* (New York, 1963); Randolph Shipley Klein, *Portrait of an Early American Family: The Shippens of Pennsylvania Across Five Generations* (Philadelphia, 1975); Louis B. Wright, *The First Gentlemen of Virginia: Intellectual Qualities of the Early Colonial*

Ruling Class (Charlottesville, Va., 1964); Pierre Marambaud, *William Byrd of Westover, 1674–1744* (Charlottesville, Va., 1971); Carl Bridenbaugh, *Myths and Realities: Societies of the Colonial South* (New York, 1963); Edmund S. Morgan, *Virginians at Home: Family Life in the Eighteenth Century* (Charlottesville, Va., 1963); and Rhys Isaac, "Evangelical Revolt: The Nature of the Baptists' Challenge to the Traditional Order of Virginia, 1765 to 1775," *WMQ*, XXXI (1974), pp. 345–68, one of the most imaginative and illuminating essays to be found concerning the Virginia gentry in the mid-eighteenth century.

In addition, evidence can be gathered from the biographies of men who graduated from Harvard College, in Clifford K. Shipton's continuation of *Sibley's Harvard Graduates*, a one-volume selection of which appeared as *New England Life in the Eighteenth Century: Representative Biographies from Sibley's Harvard Graduates* (Cambridge, Mass., 1963). A similar series of biographies has been prepared for Princeton graduates by James L. McLachlan, who very kindly permitted me to read some of the biographies for evangelicals in manuscript. Since Princeton drew upon students from the Middle colonies and the South as well as New England, their biographies ought to provide invaluable material for historians (James L. McLachlan, ed., *Princetonians, 1748–1768: A Biographical Dictionary* [Princeton, N.J., 1976]).

2 Bernard Bailyn, *The Ordeal of Thomas Hutchinson* (Cambridge, Mass., 1974), p. 30; Mary Hutchinson to Mrs. Oliver, Milton, July 24, 1772, Hutchinson-Watson Papers, MHS. I am much indebted to Bernard Bailyn for his generosity in making available to me the microfilms of the manuscripts for the Hutchinson family in the Egerton Mss., vol. 2659–74, in the British Museum, as well as the microfilm of Peter Oliver's Ms. diary (1741–1821), Egerton Mss. 2674, British Museum, a copy of which also is available at the MHS.

3 "Diary of James Allen, Esq., of Philadelphia, Counsellor-at-Law, 1770–1778," *PMHB*, IX (1885), pp. 284, 433–4, 440.

4 Postscript by Marianne Belcher in Andrew Belcher to Sister, Halifax, April 30, 1799, Belcher-Jennison-Weiss Papers, MHS.

5 See Harry S. Stout, "The Great Awakening in New England Reconsidered: The New England Clergy," *JSH*, 8 (1974), pp. 37–8, and Robert V. Wells, "Family Size and Fertility Control in Eighteenth-Century America: A Study of Quaker Families," *Population Studies*, XXV (1971), pp. 73–82.

6 Ann Head Warder, Diary, HSP (5th mo. 17th d. 1786, vol. I; 8 mo. 20 d. 1786; 8 mo 27 d. 1786, vol. IV).

7 Hunter Dickinson Farish, ed., *Journal and Letters of Philip Vickers Fithian 1773–1774: A Plantation Tutor of the Old Dominion* (Williamsburg, Va., 1957), p. 26. The theme of "indulgence" is recurrent, of course, and persists unabated to the present. For the early nineteenth century, see Anne L. Kuhn, *The Mother's Role in Childhood Education: New England Concepts 1830–1860* (New Haven, Conn., 1947); Bernard Wishy, *The Child and the Republic: The Dawn of Modern Child Nurture* (Philadelphia, 1968); Robert Elno McGlone, "Suffer the Children: The Emergence of Modern Middle-Class Family Life in America, 1820–1870" (Ph.D. thesis, University of California, Los Angeles, 1971).

8 *Virginia Gazette*, March 12, 1767, quoting the *Annual Register*.

9 Mather Byles to the Reverend Mather Byles, Sr., New London, Jan. 10, 1763, Byles Family Papers 1753–1865, typed copy, p. 49, MHS; Penuel Bowen to daughter Fanny, Charleston, July 1786, Letterbook of the Reverend Penuel Bowen, SCHS; Rev. Penuel Bowen to Mrs. [Susanna] Bowen, Savannah, Jan. 4, 1787, Bowen-Cooke Papers, typed copies, SCHS; Mrs. Sarah Gibbes to son, John, Charleston, Jan. 3, 1784, Gibbes-Gilchrist Papers 1769–1945, SCHS.

10 Andrew Belcher to Sister [Elizabeth Jennison] at Cambridge, Halifax, Aug. 22, 1794, and April 30, 1799, Belcher-Jennison-Weiss Papers, 1730–1905, MHS; Edward Chandler to Samuel Thorne, Lindsey Row, Chelsea, July 7, 1785, Sept. 28, 1785, April 28, 1786, Dec. 5, 1787, Edward and Anne Chandler Letters, 1783–1787, NYPL.

11 Anne [Willing] Francis to Husband [Tench Francis], Philadelphia, June 13, 1767; Anne Francis to Husband, Philadelphia, June 12, 1767; Tench Francis to Anne Willing [Francis], London, July 11, 1767, Oct. 3, 1767, Nov. 13, 1767; Anne Francis to Husband, Philadelphia, Feb. 8, 1768, Joshua Francis Fisher Papers, Francis Family, HSP.

12 Deborah Logan to Brother, Isaac Norris, Stenton, Aug. [?] 1784, Aug. 28, 1785, Maria Dickinson Logan Family Papers, Box II, HSP; Mary Norris to Isaac Norris, Philadelphia, March 12, 1785, Mary Norris to [?], Philadelphia, April 8, [1785?], Norris of Fairhill Family Mss., Family Letters, vol. I, HSP. See also Ethel Armes, ed., *Nancy Shippen, Her Journal Book: The International Romance of a Young Lady of Fashion of Colonial Philadelphia with Letters to Her and About Her* (New York, 1968).

13 For a fascinating and delightful analysis of surrogate parents in genteel British families, see Jonathan Gathorne-Hardy, *The Unnatural History of the Nanny* (New York, 1973).

14 Mary Norris to Isaac Norris, Philadelphia, June 3, 1785, Norris of Fairhill Family Mss., Family Letters, vol. I, HSP; Letterbook of the Rev. Penuel Bowen; Peter Orlando Hutchinson, ed., *The Diary and Letters of His Excellency, Thomas Hutchinson*, Esq., 2 vols. (London, 1883–1886), I, pp. 109, 201.

15 Farish, *Journal and Letters of Philip Vickers Fithian*, p. 39.

16 Jack P. Greene, ed., *The Diary of Colonel Landon Carter of Sabine Hall, 1752–1778*, 2 vols. (Charlottesville, Va., 1965), II, pp. 907, 997.

17 See, for instance, Eugene D. Genovese, *Roll, Jordan, Roll: The World the Slaves Made* (New York, 1974), pp. 87–91.

18 Thomas Jefferson, *Notes on the State of Virginia*, William Peden, ed. (Chapel Hill, N.C., 1955), p. 162.

19 H. Trevor Colbourn, "A Pennsylvania Farmer at the Court of King George: John Dickinson's London Letters, 1754–1756," *PMHB*, LXXXVI (1962), pp. 277–8.

20 Greene, *Diary of Landon Carter*, I, p. 310; II, pp. 646, 647, 702. For some modern studies of the consequences of physical punishments in discipline, see Wesley C. Becker, "Consequences of Different Kinds of Parental Discipline," in M. L. Hoffman and L. W. Hoffman, eds., *Review of Child Development Research* (New York, 1964), pp. 169–208; Goodwin Watson, "Some Personality Differences in Children Related to Strict or Permissive

Parental Discipline," *Journal of Psychology*, 44 (1957), pp. 227–49; Martin L. Hoffman, "Childrearing Practices and Moral Development: Generalizations from Empirical Research," *Child Development*, 34 (1963), pp. 295–318; David Mark Mantell, "Doves vs. Hawks: Guess Who Had the Authoritarian Parents?", *Psychology Today*, 8 (1974), pp. 56–62.

21 Farish, *Journal and Letters of Philip Vickers Fithian*, pp. 49–50, 116. For Carter, who was a moderate by temperament and became a Baptist during the 1770's, see Louis Morton, *Robert Carter of Nomini Hall: A Virginia Tobacco Planter of the Eighteenth Century* (Charlottesville, Va., 1964). His spiritual development and some glimpses of his family life may be seen in Carter's Day Books and Letter Books (1772–1793), Duke University.

22 Farish, *Journal and Letters of Philip Vickers Fithian*, pp. 29–30.

23 For portraits, see John Wilmerding, ed., *The Genius of American Painting* (New York, 1973), p. 33; Alice Ford, *Pictorial Folk Art New England to California* (New York, 1949), p. 51; Jules David Prown, *John Singleton Copley in America 1738–1774*, 2 vols. (Cambridge, Mass., 1966), I, p. 50 (Prown's study is invaluable as a source for the genteel subjects of Copley's paintings, as well as the moderates who had their own portraits painted but never their children's portraits—which itself suggests something about the different attitudes of parents toward their children); Agnes Halsey Jones and Louis C. Jones, *New-Found Folk Art of the Young Republic* (Cooperstown, N.Y., 1960), fig. 57; *The Catalogue of Old and New England an Exhibition of American Painting of Colonial and Early Republican Days together with English Painting of the same time*, Museum of Art of the Rhode Island School of Design (Providence, R.I., 1945), fig. 31; *American Primitive Paintings from the Collection of Edgar William and Bernice Chrysler Garbisch* (Washington, D.C., 1954), p. 73; *American Naive Paintings of the Eighteenth and Nineteenth Centuries: 111 Masterpieces from the Collection of Edgar William and Bernice Chrysler Garbisch* (New York, 1969), fig. 56.

24 For portraits, see Alan Burroughs, *Limners and Likenesses: Three Centuries of American Painting* (Cambridge, Mass., 1936), fig. 5; Albert Ten Eyck Gardner and Stuart P. Feld, *American Painting: A Catalogue of the Collection of the Metropolitan Museum of Art: I, Painters Born by 1815* (Greenwich, Conn., 1965), p. 16; *American Naive Paintings*, fig. 2; Prown, *John Singleton Copley*, I, figs. 85, 29.

25 Jones and Jones, *New England Folk Art*, figs. 30, 31; Clara Endicott Sears, *Some American Primitives: A Study of New England Faces and Folk Portraits* (Boston, 1941), p. 68.

26 Prown, *John Singleton Copley*, I, fig. 26; Gardner and Feld, *American Painting*, p. 180.

27 Mather Byles, Jr., to Sisters, Halifax, Oct. 7, 1786, Byles Family Papers (1728–1835), II, typed copy, MHS. For a similar anecdote concerning a young English gentleman in 1679, see Alice Morse Earle, *Child Life in Colonial Days* (New York, 1946), pp. 41–2.

28 Stanislaus Murray Hamilton, ed., *Letters to Washington and Accompanying Papers*, 4 vols. (Boston, 1901), III, pp. 318, 324–5.

29 Hamilton, *Letters to Washington*, IV, pp. 74, 20–2.

30 Hamilton, *Letters to Washington*, IV, pp. 84–5.

[31] Hamilton, *Letters to Washington*, IV, pp. 175–6, 232–3.

[32] Hamilton, *Letters to Washington*, IV, p. 189.

[33] Edwin Morris Betts and James Adam Bear, Jr., eds., *The Family Letters of Thomas Jefferson* (Columbia, Mo., 1966), pp. 19–20, 30, 52, 71.

[34] Farish, *Journal and Letters of Philip Vickers Fithian*, pp. 36, 48–9, 130–1.

[35] Augusta [Mary Green] to Julia [Eliza Waite], n.d., Eliza Waite Correspondence with Susan Kittredge (of Andover) and Others, 1786–1791, Essex Institute.

[36] "Journal of Miss Sally Wister," *PMHB*, IX (1885), pp. 322–3, X (1886), p. 58.

[37] Clarence Cook, ed., *A Girl's Life Eighty Years Ago: Selections from Letters of Eliza Southgate Bowne* (New York, 1887), pp. 21–2, 23, 128. For similar letters, see Harriet Wadsworth's Journal, Jan. 19, 1785–March 22, 1785, CHS, which contains copies of her letters to her mother in Hartford from New York; and Harriott Pinckney, Copy Book, 1759–1764, Pinckney Papers, photocopy, SCHS.

[38] Julia Stockton Rush to Mrs. Mary Hunter at Trenton, Philadelphia, March 13, 1798, Stockton Family Correspondence, Box III (Ms. in collection of Jeanie Miles Walker, Princeton, N.J.).

[39] Farish, *Journal and Letters of Philip Vickers Fithian*, pp. 33–4, 56–7, 58.

[40] Hamilton, *Letters to Washington*, IV, pp. 42–3.

[41] Farish, *Journal and Letters of Philip Vickers Fithian*, p. 72. For a superb analysis of this conflict between the genteel and the evangelical styles of life, see Isaac, "Evangelical Revolt: The Nature of the Baptists' Challenge to the Traditional Order in Virginia, 1765 to 1775." See also Thompson, "Patrician Society, Plebian Culture."

VII
"A Polite and Hospitable People":
Themes of Genteel Temperaments and Piety

[1] Douglass Adair, ed., "The Autobiography of the Reverend Devereux Jarratt, 1732–1763," *WMQ*, IX (1952), pp. 360–1. See also E. P. Thompson, "Patrician Society, Plebian Culture," *JSH*, 7 (1974), pp. 382–405, and Rhys Isaac, "Evangelical Revolt: The Nature of the Baptists' Challenge to the Traditional Order in Virginia, 1765 to 1775," *WMQ*, XXXI (1974), pp. 345–68, for two fascinating analyses of the dual cultures of the genteel and the nongenteel in eighteenth-century England and Virginia.

[2] See, for instance, John T. Kirk's *Early American Furniture: How to Recognize, Evaluate, Buy, and Care for the Most Beautiful Pieces—High-Style, Country, Primitive and Rustic* (New York, 1970), and *American Chairs: Queen Anne and Chippendale* (New York, 1972), for a superb analysis both of style and of regional variations in particular forms of furniture.

[3] See, for example, Bernard Bailyn, *The Ordeal of Thomas Hutchinson* (Cambridge, Mass., 1974); Carol Berkin, *Jonathan Sewall: Odyssey of an American Loyalist* (New York, 1974); Judy Mann DiStefano, "A Concept of the

Family in Colonial America: The Pembertons of Philadelphia" (Ph.D. thesis, Ohio State University, 1970).

4 Elizabeth Powel to John H. Powel, Jan. 26, 1809, Duplicates of Letters, 1768–1820, Powel Collection, HSP.

5 L. H. Butterfield, *et al.*, eds., *Adams Family Correspondence* (Cambridge, Mass., 1963–   ), I, p. 137.

6 See John F. H. New, *Anglican and Puritan: The Basis of Their Opposition, 1558–1640* (Stanford, Calif., 1964); Gerald J. Goodwin, "The Anglican Middle Way in Early Eighteenth Century America: Anglican Religious Thought in the American Colonies, 1702–1750" (Ph.D. thesis, University of Wisconsin, 1965); Carl Bridenbaugh, *Mitre and Sceptre: Transatlantic Faiths, Ideas, Personalities, and Politics, 1689–1775* (New York, 1962); C. J. Stranks, *Anglican Devotion: Studies in the Spiritual Life of the Church of England between the Reformation and the Oxford Movement* (London, 1961); Roland N. Stromberg, *Religious Liberalism in Eighteenth-Century England* (London, 1954). Keith Thomas's analysis of the traditional religious order of pre-Reformation England in *Religion and the Decline of Magic* (New York, 1971) is excellent, and very suggestive for the analysis of subsequent patterns of traditional nonevangelical modes of religious experience.

7 Louis B. Wright and Marion Tinling, eds., *William Byrd of Virginia: The London Diary (1717–1721) and Other Writings* (New York, 1958), pp. 305, 494.

8 Anne Rowe Cunningham, ed., *Letters and Diary of John Rowe, Boston Merchant, 1759–1762, 1764–1779* (Boston, 1903), p. 164.

9 Peter Orlando Hutchinson, ed., *The Diary and Letters of His Excellency, Thomas Hutchinson, Esq.*, 2 vols. (London, 1883–1886), p. 460.

10 Andrew Oliver, ed., *The Journal of Samuel Curwen, Loyalist*, 2 vols. (Cambridge, Mass., 1972), I, pp. 132–3.

11 Bailyn, *Ordeal of Thomas Hutchinson*, pp. 16–17, 23–4, 25.

12 *The Belcher Papers*, MHS *Collections*, Sixth Series, VI (1893), p. 65; VII (1894), pp. 3, 21, 216–17, 417.

13 L. H. Butterfield, *et al.*, eds., *Diary and Autobiography of John Adams*, 4 vols. (Cambridge, Mass., 1962), I, pp. 213, 294.

14 Butterfield, *Diary and Autobiography*, II, p. 105.

15 Butterfield, *Diary and Autobiography*, II, pp. 118, 127. For an analysis of the genteel non-Quakers in Philadelphia, see Stephen Brobeck, "Revolutionary Change in Colonial Philadelphia: The Brief Life of the Proprietary Gentry," *WMQ*, XXXIII (1976), pp. 410–34.

16 Carl Bridenbaugh, ed., *Gentleman's Progress: The Itinerarium of Dr. Alexander Hamilton, 1744* (Chapel Hill, N.C., 1948), p. 146.

17 Cunningham, *Letters and Diary of John Rowe*, pp. 197, 211, 212, 231.

18 John Hughes to Isaac Hughes, Piscataqua, Sept. 5, 1769, Miscellaneous Correspondence, 1763–1771, Hughes Papers, HSP. For an excellent brief study of Hughes, see Edmund S. Morgan and Helen M. Morgan, *The Stamp Act Crisis: Prologue to Revolution*, rev. ed. (New York, 1963), pp. 301–24, 371–3.

19 See, for example, Jane Carson, *Colonial Virginians at Play* (Williamsburg, Va., 1965).

20 "Journal of Miss Sally Wister," *PMHB*, IX (1885), pp. 477–8; X (1886), p. 51.

21 Edwin Morris Betts and James Adam Bear, Jr., eds., *The Family Letters of Thomas Jefferson* (Columbia, Mo., 1966), p. 360; *Belcher Papers*, VII, p. 147.

22 Bridenbaugh, *Gentleman's Progress*, p. 141.

23 For the role of furniture as sculpture, see Kirk, *Early American Furniture*, p. 9 and *passim*. My appreciation and understanding of early American furniture have been greatly enriched by many discussions with John Kirk as well as by reading his illuminating books on the subject.

24 Wright and Tinling, *William Byrd: The London Diary*, pp. 140, 505; Louis B. Wright and Marion Tinling, eds., *The Secret Diary of William Byrd of Westover, 1709–1712* (Richmond, Va., 1941), pp. 253, 272, 337, 210–11.

25 Hunter Dickinson Farish, ed., *Journal and Letters of Philip Vickers Fithian 1773–1774: A Plantation Tutor of the Old Dominion* (Williamsburg, Va., 1957), pp. 86, 184–9.

26 Stanislaus Murray Hamilton, ed., *Letters to Washington and Accompanying Papers*, 4 vols. (Boston, 1901), III, pp. 35–6; IV, pp. 24, 41–4, 191, 193.

27 Bridenbaugh, *Gentleman's Progress*, p. 177.

28 Oliver, *Journal of Samuel Curwen*, I, pp. 34, 48–9.

29 Wright and Tinling, *Secret Diary*, p. 462. See also Jack P. Greene, ed., *The Diary of Colonel Landon Carter of Sabine Hall, 1752–1778*, 2 vols. (Charlottesville, Va., 1965), for other examples of recurrent domestic disputes which always flared suddenly and then died away, the anger having been expressed openly and directly between the individuals concerned. Only Landon Carter, Sr., who was a moderate by temperament, seemed to have been concerned by these angry encounters. His sons, daughters, daughter-in-law, and grandchildren did not appear to be disturbed at all.

30 *Belcher Papers*, II, pp. 97–8, 124.

31 Isaac, "Evangelical Revolt," p. 348. See also pp. 348–53 for a fascinating discussion of sports and pastimes as expressions of the genteel style of life, and Carson, *Colonial Virginians at Play*, for descriptions of their customary behavior.

32 *Belcher Papers*, II, p. 34; "Diary of James Allen, Esq., of Philadelphia, Counsellor-at-Law, 1770–1778," *PMHB*, IX (1885), pp. 433–4.

33 Douglass Adair and John A. Schutz, eds., *Peter Oliver's Origin and Progress of the American Rebellion: A Tory View* (Stanford, Calif., 1961), p. 12.

34 See, for instance, Bailyn, *Ordeal of Thomas Hutchinson*, pp. 79–80, 164, 316–17; Berkin, *Jonathan Sewall*, p. 34.

35 See T. H. Breen, *The Character of the Good Ruler: A Study of Puritan Political Ideas in New England, 1630–1730* (New Haven, Conn., 1970), pp. 137, 141–2, 205–26, 271. For Virginians, see Charles S. Sydnor, *American Revolutionaries in the Making: Political Practices in Washington's Virginia* (New York, 1962). For a general analysis of genteel leadership, see Leonard Woods Labaree, *Conservatism in Early American History* (Ithaca, N.Y., 1959).

36 See Thomas, *Religion and the Decline of Magic*; Isaac, "Evangelical Revolt," p. 350; Rhys Isaac, "Preachers and Patriots: Popular Culture and the

Revolution in Virginia," in Alfred F. Young, ed., *The American Revolution: Explorations in the History of American Radicalism* (Dekalb, Ill., 1976).

[37] Wright and Tinling, *Secret Diary*, p. 122.

[38] Cunningham, *Letters and Diary of John Rowe*, pp. 111, 136, 224.

[39] Bridenbaugh, *Gentleman's Progress*, p. 145; Penuel Bowen to Mr. William Hill of Boston, Savannah, Aug. 7, 1786, Bowen-Cooke Papers, typed copy, SCHS.

[40] Paul F. Boller, Jr., *George Washington and Religion* (Dallas, Tex., 1963), pp. 35, 75, 39, 108.

[41] Elisha Hutchinson to Polly [Watson], April 15, [1771?], Hutchinson-Watson Papers, MHS; Mary Hutchinson to [Mrs. Mary Oliver?], Milton, July 24, 1772, Hutchinson-Watson Papers; Boller, *Washington and Religion*, p. 96.

[42] Hutchinson, *Diary and Letters of Thomas Hutchinson*, I, p. 504; Oliver, *Journal of Samuel Curwen*, I, pp. 104, 19–20; Boller, *Washington and Religion*, pp. 97–8.

[43] Bailyn, *Ordeal of Thomas Hutchinson*, p. 22; Boller, *Washington and Religion*, pp. 121, 123, 183–4.

[44] Farish, *Journal and Letters of Philip Vickers Fithian*, pp. 203, 100, 137.

[45] See, for instance, Berkin, *Jonathan Sewall*, p. 94; Bailyn, *Ordeal of Thomas Hutchinson*, pp. 21–3; Frederick B. Tolles, *Meeting House and Counting House: The Quaker Merchants of Colonial Philadelphia, 1682–1763* (New York, 1963), pp. 141–2. Anglicanism, however, also appealed to a much broader group besides the genteel, as Bruce Steiner demonstrated so ably in "New England Anglicanism: A Genteel Faith?", *WMQ*, XXVII (1970), pp. 122–35. Recently, Marc A. Mappen has examined the appeal of Anglicanism to many former Presbyterians in "Anatomy of a Schism: Anglican Dissent in the New England Community of Newtown, Connecticut, 1708–1765" (Ph.D. thesis, Rutgers University, 1976).

VIII
The Clash of Temperaments:
Some Reflections on the First American Civil War

[1] L. H. Butterfield, *et al.*, eds., *Adams Family Correspondence*, 4 vols. (Cambridge, Mass., 1963), II, pp. 27–8, 74.

[2] Worthington C. Ford, ed., *Warren-Adams Letters: Being Chiefly a Correspondence among John Adams, Samuel Adams, and James Warren*, MHS *Collections*, vols. 72–73 (Boston, 1917–1925), 72, pp. 201–2; Butterfield, *Adams Family Correspondence*, I, p. 125.

[3] Ford, *Warren-Adams Letters*, 72, pp. 201–2.

[4] Bernard Bailyn has provided us with some of the most subtle and probing analyses of the influence of temperament upon political thought and actions that we have. See, for instance, "Religion and Revolution: Three Biographical Studies," *Perspectives in American History*, IV (1970), pp. 85–169, and *The Ordeal of Thomas Hutchinson* (Cambridge, Mass., 1974).

[5] Jonathan Bouchier, ed., *Reminiscences of an American Loyalist 1738–1789,*

Being the Autobiography of The Revd. Jonathan Boucher, Rector of Annapolis in Maryland and afterwards Vicar of Epsom, Surrey, England (Boston, 1925), p. 118; Lester J. Cappon, ed., *The Adams-Jefferson Letters: The Complete Correspondence between Thomas Jefferson and Abigail and John Adams*, 2 vols. (Chapel Hill, N.C., 1959), II, p. 335.

6 Butterfield, *Adams Family Correspondence*, I, p. 392.

7 For moderates, see, for instance, Bernard Bailyn's *The Ideological Origins of the American Revolution* (Cambridge, Mass., 1967); Peter Shaw, *The Character of John Adams* (Chapel Hill, N.C., 1976); Edmund S. Morgan, "The Puritan Ethic and the American Revolution," *WMQ*, XXIV (1967), pp. 3–43; L. F. S. Upton, *The Loyal Whig: William Smith of New York and Quebec* (Toronto, 1969). For the evangelicals, whose presence and influence have yet to be measured in full, see Alan Heimert, *Religion and the American Mind from the Great Awakening to the Revolution* (Cambridge, Mass., 1966); Gordon S. Wood, *The Creation of the American Republic, 1776–1787* (Chapel Hill, N.C., 1969), especially pp. 53–70, 107–24; Pauline Maier, "Coming to Terms with Samuel Adams," *AHR*, 81 (1976), pp. 12–37; Cushing Strout, *The New Heavens and New Earth: Political Religion in America* (New York, 1974). For the genteel, see Bernard Bailyn, *The Ordeal of Thomas Hutchinson* (Cambridge, Mass., 1974); Carol Berkin, *Jonathan Sewall: Odyssey of an American Loyalist* (New York, 1974); Robert McCluer Calhoon, *The Loyalists in Revolutionary America 1760–1781* (New York, 1973). Mary Beth Norton has perceived two distinctive forms of Whig ideology in "The Loyalist Critique of the Revolution," *The Development of a Revolutionary Mentality* (Washington, D.C., 1972), pp. 127–48.

8 See Winthrop D. Jordan, "Familial Politics: Thomas Paine and the Killing of the King, 1776," *JAH*, LX (1973), pp. 294–308; Philip J. Greven, Jr., *Four Generations: Population, Land, and Family in Colonial Andover, Massachusetts* (Ithaca, N.Y., 1970), pp. 279–82; John J. Waters, "James Otis, Jr.: An Ambivalent Revolutionary," *History of Childhood Quarterly*, I (1973), pp. 142–50; Edwin G. Burroughs and Michael Wallace, "The American Revolution: The Ideology and Psychology of National Liberation," *Perspectives in American History*, VI (1972), pp. 167–306; Fawn M. Brodie, *Thomas Jefferson: An Intimate History* (New York, 1974); Jack P. Greene, "An Uneasy Connection: An Analysis of the Preconditions of the American Revolution," in Stephen G. Kurtz and James H. Hutson, eds., *Essays on the American Revolution* (Chapel Hill, N.C., 1973), pp. 61–4, 79–80. For the implications of childhood and family experiences in the early national period, see Michael Paul Rogin, *Fathers and Children: Andrew Jackson and the Subjugation of the American Indian* (New York, 1975).

9 Contrast, for example, the interpretations of "liberty" in Bailyn, *Ideological Origins*, and Wood, *Creation of the American Republic*. See also Heimert, *Religion and the American Mind*, pp. 12, 454–60.

10 Merrill Jensen, ed., *Tracts of the American Revolution, 1763–1776* (Indianapolis, 1967), p. 348. See also Edmund S. Morgan and Helen M. Morgan, *The Stamp Act Crisis: Prologue to Revolution*, rev. ed. (New York, 1963), and Douglass Adair and John A. Schutz, eds., *Peter Oliver's Origin and Progress of the American Rebellion: A Tory View* (Stanford, Calif., 1961).

11 See Bailyn, *Ordeal of Thomas Hutchinson*, pp. 17, 25–6.

12 Thomas Hutchinson, *The History of the Colony of the Province of Massachusetts-Bay*, Lawrence Shaw Mayo, ed., 3 vols. (Cambridge, Mass., 1936), III, p. 293; Adair and Schutz, *Peter Oliver's Origin and Progress*, p. 5; Edmund Burke, *On the American Revolution: Selected Speeches and Letters*, Elliott Robert Barkan, ed. (New York, 1966), pp. 82, 193–4; Hutchinson, *History of Massachusetts-Bay*, III, p. 293; and Bailyn, *Ordeal of Thomas Hutchinson*, p. 91.

13 Jensen, *Tracts*, p. 287. The disintegration of political institutions is described brilliantly in Morgan and Morgan, *Stamp Act Crisis*.

14 David L. Jacobson, ed., *The English Libertarian Heritage from the Writings of John Trenchard and Thomas Gordon in* The Independent Whig *and* Cato's Letters (Indianapolis, 1965), pp. 127–31. See also Bailyn, *Ideological Origins*, and Wood, *Creation of the American Republic*.

15 Forrest McDonald, ed., *Empire and Nation:* Letters from a Farmer in Pennsylvania, *John Dickinson;* Letters from the Federal Farmer, *Richard Henry Lee* (Englewood Cliffs, N.J., 1962), p. 68; L. H. Butterfield, *et al.*, eds., *Diary and Autobiography of John Adams*, 4 vols. (Cambridge, Mass., 1962), II, pp. 58–60.

16 See, for example, Bailyn, *Ideological Origins*, pp. vi–vii, 19–20, 302–4; Wood, *Creation of the American Republic*, pp. 53–4, 91–3, 113–17, and Heimert, *Religion and the American Mind*, p. 481, both stress the reactionary character of the revolution. Thus Bailyn's vision is attuned to the moderate temperament and perception of the political process, while Wood's and Heimert's visions are responsive to the evangelical temperament and perception of the political process.

17 *Warren-Adams Letters*, 72, p. 222; Butterfield, *Adams Family Correspondence*, I, p. 383–4. See also Wood, *Creation of the American Republic*, pp. 65–70, and R. R. Palmer, *The Age of the Democratic Revolution: A Political History of Europe and America, 1760–1800*, 2 vols. (Princeton, N.J., 1959–1964), II, pp. 124–9.

18 See Wood, *Creation of the American Republic*, for the most illuminating analysis so far of this alliance.

19 Milton M. Klein, ed., *The Independent Reflector or Weekly Essays on Sundry Important Subjects More Particularly Adapted to the Province of New York by William Livingston and Others* (Cambridge, Mass., 1963), pp. 216, 219. For a different perspective upon evangelicals, see Heimert, *Religion and the American Mind*, and William G. McLoughlin, *New England Dissent 1630–1833: The Baptists and the Separation of Church and State*, 2 vols. (Cambridge, Mass., 1971), I, pp. 335–9, 555–6, 572–6; II, pp. 1277–82.

20 See, for instance, Morgan and Morgan, *The Stamp Act Crisis*, pp. 284, 297, 303, 366; Maier, "Coming to Terms with Samuel Adams"; Adair and Schutz, *Peter Oliver's Origin and Progress*; Richard L. Bushman, *From Puritan to Yankee: Character and the Social Order in Connecticut, 1690–1765* (Cambridge, Mass., 1967). See also Michael Walzer's brilliant and suggestive study, *The Revolution of the Saints: A Study in the Origins of Radical Politics* (Cambridge, Mass., 1965). The English civil war in the mid-seventeenth century provides many analogies to the mid-eighteenth-century American civil war, although very few historians have sought to draw them forth from the sources or the secondary literature.

21 Bailyn, *Ideological Origins*, p. 150; Jensen, *Tracts*, pp. 299–300, 302.

22 Bailyn, *Ideological Origins*, p. 144, and Wood, *Creation of the American Republic*, pp. 28–43. Bailyn and Wood thus both insist upon the essentially rational and conscious intellectual and political sources of the fear of conspiracy. See Bailyn, *Ideological Origins*, pp. 94–159, and Bernard Bailyn, *The Origins of American Politics* (New York, 1968), pp. 11–14, 31–53. In addition, the persistent paranoia of many Anglo-Americans throughout the seventeenth and eighteenth centuries with respect to "popery" (of both Catholic and Anglican varieties) provides an indispensable source for the politicized paranoia of the 1760's and 1770's. See Carl Bridenbaugh, *Mitre and Sceptre: Transatlantic Faiths, Ideas, Personalities, and Politics 1689– 1775* (New York, 1962). For a discussion of political paranoia in subsequent periods, see Richard Hofstadter, *The Paranoid Style in American Politics* (New York, 1965).

23 Hezekiah Niles, ed., *Centennial Offering Republication of the Principles and Acts of the Revolution in America* (New York, 1876), p. 107; Butterfield, *Diary and Autobiography*, II, pp. 35, 75. See also John M. Murrin, "Anglicizing an American Colony: The Transformation of Provincial Massachusetts" (Ph.D. thesis, Yale University, 1966); Rowland Berthoff and John M. Murrin, "Feudalism, Communalism, and the Yeoman Freeholder: The American Revolution Considered as a Social Accident," in Kurtz and Hutson, *Essays on the American Revolution*; Kenneth A. Lockridge, "Social Change and the Meaning of the American Revolution," *JSH*, VI (1973), pp. 403–39.

24 Butterfield, *Diary and Autobiography*, II, p. 63; Butterfield, *Adams Family Correspondence*, I, p. 125; John Adams to Dr. J. Morse, Quincy, Dec. 22, 1815, *The Works of John Adams, Second President of the United States*, Charles Francis Adams, ed. (Boston, 1854), X, pp. 194–5.

25 Niles, *Principles and Acts*, pp. 42, 39.

26 See, for example, Sigmund Freud, *The Complete Introductory Lectures on Psychoanalysis*, James Strachey, ed. and trans. (New York, 1966), pp. 423–7; Otto Fenichel, *The Psychoanalytic Theory of Neurosis* (New York, 1945), pp. 427–35; David Shapiro, *Neurotic Styles* (New York, 1965), ch. 3 ("Paranoid Style"), especially pp. 73–88.

27 See Shapiro, *Neurotic Styles*, pp. 73–83, for an excellent discussion of the issue of autonomy and self-will in relation to the paranoid style of personality.

28 See, for instance, Peter H. Wood, *Black Majority: Negroes in Colonial South Carolina from 1670 through the Stono Rebellion* (New York, 1974); Edmund S. Morgan, *American Slavery—American Freedom: The Ordeal of Colonial Virginia* (New York, 1975).

29 See Wood, *Creation of the American Republic*, pp. 91–124; Maier, "Coming to Terms with Samuel Adams," pp. 34–7. See also Walzer, *Revolution of the Saints*, and Strout, *New Heavens and New Earth*, ch. IV ("Calvinist Whigs and the Spirit of '76").

30 A Mechanic to Mr. Bernardus Legrange, n.d., Barnardus La Grange Papers, Special Collections, Rutgers University. See also a similar letter from K. L., a Mechanic, to Mrs. Legrange, July 28, 1776, Special Collections, Rutgers. For other documents, see Catherine S. Crary, ed., *The Price of Loyalty: Tory Writings from the Revolutionary Era* (New York, 1973), and Leslie F. S.

Upton, ed., *Revolutionary Versus Loyalist: The First American Civil War, 1774–1784* (Waltham, Mass., 1968). See also the perceptive studies of loyalists by Mary Beth Norton, *The British-Americans: The Loyalist Exiles in England 1774–1789* (Boston, 1972), and Calhoon, *Loyalists in Revolutionary America.*

31 Adair and Schutz, *Peter Oliver's Origins and Progress,* pp. 53, 111; Moses Coit Tyler, *The Literary History of the American Revolution, 1763–1783,* 2 vols. (New York, 1897), I, pp. 365–6.

32 Hutchinson, *History of Massachusetts-Bay,* III, p. 98. The anguish of banishment and exile is portrayed in Bailyn, *Ordeal of Thomas Hutchinson,* and Norton, *British-Americans.*

33 Wood, *Creation of the American Republic,* pp. 114–18.

34 John C. Miller, *Sam Adams: Pioneer in Propaganda* (Stanford, Calif., 1964), p. 363. See also Harry Alonzo Cushing, ed., *The Writings of Samuel Adams,* 4 vols. (New York, 1904–1908), IV, pp. 236–8. Gordon Wood's analysis of the post-revolutionary period is illuminating (see *Creation of the American Republic,* pp. 393–615), and I have been greatly influenced by his interpretation of political thought after 1776. For a different perspective, see Bailyn, *Ideological Origins,* which emphasizes the continuities between the revolutionary and post-revolutionary efforts to define liberty and to establish viable forms of constitutional government.

35 Adrienne Koch and William Peden, eds., *The Selected Writings of John and John Quincy Adams* (New York, 1946), pp. 119–20.

36 Jensen, *Tracts,* p. 282. See also Wood, *Creation of the American Republic,* pp. 61–3, 608–14.

37 Edward Mead Earle, ed., *The Federalist: A Commentary on the Constitution of the United States, Being a Collection of Essays written in Support of the Constitution agreed upon September 17, 1787, by the Federal Convention* (New York, n.d.), pp. 55–8, 339–40.

❧ PERMISSIONS ❧

FOR PERMISSION TO QUOTE from manuscripts in their collections, I am most grateful to: the Andover Newton Theological School, Newton Centre, Mass.; the Beinecke Rare Book and Manuscript Library, Yale University, New Haven, Conn.; the Trustees of the Boston Public Library, Boston, Mass.; the Bryn Mawr College Library, Bryn Mawr, Pa.; the Congregational Library, Boston; the Connecticut Historical Society, Hartford, Conn.; the Dartmouth College Library, Hanover, N.H.; the Essex Institute, Salem, Mass.; the Forbes Library Northampton, Mass.; the Haverford College Library, Quaker Collection, Haverford, Pa.; the Historical Society of Pennsylvania, Philadelphia, Pa.; the Massachusetts Historical Society, Boston; the New Hampshire Historical Society, Concord, N.H.; the New-York Historical Society, New York; the New York Public Library, Astor, Lenox and Tilden Foundations, New York; Mr. John Pickering, Jr., Salem, Mass.; Miss Catherine A. Potter, North Haven, Conn.; Rutgers University Library (Special Collections, Alexander Library), New Brunswick, N.J.; the South Carolina Historical Society, Charleston, S.C.; the University of North Carolina at Chapel Hill, Southern Historical Collection; Jeanie Miles Walker (Mrs. William H. Walker II), Princeton, N.J.; the Yale University Library, New Haven.

Grateful acknowledgment is made also to the following for permission to quote from previously published material:

American Book Company: Clarence H. Faust and Thomas H. Johnson, eds., *Jonathan Edwards: Representative Selections*, copyright © 1935 by American Book Company; Perry Miller and Thomas H. Johnson, eds., *The Puritans*, copyright © 1938 by American Book Company. Used by permission of American Book Company.

The Banner of Truth Trust: Arnold A. Dallimore, *George Whitefield: The Life and Times of the Great Evangelist of the Eighteenth-Century Revival*, copyright © 1970 by Arnold A. Dallimore; *George Whitefield's Journals*, new edition, 1960.

The Bobbs-Merrill Company, Inc.: *The Great Awakening*, by Alan Heimert and Perry Miller, eds., copyright © 1967 by the Bobbs-Merrill Company, Inc., reprinted by permission of the publishers; *The English Libertarian Heritage*, edited by David L. Jacobson, copyright © 1965 by the Bobbs-Merrill Company, Inc., reprinted by permission of the publisher.

Columbia University Press: Herbert and Carol Schneider, eds., *Samuel Johnson: His Career and Writings*, New York: Columbia University Press, 1929, by permission of the publisher.

William B. Eerdmans Publishing Company: Hugh Barbour and Arthur O.

⚜ SOURCES ⚜

1. MANUSCRIPTS

SINCE MY PRINCIPAL FOCUS at the outset of my inquiry was upon the religious experiences of evangelicals, I began a search for primary sources pertaining to evangelicals in various denominations during the seventeenth, eighteenth, and early nineteenth centuries. In the course of my initial research, I discovered, however, that there was no way to find useful sources for individuals and families (much less ways to distinguish those who might be evangelicals from those who were not) without looking at a great many collections of manuscript sources in various archives. While the process was both time-consuming and often frustrating, it also had an unexpected impact upon my research, since inevitably I read sources for individuals and families who were not evangelicals. Gradually, I realized that I would have to reckon with them, too, and to try to understand their experiences, beliefs, and temperaments in order to place the evangelicals in perspective. I did not pay as close attention to the sources for the genteel as to the sources for evangelicals and moderates, however, and thus must hope that others will explore the manuscripts for the genteel more intensively and extensively than I have done.

Since historians who read manuscript sources necessarily work in one archive at a time, I have listed some of the manuscript collections that I found to be the most useful and informative in particular archives, leaving out many other collections which proved to be of little value for my particular purposes.

New England

In *Connecticut*, the Connecticut Historical Society (Hartford) has some significant collections: Canterbury Separate Papers; Nathan Cole, "Spiritual Travels"; Hannah Heaton, Spiritual Diary in Calvin Eaton's Book (photocopy of Ms. in the possession of Catherine A. Potter, North Haven); Joseph Jeslin, Diary; Benjamin Lyon, Diary, 1763–1767; Philemon and Ammi Ruhamah Robbins, Papers; Benjamin Throop, Arcana Sacra (Diary, 1741–1784); Sarah Tompson, Relation of Religious Experience, 1679; Harriet Wadsworth, Journal, 1785. At the Connecticut State Library (Hartford), Matthew Grant's diary is of interest. Yale University has a number of important collections: At the Beinecke Library are diaries by David Brainerd, Timothy Edwards (Diary and Account Book, 1711–1724), Sarah Osborn (1757–1769), Charles Jeffrey Smith (1763–1765), as well as by the following: Esther [Edwards] Burr, Journal (1754–1757); Jonathan Edwards, Miscellanies (typed copies); Timothy Edwards's Notices of his Father, Richard Edwards (on loan from Andover-

Newton); Jonathan Edwards [Jr.]'s letters to his son Jonathan Walters, 1795–1801; Jonathan Walter Edwards's letters to his son Jonathan, 1814–1819; Ezra Stiles, Birthday Reflections, 1767–1794, Memoirs of the life of the Rev. Isaac Stiles, 1760; Edward Taylor, Commonplace Book. At the Yale University Library, one finds: the Burr Family Papers; the Evarts Family Papers, including correspondence, 1753–1821; Joseph Fish, Diary, 1741–1770, in the Silliman Family Papers (Box 35), letters, 1733–1760, and sermons; the Johnson Family Papers, which include the correspondence of William Livingston and Noah Welles, 1742–1768; the Silliman Family Papers; Benjamin Wood's Journal, 1726–1730.

In *Massachusetts*, the Andover Newton Theological Seminary Library (Newton Centre) has extensive collections of papers for Isaac Backus and Jonathan Edwards. The Boston Public Library has Sarah [Prince] Gill's Journal, 1743–1764; papers of John Cotton and Cotton Mather; John Osborn. Letter to Father, 1740. At the Congregational Library (Boston) are papers relating to separatists in the First and Third Churches of Newbury, 1743–1746, and papers of separatists from the church in Sturbridge, 1745–1762. At the Essex Institute (Salem) are: John Cleaveland's Papers; Clarke Family Letters and Legal Papers, 1755–1839; Curwen Family Papers and Letters, 1672–1791; Fairfax Family Letters, 1729–1815; Pickering Family Papers, including typed copies (the Mss. in the possession of John Pickering, Jr., Salem) of Letters from John Pickering to Timothy Pickering, 1797–1817, Timothy to John, 1786–1829, Timothy to Rebecca, 1775–1827, and Timothy Pickering's Memorandum Book. Eliza Waite's correspondence, 1786–1791. At the Houghton Library, Harvard University (Cambridge), are several excellent diaries, including those of Ebenezer Bridge, 1749–1792; Henry Flynt; and Joseph Tompson (including his Commonplace Book), 1662–1726, as well as Josiah Cotton's important account of the Cotton family, 1727–1755. The collections of the Massachusetts Historical Society (Boston) are superb, but their volume makes locating significant collections of personal materials difficult. Unfortunately, the extensive collection of Winthrop Family Papers was closed to the public on each of my successive visits to the society, but no doubt it contains much useful material. Among the more interesting papers I located and used were: Hugh Adams's autobiographical narrative; Rebecca Amory, letters, Amory Papers, vol. 1, 1698–1784; Benjamin Bangs, Diary, 1742–1765; Belcher-Jennison-Weiss Papers, which includes the Belcher Family Papers, 1740–1818; Jeremy Belknap, Letter-book, 1768–1788, and observations on suckling children by "Clarissa," 1772; James Bowdoin, Letters, Bowdoin-Temple collection; Mrs. Bowers, Relation for Admission to Church Communion, 1727, Amos-Adams Papers; Byles Family Papers, 1753–1865, including letters of Mather Byles, 1762–1786, and copies of family papers, 1728–1835; Coffin Papers, 1769–1782; Cranch Family Papers, 1749–1882; Nicholas Gilman, Notes on Sermons, 1725–1784, and "Spiritualia"; David Hall, Diary, 1740–1789; Hutchinson-Watson Papers, including letters of Elisha Hutchinson to Polly Watson; Mrs. Frances Huttson, Letters to son, 1774–1782, Matthew Ridley, Ridley Papers; John Jeffries, Diary (transcript); Daniel King, Diary, 1730–1767 (copy of Ms. in Essex Institute); Mascarene Family Papers, including letters from Mrs. Margaret

[Mascarene] Hutchinson, 1780–1793; Samuel Mather, Letters to his Son, 1759–1785; Elizabeth [Cranch] Norton, Diary, 1781–1811, and Jacob Norton, Diaries, Letters, and Sermons; Peter Oliver, Letters to Miss Polly Watson, Hutchinson-Watson; Timothy Pickering, Sr., Letters to son Timothy, 1760–1781 (microfilm); Thomas Prince, letters and papers, 1683–1720; Edmund Quincy Letters to daughters, 1776–1784, in Letter Book; Samuel Quincy, Diary, 1776–1777, a loyalist exiled in London; Experience Richardson, Diary, 1745–1781 (microfilm); Robie-Sewall Papers, 1611–1789; Samuel P. Savage, Letters to Gilbert Tennant, George Whitefield, and others; Peter Thacher, Journal, 1678–1682 (microfilm); Mercy [Otis] Warren, Letterbook, 1770–1800; and Jonathan Willis, Diary, 1744–1747. At the New England Historic Genealogical Society (Boston) are several significant collections: Marston Cabot, Diary, 1740–1745; Francis Dane, Commonplace Book, which contains not only his extraordinary personal narrative but numerous poems on religious themes; Lydia Prout, Religious Thoughts, 1714–1716; William Homes, Diary; Daniel Rogers, Diary, 1730–1785.

In *New Hampshire*, the Dartmouth College Library (Hanover) has the extensive collection of Eleazar Wheelock, including letters to his son Ralph, and many others, as well as letters written to him. The New Hampshire Historical Society (Concord) has Nicholas Gilman's Diary, 1740–1744.

In *Rhode Island*, the John Hay Library, Brown University (Providence), has the Florence Backus Papers and Isaac Backus's Book Containing A Brief Account of My Life and of the Dealings of God with My Soul, vol. I, Ms., as well as typed transcripts of Isaac Backus's diaries (Mss. from Andover Newton), edited by William G. McLoughlin, who graciously permitted me to read them.

Middle Atlantic

Relatively few manuscripts of a personal nature have survived from the seventeenth and eighteenth centuries in New Jersey and New York, which makes studies of childhood, family life, or religious experiences in these areas very difficult.

In *New Jersey*, the Princeton University Library has several interesting collections, including Samuel Davies's Diaries, 1753–1755, and the Rush Family Papers. The Stockton Family Correspondence is in the possession of Jeanie Miles Walker, Princeton. At the Special Collections, Alexander Library, Rutgers University (New Brunswick), are: Samuel Allison's letters to friends, 1764–1790, Samuel Allison Papers; Anonymous letter from "A Mechanic" to Bernardus Legrange, 1776, Barnardus La Grange Papers. The New Jersey Historical Society (Newark) has a copy of the autobiography of Jacob Green.

In *New York*, the New-York Historical Society has: Elizabeth Colden DeLancey Correspondence, 1741–1784, Colden Papers; Timothy Edwards, Notebook, 1698–1738; Caroline Ludlow Frey, Spiritual Diary, 1821–1827, Frey Papers; Archibald Kennedy, Letters; John Moore, Memoir of his life and family; Daniel Rogers, Sermons, 1727–1784, and Diary, 1740–1753, Rogers Papers. The New York Public Library has: Elizabeth Bleecker, Diary, 1799–1806; Anne and Edward Chandler, Letters, 1783–1787; Mary Cooper, Diary,

1768–1773 (transcript); Livingston Family, Correspondence and Papers; Schuyler Papers, including some family letters; Wainwright Papers, with extensive correspondence *ca.* 1795–1840.

In *Pennsylvania* are to be found some of the richest collections outside New England of manuscripts containing personal materials. Bryn Mawr College has Joseph Bean's Spiritual Diary, 1741–1744, which also has been transcribed and may be published. The Quaker Collection at Haverford College has: Hannah [Peters] Bringhurst, Diary, 1781; George Churchman, Journals, 1759–1813; David Cooper, Diary; Sarah Cresson, Diary, 1789–1829; Elizabeth and Henry Drinker, Letters; Sarah [Logan] Fisher, Letterbook, 1783–*ca.* 1789; Richard Hockley, Letterbook, 1737–1742; Elizabeth [Hudson] Morris, Journal, 1743–1778; Ann Head Warder, Diary, typed copy, and Letters to husband, 1787–1788, typed copy; Ann Cooper Whitall, Diary, 1760–1762. The Historical Society of Pennsylvania (Philadelphia) has a superb collection, including: Burd-Shippen-Hubley Papers; Elizabeth Byles, Letterbook, 1757–1783, Ball Papers; Thomas Coombe, Jr., Letters, 1767–1803, Coombe Papers; Dickinson Family letters in Logan Papers; Elizabeth Drinker, Diary, 1758–1807 (Mss. and typed copies); Samuel Emlen, Letters; Elizabeth Graeme Ferguson, Correspondence; Joshua Francis Fisher Family Papers; Hughes Papers, Correspondence, 1763–1771; Deborah Norris Logan, Journal, 1815–1839, typed copy; James Logan, "The Duties of Man as they may be deduced from Nature," Logan Papers—Alverthorpe, and Letterbooks, 1735/6–1748; Maria Dickinson Logan Family Papers; Norris of Fairhill, Family Letters; Elizabeth [Willing] Powel, Duplicates of Letters, 1768–1820, and Letters 1792–1824, Powel Collection; Sarah [Pemberton] Rhoades, Notebooks, Samuel W. Fisher Mss.; Rebecca Shoemaker, Anna Rawle, and Margaret Rawle, Diaries and Letters, 1780–1786, copies, Shoemaker Papers; John Smith, Diaries, 1736–1752; Ann Warder, Diary.

South

In *North Carolina*, Duke University (Durham) has: the Ambler-Brown Family Papers, 1780–1865; Betsey Ambler Carrington, Letters, 1796–1799, 1780–1823, typed copies, and Robert Carter of Nomini Hall, Virginia, Day Books and Letter Books, 1772–1793, Mss. and typed copies. The Southern Historical Collection at the University of North Carolina (Chapel Hill) has: Mrs. Eliza Clitherall's Autobiography and Diary, 1751–1860, Mss. and typed copy; and William Wirt's Childhood Reminiscences (*ca.* 1775–1783), Wirt Family Papers.

In *South Carolina*, the South Carolina Historical Society (Charleston) has: Penuel Bowen, Letterbook, Bowen-Cooke Collection; Mrs. Sarah Gibbes, Letters to son John 1783–1784, Gibbes-Gilchrist Papers; Anne Isabella Kinlock, Diary, 1799, Cheves Collection; Harriott Pinckney, Copy Book, 1759–1764, photocopy, Pinckney Papers; Edward Rutledge, Letters to Sarah Rutledge, 1793–1799.

For *Virginia*, I have relied upon printed sources. Colonial Williamsburg, however, has an excellent collection of microfilms of manuscript collections relevant to Virginia.

II. PRINTED SOURCES

NO ONE ᵥVHO SEEKS to understand both the secular and the religious experiences of people in childhood, youth, and adulthood can fail to be deeply indebted to the transcribers and editors who have published so many sources over the past centuries. The printed sources are invaluable, since they not only are easy to read but are always available for constant perusal and reflection. I have chosen to use many of these as the sources for my arguments in the text since one of my hopes has been that others will explore these sources for themselves, and thus augment our understanding of the temperaments, the experiences, and the beliefs of the people whose lives shaped our past. We scarcely have begun to appreciate the value of many of these printed sources, since they often seem to contain so little material relevant to public events.

Among the many printed sources that I have used in addition to those cited in footnotes are the following: Bernard Bailyn, ed., *The Apologia of Robert Keayne: The Self-Portrait of a Puritan Merchant* (New York, 1965); Mark Van Doren, ed., *Correspondence of Aaron Burr and His Daughter Theodosia* (New York, 1929); Elmer T. Clark, ed., *The Journal and Letters of Francis Asbury* (Nashville, Tenn., 1958); Sheldon S. Cohen, ed., "The Diary of Jeremiah Dummer," *WMQ*, XXIV (1967), pp. 397–422; Wesley Frank Craven and Walter B. Hayward, eds., *The Journal of Richard Norwood* (New York, 1945); Richard Beale Davis, ed., *William Fitzhugh and His Cheasapeake World 1676–1701: The Fitzhugh Letters and Other Documents* (Chapel Hill, N.C., 1963); *The Diary of William Bentley* (Gloucester, Mass., 1962); Alice Earle Morse, ed., *Diary of Anna Green Winslow: A Boston School Girl of 1771* (Boston, 1894); John C. Fitzpatrick, ed., *The Diaries of George Washington, 1748–1799* (Boston, 1925); Samuel P. Fowler, "Biographical Sketch and Diary of Rev. Joseph Green, of Salem Village," *EIHC*, VIII (1868), X (1870), XXXVI (1900); Raymond C. Werner, ed., "Diary of Grace Crowden Galloway," *PMHB*, LV (1931), pp. 32–94, LVIII (1934), pp. 152–89; Mrs. Grant, *Memoirs of an American Lady* (New York, 1809); L. F. Greene, ed., *The Writings of John Leland* (New York, 1969); Philip M. Hamer, ed., *The Papers of Henry Laurens* (Columbia, S.C., 1968–   ); Richard J. Hooker, ed., *The Carolina Backcountry on the Eve of the Revolution: The Journal and Other Writings of Charles Woodmason, Anglican Itinerant* (Chapel Hill, N.C., 1953); William G. McLoughlin, ed., *Isaac Backus on Church, State, and Calvinism: Pamphlets, 1754–1789* (Cambridge, Mass., 1968); William G. McLoughlin, ed., "The Life of Elder Jabez Cottle (1747–1820): A Spiritual Autobiography in Verse," *NEQ*, XXXVIII (1965), pp. 375–86; Robert E. Moody, ed., *The Saltonstall Papers, 1607–1815*, MHS *Collections*, 80 (Boston, 1972); *Papers of the Lloyd Family of the Manor of Queens Village . . . 1654–1826*, NYHS *Collections*, vols. 59–60 (1926–1927); James Dow McCallum, ed., *The Letters of Eleazar Wheelock's Indians* (Hanover, N.H., 1932); J. D. Marshall, ed., *The Autobiography of William Stout of Lancaster, 1665–1752* (New York, 1967); Frances Norton Mason, ed., *My Dearest Polly: Letters of Chief Justice John Marshall to His Wife* (Richmond, Va., 1961); Cotton Mather, "Directions for a Son going to the Colledge," *Bulletin of the American Congregational Associa-*

tion, III (1952), pp. 16–18; "Diary of Increase Mather," MHS *Proceedings*, 2nd Ser., XIII (1899–1900), pp. 338–411; Samuel Eliot Morison, ed., "The Commonplace Book of Joseph Green (1675–1715)," Colonial Society of Massachusetts *Collections* (1938), pp. 191–253; Samuel Eliot Morison, ed., *Of Plymouth Plantation 1620–1647 by William Bradford* (New York, 1952); Samuel Eliot Morison, ed., "The Reverend Seaborn Cotton's Commonplace Book," Colonial Society of Massachusetts *Collections* (April 1925), pp. 320–52; "Deacon John Paine's Journal," *Mayflower Descendant*, VIII–IX (1906–1907); Frederick B. Tolles and E. Gordon Alderfer, eds., *The Witness of William Penn* (New York, 1957); "Extracts from the Diary of Rev. Jonathan Pierpont," *NEHGR*, XIII (1859); "Memoirs of a Senator from Pennsylvania; Jonathan Roberts, 1771–1854," *PMHB*, LXII (1938); Louis Effingham DeForest, ed., *The Journals and Papers of Seth Pomery* (n.p., 1926); Robert A. Rutland, ed., *The Papers of George Mason* (Chapel Hill, N.C., 1970–   ); Donald E. Sanford, ed., *The Poems of Edward Taylor* (New Haven, Conn., 1960); Ethel Armes, ed., *Nancy Shippen: Her Journal Book* (Philadelphia, 1935); "Some Colonial Letters" and "Some Family Letters of the Eighteenth Century," *Virginia Magazine of History and Biography*, X (1902), pp. 176–83, XV (1908), pp. 432–6; Donald E. Stanford, ed., "Edward Taylor's 'Spiritual Relation,'" *American Literature*, XXXV (1964), pp. 467–75; Theodore G. Tappert and John W. Doberstein, eds., *The Journals of Henry Melchoir Muhlenberg* (Philadelphia, 1942–1958); Henry C. Van Schaack, ed., *The Life of Peter Van Schaack, Embracing Selections from His Correspondence and Other Writings* (New York, 1842); John Telford, ed., *The Letters of the Rev. John Wesley* (London, 1931); *The Experiences of God's Gracious Dealing with Mrs. Elizabeth White* (Boston, 1741); Joseph Emerson, ed., *Writings of Miss Fanny Woodbury* (Boston, 1815).

In addition, I relied heavily upon the collections of documents pertaining both to evangelicals and to nonevangelicals in the following sources: for the seventeenth century, Hugh Barbour and Arthur O. Roberts, eds., *Early Quaker Writings, 1650–1700* (Grand Rapids, Mich., 1973), and David D. Hall, ed., *The Antinomian Controversy, 1636–1638: A Documentary History* (Middletown, Conn., 1968); for the eighteenth century, J. M. Bumsted, ed., *The Great Awakening: The Beginnings of Evangelical Pietism in America* (Waltham, Mass., 1970); Richard L. Bushman, ed., *The Great Awakening: Documents on the Revival of Religion, 1740–1745* (New York, 1970); Philip J. Greven, Jr., *Child-Rearing Concepts, 1628–1861: Historical Sources* (Itasca, Ill., 1973); Alan Heimert and Perry Miller, eds., *The Great Awakening: Documents Illustrating the Crisis and Its Consequences* (Indianapolis, 1967); David S. Lovejoy, ed., *Religious Enthusiasm and the Great Awakening* (Englewood Cliffs, N.J., 1969); Stephen Nissenbaum, ed., *The Great Awakening at Yale College* (Belmont, Calif., 1972); for the nineteenth century, William G. McLoughlin, ed., *The American Evangelicals, 1800–1900* (New York, 1968).

The microprint edition of *Early American Imprints, 1639–1800*, edited by Clifford K. Shipton, is invaluable.

III. SECONDARY WORKS

MY THOUGHT ON MANY of the issues raised by the primary sources explored in this study has been influenced continuously and profoundly by works published by countless other scholars and writers. It would be impossible, however, to acknowledge the full extent of my indebtedness to the historians, theologians, sociologists, psychologists, and others who have written on topics of interest to me since I began exploring some of these problems nearly twenty years ago. In the notes for each of the chapters, though, I have indicated a number of secondary works that seem to me to be most relevant, useful, and suggestive for particular subjects. I trust that these extensive references will serve the purpose of a general bibliography of secondary sources, guiding readers toward books and articles which might be of interest for a variety of purposes.

INDEX

authority in, 341; Pinckney on, 225; self-love and, 205; and slavery, 275, 277; *see also* authority and family government; conversion; will

Child-Rearing Concepts, 1628–1861: Historical Concepts, (Greven), 16, 160n

children: diet of, 26; feminization of, 282; genteel feelings for, 268–71; and Half-Way Covenant, 258; manners of evangelical, 46–7; of moderates, 179; mortality of, 34; portraits of, 283; physical punishment of, 50; regulation of, 48

choice: "Choice of Hercules", 243; freedom of, 218, 231, 257; importance of, to moderates, 217, 220

Christ, imagery of marriage to, 126–7

Christian Nurture (Bushnell), 168, 173

Christianity, Wesley on, 21

Christian Sparta, 358

Churchman, George, on indulgence, 166

Church of England, 198, 271, 330

church membership: boundaries of, 258, and conversion, 257; and purity, 147; and revivalism, 7n; salvation and, 87

Cities in Revolt (Bridenbaugh), 322n

civil government, and maintenance of authority, 210

civil rights, 360

civil war (English), 140, 203

Clarke, Ann Jones, 185

Clarke, Hannah, 184

Clarke, John, 184

Clarke, William, 184

class, *see* social rank

classicism, of genteel, 313

Cleaveland, John: family memories of, 23–4; parish of, 97

Clitherall, Eliza: child-rearing practices of, 165; on infant salvation, 157

Clive, John, 3n; *Macaulay: The Shaping of the Historian,* 3n

clothing: as discipline, 45, 46; and gender, 45–6, 242n, 284; of genteel children, 269, 282,

303, 304, 309, 310; moderates on, 213; plainness in, 296; and regionalism, 329; temptation of, and guilt, 60; of young women, 284, 290

coercive acts, 337

Coffin, Thomas Aston, portrait of, 283

co-habitation, and church community, 257

Cole, Nathan, 90; arminian beliefs of, 88; conversion experience of, 62, 82, 95; on purity of church membership, 147; rules of, 142; suicidal thoughts of, 83

Collected Papers (Freud), 15n

Collins, John, remembers youth, 59

commerce: and evil, 233; moderation in, 214

community: churches and, 257; evangelical households distant from, 25; genteel leadership in, 266, 286, 297, 329, 342; meaning of, to moderates, 152, 153, 178; nurture and, 257; purity in, 347; revivals disturb, 117

community (political), inclusive nature of, 259

Complete Introductory Lectures on Psychoanalysis (Freud), 15n

conformity, and evangelical union, 147–8

confusion, among evangelical children, 56

Congregationalists and Congregationalism, 7n, 12, 24, 154, 161, 167, 170, 204, 271, 330

conjugal relationships, among moderates, 180

Connecticut, 8n, 23, 62, 69, 78, 79, 114, 147, 167, 232

conscience: Chauncy on, 209; and childhood memories, 57; and conversion, 92; of evangelicals, 50–2, 59–60, 79; among genteel, 281, 292; guidance of 210; hatred and, 112; liberty of, 259–60; among moderates, 152, 187, 208, 260; among Puritans, 228; shaping of, 52, 55

conservatism: of genteel, 342; among moderates, 261, 344

residence, and church membership,
258
residence patterns, among moderates,
152
responsibility, and free will, 220
revivals and revivalism, 135, 196;
continuity in, 10; and conversion, 7n, 94, 95; English, and
origin of Methodism, 142; in
Great Awakening, 6; in Ipswich,
94; in Middleborough, 93, 95;
moderates critical of, 213;
opposed, 117; as outlet for anger,
120-1; and social conflict,
335; in Taunton, 95
revolution (American): effect on
families, 267-8, 271, 292; effect
on genteel, 310, 327; exiles from,
308; moderate and evangelical
alliance during, 354; Pickering
and, 221; as religious revival,
11n; transforming effect of, 335
revolution (French), Wollstonecraft
on, 212
*Revolution of the Saints, The: A
Study in the Origin of Radical
Politics* (Walzer), 7n, 194n,
354n
Rhoads, Sarah Pemberton, 157
Rich, Mrs. Aphia Salisbury, 283
Rich, Baby Edward, portrait of, 283
ritual, among genteel, 319-20, 324,
328, 330
Robinson, John: child-rearing advice
of, 37; fear of children, 28;
on indulgence of grandparents,
27; on physical punishment, 50;
recommends plain diet, 43-4
Robinson, William, imprisoned in
Boston, 108
Rogers, Daniel: on revivals, 94;
sense of self, 69, 70, 81
Rogers, John, on masculinity, 126
Rogers, Richard, on precision, 141;
on self-control, 207
Roman Catholics, Washington on,
328
routines: in evangelical child-
rearing, 48; among genteel, 300,
324
Rowe, John, 326; activities of, 301;
on genteel amusements, 307;
routines and piety of, 324

royal authority: collapse of, 343;
and evangelicals, 347
rules: among evangelicals, 129-30;
and government, 344; of life,
142; *see also* schedules
Rush, Benjamin, self-denial in
life of, 215-16
Rush, Julia Stockton, social life
of, 293
Rutman, Darrett B., 7n; *American
Puritanism: Faith and Practice*,
7n

sabbatarianism, and genteel, 295
sabbath breaking, in post-
revolutionary Massachusetts, 358
Sabine Hall, 190, 277, 279
sacraments: evangelicals and, 63;
genteel and, 14; moderates and,
230; and unregenerate, 258;
see also rituals
Saffin, John, on infants, 157-8
St. Augustine, 8, 13n
Salem (Mass.), 184, 222, 292, 325
Salem-Village, witchcraft in, 117,
123
salvation: among moderates, 220
226, 227; will versus conversion
in, 87
Sanford family, 266
Schaack, Peter Van, on conspiracy,
348
schedules: for children, 36; of
Jefferson, 289
science, and genteel, 298
Scotts, Morine, entertainments of,
305
*Second Look, The: The Reconstruc-
tion of Personal History in
Psychiatry and Psychoanalysis*
(Novey), 15n
seduction: and conspiracy, 350;
theme of, among moderates,
256; and republicanism, 354-5
self: chain of being and, 197; conversion and, 85, 87, 94-5, 101,
231; sexual elements of, 244;
sense of, among evangelicals,
12-13, 59-60, 65, 66, 203; and
genteel, 303, 312; and moderates,
152-3, 191, 206-7, 234, 261;
shaping of, 4; source of sin,
65-73, 76

About the Author

Philip Greven was born in New Orleans in 1935. He received his B.A. from Harvard College, a master's degree from Columbia University, and a Ph.D. in 1964 from Harvard University. He is currently a Professor in the Department of History at Rutgers College. He has been the recipient of several awards and grants, among them a National Endowment for the Humanities fellowship in 1970 and an American Council of Learned Societies fellowship in 1974. From 1974 to 1975 he was a Visiting Fellow at the Institute for Advanced Study in Princeton. His works include *Four Generations: Population, Land, and Family in Colonial Andover, Massachusetts* (1970) and *Child-Rearing Concepts, 1628–1861: Historical Sources* (1973). He is married to Helen Stokes Greven, and they have two children, Philip III and Hannah.